Cyber–Physical Systems for Social Applications

Maya Dimitrova
Bulgarian Academy of Sciences, Bulgaria

Hiroaki Wagatsuma
Kyushu Institute of Technology, Japan

A volume in the Advances in Systems Analysis, Software Engineering, and High Performance Computing (ASASEHPC) Book Series

Published in the United States of America by
  IGI Global
  Engineering Science Reference (an imprint of IGI Global)
  701 E. Chocolate Avenue
  Hershey PA, USA 17033
  Tel: 717-533-8845
  Fax: 717-533-8661
  E-mail: cust@igi-global.com
  Web site: http://www.igi-global.com

Library of Congress Cataloging-in-Publication Data

Names: Dimitrova, Maya, 1961- editor. | Wagatsuma, Hiroaki, editor.
Title: Cyber-physical systems for social applications / Maya Dimitrova and
  Hiroaki Wagatsuma, editors.
Description: Hershey, PA : Engineering Science Reference, an imprint of IGI
  Global, [2019] | Includes bibliographical references and index.
Identifiers: LCCN 2018037299| ISBN 9781522578796 (hardcover) | ISBN
  9781522578802 (ebook)
Subjects: LCSH: Automation. | Cooperating objects (Computer systems) |
  Robotics--Social aspects. | Robotics in medicine.
Classification: LCC TJ213 .C8855 2019 | DDC 303.48/3--dc23 LC record available at https://lccn.loc.gov/2018037299

This book is published in the IGI Global book series Advances in Systems Analysis, Software Engineering, and High Performance Computing (ASASEHPC) (ISSN: 2327-3453; eISSN: 2327-3461)

British Cataloguing in Publication Data
A Cataloguing in Publication record for this book is available from the British Library.

All work contributed to this book is new, previously-unpublished material. The views expressed in this book are those of the
authors, but not necessarily of the publisher.

For electronic access to this publication, please contact: eresources@igi-global.com.

Advances in Systems Analysis, Software Engineering, and High Performance Computing (ASASEHPC) Book Series

Vijayan Sugumaran
Oakland University, USA

ISSN:2327-3453
EISSN:2327-3461

MISSION

The theory and practice of computing applications and distributed systems has emerged as one of the key areas of research driving innovations in business, engineering, and science. The fields of software engineering, systems analysis, and high performance computing offer a wide range of applications and solutions in solving computational problems for any modern organization.

The **Advances in Systems Analysis, Software Engineering, and High Performance Computing (ASASEHPC) Book Series** brings together research in the areas of distributed computing, systems and software engineering, high performance computing, and service science. This collection of publications is useful for academics, researchers, and practitioners seeking the latest practices and knowledge in this field.

COVERAGE

- Engineering Environments
- Network Management
- Computer Networking
- Performance Modelling
- Human-Computer Interaction
- Enterprise Information Systems
- Computer System Analysis
- Storage Systems
- Virtual Data Systems
- Software Engineering

IGI Global is currently accepting manuscripts for publication within this series. To submit a proposal for a volume in this series, please contact our Acquisition Editors at Acquisitions@igi-global.com or visit: http://www.igi-global.com/publish/.

Titles in this Series

For a list of additional titles in this series, please visit: www.igi-global.com/book-series

Integrating the Internet of Things Into Software Engineering Practices
D. Jeya Mala (Thiagarajar College of Engineering, India)
Engineering Science Reference • copyright 2019 • 293pp • H/C (ISBN: 9781522577904) • US $215.00 (our price)

Analyzing the Role of Risk Mitigation and Monitoring in Software Development
Rohit Kumar (Chandigarh University, India) Anjali Tayal (Infosys Technologies, India) and Sargam Kapil (C-DAC, India)
Engineering Science Reference • copyright 2018 • 308pp • H/C (ISBN: 9781522560296) • US $225.00 (our price)

Handbook of Research on Pattern Engineering System Development for Big Data Analytics
Vivek Tiwari (International Institute of Information Technology, India) Ramjeevan Singh Thakur (Maulana Azad National Institute of Technology, India) Basant Tiwari (Hawassa University, Ethiopia) and Shailendra Gupta (AISECT University, India)
Engineering Science Reference • copyright 2018 • 396pp • H/C (ISBN: 9781522538707) • US $320.00 (our price)

Incorporating Nature-Inspired Paradigms in Computational Applications
Mehdi Khosrow-Pour, D.B.A. (Information Resources Management Association, USA)
Engineering Science Reference • copyright 2018 • 385pp • H/C (ISBN: 9781522550204) • US $195.00 (our price)

Innovations in Software-Defined Networking and Network Functions Virtualization
Ankur Dumka (University of Petroleum and Energy Studies, India)
Engineering Science Reference • copyright 2018 • 364pp • H/C (ISBN: 9781522536406) • US $235.00 (our price)

Advances in System Dynamics and Control
Ahmad Taher Azar (Benha University, Egypt) and Sundarapandian Vaidyanathan (Vel Tech University, India)
Engineering Science Reference • copyright 2018 • 680pp • H/C (ISBN: 9781522540779) • US $235.00 (our price)

Green Computing Strategies for Competitive Advantage and Business Sustainability
Mehdi Khosrow-Pour, D.B.A. (Information Resources Management Association, USA)
Business Science Reference • copyright 2018 • 324pp • H/C (ISBN: 9781522550174) • US $185.00 (our price)

Optimizing Contemporary Application and Processes in Open Source Software
Mehdi Khosrow-Pour, D.B.A. (Information Resources Management Association, USA)
Engineering Science Reference • copyright 2018 • 318pp • H/C (ISBN: 9781522553144) • US $215.00 (our price)

701 East Chocolate Avenue, Hershey, PA 17033, USA
Tel: 717-533-8845 x100 • Fax: 717-533-8661
E-Mail: cust@igi-global.com • www.igi-global.com

Table of Contents

Detailed Table of Contents

Section 1
Social and Empirical Foundations of Cyber-Physical Systems for Social Applications

> *Vassilis G. Kaburlasos, Eastern Macedonia and Thrace Institute of Technology (EMaTTech), Greece*
> *Eleni Vrochidou, Eastern Macedonia and Thrace Institute of Technology (EMaTTech), Greece*

The use of robots as educational learning tools is quite extensive worldwide, yet it is rather limited in special education. In particular, the use of robots in the field of special education is under skepticism since robots are frequently believed to be expensive with limited capacity. The latter may change with the advent of social robots, which can be used in special education as affordable tools for delivering sophisticated stimuli to children with learning difficulties also due to preexisting conditions. Pilot studies occasionally demonstrate the effectiveness of social robots in specific domains. This chapter overviews the engagement of social robots in special education including the authors' preliminary work in this field; moreover, it discusses their proposal for potential future extensions involving more autonomous (i.e., intelligent) social robots as well as feedback from human brain signals.

> *Aneta Petrova Atanasova, Sofia University "St. Kliment Ohridski", Bulgaria*
> *Aleksandra Ivaylova Yosifova, New Bulgarian University, Bulgaria*

The focus of the current chapter is on humanoid robots as part of inclusive education. The investigation of the perception of and attitude of children and teachers to the application of cyber physical systems in education is essential. The data of a survey of the perception and attitude to the application of cyber physical systems in education of teachers and students from several Bulgarian schools are currently being examined. The attitude of teachers in the current study towards robots is positive. The attitude of students is rather neutral, and the difference between the two populations is statistically significant. Both teachers and students think of the robot as of a humanoid, capable of expression emotions. There is no difference between the attitudes towards the role and appearance of the robot of boys and girls. However, older children demonstrate a more negative attitude than younger children.

Chapter 3

Roman Zahariev Zahariev, Bulgarian Academy of Sciences, Bulgaria
Nina Valchkova, Bulgarian Academy of Sciences, Bulgaria

Collaborative robots (Cobots) are described from the point of view of the cognitive processes underlying the perception and emotional expression of learners based on individual human interacting with non-humanoid robots. The chapter describes a project that is aimed at the development and prototyping of mobile cognitive robotic system designed for service and assistance to people with disabilities. In creating this robot called "AnRI" (anthropomorphic robot intelligent) the experience from building the previous one was used, and it was used in the project Conduct Research into the Adoption of Robotic Technologies in Special Education by Children, Young People, and Pedagogical Specialists. It is described as a device of the robot and realization of cognitive processes to integrate knowledge-related information from sensors, actuators, and multiple sources of information vital to the process of serving people with disabilities.

Chapter 4

Maya Dimitrova, Bulgarian Academy of Sciences, Bulgaria
Hiroaki Wagatsuma, Kyushu Institute of Technology, Japan
Gyanendra Nath Tripathi, Renesas Electronics, Japan
Guangyi Ai, Neusoft Institute Guangdong, China

A novel framework for investigation of the learner attitude towards a humanoid robot tutoring system is proposed in the chapter. The theoretical approach attempts to understand both the cognitive motivation as well as the social motivation of the participants in a teaching session, held by a robotic tutor. For this aim, a questionnaire is delivered after the eye tracking experiment in order to record the type and amount of the learned material as well as the social motivation of the participants. The results of the experiments show significant effects of both cognitive and social motivation influences. It has been shown that cognitive motivation can be observed and analyzed on a very individual level. This is an important biometric feature and can be used to recognize individuals from patterns of viewing behaviors in a lesson. Guidelines, drawn from first-person accounts of learner participation in the study, are also formulated for achieving more intuitive interactions with humanoid robots intended to perform social jobs like being teachers or advisors.

Chapter 5

Gyanendra Nath Tripathi, Renesas Electronics, Japan

Humans have several kinds of intelligence like logical thinking, decision making, social and behavioral intelligence, and many more. However, above all, emotional intelligence plays a vital role to drive action and event. To analyze the need of emotion for robot, it is required to investigate emotion in human and its socio-cognitive effect on event-action relation and behavior. Emotion is not required for a robot that is programmed just to perform certain commanded tasks. However, for a socially interactive assist robot in an environment of home, hospital, office, etc., emotion is important for decision making and to perform action. Moreover, emotion for robot is helpful to define the behavior and even to personalize the robot for its owner. The chapter aims to discuss three prominent questions regarding "emotion for a robot": 1) why we need emotion for robot, 2) what can be a probable solution as an emotion model, and 3) how emotion model can be devised for robot in a real-time environment.

Chapter 6

    Marina Santini, RISE Research Institutes of Sweden, Sweden
    Arne Jönsson, RISE Research Institutes of Sweden, Sweden & Linköping University, Sweden
    Wiktor Strandqvist, RISE Research Institutes of Sweden, Sweden & Linköping University, Sweden
    Gustav Cederblad, Linköping University, Sweden
    Mikael Nyström, RISE Research Institutes of Sweden, Sweden & Linköping University, Sweden
    Marjan Alirezaie, Örebro University, Sweden
    Leili Lind, RISE Research Institutes of Sweden, Sweden & Linköping University, Sweden
    Eva Blomqvist, RISE Research Institutes of Sweden, Sweden & Linköping University, Sweden
    Maria Lindén, Mälardalen University, Sweden
    Annica Kristoffersson, Örebro University, Sweden

In the era of data-driven science, corpus-based language technology is an essential part of cyber physical systems. In this chapter, the authors describe the design and the development of an extensible domain-specific web corpus to be used in a distributed social application for the care of the elderly at home. The domain of interest is the medical field of chronic diseases. The corpus is conceived as a flexible and extensible textual resource, where additional documents and additional languages will be appended over time. The main purpose of the corpus is to be used for building and training language technology applications for the "layfication" of the specialized medical jargon. "Layfication" refers to the automatic identification of more intuitive linguistic expressions that can help laypeople (e.g., patients, family caregivers, and home care aides) understand medical terms, which often appear opaque. Exploratory experiments are presented and discussed.

Chapter 7

    Lyuba Alboul, Sheffield Hallam University, UK
    Martin Beer, Sheffield Hallam University, UK
    Louis Nisiotis, Sheffield Hallam University, UK

The rapid developments in online technology have provided young people with instant communication with each other and highly interactive and engaging visual game playing environments. The traditional ways of presenting museum and heritage assets no longer, therefore, hold their attention and provide them with an exciting and dynamic visitor experience. There is considerable interest in the use of augmented reality to allow visitors to explore worlds that are not immediately accessible to them and relating them to the real worlds around them. These are very effective in providing much needed contextual information, but appear rather static when compared with multi-player games environments where players interact with each other and robotic characters (non-player characters) in real time. By fusing these technologies, the authors postulate a new type of conceptually-led environment (cyber museum) that fuses real (physical), virtual worlds and cyber-social spaces into a single dynamic environment that provides a unique experience of exploring both worlds simultaneously.

Chapter 8

Galina T. Bogdanova, Bulgarian Academy of Sciences, Bulgaria
Nikolay Genchev Noev, Bulgarian Academy of Sciences, Bulgaria

This chapter explores digital technologies and their use in social applications for blind people. The digitization, creation, and indexing of digital resources aimed at using these resources for the needs of visually impaired people are presented. Standards for digitization, metadata, digital media storage, and media resources are presented. Internet technologies, semantic networks, and ontologies are of particular importance and can be used for blind learners. 3D technologies and 3D models are particularly suitable tools and give new opportunities for blind people. Website standards and website accessibility standards, as well as accessibility technologies for people with disabilities, are a means and a way of socializing. Both digital resources and robots are considered inaccessible to people with visual limitations. They are widespread on a global scale, but their use is rather limited in people with disabilities and in their special education. Particular attention is paid to the interdisciplinary use of digital technologies and social robots as training tools.

Chapter 9

Mamata Rath, Birla Global University, India

A social network is a portrayal of the social structure between actors, mostly individuals or organizations. It indicates the ways in which they are connected through various social familiarities ranging from casual acquaintance to close familiar bonds. This chapter exhibits an exhaustive review of various security and protection issues in social networks that directly or indirectly affect the individual member of the network. Furthermore, different threats in social networks have been focused on that appear because of the sharing of interactive media content inside a social networking site. Additionally, the chapter also reports current cutting-edge guard arrangements that can shield social network clients from these dangers.

Section 2
Engineering and Mathematical Foundations of Cyber-Physical Systems for Social Applications

Chapter 10

T. V. Gopal, Anna University, India

Human beings are always attracted to patterns, designs, and shapes. Even infants are attracted to the geometry around them. Angles, shapes, lines, line segments, curves, and other aspects of geometry are ubiquitous. Even the letters are constructed of lines, line segments, and curves. Nature also has an abundance of geometry. Patterns can be found on leaves, in flowers, in seashells, and many other places. Even the human bodies consist of patterns, curves, and line segments. Therefore, like many professions, the cyber-physical systems also require at least a foundational understanding of geometry. This chapter elucidates the use of geometry to simplify the design and analysis of cyber-physical systems to enhance the efficiency in social applications. The knowledge learned through the understanding of geometric principles provides not only an increase in safety but also an increase in the creation of tools, skill level enhancement, and aesthetically pleasing arrangements.

Chapter 11

Mitko Gospodinov, Bulgarian Academy of Sciences, Bulgaria
Galya Nikolova Georgieva-Tsaneva, Bulgarian Academy of Sciences, Bulgaria
Evgeniya Gospodinova, Bulgarian Academy of Sciences, Bulgaria
Krasimir Cheshmedzhiev, Bulgarian Academy of Sciences, Bulgaria

The implementation of photoplethysmographic sensors in the data capture and data storage to analyze the cardiovascular condition of the patient is a new direction in automatized diagnosis of the cardiovascular system. This chapter contains a description of the use of photoplethysmographic sensors in a computerized patient cardiac monitoring system. The system consists of a portable device for collection of patient's cardiac data by applying photopletithysmographic method and software for mathematical analysis. An important diagnostic parameter that can be determined by the photoplethysmographic signal is the heart rate variability. The current application of the photoplethysmographic sensors in portable automatized system is of particular importance because the results of cardiac data analysis with these methods can provide not only detailed information about the cardiovascular status of the patients but also provide the opportunity to generate new knowledge about the diagnosis, and the prevention of pathology in cardiovascular diseases.

Chapter 12

Galya Nikolova Georgieva-Tsaneva, Bulgarian Academy of Sciences, Bulgaria

The study of human cardiovascular activity is one of the main methods for assessing the health of the human. It is performed in clinical conditions via electrocardiographic devices and in the daily life of a individuals through Holter monitoring. An important diagnostic parameter that can be determined by an electrocardiogram, taking into account the difference between successive heartbeat is heart rate variability – a widely used non-invasive method of measuring heart rate. This parameter makes it possible to assess the risk of various cardiac diseases such as angina, cardiac infarction, life-threatening arrhythmias, etc. This chapter presents the morphological bases of the cardio records, heart rate variability, and its impact on the healthy status of the individual. It describes the created cardiology base of prolonged Holter recordings for the purposes of scientific research project. Presented are internationally approved standards to provide web accessibility to internet-based data bases and other resources for people with disabilities.

This chapter is a general introduction to electroencephalography and popular methods used to manipulate EEG in order to elicit markers of sensory, cognitive perception, and behavior. With development of interdisciplinary research, there is increased curiosity among engineers towards biomedical research. Those using signal processing techniques attempt to employ algorithms to the real-life signals and retrieve characteristics of signals such as speech, echo, EEG, among others. The chapter briefs the history of human EEG and goes back to the origins and fundamentals of electrical activity in brain, how this activity reaches the scalp, methods to capture this high temporal activity. It then takes the reader through design methodology that goes behind EEG experiments, general schema for analysis of EEG signal. It describes the concept of early evoked potentials, which are known responses for study of sensory perception and are used extensively in medical science. It moves on to another popular manipulation of EEG technique used to elicit event related potentials.

Chapter 14

Electroencephalogram (EEG) is one of the most popular approaches for brain monitoring in many research fields. While the detailed working flows for in-lab neuroscience-targeted EEG experiments conditions have been well established, carrying out EEG experiments under a real-life condition can be quite confusing because of various practical limitations. This chapter gives a brief overview of the practical issues and techniques that help real-life EEG experiments come into being, and the well-known artifact problems for EEG. As a guideline for performing a successful EEG data analysis with the low-electrode-density limitation of portable EEG devices, recently proposed techniques for artifact suppression or removal are briefly surveyed as well.

Chapter 15

This chapter explains the removal of artifacts from the multi-resource biological signals. Morphological components can be used to distinguish between the brain activities and artifacts that are contaminated with each other in many physical situations. In this chapter, a two-stage wavelet shrinkage and morphological component analysis (MCA) for biological signals is a sophisticated way to analyze the brain activities and validate the effectiveness of artifacts removal. The source components in the biological signals can be characterized by specific morphology and measures the independence and uniqueness of the source components. Undecimated wavelet transform (UDWT), discrete cosine transform (DCT), local discrete cosine transform (LDCT), discrete sine transform (DST), and DIRAC are the orthonormal bases function used to build the explicit dictionary for the decomposition of source component of the biological signal in the morphological component analysis. The chapter discusses the implementation and optimization algorithm of the morphological component analysis.

Chapter 16

The methods that have been used in navigation over the centuries have changed as have the goals they serve. One of these methods is inertial navigation. Nowadays inertial navigation offers many advantages over other types of navigation. A major advantage is the lack of dependence on external transmitters or other devices, which means independence of the system. With the development of new technologies, the accuracy of these systems is increasing, which increases their applicability. An important aspect is the reduction in the price of sensors, which is a prerequisite for their application in new areas where they have not yet been offered. An important advantage of inertial navigation is the ability to give in real-time information about acceleration, speed, and location and the possibility of autonomous operation of the object.

Chapter 17

In this chapter, the problem of controlling bipedal walking robots with integrated elastic elements is considered. A survey of the existing control methods developed for walking robots is given, and their applicability to the task of controlling the robots with elastic elements is analyzed. The focus of the chapter lies with the feedback controller design. The chapter studies the influence that the elastic elements modelled as a spring-damper system have on the behavior of the control system. The influence of the spring-damper parameters and the inertial parameters of the actuator gear box and the motor shaft on the generated control laws and the resulting peak torques are discussed. The changes in these effects associated with motor torque saturation and sensors nonlinearities are studied. It is shown that the introduction of torque saturation changes the way the elastic drive parameters affect the resulting behavior of the control system. The ways to use obtained results in practice are discussed.

Foreword

It is a great pleasure to introduce this new book edited by two eminent scientists. I am aware of their scientific achievements, since I have collaborated with them, in recent years, towards investigating novel highly intelligent cyber-physical systems (CPSs).

By far, the most important success factor in the publication of a scientific book is the scientific quality of the authors/editors. This book was compiled by the efforts and supervision of Professor Maya Dimitrova, a psychologist with expertise in human-computer interaction systems design and Professor Hiroaki Wagatsuma, an A.I. engineer specialized in neuroscience. These two brilliant scientists are characterized by enthusiasm, scientific consistency and their high committed to their thoughts and novel scientific ideas. Thus, there is no doubt that this book constitutes a product of high quality enough to inspire scientists all over the globe, capable to stimulate them with some new ideas in designing cyber-physical systems in a social framework.

This book opens a wide window on cyber-physical systems, a hot multidisciplinary topic in recent years, with emphasis to CPSs integration embodying robotic technology. It is worth to note that CPSs constitute an inevitable component of Industry 4.0 (Europe), Industrial Internet of Things (IIoT – USA) and Society 5.0 (Japan) development frameworks, consequently they help towards the industrial and social evolution of modern human societies.

In the light of this emerging technology, the book provides to the reader some innovative cases of integrating CPSs in human-centric applications characterized by a high degree of social interaction. Considering that science is evolved by searching towards the theoretical and practical directions, this book aims to keep a remarkable balance between research and development production phases of social CPSs. In this context, new social and empirical foundations in CPSs are presented in the first part, while engineering and mathematical tools, capable to implement CPSs, are proposed in the second part. This balance was exceptionally managed by the two editors, through appropriate selection of the book chapters without diminishing the quality of the final outcome.

For sure, this book constitutes the first attempt to collect the emerged trends in social CPSs and provides an exciting journey to the experienced as well as the early stage researchers, starting from the theoretical aspects of CPSs design and continuing to novel social application avenues.

George A. Papakostas
Eastern Macedonia and Thrace Institute of Technology, Greece

Preface

Consider present day social institutions like a school, or a municipal social service. A school is a complex hierarchical organisation of many functional levels; its operation is based on planned activities aimed at achieving certain goals within fixed time constraints. From a managerial point of view a school resembles an industrial enterprise - therefore it can be modelled like a cyber-physical system (CPS), designed to accomplish some production mission within a networked environment with humans in the information and control loop. The same logic applies to a social service institution.

Present day sophisticated, adaptive and autonomous to a certain degree robotic technology is a radically new stimulus for the cognitive system of the human learner from the earliest to the oldest age and deserves extensive, thorough and systematic research, based on novel frameworks for analysis, modelling, synthesis and implementation of CPSs for social applications.

This book aims to provide relevant theoretical frameworks and the latest empirical findings in the areas of designing socially-oriented cyber-physical systems. Instead of being trapped by the debate human against the robot in the social sphere, it aims at forwarding the symbiotic human-robot perspective in areas like education, social communication, entertainment and health monitoring. The intelligence of the CPS is augmented by the advances in communication sciences, medical diagnosis and visualisation, information retrieval and the semantic web. At the same time simplification and adaptation to the 3D mental representation of the human mind of the reality is necessary to be able to maintain mutually understandable human-robot and human-system dialogue.

The emergence of this book was inspired by the "3rd European Network for the Advancement of Artificial Cognitive Systems, Interaction and Robotics, Project no.: 269981, Coordination Action, European Commission, 7th Research Framework Programme, Information and Communication Technologies" - in particular the idea to explore multi-level pedagogical potential of robotic technology, including understanding social mechanisms by artificial agents/robots. It is also inspired by COST Action IC1404 Multi-Paradigm Modelling for Cyber-Physical Systems (MPM4CPS) (2015-2018) and the formalisms, proposed to address the complexity of building a CPS in the social sphere. An attempt to build such a system is the ongoing project CybSPEED funded by H2020-MSCA-RISE-2017 No 777720 via proposing a novel framework for analysis, modelling, synthesis and implementation of Cyber-Physical Systems for pedagogical rehabilitation in special education, based on a combination of the best of experience and achievements of the partners in the domains of brain-aware robotics, cognitive biometrics, computational intelligence and reasoning in humanoid and non-humanoid robots for education. Many of these ideas are further developed in the chapters of this book. The individual chapters try to open novel perspectives on design of CPSs for social applications where people with different learning aspirations and needs are being supported by intelligent and empathic technology.

The book consists of two major parts, dealing with the social and empirical foundations of cyber-physical systems for social applications: Section 1; and the mathematical and engineering foundations of Cyber-Physical Systems for social applications: Section 2.

SECTION 1: SOCIAL AND EMPIRICAL FOUNDATIONS OF CYBER-PHYSICAL SYSTEMS FOR SOCIAL APPLICATIONS

Chapter 1 discusses at length the potential of social robotics to provide various means for pedagogical and psycho-social rehabilitation of children, possible vulnerable due to preexisting conditions. It proposes the novel Lattice Computing (LC) framework for modelling of CPSs, where the "cyber" component is modelled via non-numerical, e.g. symbolic, data representations, whereas the "physical" component is modelled via numerical data representations. LC, as proposed by the authors, is a candidate for a mathematically rigorous modelling of CPSs in social applications without the need to translate non-numeric values in numeric or vice versa. Therefore, it can implement natural ways to describe the child-robot interaction in teaching children via technology.

Chapter 2 discusses a variety of means that cyber-physical and robotic technology can provide to special education. An empirical study is presented, which reveals the complexity of the ad-hoc assumptions of teachers and students towards the robotic potential in class with children with special learning aspirations and needs. The study provides initial assessment of the expectations of teachers and children of the role of the robots at school.

Chapter 3 provides and extensive historical review on service robotics and its potential for implementation in various social activities. It discusses issues of acceptance and safety of the mechanical parts of the device, as well as of its embedded intelligence, based on the authors' own experience in working in the field.

Chapter 4 presents an experimental framework for studying learners' attitudes towards robots as tutors in the classroom. The framework presents a procedure for studying both the cognitive and social motivation of the learners when presented with a lesson delivered by a humanoid robot NAO. The results of an experimental study are given, which has encountered that socially-motivated people report reliably higher number of positive opinions on robot performance, whereas socially-indifferent people are more critical in their opinions on robot performance. These results provide a strong argument in favour of the socialising role of technology in general, and humanoid robots, in particular, contrary to some common opinions.

Chapter 5 proposes a novel conceptual model of behavior design for a humanoid robot to reinstate the reactions on an intelligent agent when perceived as expressing emotions. It builds on a psychological theory of emotions and provides a framework, aiming to represent by a robot the reactions, often associated with experienced emotions.

Chapter 6 presents an extensive study of medical terminology classification based on its explanatory level for medical professionals versus non-professionals, retrieved from health-related sites on the web. The implemented algorithms are novel and suitable for cases of including robot "encyclopaedic" knowledge in the robot maintained dialogue. A lot of applications like social robots would benefit from using the methodology for domain-specific web corpus generation in the process of online communication with a person at home, who seeks assistance with monitoring and explaining health related issues.

Chapter 7 is a literature review on methods for digitalisation of visual information, and in particular the three dimensional relations among these. The authors discuss them from the point of vie of the existing accessibility standards for web site design for people with visual impairment. The approach provides useful means to address the issue of generating common mental representations among all users of the CPS.

Chapter 8 proposes a new framework for generating augmented reality, which, from the user perceptual point of view transcends through both space and time. The user can travel back and forth in history in a way, similar to browsing around the surrounding present-day environments. This is a step, according to the authors, towards the emergence of the cyber-physical eco-society of the future.

Chapter 9 discusses the information security problem in CPSs for social applications. In these systems the user is exposed to a number of possible influences - explicit and implicit. Different threats in social networks are formulated, falling out from sharing of interactive media content inside a social networking site. The chapter also reports current cutting edge protection arrangements that can shield social network clients from these dangers.

SECTION 2: ENGINEERING AND MATHEMATICAL FOUNDATIONS OF CYBER-PHYSICAL SYSTEMS FOR SOCIAL APPLICATIONS

Chapter 10 introduces a philosophical discourse of geometry as defined in mathematical theories and in visualisation oriented computer algorithms. It emphasises that geometry is meaningful in CPSs if adapted to the human way of perceiving geometrical objects - how these can be imagined and communicated between the agents in the CPS. The phenomenon of traversing within the different levels of abstraction of the numerous world representations in a CPS is described in its complexity.

Chapter 11 describes a novel medical interface for recording cardiological data based on photoplethysmographic sensors. The interface itself is extremely appropriate for inclusion in CPSs or robotic technologies for enabling individual users monitor their health condition and also for robot alerting on user change in health condition. Analysis of real data is performed and proven fast and precise in predicting cardiological conditions.

Chapter 12 aims at creation of annotated physiological databases that can be used by people with special needs and especially people with visual deficits. It emphasises the diagnostic potential of heart rate variability and the possibility to implement wavelet-based algorithms for diagnostics -on the one hand - and conveying this information in semantically consistent form to the user - on the other.

Chapter 13 discusses the cognitive correlates of brainwaves received from EEG records aimed at monitoring mental and emotional states of users of CPSs. It introduces a systematic approach to human EEG, which can be the basis for creating models of human cognition and affect in contexts relevant to design of social interaction modules such as cobots, and robotic systems within the social sphere.

Chapter 14 presents an expert analysis on problems, arising in using present-day portable EEG recording datasets in order to obtain a relevant EEG signal. It can serve as a handbook for learners, who want to obtain data outside laboratory settings and the discussed heuristics form a basic guideline for real-life EEG research.

Chapter 15 presents detailed mathematical description of the application of morphological component analysis to neurological data, aiming to predict epilepsy. The entire methodology provides a promising method to be implemented in a CPS when unexpected neurological phenomena have to be detected and signalled - for example when the vulnerable person is alone.

Chapter 16 discusses an attitude and heading reference system designed to maintain a videocamera to produce video streams, adapted to the dynamics of the human vision in a constantly changing environment. With such systems the CPS and the human can "see" identical images from streams of data in order to perform in synergy.

Chapter 17 gives an answer to the question why robots need walking instead of rolling around on platforms. The universality in obstacle avoidance via walking mechanisms gives a humane aspect of the robot, in addition to being able to overcome the clumsy locomotion style of bipedal robots. The focus of the chapter is on aspects that are specific to robots with elastic elements, rather than on ones that are general for all types of walking robots, providing an implementable model for a CPS, capable of controlling robot locomotion.

The book is intended for both researchers and practitioners, who aim at building cyber-physical systems for social applications, for postgraduate students and for anyone, interested in the topic of the humanising, socialising and inspirational role of technology in the life of people around the World.

We hope the readers will find the book exciting and inspiring.

Maya Dimitrova
Bulgarian Academy of Sciences, Bulgaria

Hiroaki Wagatsuma
Kyushu Institute of Technology, Japan
January 2019

Section 1
Social and Empirical Foundations of Cyber–Physical Systems for Social Applications

Chapter 1
Social Robots for Pedagogical Rehabilitation:
Trends and Novel Modeling Principles

Vassilis G. Kaburlasos
Eastern Macedonia and Thrace Institute of Technology (EMaTTech), Greece

Eleni Vrochidou
Eastern Macedonia and Thrace Institute of Technology (EMaTTech), Greece

ABSTRACT

The use of robots as educational learning tools is quite extensive worldwide, yet it is rather limited in special education. In particular, the use of robots in the field of special education is under skepticism since robots are frequently believed to be expensive with limited capacity. The latter may change with the advent of social robots, which can be used in special education as affordable tools for delivering sophisticated stimuli to children with learning difficulties also due to preexisting conditions. Pilot studies occasionally demonstrate the effectiveness of social robots in specific domains. This chapter overviews the engagement of social robots in special education including the authors' preliminary work in this field; moreover, it discusses their proposal for potential future extensions involving more autonomous (i.e., intelligent) social robots as well as feedback from human brain signals.

INTRODUCTION

A percentage around 4% of the students in member countries of the European Union (EU) are registered in special education programs according to Special Needs Education (2012) European data. At least 10% has been reported in the USA regarding children characterized by a learning difficulty (Cortiella, & Horowitz, 2014), while in Finland a reported 17% of students are enrolled in special education (Meijer, Soriano, & Watkins, 2003). Special scientists such as educators, pedagogues, psychologists and speech therapists suggest that the percentage of children in need for special education is higher than reported, since many cases are not recorded for various reasons (Pastor, & Reuben, 2008). Furthermore, if we also consider the families of children then the percentage of people involved in special education is even

DOI: 10.4018/978-1-5225-7879-6.ch001

higher. For the aforementioned reasons, the support of children with Special Education Needs (SEN) is included in national /European /world policies (UNESCO, 1994). Children with SEN are experiencing a variety of difficulties in family as well as at school. Effective special education at an early stage may improve the emotional and social development of children with SEN, their learning capacity, and, finally, improve the quality of life for a significant part of the population. Furthermore, special education may also improve the work skills of people with SEN thus enhancing a nation's workforce. There is a need for a policy framework regarding SEN. The latter has been a subject of debate in particular regarding whether special education itself is a problem of, or the solution to, issues of social justice (Norwich, 2007).

During the last decades robots seem to leave the industrial manufacturing floor and enter other domains such as farming, surveillance, entertainment, education, etc. Educational robotics are used worldwide as learning tools (Miller, Church, & Trexler, 2000) but surprisingly rarely in special education. At the moment, the demand for special education services remains high, yet unsatisfied due to the high cost involved. However, the benefits surpass all costs. Lately, Cyber-Physical Systems (CPSs), including social robots, have been proposed in education with emphasis on special education (CybSPEED, 2017). Note that the concept of CPSs has been introduced to account for technical devices with both sensing and reasoning abilities including a varying degree of autonomous behavior. There are a lot of expectations from CPSs (Serpanos, 2018). Seven types of CPSs are most often discussed, focusing on Disabled People, Healthcare, Agriculture and Food Supply, Manufacturing, Energy and Critical Infrastructures, Transport and Logistics, and Community Security and Safety. To them one additional type has been proposed lately, namely Education & Pedagogical Rehabilitation (CybSPEED, 2017). The CPSs we are interested in here include Social Robots in (special) education such as NAO, Pepper, Jibo, Leka etc. (Papakostas et al., 2018; Ueyama, 2015). In particular, humanoid robots such as NAO are already employed in various contexts for the treatment of children with Autism Spectrum Disorder (ASD) (Amanatiadis et al., 2017; Kaburlasos et al., 2018 January; Lytridis et al., 2018; Ueyama, 2015).

Despite reported evidence, the majority of people are still skeptical regarding the application of robots in Special Treatment and Education (STE) of children. For example, according to a recent survey (Eurobarometer, 2012), European responders appear positive towards robots but 60% of them believe that robots should be banned from taking care of children, the elderly as well as the disabled. Furthermore, only 3% said that robots should be a priority in education, while 34% maintained that robots should be banned from education altogether. All the aforementioned responses were attributed to the people's belief that robots may be dangerous for certain, sensitive categories of people. A more recent survey conducted simultaneously in three Balkan countries (Kostova et al., 2018) has confirmed the aforementioned results, and furthermore it recorded responses encouraging the joint engagement of robots and information technologies. An important question is posed next.

How far can a social robot interact with a child without raising ethical questions? General public opinion is important toward answering the latter question. Note that studies based on public surveys regarding the use of robots in eldercare revealed high acceptance of pet-like therapeutic robots, for humanoid caretaker robots as well as for surveillance care robots (Moon, Danielson, & Van der Loos, 2012). However, rejection of robots is reported occasionally because people often think that robots might replace humans and take their jobs. It seems that negative public opinion is probably the biggest challenge the scientific community must overcome in order to introduce social robots in the field of STE. Adaptation of a robot's appearance and/or behavior would improve the acceptance of robots by human users (Kanda et al., 2008).

The next generation of robot assistants in STE calls for robots tailored to individual needs. Currently, the robots used in special education are semi-autonomous, in sense that a robot has some autonomy from the manufacturer, for example to turn its head or to pronounce certain words, but there is always a human tele-operator in the background that controls the robot. An increased autonomy is expected to increase the usability of a robot. It is expected that providing robots with more intelligence, would make robots more useful. Preliminary application results suggest that robot technology could have a great impact on STE as an assisting tool for both teachers and therapists (Tanaka, Cicourel, & Movellan, 2007). In particular, educational applications of robots are promising for students with disabilities in two different manners: first, the robots can motivate students undertake a wide range of tasks that would otherwise refuse due to their disability and, second, the use of robots may result in an equal participation with peers in robot-based learning activities (Martyn Cooper, & William Harwin, 1999).

SPECIAL EDUCATION FROM AN ENGINEERING POINT OF VIEW

Special education is defined as the education of students with special educational needs in a way that addresses their individual differences. It involves individually planned and systematically monitored arrangement of various teaching procedures and scenarios, suitably adapted equipment as well as alternative materials. Such interventions are designed to support individuals with STE in order to achieve a higher level of personal self-sufficiency and success both at school and in the community that would not had been possible were the students only given access to typical education.

Common special needs include learning disabilities (e.g. dyslexia), communication disorders, emotional and behavioral disorders (e.g. attention deficit hyperactivity disorder), physical disabilities and development disabilities (e.g. ASD and intellectual disabilities). Students with special needs are likely to improve on their learning capacity and benefit from additional educational services based on different teaching approaches, the use of technology and especially adapted areas or resource rooms (Smith, 2007).

One way to study learning disabilities is by the analytic information processing model (i.e., block-diagram) in Figure 1 that explains how students interact with their external world during learning (Kirk et al., 2011). More specifically, first, the children receive information from their senses (vision, hearing etc.); then, they process this information by their memory, classification and reasoning capacities; finally, they respond to the input information by an output (i.e. speaking, writing, action).

This information processing is driven by the Executive Function which is the ability to decide which information to attend, how to interpret it and how to respond to it. Information processing takes place within an Emotional Context that influences every aspect of the proposed model shown in Figure 1.

Special education is necessary when a child is unable to process information effectively. In the latter case the problem might be either in the information input or in the internal processing of information or in the output response. The executive function is the decision-making part of the model that directs a child's attention to an input by choosing the thinking process to be called upon and decide how to respond. All this information processing is carried out within an emotional context which can activate various modules of the model conditioned on stress, anxiety, calmness, confidence, etc. Any deviation from the "typical" information processing described in Figure 1 calls for special education. For instance, autism spectrum disorder (ASD) is a developmental disorder characterized by impairments in communication, social interaction and imagination that may occur to different degrees and in a variety of forms. Children with ASD often have: accompanying learning disabilities and experience inability to relate to

Figure 1. The information processing model assumed during student learning

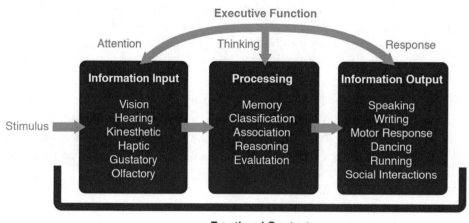

other people, rare eye contact, difficulty in verbal and non-verbal communication and tendencies towards repetitive behavior patterns (Jordan, 2013). In all, the analytic model of Figure 1 can be used toward analytically designing educational interventions by Social Robots as explained next.

SOCIAL ROBOTS IN SPECIAL EDUCATION

The term "social robots" typically refers to robots engaged in some form of social interaction with humans through speech, gestures, or other means of communication. Moreover, the term "assistive robots" refers to robots that aid people mainly with physical and neuro-developmental disabilities. In conclusion, the term Social Assistive Robots (SARs) has been proposed as the intersection of the previous two families of robots and it refers to robots designed to assist humans via interaction driven by user needs (e.g. for tutoring, physical therapy, emotional expression) using multimodal interfaces involving speech, gestures and various input devices (Fong, Nourbakhsh, & Dautenhahn, 2003). Our interest here is in SARs for pedagogical rehabilitation in special education with special attention to ASD.

In the aforementioned context, our basic Working Hypothesis, namely WH, is the following:

WH: SARs can be used by human teachers as sophisticated stimuli to multiple levels of cognitive processing in children with learning difficulties (also possibly due to preexisting conditions) toward modifying the processing within those levels by triggering underlying brain compensatory mechanisms and, consequently, improve a child's learning behavior based on education delivery methods alone.

We remark that our long-term objective is to improve the learning capacity of an individual human brain by non-invasive methods, namely by educational methods exclusively.

SARs face challenges different from those faced by social or assistive robots alone. For instance, social or assistive robots alone typically focus on reliability, precision of motion and repeatability since they interact physically with a person, whereas SARs emphasize emotional expressiveness, user engagement, physical appearance and robustness during interaction. The social features of SARs are particularly important because they are expected to support the user by coaching, motivating and directing change.

SARs pose important questions regarding how to design an effective, user-friendly system suitable for STE needs. Note that children with STE are sensitive to novel stimuli and have substantial difficulties with attention and engagement. In particular, SARs for autism must balance between non-threatening, goal-oriented treatment and productive interaction (Scassellati, Admoni, & Matarić, 2012).

Physical Appearance of Robots

The first that captures a user's attention is the robot's physical appearance (Tanaka, Cicourel, & Movellan, 2007). The appearance of SARs may range across many patterns including anthropomorphic, humanoid, animal-like, and non-biological. Due to the shortage of standards, different research groups often propose different robot designs. Nevertheless, in all variations, certain physical appearance standards have been adopted. For instance, a SAR cannot appear both extremely human-like and socially simple. A robot that resembles a human might facilitate the transfer of skills in human-robot interactions (van Straten et al., 2017), whereas a less human-like robot might contain distraction thus helping children focus attention on particular skill learning (Lord, & Bishop, 2010). In this context, of particular interest is the so called "uncanny valley" phenomenon, that is a feeling of unpleasantness and fear emerging in people communicating with robots when the physical attributes of a robot exceed a certain degree of resemblance to the human (Mori, 1970/2012; Dimitrova, & Wagatsuma, 2015).

In addition to the physical appearance, realism can be pursued by varying levels of biological motion. A robot that moves its head (Dachkinov et al., 2019) and/or its arms with multiples degrees of freedom looks more human-like than one that moves solely its arms up and down. The level of the capacity to move is dictated by the goals of human-robot interaction. Note that an increased actuation enables more complex expressions, thus increasing anthropomorphism, whereas a deceased actuation reduces the cost of development but it also simplifies the sophistication of interaction.

Designers must also decide about the extent of a robot ability to move around in its environment. For instance, most robots used in ASD therapy research typically involve motion of their body limbs such as arms and head, but other robots are fixed upright on the floor or on a table (Kozima, Nakagawa, & Yasuda, 2007). More rarely robots can move around freely in their working environment. Mobility allows for a greater flexibility in human-robot interaction by increasing the number as well as the types of collaborative activities that can be carried out. Nevertheless, mobility increases the number of parameters to be controlled during interaction thus increasing technical design difficulties (Michaud et al., 2007).

Children-Robot Interaction

Together with physical appearance, a robot's behavior is also important as to how well it can be accepted by humans as well as how effective it can be during a therapeutic session. Despite variations in robots' physical appearance, all SARs aim at generating therapeutic interactions such as elicitation, coaching, and reinforcement of social behaviors with human users. Human-robot interaction is described by the behaviors produced both by the user and by the robot during a session. The goal of an interaction might be to elicit joint attention, to mediate sharing and turn-taking between the user and others, to encourage imitation, etc. The robot can act as a teacher in an authoritative role, as a toy intending to mediate behaviors, or as a proxy to allow the user express emotions or goals (Scassellati, Admoni, & Matarić,

2012). A superb feature of robots is their capacity for repeatability and work without getting tired or complaining. Since robots do not humiliate or belittle people, it occurs that people in special conditions, e.g. autism, have less anxiety in interacting with robots and they are more willing to participate in learning exercises with robots rather than with humans.

Developing robots that socialize with people for sustained periods of time is technologically demanding (Kanda et al., 2004). Nevertheless, recent years have witnessed progress in this area. For instance, in a recent study, a state-of-the-art social robot was introduced in a classroom of toddlers for more than 5 months with the following results. The quality of the interaction between children and robots improved steadily for 27 sessions; then quickly dropped for 15 sessions when the robot was reprogrammed to behave in a predictable manner and finally it improved in the last three sessions when the robot displayed again its full behavioral repertoire. Note that, initially, the children treated the robot very differently than they treated one another. Application results have also demonstrated that current robot technology is surprisingly close to achieving bonding and socialization with human toddlers for sustained periods of time. More specifically, quantitative behavioral studies have demonstrated that in a period of 5 months, long-term bonding and socialization took place between toddlers and the social robot. Rather than decreasing, the interaction between children and the robot increased over time. In particular, children exhibited a variety of social and care-taking behaviors towards the robot and progressively treated it more as a peer than as a toy (Tanaka, Cicourel, & Movellan, 2007).

As mentioned above, the goal of using robots in STE is to encourage children to both engage and develop social skills. Thus, robots used in therapy are designed to take part in different interaction goals such as attract/maintain attention, evoke joint attention, suggest imitation, facilitate turn-taking, etc. Many studies have reported positive effects regarding robot presence on attention and/or engagement therapy scenarios with children (Barakova et al., 2018; Dautenhahn et al., 2009; Feil-Seifer, & Mataric, 2008; Ferrari, Robins, & Dautenhahn, 2009; Kozima, Nakagawa, & Yasuda, 2007; Michaud, & Caron, 2002; Pioggia et al., 2006). Some research provides evidence that robot behavior must be correlated or depend on the users' actions so as to elicit prolonged engagement (Feil-Seifer, & Mataric, 2008; Goan, Fujii, & Okada, 2006; Stanton et al., 2008), whereas other studies fail to confirm such a connection (Scassellati, 2005). However, any engagement recorded is social in nature, and despite social impairment, children with autism are statistically as engaged as typical children during robot interaction (Kim et al., 2012).

Joint attention is omnipresent in typical human communication and essential for learning collaborative skills (Johnson, & Myers, 2007). Some social robots, such as Keepon and NAO, are programmed toward successively searching for a user's eyes and then for an object thus seeking to engage joint attention. Such behaviors performed by robots are likely to evoke joint attention regarding children with ASD. Many studies confirm that children with autism demonstrate spontaneous joint attention behavior when interacting with a robot, for example when looking to an adult and back to the robot or when pointing to the robot and looking to an adult or to another child with the intention of sharing some feature with that person (Dautenhahn et al., 2009; Ferrari, Robins, & Dautenhahn, 2009; Kozima, Nakagawa, & Yasuda, 2005; Kozima, Nakagawa, & Yasuda, 2007; Pioggia et al., 2006; Robins et al., 2005; Werry et al., 2001). Children display the aforementioned behavior despite their previous tendency of avoiding eye contact and/or any engagement with unknown adults.

Imitation is an additional essential mechanism for learning an appropriate behavior. Children with autism face difficulties to imitate other people's social behavior such as wave hello or goodbye (Williams, Whiten, & Singh, 2004). Imitation seems to arise naturally in many child-robot interactions in STE research. In particular, sometimes the children are encouraged by adults or by a robot to imitate the robot's actions (Duquette, Michaud, & Mercier, 2008; Ferrari, Robins, & Dautenhahn, 2009; Robins et al., 2004; Robins et al., 2005); other times imitation occurs spontaneously and develops into a game with the child imitating the robot's behavior and vice versa (Kozima, Nakagawa, & Yasuda, 2005; Kozima, Nakagawa, & Yasuda, 2007; Robins, Dautenhahn, & Dickerson, 2009).

Turn-taking and sharing introduce challenges during social interactions with children with autism. More specifically, children can learn important life skills through social games that involve turn-taking. Robots by their nature, that renders them more animate than typical toys but less socially complex than humans, can elicit turn-taking with children who tend not to engage easily in such a behavior (Dautenhahn et al., 2009; Kozima, Nakagawa, & Yasuda, 2007; Ferrari, Robins, & Dautenhahn, 2009; Robins et al., 2005). For instance, social robot Kaspar has been employed in a turn-based imitation game that resulted in a sensible interaction between two children with ASD (Robins, Dautenhahn, & Dickerson, 2009).

Roles of the Robot

Robots in STE can assume different roles, even during a single therapy session. For example, a robot can act as a teacher or a leader that guides the interaction, as a toy that responds to the child and mediates social behavior between child and others (Vrochidou et al., 2018), as a peer or a proxy that encourages children to express their emotions and/or desires, etc.

Playing is important for the development of children. Robots designed for therapy are presented to children as toys during special therapy sessions. The fact that robots can capture attention, act autonomously and move distinguishes them from conventional toys. In some cases, robots in STE are combined with conventional toys (Kozima, Nakagawa, & Yasuda, 2007), whereas in other cases they are presented in a free-form play session individually (Feil-Seifer, & Matarić, 2009; Kim et al., 2012; Michaud, & Caron, 2002). Robots can also be engaged as peers of children, especially in imitation games (Duquette, Michaud, & Mercier, 2008; Robins et al., 2004). Recall that joint attention is a context where robots can act as effective social mediators. By extending social mediation further, robots can initiate turn-taking games between children with ASD. For example, researchers have reported the case of a teenager who, although previously could not tolerate another child in any playing activity, he was progressively introduced to a turn-taking imitation game first with his therapist and then with another child (Robins, Dautenhahn, & Dickerson, 2009).

Robots can act as teachers taking the lead and guiding social interactions. A robot can verbally ask a child to carry out certain behaviors such as spinning (Michaud et al., 2005), to guide the child through predefined play scenarios (Duquette, Michaud, & Mercier, 2008; Ferrari, Robins, & Dautenhahn, 2009), or to move autonomously in order to engage the child either in an imitation game (Robins et al., 2005) or in free-play interactions on will (Feil-Seifer, & Matarić, 2011). In most cases, a therapist or teacher instructs a child during interaction sessions with robots by explaining and giving instructions, e.g. "touch the robot" or "imitate the robot's behavior" (Robins et al., 2005; Stanton et al., 2008).

More rarely, robots appear to act as proxies or receptacles of emotions or intentions of children. For instance, Kozima, Nakagawa, & Yasuda (2005) have reported cases where children express emotional behaviors toward a robot in the absence of other people; for example, they hit the robot on the head, they stroke it and/or try to comfort it, they wrap the robot with clothes so that it does not get cold etc.

Introducing robots in entertainment, e.g. in the theater, is a promising alternative toward CPSs for pedagogical rehabilitation in special education that needs to be investigated.

Robot Autonomy

Children with learning difficulties, also due to preexisting conditions, might not behave consistently from day to day. More specifically, a child may be highly engaged one day during a therapy session and distracted the very next day. Therapists are ready to handle changes in a child's behavior, therefore so should robots be, if they are to be engaged constructively in therapy.

Very often robots in therapy are controlled remotely by the so-called Wizard of Oz (WOZ) technique (Kahn et al., 2008). More specifically, a human programmer controls the robot remotely either from a different room or from the same room. The programmer can monitor human-robot interaction via cameras in the room (Kim et al., 2012; Robins et al., 2004) or via cameras mounted on the robot in order to observe the interaction more closely (Kozima, Nakagawa, & Yasuda, 2005). The WOZ technique makes the robot more adaptive in line to the robot's technical capacities. Although WOZ is effective toward quickly introducing robots in complex environments, it is not considered effective for long-term and/or large-scale use. By designing autonomous robots that could interact socially with individuals, researchers hope to achieve a seamless integration of SARs in therapies. Autonomous robots are only partly designed, since it is difficult to design robots that operate adequately in complex, dynamic and unpredictable environments such as those during therapy. Researchers aim at developing robust and flexible robot controls for real-world-applications (Scassellati, Admoni, & Matarić, 2012).

A control architecture, namely B³IA, that is a behavior-based architecture designed to address the challenges of autonomous robots as tools for children with ASD, has been proposed by Feil-Seifer & Mataric (2008). The robots possess an array of capabilities including sensing and interpreting the actions of children, processing of sensed data, evaluating the interaction, and changing the behavior by user-defined parameters. Figure 2 shows a block-diagram of the B³IA architecture, where each module corresponds to one of the capabilities required by an autism intervention robot. The suggested architecture has been implemented successfully on a wheeled, non-humanoid bubble blowing robot and pilot experimental results have demonstrated improvements in the social behavior of children with autism.

Increased robot autonomy is expected to increase the operational capacities of SARs and thus enhance their potential in (special) education applications. One way of increasing robot autonomy is by making a robot more intelligent. The latter can be pursued by effective mathematical models implementable mainly in software. In particular, SARs call for an enhanced mathematical modeling paradigm due to their interaction with humans according to the following rationale.

The operation of conventional, i.e. non-social, robots typically occurs in a physical environment excluding humans and based solely on electronic sensors; hence, numerical models suffice to drive conventional robots. Nevertheless, when humans are involved, non-numerical data emerge such as words. In the latter context, the Lattice Computing (LC) paradigm has been proposed for modeling based on numerical and/or non-numerical data in any combination for social robot applications (CybSPEED, 2017). Recall that LC has been defined as "an evolving collection of tools and methodologies that process lattice ordered data including logic values, numbers, sets, symbols, graphs, etc" (Kaburlasos, & Papakostas, 2015). LC models can rigorously involve numeric data and/or non-numeric data *per se* without transforming one to another. In this manner it also becomes feasible to compute with semantics represented by a partial (lattice) order relation. Trends in LC appear in (dos Santos, & Valle, 2018; Kaburlasos, 2011; Papakostas, & Kaburlasos, 2018; Sussner, & Schuster, 2018; Valle, & Sussner, 2013). LC models are expected to be instrumental in optimal CPS modeling applications because LC models can (1) deal with both numerical data (regarding any physical system component) and non-numerical data (regarding any cyber system

Figure 2. Schematic of (a) the control architecture and (b) the behavior network of architecture B³IA

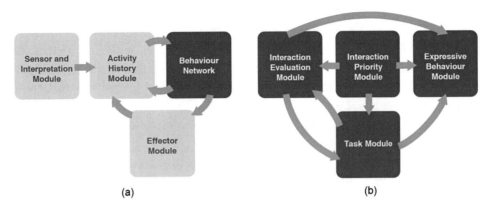

component), (2) compute with semantics, (3) rigorously deal with ambiguity, (4) naturally engage logic and reasoning and (5) process data fast (Papakostas, & Kaburlasos, 2018).

CHALLENGES IN THE STATE-OF-THE-ART

Control architectures for SARs must include sensors as well as efficient software in order to also interpret the intention of children by monitoring them. Sensors could include physiological /biometrics detectors such as blood pressure, pulse, skin conductance and brain activity (Liu et al., 2008) or cameras that detect behavior (Feil-Seifer, & Matarić, 2011). Contact sensors that measure physiological /biometrics data are difficult to apply to people with autism because those people are sensitive to touch; nevertheless, the aforementioned sensors supply more precise information than non-contact sensors.

Interaction with autonomous robots that sense and respond to user behavior is an emerging field of scientific interest (de Haas et al., 2016; Kaburlasos et al., 2018 June). The development of effective robot controls for autism therapy applications might enable consistency of robot behavior, which is important in social assistive applications. Hence, human presence might be restricted, even substantially. Lately, scientific interest focuses on the design of SARs that response to high-level commands, such as verbal commands, from therapists in order to avoid awkward tele-operation of the robot.

In addition to robots that detect and respond to users' actions, an emerging field in robots for STE regards detection of user mood and/or preferences so that robots adapt their behavior in real time accordingly. For instance, a child with sensitivity to bright lights will be negative to therapies involving bright colored videos or images. Human therapists readily recognize and adapt to such circumstances. Robots need also to be flexible likewise during therapies. Significant work is still required before effective / efficient control architectures for autonomous robots are integrated into real-world therapy sessions.

A recent work has proposed a behaviour modulation system for social robots based on emotional speech recognition. In particular, human emotion cues were detected using linguistic features in order to direct the robot towards appropriate behaviours (Lytridis, Vrochidou, & Kaburlasos, 2018). Note that commercial social robots such as NAO have embedded cameras that can detect behaviors; however, the low processing power of commercially available social robots as well as their low-resolution embedded cameras constitute substantial obstacles to overcome for real-time object recognition.

EVALUATION STUDIES

Socially interactive robots can be useful in therapy as well as in special education for a number of reasons (Boucenna et al., 2014). For instance, it might be easier for children with STE needs to interact with robots rather than with humans because robots are less complex yet they are controllably sophisticated enough so as to provide sensory stimuli toward enabling embodied interactions that are appealing to children (Scassellati, Admoni, & Matarić, 2012). Note that Thill et al. (2012) suggest that robots need to be applied in a controlled manner such that only relevant information is presented to the users, furthermore robots are better than people in endless repetition.

Scassellati, Admoni, & Matarić (2012) report encouraging results when children interact with robots regarding engagement, level of attention and novel social behaviors including joint attention and imitation. Cabibihan et al. (2013) present a number of benefits and roles that robots could have; these roles range from friend to therapist. Another study identifies four roles for the interactive robots in clinical applications (Aresti-Bartolome, & Garcia-Zapirain, 2014). More specifically, robots are used to (1) investigate robot-like behavior of children with STE in comparison to human behavior, (2) elicit behaviors, (3) model, teach or practice a skill, and (4) provide feedback on performance. Although most studies report positive effects regarding the use of robots in STE, it is also demonstrated that not all children can benefit from robotic support or can perform better than with a human (Diehl et al., 2012). Mixed results and variability in the nature of affective response is also reported (Kahn et al., 2008).

Regarding teacher acceptance of robots in STE, a recent study (Fridin, & Belokopytov, 2014) indicates that teachers in pre-schools and elementary schools accept the use of a humanoid robot as an interactive tool in the teaching process. Other studies (Costescu, & David, 2014; Oros et al., 2014) report a positive attitude towards the use of robots in (psycho) therapy and education, considering them as useful and potentially effective tools in STE. Recent survey results seem to encourage the joint engagement of robots and information technologies (Kostova et al., 2018). Despite the promising results, the actual current state of the application of robots in STE is still in early stages. More research is required to comprehend the clinical effects as well as the added value of robots in therapy and education. Note that a review by Diehl et al. (2012) has concluded that many studies are explorative; they also have methodological limitations and do not focus on the clinical application of technology. The exploration of robot-based autism interventions is more directed to clinical or to therapy applications, and less to educational applications where children might also benefit from the use of robots for education delivery (Shamsuddin et al., 2015).

POTENTIAL FUTURE RESEARCH

Future advances regarding SARs in education applications call for improvements in both hardware and software as explained next. Currently, there are many open-source projects that can help beginners to get started. A number of open-source hardware platforms (Sparki, Hexy, OpenPilot, Arduipilot, TurtleBot etc.) and open-source software projects (LeJOS, Rock, ROS etc.) already exist and can support robotic research, education and product development (Pachidis et al., 2018).

On one hand, effective hardware design calls for the following specifications: (1) low cost in order to support the pedagogical model of one robot per student, (2) versatility so as to support a variety of curricula, i.e. engage an array of sensors for a broader range of applications, and (3) usability so as the robot has a simple, easy-to-explain design. Design is often the last consideration when incorporating robots in an application; yet studies indicate that the design can make the difference regarding robot acceptance and encourage children participation. Due to the shortage of commercially available robot platforms for education, many research groups design their own robots. Note that most of the reported bibliography applications use either Lego in typical education applications or NAO in special education applications. On the other hand, effective software design needs to support several development environments from block programming to script (Barakova et al., 2013). Furthermore, the software, that is the principal means for making a SAR more intelligent, should support innovative teaching and therapeutic methodologies transferable across geographical and cultural regions. The design of complex activities for a robot to perform cannot be easily supported by current robot intelligence (Serholt, 2018). There is a need to increase SAR intelligence. In the latter context, the aforementioned LC (information processing) paradigm emerges promising according to the following rationale.

Conventional robot interaction applications with the physical environment are typically pursued based on a 3D digital representation of the physical environment induced from measurements. Likewise, we suggest SAR interaction with a human based on a (structured) lattice data representation of a human's "world model" of perceptions induced likewise from measurements. Note that a number of techniques for inducing lattice-ordered representations of perceptions/concepts has already been presented in the context of Formal Concept Analysis (Ganter, & Wille, 1999). Furthermore, recent work has considered the potential of representing psychological "gestalts" by lattice elements in social robot applications regarding autism treatment (Kaburlasos et al., 2018 January). What might be important is to further associate abstract notions of the human mind with specific brain activity patterns as well as with human behavior as shown in Figure 3. For simplicity here by "Mind" we mean a set of computer algorithms that process information, by "Brain" we mean a set of neurophysiology equations that describe brain activity, whereas by "Behavior" we mean a set of valid descriptions from human psychology – Note that Behavior could be as simple as eye blinking or gaze etc. In any case, lattice-order isomorphisms between Mind, Brain and Behavior are especially meaningful (Kaburlasos, 2004). Furthermore, LC models could be used inside the Mind /Brain /Behavior blocks according to the needs. It is understood that Figure 3 may raise ontological-, philosophical- as well as practical implementation questions which we ignore here. In particular, here we simply assume all the required mathematical functions. Apparently, any implementation of the scheme in Figure 3 calls for interdisciplinary collaboration.

Figure 3 might also be a guideline for developing algorithms toward sharing (subjective) value systems such as intensions (Okanoya, 2018). Recall that the LC paradigm lends itself for developing algorithms that compute with semantics instead of computing solely by number crunching. In addition, due to the inherent hierarchy of lattice-ordered data, a learning algorithm in the LC paradigm has the potential for inducing structures in its application environment be it language, or emotions, etc.

A convenient starting point can be electroencephalography (EEG) signals. For example, Figure 4 shows EEG signals from the UCI repository of machine learning databases (Dua, & Karra Taniskidou, 2017) – This particular data arose from a study that examines EEG correlates of genetic predisposition to alcoholism. It contains measurements from 64 electrodes placed on the scalp sampled at 256 Hz. In particular, Figure 4 shows example plots of a control (i.e., non-alcoholic) subjects; the plots indicate voltage, time, and channel and are averaged over 10 trials for the single stimulus condition.

It is understood that EEG signals record, quite restrictively, integrated neuron activity in selected points on the surface of the brain, therefore EEG signals might miss subtle brain activity patterns. Nevertheless, in carefully designed experiments, EEG signals could provide initial evidence that abstract notions may be associated with specific brain activity patterns. In the aforementioned context, lattice-ordered

Figure 3. Pair-wise interactions, tentatively designed analytically by Lattice Computing (LC) techniques, between Mind, Brain and Behavior might drive social robots

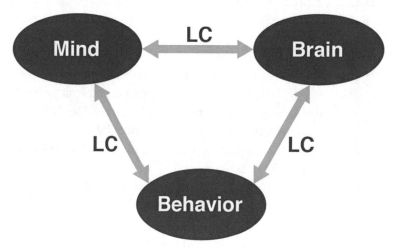

Intervals' Numbers (INs) (Kaburlasos, & Papakostas, 2015) might be useful for representing EEG big data patterns; furthermore, deep learning can be pursued based on several layers of IN processing.

Recall that our objective here is to change the brain toward improving its capacity according to the Working Hypothesis WH that is by educational methods alone without resorting to any surgery and/ or medicament. Substantial preliminary work needs to be carried out toward providing clear evidence regarding any utility of Social Robots in (special) education as described next.

Large numbers of brain activity (response) patterns need to be matched painstakingly to the content of (evoking) "story telling" by a human narrator; the latter data are to be used as the Control Group in a number of statistical hypothesis testing experiments. Then, additional brain activity patterns should be recorded likewise by a programmable robot narrator; the latter data are to be used as the Treatment Group in the aforementioned statistical experiments toward identifying specific advantages of social robots in (special) education. For example, Figure 5 proposes tentatively a closed-loop control scheme as an implementation of educational scenarios. Recall that a Social Robot is to be employed as a sophisticated stimulus of the Mind toward changing the Brain and, ultimately, toward changing the Behavior of a human student by educational methods alone. Note that all previous explanations hold even after dropping the "Brain" block either in Figure 3 or in Figure 5. Nevertheless, the engagement of brain signals is expected to increase the robustness of information processing.

CONCLUSION

This paper has described the potential of Social Assistive Robots (SARs) applications in pedagogical rehabilitation. SARs were presented as a subset of the more general and rapidly emerging technology of social robots. Moreover, pedagogical rehabilitation was presented as a specific domain in the more general framework of special education. Trends have been outlined.

Figure 4. EEG signals in 64 channels averaged over 10 trials
(Dua, & Karra Taniskidou, 2017)

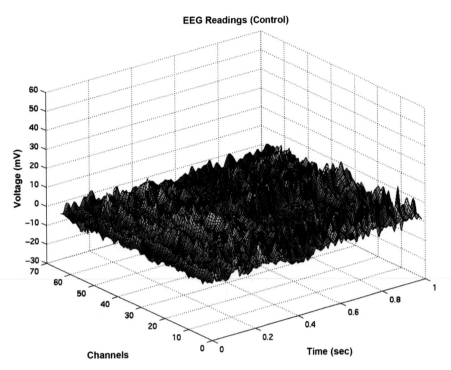

Figure 5. A tentative implementation of educational scenarios

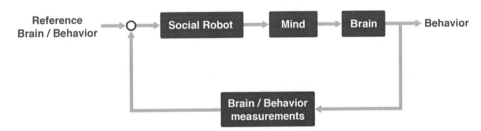

Central in this paper has been the Working Hypothesis WH, which can be summarized as follows: SARs can be used as sophisticated stimuli to multiple levels of cognitive processing in children with learning difficulties toward modifying the cognitive processing, by triggering underlying brain's compensatory mechanisms, and improve a child's learning behavior based on education delivery methods alone.

Apart from improved hardware, the effectiveness of future SARs in pedagogical rehabilitation also depends on improved (intelligent) software. In turn, since the software typically implements mathematical models, effective mathematical modeling techniques are required. In this paper we proposed using models from the Lattice Computing (LC) information processing paradigm toward also computing with semantics represented by partial (lattice) order relation. Future work calls for systematic experimental testing toward demonstrating the validity of specific hypotheses.

ACKNOWLEDGMENT

This project has received funding from the European Union's Horizon 2020 research and innovation programme under the Marie Skłodowska-Curie grant agreement No 777720. The contribution of author Vassilis Kaburlasos was made while he was on a secondment in the Graduate School of Life Science and System Engineering of Kyushu Institute of Technology at Hibikino, Japan during July and August 2018.

REFERENCES

Amanatiadis, A., Kaburlasos, V. G., Dardani, C., & Chatzichristofis, S. A. (2017, September). Interactive social robots in special education. In *2017 IEEE 7th International Conference on Consumer Electronics-Berlin (ICCE-Berlin)* (pp. 126-129). IEEE. 10.1109/ICCE-Berlin.2017.8210609

Aresti-Bartolome, N., & Garcia-Zapirain, B. (2014). Technologies as support tools for persons with autistic spectrum disorder: A systematic review. *International Journal of Environmental Research and Public Health*, *11*(8), 7767–7802. doi:10.3390/ijerph110807767 PMID:25093654

Barakova, E. I., De Haas, M., Kuijpers, W., Irigoyen, N., & Betancourt, A. (2018). Socially grounded game strategy enhances bonding and perceived smartness of a humanoid robot. *Connection Science*, *30*(1), 81–98. doi:10.1080/09540091.2017.1350938

Barakova, E. I., Gillesena, J. C. C., Huskens, B. E. B. M., & Lourens, T. (2013). End-user programming architecture facilitates the uptake of robots in social therapies. *Robotics and Autonomous Systems*, *61*(7), 704–713. doi:10.1016/j.robot.2012.08.001

Boucenna, S., Narzisi, A., Tilmont, E., Muratori, F., Pioggia, G., Cohen, D., & Chetouani, M. (2014). Interactive technologies for autistic children: A review. *Cognitive Computation*, *6*(4), 722–740. doi:10.100712559-014-9276-x

Cabibihan, J. J., Javed, H., Ang, M., & Aljunied, S. M. (2013). Why robots? A survey on the roles and benefits of social robots in the therapy of children with autism. *International Journal of Social Robotics*, *5*(4), 593–618. doi:10.100712369-013-0202-2

Cortiella, C., & Horowitz, S. H. (2014). *The state of learning disabilities: Facts, trends and emerging issues*. New York: National Center for Learning Disabilities.

Costescu, C. A., & David, D. O. (2014). Attitudes toward Using Social Robots in Psychotherapy. *Transylvanian Journal of Psychology, 15*(1).

CybSPEED. (2017). *Cyber-Physical Systems for PEdagogical Rehabilitation in Special EDucation*. Horizon 2020 MSCA-RISE Project no. 777720, 1 Dec 2017 – 30 Nov 2021.

Dachkinov, P., Lekova, A., Tanev, T., Batbaatar, D., & Wagatsuma, H. (2019). Design and Motion Capabilities of an Emotion-Expressive Robot, "EmoSan". *Proceedings of the Joint 10th International Conference on Soft Computing and Intelligent Systems (SCIS) and 19th International Symposium on Advanced Intelligent Systems (ISIS) in conjunction with Intelligent Systems Workshop (ISWS)*.

Dautenhahn, K., Nehaniv, C. L., Walters, M. L., Robins, B., Kose-Bagci, H., Mirza, N. A., & Blow, M. (2009). KASPAR–a minimally expressive humanoid robot for human–robot interaction research. *Applied Bionics and Biomechanics*, *6*(3-4), 369–397. doi:10.1155/2009/708594

de Haas, M., Aroyo, A. M., Barakova, E., Haselager, W., & Smeekens, I. (2016). The effect of a semi-autonomous robot on children. In *Intelligent Systems (IS), 2016 IEEE 8th International Conference on* (pp. 376-381). IEEE. 10.1109/IS.2016.7737448

Diehl, J. J., Schmitt, L. M., Villano, M., & Crowell, C. R. (2012). The clinical use of robots for individuals with autism spectrum disorders: A critical review. *Research in Autism Spectrum Disorders*, *6*(1), 249–262. doi:10.1016/j.rasd.2011.05.006 PMID:22125579

Dimitrova, M., & Wagatsuma, H. (2015). Designing Humanoid Robots with Novel Roles and Social Abilities. *Lovotics*, *3*(112), 2.

dos Santos, A. S., & Valle, M. E. (2018). Max-plus and min-plus projection autoassociative morphological memories and their compositions for pattern classification. *Neural Networks*, *100*, 84–94. doi:10.1016/j.neunet.2018.01.013 PMID:29477916

Dua, D., & Karra Taniskidou, E. (2017). *UCI Machine Learning Repository*. Irvine, CA: University of California, School of Information and Computer Science.

Duquette, A., Michaud, F., & Mercier, H. (2008). Exploring the use of a mobile robot as an imitation agent with children with low-functioning autism. *Autonomous Robots*, *24*(2), 147–157. doi:10.100710514-007-9056-5

Eurobarometer, S. (2012). *382 'Public Attitudes Towards Robots'*. Academic Press.

Feil-Seifer, D., & Mataric, M. J. (2008). B 3 IA: A control architecture for autonomous robot-assisted behavior intervention for children with Autism Spectrum Disorders. In *Robot and Human Interactive Communication, 2008. RO-MAN 2008. The 17th IEEE International Symposium on* (pp. 328-333). Academic Press.

Feil-Seifer, D., & Matarić, M. J. (2009). Toward socially assistive robotics for augmenting interventions for children with autism spectrum disorders. In *Experimental robotics* (pp. 201–210). Berlin: Springer. doi:10.1007/978-3-642-00196-3_24

Feil-Seifer, D., & Matarić, M. J. (2011). Automated detection and classification of positive vs. negative robot interactions with children with autism using distance-based features. In *Human-Robot Interaction (HRI), 2011 6th ACM/IEEE International Conference on* (pp. 323-330). ACM. 10.1145/1957656.1957785

Ferrari, E., Robins, B., & Dautenhahn, K. (2009). Therapeutic and educational objectives in robot assisted play for children with autism. In *Robot and Human Interactive Communication, 2009. RO-MAN 2009. The 18th IEEE International Symposium on* (pp. 108-114). IEEE. 10.1109/ROMAN.2009.5326251

Fong, T., Nourbakhsh, I., & Dautenhahn, K. (2003). A survey of socially interactive robots. *Robotics and Autonomous Systems*, *42*(3), 143–166. doi:10.1016/S0921-8890(02)00372-X

Fridin, M., & Belokopytov, M. (2014). Acceptance of socially assistive humanoid robot by preschool and elementary school teachers. *Computers in Human Behavior*, *33*, 23–31. doi:10.1016/j.chb.2013.12.016

Ganter, B., & Wille, R. (1999). *Formal Concept Analysis*. Heidelberg, Germany: Springer. doi:10.1007/978-3-642-59830-2

Goan, M., Fujii, H., & Okada, M. (2006). Child–robot interaction mediated by building blocks: From field observations in a public space. *Artificial Life and Robotics*, *10*(1), 45–48. doi:10.100710015-005-0375-3

Johnson, C. P., & Myers, S. M. (2007). Identification and evaluation of children with autism spectrum disorders. *Pediatrics*, *120*(5), 1183–1215. doi:10.1542/peds.2007-2361 PMID:17967920

Jordan, R. (2013). *Autistic spectrum disorders: an introductory handbook for practitioners*. Routledge. doi:10.4324/9780203827352

Kaburlasos, V., Bazinas, C., Siavalas, G., & Papakostas, G. A. (2018, June). Linguistic social robot control by crowd-computing feedback. In *Proceedings of the 2018 JSME Conference on Robotics and Mechatronics*. Academic Press. 10.1299/jsmermd.2018.1A1-B13

Kaburlasos, V. G. (2004). A device for linking brain to mind based on lattice theory. In *Proceedings of the 8th International Conference on Cognitive and Neural Systems (ICCNS 2004)*. Boston University.

Kaburlasos, V. G. (2011). Special issue on: Information engineering applications based on lattices. *Information Sciences*, *181*(10), 1771–1773. doi:10.1016/j.ins.2011.01.016

Kaburlasos, V. G., Dardani, C., Dimitrova, M., & Amanatiadis, A. (2018, January). Multi-robot engagement in special education: a preliminary study in autism. In *2018 IEEE International Conference on Consumer Electronics (ICCE)* (pp. 1-2). IEEE. 10.1109/ICCE.2018.8326267

Kaburlasos, V. G., & Papakostas, G. A. (2015). Learning distributions of image features by interactive fuzzy lattice reasoning in pattern recognition applications. *IEEE Computational Intelligence Magazine*, *10*(3), 42–51. doi:10.1109/MCI.2015.2437318

Kahn, P. H., Freier, N. G., Kanda, T., Ishiguro, H., Ruckert, J. H., Severson, R. L., & Kane, S. K. (2008). Design patterns for sociality in human-robot interaction. In *Proceedings of the 3rd ACM/IEEE international conference on Human robot interaction* (pp. 97-104). ACM. 10.1145/1349822.1349836

Kanda, T., Hirano, T., Eaton, D., & Ishiguro, H. (2004). Interactive robots as social partners and peer tutors for children: A field trial. *Human-Computer Interaction*, *19*(1), 61–84. doi:10.120715327051hci1901&2_4

Kanda, T., Miyashita, T., Osada, T., Haikawa, Y., & Ishiguro, H. (2008). Analysis of humanoid appearances in human–robot interaction. *IEEE Transactions on Robotics*, *24*(3), 725–735. doi:10.1109/TRO.2008.921566

Kim, E., Paul, R., Shic, F., & Scassellati, B. (2012). *Bridging the research gap: Making HRI useful to individuals with autism*. Academic Press.

Kirk, S., Gallagher, J. J., Coleman, M. R., & Anastasiow, N. J. (2011). *Educating exceptional children*. Cengage Learning.

Kostova, S., Dimitrova, M. I., Saeva, S., Zamfirov, M., Kaburlasos, V., Vrochidou, E., ... Papić, V. (2018). Identifying needs of robotic and technological solutions for the classroom. *Proceedings of the 26th International Conference on Software, Telecommunications and Computer Networks (SoftCOM 2018), Symposium on: Robotic and ICT assisted wellbeing.* 10.23919/SOFTCOM.2018.8555751

Kozima, H., Nakagawa, C., & Yasuda, Y. (2005). Interactive robots for communication-care: A case-study in autism therapy. In *Robot and human interactive communication, 2005. ROMAN 2005. IEEE International Workshop on* (pp. 341-346). IEEE. 10.1109/ROMAN.2005.1513802

Kozima, H., Nakagawa, C., & Yasuda, Y. (2007). Children–robot interaction: A pilot study in autism therapy. *Progress in Brain Research, 164,* 385–400. doi:10.1016/S0079-6123(07)64021-7 PMID:17920443

Liu, C., Conn, K., Sarkar, N., & Stone, W. (2008). Online affect detection and robot behavior adaptation for intervention of children with autism. *IEEE Transactions on Robotics, 24*(4), 883–896. doi:10.1109/TRO.2008.2001362

Lord, C., & Bishop, S. L. (2010). Autism Spectrum Disorders: Diagnosis, Prevalence, and Services for Children and Families. *Social Policy Report, 24*(2). doi:10.1002/j.2379-3988.2010.tb00063.x

Lytridis, C., Vrochidou, E., Chatzistamatis, S., & Kaburlasos, V. G. (2018). Social engagement interaction games between children with autism and humanoid robot NAO. In *Proceedings of the 9th International Conference on EUropean Transnational Educational.* Springer.

Lytridis, C., Vrochidou, E., & Kaburlasos, V. G. (2018). Emotional Speech Recognition toward Modulating the Behavior of a Social Robot. *Proceedings of the 2018 JSME Conference on Robotics and Mechatronics.* 10.1299/jsmermd.2018.1A1-B14

Martyn Cooper, D. K., & William Harwin, K. D. (1999). Robots in the classroom-tools for accessible education. *Assistive Technology on the Threshold of the New Millennium, 6,* 448.

Meijer, C. J., Soriano, V., & Watkins, A. (Eds.). (2003). *Special needs education in Europe: Thematic publication.* European Agency for Development in Special Needs Education.

Michaud, F., & Caron, S. (2002). Roball, the rolling robot. *Autonomous Robots, 12*(2), 211–222. doi:10.1023/A:1014005728519

Michaud, F., Laplante, J. F., Larouche, H., Duquette, A., Caron, S., Létourneau, D., & Masson, P. (2005). Autonomous spherical mobile robot for child-development studies. *IEEE Transactions on Systems, Man, and Cybernetics. Part A, Systems and Humans, 35*(4), 471–480. doi:10.1109/TSMCA.2005.850596

Michaud, F., Salter, T., Duquette, A., Mercier, H., Lauria, M., Larouche, H., & Larose, F. (2007). Assistive technologies and child-robot interaction. AAAI spring symposium on multidisciplinary collaboration for socially assistive robotics.

Miller, G., Church, R., & Trexler, M. (2000). *Teaching diverse learners using robotics.* Morgan Kaufmann.

Moon, A., Danielson, P., & Van der Loos, H. M. (2012). Survey-based discussions on morally contentious applications of interactive robotics. *International Journal of Social Robotics*, 4(1), 77–96. doi:10.100712369-011-0120-0

Mori, M. (1970/2012). The uncanny valley (K. F. MacDorman & N. Kageki, Trans.). *IEEE Robotics & Automation Magazine*, 19(2), 98–100. doi:10.1109/MRA.2012.2192811

Norwich, B. (2007). *Dilemmas of difference, inclusion and disability: International perspectives and future directions.* Routledge. doi:10.4324/9780203938867

Oros, M., Nikolić, M., Borovac, B., & Jerković, I. (2014). Children's preference of appearance and parents' attitudes towards assistive robots. In *Humanoid Robots (Humanoids), 2014 14th IEEE-RAS International Conference on* (pp. 360-365). IEEE.

Pachidis, T., Vrochidou, E., Kaburlasos, V. G., Kostova, S., Bonković, M., & Papić, V. (2018). Social Robotics in Education: State-of-the-Art and Directions. *Proceedings of the 27th International Conference on Robotics in Alpe-Adria-Danube Region.*

Papakostas, G., Sidiropoulos, G., Bella, M., & Kaburlasos, V. (2018). Social robots in special education: current status and future challenges. *Proceedings of the 2018 JSME Conference on Robotics and Mechatronics.* 10.1299/jsmermd.2018.1P1-A15

Papakostas, G. A., & Kaburlasos, V. G. (2018). Modeling in cyber-physical systems by lattice computing techniques: the case of image watermarking based on intervals' numbers. *Proceedings of the World Congress on Computational Intelligence (WCCI) 2018, FUZZ-IEEE Program,* 491-496. 10.1109/FUZZ-IEEE.2018.8491653

Pastor, P. N., & Reuben, C. A. (2008). Diagnosed Attention Deficit Hyperactivity Disorder and Learning Disability: United States, 2004-2006. Data from the National Health Interview Survey. Vital and Health Statistics. Series 10, Number 237. Centers for Disease Control and Prevention.

Pioggia, G., Ferro, M., Sica, M. L., Dalle Mura, G., Casalini, S., De Rossi, D., & Muratori, F. (2006). Imitation and learning of the emotional behaviour: towards an android-based treatment for people with autism. In *Proc. Sixth Int. Workshop Epigenet. Robot.* (pp. 119-25). Lund, Sweden: LUCS.

Robins, B., Dautenhahn, K., & Dickerson, P. (2009). From isolation to communication: a case study evaluation of robot assisted play for children with autism with a minimally expressive humanoid robot. In *Advances in Computer-Human Interactions, 2009. ACHI'09. Second International Conferences on* (pp. 205-211). Academic Press. 10.1109/ACHI.2009.32

Robins, B., Dautenhahn, K., Te Boekhorst, R., & Billard, A. (2004). Effects of repeated exposure to a humanoid robot on children with autism. *Designing a more inclusive world*, 225-236.

Robins, B., Dautenhahn, K., Te Boekhorst, R., & Billard, A. (2005). Robotic assistants in therapy and education of children with autism: Can a small humanoid robot help encourage social interaction skills? *Universal Access in the Information Society*, 4(2), 105–120. doi:10.100710209-005-0116-3

Scassellati, B. (2005). Quantitative metrics of social response for autism diagnosis. In *Robot and Human Interactive Communication, 2005. ROMAN 2005. IEEE International Workshop on* (pp. 585-590). IEEE. 10.1109/ROMAN.2005.1513843

Scassellati, B., Admoni, H., & Matarić, M. (2012). Robots for use in autism research. *Annual Review of Biomedical Engineering, 14*(1), 275–294. doi:10.1146/annurev-bioeng-071811-150036 PMID:22577778

Serholt, S. (2018). Breakdowns in children's interactions with a robotic tutor: A longitudinal study. *Computers in Human Behavior, 81*, 250–264. doi:10.1016/j.chb.2017.12.030

Serpanos, D. (2018). The Cyber-Physical Systems Revolution. *Computer, 51*(3), 70–73. doi:10.1109/MC.2018.1731058

Shamsuddin, S., Yussof, H., Hanapiah, F. A., Mohamed, S., Jamil, N. F. F., & Yunus, F. W. (2015). Robot-assisted learning for communication-care in autism intervention. In *Rehabilitation Robotics (ICORR), 2015 IEEE International Conference on* (pp. 822-827). IEEE. 10.1109/ICORR.2015.7281304

Smith, P. (2007). Have we made any progress? Including students with intellectual disabilities in regular education classrooms. *Intellectual and Developmental Disabilities, 45*(5), 297–309. doi:10.1352/0047-6765(2007)45[297:HWMAPI]2.0.CO;2 PMID:17887907

Special Needs Education. (2012). European Agency for Development for Special Needs and Inclusive Education. Country Data.

Stanton, C. M., Kahn, P. H., Severson, R. L., Ruckert, J. H., & Gill, B. T. (2008). Robotic animals might aid in the social development of children with autism. In *Human-Robot Interaction (HRI), 2008 3rd ACM/IEEE International Conference on* (pp. 271-278). ACM. 10.1145/1349822.1349858

Sussner, P., & Schuster, T. (2018). Interval-valued fuzzy morphological associative memories: Some theoretical aspects and applications. *Information Sciences, 438*, 127–144. doi:10.1016/j.ins.2018.01.042

Tanaka, F., Cicourel, A., & Movellan, J. R. (2007). Socialization between toddlers and robots at an early childhood education center. *Proceedings of the National Academy of Sciences of the United States of America, 104*(46), 17954–17958. doi:10.1073/pnas.0707769104 PMID:17984068

Thill, S., Pop, C. A., Belpaeme, T., Ziemke, T., & Vanderborght, B. (2012). Robot-assisted therapy for autism spectrum disorders with (partially) autonomous control: Challenges and outlook. *Paladyn: Journal of Behavioral Robotics, 3*(4), 209–217. doi:10.247813230-013-0107-7

Ueyama, Y. (2015). A bayesian model of the uncanny valley effect for explaining the effects of therapeutic robots in autism spectrum disorder. *PLoS One, 10*(9), e0138642. doi:10.1371/journal.pone.0138642 PMID:26389805

UNESCO. (1994). *World Conference on Special Needs Education: Access and Quality*. The Salamanca Statement. Retrieved from http://www.unesco.org/new/en/social-and-human-sciences/themes/

Valle, M. E., & Sussner, P. (2013). Quantale-based autoassociative memories with an application to the storage of color images. *Pattern Recognition Letters, 34*(14), 1589–1601. doi:10.1016/j.patrec.2013.03.034

van Straten, C. L., Smeekens, I., Barakova, E., Glennon, J., Buitelaar, J., & Chen, A. (2017). Effects of robots' intonation and bodily appearance on robot-mediated communicative treatment outcomes for children with autism spectrum disorder. *Personal and Ubiquitous Computing*, 1–12.

Vrochidou, E., Najoua, A., Lytridis, C., Salonidis, M., Ferelis, V., & Papakostas, G. A. (2018). Social Robot NAO as a self-regulating didactic mediator: a case study of teaching/learning numeracy. *Proceedings of the 26th International Conference on Software, Telecommunications and Computer Networks (SoftCOM 2018), Symposium on: Robotic and ICT assisted wellbeing*. 10.23919/SOFTCOM.2018.8555764

Werry, I., Dautenhahn, K., Ogden, B., & Harwin, W. (2001). Can social interaction skills be taught by a social agent? The role of a robotic mediator in autism therapy. *Cognitive technology: instruments of mind*, 57-74.

Williams, J. H., Whiten, A., & Singh, T. (2004). A systematic review of action imitation in autistic spectrum disorder. *Journal of Autism and Developmental Disorders*, *34*(3), 285–299. doi:10.1023/B:JADD.0000029551.56735.3a PMID:15264497

ADDITIONAL READING

Amanatiadis, A., Gasteratos, A., Papadakis, S., & Kaburlasos, V. (2010). Image stabilization in active robot vision. In *Robot Vision*. InTech. doi:10.5772/9298

Barakova, E. I., Bajracharya, P., Willemsen, M., Lourens, T., & Huskens, B. (2015). Long-term LEGO therapy with humanoid robot for children with ASD. *Expert Systems: International Journal of Knowledge Engineering and Neural Networks*, *32*(6), 698–709. doi:10.1111/exsy.12098

Dimitrova, M., Lekova, A., Chavdarov, I., Kostova, S., Krastev, A., Roumenin, C., . . . Pachidis, T. A. (2016). Multidisciplinary Framework for Blending Robotics in Education of Children with Special Learning Needs. In *Proceedings of the International Association for Blended Learning Conference (IABL 2016)*, Kavala, Greece, 22-24 April 2016, pp. 152-155.

Dimitrova, M., Vegt, N., & Barakova, E. (2012). Designing a system of interactive robots for training collaborative skills to autistic children. In *Interactive Collaborative Learning (ICL), 2012 15th International Conference on* (pp. 1-8). 10.1109/ICL.2012.6402179

Gillesen, J. C., Barakova, E. I., Huskens, B. E., & Feijs, L. M. (2011). From training to robot behavior: Towards custom scenarios for robotics in training programs for ASD. In *Rehabilitation Robotics (ICORR), 2011 IEEE International Conference on* (pp. 1-7).

Huskens, B., Verschuur, R., Gillesen, J., Didden, R., & Barakova, E. (2013). Promoting question-asking in school-aged children with autism spectrum disorders: Effectiveness of a robot intervention compared to a human-trainer intervention. *Developmental Neurorehabilitation*, *16*(5), 345–356. doi:10.3109/17518423.2012.739212 PMID:23586852

Mwangi, E. N., Barakova, E. I., Díaz, M., Mallofré, A. C., & Rauterberg, M. (2017). Who is a better tutor?: gaze hints with a human or humanoid tutor in game play. In *Proceedings of the Companion of the 2017 ACM/IEEE International Conference on Human-Robot Interaction* (pp. 219-220). ACM.

KEY TERMS AND DEFINITIONS

Autism: An early childhood mental condition, characterized by difficulty in communication, in forming relations with others and in using language and abstract concepts.

Educational Robotics: Robots provided to facilitate student's development of knowledge, skills, and attitudes.

Human-Robot Interaction: Is the study of interaction between humans as a multidisciplinary field with contributions from human-computer interaction, artificial intelligence, design and social sciences.

Robot Autonomy: The ability of a robot to possess the necessary computational resources when functioning, in terms of hardware and software, so as to be physically embedded in the environment.

SEN: Special education needs refer to people who have learning difficulties or disabilities that makes it harder for them to learn than most people of the same age, which calls for special educational provision.

Social Robots: Is a robot that interacts and communicates with humans by following social behaviors and rules attached to its role.

STE: Special treatment and education is defined as the treatment and education of students with special educational needs in a way that addresses their individual differences.

Chapter 2
Addressing Special Educational Needs in Classroom With Cyber Physical Systems

Aneta Petrova Atanasova
Sofia University "St. Kliment Ohridski", Bulgaria

Aleksandra Ivaylova Yosifova
New Bulgarian University, Bulgaria

ABSTRACT

The focus of the current chapter is on humanoid robots as part of inclusive education. The investigation of the perception of and attitude of children and teachers to the application of cyber physical systems in education is essential. The data of a survey of the perception and attitude to the application of cyber physical systems in education of teachers and students from several Bulgarian schools are currently being examined. The attitude of teachers in the current study towards robots is positive. The attitude of students is rather neutral, and the difference between the two populations is statistically significant. Both teachers and students think of the robot as of a humanoid, capable of expression emotions. There is no difference between the attitudes towards the role and appearance of the robot of boys and girls. However, older children demonstrate a more negative attitude than younger children.

INTRODUCTION

The focus of the current chapter is on humanoid robots as part of inclusive education. The field of CPS in the form of socially assistive robots in education is developing quickly. Although still practically non-existing, this seems to be the natural course of events, considering the fast development of technology and its application in education and therapy. Efforts in the fields of mainstream education and assistive therapy have already been made and the results are promising. Robots could support the learning of children (Kory Westlund et al. 2017), personalize it to their needs (Leyzberg et al. 2014) and reduce the teachers' workload (Movellan et al. 2005). However, thorough research is necessary before the application of CPS with SEN children in schools.

DOI: 10.4018/978-1-5225-7879-6.ch002

Children With Special Educational Needs (SEN)

The integration of children with special educational needs (SEN) and the creation of appropriate, accepting and supportive environment is one of the main challenges in the contemporary educational system.

The main groups of SEN include autistic spectrum disorder (ASD), dyslexia, physical disability, hearing and vision impairment, hyperactivity, and intellectual disability. The specific characteristics of each condition require modification of the learning environment and teaching methods in order to meet the needs of the child.

Autistic Spectrum Disorder (ASD)

ASD is a neurodevelopmental disorder which impairs the social communication skills of the children. The number of children with autism has increased significantly during the last few years. Respectively – so did the need to find appropriate ways for them to be included in the educational process. ASD is a condition, which continues throughout the whole lifespan of the person. It is characterised by the typical specifics and the necessity to apply the appropriate intervention at every age. The stage of school education represents a great challenge to children with autism due to the need to cope with a variety of demands. The typical difficulties experienced by children with ASD in school include discomfort from physical stimuli in the environment, such as noise, light, temperature. The understanding of the group norms and social rules of conduct could also be a challenge. In addition, children with autism do not follow/ imitate others spontaneously; often fail to understand that the instructions of the teacher apply to them. Some peculiarities in eye contact (inability to maintain appropriate eye contact, the predominant use of peripheral sight, etc.) are typical for people with ASD. It is possible that some children with autism prefer to be left alone, while others insist to be part of the group but are unable to achieve that. In many cases it is difficult for them to control their emotions and behaviour. They could have ritualised behaviour, characterised by repetitive movement of parts of or the whole body and manipulation of objects. These challenges could be addressed by following a consistent, clearly structured visual program and regular reminding of the order of the daily responsibilities.

The structured behavioural programme, based on ABA (Applied Behavioural Analysis), is usually applied by therapists trained in the work with children with ASD. Its aim typically includes the training of certain capabilities, such as social skills (Reid, Lannen & Lannen, 2016). Some aspects of the behavioural programme, designed for concrete children with autism, could be applied with the assistance of a robot. The programme requires the representation of the target skills in small chunks. For example, the child needs to tell his/her name, age, address and receives a reinforcement for every right response. Common social situations and the accompanying conversations could also be trained with the help of a robot. Examples of such situations are borrowing books from the library, buying food for lunch or stationery from the bookshop.

Attention Deficit Hyperactivity Disorder (ADHD)

ADHD is a neurodevelopmental disorder associated with difficulties in concentration, attention, impulsivity and inhibition of undesirable behavior. Remaining immobile in their seat in the classroom for long periods of time could be challenging for children with ADHD. Their attention is easily captured by distractions or spontaneously diverted without any apparent external stimuli in the environment. They need breaks between activities more often than other children; alternation of physical activity with learning could relieve the monotony of the process. In some cases, children could learn how to identify the increase in their tension, signalise and receive permission to take a break. In other cases, self-reflection is more difficult to achieve and stress is manifested in the form of behavioral issues, which could disturb the learning environment. Dealing with crises in undesired behavior of children with autism and ADHD is among the biggest challenges for teachers. Children with ADHD need well-structured environment and workload, which could be implemented and successfully maintained by CPS.

According to Brown (in Soppit, 2016) the main deviations from the norm of children with ADHD are in the following six areas of executive functioning: 1) organise, prioritise, activate; 2) focus, shift and sustain attention; 3) regulate alertness, effort, processing speed; 4) manage frustration, modulate emotion; 5) working memory, accessing recall; 6) monitor and regulate action. With the assistance of cyber physical robots, each of these main difficulties of children with ADHD could be addressed. The problems with organisation and prioritising could be managed through individually designed programme with a sequence of actions, which accomplishment could be monitored and assisted by the robot. Attention deficits (typical not only for children with ADHD, but with other developmental disorders as well) could be regulated by reminders and maintenance of the attention with symbols, presented to the child by the robot. Problems with the speed of processing and working memory (also characteristic of dyslexia) could be addressed by repetition of instructions, divided into small steps, for one or several children. Behavioural problems could be faced by the robot by different strategies: detecting early signals of potential problems and prevention (for example, the child could be taken out of the classroom temporarily); timely intervention at the moment of the emergence of the undesirable behaviour; warning (by a preliminary established signal) at the first sign of a problem; reinforcement (or the accumulation of a certain number of tokens in order to receive the reinforcement) in case of a positive achievement. In order to monitor and regulate action, the robots could give individual instructions (visual or auditory) to help the work of the child.

Behavioural therapies, and the chief technique in particular, which involves the use of rewards or positive reinforcers, is often applied with children with ADHD (Soppit, 2016). The implementation of this technique could be managed by a robot. It could give regular positive feedback to the child; be its partner in the completion of certain tasks; take the child out of the classroom when he/she demonstrates inappropriate behaviour; distribute tokens as reinforcement for positive behaviour. All of the techniques mentioned above are appropriate for application in the classroom.

Dyslexia

Dyslexia is a neurodevelopmental disorder, which affects reading and other fundamental school skills, while the overall intellectual potential, creativity and high capabilities in other areas remain intact. Approximately 2% of people have severe form of dyslexia, around 15% - mild (Soppit, 2016). Children with dyslexia could experience difficulties with copying from the board, keeping up with rapid dictation, reading text exercises in mathematics and instructions in tests, and the independent work in class. Sometimes they need additional time to complete a particular task. Organising stationery on the desk or in their bag could also be a challenge.

Nowadays literacy is an essential factor for the achievement of professional and personal realisation and adaptation. Children with dyslexia possess intellectual abilities, self-criticism, sensitivity towards their own difficulties and failures. As a result, they often develop secondary negative emotional symptoms, such as anxiety, low self-esteem, learned helplessness. It is crucial for their work in the classroom and learning to be supported in a positive manner. One of the ways to help children with dyslexia in the classroom is to present texts digitally with the help of CPS. In addition, the lessons could be told and audio recorded by the teacher for the use of children at home. That way, the child could still learn the material without struggling with reading.

Intellectual Disability

Children with intellectual disability need more repetitions in order to master the school material, assistance in the preparation of lessons and individual work. It is possible that they experience difficulties understanding certain norms and rules of conduct. Sustained mental activity causes fatigue and could easily lead to unstable emotional states – anxiety, crying, aggression, resistance.

Remembering the learned material is one of the main weaknesses of children with intellectual disabilities. The robot could help the child by giving him/her cues: e.g. for the multiplication table, the next word in a learned poem, the name of the country, river, etc. That way the child could continue working with the pace of the class and advance instead of wasting time in attempts to cope with the difficulties, which objectively could not be overcome completely.

Other areas in which the child could experience difficulties in school are verbal skills, understanding abstract concepts, organisation and planning of activities. Children with mild disabilities could learn how to read but the process might take longer than the usual. They also have delayed motor development. The strategies proposed for children with dyslexia and other SEN to overcome the aforementioned difficulties (reading, motor skills, attention, planning, language) could be applied with children with intellectual disabilities as well.

Physical Disability

It is essential to provide children with physical disability with the necessary space for their special assisting equipment. They need assistance not only for moving around the school, but for the preparation of books and stationery, and the execution of daily routine tasks (drinking water, eating, using the toilet, changing clothes). According to the level of their mobility, their capability to participate in physical activity, sport and PE classes could vary. Their writing ability could also be affected to different extent.

Children with physical disabilities could have a variety of accompanying problems, related to delays in their cognitive and social development. Attention deficits, problems with memory, understanding, executive functions, language development and others could often emerge as secondary to the physical deficit issues. These challenges, in addition to assistance with their physical need, could be handled by CPS.

Hearing Disability

According to the level of visual impairment, children could need auditory augmentation of the acoustic signal or translation of auditory into visual information (in the form of written text or sign language). Children with hearing disability could experience difficulty participating in group activities due to their inability to hear the instructions. They could not orient in the environment by auditory signals, such as bells, whistles, or calling their name.

According to the level of the hearing impairment and/or the level of correction, the child could hear sounds with different frequency and intensity, or not hear at all. In that sense, he/she could only need augmentation of the signal or an entirely new channel of information – light, symbols, or sign language. Some children with hearing disabilities could use sign language, others – oral speech or a combination between both (Duncan, 2016). Others could read on the lips at least to some extent. Reading, writing and other academic achievements could be impaired in children with hearing difficulties (Duncan, 2016).

CPS could offer to the children with hearing disabilities simultaneous sign language translation or representation of the information in other form. They could help the interaction between the child and other children and adults. The opportunity to communication between a child with hearing disability and his/her peers and teacher is crucial for the successful integration in school (Duncan, 2016). The robot could also demonstrate the exercises for children with hearing disabilities, while the teacher gives verbal instructions.

Visual Disability

In order to determine the level of visual disability, visual acuity has to be assessed with an eye chart with big and small letters and symbols. Similar to hearing disability, the level of visual disability could vary. Full blindness occurs very rarely (Ravenscroft, 2016). The majority of children still possess some level of sight and that facilitates their inclusion in the education system. Regardless of the level of their ability to see, children with visual disability need assistance, like those with physical impairments, with some daily routine tasks (drinking water, eating, using the toilet, changing clothes). Orientation in the environment and mobility are among the main difficulties they could experience, which could be addressed with the assistance of a robot.

A great part of the child's development is based on what he/she sees, exploration of the organisation of the world of objects and models of behaviour. Since the majority of visual disability is due to brain damage, not eye damage, many children have accompanying impairments (Ravenscroft, 2016). CPS could help both with visual and other impairments and difficulties.

There is a high comorbidity between children with ASD and other specific learning difficulties, such as dyslexia, ADHD, dyspraxia, dyscalculia, SLI (Reid, Lannen & Lannen, 2016) . 86% of children with ADHD have another comorbid disorder, 67% of them – two or more (Soppit, 2016). In addition, the demonstrated difficulties of children with different diagnoses could overlap significantly (Macintyre & Deponio, 2015). For example, attention and memory deficits could be typical for dyslexia, dyspraxia and ADHD. Hyperactivity and hypersensitivity to certain stimuli are characteristic for ADHD and autism. Children with specific language disorders, dyslexia, dyspraxia and ASD could exhibit difficulties with the following of verbal instructions. Problems related to motor skills could be evident among children with intellectual, physical and sensor disabilities. Reading difficulties are common among children with dyslexia, autism, intellectual and hearing impairments and others.

The increasing number of children with SEN requires more resources to handle their needs. The advance in technology gives one opportunity to meet these requirements adequately and with less human resources.

Cyber Physical Systems (CPS)

The development of technology has created new possibilities for the development of the society in any aspect of the human life. The application of computers, robotics and cyber physical systems (CPS) in engineering, medicine, therapy and other areas is being thoroughly investigated. The application of computers and robots in schools has also been a topic of investigation. However, the application of CPS in special education has not been examined in detail.

CPS is a heterogeneous system of systems, which integrates physical, computer and communication components (Tan et al. 2009). These components are inter-connected by feedback loops and act autonomously to produce a consistent response (Lee 2008). In other words, computer systems recognize characteristics from the physical world, analyze them and produce the pre-programmed appropriate reaction. Computers recognize and react to physical activity by embedded systems, such as actuators and sensors (Tan et al. 2009). Sensors detect physical activity and convert it into information. Actuators receive signals and convert their energy into motion. Physical processes affect cyber mechanisms and vice versa. This interaction is characterized by time and spatial sensitivity (physical changes are reflected in the cyber space when and where they occur) (Tan et al. 2009). However, not all changes need to be reflected. Therefore, by pre-programming the parameters of the conditions of interest into the computer, the important changes are recognized by the cyber system as *events*. The detection of *event* results in *action*, or predefined reaction.

These characteristics give advantage to CPS to other technology. In addition, the variety of mechanisms of activation could facilitate the adaptation of children with special needs to their daily use. For example, robots operated by CPS rely upon visual and auditory recognition mechanisms, pressure sensors responding to tactile stimulation, wireless control (from computers, smartphones, tablets). Children with special needs could experience difficulties with the activation of the robots (for example, due to motor control difficulties). The possible solutions of this problem include activation by the teacher or pre-set adjustments of the robot to activate as a response to different triggers (to execute a particular behavior at a set period of time, as a reaction to specific command or physical response by the child, such as eye movement). Alternatively, it could be activated by a push switch (large button or joystick) on the robot or on a remote control, by vocalization, or by pressure sensors on the armrest of a wheelchair, by chin or eyelid movement as an adaptation for children with severe motor deficits (Standen et al. 2016).

Based on behavioral methods, the robots could be programmed to produce reactions to specific responses or behaviors of the children to reward them. For example, a correct response could be reinforced by clapping hand, singing a song, playing music, saying an encouraging phrase, and others. According to the necessities of the children and teachers, the robots could be programmed to follow and/or issue commands. Recognition of fingerprints could be used to identify the child and activate user-specific features (Poovendran 2010). Application of cyber physical robots could be facilitated by the mood recognition features of the robot. However, these advantages of CPS have also become the biggest challenge to design. The predictability and reliability of CPS are essential in health care and education and more difficult to achieve due to the unpredictability of behavior of SEN children (Lee 2008).

Challenges

Considering all the changes CPS have to undergo in order to fulfill the desired functions, several factors should be taken into account in their design and application in schools. The robot's physical appearance geared to the needs and preferences of the students; the robot's personal characteristics, such as personality (Shen et al. 2001) or degree of extroversion (Kang et al. 2007); social behaviour, such as initiating and maintaining communication, showing empathy, understanding and expressing verbal and non-verbal cues (Kang and Son 2008) and others.

The accomplishment of all this would impose on the system great demands in terms of data storage capacity. One way to handle this is Cloud Computing – a wireless storage system applied in healthcare that offers computing, storage, networking, and software (Kang and Son 2008). In other words, data could be accessed by any computer via Internet by parents, teachers, educational psychologists, the school and the government to improve interventions and to retrieve data for statistical reports, for example. However, this raises the issue of data protection. Serious measures in terms of access and data use should be taken to assure confidentiality of the children. First, privacy could be achieved by careful control of access. Second, data could be encrypted at the user level to improve security (Ramamritham et al. 2004).

Application

The investigation of the possible applications of CPS in the education of children with SEN and the development of cyber physical technology to facilitate this process is essential. Engagement was found to be one of the main predictors of learning for children with difficulties. The predictability of such interactions increases the interest and playfulness of SEN children. As a result, their motivation to learn is higher with robots compared to teachers. Robots could also be used to increase engagement by applying behavioral techniques, such as reinforcement by encouragement, praising positive behavior and others. The main domains in which robots have been applied so far in mainstream education are technical education, science and language (Mubin et al. 2013). According to Han et al. (2008), learning English with an interactive robot was more effective (higher concentration, interest and academic achievement) than books with audiotape and web-based instruction methods for a group of Korean children.

Another domain of application of robots is assistive learning. Ibrani et al. (2011) suggested that young children with austim, Down syndrome and mild learning disabilities were capable of using mobile robots as learning aids and demonstrated high engagement and motivation. In addition, the short-term effect of robot toys on playfulness in therapy with children with developmental disabilities was positive (Klein et al. 2011). Longitudinal studies are scarce, but clearly demonstrating the benefits of robots on the communication skills of children with autism (Robins et al. 2005). Although currently the main application of socially assistive robots is with children with autism, the benefits for children with other disabilities have been demonstrated. Research suggested that engagement with the learning process of children with profound and multiple disabilities was higher with a robot than in the classroom (Hedgecock et al. 2014; Standen et al. 2014).

Robots could be used to identify and predict undesirable behavior and prevent it by engaging the child more actively in the educational process. This could be achieved by pre-programming the robot to react to excessive movement when relative immobility is required (notice the moving child among the static children in the classroom), or recognizing repetitive strong noise when silence is required (identify the noisy child in the classroom). In addition, robots could be pre-programmed to demonstrate empathy when one of the children shows signs of emotional or psychological distress. This could be applied to assist hyperactive children by engaging their attention when necessary. In addition, it would prevent disruption of the overall educational processes in the class.

A fingerprint recognition system could be applied to identify the student and activate the pre-set behavior tailored to the specific need of that student. In other words, apart from group work, robots could be used to target individual needs and enable the development and work on individual programs (focused on reading for children with dyslexia and visual impairments, communication for autism, mathematics for dyspraxia, and others). They could also accompany children outside the classroom when they need to visit a specialist's room, or to have a short break. The children's oral speech could be transformed into written text by voice recognition in order to assist children with physical disabilities, visual impairments, dyslexia, or some children with autism. The robot could be used as an individual assistant of certain children – to accompany them outside the classroom, to read to them and help them organize their desks and bags, to show them the schedule (with visual representations for children with autism), to translate speech into sign or written language for children with hearing disability. Cyber physical robots could draw the attention to certain events, such as beginning and end of a class, breaks and lunch time by light signals, which would help children with hearing disability, autism, or hyperactivity to orient in the environment.

Robots could also be used to alleviate the tension created by the bell or other sounds for children with sensory hypersensitivity. Apart from reducing the intensity of the sound of the bell, the robot could notify the child (with light signal, visual symbol or other) of the forthcoming sound.

The child could also be trained to apply other strategies with the assistance of the robot. For example, using headphones to reduce the sound; listening/ watching short video clips from his/her favorite film while the bell is ringing to compensate for the uncomfortable feeling, etc.

CPS have a rich potential to address attention problems. The attention span of children with deficits in this area could be increased by sporadic attractive stimuli, applied by the robot in order to sustain and redirect the attention when it is shifting. Another way of using robots to help in such cases is giving a desired reward when attention is sustained successfully for a certain amount of time.

The main educational topics in which robots are used to assist learning are technology (knowledge about robots and computers), science (engineering, mathematics, and physics) and language. However, the use of robots to teach biology, chemistry, geography, history, to improve social skills and cognitive functioning, to increase creativity (writing, painting) was not explored.

Parts of the school material (new terms, words, places, names) could be embedded in the computer system of a robot. The child could then think of a word and the robot has to guess it by asking questions, or vice versa. This could give children the opportunity to practice new material through playing. It could be useful for children with dyslexia because it does not involve reading or writing. To children which have difficulties grasping abstract concepts (like children with autism or intellectual disabilities), the robot could offer illustrations, examples, applications, algorithms to facilitate the understanding.

Many children (with autism, dyspraxia and other) have difficulties understanding the concept of time. It is difficult for them to follow the duration of lessons and breaks, the sequence of events and activities during the day. CPS could be applied to assist these children with visual representation of the daily schedule; marking the duration of certain activities with symbols and reminders of upcoming events (or the beginning and end of things).

Children with autism and intellectual impairments could experience difficulties with social norms and appropriate use of language. CPS could assist such children in social situations. Video modeling is a technique, successfully applied in such cases – the child watches a video modeling concrete behaviours and is expected to apply it after that in practice.

Robots could also be used in PE classes. For example, they could demonstrate exercises tailored to the specific needs of children (mild, more static exercises to children with physical disabilities, relaxation techniques to children with ADHD, verbal instructions to children with impaired vision, visual modeling for children with hearing disability and others).

Diving the new tasks in chunks and the regular representation with different materials could help all students in the learning of new skills (Strnadova & Evans, 2016). All children – SEN or typical development, could take advantage of these strategies, and robots could be responsible for their application.

Some children with SEN (usually with autism and ADHD) have specific dietary requirements, related to food intolerance or allergic reactions. CPS could help following their diet by analysing the ingredients and detecting the appropriate and inappropriate foods.

Least but not last, part of the great potential of robots is due to the high motivation of people to use them Technology has become an inseparable part of the modern world and their application in the educational system came naturally. In spite of this, the introduction of technological novelties in the relatively conservative environment of the school poses many questions to the way they will be accepted. In order to use the full potential of CPS in education, it is necessary to take into account the attitudes of the main users of the new technology – students and teachers.

Perception and Attitude of Children and Teachers

The rapid technological development led to the application of such systems in a variety of areas. Despite the undeniable benefits, this advance also caused many unpredictable changes. The negative attitude of people associated with the fast change could decrease the introduction of technology to aspects of the everyday life where it could be beneficial. In that sense, the investigation of the perception of and attitude of children and teachers to the application of CPS in education is essential.

Although human-robot interactions are not part of the everyday life of people yet, their presence in the modern world became more evident over the past few years. 87% of European citizens claimed they have never used a robot (European Commission 2012). Instead, most people's mental representations of robots have been formed by encounters with films and literature. Although robots are not social in nature, people's attitudes towards them are a social construct, influenced by the user's personal characteristics and environmental factors. The quality of the human-robot interaction (HRI), in turn, depends on the person's expectation of it and the robot's capabilities. A study by Höflich & El Bayed (2015), investigating people's attitudes towards robots, revealed that children and adults represent robots in a similar manner, resembling children book illustrations and always with a switch-off button (desire for control). In terms of application, the general belief is that robots could be used to benefit humans in domains requiring mechanical work, while people are seen as more experienced in medical health care, teaching, etc., which could be an indication of the underestimation of modern technology, or fear of unemployment (Höflich & El Bayed 2015). However, previous experience with robots was associated with more positive attitudes. Overall, teachers are more cautious towards the use of robots in education than parents and children. Younger children were more enthusiastic about robots and more likely to perceive them as peers, while older children saw robots mainly as tools (Shin & Kim 2007). An essential characteristic of robots according to students is human-like behavior. Social interaction (Shin & Lee 2008), human-like voice (Okita et al. 2009) and eye contact (Johnson et al. 2000) were demonstrated to increase engagement.

Children's perception of robots is closely related to their understanding of the robot's characteristics and capabilities. Toddlers treated robots as peers rather than toys and socialised with them in a similar way as between each other (Tanaka et al. 2007). This interaction was characterised by touch and care-taking behaviours and increased over time. In a group of Taiwan children, the capabilities of robots were exaggerated and influenced by fictitious images; robots were seen as servants or companions; an equal number of children approved and disapproved robots as teachers; the reason for disapproval was their lack of emotions (Lin et al. 2009). When actual child-robot interactions were observed, similar results were obtained – children treated the robots as peers (Alves-Oliveira et al. 2016) and engaged with them socially (Serholt & Barendregt 2016). A study on the perception of animacy of robots of pre-school children revealed that older children were less likely to attribute biological properties to the robots, and this tendency depended on the interactivity of the robot (Okita & Schwartz 2006). However, for younger children the attribution of animacy did not depend on the actions of the robot. This suggests that the theory of animacy of children develops over time, and earlier perceptions depend on embedded beliefs. However, realism is not the most important feature of a robot for children. Instead, Okita et al. (2009) suggested that familiar and engaging scripts would improve the child-robot interaction. Other factors that increased the positive perception and learning of children were anthropomorphic features (human-like voice and gesture, movement of the mouth when speaking, lack of prolonged pauses) and cooperative learning style (Okita et al. 2009).

The biggest challenge is to create a robot that could respond to the needs of all children in a class. In order to avoid stigma and the negative perception of robots as tools for "special assistance for different children", all children should engage and be approached by the robot. Therefore, it should be customized to recognize the individual and adapt its behavior to the needs, personality and mood of the child. At the same time, the same program should be followed for all children, thus providing equal opportunities and treatment.

Based on the research mentioned above, it is only logical that the main focus of the development of CPS is towards believable and timely interactions with the environment. People's perceptions of robots depend on many factors, such as empathy, behaviour and anthropomorphism of the robot, age and gender of the user and others. Their physical presence in the same environment and human-likeness are the main reasons for the high expectations for interaction (Höflich 2013).

The ability of the robot to express empathy increase the users' satisfaction (Prendinger et al. 2005), engagement (Ochs et al. 2008), performance on tasks (Partala & Surakka 2004) and overall positive perception (Picard & Liu 2007). However, this relationship is not simple and independent. On one hand, robots are perceived more positively when they express both positive and negative emotions compared to no emotions when the user is looking for information in particular domain, but when the expressed emotion is incongruent with the situation, the reverse effect becomes evident (Ochs et al. 2008). On the other hand, in a game-playing context, incongruent reactions could increase the negative perception of the robot, but positive reactions are preferred when losing the game (Cramer et al. 2010).

Other factors that influence perceptions are age and gender. Generally, younger children are more enthusiastic about learning with robots (Shin and Kim 2007). In addition, women feel closer to and accept better robots with female human-like voice, and the same relationship was found for men and male human-like voice (Eyssel et al. 2012). However, no such difference existed for robot voice.

The data of a survey of the perception and attitude to the application of CPS in education of teachers and students from several Bulgarian schools are currently being examined.

EMPIRICAL RESEARCH

Aim of the Study

The current study has the purpose of investigating the attitudes towards and perceptions of teacher and student of the role of the robot in the classroom.

Materials

A survey with 20 statements has been designed; 15 of which aim to evaluate the attitude toward the presence of the robot in the classroom (e.g.: "I would enjoy to have a robot in the classroom very much.") and the perception of its role (e.g.: "The robot in the classroom could give children the rewards they deserve."). The remaining five questions are related to the understanding of the way the robot should be present in the classroom (the whole time or only temporarily; the degree of its autonomy or dependence on the teacher) and it appearance (human-likeness; ability to express emotions). The answers to this set of questions could not be evaluated as positive or negative attitudes toward the robot.

The questionnaire consists of two parts – for students (Appendix A) and teachers (Appendix B). Participants respond to every statement using the scale from 1 (strongly disagree) to 4 (strongly agree).

The study was conducted between 15/05/2018 and 30/05/2018. The data has been gathered from a secondary public school in the town of Kostinbrod, Bulgaria.

Results

Participants include 17 teachers in primary and secondary school and 119 students from 2nd to 11th grade. Due to missing data in the survey, 11 students and five teachers have been excluded from the analysis.

Data Analysis of Students' Responses

The number of participants is unequally distributed among the 2nd, 4th, 5th, 7th and 11h grades (Table 1). The highest number of students are in the 7th (41%) and 4th grades (31%).

The distribution of students by gender is relatively equal.

The inter reliability of the 14 items of the study of attitudes has been analysed. The reliability of the questionnaire for students measured with Cronbach's Alpha, is high (Table 3).

Table 1. Distribution of students by grades

Grade	Frequency	Percent
2	1	0.9
4	33	30.6
5	16	14.8
7	44	40.7
11	14	13.0
Total	108	100.0

Table 2. Distribution of students by gender

Gender	Frequency	Percent
Boys	55	50.9
Girls	53	49.1
Total	108	100.0

Table 3. Inter reliability of the questionnaire for students

Cronbach's Alpha	Cronbach's Alpha Based on Standardized Items	N of Items
.806	.819	14

The mean value of the students' attitudes toward a robot in the classroom has been calculated, as well as a mean value for each of the items on the questionnaire (Table 4). Since responses 1 and 2 indicate negative attitudes, and 3 and 4 – positive attitudes, the mean value (M = 2. 26; SD = 0. 71) indicates a rather neutral overall attitude with a slight tendency towards the positive.

The analysis by items indicated that the perception of the robot as assistant for children with physical disabilities and difficulties in understanding are highest (item 2 and 13 respectively). According to children, the robot is a teacher assistant (item 10). In addition, the expectation is that teachers (item 5), parents (item 6) and students (item 1) would like the presence of a robot in the classroom. Students also perceived the role of the robot as an assistant for children with learning difficulties (item 3), behavioural problems (item 4) and giving reinforcement to the children who deserve it (item 12) positively. Generally, children do not perceive the robot as a distraction (item 8), although the value is rather close to neutral. The high standard deviation suggests that the range of opinions on this item varies significantly among students. See the analysis of opinions on this item in the text below (Table 5 indicates the percentage of the distribution of responses by grades). The responses of children on the question of fear of the robot are also controversial (item 11), resulting in a mean response close to neutral. However, the difference in the responses between children in different grades is not significant.

The analysis of responses on item 8 ("The robot in the classroom will distract children") revealed a significant difference between children in different grades (t (12) = 25.78, p < .05). Although the number of children who think that the robot will not be a distraction is the highest (38.9% disagreed with the statement), the number of children from the higher grades who think it will be a distraction is bigger (42.9% of children in the 11th grade agreed with the statement).

The attitude of students toward the rest of the items, corresponding to questions on the presence and appearance of the robot, were also investigated. Children believe that the teacher should be in charge of the robot, which could sometimes be a substitute, but should not be present in the classroom during the whole time (Table 6).

According to children, the robot is a humanoid that can express emotions (Table 7).

No significant differences were detected between the mean answers of boys and girls overall or separately by items.

Table 4. Distribution of Responses of children in different grades by items

Item	M	SD
Total 1-14	*2.26*	*0.71*
2) The robot can help children that cannot walk alone to move.	3.51	0.81
13) The robot can repeat what the teacher said to children who did not understand it.	3.18	1.03
7) It will be fun to have a robot in the classroom.	3.18	1.08
10) The robot will be assistant to the teacher.	3.14	1.02
5) The teacher would like to have an assistant robot.	3.11	1.03
3) The robot can help children that cannot learn independently.	3.10	1.00
12) The robot can give rewards to children who deserve it.	3.05	1.19
4) The robot can help children who misbehave in class.	2.94	1.19
1)I would enjoy having a robot in the classroom very much.	2.94	1.11
9) The robot in the classroom will be our friend.	2.88	1.15
6) Parents would like to have a robot in the classroom very much.	2.53	1.12
8) The robot in the classroom will distract the children. (*reverse item*)	2.31	1.26
11) Some children will be afraid of the robot in the classroom.	2.16	1.12
14) If there is a robot in the classroom, children will be more obedient.	1.03	1.16

Table 5. Distribution on Item 8 (The robot in the classroom will be a distraction for children)

Grade	Response 1	Response 2	Response 3	Response 4
2	100%	0.0%	0.0%	0.0%
4	66.7%	21.2%	3.0%	9.1%
5	43.8%	12.5%	6.2%	37.5%
7	22.7%	22.7%	18.2%	36.4%
11	14.3%	21.4%	21.4%	42.9%
Total	38.9%	20.4%	12.0%	28.7%

Table 6. Perceptions of students of the presence of the robot in the classroom and its relationship with the teacher

Item	M	SD
20) The robot in the classroom can sometimes substitute the teacher.	2,95	1,23
16) Only the teacher can control the robot.	2,81	1,23
15) The robot cannot stay in the classroom during the whole time.	2,55	1,17
17) The robot can decide what to do on its own.	2,08	1,17

Table 7. Students' Perceptions of the Appearance of the Robot

Item	M	SD
19) If the robot is in the classroom, it should be able to smile and frown.	2,92	1,16
18) The robot should look like a human.	2,66	1,14

Table 8. Significant correlations between age and items measuring attitudes towards the role and appearance of the robot

Item	Correlation with age (r)
19) If there is a robot in the classroom, it should be able to smile and frown.	1*
20) The robot in the classroom can sometimes be a substitute for the teacher.	1**

* - p<0,05; ** - p<0,001

The correlation between the overall attitude toward the robot and the age of the students was significant ($r = -.564$, $p < .01$): the younger the child, the more positive the attitude. A positive correlation was also detected between age and one of the items, measuring the attitude of children toward the relationship between the teacher and the robot (Table 8). Older students believe that the robot can sometimes be a substitute for teachers, while in the perceptions of younger children the teacher is irreplaceable. In addition, there is a significant correlation between age and one of the items related to the appearance of the robot (Table 8). Older children believe that the robot should be able to express emotions.

All the items measuring the attitude (items 1-14), except item 11 ("Some children will be afraid of the robot in the classroom") are positively correlated to the age of children ($p < .01$).

Analysis of the Responses of Teachers

Twelve of the teachers (100% female) have completed the questionnaire without any missing data. Six of them teach in classes with children with SEN, and six in classes without SEN.

The inter reliability of the questionnaire of 14 items measuring the attitude of teachers towards robots is high (Table 9).

The mean value of teachers' attitude toward the presence of the robot in the classroom is rather positive ($M = 2.77$; $SD = 0.60$). Compared to the students' attitudes ($M = 2.26$; $SD = 0.71$), this value is significantly higher ($t (119) = 2. 48$, $p < .05$).

Teachers believe (Table 10) that children will like having a robot in the classroom very much (item 5); they perceive the robot as their assistant (item 10) who can repeat what they said to certain students

Table 9. Inter reliability of the questionnaire for teachers

Cronbach's Alpha	Cronbach's Alpha Based on Standardized Items	N of Items
,898	,897	14

(item 13) and reward children who deserve it (item 12); to accompany children with physical disabilities outside the classroom (item 2). According to teachers, some children might be afraid (item 11), but not distracted by the robot (item 8). Teacher do not believe that the robot will make children more obedient (item 14) and are skeptical toward the attitudes of parents (item 6). The latter item 6 is rather positive but close to neutral (M = 2. 25).

The attitude of teachers toward the way the robot should be present in the classroom and its appearance was also examined. Teachers believe that they should control the robot during the whole time and it should not be able to decide what to do on its own. According to them, the robot cannot be present in the classroom during the whole time, can substitute them sometimes but the teacher should continue having the control (Table 11).

According to teachers, the robot should be able to express emotions (Table 12).

The attitudes of teachers in classes with children with and without SEN were compared. The number of teachers in both groups is 6. The difference is of statistical significance (t (10) = 2. 902, p < .05). The attitude of SEN teachers is more negative (M = 2.17; SD = 0.98) than the attitude of teachers in classes without SEN (M = 3.50; SD = 0.55). Overall, the attitude toward robots of the latter group is generally positive.

Discussion

The attitude of teachers in the current study towards robots is positive. The attitude of students is rather neutral, and the difference between the two populations is statistically significant. These findings are surprising, considering that the expectations are that adults will be more skeptical on this matter. However,

Table 10. Distribution of teachers' means by item

Item	M	SD
Statements 1-14	2.77	.600
5) The children will like having a robot in the classroom very much.	3.33	.778
13) The robot can repeat what the teacher said to children who did not understand.	3.25	.866
10) The robot can be an assistant to the teacher.	3.17	.718
12) The robot can give rewards to children who deserve it.	3.00	.953
7) It will be fun to have a robot in the classroom.	2.92	.900
11) Some children will be afraid of the robot in the classroom.	2.92	.900
2) The robot can help children who cannot walk alone to move.	2.83	1.030
8) The robot in the classroom will distract children. *(reverse item)*	2.67	.985
3) The robot can help children who cannot learn independently.	2.58	.996
9) The robot in the classroom will be a friend.	2.58	1.165
4) The robot can assist with children who misbehave in class.	2.50	1.000
1) I would like having a robot in the classroom very much.	2.42	.996
6) The parents would like having a robot in the classroom.	2.33	.778
14) If there is a robot in the classroom, children will be more obedient.	2.25	1.138

Table 11. Teachers' attitudes toward the presence of the robot in the classroom and their relationship to it

Item	M	SD
16) Only the teacher can control the robot.	3.58	.51
15) The robot can stay in the classroom at all times.	2.42	.99
20) The robot in the classroom can sometimes substitute the teacher.	2.08	.79
17) The robot can decide what to do on its own.	1.58	.67

Table 12. Teachers' perception of the robot's appearance

Item	M	SD
19) If there is a robot in the classroom, it should be able to smile and frown.	3.17	.83
18) The robot should look like a human.	2.83	.83

this difference could be due to the difference of the number of participants in each group (12 teachers and 108 students).

The difference between the attitudes of teachers with and without SEN in the class is statistically significant to the advantage of the latter group. Considering the potential of robots to assist this particular group of children, this result is also surprising and could be due to the small number of participants (N = 12). Alternatively, the experience of teacher with SEN could have been rather challenging and negatively influencing their perception of the potential benefits of the assistance of robots. Possibly, after a demonstration of the abilities of the robot this attitude could change.

In a study by Stander et al. (2014) teachers generated a long list of suggestions for applications of robots in education after a demonstration of its capabilities. Among the suggestions are giving reinforcement (as part of behavioural therapy); making dancing and music more desirable for children; aiding the achievement of targets of the learning material, giving commands.

According to teachers in the current empirical study, the children would like to have a robot in the classroom. They perceived the robot as a potential assistant who can repeat information for children who need it and reward children who deserve it; it could also help children who need physical support.

Children's perception of the role of the robot is similar – assistant for children with physical disabilities, difficulties in understanding, teacher assistant and a source of rewards.

Both teachers and students believe that the robot could substitute the teacher to some extent, but the teacher should remain in control and cannot be present in the classroom at all times. Both teachers and students think of the robot as of a humanoid, capable of expression emotions.

There is no difference between the attitudes towards the role and appearance of the robot of boys and girls. However, older children demonstrate a more negative attitude than younger children.

CONCLUSION

The number of children with SEN in the classroom increased during the last few years, which augmented the requirements towards teachers. The advance of technology and the development of CPS led to an increase in attention toward its application in education. However, the issue of the perception of teachers and students of this tendency remains unanswered.

The current empirical research could be perceived as a pilot study of the attitudes of teachers and students towards the presence of a robot in the classroom, as well as the role it could perform and its appearance. Due to the small number of teacher responding to the questionnaire and the limitation of the study to data from one particular school, the results should be interpreted cautiously. The attitudes of teachers and students are rather positive, but this tendency decreases with age among students. Both students and teachers perceive the robot as s humanoid, capable of expressing emotions. They see it as teaching assistant who can substitute the teacher if necessary.

The great potential of the use robots in special education is not fully examined and acknowledged. The application of CPS in the classroom requires specific programming, resources and the laying of positive foundations in order to fulfill their potential. This process is a matter of time, but also thorough research.

REFERENCES

Alves-Oliveira, P., Sequeira, P., & Paiva, A. (2016). *The role that an educational robot plays*. Paper presented at the 2016 25th IEEE International Symposium on Robot and Human Interactive Communication (RO-MAN).

Cramer, H., Goddijn, J., Wielinga, B., & Evers, V. (2010). Effects of (in) accurate empathy and situational valence on attitudes towards robots. In *Human-Robot Interaction (HRI), 2010 5th ACM/IEEE International Conference on* (pp. 141-142). IEEE.

Duncan, J. (2016). Incusive Education for Students who are Deaf or Hard of Hearing. In L. Peer & G. Reid (Eds.), *Special Educational Needs. A Guide for Inclusive Practice* (pp. 250–267). Los Angeles, CA: SAGE.

European Commission. (2012). *Special Eurobarometer/Wave EB77.1: Public attitudes towards robots*. Report. Retrieved from http://ec.europa.eu/public_opinion/archives/ebs/ebs_382_en.pdf

Eyssel, F., De Ruiter, L., Kuchenbrandt, D., Bobinger, S., & Hegel, F. (2012). 'If you sound like me, you must be more human': On the interplay of robot and user features on human-robot acceptance and anthropomorphism. In *Human-Robot Interaction (HRI), 2012 7th ACM/IEEE International Conference on* (pp. 125-126). IEEE.

Han, J., Jo, M., Jones, V., & Jo, J. (2008). Comparative Study on the Educational Use of Home Robots for Children. *Journal Of Information Processing Systems, 4*(4), 159–168. doi:10.3745/JIPS.2008.4.4.159

Haque, S., Aziz, S., & Rahman, M. (2014). Review of Cyber-Physical System in Healthcare. *International Journal of Distributed Sensor Networks, 10*(4), 217415. doi:10.1155/2014/217415

Hedgecock, J., Standen, P., Beer, C., Brown, D., & Stewart, D. (2014). Evaluating the role of a humanoid robot to support learning in children with profound and multiple disabilities. *Journal of Assistive Technologies, 8*(3), 111–123. doi:10.1108/JAT-02-2014-0006

Höflich, J., & El Bayed, A. (2015). Perception, Acceptance, and the Social Construction of Robots—Exploratory Studies. *Social Robots From A Human Perspective*, 39-51. doi:10.1007/978-3-319-15672-9_4

Höflich, J. R. (2013). Relationships to Social Robots: Towards a Triadic Analysis of Media-oriented Behavior. *Intervalla: Platform for Intellectual Exchange, 1*, 35–48.

Ibrani, L., Allen, T., Brown, D., Sherkat, N., & Stewart, D. (2011). *Supporting students with learning and physical disabilities using a mobile robot platform. In Interactive Technologies and Games* (pp. 84–265). Nottingham, UK: ITAG.

Johnson, W. L., Rickel, J. W., & Lester, J. C. (2000). Animated pedagogical agents: Face-to-face interaction in interactive learning environment. *International Journal of Artificial Intelligence in Education, 11*(1), 47–78.

Kang, K. D., & Son, S. H. (2008). Real-time data services for cyber physical systems. In *Distributed Computing Systems Workshops, 2008. ICDCS'08. 28th International Conference on* (pp. 483-488). IEEE. 10.1109/ICDCS.Workshops.2008.21

Kang, W., Son, S. H., Stankovic, J. A., & Amirijoo, M. (2007). I/O-aware deadline miss ratio management in real-time embedded databases. In *Real-Time Systems Symposium, 2007. RTSS 2007. 28th IEEE International* (pp. 277-287). IEEE. 10.1109/RTSS.2007.19

Klein, T., Gelderblom, G., de Witte, L., & Vanstipelen, S. (2011). Evaluation of short term effects of the IROMEC robotic toy for children with developmental disabilities. *2011 IEEE International Conference On Rehabilitation Robotics.* 10.1109/ICORR.2011.5975406

Kory Westlund, J. M., Dickens, L., Jeong, S., Harris, P. L., DeSteno, D., & Breazeal, C. L. (2017). Children use nonverbal cues to learn new words from robots as well as people. *International Journal of Child-Computer Interaction*, 1-9. doi:10.1016/j.ijcci.2017.04.001

Lee, E. A. (2008). *CyberPhysicalSystems: DesignChallenges.* Electrical Engineering and Computer Sciences University of California at Berkeley.

Leyzberg, D., Spaulding, S., & Scassellati, B. (2014). *Personalizing robot tutors to individuals' learning differences.* Paper presented at the 2014 ACM/IEEE international conference on Human-robot interaction, Bielefeld, Germany. 10.1145/2559636.2559671

Lin, Y., Liu, T., Chang, M., & Yeh, S. (2009). Exploring Children's Perceptions of the Robots. Learning By Playing. *Game-Based Education System Design And Development*, 512-517. doi:10.1007/978-3-642-03364-3_63

Macintyre, Ch., & Deponio, P. (2015). Identifying and supporting children with specific learning difficulties. In Looking beyond the label to assess the whole child. Sofia: Iztok-Zapad; Centar za priobshtavashto obrazovanie.

Movellan, J. R., Tanaka, F., Fortenberry, B., & Aisaka, K. (2005). *The RUBI/QRIO Project: Origins, Principles, and First Steps.* Paper presented at the 4th International Conference on Development and Learning. 10.1109/DEVLRN.2005.1490948

Mubin, O., Stevens, C., Shahid, S., Mahmud, A., & Dong, J. (2013). A review of the applicability of robots in education. *Technology For Education And Learning, 1*(1). doi:10.2316/Journal.209.2013.1.209-0015

Ochs, M., Pelachaud, C., & Sadek, D. (2008). An empathic virtual dialog agent to improve human-machine interaction. In *Proceedings of the 7th international joint conference on Autonomous agents and multiagent systems* (vol. 1, pp. 89-96). International Foundation for Autonomous Agents and Multiagent Systems.

Okita, S. Y., Ng-Thow-Hing, V., & Sarvadevabhatla, R. (2009). Learning together: ASIMO developing an interactive learning partnership with children. In *Robot and Human Interactive Communication, 2009. RO-MAN 2009. The 18th IEEE International Symposium on* (pp. 1125-1130). IEEE.

Okita, S. Y., & Schwartz, D. L. (2006). Young children's understanding of animacy and entertainment robots. *International Journal of Humanoid Robotics*, *3*(3), 393-412.

Partala, T., & Surakka, V. (2004). The effects of affective interventions in human–computer interaction. *Interacting with Computers*, *16*(2), 295–309. doi:10.1016/j.intcom.2003.12.001

Picard, R. W., & Liu, K. K. (2007). Relative subjective count and assessment of interruptive technologies applied to mobile monitoring of stress. *International Journal of Human-Computer Studies*, *65*(4), 361–375. doi:10.1016/j.ijhcs.2006.11.019

Poovendran, R. (2010). Cyber–Physical Systems: Close Encounters Between Two Parallel Worlds. *Proceedings of the IEEE*, *98*(8), 1363–1366. doi:10.1109/JPROC.2010.2050377

Prendinger, H., Mori, J., & Ishizuka, M. (2005). Using human physiology to evaluate subtle expressivity of a virtual quizmaster in a mathematical game. *International Journal of Human-Computer Studies*, *62*(2), 231–245. doi:10.1016/j.ijhcs.2004.11.009

Ramamritham, K., Son, S. H., & Dipippo, L. C. (2004). Real-time databases and data services. *Real-Time Systems*, *28*(2-3), 179–215. doi:10.1023/B:TIME.0000045317.37980.a5

Ravenscroft, J. (2016). Visual Impairment and Mainstream Education: Beyond Mere Awareness Raising. In L. Peer & G. Reid (Eds.), *Special Educational Needs. A Guide for Inclusive Practice* (pp. 232–249). Los Angeles, CA: SAGE.

Reid, G., Lannen, S., & Lannen, C. (2016). Autistic Spectrum Disorder. Challenges, Issues and Responses. In L. Peer & G. Reid (Eds.), *Special Educational Needs. A Guide for Inclusive Practice* (pp. 268–286). Los Angeles, CA: SAGE.

Robins, B., Dautenhahn, K., Boekhorst, R., & Billard, A. (2005). Robotic assistants in therapy and education of children with autism: Can a small humanoid robot help encourage social interaction skills? *Universal Access in the Information Society*, *4*(2), 105–120. doi:10.100710209-005-0116-3

Serholt, S., & Barendregt, W. (2016). *Robots Tutoring Children: Longitudinal Evaluation of Social Engagement in Child-Robot Interaction.* Paper presented at the 9th Nordic Conference on Human-Computer Interaction (NordiCHI'16), Gothenburg, Sweden. 10.1145/2971485.2971536

Shen, C. C., Srisathapornphat, C., & Jaikaeo, C. (2001). Sensor information networking architecture and applications. *IEEE Personal Communications, 8*(4), 52-59.

Shin, N., & Kim, S. (2007). Learning about, from, and with Robots: Students' Perspectives. *RO-MAN 2007 - The 16Th IEEE International Symposium On Robot And Human Interactive Communication.* doi: 10.1109/roman.2007.4415235

Shin, N., & Lee, S. (2008). The effects of appearance and interface design on user perceptions of educational robots. *Proc. URAI 2008.*

Soppit, R. (2016). Attention Deficit Hyperactivity Disorder (or Hyperkinetic Disorder). In L. Peer & G. Reid (Eds.), *Special Educational Needs. A Guide for Inclusive Practice* (pp. 216–231). Los Angeles, CA: SAGE.

Standen, P., Brown, D., Hedgecock, J., Roscoe, J., Galvez, T., & Elgajiji, E. (2014). *Adapting A Humanoid Robot for Use with Children with Profound and Multiple Disabilities.* 10th Internasional Conference of Disability, Virtual Reality & Associated Technologies, Gothenberg, Sweden.

Standen, P., Brown, D., Roscoe, J., Hedgecock, J., Stewart, D., Trigo, M. J. G., & Elgajiji, E. (2014). Engaging students with profound and multiple disabilities using humanoid robots. In *International Conference on Universal Access in Human-Computer Interaction* (pp. 419-430). Springer. 10.1007/978-3-319-07440-5_39

Strnadova, I., & Evans, D. (2016). Students with Down Syndrome in Inclusive Classrooms. Using Evidence-Based Practices. In L. Peer & G. Reid (Eds.), *Special Educational Needs. A Guide for Inclusive Practice* (pp. 201–215). Los Angeles, CA: SAGE.

Tan, Y., Vuran, M. C., & Goddarrd, S. (2009). Spatio-Temporal Event Model for Cyber-Physical Systems. *CSE Conference and Workshop Papers*, 147.

Tanaka, F., Cicourel, A., & Movellan, J. (2007). Socialization between toddlers and robots at an early childhood education center. *Proceedings of the National Academy of Sciences of the United States of America, 104*(46), 17954–17958. doi:10.1073/pnas.0707769104 PMID:17984068

APPENDIX A

Questionnaire for Teachers

You are: male__ female____ Teaching: _____ Are there any children with SEN in you class? ___
(please specify what)_____

    School:_____ Town:_____ Date:_____

    Nowadays, technology develops quickly. The time when a robot could be present in the classroom is approaching. Imagine this situation and answer the questions below.

    1 – strongly disagree 2 – disagree 3 – agree 4 – strongly agree

Table 13.

1	I would like to have a robot in the classroom.	1	2	3	4
2	The robot can help children who cannot walk alone to move.	1	2	3	4
3	The robot can help children who cannot learn independently.	1	2	3	4
4	The robot can help children who misbehave in class.	1	2	3	4
5	Children would like to have a robot in the classroom very much.	1	2	3	4
6	Parents would like to have a robot in the classroom.	1	2	3	4
7	It will be fun to have a robot in the classroom.	1	2	3	4
8	The robot in the classroom will distract children.	1	2	3	4
9	The robot in the classroom will be a friend.	1	2	3	4
10	The robot in the classroom will help the teacher.	1	2	3	4
11	Some children will be afraid of the robot.	1	2	3	4
12	The robot can reward children who deserve it.	1	2	3	4
13	The robot can repeat what the teacher said to children who did not understand.	1	2	3	4
14	If there is a robot in the classroom, children will be more obedient.	1	2	3	4
15	The robot can stay in the classroom at all times.	1	2	3	4
16	Only the teacher can control the robot.	1	2	3	4
17	The robot can decide what to do on its own.	1	2	3	4
18	The robot should look like a human.	1	2	3	4
19	If there is a robot in the classroom, it should be able to smile and frown.	1	2	3	4
20	The robot in the classroom can substitute the teacher.	1	2	3	4

APPENDIX B

Questionnaire for Students

You are: male___ female_____ Age: _____Class:_____

   School:_____ Town:_____ Date:_____

   Nowadays, technology develops quickly. The time when a robot could be present in the classroom is approaching. Imagine this situation and answer the questions below.

   1 – strongly disagree 2 – disagree 3 – agree 4 – strongly agree

Table 14.

1	I would like to have a robot in the classroom.	1	2	3	4
2	The robot can help children who cannot walk alone to move.	1	2	3	4
3	The robot can help children who cannot learn independently.	1	2	3	4
4	The robot can help children who misbehave in class.	1	2	3	4
5	Teachers would like to have a robot in the classroom very much.	1	2	3	4
6	Parents would like to have a robot in the classroom.	1	2	3	4
7	It will be fun to have a robot in the classroom.	1	2	3	4
8	The robot in the classroom will distract children.	1	2	3	4
9	The robot in the classroom will be a friend.	1	2	3	4
10	The robot in the classroom will help the teacher.	1	2	3	4
11	Some children will be afraid of the robot.	1	2	3	4
12	The robot can reward children who deserve it.	1	2	3	4
13	The robot can repeat what the teacher said to children who did not understand.	1	2	3	4
14	If there is a robot in the classroom, children will be more obedient.	1	2	3	4
15	The robot can stay in the classroom at all times.	1	2	3	4
16	Only the teacher can control the robot.	1	2	3	4
17	The robot can decide what to do on its own.	1	2	3	4
18	The robot should look like a human.	1	2	3	4
19	If there is a robot in the classroom, it should be able to smile and frown.	1	2	3	4
20	The robot in the classroom can substitute the teacher.	1	2	3	4

Chapter 3
Existing Robotics Technologies for Implementation of Special Education

Roman Zahariev Zahariev
Bulgarian Academy of Sciences, Bulgaria

Nina Valchkova
Bulgarian Academy of Sciences, Bulgaria

ABSTRACT

Collaborative robots (Cobots) are described from the point of view of the cognitive processes underlying the perception and emotional expression of learners based on individual human interacting with non-humanoid robots. The chapter describes a project that is aimed at the development and prototyping of mobile cognitive robotic system designed for service and assistance to people with disabilities. In creating this robot called "AnRI" (anthropomorphic robot intelligent) the experience from building the previous one was used, and it was used in the project Conduct Research into the Adoption of Robotic Technologies in Special Education by Children, Young People, and Pedagogical Specialists. It is described as a device of the robot and realization of cognitive processes to integrate knowledge-related information from sensors, actuators, and multiple sources of information vital to the process of serving people with disabilities.

INTRODUCTION

The first service applications of the mobile robots were very successful and soon the robotic community become aware of the great future of this new branch of robotics – service robotics, stating that their positions promises to be even stronger than those of the industrial ones in the near future. At the beginning of service robotics they were developments mostly of single purpose (specialized) mobile robots able to be used only for specific tasks. Many designers and companies today are changing their design and production strategies in service robotics towards modularization in order to become more flexible and competitive on the market (Bjoern M., 2015).

DOI: 10.4018/978-1-5225-7879-6.ch003

As stated in the Cybernetics of Norbert Wiener (Wiener N., 1961), man is a purposeful system, the behavior of which is determined by the set of tasks. The process of successful pursuit and achievement of the set goals, without prejudice to the pre-set restrictions, is determined to a large extent by the learner's desire and interest. The learner's interests are a powerful stimulus in the processes of education, learning the information on the path of pursuing the strategic task (Smith, P., 2007). At the modern stage of human society development, with the introduction of new ultramodern technologies, including robotics, it is possible to challenge the interest of the learners, thereby enlivening the perception of such important information in the process of education. It is possible to use the Service Robots like Assistant Teachers in the process of special education (Kaburlasos, V.G., Dardani, Ch., Dimitrova, M., & Amanatiadis, A. 2018).

Using better and better cheap sensors and sensor systems, robots become easily adaptable to a large variety of industrial processes. The simple mobile robots called in the industry as Automated Guided Vehicles (AGV's) have entered the production systems firmly and have helped the creation of the Flexible Manufacturing Systems (FMS) and later on the Computer Integrated Manufacturing (CIM). Giving to the AGV's some more sensors and intelligent functions, they become the first's service robots operating in warehouses, shops, supermarkets etc. The degree of intelligence of the universal mobile robots, developed for R&D and scientific applications by the world leading universities and laboratories, is growing very fast (GNU ARM, 2015). This is possible with the development of modern microprocessor based control systems, and thanks to the use of sophisticated yet comparatively cheap sensors (like mono and stereo, colour CCD video-systems, laser based sensors and a large variety of other types) and remarkable achievements in the software (Zahariev R., N.Valchkova., 2004).

Data from the US Census Bureau Statistical Brief of 1993 showed that over 34 million Americans had difficulty performing functional activities. Of this number, over 24 million were considered to have severe disabilities. Every year more and more people become disabled in a way which minimizes their use of upper extremities. These can be motor dysfunctions due to accidents, disease, or genetic predispositions (Mitchell R. L., 2012).

The field of Rehabilitation Robotics has emerged in an attempt to increase the quality of life and to assist in the activities of daily living. Rehabilitation Robotics addresses assistive technologies as well as the traditional definition of rehabilitation: increasing or expanding the individual's mental, physical, or sensory capabilities. The primary focus of Rehabilitation Engineering and robotics is to increase the quality of life of individuals through increasing functional independence and decreasing the costs associated with the assistance required by the individual (Scassellati B., H.Admoni, & M.Matarić, 2012).

Robotic aids used in these applications vary from advanced limb orthosis to robotic arms. These devices can help in everyday activities for persons with severe physical disabilities limiting their ability to manipulate objects by reducing their dependency on caregivers (Serpanos, D., 2015).

Often but not always the service robots are mobile. Service robots usually consist of a mobile platform on which one or several arms are attached and controlled in the same mode as the arms of the industrial robots. With this definition manipulating industrial robots could also be regarded as service robots provided they are installed for non manufacturing operations (Liu C., and all 2008).

In overall, people are generally content with the intelligent sensing and performance of robots at work, even become emotionally to them and accept them as partners - they even prefer robots repaired rather than replaced (Prescott T. & Szollosy M.,2017).

BRIEF HISTORY OF THE FIRST ROBOTS

The word "robot" was invented in 1920 by the Czech writer Karel Chapek who used it for the first time in the science fiction RWR or Rosum's Universal Robots. In 1954, the world's first robot IC industrial arm, called the Programmed Transfer Device, was patented by George Devol. In partnership with Joseph Engelberger, in 1959 it was marketed under the name "Unimate". Then for the first time a robot was successfully installed in a General Motors plant. Joseph F. Engelberger, an American physicist, engineer, and businessman, was responsible for the birth of one the most important and impactful industries, gaining him global recognition as the Godfather of Robotics. It is very fames his remark "I can't define a robot, but I know one when I see one." (Engelberger,J.1983).

In the period from 1960 to 2000, industrial robots became robotic cells as complete systems that include the robot, controller, and other peripherals, requiring considerable investment and programming knowledge, and became widely known in automation and other industrial sectors. Since 1979 was started work in the field of Robotics at Bulgarian Academy of Sciences (BAS), Institute of Technical Cybernetics and Robotics, which successor is at present Institute of Robotics – BAS (IR-BAS). As an illustration on Figure 1, a historical view of the robots from the Institute of Robotics-BAS is presented.

BRIEF HISTORY OF THE FIRST COLLABORATIVE ROBOTS (COBOTS)

In 1989 Joseph F. Engelberger in the book "Robots in Service" place the Idea for used the robots for human service (Engelberger,J.1989). In 2001-2005, a research team at the University of Southern Denmark compared existing automation solutions to market needs and opened up a new era for industrial robots. In 2005, Universal Robots A/S was founded by three specialists from the University of Southern Denmark's research team to develop a flexible, collaborative, and light-weight, robust robot with a fast return on investment.

In 2008, Universal Robots launched UR 5 - the world's first collaborative robot to work well, reliably and safely, side by side with the human. In 2012, the new collaborative robot UR 10 with greater reach and payload makes its world debut. In the years 2012-2016 "Collaborative Robots" are recognized as a

Figure 1. Historical view of the robots of IR-BAS

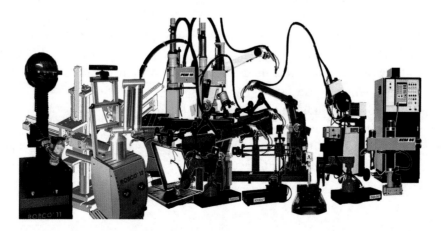

fully applicable, new class of robots. A major robot maker and robotic technician began to develop and produce robots.

In 2014, TÜV NORD (German Product Validation Organization) certifies the safety system of the 3rd Generation UR Cobbies. In 2015, Universal Robots released UR3 on the world market - the first desktop tabletop robot. In 2016, ISO publishes the long-awaited ISO/TS 15066:2016 specification containing instructions on how to ensure employee safety when handling robotic collaborative systems. With the new third-generation Cobots, robotics has a real opportunity to be used where both flexibility and safety are required ISO 10218-1:2011. The new robots offer up-to-date hardware technology and an improved security system.

ADVANTAGES OF COLLABORATIVE ROBOTS

Collaborative robots are a natural evolutionary branch in robotics. They save a valuable place in factories, making them suitable for implementation even in the most space-related applications (Bjoern M. 2015). At the same time, it is becoming easier for such a robot to be programmed and adapted to a specific task, even to the most specific processes, by not requiring a specially trained programmer. Configuration can be done quickly and easily by anyone via the robot's touch screen (Figure 2).

Among the most serious arguments in favor of collaborative robots is safety. These robots have integrated sensors, soft and rounded surfaces and a number of other ways to minimize the risk of impact, breaking down or crushing the user. The most significant distinguishing feature of collaborative robots in terms of safety is the limitation of force in the moving joints (hinges, joints). Additionally, the robot is typically programmed to immediately stop touching a person or shortening the distance to the person to avoid possible collisions and injuries.

Figure 2. Configuration of the collaborative robot

ORIGIN OF SERVICE ROBOTS

Service robots assist human beings, typically by performing a job that is dirty, dull, distant, dangerous or repetitive, including household chores. They typically are autonomous and/or operated by a built-in control system, with manual override options. The term "service robot" does not have a strict technical definition. The International Federation of Robotics (IFR) preliminary definition of service robotics states: "Service robot – a robot which operates semi or fully autonomously to perform services useful to the well-being of humans and equipment excluding manufacturing operations". Service robots may or may not be equipped with an arm structure as the industrial robots (Bjoern M., Th.Reisinger, 2016).

DEFINITION OF "SERVICE ROBOTICS"

In a joint effort started in 1995, the United Nations Economic Commission for Europe (UNECE) and IFR engaged in working out a first service robot definition and classification scheme which has been adopted by the current ISO Technical Committee 184 / Subcommittee 2 resulting in a novel ISO-Standard ISO8373:2012 which became effective in 2012. This International Standard specifies a vocabulary to be used in relation to robots and robotic devices operating in both industrial and non-industrial environments. It provides definitions and explanations of the most commonly used terms, which are grouped into clauses of the main topics of robotics. Its vocabulary definitions relate to industrial as well as to service robotics. Relevant robotics related definitions are (Provisional definition of Service Robots, 2012):

- A robot is an actuated mechanism programmable in two or more axes with a degree of autonomy, moving within its environment, to perform intended tasks. Autonomy in this context means the ability to perform intended tasks based on current state and sensing, without human intervention.
- A service robot is a robot that performs useful tasks for humans or equipment excluding industrial automation application. Note: The classification of a robot into industrial robot or service robot is done according to its intended application.
- A personal service robot or a service robot for personal use is a service robot used for a non-commercial task, usually by lay persons. Examples are domestic servant robot, automated wheelchair, and personal mobility assisting robot.
- A professional service robot or a service robot for professional use is a service robot used for a commercial task, usually operated by a properly trained ◊operator. Examples are cleaning robot for public places, delivery robot in offices or hospitals, fire-fighting robot, rehabilitation robot and surgery robot in hospitals. In this context, an operator is a person designated to start, monitor and stop the intended operation of a ◊robot or a ◊robot system.
- A robot system is a system comprising robot(s), end-effector(s) and any machinery, equipment, devices, or sensors supporting the robot performing its task.

Please note: According to the definition, "a degree of autonomy" is required for service robots ranging from partial autonomy (including human-robot interaction) to full autonomy (without operational human-robot intervention). Therefore, in addition to fully autonomous systems, service robot statistics include systems which may also be based on some degree of human-robot interaction (physical or informational) or even full teleoperation. In this context, human-robot interaction means information and action exchanges between human and robot to perform a task by means of a user interface (Dimitrova, M., N. Vegt, N., & E.Barakova, 2012).

AUTONOMOUS ROBOT

An autonomous robot is a robot that performs behaviors or tasks with a high degree of autonomy. This feature is particularly desirable in fields such as spaceflight, household maintenance and delivering goods and services.

A fully autonomous robot cans (Fasola J, Mataric M. J., 2010):

- Gain information about the environment.
- Work for an extended period without human intervention.
- Move either all or part of itself throughout its operating environment without human assistance.
- Avoid situations that are harmful to people, property, or itself unless those are part of its design specifications.

An autonomous robot may also learn or gain new knowledge like adjusting for new methods of accomplishing its tasks or adapting to changing surroundings.

Like other machines, autonomous robots still require regular maintenance.

The first requirement for complete physical autonomy is the ability for a robot to take care of itself. Many of the battery-powered robots on the market today can find and connect to a charging station, and some toys like Sony's "Aibo" are capable of self-docking to charge their batteries.

Self-maintenance is based on "proprioception", or sensing one's own internal status. In the battery charging example, the robot can tell proprioceptively that its batteries are low and it then seeks the charger. Another common proprioceptive sensor is for heat monitoring. Increased proprioception will be required for robots to work autonomously near people and in harsh environments. Common proprioceptive sensors include thermal, optical, and haptic sensing, as well as the "Hall's effect" (electric).

COLLABORATIVE FUNCTIONS

According to the international standard ISO 10218-1:2011, "Robots and Robotic Devices - Safety Requirements for Industrial Robots", Part 1 Part 2, there are four types of Collaborative Functions:

- Safe braking. This collaborative function is mainly used when the robot works mostly on its own, but it is possible for the user to enter its workspace. When the user enters the secure, virtually restricted work zone, the robot immediately stops, not shutting down, but stays in the standby mode.
- Direction of manual operations. This collaborative application is used to guide the hand when working with robotic tools or to train the robot on the desired trajectories in pick-and-place and other similar operations.

The technology allows the robot to engage in collaborative activities through additional force-sensing devices by means of force, compression, torque and torque sensors, and so on.

- Speed monitoring and redefined work area. In this type of collaborative applications, the robot's working environment is monitored by lasers or a machine vision system that track the user's position in space.

The robot operates only within the scope of the predefined work area. When the user enters this zone, the robot reacts with a significant decrease in its speed of operation, and when a person enters a predefined smaller perimeter around the robot, it stops completely. Typically, to resume work in Safe Shutdown and Safe Mode modes, the robot waits for a feedback (command or signal) from the operator.

Work areas and safety zones are classified so that the robot reproduces different responses to the human situation in space.

- Power and power limitation. Collectible robots with power and power limitation function are considered to be the safest as they can work side by side with no additional devices or restraint systems.

The robot is programmed to "recognize" unusual (too big) efforts and to stop instantaneously in the presence of such. This type of robot is designed to "distract" the force in the event of a collision with a person on a larger area, and therefore have rounded shapes. In addition, this type of robots has no display cables and other moving parts.

A large number of collaborative robots are certified by the relevant authorities in accordance with industrial safety standards for human and robot collaboration. In this respect, the Technical Specification ISO/TS 15066:2016 "Robots and Robotic Devices - Collaborative Robots" defines the maximum force and energy that can be applied to a person without causing him physical harm.

ISO/TS 15066:2016 specifies safety requirements for collaborative industrial robot systems and the work environment, and supplements the requirements and guidance on collaborative industrial robot operation given in ISO 10218-1 and ISO 10218-2. ISO/TS 15066:2016 apply to industrial robot systems as described in ISO 10218-1 and ISO 10218-2. It does not apply to non-industrial robots, although the safety principles presented can be useful to other areas of robotics.

This Technical Specification provides guidance for collaborative robot operation where a robot system and people share the same workspace. In such operations, the integrity of the safety-related control system is of major importance, particularly when process parameters such as speed and force are being controlled. It is applicable to human-robot collaboration with both conventional industrial robots and collaborative robots with power constraints.

DEVELOPMENT OF SENSOR TECHNOLOGIES FOR COLLABORATIVE ROBOTS

Sensor devices are keys to integrating robots into industrial machinery and equipment. Mass presence sensors, including capacitive and inductive proximity sensors and distance sensors, ultrasonic and photoelectric sensors, are widely used.

Generally, all robots incorporate feedback devices - encoders, resolvers and electromechanical angular or revolution measuring devices. Additionally, depending on the particular purpose, the collaborative robots are equipped with three categories of sensor technology - Snap Sensors and other End-of-Arm

Tooling devices (EOAT); preventive sensors (to prevent damage to the robots themselves) and safety sensors that take care of the security of people near robots on the move.

- **EOAT Sensors:** Typically photoelectric sensors, proximity sensors or video sensors that detect when an object is caught by the grippers or other robot tools associated with system logic. If the griper sensor is not active, the robot programming will instruct the robot to take another trajectory or to alert the operator that something is wrong.

This type of reporting has two distinct aspects - registering an object's presence in the gripper in order to safely continue the sequence of operations as well as qualitatively assessing an object when it enters the robot's workspace, verifying and deciding whether to be captured by tools and manipulation with it to continue.

- **Prevention Sensors:** Prevention sensors are usually analog sensors. They are used to detect small deviations in the robot's work by analogue measurements, which he is not able to account for as errors. Such are, for example, attempts to assemble two parts that do not fit in assembly operations.

In such cases, the sensor sensing system detects more effort than is typically required by the load sensors and instructs the robot to stop trying to perform the processes. This type of reading prevents breakage or other damage to the clamps and other robot tools and systems.

- **Safety Sensors:** The sensor systems for industrial robots have undergone significant development over the years. Among the most advanced technology to provide staff safety today are 3D scanners and video sensors. Usually, they are positioned next to the robot perimeter of the operating area and programmed to register the entry of a person into predefined range of the system. This technology is suitable for ensuring robot safety, which is triggered automatically.
- **Proximity Sensors:** Proximity sensors have the main function to register the presence or absence of an object (device, product, component, tool) at a certain stage of the robotic processes necessary for the safe performance of the desired subsequent operations. Installed mainly of buckles or the relevant enforcement tools (end effectors) on top of the robotic arm/hand, this type of sensors take into account whether they were engaged with the right object, and whether it was engaged in a correct way. For this purpose different solutions exist - from simple discrete sensors that only turn on and off to more sophisticated sensors that send information to the controller about the constant spatial position and size of the object via analog or serial digital outputs.
- **Precision Sensors:** By reducing the gauges of the objects with which the industrial robots handle, as well as the working cells themselves, they require ever higher accuracy and precision in their work. As a result, miniature sensors are becoming more and more sophisticated in automated production.

In addition to obvious advantages, such as extremely small dimensions and weight, this category of sensors also ensures much higher accuracy of reading. The term "precision readout" is used to define the ability of miniature sensors to provide more stable reading points even at temperature fluctuations. Sensors of this type are also more repetitive, with shorter hysteresis windows, the difference between switching and switching points, and a better ability to detect the presence of very small objects, often "invisible" for larger sensors. Precision miniature sensors provide robots with spatial information about the positioning of the object being handled. Through technologies such as laser distance sensors and machine vision systems, robots can precisely handle the desired product or component, as well as avoid collisions with workers or different objects in the work area.

- **Machine Vision Systems:** Machine Vision Systems in the last years has been developing very much. They are a separate category of sensors with very rich capabilities. Due to their wide-range functionality, they can be used to perform all of the above-mentioned types of robot sensor systems. The problem is that the robot is run in real-time mode and sometimes does not reach the machine's time to perform the task. Therefore, the combination with other types of sensors is very successful in identifying certain obstacles or objects with which the robot will interact. By using the Sensors Fusion processes, the tasks of the Video System are minimized by alleviating its activity and utilizing the information from other more profiled sensors in order to make a successful decision for the realization of certain actions of the robot in real time mode.

By using the Sensors Fusion processes, the tasks of the Video System are minimized by alleviating its activity and utilizing the information from other more profiled sensors in order to make a successful decision for the realization of certain actions of the robot in real time mode.

By using Artificial Intelligence elements such as "Detecting" and "Identifying" objects from the robot's workspace using predefined "Knowledge" in the Environmental Database, the Video System is greatly facilitated and so it is possible used in the process of managing the robot in real-time mode. When making a successful decision in the management process, the resulting is recorded in the Database for future use in a similar situation so could "Self Learning Procedure".

Indisputable benefits from the collaborative robots are:

- **Fast Installation:** Collectable robots can be installed by untrained staff and put into service only within a few hours.
- **Easy Programming:** The innovative collaborative robot technology enables anyone without pre-training or experience to program the system quickly and seamlessly with intuitive tools and logical steps through an easy-to-use software programming wizard.
- **Improved Safety:** Collaborative robots, on the other hand, can work side by side with no safety equipment and no need for large space to install.
- **Flexible Adaptation:** to multiple applications. The collaborative robots are lightweight, small-sized, save space and are suitable for deployment in different areas of the technological lines and can be easily moved. Capable of repeatedly using recurrent operations, they require minimal reset time and effort.

Technavio, ABB, Kuka, Rethink Robotics, Universal Robotics, Adept Technology, Fanuc, Yaskawa Motoman and some others are the biggest suppliers of robot products and solutions. ABB has announced the acquisition of the German company Gomtec, which will expand its portfolio of collaborative robots. Collaboration with Gomtec will extend our range of collaborative automation technologies, which already includes the first YuMi industrial two-handed robot developed specifically for small-part assembly applications.

- **Sensing the Environment:** Exteroception is sensing things from the environment. Autonomous robots must have a range of environmental sensors to perform their task and stay out of trouble. Common exteroceptive sensors include the electromagnetic spectrum, sound, touch, chemical (smell, odour), temperature, range to various objects, and altitude.
- **Task Performance:** The next step in autonomous behavior is to actually perform a physical task. A new area showing commercial promise is the area of domestic robots. While the level of intelligence is not high in these systems, they navigate over wide areas and pilot in tight situations around homes using contact and non-contact sensors. Both of these robots use proprietary algorithms to increase coverage over simple random bounce. The next level of autonomous task performance requires a robot to perform conditional tasks. For instance, security robots can be programmed to detect intruders and respond in a particular way depending upon where the intruder is.

AUTONOMOUS NAVIGATION

For a robots which are used behaviors and need with a place (localization) requires it to know where it is possible to be able to navigate "point-to-point". Such navigation began with wire-guidance in the 1970-s and progressed in the early 2000-s to "beacon-based" triangulation. Current commercial robots autonomously navigate based on sensing natural features. The first commercial robots to achieve this were Pyxus' HelpMate Hospital Robot and the Cyber Motion Guard Robot, both designed by robotics pioneers in the 1980-s. These robots originally used manually created CAD floor plans, sonar sensing and wall-following variations to navigate buildings. The next generation, such as Mobile Robots' Patrol Bot and Autonomous Wheelchair, both introduced in 2004, have the ability to create their own laser-based maps of a building and to navigate open areas as well as corridors. Their control system changes its path on the fly if something blocks the way.

At first, autonomous navigation was based on planar sensors, such as laser range-finders, that can only sense at one level. The most advanced systems now fuse information from various sensors for both localization (position) and navigation. Systems such as "Motivity" can rely on different sensors in different areas, depending upon which provides the most reliable data at the time, and can re-map a building autonomously (Zahariev R., N.Valchkova., 2009).

Rather than climb stairs, which requires highly specialized hardware, most indoor robots navigate areas, which are accessible for people with special needs like controlling elevators, and electronic doors. With such electronic access-control interfaces, robots can now freely navigate indoors. Autonomously climbing stairs and opening doors manually are topics of research at the current time. As these indoor techniques continue to develop, vacuuming robots will gain the ability to clean a specific user-specified room or a whole floor. Security robots will be able to cooperatively surround intruders and cut off exits. These advances also bring concomitant protections: robots' internal maps typically permit "forbidden areas" to be defined to prevent robots from autonomously entering certain regions (Valchkova N., R. Zahariev, 2016).

During the final NASA Sample Return Robot Centennial Challenge in 2016, a rover, named Cataglyphis, successfully demonstrated fully autonomous navigation, decision-making, and sample detection, retrieval, and return capabilities (Hall R. L.,N. Loura, 2016). The rover relied on a fusion of measurements from inertial sensors, wheel encoders, "Lidar", and Video camera for navigation and mapping, instead of using GPS or magnetometers. During the 2 hour challenge, Cataglyphis traversed over 2.6 km and returned five different samples to its starting position.

SERVICE MOBILE ROBOTS FOR HELP OF PEOPLE WITH SPECIAL NEEDS

The creation of Cognitive Mobile Service Robots for help of disabled people aims explicitly at fostering the scientific, innovation and patenting excellence of a leading Bulgarian institute – the Institute of Robotics of the Bulgarian Academy of Sciences (IR-BAS) in its striving for European and World Recognition in the area of research, being unique for the Region and acting as a Center of Innovation in: Innovative solutions of advanced system engineering and robotics for supporting independent living.

There is an emerging need worldwide for „Personal Robots", following the development of personal computers and personal devices like tablets, iPad, touch screen GSMs, etc. It is widely accepted that Service Robots can significantly contribute to better human working conditions, improved quality, profitability and availability of services (Serholt S., 2018). Some visions depict these robots as companions for household tasks like fetch-and-carry-services, maintenance, cleaning, entertainment, elderly care and even care for disabled persons, which on its own right – is no longer a matter of fiction in view of the recent advances in robotics of Honda, Sony, European robotics and many others (Smith,P. 2007).

Present day systems engineering and robotics research aims at implementing cost oriented innovative approaches to build smart, robust, reliable and understandable robotic devices and technological systems serving better the needs of people and creating conditions for a better quality of life for the future generations (Valchkova N., R. Zahariev,2016). These systems have to be projective – not replicating the existing solutions - implementing excellence and innovation based scientific thinking in the socio-economical context of the current world crisis. This is crucially important for countries from the region of South East Europe – where short-cut technologies have to be newly designed and made cost-oriented in order to converge faster to the standards of the European Union and be competitive on the international market (Angelov G., R. Zahariev, 2017) (Figure 3).

DESCRIPTION OF THE ROBOTS "ANRI-0" AND "ANRI-1"

The Robots from series AnRI (Anthropomorphic Robot with Intelligence) was developed based on the Robots from the family "ROBCO" at the Institute of Robotics – Bulgarian Academy of Sciences. (Chivarov N., Penkov Sv., Angelov G., at all, 2012), (Chivarov N,, Paunski Y., at all, 2012). The Robots "AnRI-1" and "AnRI-0" (Figure 4 and Figure 5) are on the base of mobile platforms with four wheels, of which two are driven and two are independent "free" wheels. In the Robot "AnRI-1" the wheels are located in the form of a cross. The driven wheels are at two sides of the platform and the "free" wheels are at the rear and front sides.

With the help of this location of the wheels it is possible to realize the Robots movements around the vertical axis at geometrical centre of construction in the left and right sides. At the hub of the driven wheels are built electric motors, DC powered by a rechargeable battery. The robot is equipped with a manipulator of anthropomorphic type, situated on the platform with three regional and three local degrees of mobility and gripper with separate drive and with three fingers. The same construction has the Robot

Figure 3. Experience of IR-BAS - Mobile service robots "AnRI" for help of people with special needs

"AnRI-0" with the difference is of situation of the wells, which are in the form of "triangle". At the two tops of the triangle are located the driven wheels and at the third top is the "free" wheel.

After experiments with Mobile service robot "AnRI-0", serving people with special needs, it was observed phenomena "The uncanny valley", defined bay Professor Mori (Japan) in 1970 (Mori, M. 1970/2012). This is negative reaction in behavior of the serving people provoke from the anthropoid image of the robot. To avoid this phenomena Mobile service robot "AnRI -1" was constructively formed without anthropoid had.

The drive of the robots is realized, based on "servo" controllers with feedback from incremental sensors, located in each degree of mobility of the manipulator. Regional levels are equipped with electromagnetic brakes and drive wheels of the platform are equipped with worm gearboxes that do not allow movement back using their braking effect.

The Control System of the robot is hierarchical, distributed, microprocessor type (Trevor Martin, 2016) and includes different levels, different devices and systems and corresponding software modules. (Angelov G., R. Zahariev, 2017) The connection between all devices on the management takes place via the serial interface RS 232. The total control module is based on 32 bit microprocessor embedded in the CPU module (Paunski Y., R.Zahariev, 2017).

Figure 4. Service Robot "AnRI-1"

Figure 5. Service Robot "AnRI-0"

PLANNING TRAJECTORY OF THE ROBOTS USING THE FUSION OF THE SENSORS INFORMATION

The Sensors Informational System of the robot converts various values (most often physical) into an information signal (most commonly electrical) that gives an idea of the quantity and quality of the measured parameters.

The mobile service robot is subject to specific requirements for the sensor information system, dictated, in particular, by the following features of the robot:

- Heterogeneity of the system: it must combine elements that function in different ways, communicate on different protocols and fulfill different purposes.
- Heteroarchism, heterogeneity of the organization of the system: some of the elements are centralized and hierarchically organized, while others are distributed with a high degree of autonomy:
- Work in conditions of uncertainty: since dynamics of change leads to reaching the limits of knowledge, it is often necessary for the system to use probabilistic or fuzzy methods.
- Working in real-time mode: all changes to the structure and functions of the system must be embedded within real-time mode (Adam Dunkels and all, 2002).

The coherence between the sensors and the mechanical units for which they are to provide information is not unambiguous. For example, one sensor is connected to a mechanical link (robot encoder), in other cases several sensors measure the same magnitude (radar, optical sensor, infrared sensor), in the third case the same sensor gives information about several mechanical components (Video sensor and multiple point tracking in space), and so on.

It is important to note the dynamics of the configuration, which requires a rapid change in the overall functioning of the Sensor System under the influence of the mobile robot coordination unit (Figure 6).

Figure 6. Experimental use of robot "AnRI-0" by people with special needs

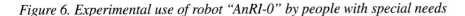

This ambiguity and dynamics of the sensor flow implies the need to integrate information, merging, sorting, filtering and completing the data needed to meet the current goal.

The dynamics of changing the environment requires the integration of information from new sensors connected in a new way to new mechanical units, new algorithms and approaches (Joseph Yiu, 2013). In practice, there is a large arsenal of approaches and methods for integrating information into the mobile service robot. The question of strategy and tactics of the particular implementation is what combination of such methods will be applied. (Dimitrova, M., & Wagatsuma, H. 015). The sensor subsystem merges the signals from all the sensors and, after processing, outputs information about the situation in which the robot is at all times.

CONCLUSION

The main challenge of the Project is to make personal robots affordable to people – which is to be achieved by implementing innovations in all aspects of functioning of the robotic device – materials, sensors, cognitive, communication, actuators, energy consumption, etc. In the extremely complicated process of education, an essential point is the definition of clear work and tactical goals (Shamsuddin, S., and all. 2015). With a certain clarity, the teacher should be aware of the goals set and be able to create an interest and desire in learners to absorb information based on key elements. These elements are also keywords that make it easier for learners to perceive the matter and create the prerequisite for higher learning efficiency.

According to M. Minsky's Theory of Framework for Representing Knowledge, (Minsky M., 1974) the information can be organized by the robot in separate frames, each subsequent frame inserted in the previous one clarifying and specifying it and thus progressing to a deep penetration of the problem. The information displayed in this way by a robot will cause interest in learners, which will be a powerful stimulus in the role of absorbing matter on the way to reaching the goals.

The innovations in their concerted design will bring cost efficiency in order to make the product complying with the market demand. That is why the main purpose of the project of conducting research into the adoption of Robotic Technologies in Special Education by children, young people and pedagogical specialists in the Implementation of the EC-funded program "Marie Curie" Project H2020-MSCA-RISE-2017, ID No 77720 "CybSPEED: "Cyber-Physical Systems for Pedagogical Rehabilitation in Special Education", was to examine to what extent the developed robots contribute to ensuring a dignified and independent life for (with a focus on young) people with special needs (CybSPEED, 2017).

On the basis of the studied necessary robots behavioral models, the hardware part should be further developed, which can provide the necessary basis for further development of the program platform in order to better meet the service needs of the same users. In this respect, advances in modern technologies are developing and increasing the capabilities of the used equipment for robots control in "real time" mode. Here, not only the rapid development of digital technology has led to an unprecedented rise in communication tools in society.(Barakova, E. and all. 2015). There is already a new technical revolution with the possibilities for developing analog technology. In this way, extremely fast processes for collection of analogue information from the environment are obtained, without having to transfer it in digital form in order to process it properly and then to decide on the implementation of a given task.

These two processes of development of the hardware and the software part of the robot should go in parallel and iteratively with the development of one part implying a jump in the development of the other part, which in turn puts its own possibilities and requirements that catalyze the development of the other part.

ACKNOWLEDGMENT

The authors acknowledge the financial support of the European Union's Horizon 2020 Research and Innovation Programme under the Marie Skłodowska-Curie Grant Agreement No 777720 (H2020-MSCA-RISE-2017 for project "Cyber-Physical Systems for PEdagogical Rehabilitation in Special Education". CybSPEED.

REFERENCES

Angelov, G., & Zahariev, R. (2017) Research and realization of TCP/IP communication with user interface in service robot, based on ROS node. *Pr. TUSofia, XXVI International Conference ADP-2017*, 304-308.

Barakova, E. I., Bajracharya, P., Willemsen, M., Lourens, T., & Huskens, B. (2015). Long term LEGO therapy with humanoid robot for children with ASD. *Expert Systems: International Journal of Knowledge Engineering and Neural Networks*, *32*(6), 698–709. doi:10.1111/exsy.12098

Bjoern, M. (2015). *ISO/TS 15066 - Collaborative Robots - Present Status*. Conference: European Robotics Forum 2015, ABB Germany, Corporate Research, Vienna, Austria.

Bjoern, M., & Reisinger, Th. (2016). *Example Application of ISO/TS 15066 to a Collaborative Assembly Scenario*. 47th International Symposium on Robotics (ISR 2016), Munich, Germany.

Chivarov, N., Paunski, Y., Ivanova, V., Vladimirov, V., Angelov, G., Radev, D., & Shivarov, N. (2012). Intelligent modular service mobile robot controllable via internet. *IFAC International Conference "SWIIS 2012"*, 149-153.

Chivarov, N., Penkov, Sv., Angelov, G., Radev, D., Shivarov, N., & Vladimirov, V. (2012). Mixed Reality Server and Remote Interface Communication for ROS Based Robotic System. *International Journal Automation Austria*, 144-155.

CybSPEED. (2017). *Cyber-Physical Systems for PEdagogical Rehabilitation in Special Education*. Horizon 2020 MSCA-RISE Project no. 777720, 1 Dec 2017 – 30 Nov 2021.

Dimitrova, M., Vegt, N. N., & Barakova, E. (2012). Designing a system of interactive robots for training collaborative skills to autistic children. *Interactive Collaborative Learning (ICL), 2012, 15th International Conference*, 1-8.

Dimitrova, M., & Wagatsuma, H. (2015). Designing Humanoid Robots with Novel Roles and Social Abilities. *Lovotics*, *3*(112), 2.

Dunkels. (2002). *lwIP - A Lightweight TCP/IP stack*. Retrieved from https://savannah.nongnu.org/projects/lwip

Engelberger, J. (1983). *Robots in Practice: Management and Applications of Industrial Robots*. Berlin: Springer. doi:10.1007/978-1-4684-7120-5

Engelberger, J. (1989). *Robots in Service*. MIT Press.

Fasola, J., & Mataric, M. J. (2010). Robot exercise instructor: A socially assistive robot system to monitor and encourage physical exercise for the elderly. RO-MAN, IEEE, 416-421.

GNU ARM. (2015). *Embedded Toolchain*. Retrieved from https://launchpad.net/gcc-arm-embedded/4.9/4.9-2015-q3-update

Hall & Loura. (2016). *NASA Awards $750K in Sample Return Robot Challenge*. Academic Press.

ISO 10218-1:2011. (2011). *Robots and robotic devices – Safety requirements for industrial robots – Part 1: Robots*. ISO.

ISO 8373:2012. (n.d.). *Robots and robotic devices – Vocabulary*. Retrieved from http://www.iso.org/iso/iso_catalogue/catalogue_tc/catalogu.e_detail.htm?csnumber=55890

ISO/TS 15066:2016. (2016). *Robots and robotic devices – Collaborative robots*. ISO.

Kaburlasos, V. G., Dardani, Ch., Dimitrova, M., & Amanatiadis, A. (2018). Multi-robot engagement in special education: a preliminary study in autism. *Proceedings of the 36th IEEE International Conference on Consumer Electronic (ICCE)*, 995-996. 10.1109/ICCE.2018.8326267

Liu, C., Conn, K., Sarkar, N., & Stone, W. (2008). Online affect detection and robot behavior adaptation for intervention of children with autism. *IEEE Transactions on Robotics*, *24*(4), 883–896. doi:10.1109/TRO.2008.2001362

Martin. (2016). Designer's Guide to the Cortex-M Processor Family (2nd ed.). Academic Press.

Minsky, M. (1974). *A Framework for Representing Knowledge*. Retrieved from dspace.mit.edu

Mitchell, R. L. (2012). Robots Move Into Corporate Roles: Active Media's Jeanne Dietsch says mobile robots make good corporate citizens. *Computer World*.

Mori, M. (1970/2012). The uncanny valley (K. F. MacDorman & N. Kageki, Trans.). *IEEE Robotics & Automation Magazine*, *19*(2), 98–100. doi:10.1109/MRA.2012.2192811

Paunski, Y., & Zahariev, R. (2017). Service robots control system, based on "Arm cortex M" architecture microprocessor system. *Pr. TUSofia, XXVI International Conference ADP-2017*, 300-304.

Prescott, T., & Szollosy, M. (2017). Ethical principles of robotics. *Connection Science*, *29*(2), 119–123. doi:10.1080/09540091.2017.1312800

Scassellati, B., Admoni, H., & Matarić, M. (2012). Robots for use in autism research. *Annual Review of Biomedical Engineering*, *14*(1), 275–294. doi:10.1146/annurev-bioeng-071811-150036 PMID:22577778

Serholt, S. (2018). Breakdowns in children's interactions with a robotic tutor: A longitudinal study. *Computers in Human Behavior, 81*, 250–264. doi:10.1016/j.chb.2017.12.030

Serpanos, D. (2015). The Cyber-Physical Systems Revolution. *J. Computer, 51*(3), 70-73.

Shamsuddin, S., Yussof, H., Hanapiah, F. A., Mohamed, S., Jamil, N. F. F., & Yunus, F. W. (2015). Robot-assisted learning for communication-care in autism intervention. In *Rehabilitation Robotics (ICORR), 2015 IEEE International Conference*, 822-827.

Smith, P. (2007). Have we made any progress? Including students with intellectual disabilities in regular education classrooms. *Intellectual and Developmental Disabilities, 45*(5), 297–309. doi:10.1352/0047-6765(2007)45[297:HWMAPI]2.0.CO;2 PMID:17887907

Valchkova, N., & Zahariev, R. (2016). Cognitive Service Robot For Help Of Disabled People. *Pr. TU-Sofia, XXV International Conference ADP-2016*, 168-173.

Wiener, N. (1961). *Cybernetics: Or Control and Communication in the Animal and the Machine*. MIT Press.

Yiu. (2013). Definitive Guide to the ARM Cortex-M3 and Cortex-M4 Processors (3rd ed.). Academic Press.

Zahariev, R., & Valchkova, N. (2004). *Assembly Mechatronic System with Flexible Organisation*. University of Technology.

Zahariev, R., & Valchkova, N. (2009). Perturbation Approach for Trajectory Planning of Technological Robot with Analyze of Task Accuracy Performance. *J. Scientific Announcement, 16*(2), 20-24.

Chapter 4
Learner Attitudes Towards Humanoid Robot Tutoring Systems:
Measuring of Cognitive and Social Motivation Influences

Maya Dimitrova
ⓘD https://orcid.org/0000-0002-9975-1255
Bulgarian Academy of Sciences, Bulgaria

Gyanendra Nath Tripathi
ⓘD https://orcid.org/0000-0001-9914-3789
Renesas Electronics, Japan

Hiroaki Wagatsuma
Kyushu Institute of Technology, Japan

Guangyi Ai
Neusoft Institute Guangdong, China

ABSTRACT

A novel framework for investigation of the learner attitude towards a humanoid robot tutoring system is proposed in the chapter. The theoretical approach attempts to understand both the cognitive motivation as well as the social motivation of the participants in a teaching session, held by a robotic tutor. For this aim, a questionnaire is delivered after the eye tracking experiment in order to record the type and amount of the learned material as well as the social motivation of the participants. The results of the experiments show significant effects of both cognitive and social motivation influences. It has been shown that cognitive motivation can be observed and analyzed on a very individual level. This is an important biometric feature and can be used to recognize individuals from patterns of viewing behaviors in a lesson. Guidelines, drawn from first-person accounts of learner participation in the study, are also formulated for achieving more intuitive interactions with humanoid robots intended to perform social jobs like being teachers or advisors.

DOI: 10.4018/978-1-5225-7879-6.ch004

INTRODUCTION

Trying to 'see' the robot tutor through the eyes of the learners by capturing the eye movements in an eye tracking experimental framework is a novel approach towards understanding the learners' attitude to inclusion of robots as teachers in the classroom. We propose a framework for testing the learner attitude towards a humanoid robot tutoring system that attempts to capture both the *cognitive motivation* as well as the *social motivation* of the participants in a teaching session, held by a robotic tutor. The important role of humanoid robots as technological support in the classroom has been extensively investigated recently both with typically developing children and children with learning difficulties (Lourens & Barakova; 2009; Krichmar & Wagatsuma, 2011; Leyzberg, Spaulding, Toneva, & Scassellati, 2012; Belpaeme et. al, 2013; Feng, Gutierrez, Zhang, & Mahoor, 2013; Huskens, Verschuur, Gillesen, Didden, & Barakova, 2013; Kim et. al, 2013; Anzalone et. al, 2014; Barakova, Kim, & Lourens, 2014). The aspects of being different from a human tutor and therefore more patient, less emotional, more amusing and drawing child's attention have been emphasized in these studies. The present study explicitly addresses the investigation of the 'social nature' of the learning process modulated by a humanoid robot in the classroom. Some results from the behavioral aspect of the current study were published in (Dimitrova, Wagatsuma, Tripathi, & Ai, 2015; Dimitrova, Wagatsuma, Kaburlasos, Krastev, & Kolev, 2018). Here we present in detail the novel experimental framework, proposed to investigate aspects of the attitude towards humanoid robot tutors combined with a 'viewing timeline analysis' (VTA) of eye-tracking data.

The inspiration for the experiment described in the paper has come from recent neuroscience research on the importance of the underlying brain mechanisms of 'social cognition' for shaping the cognitive abilities of the learner (Pfeiffer, Vogeley, & Schilbach, 2013; Schilbach, 2014). These studies can provide novel pedagogical insights towards designing robots to assist the teaching process in the classroom in order to achieve smooth and intuitive interaction of the robot with the learner at hand.

A promising novel trend of research on understanding the brain mechanisms of learning (in cognitive and social contexts) is "social cognitive neuroscience", which provides evidence of the primary role of social interaction in the developmental process of shaping cognition (Ochsner & Lieberman, 2001). M.D. Lieberman (2012) has proposed the concept of "social working memory" as distinct in its neurological basis from the commonly assumed cognitive 'working memory'. The areas of the brain that get involved while attending to a lesson, which is being explained with emphasis on its social relevance or historical context, are broader and involve the cognitive 'working memory' areas as well. Moreover, memories, created with the participation of 'social working memory areas' are much more durable than without them (which is actually a pedagogical aim by itself). Therefore, the social cognitive neuroscience forwards the idea of the emotion-cognition unity, where learning is driven by the rewarding role of the communication with the teacher and the peers or by the so called "intrinsic motivations" (e.g. Baldassarre & Mirolli, 2013), rather than by some functional self-realization notion. This requires designing innovative experimental paradigms to investigate the learners' attitudes towards humanoid robot tutoring systems, which aim at being more competent about the explicit and implicit aspects of the social communication process involved in education.

In respect to the issue of implementing social communication competence, K. Dautenhahn (2007) has summarized some of the existing definitions of a social robot and outlined five functional roles of being: "socially evocative", "socially situated", "sociable", "socially intelligent" and "socially interactive".

Figure 1. A humanoid robot tutoring framework implementing competence about the explicit and implicit aspects of the social communication process

According to Dautenhahn (2007, p. 584), the socially interactive robots can perform the following behaviors: "express and/or perceive emotions; communicate with high level dialogue; learn models of, or recognize other agents; establish and/or maintain social relationships; use natural cues (gaze, gestures, etc.); exhibit distinctive personality and character; and may learn and/or develop social competencies". Within this list of characteristic features of a 'social robot', the proposed experimental framework is focused on using 'natural cues' to 'develop social competencies' in the social situation of introducing a robot as a tutor in the classroom (Figure 1). The central point of the proposed novel experimental framework is measuring in *parallel* the *cognitive* and *social* motivation influences during learning from a humanoid robot tutor.

Cognitive Motivation Influences

Responses, triggered usually by physical stimulation, are considered cognitive in their nature and are processed by the mechanisms of overt attention under natural conditions (Taylor, Spehar, Donkelaar & Hagerhall, 2011; Kaspar & Konig, 2011; Borji, Sihite, & Itti, 2013). The human natural inclination to perceive, memorize and recollect physical events and objects from the surrounding environment comprises the spontaneous learning process. The curiosity, considered a fundamental orienting feature of human intelligence, is a feature that often can be attributed to a person (i.e. student) and has a gradation of being expressed in the classroom. Such aspects, guiding human behavior in the learning process, are manifestation of the *cognitive motivation* of the student to learn. Automatic processing such as *priming* or pre-exposure to a physical stimulus, event or objectified environment, belongs to this category of psychological processing, including perceiving people and their actions as physical objects (Oliva & Torralba, 2007; Sanada, Ikeda, Kimura, & Hasegawa, 2013; Dimiccoli, 2015). We refer to the analysis of the eye gaze behavior as to investigation of the *cognitive motivation* of the participants in the present experiment (Wykowska, Anderl, Schubo & Hommel, 2013).

Social Motivation Influences

In recent studies evidence is being accumulated about the neurological basis of social influences of the learning situation, within a novel theoretical framework called social-cognitive neuroscience in Ochsner & Lieberman (2001). A social motivation theory has been proposed by Chevallier, Kohls, Troiani, Brodkin, & Schultz (2012), stating that some aspects of the 'natural' human behavior are guided by seeking social contact and feeling pleasure solely by being in the company of other people. Novel studies reveal 'natural', i.e. 'hard-wired' in the neuronal activity processes such as "social perception" (e.g. Barraclough & Perrett, 2011), "social working memory" (Lieberman, 2012), "social gaze" of e.g. Emery (2000) and "social attention" of Langton, Watt, & Bruce (2000). It has been shown that the cues to the direction of social attention are not limited to eye gaze direction, but are combined with other cues, such as head orientation and pointing gestures. Moreover, it is concluded in Langton, Watt, & Bruce (2000, p. 56) that "…secondary cues, such as head orientation and pointing gestures, might provide more salient signal to the direction of another's attention than eye-gaze direction alone".

Viewing Timeline Analysis (VTL)

In the present study the fine grained eye gaze behaviors are investigated of the listeners to a lesson, delivered by a humanoid robot NAO, who is imitating the human teacher by using pointing gestures, head movement and eye-gaze direction when attempting an eye contact with the student. The point of interest is the relative amount of time spent on viewing these activities, performed by NAO, in order to propose a method called "Viewing timeline analysis" (VTL). The paper presents the main idea of this method, which will be developed in future studies.

The chapter presents a robotic-tutor scenario to investigate fine-grained gaze behavior of students when taught by a humanoid robot NAO, the obtained results from an experimental study and the design implications for pedagogical aims.

BACKGROUND

The experiments with unimodal and multimodal communication cues in human-robot interaction, presented by Torta, van Heumen, Piunti, Romeo, & Cuijpers (2015) are closely related to the present study. A NAO robot attempted to attract attention of a viewer of a TV show in a home environment. Three visual and one auditory actions were manipulated – NAO attempting to establish eye contact, waving gesture, blinking NAO's eyes and uttering the word "Hello". Reaction time was measured from the moment of noticing NAO in the periphery of one's vision by pressing the spacebar of a computer keyboard. Contrary to the expectations, reaction time was faster in the unimodal sound conditions than in the conditions of combined visual and sound effects to capture attention. In our study information was presented in a multimodal form – NAO explaining and pointing to an illustration. We expect to observe the normal student viewing behavior, on the one hand, and on the other – to try and explore comprehensively the fine grained gaze behavior of the student in the multimodal mode of information presentation. Hypothesis 1 is formulated in the next section based on the assumption that the dynamical behavior of the robot NAO is a holistic stimulus presenting a lesson in the classroom where multimodality is a precondition to the lesson presentation.

Eye tracking data is used to obtain deeper understanding of the actual visual processes during viewing NAO tutoring. In a study of Taylor, Spehar, Donkelaar & Hagerhall (2011) natural and artificial scenes as well as fractals and pink noise were presented successively. The results showed that the "biggest change occurred between initial and second observation and is expressed by a result pattern of increasing fixation durations, a decrease of saccade frequency and saccade length, and a reduced individual fixation distribution" (p. 4). We expect to obtain a similar pattern of saccadic eye movement change from the first to the second picture of the presented animals (based on their visual similarity) and formulated on this assumption Hypothesis 2.

In a study of Ai, Shoji, Wagatsuma, & Yasukawa (2014) participants viewed photographs with different figure-ground organization to extract profiles of spontaneous observation. Similarly, we want to extract profiles of gaze behaviors (as indicators of cognitive motivation) during viewing the actual robot and the illustrations of the lesson in the further analysis of the experimental data. Hypothesis 3 forwards the idea that the pattern of eye gaze can be assumed a biometric indicator which can bring new applications of the proposed approach. By applying the "viewing timeline analysis" (VTA) features can be extracted of individual viewing behavior for the purposes of the individualized tutoring in typical children and children with special needs.

Robotic reflexive cueing of attention was investigated by Admoni, Bank, Tan, Toneva, & Scassellati (2011) by implementing psychophysical methods. The participants viewed briefly on a laptop screen cues that were photographs of a human face, line drawing of a human face, arrow and two robotic faces with different degrees of anthropomorphism - Zeno (high) and Keepon (low), gazing in different directions. They were informed that a flashing stimulus will appear in the periphery of their viewing focus. The probability of the probe to appear in a location that is opposite to the cuing gaze was three times higher than to appear anywhere else on the screen, which was also explained to the participants. The theoretical hypothesis was that the response time will reflect the level of anthropomorphism of the cue. It was expected to observe that the information about probe appearing more often to the opposite of the gaze direction of the cue (human face, drawing of a human face, two types of robot faces or abstract drawing of an arrow) will result in different speed of responding to the probe, influenced by the level of human-likeness of the cue. This was not observed. Viewers' attention was reflexively cued by all stimuli except for the robotic faces. The robotic faces gaze did not interfere with the intentional orienting of the participants' gaze following the given instructions. Although this result may seem unexpected, it gives useful design clues for using robots in the classroom. We assume that the main potential of the robotic technology is in the ability to adapt the dynamics of its behavior to the most subtle human viewers' dynamics. The adaptive potential of the robot, especially in the time dynamics domain, is limitless and is of the kind that is not possible to expect from a human tutor. In the present study, we expect to observe robot cuing and capturing the attention of the viewer, which we attribute to the robot motion as temporal stimulus and use to formulate Hypothesis 4, unlike the static case of viewing snapshots of robot gaze in predicted directions as in (Admoni, Bank, Tan, Toneva, & Scassellati, 2011)

Not many studies attempt to relate cognitive and personality aspects of experiments on viewing behavior. In the study of Kaspar & Konig (2011) the participants in an experiment on focus of attention with an eye tracking system were delivered a personality test before the experiment. The test divided the participants into two groups of action- or state- oriented. A separate factor was introduced dividing the participants into a group, rating the viewed pictures as more interesting than the second group being less interested (by median splitting of the interestingness ratings). The main outcome was the three way interaction of the factors type of image viewed, action orientation and rating of the image. The action orientation in combination with high interestingness of the images had lowest saccade fixation and highest saccade frequency especially during viewing fractals or pink noise. The authors call it influence of "motivational disposition" on viewing behavior (p. 13). After rejection of pink noise images, the effects remained significant, which validated the subjective motivation influence on viewing behavior in general. However, it is important to note that the first two second's viewing revealed no effect of subject's interest in images on saccade length. Therefore, the subjective motivation is revealed at longer duration of viewing the images (6 sec) and may reflect the temporal dynamics of processing in the brain (Wagatsuma & Yamaguchi, 2001). Also, it seems that interestingness and action orientation may not be independent from each other, since they are revealed by similar questions. In our experiment, NAO took less than a minute to direct student attention to each of the pictures, so we did not expect differences due to the social motivation trait of the person. Rather, we expect independence relation (i.e. Dimitrova & Wagatsuma, 2011) between the cognitive and social motivation of a person, which can be considered features of the individual profile of the viewer and base the formulation of Hypothesis 5 on this assumption.

The aim of proposing a framework for relating the influences of the cognitive and the social motivation in studies on eye movement analysis is to extend the current approaches to extract features of scan path patterns (e.g. Kang & Landry, 2015) that are used to predict performance of novices vs. experts in aircraft conflict detection, for example. Another practical application is robot recognizing user focus of attention in order to support user intention by distinguishing sustained (longer duration) from shifted (brief) attention (e.g. Das, Rashed, Kobayashi, & Kuno, 2015). We propose an approach to predict the user's learning style, based on the analysis of the timeline of user viewing behavior for designing robot led learning courses tailored to the individual dynamics underlying the attentive processes (and to our knowledge is proposed for the first time). This approach can be extended even to special education, where robots can be pedagogical assistants to the teacher in the effort to overcome the learning limitations, which are due to scarce cognitive resource available to the individual learner.

AN EXPERIMENTAL DESIGN OF A NAO HUMANOID ROBOT TEACHER SCENARIO TO INVESTIGATE FINE-GRAINED STUDENT GAZE BEHAVIOR

The educational interaction process is assumed an interplay between joint attention and gaze-based interaction in a social communication scenario. A teacher captures the gaze of the child, then points to some illustrative material (joint attention), then gazes again at the child to find out if the point made has been understood by the learner. This constant interaction process is being paused periodically because the attention focus is tiring for the child and some rest is needed to accumulate some new attentional resource. The tutor, adapting to the dynamics of the child's attention, and the child, intuitively feeling comfortable with the tutor's teaching style, are both sides of a single educational process based on social communication competence at a very subtle level. This process is being reinstated in a NAO robot pedagogical framework in the present chapter.

Main Hypotheses of the Study

The following hypotheses are formulated within the proposed experimental design:

Hypothesis One: The fine grained gaze behavior of the student in the multimodal mode of information presentation will, in general, be consistent with the expectation that a robot tutor can be a successful substitute for a human tutor based on the analysis of eye tracking data, the recall test and the subjective reports.

Hypothesis Two: The pattern of saccadic eye movements change from the first to the second picture of the presented animals, based on their visual similarity, is expected to take place towards longer fixations as well as fewer and shorter saccades as a sign of transition from global to local processing.

Hypothesis Three: We expect to extract profiles of gaze behaviors (as indicators of cognitive motivation) during viewing the actual robot and the illustrations of the lesson in the analysis of the experimental data.

Hypothesis Four: We expect to observe robot cuing and capturing the attention of the viewer, which we attribute to the robot motion as a temporal stimulus, unlike the static case of viewing snapshots of robot gaze in predicted directions.

Hypothesis Five: We expect independence of the factors cognitive and social motivation, which can be considered features of the individual biometrics of the viewer. By establishing this, novel pedagogical strategies can be designed and implemented in a robot tutor for more adaptive and intuitive interaction with the current student.

Hypothesis Six: Cuing and capturing attention (indicators of learner attitude to the robot tutor) can be predicted based on a novel combination of features expressing the cognitive and social motivation for the individual learner by applying VTA.

Experimental Procedure

An experimental design was set up for demonstrating that a humanoid robot NAO can be used to modulate students' attention during a lesson. We investigated the spontaneous viewing behavior of typical students from University being taught by NAO by collecting eye tracking data (Figures 2 and 3).

Figure 2. Recording gaze behavior in a NAO tutor experimental framework using the AR system

Participants

Participants were eleven pairs of students and staff (17 male and 5 female students and staff) who knew English and were naïve to the purpose of the study. The average age was 32.6 years (23-55; SD = 9, 92).

The main selection criterion was to test viewing behavior of typical adults in order to obtain baseline levels of performance in human-robot context. Half of the participants had normal or corrected to normal vision via lenses (11 subjects). Having normal vision was not a prerequisite for the particular study because it tested a natural classroom situation with students adjusting their cognitive abilities to the multimodal style of the teacher. The other half of the participants wore glasses and took them off for the eye tracking part of the experiment. This did not change any of the dependent variables of the experiment.

Experimental Set Up

Figure 4 presents a diagram of the experimental setup with respect to the position, device and gender of the participants (blue for female). The yellow area represents the spatial organization of the experimental set up. The participants are invited in pairs and situated at 90 degrees to each other, and the robot is placed facing the diagonal line. In this way NAO can successively point out to one or the other board with displayed pictures of two classes of animals – forest animals on one of the boards and sea animals on the second.

Ethics

The study conformed to the national and EU guidelines for conducting experiments with human subjects. Written consent was obtained from all participants and they received a gift coupon as award after the experiment. The study was approved by the Ethics Committee of the Kyushu Institute of Technology, Japan, where the experiment took place.

Figure 3. Recording gaze behavior in a NAO tutor experimental framework using Takei Device

Figure 4. Diagram of the experimental setup with respect to position, device and gender of the participants (blue for female, white for male)

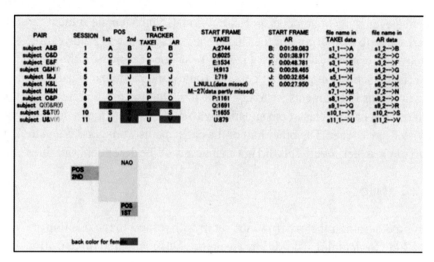

Instructions and Behavioral Test

The instructions to the participants in the experiment are given in Table 1.

Apparatuses

For recording data of eye gaze behavior AR ViewPoint PC-60 Scene Camera with EyeFrame PCI digitizer was used, with scanning at 30 Hz. The system mainly provides positions of the gaze (x, y) and the height and width of the pupil of the right eye (Figure 2, a). As a second device was used Takei TalkEye Lite T.K.K. 2950 system with same frequency and recording x and y angles and pupil size (x, y) of the right eye (Figure 2, b).

Table 1. Instructions to the participants

No	Steps	Instructions
1.	Informed Consent Form	You are going to participate in a study on using the humanoid robot NAO as a tutor in the classroom. Imagine NAO is teaching a zoology lesson. We are interested in the spontaneous gaze behavior while watching a teacher. Please, make yourself comfortable in the chair. The session will take a few minutes. Please sign this form as consent to participate in the study.
2	Free Recall Test (random order of presentation)	1. Please, write down the main differences between a Shark and a Dolphin as explained by NAO. 2. Please, write down the main differences between a Panda and a Koala as explained by NAO.
3	Feedback on the Experiment	Please, write any comments if you have, about the NAO robot teacher
4	Social Motivation Question	Was it better to listen to NAO in the presence of another person or indifferent? (Please circle the correct answer) A) Better B) Indifferent

Figure 5 presents a snapshot of the visualization interface of the Takei TalkEye Lite T.K.K. 2950 system.

Procedure

The participants were given instructions to imagine NAO as a zoology teacher. NAO presented in a synthetic voice 7 sentences comparing two forest animals - panda and koala - and 7 sentences comparing two sea animals in English - shark and dolphin (Table 2). During pointing out to the first pair of animals, NAO was making eye contact with one of the participants, and during pointing out to the second – with the other participant.

The total time NAO presented each pair of animals was 40 seconds, so the learning session took 1 min 20 seconds in total with 10 seconds pause after each pair (memory consolidation time). The preparation phase with the eye tracking glasses adjustment took 5-6 min.

The text included features of animals of the following categories – geographical location, habits, appearance and species information (in this order). The photographs were taken from the respective entries

Figure 5. Visualization interface of the Takei TalkEye Lite T.K.K. 2950 system

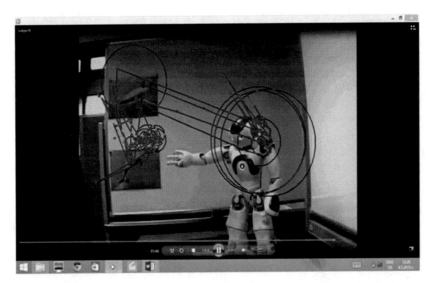

Table 2. Text pronounced by NAO

Condition	Text, Spoken by Nao about Forest Animals	Text, Spoken by Nao about Sea Animals
First animal presented and pointed at Text after making eye contact	This is a Panda. It leaves in China and eats bamboo leaves. Its color is white and black. Panda is a bear.	This is a Shark. It lives in the ocean and is dangerous. Its color is silver and white. Shark is a fish.
Second animal presented and pointed at Text after making eye contact	This is a Koala. It lives in Australia and eats eucalyptus leaves. Koala is not a bear.	This is a Dolphin. It lives in the sea and is not dangerous. Dolphin is not a fish.

in Wikipedia. The text about the appearance of the second presented animal was omitted in order to trace if previous knowledge would be used during recall. Due to the organization of the experiment, where pictures of the animals are presented like in a standard classroom – on a white board (instead on the computer screen) - it was not possible to exchange places and the order of presentation. Instead, the eye tracking systems were used in a counterbalanced order in respect to the presented animal photographs. The animal photographs were covered with a white sheet before the experiment.

After signing the informed consent form, the experimenter calibrated the eye tracking systems of the participants. During the calibration the participants were asked to focus at NAO's face, so using the robot as a vision focus became naturally. The photographs were uncovered and the experiment started. NAO stood up and pronounced the text about Panda while pointing at it and looking at it. Then it looked at the participant that was facing the forest animals and pronounced the rest of the text about Panda after making eye contact. Next NAO pointed out to the second forest animal (below the first one) and repeated the procedure. Then 10 seconds were allowed as memory consolidation time and NAO pronounced the text about the sea animals, addressing the participant, sitting facing the sea animals. In 10 more seconds' memory consolidation time, NAO pronounced the final words, waving its hand: "Have a good day! Bye!" and sat down. This was the end of the eye tracking part of the experiment.

Experimental Design

The experimental design is 2X2X2 factorial design with levels *type of attention modulation* (cuing vs. capturing attention*), type of communication signaling* (joint attention vs. eye-contact) and *stimulus exposure type* (exposed vs. pre-exposed stimulus). This design aims to capture the influences of the cognitive motivation to learn from NAO. The experiment investigates the *cognitive motivation and* the *social motivation* of the participants when taught by a robot in the presence of a classmate by asking a specially formulated social motivation question after the recall test (Question 4 in Table 2).

Independent and Dependent Variables

It was pre-tested if the type of attention modulation (cuing vs. capturing attention) interacted with the type of communication signaling (joint attention vs. eye-contact) in a 2X2 ANOVA. The type of attention modulation in terms of cuing vs capturing attention is related to the sitting position of the participant in respect to the position of the presented pictures and, in a way, represents the influence of a somewhat quasi-independent (or extrinsic) variable. Therefore, the independent variables of interest in the present experiment are the *type of communication signaling* (joint attention vs. eye-contact) and the *stimulus exposure type* (exposed vs. pre-exposed stimulus) and the dependent variables are the *level of recall* of features of the presented animals in the robot-performed zoology lesson (behavioral test) and *the nature of the saccadic eye movements* (cognitive test) – overall viewing time and individual viewing patterns.

Behavioral Test

After finishing the task, the participants were given a questionnaire, consisting of an unexpected free recall test, a question if they had comments about NAO as a robot teacher and a social motivation question if they were more comfortable in the presence of another person during a lesson delivered by a robot or indifferent.

RESULTS AND DISCUSSION

Results From the Behavioral Part of the Experiments

The behavioral part of the experiment was designed to provide a broader context to testing the operational hypotheses from One to Six. The results of the pre-test to see if the sitting position (view point) and type of stimulus (forest vs. sea animals) influenced the level of retention of the presented animal features in the zoology lesson are given in Table 3.

Table 3. Level of retention of the presented animal features in the zoology lesson

		Subject	Type of Stimulus (Forest vs. Sea Animals)			
			No	Sea Animals	No	Forest Animals
View point	Viewing sea animals first AR device T device	C G K O S		2 - habit, appearance 4 - appearance, habit, location, *species* 2 - habit, *species* 2 - habit 1 - <u>species</u>		1- location 4 - location, habit, appearance, *species* 3 location, appearance, *species* 2 location, appearance 1 <u>species</u>
		Mean$_{AR}$ = Mean$_{AR}$/n = Mean$_{AR}$ eye=		2,2 0,44 0,60		2,2 0,44 0,60
		A E I M Q U		1 – appearance 1 – *species* 1 – *species* 1 – *species* 1 – *species* 2 – location, habit		2 – location, habit 2 - appearance, habit 2 – location, habit - 1 – appearance -
		Mean$_T$ = Mean$_T$/n= Mean$_T$ eye =		1,4 0,23 0,67		1,4 0,23 0,00
	Viewing forest animals first AR device T device	B F J N R V		2 habit, *species* 1 *species* 4 appearance, habit, location, *species* 2 location, *species* 2 habit, *species* 1 habit		2 appearance, *species* 0 - 3 appearance, habit, location 2 location, *species* 2 appearance 0 -
		Mean$_{AR}$ = Mean$_{AR}$/n = Mean$_{AR}$ eye=		2,00 0,33 0,83		1,5 0,25 0,33
		D H L (f) P T		2 – habit, *species* 1 – location 1 – habit 1 – habit 1 – *species*		2 – location, habit 2 – appearance, habit 1 – location 2 – location, habit 1 - location
		Mean$_T$ = Mean$_T$/n= Mean$_T$ eye =		1,2 0,24 0,40		1,6 0,32 0,00
Mean$_{Total}$ = SD$_{Total}$ = Mean$_{Total}$/n=				1,64 0,90 0,41		1,59 1,05 0,40
M$_{Total}$eye = SD$_{Total}$eye =				0,64 0,49		0,23 0,43

The two-way ANOVA revealed a main effect of the type of sitting position used for viewing the lesson $F(1, 21) = 4,40$, $p = 0,0006$, but not type of the animals viewed first $(1, 21) = 0,06$, $p = 0,80$. The type of animal viewed first we have called influence of cued vs. captured attention. The first viewed animal is seen by captured attention by the robot pointing with its hand, and the second viewed animal is being cued by the robot pointing to the picture and looking at the other participant. Therefore it did not matter if the viewer was sitting frontal to the educational material that NAO was explaining, or was turning eyes to see what NAO was explaining. In this way a realistic classroom situation was reinstated with the robot-teacher being able to both cue and capture viewers' attention.

The remembered information after the eye contact was influenced by the attention being cued or captured in the total group of participants as revealed by a 2 way ANOVA, $F(1,21) = 14,54$, $p = 0,001$. The influence of the sitting position factor reached significance, too, $F(1,21) = 2,37$, $p = 0,027$. Since part of the participants on a sitting position wore one of the devices and part – the other, we tested the influence of the individual device on this pattern of results. The number of remembered animal features did not depend on the cueing vs. capturing attention in the group of subjects, sitting in position 1 (see figure 2) $F(1, 11) = 0,80$, $p = 0,39$, but depended on the type of device that was used for eye gaze recording AR vs. Takei $R(1,11) = 0,032$ (2 way ANOVA). Similar were the results from the 2 way ANOVA on the remembered items in the group of subjects sitting in position 2 with cueing vs. capturing attention being non-significant $F(1,8) = 1$, $p = 0, 35$, but type of device influencing the results, $F(1,8) = 8,5$, $p = 0,003$.

It seems that there was some problem with the Takei device for providing optimal view for the participants, so in our further analysis the examples are taken from the AR group. For example, the group wearing the Takei device and viewing the sea animals first recollected only the information from NAO making an eye contact, whereas the group wearing the Takei device and viewing the forest animals first did not recollect at all the information presented by NAO after making and eye contact. This can be due to the device itself being an obstacle to the proper vision of the participants. The pattern of data from the AR device favor the view that this is most probably an artefact from using the Takei device rather than a regularity in the group (see Table 4). In further experiments we recommend using the AR device as more reliable for the purpose of investigating the eye gaze behavior of students during a lesson, presented by a humanoid robot.

The pattern of recollection in the AR group was much more consistent than in the Takei group. Regarding the level of recollection of the information presented after the robot making an eye contact, the mean values of items remembered from the presented before and after making the eye contact were equal in the AR group, suggesting similar influences on the remembering of the information presented with robot pointing at pictures or during looking in the eyes of the listener. Therefore, the students felt comfortable as in a classroom where the teacher is using gaze behavior and pointing gestures to hold students' attention during the episode of presented information (which normally is made by the teacher between the natural pauses of the lesson).

As a primacy effect (see also Figure 6) the forest animals were less well remembered in the entire group. From the mean values of recall of sea and forest animals as well as the mean recalled after being presented after the eye contact of the robot with the students in the AR group it is evident that almost no influence is observed (i.e. values are similar in both conditions), which validates the experimental results in respect to the quasi-independent variable sitting position in the experimental 'classroom' being non-influential in the current experimental setting.

Table 4. Level of retention of the presented animal features in the zoology lesson in the AR group

		Subject	Type of Stimulus (Forest vs. Sea Animals)			
			No	Sea Animals	No	Forest Animals
View point	Viewing sea animals first	C G K O S		2 - habit, appearance 4 - appearance, habit, location, *species* 2 - habit, *species* 2 - habit 1 - <u>species</u>		1- location 4 - location, habit, appearance, *species* 3 location, appearance, *species* 2 location, appearance 1 *species*
	M = M/n = M eye =			2,2 0,55 0,6		2,2 0,55 0,6
	Viewing forest animals first	B F J N R V		2 habit, *species* 1 *species* 4 appearance, habit, location, *species* 2 location, *species* 2 habit, *species* 1 habit		2 appearance, *species* 0 - 3 appearance, habit, location 2 location, *species* 2 appearance 0 -
	M= M/n = M eye =			2,09 0,52 0,83		1,56 0,39 0,33

Recollection of the Study Episode

The participants were university students and staff and the teaching material was selected for children in early school. Table 5 presents the mean items recollected by the participants in total, being at the level of about 40% of the presented information.

The similar M_{Total} and SD_{Total} values of remembering information about the forest animals and the sea animals support the above conclusion that the setup has provided a realistic reinstatement of the classroom situation where a humanoid robot NAO plays successfully the role of a teacher. Figure 6 presents the proportions (in terms of percentage of the difference between animal features) recalled by the participants. It is important that they did not substitute the information, provided by NAO, with preexisting knowledge or from the visual memory. The standard primacy and recency effects are clearly observed: the geographical location of the forest animals was presented first, whereas the species information of the sea animals was presented last (the first and the last bars in the chart on recall in Figure 6). This validates the experimental results, as it is well known that information presented early during an experimental trial is well remembered as rehearsed longer than the rest, whereas the information, presented last stays in the working memory after the end of the trial (e.g. Baddeley, 1997).

Table 5. Mean feature items recollected by the participants in total

	Sea Animals	Forest Animals
M_{Total}	1,59 (40%)	1,55 (0,39%)
SD_{Total}	0,89	1,03

Figure 6. Recalled features per category (see text)

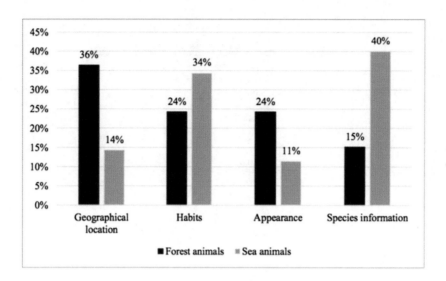

In the subjective reports the participants paid more attention to the human-robot interaction aspect of the study and commented how to improve robot performance to make it more intuitive. Some of the comments are related to the long 10 second pause after the presentations of the pairs of animals. The pause was made on purpose for memory consolidation after the presentation of the pairs of animals' text, so photos and mentioning it was omitted from the transcript of the protocols.

Social Motivation Results

Table 6 summarizes the comments of the participants regarding the robotic tutoring framework. Some participants gave positive comments and some commented on the performance of the actual robot as an imitation of a teacher. In overall, participants' comments addressed the way a robot interaction with the human should become more 'natural', i.e. more anthropomorphic as sound, posture, movement, etc. One explanation is that all participants were engineering and computer science students and staff, who were interested in designing user-friendly technological devices.

The observation of the participant behavior in the experiment demonstrates the relaxed way people perceive the option of having a robot teacher and the amusement this can bring to the educational process.

The participants, who reported that they preferred the presence of a classmate during the session were 13 (the socially motivated group), in comparison with the indifferent ones, who were 9 (the socially indifferent group). One particular result deserves special attention. Interestingly, the socially-motivated participants gave more positive comments and less recommendations to the robot teacher than the indifferent as illustrated in Figure7.

The type of device did not influence the number of positive comments or recommendations towards the humanoid robot teacher revealed by a 2 way ANOVA, $F(1,21) = 0,327$, $p = 0, 223$. The socially motivated group gave comparable amount of positive comments and recommendations as revealed by a single factor ANOVA, $F(1, 24) = 0,69$, $p = 0,416$. The socially indifferent group, however, gave sig-

Table 6. Text pronounced by NAO

Parti-Cipant	Positive Comment	Recommendation
A		"May lip movements and more human-like gestures can help in the retention".
B		"The direction to the picture it points is not accurate. Sometimes if user has no knowledge about pictures may find hard to distinguish which one it is pointing to."
D	"Interesting to listen from a robot teacher."	
E	"I like the flashing light on the robot."	"May need some more movement for more interesting attraction."
F	"Very good of teaching."	"Sometimes voice in not much understandable."
G	"It is very nice to look at. When it makes eye contact, its influence is huge."	"Maybe its going too fast."
H	"It is easy for me to understand."	
I	"The NAO robot is a good teacher."	
J	"Interested to know how it follows the motion of the human."	
K	"The explanations were nice," but the interval between them was unnatural.	
L	"It was awesome to experience listening NAO robot teacher"	
M		"I think speaking (can be) more clearly."
N		"I heard some audio noise on his/her voice, which was a little bit disturbing to listen to his/her voice."
O	"NAO robot is an intelligent robot."	
P	"Nearly very good."	"If it is possible more clear speaking form NAO."
Q	"Robot teacher is very good, but ..."	"... speaking is not clear."
R	"It is more interesting to listen to NAO" "And if it can say some jokes like person, I think it will make the phenomenon more comfortable and relaxible."	"I think it can explain more and more active" Sometimes it can point to the right direction of the picture"
U		"Well, it's better to give instruction by robot to listen carefully."
V		"NAO's way of speaking was a bit unnatural."

nificantly higher number of recommendations, than of positive comments as revealed by a single factor ANOVA, $F(1,16) = 7,69$, $p = 0,14$.

The finding that *the socially-motivated participants were more positive overall* towards the robot tutor than those who were socially-indifferent deserves further investigation with more participants, yet it provides support to the proposed in the present chapter framework that social interaction is an essential (and broader) concept for education than making mere attempts for memorizing the contents of the lesson. It confirms in a behavioral setting the 'social working memory' proposal of M.D. Lieberman (2012). With a human teacher, people are usually more attentive to the actual information presented in verbal and pictorial forms. With NAO tutoring it seems that the participants focus on the entertaining and the communicative aspects of the human-robot interaction process, rather than on the information

Figure 7. Percent positive comments (dark bar) and percent recommendations (light bar) made by the socially motivated participants vs. the indifferent

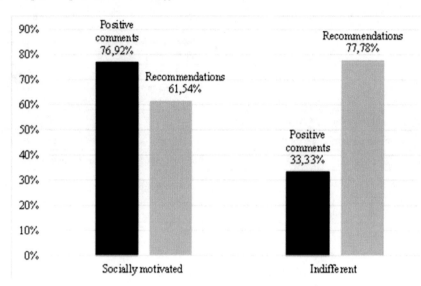

that NAO is giving by speaking and by pointing to pictures. This is also found in the subjective reports after the session with NAO.

Analysis of the Eye Tracking Data

Figure 9 presents example of a pie chart obtained about time devoted to viewing the robot or the pictures, demonstrated by the robots. Figure 10 present an example of the timeline diagrams of the viewing behavior. Both represent the data received from the AR ViewPoint PC-60 Scene Camera. It was evident that there is no dependency between any indicators of the social and cognitive motivation. Therefore, these two aspects of user behavior towards a robot appear orthogonal and fit well with a novel human-robot interaction account, where the *cognitive* and *social* motivation of a person can be considered independent dimensions. For a human-robot system, diagnostic of the user, this finding is important in order to make possible to draw a relevant profile of each individual user and be able to predict behavior based on both qualitative and quantitative indicators.

Testing the Individual Hypotheses

Hypothesis One: The fine grained gaze behavior of the student in the multimodal mode of information presentation will, in general, be consistent with the expectation that a robot tutor can be a successful substitute of a human tutor based on the analysis of eye tracking data, the recall test and the subjective reports. Table 7 displays the amount of time devoted to viewing robots' hand and robot's face in the AR group.

Students are attentive to the lesson and focus on the pointing gestures of the robot-tutor, which is in agreement with the expectation that pointing gestures and face movements are important to direct one's

Table 7. Amount of time (%) devoted to viewing robots' hand vs. robot's face in the AR group

	Robot's Hand	Robot's Face
M_{AR}	42,90%	24,51%
SD_{AR}	34,21%	31,49%

social attention, not just seeing it as a physical object. The amount of time viewing the robot hand did not differ significantly from the amount of time viewing the robot's face, as revealed by ANOVA, $F(1,20)$ $=1,56$, $p = 0,2255$. It is shown that robots are not stereotypically defined by their face in a study comparing user attitude towards a human, a robot and a computer (Ramey, 2006). This is in agreement with the present finding of feeling comfortable with a robot taking over a human profession like a teacher.

Hypothesis Two: The pattern of saccadic eye movements change from the first to the second picture of the presented animals, based on their visual similarity, is expected to take place towards longer fixations as well as fewer and shorter saccades as a sign of transition from global to local processing. Figure 8 presents the amount of time devoted to viewing the first presented animal compared to the second in the AR group.

The time spent viewing 4 pictures of animals differed from one to another in the AR group as revealed by one way ANOVA, $F (3, 40) = 6,29$, $p = 0,001$. The time spent viewing Panda differed significantly from the time spent viewing Koala as revealed by ANOVA, $F (1, 20) = 8,64$, $p = 0,008$. The time spent viewing Shark did not differ significantly from the time spent viewing Dolphin as revealed by ANOVA $F (1, 20) = 0, 36$, $p = 0,5556$ (see Figure 8).

Figure 8. Pre-exposure effect of a similar category

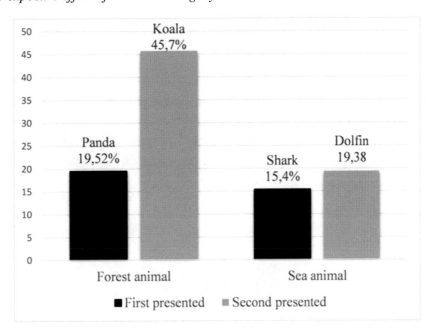

Figure 8 illustrates the pre-exposure effect of the similar category for both types of animals. As expected, the pre-exposure to Panda leads to bigger time devoted to viewing Koala and the pre-exposure to Shark leads to bigger time devoted to viewing Dolphin (although insignificant in the second case).

The pie chart in Figure 9 represents example of the individual proportions of viewing times in the AR group. Subjects B, C and J (Figure 4) are the group devoting most of their attention to viewing the pictures, whereas the rest devote most of their attention to viewing the robot. No other similarities can be observed among them. Evidently, cognitive motivation can be observed and analyzed on a very individual level in a way similar to reading the fingerprints of a person. This is an important biometric feature and can be used to recognize individuals based on patterns of viewing behaviors in a lesson, as well as to predict motivation to focus on the lesson via VTA ("viewing timeline analysis").

Robot cuing and capturing attention is seen from the pattern of individual timelines of viewing behavior (Figure 10). Subjects followed the pointing behavior of the robot from one picture to another and spent almost all of the time in viewing the teacher and the lesson. Formal analyses will be performed in future studies. The final sentence of the presented information about each animal is made in a mode of robot attempting eye contact. With a robot teacher, students behaved in full awareness that the robot is not a substitute for a human, but is performing a human role of a professional for a special reason. This is a conclusion that has to be accounted for when designing humanoid robots for playing different roles in human society that are not attempting to substitute the humans, but to assist them in their professional work.

Figure 9. Example pie chart of % individual viewing time during the robot lesson

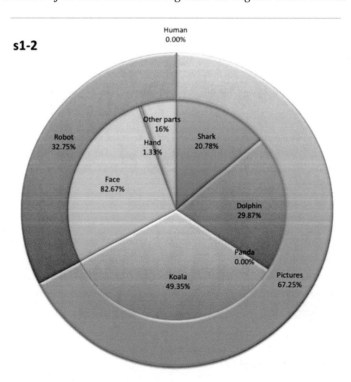

Figure 10. Example of a personal timeline of a learner viewing Panda first

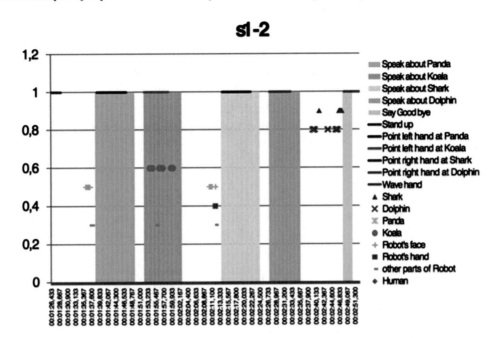

CONCLUSION AND FUTURE WORK

With the inclusion of robots in the educational and instructional activities of all possible aspects of life in the near future, and with the increased cognitive competence implemented in technology, people of different learning styles and educational needs will rely on learner-adaptive instruction and intuitive human-robot interface. This is particularly valuable if the robotic technology is implemented in adaptive and intuitive learning settings for children with special educational needs, but also in the classroom in general.

The eye tracking data revealed the expected effects of attention cueing of the first participant to the first pair of animals, and of the second participant to the second pair of animals. Also the expected effect of attention capturing of the second participant by pointing to the first pair of animals, or attention capturing of the first participant to the second pair of animals was observed.

As a novel finding we established the participation of *both* social motivation and cognitive motivation in the process of perceiving a robot tutor. People demonstrated main concern with robot social communication competence/ability before actually paying attention to the contents of the lesson to be learned. This is an outcome that has to be taken into account when designing novel robotic tutoring systems.

It has become evident in this study that cognitive motivation can be observed and analyzed on a very individual level in a way similar to reading the fingerprints of a person. This is an important biometric feature and can be used to recognize individuals from patterns of viewing behaviors in a lesson for robotic implementation. Future work will include tests of the VTA approach and implementation of the proposed framework in different educational settings.

ACKNOWLEDGMENT

This work is partially supported by Grant 777720 of H2020-MSCA-RISE-2017 for project CybSPEED (2017 - 2021), MEXT/JSPS KAKENHI 15H05878, 16H01616, 17H06383 and the New Energy and Industrial Technology Development Organization (NEDO). The actual experiment was performed in 2015 while Maya Dimitrova was on a FY2014 JSPS Invitation Fellowship Program (Short-Term) for Research in Japan ID No. S-14156 at Kyushu Institute of Technology (KYUTECH). The authors are grateful to MSc Mayu Ichiki, who encoded the data for the timeline analysis.

REFERENCES

Admoni, H., Bank, C., Tan, J., Toneva, M., & Scassellati, B. (2011, January). Robot gaze does not reflexively cue human attention. In *Proceedings of the Annual Meeting of the Cognitive Science Society* (*Vol. 33*, No. 33). Academic Press.

Ai, G., Shoji, K., Wagatsuma, H., & Yasukawa, M. (2014). A Structure of Recognition for Natural and Artificial Scenes: Effect of Horticultural Therapy Focusing on Figure-Ground Organization. In *Advanced Intelligent Systems* (pp. 189–196). Cham: Springer. doi:10.1007/978-3-319-05500-8_18

Anzalone, S. M., Tilmont, E., Boucenna, S., Xavier, J., Jouen, A. L., Bodeau, N., ... Chetouani, M. (2014). How children with autism spectrum disorder behave and explore the 4-dimensional (spatial 3D+ time) environment during a joint attention induction task with a robot. *Research in Autism Spectrum Disorders*, *8*(7), 814–826. doi:10.1016/j.rasd.2014.03.002

Baddeley, A. D. (1997). *Human Memory: Theory and Practice*. Psychology Press.

Baldassarre, G., & Mirolli, M. (2013). Intrinsically motivated learning systems: an overview. In *Intrinsically Motivated Learning in Natural and Artificial Systems* (pp. 1–14). Berlin: Springer. doi:10.1007/978-3-642-32375-1_1

Barakova, E. I., Kim, M. G., & Lourens, T. (2014, June). Development of a robot-based environment for training children with autism. In *International Conference on Universal Access in Human-Computer Interaction* (pp. 601-612). Springer. 10.1007/978-3-319-07446-7_58

Barraclough, N. E., & Perrett, D. I. (2011). From single cells to social perception. *Philosophical Transactions of the Royal Society of London. Series B, Biological Sciences*, *366*(1571), 1739–1752. doi:10.1098/rstb.2010.0352 PMID:21536557

Beach, P., & McConnel, J. (2018). Eye tracking methodology for studying teacher learning: A review of the research. *International Journal of Research & Method in Education*, 1–17. doi:10.1080/1743727X.2018.1496415

Belpaeme, T., Baxter, P., De Greeff, J., Kennedy, J., Read, R., Looije, R., ... Zelati, M. C. (2013, October). Child-robot interaction: Perspectives and challenges. In *International Conference on Social Robotics* (pp. 452-459). Springer. 10.1007/978-3-319-02675-6_45

Borji, A., Sihite, D. N., & Itti, L. (2013). What stands out in a scene? A study of human explicit saliency judgment. *Vision Research*, *91*, 62–77. doi:10.1016/j.visres.2013.07.016 PMID:23954536

Cantoni, V., Galdi, C., Nappi, M., Porta, M., & Riccio, D. (2015). GANT: Gaze analysis technique for human identification. *Pattern Recognition*, *48*(4), 1027–1038. doi:10.1016/j.patcog.2014.02.017

Chevallier, C., Kohls, G., Troiani, V., Brodkin, E. S., & Schultz, R. T. (2012). The social motivation theory of autism. *Trends in Cognitive Sciences*, *16*(4), 231–239. doi:10.1016/j.tics.2012.02.007 PMID:22425667

Das, D., Rashed, M. G., Kobayashi, Y., & Kuno, Y. (2015). Supporting human–robot interaction based on the level of visual focus of attention. *IEEE Transactions on Human-Machine Systems*, *45*(6), 664–675. doi:10.1109/THMS.2015.2445856

Dautenhahn, K. (2007). Socially intelligent robots: Dimensions of human–robot interaction. *Philosophical Transactions of the Royal Society of London. Series B, Biological Sciences*, *362*(1480), 679–704. doi:10.1098/rstb.2006.2004 PMID:17301026

Diehl, J. J., Crowell, C. R., Villano, M., Wier, K., Tang, K., & Riek, L. D. (2014). Clinical applications of robots in autism spectrum disorder diagnosis and treatment. In *Comprehensive Guide to Autism* (pp. 411–422). New York, NY: Springer. doi:10.1007/978-1-4614-4788-7_14

Dimiccoli, M. (2016). Figure–ground segregation: A fully nonlocal approach. *Vision Research*, *126*, 308–317. doi:10.1016/j.visres.2015.03.007 PMID:25824454

Dimitrova, M., & Wagatsuma, H. (2011). Web agent design based on computational memory and brain research. *Information Extraction from the Internet*, 35-56.

Dimitrova, M., Wagatsuma, H., Kaburlasos, V., Krastev, A., & Kolev, I. (2018). Towards Social Cognitive Neuropsychology Account of Human-Robot Interaction. *Complex Control Systems*, *1*, 12-16. Retrieved from http://ir.bas.bg/ccs/2018/2_dimitrova.pdf

Dimitrova, M., Wagatsuma, H., Tripathi, G. N., & Ai, G. (2015, June). Adaptive and intuitive interactions with socially-competent pedagogical assistant robots. In *Proc. 6th International Workshop on Interactive Environments and Emerging Technologies for eLearning (IEETeL 2015)* (pp. 1-6). IEEE. 10.1109/ITHET.2015.7218031

Emery, N. J. (2000). The eyes have it: The neuroethology, function and evolution of social gaze. *Neuroscience and Biobehavioral Reviews*, *24*(6), 581–604. doi:10.1016/S0149-7634(00)00025-7 PMID:10940436

Feng, H., Gutierrez, A., Zhang, J., & Mahoor, M. H. (2013, September). Can NAO robot improve eye-gaze attention of children with high functioning autism? In *2013 IEEE International Conference on Healthcare Informatics* (pp. 484-484). IEEE. 10.1109/ICHI.2013.72

Huskens, B., Verschuur, R., Gillesen, J., Didden, R., & Barakova, E. (2013). Promoting question-asking in school-aged children with autism spectrum disorders: Effectiveness of a robot intervention compared to a human-trainer intervention. *Developmental Neurorehabilitation*, *16*(5), 345–356. doi:10.3109/175 18423.2012.739212 PMID:23586852

Ichiki, M., Ai, G., Ooi, J. S., & Wagatsuma, H. (2016). A Comparative Analysis of Indexing of Mental Workload by using Neuro-Driving Tools based on EEG Measurements Coupling with the Eye-Tracking System. *Frontiers in Neuroinformatics. Conference Abstract: Neuroinformatics, 2016*. doi:10.3389/conf. fninf.2016.20.00041

Kang, Z., & Landry, S. J. (2015). An eye movement analysis algorithm for a multielement target tracking task: Maximum transition-based agglomerative hierarchical clustering. *IEEE Transactions on Human-Machine Systems, 45*(1), 13–24. doi:10.1109/THMS.2014.2363121

Kaspar, K., & König, P. (2011). Overt attention and context factors: The impact of repeated presentations, image type, and individual motivation. *PLoS One, 6*(7), e21719. doi:10.1371/journal.pone.0021719 PMID:21750726

Kim, E. S., Berkovits, L. D., Bernier, E. P., Leyzberg, D., Shic, F., Paul, R., & Scassellati, B. (2013). Social robots as embedded reinforcers of social behavior in children with autism. *Journal of Autism and Developmental Disorders, 43*(5), 1038–1049. doi:10.100710803-012-1645-2 PMID:23111617

Krichmar, J. L., & Wagatsuma, H. (Eds.). (2011). *Neuromorphic and Brain-Based Robots*. Edinburgh, UK: Cambridge University Press. doi:10.1017/CBO9780511994838

Langton, S. R., Watt, R. J., & Bruce, V. (2000). Do the eyes have it? Cues to the direction of social attention. *Trends in Cognitive Sciences, 4*(2), 50–59. doi:10.1016/S1364-6613(99)01436-9 PMID:10652522

Leyzberg, D., Spaulding, S., Toneva, M., & Scassellati, B. (2012, January). The physical presence of a robot tutor increases cognitive learning gains. In *Proceedings of the Annual Meeting of the Cognitive Science Society* (*Vol. 34*, No. 34). Academic Press.

Lieberman, M. D. (2012). Education and the social brain. *Trends in Neuroscience and Education, 1*(1), 3–9. doi:10.1016/j.tine.2012.07.003

Lourens, T., & Barakova, E. (2009, June). My sparring partner is a humanoid robot. In *International Work-Conference on the Interplay between Natural and Artificial Computation* (pp. 344–352). Berlin: Springer. doi:10.1007/978-3-642-02267-8_37

Ochsner, K. N., & Lieberman, M. D. (2001). The emergence of social cognitive neuroscience. *The American Psychologist, 56*(9), 717–734. doi:10.1037/0003-066X.56.9.717 PMID:11558357

Oliva, A., & Torralba, A. (2007). The role of context in object recognition. *Trends in Cognitive Sciences, 11*(12), 520–527. doi:10.1016/j.tics.2007.09.009 PMID:18024143

Pfeiffer, U. J., Vogeley, K., & Schilbach, L. (2013). From gaze cueing to dual eye-tracking: Novel approaches to investigate the neural correlates of gaze in social interaction. *Neuroscience and Biobehavioral Reviews, 37*(10), 2516–2528. doi:10.1016/j.neubiorev.2013.07.017 PMID:23928088

Ramey, C. H. (2006). An inventory of reported characteristics for home computers, robots, and human beings: Applications for android science and the uncanny valley. In *Proceedings of the ICCS/CogSci-2006 long symposium "Toward social mechanisms of android science"* (pp. 21-25). Academic Press.

Sanada, M., Ikeda, K., Kimura, K., & Hasegawa, T. (2013). Motivation enhances visual working memory capacity through the modulation of central cognitive processes. *Psychophysiology, 50*(9), 864–871. doi:10.1111/psyp.12077 PMID:23834356

Schilbach, L. (2014). On the relationship of online and offline social cognition. *Frontiers in Human Neuroscience, 8,* 278. doi:10.3389/fnhum.2014.00278 PMID:24834045

Taylor, R., Spehar, B., Hagerhall, C., & Van Donkelaar, P. (2011). Perceptual and physiological responses to Jackson Pollock's fractals. *Frontiers in Human Neuroscience, 5,* 60. doi:10.3389/fnhum.2011.00060 PMID:21734876

Torta, E., van Heumen, J., Piunti, F., Romeo, L., & Cuijpers, R. (2015). Evaluation of unimodal and multimodal communication cues for attracting attention in human–robot interaction. *International Journal of Social Robotics, 7*(1), 89–96. doi:10.100712369-014-0271-x

Wagatsuma, H., & Yamaguchi, Y. (2007). Neural dynamics of the cognitive map in the hippocampus. *Cognitive Neurodynamics, 1*(2), 119–141. doi:10.100711571-006-9013-6 PMID:19003507

Wykowska, A., Anderl, C., Schubö, A., & Hommel, B. (2013). Motivation modulates visual attention: Evidence from pupillometry. *Frontiers in Psychology, 4,* 59. doi:10.3389/fpsyg.2013.00059 PMID:23407868

Chapter 5
Emotion Model for a Robot

Gyanendra Nath Tripathi
https://orcid.org/0000-0001-9914-3789
Renesas Electronics, Japan

ABSTRACT

Humans have several kinds of intelligence like logical thinking, decision making, social and behavioral intelligence, and many more. However, above all, emotional intelligence plays a vital role to drive action and event. To analyze the need of emotion for robot, it is required to investigate emotion in human and its socio-cognitive effect on event-action relation and behavior. Emotion is not required for a robot that is programmed just to perform certain commanded tasks. However, for a socially interactive assist robot in an environment of home, hospital, office, etc., emotion is important for decision making and to perform action. Moreover, emotion for robot is helpful to define the behavior and even to personalize the robot for its owner. The chapter aims to discuss three prominent questions regarding "emotion for a robot": 1) why we need emotion for robot, 2) what can be a probable solution as an emotion model, and 3) how emotion model can be devised for robot in a real-time environment.

INTRODUCTION: BRIEF BACKGROUND OF EMOTION

When 'Emotion for Robot' is considered as a philosophical discussion, it can include two main attributes one is to have a model representing the phenomenal occurrence of emotion, representing process explained on scientific basis. The second attribute is from engineering point of view, to have a model that is implementable for real time environment of robot inclusive to the first attribute. This section of chapter gives philosophical view point and theoretical scientific background of emotion. Next section of chapter will further discuss the implementation of emotion for robot from engineering view point.

PHILOSOPHICAL UNDERSTANDING OF EMOTION

As 'Emotion' is considered from view point of state of feeling of emotion in an individual, as a result of situation and event occurred in environment, or with virtual realization of situation and event based on

DOI: 10.4018/978-1-5225-7879-6.ch005

memory from past, and also a realization due to thoughtful consideration of its prospective occurrence in future. An analytical discussion regarding feeling of emotion in an individual becomes more subjective. Griffiths (2002) explained that 'Emotions' is not the 'natural kind', and by that he want to explain that different kind of emotions cannot be explained with single and unified theory. Further, the normative behavior of emotion(s), is detailed by Griffiths (2004) and elaborated that an objective analysis is not capable of explaining adequately due to its incomplete view point for human emotion. In a contemporary definition by Prinz (2004) explained that there is common basis of embodied phenomenon for emotion, which explains the common nature and phenomenal occurrence of emotion. In the review paper, 'current emotion research in philosophy' Griffiths (2013) discussed the view of memory based arousal of emotion, as it happens due to recall of event or object between long term memory, or procedural and episodic memory to working memory, and this eventual phenomenon of memory recall shows the different way the feeling of emotion occurs, which not be the same all the time.

With the advancement scientific understanding of human brain and mind, the purpose of both scientific and philosophical argument for emotion and nature of emotion(s) is to find the diverse but wholesome view. This wholesome view is helpful to propose a phenomenal model of emotion, representing feeling of emotion in human, in a real time environment of object and event. Recent philosophical argument also based on the affective neuroscience, and explains the process of arousal of emotion, Barrett (2009). Figure 1 explains the real-time environment phenomenon of emotion based on memory of emotion related to event and object.

NEUROSCIENCE OF EMOTION

Attention towards object and event driven by feeling of emotion attached to object and event, which further decide our action in the environment. An integrated sensory response system of emotion, attention, and action defines the overall behavior. Charles Darwin (1872) explained that emotion of fear to escape and aggression to attack are important for the drive action of survival and thus evolution of species. Darwin further emphasized the presence of basic emotion across species and cultures, which became a broad basis for neuroscientific findings by doing research on animal brains. However, at the same time it was

Figure 1. Figure explaining memory of emotion and event/object relation in real-time environment

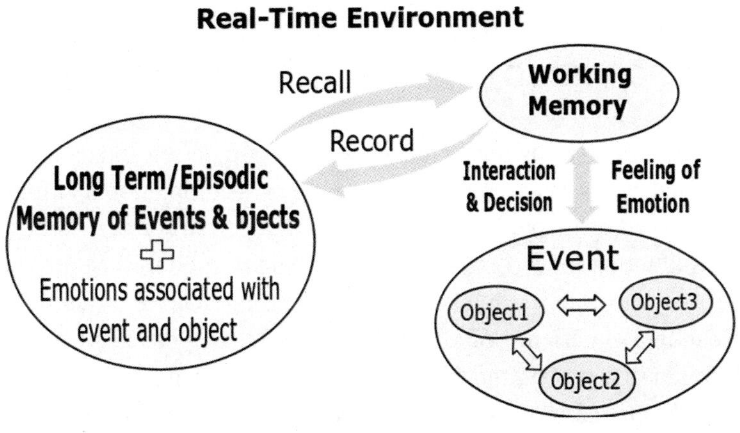

also considered that the emotions are result of physiological changes in body, experienced by object or event based stimulus that causes these bodily changes to happen, William James (1884), Carl Lange (1885). With a detailed historical development ground, Dalgleish (2004) review paper "The emotional brain", explained about the Cannon-Bards (1927) theory which counters the James (1884) idea of emotion being merely experience of bodily changes, and further explained Papez (1937) circuit with top-down and bottom-up emotion circuit of brain, the theory further strengthened by limbic system proposed by Kluver & Bucy (1937) brain and MacLean (1949) anatomy based theory of emotion.

This affective neuroscience development with century explains different part of brain anatomy which involve in generation of emotion. Dalgleish (2004) detailed about experimental basis of affective neuroscience defines the role of brain areas (Amygdala, Thalamus, Hippocampus, Prefrontal cortex, Anterior cingulate cortex) for generation of emotion. Such experimentally verified brain circuit theory involving brain anatomy parts helps to understand the phenomenon process of feeling emotion. This understanding is useful to develop a model based on brain circuit theory of emotion and its execution for robot as likely to be happening eventually, in human environment with several objects and events.

COGNITIVE NEUROSCIENCE OF EMOTION

Cognition of emotion explains the mental process involved in feeling of emotion. Gazzaniga (2014), emotion had been one of the great points of interest from beginning of the cognitive neuroscience field. By explaining reward and punishment theory, Lazarus & Folkman (1987) explained the cognitive basis of emotion. In cognition of emotion, Lazarus further explained the occurrence of physiological changes (change of heart rate, sweating etc.) driving decision making for action. Lazarus theory supported the James (1884) - Lange (1885) theory of emotion as physiological phenomenon, which was countered by Cannon-Bards (1927). Emotion is inclusive to other cognitive processes of brain like attention, decision making, learning, memory, perception etc. so potentially considered as interaction of emotion and meta-cognition process, by Dolan (2002), Bjork et.al. (1994), Gross (2002), Bechara & Damasio (2000).

A neuroscientific approach for emotion evolved with total view point of affective neuroscience as well as cognitive process of emotion. LeDoux (1989), LeDoux & Phelps (1993) talked about high road and low road neural pathway with neural anatomy point of view, however explaining the explaining process of feeling the emotion inclusive of cognition of emotion. Damasio, also explained the emotion model for feeling of emotion with inclusive approach to both neuroanatomy and cognition Damasio (1998, 1994).

EMOTION MODEL FOR ROBOT

David et.al.(2013), pointed out worldwide increasing elderly population and requirement of care at places like home, office hospital etc., service robots supposed to be a companion and for care giving. Tripathi (2013) explained about need of model for emotional intelligence in service robot to understand the human emotion and having action in working environment. Such a model is useful to implement in a robot to foster the robot-robot, and robot-human interaction. The interactive emotion model should further have capability to lead into experience of affect. Höök (2009) emphasized that model requires having representation of emotion as memory, and the recall of memory during real time interaction as cognition of feeling emotion, which inclusively develops affective experience loop of emotion with interactive real time response. Ana Paiva et. al. (2014) and Höök (2008) explained three steps of human-robot interaction activity that complete the affective loop of human emotion. Detailed explanation of feeling, emotion, affect and their inter-relation by Shouse (2005), gives in-depth understanding about these steps. Figure 2 illustrates the three steps involving the recognition of human affect state by robot, decision making for appropriate emotion action by robot, and robot interactive action with user.

Emotional Robots

Facial expression being one of the most effective ways of communication in human also plays a key factor in human robot interaction. Happiness, sadness, anger, fear, disgust, and surprise been illustrated as the six most basic emotion in human, by Ekman et.al (1978). Robot 'Kismet', with these basic human like expressions, been developed by Breazeal (2002) and his group as 'Sociable Machines Project'. At the same period seal robot 'Paro' been developed for pain management and anti-depression therapy solution, explained by Shibata et.al (2002) and Wada et.al (2005), beside facial Paro's emotion expression been performed by head, eyelids, front paws and tail. A both top-down and bottom-up emotion is devisable for human, in a interactive environment of human and robot. Humanoid robot like NAO (developed by Aldebaran) is an efficient platform to implement the emotion model with an interactive environment between human and robot. Another humanoid 'Pepper' been developed by Aldebaran been more popular for the movement, expression and cloud based speech communication capability. Beside the facial expressions, robot arms, humanoid NAO, and fun-bots by Wendt (2009), have more action based human interaction, to further enhance the affect loop communication by empathic touch as fellow and companion.

As explained in section: Cognitive neuroscience of Emotion, beside expression and action, another important aspect of the emotional interaction is the activity level and attention involvement of human towards robot as well as robot sensory attention to user. The model of internal representation and execution should incorporate the attention and activity level representation. The model proposed in the next section is includes the activity level and attention in robot and its association to object and event. Figure 3 shows overview of interactive model.

Figure 2. Event/object based human robot interaction in real-time environment

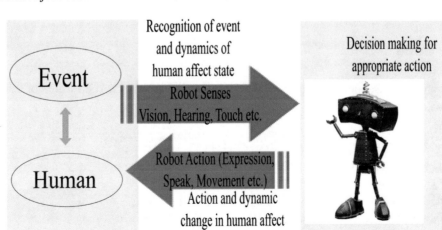

Figure 3. Overview of proposed model

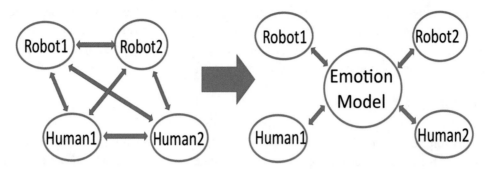

THE PROPOSED MODEL OF EMOTION

The model based on Plutchik's wheel (1991) of emotions is proposed with aim to internal representation of emotion for robot. The internal representation of emotion is based on classification of event and object against the type of emotion evoked by that event or object. The classification of event and object against human emotion is referred from previous research and event and object in prospective robot environment are listed accordingly. Model represents different modalities of emotion by value of signal θ as $\theta : -180 < \theta < 180$. Variable 'r' representing the level of primary or secondary emotion at particular time, and $z : 0 < V < 1$ is showing the level of attention, as level of emotion affectively associated with level of attention. Occurrence of change in emotion state appears due to an event or object appearance in the environment. The internal representation of object in robots memory associates the values θ, r and z as $Obj.(r, \theta, z)$. The associated value r, θ is corresponding to the emotion that object or event evokes in robot. Figure 4 shows the way of graphical 3D representation of object or event by (r, θ, z). The variable r, θ represent the type of emotion on a 2D plane corresponding to Plutchik's wheel and variable z specifies level of awareness, to make decision of next robot action. Object or event representation as (r, θ, z) is required to map the change in emotion state caused by object or event. Overall model takes up three steps taking input information from robot regarding event or object, representing current emotional state and next emotion state due to event or object appearance including decision making for action, perform time based action sequence.

Computer Code

Robot routine behavior sequenced (observing and sensing environment, keep watch on critical activity, attention to voice etc.)

if: Event:(r, θ, z) or appearance of object:(r, θ, z) occurs
Robot re-calls the emotion:(r, θ, z) associated to event and object
Robot makes decision action according to event/ object
when: action/ behavior performed
Robot may update emotion:(r, θ, z) associated to event and object
Robot retrieves the routine behavior back

Robot get back to routine behavior sequenced (observing and sensing environment, keep watch on critical activity, attention to voice etc.)

Classification of human emotion and corresponding implementation in robot is given in table 1~5. The tables 1~5 are corresponding to five prime emotion (fear, sadness, anger, joy, love) and represents the cause and reaction in human corresponding to these emotion as example. Further, corresponding cause and reaction is proposed in view of robotic work space environment. The proposed cause and reaction for robot has been exemplified by considering humanoid robot NAO work space. For other robots these cause and reaction may be mapped considering the robot's work space environment. Moreover, the cause and reaction table can be extended for other types of emotion.

FUTURE RESEARCH DIRECTION

The proposed model in this chapter emphasizes on attention and activity level mapping to representation of object and event on a three-dimensional conical space by representing point of the cone as tip of iceberg of attention. There can be further extensive emotion representation model with time-line based memory (short and long memory) and bottom up emotion model in robot, resulting from the affect loop interaction. Moreover, sentiment behind an emotion state is an attribute related to the cause of emotion, inclusion of sentiment map in the model is to be considered for the future work. Another direction is to use complex dynamic model for execution of emotion based on oscillators, which can be implemented as emotion loop.

Figure 4. 3D-emotion mapping using 3rd dimension of attention/awareness to 2D-wheel of Plutchik

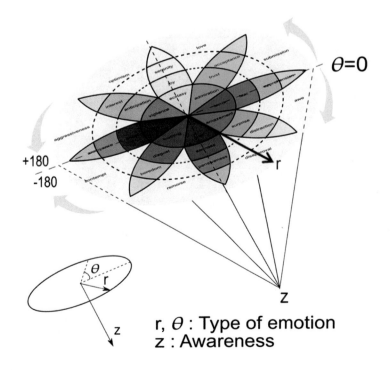

Table 1. Emotion of fear in human: cause-reaction, proposed cause and reaction for robot

Human			Robot	
Emotion	**Cause**	**Reaction**	**Environmental Cause**	**Reaction**
Fear	Threat of social rejection	Sweating, perspiring	Fear of collision or fall	Stop action, Sense the environment showing fear
	Possibility of lose and failure	Feeling nervous, jittery, jumpy	Being In Dark	Sitting on same position Freezing
	Losing control or competence	Shaking, quivering, trembling	Possibility of failure (Battery Low)	Freezing and Asking someone to put on charging
	Threat of harm or death	eye darting looking quickly around	Losing control (Battery Low)	Freezing and Asking someone to put on charging, or having self-motion to charging point
	Novel unfamiliar situation	nervous fearful talk		
	Being Alone	shaky trembling voice		
	Being in Dark	crying whimpering		

Table 2. Emotion of sadness in human: cause-reaction, proposed cause and reaction for robot

Human			Robot	
Emotion	**Cause**	**Reaction**	**Environment Cause**	**Reaction**
Sadness	Undesirable outcome, negative surprise	Sitting or lying down(being inactive)	Failure attempt	sad expression for moment, If battery ok try again,
	Death of Loved one	Tired rundown low energy	Power less	sadly asking for charging and sit
	Rejection Exclusion Disapproval	Slow, shuffling movement	Empathy with someone sad	Trying to make happy by dance and song
	Not getting what was wanted	slumped droofing posture	Empathy with someone sad	
	loss of relationship separation	Withdraw from social contact		
	reality falling short of expectation	Talking little or not		
	Finding oneself power less or help less	Low quite slow monotonous		
	Empathy with someone who is sad, hurt	saying sad things		

Table 3. Emotion of anger in human: cause-reaction, proposed cause and reaction for robot

Human			Robot	
Emotion	**Cause**	**Reaction**	**Environment Cause**	**Reaction**
Anger	predisposition of anger	Obscenities, cursing	Unwanted touch	Annoyed showing anger
	reversal of loss of power, status	verbally attacking the cause of anger	Someone touching or taking the Liked thing	Annoyed showing anger
	violation of expectation	Loud voice, yelling, Screaming	Calling but no answer	Annoyed showing anger
	frustration/ interruption of activity	complaining, bitching		
	Real or threatened pain	Hands or fists clenched		
	Judgement of illegitimacy, unfairness	Aggressive threatening gestures		

Table 4. Emotion of joy in human: cause-reaction, proposed cause and reaction for robot

Human			Robot	
Emotion	**Cause**	**Reaction**	**Environmental Cause**	**Reaction**
Joy	Task success achievement	Being courteous, friendly to others	Task success full	Showing joyful action
	Desirable out com; getting what was wanted	Doing nice things for others	Master praising	Joyful attention
	Receiving esteem, respect, praise	Communicating the good feeling	Getting red ball	Happiness with joy
	getting something striving for	sharing the feeling	Receiving love and affection from master	Happiness with joy
	reality exceeding expectation	Hugging the people		
	Receiving wonderful surprise	positive outlook seeing the bright side		
	Experiencing pleasurable stimuli	High threshold for worry, annoyance		
	Being accepted belonging	giggling laughing		
	receiving love liking affection	feeling excited		

Table 5. Emotion of love in human: cause-reaction, proposed cause and reaction for robot

	Human		Robot	
Emotion	**Cause**	**Reaction**	**Environmental Cause**	**Reaction**
Love	Other offer something wanted	wanting the best for other	Someone giving something wanted (Red Ball)	Thank you showing feeling
	Person knows other loves, needs him or her	Wanting to see and spend time with other	Someone known shows affection and Love	I love you. Love feeling
	person find other attractive	Saying I love you	Someone plays with	Thank you showing feeling
	exceptionally good communication	Expressing positive feeling to others	Talking politely and showing love	I love you. Love feeling
	other inspires openness trust	Wanting physical closeness or sex		
	Having shared time, experiences	kissing		
	Being forgetful distracted	touching petting		
		Hugging holding cuddling		

CONCLUSION

The chapter aimed to explain 'why we need emotion for robot' by explaining the philosophical and neuro-cognitive explanation of emotion as need for human and an implementable model for robot that is needed for social robots as assistive, entertainer and help in an environment like hospital, office and domestic etc. Section 'emotion model for robot' and subsection 'emotional robots' explain about emotion robots and probable solution for a socially intractable emotional robot. In subsection 'the proposed model of emotion' a devised emotion model is explained, the model focused on attention and active level representation of emotion associated with event and object of work space. Regarding practical implementation, the proposed emotion model can potentially be used in a wide variety of robot, with desirable response against event and object appearance in environment of robot.

ACKNOWLEDGMENT

Author takes this as an opportunity to show gratitude towards professor for their guidance and providing facilities of lab environment, moreover giving space of free and creative thinking during my association with Kyushu Institute of Technology as PhD student. I like to thank KIT staff for their great support in every aspect of academic life.

REFERENCES

Aldebaran - SoftBank Robotics. (n.d.). Retrieved from https://www.softbankrobotics.com/emea/ja

Barrett, L. F. (2009). The future of psychology: Connecting mind to brain. *Perspectives on Psychological Science, 4*(4), 326–339. doi:10.1111/j.1745-6924.2009.01134.x

Bechara, A., Damasio, H., & Damasio, A. R. (2000). Emotion, decision making and the orbitofrontal cortex. *Cerebral Cortex, 10*(3), 295–307. doi:10.1093/cercor/10.3.295

Bjork, R. A., Metcalfe, J., & Shimamura, A. P. (1994). *Metacognition: Knowing about knowing.* Academic Press.

Breazeal, C. (2002a). *Designing Sociable Robots.* Cambridge, MA: MIT Press.

Cannon, W. B. (1927). The James-Lange theory of emotions: A critical examination and an alternative theory. *The American Journal of Psychology, 39*(1/4), 106–124. doi:10.2307/1415404

Chik, D., Tripathi, G. N., & Wagatsuma, H. (2013, November). A Method to Deal with Prospective Risks at Home in Robotic Observations by Using a Brain-Inspired Model. In *International Conference on Neural Information Processing* (pp. 33-40). Springer. 10.1007/978-3-642-42051-1_5

Dalgleish, T. (2004). The emotional brain. *Nature Reviews. Neuroscience, 5*(7), 583–589. doi:10.1038/nrn1432

Damasio, A. R. (1994). *Descartes' error: Emotion, rationality and the human brain.* Academic Press.

Damasio, A. R. (1998). Emotion in the perspective of an integrated nervous system. *Brain Research. Brain Research Reviews, 26*(2-3), 83–86. doi:10.1016/S0165-0173(97)00064-7

Darwin, C. (2007). *The expression of the emotions in man and animals.* New York: Filiquarian.

Dolan, R. J. (2002). Emotion, cognition, and behavior. *Science, 298*(5596), 1191-1194.

Ekman, P., & Friesen, W. V. (1978). *Facial action coding system: Investigator's guide.* Consulting Psychologists Press.

Gazzaniga, M. S. (Ed.). (2014). *Handbook of cognitive neuroscience.* Springer.

Griffiths, P. E. (2002). *Emotion is still not a natural kind.* Academic Press.

Griffiths, P. E. (2004). Emotions as natural and normative kinds. *Philosophy of Science, 71*(5), 901–911. doi:10.1086/425944

Griffiths, P. E. (2013). Current emotion research in philosophy. *Emotion Review, 5*(2), 215–222. doi:10.1177/1754073912468299

Gross, J. J. (2002). Emotion regulation: Affective, cognitive, and social consequences. *Psychophysiology, 39*(3), 281–291. doi:10.1017/S0048577201393198

Höök, K. (2008, June). Affective loop experiences–what are they? In *International Conference on Persuasive Technology* (pp. 1-12). Springer.

Höök, K. (2009). Affective loop experiences: Designing for interactional embodiment. *Philosophical Transactions of the Royal Society of London. Series B, Biological Sciences*, *364*(1535), 3585–3595. doi:10.1098/rstb.2009.0202

James, W. (1884). What is an emotion? *Mind*, *9*(34), 188–205. doi:10.1093/mind/os-IX.34.188

Klüver, H., & Bucy, P. C. (1937). Psychic blindness and other symptoms following bilateral temporal lobectomy in Rhesus monkeys. *The American Journal of Physiology*.

Lange, C. (1885). *The Emotions*. Baltimore, MD: Williams & Wilkins.

Lazarus, R. S., & Folkman, S. (1987). Transactional theory and research on emotions and coping. *European Journal of Personality*, *1*(3), 141–169. doi:10.1002/per.2410010304

LeDoux, J. E. (1989). Cognitive-emotional interactions in the brain. *Cognition and Emotion*, *3*(4), 267–289. doi:10.1080/02699938908412709

LeDoux, J. E., & Phelps, E. A. (1993). Emotional networks in the brain. Handbook of Emotions, 109, 118.

MacLean, P. D. (1949). Psychosomatic disease and the" visceral brain"; recent developments bearing on the Papez theory of emotion. *Psychosomatic Medicine*, *11*(6), 338–353. doi:10.1097/00006842-194911000-00003

Paiva, A., Leite, I., & Ribeiro, T. (2014). Emotion modelling for social robots. In R. A. Calvo, S. K. D'Mello, J. Gratch, & A. Kappas (Eds.), *Handbook of affective computing*. Oxford University Press.

Papez, J. W. (1937). A proposed mechanism of emotion. *Archives of Neurology and Psychiatry*, *38*(4), 725–743. doi:10.1001/archneurpsyc.1937.02260220069003

Plutchik, R. (1991). *The emotions*. University Press of America.

Prinz, J. (2004). Embodied emotions. In R. C. Solomon (Ed.), *Thinking about feeling: Contemporary philosophers on the emotions* (pp. 44–59). Oxford, UK: Oxford University Press.

Shibata, T., Mitsui, T., Wada, K., Touda, A., Kumasaka, T., Tagami, K., & Tanie, K. (2001) Mental commit robot and its application to therapy of children. *Proceedings of the IEEE/ASME International Conference on Advanced Intelligent Mechatronics*, 2, 1053-1058. 10.1109/AIM.2001.936838

Shouse, E. (2005). Feeling, emotion, affect. *M/C Journal, 8*(6), 26.

Tripathi, G. N., Chik, D., & Wagatsuma, H. (2013, January). How Difficult Is It for Robots to Maintain Home Safety?–A Brain-Inspired Robotics Point of View. In Neural Information Processing (pp. 528-536). Springer Berlin Heidelberg.

Wada, K., Shibata, T., Saito, T., Sakamoto, K., & Tanie, K. (2005). Psychological and social effects of one year robot assisted activity on elderly people at a health service facility for the aged. *Proceedings of the IEEE International Conference on Robotics and Automation (ICRA)*, 2785-2790. 10.1109/ROBOT.2005.1570535

Wendt, C., & Berg, G. (2009) Nonverbal humor as a new dimension of HRI. *Proceedings of the 18th IEEE International Symposium on Robot and Human Interactive Communication (RO-MAN) 2009*, 183–188. 10.1109/ROMAN.2009.5326230

Chapter 6
Designing an Extensible Domain–Specific Web Corpus for "Layfication":
A Case Study in eCare at Home

Marina Santini
RISE Research Institutes of Sweden, Sweden

Marjan Alirezaie
Örebro University, Sweden

Arne Jönsson
*RISE Research Institutes of Sweden, Sweden &
Linköping University, Sweden*

Leili Lind
*RISE Research Institutes of Sweden, Sweden &
Linköping University, Sweden*

Wiktor Strandqvist
*RISE Research Institutes of Sweden, Sweden &
Linköping University, Sweden*

Eva Blomqvist
*RISE Research Institutes of Sweden, Sweden &
Linköping University, Sweden*

Gustav Cederblad
Linköping University, Sweden

Maria Lindén
Mälardalen University, Sweden

Mikael Nyström
*RISE Research Institutes of Sweden, Sweden &
Linköping University, Sweden*

Annica Kristoffersson
Örebro University, Sweden

ABSTRACT

In the era of data-driven science, corpus-based language technology is an essential part of cyber physical systems. In this chapter, the authors describe the design and the development of an extensible domain-specific web corpus to be used in a distributed social application for the care of the elderly at home. The domain of interest is the medical field of chronic diseases. The corpus is conceived as a flexible and extensible textual resource, where additional documents and additional languages will be appended over time. The main purpose of the corpus is to be used for building and training language technology applications for the "layfication" of the specialized medical jargon. "Layfication" refers to the automatic identification of more intuitive linguistic expressions that can help laypeople (e.g., patients, family caregivers, and home care aides) understand medical terms, which often appear opaque. Exploratory experiments are presented and discussed.

DOI: 10.4018/978-1-5225-7879-6.ch006

INTRODUCTION

Cyber-Physical Systems (CPSs) denote an emergent paradigm that combines most advanced technological approaches and computational tools to solve complex tasks. CPSs are domain-independent and have penetrated diversified disciplines, such as healthcare and self-driving vehicles. Corpus-based Language Technology is an essential component of many CPSs, where linguistic knowledge is indispensable to prevent failures or fatal errors due to misunderstandings or poor understanding.

Web corpora are the bedrock underlying modern real-world corpus-based Language Technology applications (henceforth LT applications), such as terminology extraction, ontology learning, text simplification, automatic summarization and machine translation. In this chapter, we describe the design and the development of an extensible domain-specific web corpus to be used in a distributed social application for the care of the elderly at home.

Web corpora are text collections made of documents that have been automatically retrieved and downloaded from the web. Generally speaking, building web corpora is convenient because the whole process of corpus creation is automated, fast and inexpensive. In contrast, the construction of traditional corpora– such as the British National Corpus (BNC) (Burnard, 2007) or the Corpus of Contemporary American English (COCOA) (Davies, 2009) or the recent iWeb corpus[L] normally spans over several years, relies on considerable amount of human expertise to decide the ideal combination of documents that is worth storing in the corpus and, last but not least, necessitates substantial funding. It goes without saying that the investments in time, financial resources and human knowledge required by traditional corpora are well paid-off because such an effort amounts to high-quality and long-lasting collections, that are extensively used by teachers, students, researchers and system developers. For instance, the Brown corpus created in the 60's (Kucera & Francis, 1979) is still valuable today, especially for monitoring how the language has changed in the last decades (e.g. Malá, 2017).

While traditional corpora are a shrine of hand-crafted qualities, the added value of web corpora is in their malleability. Similar to traditional corpora, web corpora can be general-purpose or specialized (Barbaresi, 2015) and may serve different purposes, such as linguistic studies (e.g. Schäfer & Bildhauer, 2013; Biemann et al., 2007; Lüdeling et al. 2007) and professional uses (Goldhahn et al., 2012; Baroni et al., 2006). However, the unique and unprecedented potential of web corpora is that they can promptly and inexpensively account for virtually any domain, topic, genre, register, sublanguage, style and emotional connotation, since the web itself is a panoply of linguistic and textual varieties. This potential can be profitably exploited for domain-specific projects that require specialized text collections to implement corpus-based LT applications. Examples of these types of LT applications are those implemented in projects like *DigInclude*[2] and *E-care@home*[3] in Sweden or those that have been developed for European projects, such as *SEMANTICMINING*[4] and *SemanticHealthNet*[5] in the semantic interoperability field, as well as *Accurat*[6], *TTC*[7] and *EXPERT*[8] in Natural Language Processing (NLP), Computational Linguistics and Information Retrieval.

Arguably, traditional corpora and web corpora are complementary and allow for a wide spectrum of possible linguistic, empirical and computational studies and experiments.

Since web corpora are often at the core of LT applications, seemingly the design and the quality of web corpora affect the reliability and the performance of final applications. Building a 'clean' corpus with selected documents requires time, careful planning, long-term decision-making and extensive funding. Frequently, in the implementation of LT applications, the corpus is only a single piece (even though an important one) of a complex pipeline, and often the time and financial resources allocated for corpus creation are limited. For this reason, bootstrapping corpora from the web (either via web crawling or via search engines) has become normal practice. Corpora built from the web are convenient because their creation is fast and inexpensive, although corpus evaluation is not yet fully standardized (cf. Kilgarriff et al. 2011), and it is hard to replicate results or to generalize on the findings, especially when web corpora are domain-specific.

The Whys and Wherefores

The version of the web corpus described in this chapter is known as *eCare_Sv-En_03*. It contains web documents written in English and in Swedish. We propose the construction of an extensible web corpus which should be seen as an ever-changing textual resource, i.e. as a corpus that is constantly in-progress, where web texts can be added when needed and where a light set of metadata keeps track of updates and allows for the extraction of virtual sub-corpora.

The rationale underlying the creation of *eCare_Sv-En_03* stems from the following needs: (1) having publicly-available medical web documents to represent a fine-grained medical domain (e.g. chronic diseases); (2) having a corpus with a design and a structure that allows for expansion with additional documents and languages to account for research, development and commercialization; (3) accounting for very specific technical terms, in our case both specialized and lay medical terms, that can meet the needs of two broad user groups, namely medical professional staff and health consumers, like patients, family caregivers and home-care aides, who are not expected to have any specific medical education.

Our perspective on web corpora is from the point of view of the implementation of corpus-based real-world LT applications in specialized domains. Our ambition is to find ways to build LT applications that are efficient in terms of time and financial resources, and that require the least implementation effort.

Essentially, we take a *minimalist* approach. Our assumption is that not all applications need large and clean corpora, and our ambition is to understand to what extent a corpus can be small and noisy without negatively affecting the performance of an application. More prosaically, we would like to save time and economic resources because building large corpora and cleaning them require time and funding that are not always available in real-world settings.

In practical terms, this means that we try to identify the corpus critical mass for a specific LT application. In this context, critical mass indicates the minimal corpus size that an LT application needs to achieve a "good enough" performance. We also try to understand whether we can build LT applications using noisy documents. In short, we would like to build reliable LT applications using small corpora containing noisy documents.

Our research is somewhat complementary to the current challenge being met by other research lines, which focus on the construction of large-scale web corpora. Examples of this corpus typology include enC[3] (Kristoffersen, 2017), C4Corpus (Habernal et al. 2016), the web corpora created within the COW initiative (Schäfer & Bildhauer, 2012), and those constructed in the WaCky project (Baroni et al. 2009). These large-scale web corpora will certainly help the progress of NLP, as pointed out by Biemann et al. (2013) and Habernal et al. (2016), especially when using neural networks for deep learning or word embedding, since these algorithms require a large quantity of data in order to be effective.

Meeting such a challenge often implies an impressive distributed architecture (such as the Hadhoop MapReduce framework, e.g. see Biemann et al., 2013) that in certain cases is impractical. What is more, large-scale web corpora are "static" (as pointed out in Biemann et al.; 2013, see also Schäfer & Bildhauer, 2013). In this respect, their design is similar to traditional corpora, which are not designed to be extended (although some of them are available in several releases). These corpora are more of a huge snapshot of the language of the web at a certain point in time. For example, the C4Corpus has been built with a CommonCrawl dating from 2007 to 2015 and has not been updated by adding new texts after 2016-04-14[9]. The static corpus design is certainly beneficial for many empirical studies and NLP tasks. It is be less beneficial for a live real-world LT application that thrives on frequent updates of the underlying corpus to encompass the new terms and the new findings that are constantly being produced by modern science. In a word, the language of static corpora "age" over the years. Even the much welcome CommonCrawl data is affected by this "aging" process, as pointed out by Barbu (2016) who writes: "the way that Common Crawl collects data is not by crawling live sites". Barbu himself uses a list of web urls provided by the defunct searching engine Blekko[10] and downloads the pages corresponding to those links. This means that for some sites there is a huge gap between the content of the site in Common Crawl and the live content of the site." This aging factor may be irrelevant for some tasks (such as morphology, syntax or discourse analysis), while it may not be ideal for some others (e.g. terminology extraction or ontology learning from text).

It is indeed the case that, in some subject fields and for some topics, there is often the need to update a document collection with the most recent texts, containing novel findings, new issues or unprecedented cases, new terms, new medical devices, new medications, as well as the latest discoveries. For this reason, we propose a corpus design and a corpus structure that can accommodate incremental corpus extension over time and when needed, and where documents, languages, metadata and specific topics can be smoothly added or rearranged.

In summary, we need a corpus design that is flexible, replicable and "good enough" to: 1) keep track of diversified textual traits and 2) orderly stratify the successive corpus developments. Depending on the purpose of a specific LT application, a corpus designed in this way will allow for either the use of the corpus as a whole, or of portions (sub-corpora), thus facilitating corpus re-use.

Importantly, the texts in the corpus do not need to be uniformly annotated. For example, a portion of the corpus may be annotated as lay or specialized, while another part may be annotated by readability or genre. What is important is that the subpart of interest can be easily identified and extracted from the whole corpus, thus creating virtual textual collections that serve specific purposes.

To build such a corpus, we were inspired by the Agile methodologies[11] that are based on iterations and incremental developments. To the best of our knowledge, such a corpus design has not been proposed to date. We present the construction of our corpus in Section 5.

A Corpus for Layfication

The medical domain centers upon specialized and technical notions elaborated and usually disseminated by healthcare professionals. These notions often remain opaque and incomprehensible for non-expert users, and especially for patients (Berland et al., 2001). Despite it is acknowledged that understanding what the doctor says has an important influence on the success of treatments, in many cases medical terminology hinders the comprehension of various groups of people (such as non-native speakers, people with low-education, etc.), and has negative effects on the health consumer user group (e.g. patients and caregivers). The main actors of the medical field are physicians and patients. However, also students, pharmacists, managers, biologists, nurses who have different levels of expertise need to interact and understand each other (Tchami & Grabar, 2014). We focus on two broad user groups. The first group (the expert) includes those who use and understand medical specialized terminology, such as healthcare professionals. The second group encompasses "ordinary people" (the lay), i.e. people without medical education, who struggle to get a grip on the medical jargon. It is true that "ordinary people" are exposed to medical terms through the media (e.g. radio, TV and newspapers) and some of them who suffer from a chronic disease may become experts on their own illness. This knowledge, however, is not reliable, since, as observed in several studies, "ordinary people" might misunderstand medical information in good faith (Claveau et al., 2015; Bigeard et al., 2018).

In this chapter the term "layfication" refers to the automatic identification of more intuitive linguistic expressions that can help laypeople (mostly patients and family, family caregivers and home-care aides) understand medical terms, which often appear neboulous and incomprehensible. Typical examples of the linguistic dichotomy existing in the medical field are words like "anemia" -- also written anaemia -- (a specialized term) vs. "lack of iron" or "iron deficiency" (lay synonyms). Lay synonyms are lexical items that are based on common words, so that an expression like "lack of iron" is more intuitive than the medical term "anemia".

Although medical terms are more precise and less ambiguous than their lay counterpart, it has been widely acknowledged that consumer health information is often inaccessible to healthcare consumers (Miller et al., 2007). When dealing with the lay user group, it becomes apparent that the precision and lack of ambiguity of the medical term does not necessarily benefit the laypeople since it creates a communication gap that entails detrimental consequences for the patient's health due to misunderstandings or partial understanding. It has been repeatedly stressed that it is important that people who receive health care and medical treatments but do not have a medical education (normally patients and caregivers) are helped to fully understand the medical language used by healthcare professionals. Helping laypeople by providing them with lay synonyms (e.g. using "lack of iron"[12] rather than "anemia") or reformulation (e.g. "Anaemia is a lack of red blood cells"[13]) can help prevent unwanted consequences such as the misunderstandings (Claveau et al., 2015) that may cause medication misuses (Bigeard et al., 2018). A better understanding of medical jargon is especially important for elderly people affected by chronic diseases because it facilitates a proactive behaviour and fosters self-empowerment, which has proven to be beneficial for long-term successful treatment (Fotokian et al., 2017).

Nowadays, the creation of medical lay variants is mostly corpus-based (see Section 4). Normally, the corpora for this task are created by going to specific pre-defined web sites and downloading lay and specialized medical texts. Using this approach is theoretically profitable because corpora can be built with the material available. However, it has a reduced applicability in real-world domain-specific LT applications because these websites do not contain all the illnesses but only the most common ones, like "fever" or "allergy". The same is true for user-generated texts, such as those that can be found in forums and blogs, since users mostly talk about general problems or common diseases. Another common approach to build medical corpora has been to focus on journals or, more rarely, on patient record collections but in these cases, there exist copyright, ethical and legal restrictions that limit the shareability and experimental replicability.

For all these reasons, with *eCare_Sv_En_03* we are exploring a different avenue. More specifically, with *eCare_Sv_En_03* the idea is to pre-select some very specific medical terms (not just the most common illnesses) that represent the granularity of domain of interest, use them as seeds in a search engine and download only the pages that are related to the specific terms we focus on. In practice, we aim at building a corpus that contains documents that are related only to specific medical terms that indicate chronic diseases, and that are not always documented in medical websites, such as the Swedish medical information portal called "1177 Vårdguiden[14]".

eCare_Sv_En_03, the current version of the *E-care@home Corpus*, does *not* rely for its annotation on documents coming from specific sources (a method that was also used in Santini, 2006 and referred to as "annotation by objective sources"). Here, we reverse the approach. We start from our topics of interest (i.e. chronic illnesses) and search for the material that is available on the web at a certain point in time. At retrieval time, we make no distinction between lay and specialized web sites. Rather, we follow the approach initiated by Glavas and Stajner (2015) within text simplification. These authors observe that "'simple' words, besides being frequent in simplified text, are also present in abundance in regular text. This would mean that we can find simpler synonyms of complex words in regular corpora, provided that reliable methods for measuring (1) the 'complexity' of the word and (2) semantic similarity of words are available.". Inspired by this remark, we build a web corpus of domain-specific documents retrieved by search engines in the searchable web. Then, we put forward the hypothesis that in this way the corpus include both lay and specialized documents and, consequently, lay and specialized terms. This hypothesis will be tested in Section 5.1.

Research Questions and Objectives

The research questions motivating this work relate to the creation of real-world, domain-specific and corpus-based LT applications. We investigate whether it is possible to:

- Find an agile corpus design that accounts for incremental expansions according to real-word needs that may occur over time (e.g. multilinguality and additional text types);
- Use a minimalist approach to LT applications that ensure good enough performance and easy replicability and/or portability to other domains (application of Occams's razor law as used in the context of machine learning and data science[15]).
- Downplay the effects of noise and corpus size variations.

We investigate possible answers to these research questions by carrying out a number of experiments with clear objectives, namely by:

1. Implementing the design of a web corpus that is conceived as "work-in-progress", i.e. an *extensible, open-ended and multilingual* textual resource, where each stage of the construction is useful to gain insights into some aspects of language and/or language technology (Section 5.1).
2. Automatically classifying texts written for laypeople from those written for the expert and explore the effect of noise and corpus size variations (Section 5.2)
3. Creating a distributional thesaurus by inducing words related to chronic illnesses from a small corpus in Swedish (Section 5.3);
4. Expanding the corpus with documents in English and assessing the domain-specificity, or domain-hood, of the English sub-corpora using well-established language independent statistical measures (Section 5.4).

The experimental investigations presented in this chapter are still exploratory but lay the groundwork for further research and future development.

The chapter is organized as follows: Section 2 briefly describes a distributed CPS where the Internet of Things (IoT) and Language Technology (LT) meet each other to support elderly eCare at home for chronic diseases; in Section 3 the working hypothesis underlying our investigation is set out, and the intrinsic challenges are spelled out; in Section 4, previous research on layfication is summarized; Section 5 subsumes four subsections, each one presenting experiments and discussions; finally in Section 6 conclusions are drawn and future directions are outlined.

THE INTERNET OF THINGS IN E-CARE: TOWARDS SEMANTIC INTEROPERABILITY

Prevention and adaptive support to ageing population is an important objective in today's society. Telemedicine, robotics and the IoT (Internet-of-Things) have made a giant leap forward in providing solutions to overcome the challenge of helping patients who live alone.

Telemedicine is the use of telecommunication and information technology to provide clinical health care from a distance. It has been used to overcome distance barriers and to improve access to medical services that would often not be consistently available in distant rural communities. Telemedicine is a field that is widely developed in geographically extended countries, like the United States and Sweden (for recent advances in this field, see Lilly et al., 2014 and Lind & Karlsson, 2018 respectively).

In addition, robotics has provided intelligent machines that help patients to be more independent. For instance, the EU research project GiraffPlus[16] (Coradeschi et al., 2014; Coradeschi et al., 2013) monitored activities and physiological parameters in the home using a network of sensors. The telerobot Giraff was used to communicate with elderly patients. Recently, also social robots for home (e.g. Jibo and Buddy) have been launched as context-based social artificial companions that verbally interact with humans and help them in several activities (Quintas, 2018).

Extending previous experience in telemedicine and robotics, *E-care@home* (a Swedish research project running from 2015 to 2020), is creating new knowledge and exploring novel avenues for the smooth and robust implementation of eCare for the multimorbid and frail elderly living at home.

E-care@home is a multi-disciplinary project that investigates how to ensure medical care at home and avoid long-term hospitalization in the eldercare (Loutfi et al., 2016). Long hospitalizations are discomforting for elderly patients and expensive for the national healthcare systems. Providing medical care at home to the elderly can be effective by populating the home with electronic devices ("things"), i.e. sensors and actuators, and linking them to the Internet. Creating such an IoT infrastructure is done with the ambition to provide automated information gathering and processing on top of which e-services can be built trough reasoning (Sioutis et al., 2017). The rapid growth of data from sensors can potentially enable a better understanding and awareness of the environment for humans. For example, "[i]n Japan, an estimated 6.24 million people aged 65 or older were living alone in 2015, exceeding the 6 million mark for the first time, according to a welfare ministry survey released in July 2016."[17].

E-care@home: Semantic Interoperability

The interpretation of sensor data needs to be both machine-readable and human understandable. In order to be understandable for humans, interpretation of data may include semantic annotations in the form of context-dependent terms that hold the meaning of numeric data. Information gathered by sensors are lists of numbers. It is possible however to convert these bare numbers into specialized semantic concepts (Alirezaie, 2015). This conversion complies to one of major objectives of *E-care@home*, i.e. to represent information in a "human consumable way", since the project focuses on technological solutions and uses artificial intelligence for creating a semantic interoperability between sensor data, systems and humans (Kristoffersson and Lindén, 2017). The international challenge of "Patient Empowerment" implies that patients should contribute to their health and include their perspectives for shared decision making with clinicians. Standard international classifications or terminologies are also needed to implement semantic interoperability of the whole system (Cardillo, 2015). This implies using and creating different types of terminologies for different levels of medical expertise and for multiple languages.

A simplified version of the architecture for *E-care@home* semantic interoperability that would allow for all the different data sources to talk to each other is shown in Fig 1. Fig 1 is a conceptual system overview completed by balloons showing where all the data would come from. Data has here been placed as far out towards the sides of the picture as possible, e.g. we imagine that all the sensor data and the reports from the patient would then be stored in the central Knowledge Base (KB) of the home system, but in the picture we show where it entered the system, because that says more about its potential format, how reliable it may be etc. than placing everything at the center. What is placed at the center of the picture is such things that have to be derived from other data that comes in, and hence, actually originates from some of the processing components that would directly operate on the KB content. The semantic interoperability of several data sources has already been implemented in a series of ontologies (Alirezaie et al., 2018a; Alirezaie et al., 2018b). Lay medical vocabulary is also going to be integrated in the whole architecture.

Figure 1. Simplified semantic interoperability architecture

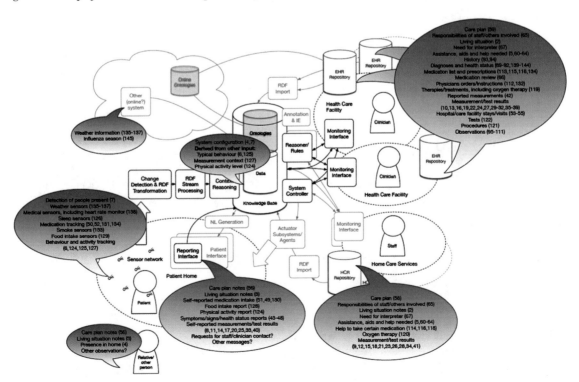

The Contribution of Language Technology

Language Technology is an essential part of an eCare solution, since it empowers patients and other non-professional actors to understand medical information. The focus is on medical terminology that is sorted out based on its explanatory level, either for medical professionals (the expert) or for non-professionals (the lay). The terminology is extracted from documents retrieved from health-related sites on the web. Other applications, like social robots, can benefit from using the methodology for domain-specific web corpus generation in the process of online communication with a person at home, who seeks assistance with monitoring and explaining health related issues.

To date, linguistic understanding of sensor data targets clinicians and other professional staff[18]. To our knowledge, very little research exists on the conversion of sensor data targeted to patients. In *E-care@home*, Language Technology helps enhance patients' self-empowerment. In the project, a lay-specialized textual corpus is being prepared for the automatic extraction of lay terms and paraphrases that match specialized medical terminology used by healthcare professionals. "Lay" means that a document has been written for readers who do not need to have a domain-specific knowledge (e.g. patients, their relatives, home-care aides, etc.). "Specialized" means that a document is written for professional staff (e.g. physicians, nurses, etc.). Research on lay-specialized sublanguages is long-standing and spawn by the need to improve communication between two specific user groups: the layman on one side, and the expert on the other side. A classic example of a specialized term is "varicella", which patients often call "chicken pox". The word "varicella" is a medical term used by healthcare professionals (experts), while "chicken pox" (together with its graphical variant "chickenpox") is a lay paraphrase commonly used by patients (laypeople). Within the *E-care@home* project, the Language Technology group is working to provide methods and tools for the automatic extraction of the lay-specialized linguistic variations.

Converting numbers into concepts expressed in a natural language that experts can understand is certainly a big step forward and it is especially valuable for healthcare professionals, who can use this converted information for timely decision-making. However, since in the *E-care@home* framework patients are empowered and take active part in the management of their illnesses, it is no longer enough to convert sensor data to a medical language that only experts understand. Patients too should be included in the information cycle. There are linguistic hinders, though, as highlighted earlier.

CHALLENGES AND OPEN ISSUES

The research questions and the experiments presented in this chapter contribute to the design and implementation of LT applications for E-care@home. However, several challenges lie on the way. We briefly discuss them below.

Corpus Design: An Extensible Web Corpus

As mentioned above, the purpose of the *E-care@home Corpus* is to be used to build and/or train domain-specific LT applications for eCare and eHealth. We need a corpus whose design is dynamic and flexible, and where additional documents and several languages will be appended over time. Currently, corpus construction practice is still in a stage where a corpus is built as a "static" collection, that is a representative text collection of one or multiple languages of one or several domains at a certain point in time. Methods have been proposed to expand corpora for specific purposes, e.g. for Statistical Machine Translation (Gao & Vogel, 2011) or for paraphrase generation (Quirk et al., 2004). However, these corpora expansions are made of artificial sentences, generated by algorithms trained on large volumes of sentence pairs, and not by adding running texts. Similarly, the approach used by Zadeh (2016) to study the effect of corpus size on the parameters of a distributional model is ad-hoc and one-off rather than driven by a long-lasting design. The first challenge is then to figure out how to design a dynamic, extensible corpus. As explained in Section 5.1, we propose an agile approach based on iteration and incremental developments to meet the needs when they arise. Therefore, at this stage, *eCare_Sv_En_03* is not incomplete or unfinished: it is at an early stage and has its own validity and usage.

Domain-Granularity

We claim that being focused around specific medical terms, and not common diseases, is important for real-word LT applications that aim at solving very specific problems in our society. Although common medical words are important for many purposes, fine-grained domain granularity plays an important role too. As pointed out by Lippincott et al. (2011) "while variation at a coarser domain level such as between newswire and biomedical text is well-studied and known to affect the portability of NLP systems, there is a need to develop an awareness of subdomain variation when considering the practical use of language processing applications [...]". Essentially, we are pushing the limit of domain granularity towards subdomains, and this is our second challenge.

Language Varieties: Lay vs. Specialized

Medicine is a domain where there exists a divide between the language used by healthcare professionals and the language normally used and understood by patients, family caregivers or home-care aides. This is a well-known problem that is extensively researched (see Section 4).

The need of lay synonyms or lay paraphrases that match specialized medical terminology used by healthcare professionals has been the focus of recent research, both in Language Technology (Deléger et al. 2013), and in the clinical community (Seedor et al. 2013). Research on lay-specialized sublanguages is brought about by the need to improve communication between two specific user groups: the layman on one side, and the domain expert on the other side (Miller & Leroy, 2008; Smith & Wicks, 2008; Soergel & Slaughter, 2004). Solid studies show that the gap exists and is detrimental for patients (e.g. Chapman et al., 2003). The importance of matching lay and specialized vocabulary is emphasized by Williams & Odgen (2004) whose study shows that "a doctor's choice of vocabulary affects patient satisfaction immediately after a general practice consultation and that using the same vocabulary as the patient can improve patient outcomes". Thus, the issue of patient empowerment, as well as the development and evaluation of generic methods and tools for assisting patients to better understand their health and healthcare, has been the goal of several EU-funded projects[19]. Unfortunately, while the language and terminology used by professionals are subject to control by continuously evolving standardization, usage of medical terms on the part of laypeople is much more difficult to capture[20].

To date, there is no agreed lexical expression that subsumes concepts such as "lay", "normal", "simplified", "expert", "specialized", "consumer health vocabulary", "consumer terminology", "in plain language", and the like. Researchers use different expressions to indicate these kinds of language varieties, for instance, "different genres (such as specialized and lay texts)" (Deléger et al., 2009); "discourse types (lay and specialized)" (Deléger et al. 2013); or "registers" (Heppin, 2010). Most commonly, however, researchers do not relate the specialized-lay varieties to any superordinate category (as in Abrahamsson et al., 2014).

Classifying language varieties into categories is a difficult exercise. This is not only the case for the "lay variety" but for any textual dimensions, such as style, genre, domain, register and similar. Dozens of definitions exist for each of these textual varieties (as appropriately pointed out in Lee, 2001), and a common conclusion is that the classification into these textual categories is slippery, since no standard and agreed upon characterization is currently available, but there exist different schools of thought and different needs.

Lay vs. specialized language varieties could go under umbrella terms like "discourse" or "communication" or "language for special purposes", or referred to as "register" or "genre" or "sublanguage", and more. Any of these categories do not fully capture the lay-specialized distinction, and any ontological decision may be either questioned or supported, depending on the researchers' personal stances on textual classification schemes.

Since this long-standing discussion is still ongoing, we contribute to it by suggesting the adoption of the category "sublanguage" to refer to the different language varieties employed by user groups when they talk about topics that belong to specialized disciplines, such as medicine and law.

Normally, a sublanguage refers to a technical language (Kittredge & Lehrberger, 1982; Grishman & Kittredge, 2014) or jargon used in restricted communities (e.g. the jargon used by teenagers stored in the Corpus of London Teenagers (Haslerud and Stenstöm, 1995) or to a very specialized domain-specific communication style (e.g. the "notices to skippers"). Both in linguistics and in computational linguistics, a sublanguage is characterized by domain-specific terms (or word co-occurrences) and syntactic cues that deviate from normal language use (Kittredge, 2003: 437; Basili et al. 1993; O'Brien, 1993 lists several definitions of sublanguage). We can safely say that the medical jargon used by physicians and other healthcare professional staff is a sublanguage. What about the language used and understood by patients when they talk about medical topics? It is not properly speaking "general language", it is not a "register"[21], i.e. a language variety used in special situations or contexts as listed in the standard ISO 12620 on Data Category Registry[22], it is not a genre, and it is not a domain. It is indeed a type of discourse. To be fair, we should call it "layspeech" or "patientspeak" as proposed by Scott & Weiner (1984). Although less restricted than the domain-specific technical sublanguage used by professional staff, the layspeech is also domain-specific. According to Kittredge (2003): "Restricted subsystems of language can arise spontaneously in a subject-matter domain where speech or writing is used for special purposes". Leveraging on this observation, we broaden the definition of sublanguage in order to encompass the non-overlapping language varieties that are commonly used when two or more user groups communicate in specific domains on certain topics. While in previous definitions, the notion of sublanguage indicated either a domain-specific jargon or a community jargon, in the sublanguage definition proposed here we combine the connotation of domain specificity and user group usage. This definition of sublanguage is more flexible and more accurate because it has two attributes, the domain (e.g. medicine, law, etc.) and the user group (e.g. experts, laypeople, novices, learners etc.). It is worth noting that although in the experiments presented here we are using only the lay vs specialized categories, healthcare actors are heterogeneous, including a wide variety of backgrounds, levels of medical literacy and ages.

In this complex landscape, a more flexible characterization of sublanguage allows us to refer to a language variety so that we can use formulations such as: "medical professional and lay sublanguages" or "medical professional, learners' and lay sublanguages", where "medical" refers to the domain, and "professional", "learners" and "lay" indicate the levels of medical literacy of a user group whose language use is going to be analyzed (cf. Zheng et al., 2002; Miller et al., 2007). This modularity can be easily exported to other domains (e.g. the legal domain, see Heffer et al., 2013 or the business domain[23] or the marketing domain[24]), so we can say "legal lay sublanguage" or "business specialized sublanguage" and so on.

Arguably, this definition of sublanguage is more flexible and applicable to all the domains where the domain-specificity of a jargon causes some kind of "diglossia" or "polyglossia" that causes a gap in human communication. Following the extended definition, we can then say that in the medical domain, two sublanguages normally come in contact, namely the lay sublanguage used by patients and their relatives (the lay) and the specialized sublanguage used by healthcare professionals (the expert).

Normally, lay synonyms are based on everyday language, and are easier to read and to understand than medical terminology, which conversely have highbrow connotation. For ordinary people without a medical education or background, medical terms are often opaque or hard to remember due to the Greek and/or Latin etymology. These terms are called "neoclassical" terms, and, interestingly, recent research shows that also healthcare professionals tend to "normalize" this type of lexicon to everyday language, as in the case of "Swedification" of Latin and Greek affixes in patient records (Grigonyte et al., 2016). Generally speaking, it seems that the layfication of medical language is an extensive phenomenon that affects, in different ways, several user groups. It must be emphasized that the lay sublanguage is not as accurate as the specialized sublanguage. Lay medical terms, when they exist, are indeed more transparent and more easily understood by laypeople. Again, consider the specialized medical term "varicella" and its lay synonym "chickenpox". Both varicella and chickenpox are medical terms, one highbrow and the other one colloquial. The same high-low connotation can be found in the words surrounding the medical terms, e.g. the verb "alleviate" can be rendered by "decrease" in lay texts. Presumably, the lay sublanguage shares similarities across all languages (cf. also Grabar et al. (2007), since it is a phenomenon of text simplification.

Noise

The concept of noise is tightly linked to the concept of quality. Recently, several researchers have investigated this aspect of web texts (e.g. Biemann et al. 2013; Barbaresi, 2015). In particular, Schäfer et al., 2013 have proposed text quality evaluation in the form of the so-called Badness score. That is, a document receives a low Badness score if the most frequent function words of the target language have a high enough frequency in the document. The Badness score is based on research findings in language identification and web document filtering (Grefenstette, 1995; Baroni et al., 2009).

In this chapter, we consider two main forms of noise. The first type of noise (cf. also Versley & Panchenko, 2012) is in the form of misspellings, mis-tokenizations, encoding problems, scattered html tags, residual url chunks and incoherent punctuation caused by boilerplate removal. The second form of noise refers to badly written texts and more precisely noise caused by the presence of automatically translated texts, which have been published on the web without post-editing or proofreading. Since we aim at finding a quick and replicable methodology to compile reliable web corpora with minimum curation, we wish to explore to what extent corpus-based LT applications are tolerant to these kinds of noise. We are aware that certain LT applications require corpora that meet certain quality requirements, for example in Machine Translation, as pointed out by Escartin and Torres (2016). However, our effort is geared towards noise-resistant applications. For example, as presented in Section 5.2, we noticed that noise become irrelevant and neutralized when using a bag-of-words approach combined with the StringsToVector filter as explained in Section 5.2.

Small (Data) Is Beautiful: The Minimalist Approach

Many recent web corpora have been built using data from the CommonCrawl Foundation, which is the largest crawl in the world (e.g. Kristoffersen, 2017; Habernal et al., 2016; Schäfer, 2016). However, size is not everything. As pointed out by Kistoffersen (2017:1), large corpora are time-consuming. This author reports that it takes some 18 hours just to read a snapshot of web content distributed by the CommonCrawl Foundation. Additionally, Remus & Biemann (2016) highlight that "large-scale data is largely collected without notions of topical interest. If an interest in a particular topic exists, corpora have to undergo extensive document filtering with simple and/or complex text classification methods. This leads to a lot of downloaded data being discarded with lots of computational resources being unnecessarily wasted".

Up to few months ago, the ruling catchphrase was *big data*. Now the opposite concept starts gaining momentum: *small data*. The concept has been created for sales or customer analytics, but now it has expanded not only to healthcare[25] but also to text analytics and corpus construction.

In this work, we wish to strike the balance between corpus size (as small as possible depending on the application), time (as short as possible) and speedy portability (as fast as possible) of LT models to other domains.

Regardless of the current size of the *eCare_Sv_En_03*, small data is an interesting concept in itself. According to current definitions small data is data that has small enough size for human comprehension. As a matter of fact, the small size of *eCare_Sv_01* (one of *eCare_Sv_En_03*'s sub-corpora) has given us the opportunity to detect phenomena such as the noise caused by automatically translated web pages and the inter-rater disagreement due to user group bias. With a much larger corpus, these fine-grained phenomena would go unnoticed or it would have taken much more time to be identified. We argue that for many problems and questions, small data in itself is enough. The challenge of small data is to find the ideal "critical mass" that benefits the application of interest. This critical mass changes from application to applications (see Section 5).

PREVIOUS WORK: LAYFICATION

By layfication, we refer to empirical and computational approaches to the automated identification, extraction, classification of lay and specialized sublanguages. In this section, we summarize research efforts made to characterize, detect or discriminate lay vs. specialized texts in the medical field. Previous work in this area is extensive, although not exhaustive, since more research is still needed.

In this cursory overview, we divide previous work in three broad areas, namely studies focusing on the relationships between readability and lay sublanguage; automatic induction of lay terminology; and finally, automatic lay-specialized text classification. For a more exhaustive overview of previous work in this field, see Åhlfeldt et al. (2006).

As pointed out by Zeng et al. (2007), lay terminology is more challenging to identify than professional health vocabulary and medical terminology. This is because lay terms are more ambiguous and more heterogeneous than medical technical terms. This state of affairs is well-described by Zeng and Tze (2006): "When producing words to describe health-related concepts, a lay person may use terms such as hair loss and heart failure without knowing their technical definitions or use general language expressions to describe familiar concepts (e.g., loss of appetite for anorexia and pain killer for analgesic). The range of lay expressions seems to vary from general and descriptive (e.g., device to look inside my ear for otoscope) to specific, but colloquial (e.g., sugar for diabetes). Thus, lay discourse on the health-related topics often includes a combination of technical terminology and general language expressions, with many possible interpretations based on individual, contextual, societal, and cultural associations. The challenge is to sort out the different ways consumers communicate within distinct discourse groups and map the common, shared expressions and contexts to the more constrained, specialized language of professionals, when appropriate.". The difficulty is not only about medical expressions per se but also in words that are not technical, but are used as technical terms in the medical jargon, e.g. "alleviate" or "apprehensive" etc. (Scott & Weiner, 1984).

Several researchers have investigated the relation between *readability* and lay/specialized sublanguage (e.g. Ownby, 2005; Zeng-Treitler et al., 2007; Kunz &Osborne, 2010). The general assumption is that the use of specialized vocabulary hinders the comprehension of patients with lower reading skills, thus more "readable" texts are more comprehensible for those who have lower reading proficiency. However, this assumption is challenged by several scholars. For instance, Miller et al. (2007) argue that "traditional readability formulas examine syntactic features like sentence length and number of syllables, ignoring the target audience's grasp of the words themselves". Several studies indicate that standard readability formulas might not be of help when assessing the difficulty of medical texts. Leroy et al. (2008) found that readability differs by topic and source. They proposed metrics different from readability formulas and argued that these metrics were more precise than readability scores. They compared two documents in English for three groups of linguistic metrics and conducted a user study evaluating one of the differentiating metrics, i.e. the percentage of function words in a sentence. Their results showed that this percentage correlates significantly with the level of understanding as indicated by users but not with the readability formula levels. On the same line, Zheng & Yu (2017) found that the correlations of readability predictions and laypeople's perceptions were weak. Their study with English texts explored the relationship between several readability formulas and the laypeople's perceived difficulty on two genres of text: general health information and electronic health record (EHR) notes. Their findings suggested that "the readability formulas' predictions did not align with perceived difficulty in either text genre. The widely used readability formulas were highly correlated with each other but did not show adequate correlation with readers' perceived difficulty. Therefore, they were not appropriate to assess the readability of EHR notes."

The construction of *lay corpora and lay terminology extraction* is advanced for the French language. Several experiments have been carried out by Deléger et al. (2013) based on lay-specialized monolingual comparable corpora which were built using web documents belonging to specific genres from public websites in the medical domain. Grabar & Hamon (2014b) proposed an automatic method based on the morphological analysis of terms and on text mining for finding the paraphrases of technical terms in French. Their approach relies on the analysis of neoclassical medical compounds and for searching their non-technical paraphrases in corpora. Depending on the semantics of the terms, error rate of the extractions ranges between 0 and 59%. Antoine & Grabar (2017) focused on the acquisition of vocabulary by associating technical terms with layman expressions. They proposed exploiting the notion of "reformulation" through two methods: extraction of abbreviations and their extended forms, and of reformulations introduced by markers. Tchami & Grabar (2014) described a method for a contrastive automatic analysis of verbs in French medical corpora, based on the semantic annotation of the verbs' nominal arguments. The corpora used are specialized in cardiology and distinguished according to their levels of expertise (high and low). The semantic annotation of these corpora was performed using existing medical terminology. The results suggest that the same verbs occurring in the two corpora show different specialization levels, which are indicated by the words with which they co-occur.

Lay terminology extraction methods for the English language were proposed by Elhadad and Sutaria, (2007) who mined a lexicon of medical terms and lay equivalents using abstracts of clinical studies and corresponding news stories written for a lay audience. Their collection is structured as a parallel corpus of documents for clinicians and for consumers. Zeng et al. (2007) explored several term identification methods for the English language, including collaborative human review and automated term recognition methods. The study identified 753 consumer terms and found the logistic regression model to be highly effective for lay term identification. Doing-Harris & Zeng-Treitler (2011) presented the CAU system which consisted of three main parts: a Web crawler and an HTML parser, a candidate term filter that utilizes natural language processing tools including term recognition methods, and a human review interface. In evaluation, the CAU system was applied to the health-related social network website PatientsLikeMe.com. The system's utility was assessed by comparing the candidate term list it generated to a list of valid terms manually extracted from the text of the crawled webpages. Soergel, Tse & Slaughter (2004) proposed an interpretive layer framework for helping consumers find, understand and use medical information. Seedorff et al. (2013) introduced the Mayo Consumer Health Vocabulary (MCV)—a taxonomy of approximately 5,000 consumer health terms and concepts—and developed text-mining techniques to expand its coverage by integrating disease concepts (from UMLS[26]) as well as non-genetic (from deCODEme[27]) and genetic (from GeneWikiPlus[28] and PharmGKB[29]) risk factors to diseases. Jiang and Yang (2013) used co-occurrence analysis to identify terms that co-occur frequently with a set of seed terms. A corpus containing 120,393 discussion messages was used as a dataset and co-occurrence analysis was used to extract the most related consumer expressions. The study presented in Vydiswaran et al. (2014) focused on the linguistic habits of consumers. In their study, the authors empirically evaluate the applicability of their approach using a large data sample consisting of MedLine abstracts as well as posts from a popular online health portal, the MedHelp forum. The "propensity of a term", which is a measure based on the ratio of frequency of occurrence, was used to differentiate lay terms from professional terms.

In Sweden, research on medical language is also strong. Kokkinakis (2006) described efforts to build a Swedish medical corpus, namely the MEDLEX Corpus, where generic named entity and terminology recognition for the detailed annotation of the corpus are combined. Kokkinakis & Gronostaj (2006) carried out a corpus-based, contrastive study of Swedish medical language focusing on the vocabulary used in two types of medical textual material: professional portals and web-based consumer sites within the domain of cardiovascular disorders. Linguistic, statistical and quantitatively based readability studies are considered in order to find the typical language-dependent and language independent characteristics. Heppin (2010) created a unique medical test collection for Information Retrieval to provide the possibility to assess the document relevance to a query according to two user groups, namely patients or physicians. The focus of Abrahamsson et al (2014) was on the simplification of one single genre, namely the medical journal genre. To this purpose, the authors used a subset of a collection built from the journal Svenska Läkartidningen, i.e. the Journal of the Swedish Medical association, that was created by Kokkinakis (2012). Another unique language resource is the Stockholm EPR (Electronic Patient Records) Corpus (Dalianis et al., 2009; and Dalianis et al., 2015), which comprises real data from more than two million patient records. Johansson & Rennes (2016) presented results from using two methods to automatically extract Swedish synonyms from a corpus of easy-to-read texts. They used two methods, based on distributional semantic models (more specifically word2vec), one inspired by Lin et al. (2003) and the other by Kann and Rosell (2005). The methods were evaluated using an online survey, in which the perceived synonymy of word pairs, extracted by the methods, was graded from "Disagree" (1) to "Totally agree" (4). The results were promising and showed, for example, that the most common grade was "Sometimes" (3) for both methods, indicating that the methods found useful synonyms.

Previous research in *automatic supervised lay-specialized text classification* show that simple methods yield good performance.

As for English, Zheng et al. (2002) addressed the problem of filtering medical news articles for lay and expert audiences. They used two supervised machine learning techniques, Decision Trees and Naive Bayes, to automatically construct classifiers on the basis of a training set, in which news articles have been pre-classified by a medical expert and four other human readers. The goal is to classify the news articles into three groups: non-medical, medical intended for experts, and medical intended for other readers. While the general accuracy of the machine learning approach is around 78% (three classes), the accuracy of distinguishing non-medical articles from medical ones is shown to be approximately 92% (two classes). Miller et al. (2007) created a Naive Bayes classifier for three levels of increasing medical terminology specificity (consumer/patient, novice health learner, medical professional) with a lexicon generated from a representative medical corpus. 96% accuracy in classification was attained. The classifier was then applied to existing consumer health web pages, but only 4% of the pages were classified at a layperson level, regardless of the Flesch reading ease scores, while the remaining pages were at the level of medical professionals. This finding seems to indicate that consumer health web pages are often not using appropriate language for their target audience. In order to recommend health information with appropriate reading level to consumers, Support Vector Machine (SVM) is used to classify consumer health information into easy to read and reading level for the general public by Wang (2006). He used three feature sets: surface linguistic features, word difficulty features, unigrams and their combinations were compared in terms of classification accuracy. Unigram features alone reached an accuracy of 80.71%, and the combination of three feature sets was the most effective in classification with an accuracy of 84.06%. They are significantly better than surface linguistic features, word difficulty features and their combination. Miller & Leroy (2008) created a system that dynamically generates a health topics overview for consumer health web pages that organizes the information into four consumer-preferred categories while displaying topic prevalence through visualization. The system accesses both a consumer health vocabulary and the Unified Medical Language System (UMLS). Overall, precision is 82%, recall is 75%, and F-score is 78%, and precision between sites did not significantly differ.

Multilingual approaches to lay vs. specialized text classification exhibit interesting findings. For example, Porrat et al. (2006) proposed a pipelined system for the automatic classification of medical documents according to their language (English, Spanish and German) and their target user group (medical experts vs. health care consumers). They used a simple n-gram based categorization model and presented promising experimental results for both classification tasks. Seljan et al., (2014)'s research to understand the role of terminology in online resources, was conducted on English and Croatian manuals and Croatian online texts and divided into three interrelated parts: i) comparison of professional and popular terminology use; ii) evaluation of automatic statistically-based terminology extraction on English and Croatian texts; and iii) comparison and evaluation of extracted terminology performed on an English manual using statistical and hybrid approaches. Extracted terminology candidates were evaluated by comparison with three types of reference lists: a list created by a professional medical person, a list of highly professional vocabulary contained in MeSH and a list created by non-medical persons, made as intersection of 15 lists.

A set of experiments on multilingual lay-specialized medical corpora are presented in Borin et al. (2007). They investigated readability in English, Swedish, Japanese and Russian. They explored variations in readability, lexicon and lexical-semantic relations, grammar, semantic and pragmatics, as well as layout and typography. On the basis of the findings, the authors proposed a set of recommendations per language for adapting expert clinical documents for patients.

On the cross-lingual side, Grabar et al. (2007) put forward the hypothesis that discrimination between lay vs. specialized documents can be done using a small number of features and that such features can be language- and domain-independent. The features used were acquired from a source corpus (Russian language, diabetes topic) and then tested on target (French language, pneumology topic) and source corpora. These cross-language features showed 90% precision and 93% recall with non-expert documents in the source language; and 85% precision and 74% recall with expert documents in the target language.

The medical text collections briefly mentioned above are important language resources, but their construction and usage seem to be contingent to specific experiments, rather than designed for a long-term deployment and continuous enhancement. For this reason, we propose a new kind of design for a domain-specific corpus with the intent to be re-used, easily updatable and hopefully long-lasting.

In the experiments presented in this chapter, we do not compare our results with readability scores. It would be interesting to compare the different readability levels of web documents on chronic diseases. Stable sets of readability assessment features exist both for English and Swedish (i.e. the language included in eCare Sv_En_03). Unfortunately, texts crawled from the web are noisy. For instance, texts may contain informal language (e.g. sv: "nå'n annan som hatar utredningen?" English: "somebody else who hates the investigation"), and unpredictable combinations of English words (e.g. "therapycounseling") are numerous. This means that the automatic extraction of readability assessment features from eCare Sv_En_03 would imply a regularization of the corpus that we have not planned for yet. At this stage, we focus on how to leverage on noisy texts rather than on how to regularize them.

Simple methods based on distributional semantics and automatic lay-specialized text classification are promising and easy to implement. For this reason, we continue along this line (Section 5).

RETHINKING WEB CORPORA: THE WORK-IN-PROGRESS DESIGN

In this section, we describe the *current* implementation of the design of a work-in-progress web corpus. We stress the word "current" because it is our ambition to explore several different approaches that can all be conflated into the same design of a corpus conceived as extensible, updatable and open-ended. The experiments described in this section are based on a version of the corpus that **is not** "unfinished" or "incomplete". Rather, it must be seen as the first iteration of an incremental strategy. The inspiration for this approach comes from the Agile Methodologies used in software development and project management, where the implementation of a plan is based on cycled iterations that ensure a seamless incremental progress. *Agile* is a process that "advocates adaptive planning, evolutionary development, early delivery, and continual improvement, and it encourages rapid and flexible response to change"[30]. This source of inspiration provided a framework for the idea of the work-in-progress corpus. The construction of a corpus is based on iteration which ensures a continual improvement. Since the agile approach is based on incremental deliveries, each successive version of the corpus is usable, and each version builds upon the previous one. Such a process is adaptive to changes, flexible and open-ended.

For the bootstrapping of *eCare_Sv_En_03*, we followed the general approach initiated by Baroni & Bernardini (2004) and widely used all over the world.

Starting Off: BootCaT-ing the Swedish Corpus About Chronic Diseases

eCare_Sv_01 (see also Santini et al., 2017) is a small text collection bootstrapped from the web. It contains 801 web documents that have been labelled as *lay* or *specialized* by two annotators. In the following subsections, we describe its construction and the actual corpus.

The Seeds

We started off with approximately 1300 term seeds designating chronic diseases in the Swedish SNOMED CT. A qualitative linguistic analysis of the term seeds revealed a wide range of variation as for number of words and syntactic complexity. For instance, multiword terms (n-grams) are much more frequent than single-word terms (unigrams).

We counted 13 unigrams (i.e. one-word terms) (see Table 1), 215 bigrams (i.e. two-words terms), and the rest of the seeds were characterized by specialized terms and complex syntax, such as: "kronisk inkomplett tetraplegi orsakad av ryggmärgsskada mellan femte och sjunde halskotan" (English: "Chronic incomplete quadriplegia due to spinal cord lesion between fifth and seventh cervical vertebra"). Another example is shown in Figure 2.

To bootstrap this version of the corpus, we used unigrams and bigrams only. This decision was based on the assumptions that (1) unigram- and bigram-terms are more findable on the web than syntactically complex keyword seeds, and (2) complex multiword terms are less likely to have a lay synonym or paraphrase. It should be noticed however that Swedish is a compound language where several words are united in one single graphical unit, thus the distinction between unigrams and bigrams is sometimes blurred.

Table 1. Unigram seeds

Seeds (Swedish)	Translation (English)	SCTID
ansiktstics	Facial tic disorder	230335009
bukangina	Abdominal angina	241154007
chalcosis	Chalcosis	46623005
fluoros	Fluorosis	244183009
kromoblastomykos	Chromoblastomycosis	187079000
lipoidnefros	Minimal change disease	44785005
lungemfysem	Pulmonary emphysema	87433001
mycetom	Mycetoma	410039003
ozena	Ozena	69646003
polyserosit	Polyserositis	123598000
postkardiotomi-syndrom	Postcardiotomy syndrome	78643003
Swimmingpool-dermatit	Swimming pool dermatitis	277784005
trumhinneatelektas	Tympanic atelectasis	232258001

Figure 2. Example of long medical term as it is displayed in the SNOMED CT browser

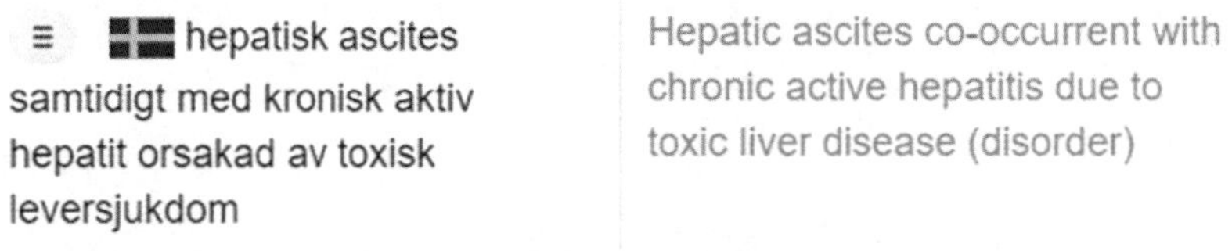

≡　🔳 hepatisk ascites
samtidigt med kronisk aktiv
hepatit orsakad av toxisk
leversjukdom

Hepatic ascites co-occurrent with
chronic active hepatitis due to
toxic liver disease (disorder)

Pre-Processing and Download

Using regular search engines (like Google, Yahoo or Bing) and term seeds (as queries) to build a corpus is handy, but it also has some caveats that depend on the design or distortion of the underlying search engine (Wong et al., 2011). These caveats affect the content of web corpora since it might happen that irrelevant documents are included in the collection, especially when searching for very specialized terms. For the construction of *ecare_Sv_01,* we decided to use seeds in the following way to have a better insight of the content of the corpus that was going to be built. Each seed was used as a search keyword in *Google.se*, i.e. Google web domain for Sweden. The searches were carried out from within Sweden (namely Stockholm and Örebro). Each of the preselected SNOMED CT terms were used individually, i.e. one seed term per query. This means that we launched 228 queries. For each seed/query, Google returned a number of hits. We limited our analysis to hits on the first page (we extended the visualization of the results to 20 hits per page). We manually opened each snippet to have an idea of the type of web documents that were retrieved. For each search lap, several documents were irrelevant (presumably as an unwanted effect of query expansion) and several were duplicated. 74 keyword seeds were discarded because the retrieved documents were irrelevant or contained passages not written in Swedish.

Unsurprisingly, we also noticed that the number of retrieved pages depends on how common a disease is for web users. For instance, "ansiktstics" (English: "facial tics") had many hits, while "chalcosis" (en: "chalcosis") had very few. As a rule of thumb, we decided to select a maximum of 20 documents for the most common illnesses, and as many as we could for rarer diseases. This observation about common and rare illnesses, is merely based on the number of hits retrieved by the search engine. We do not rely on medical statistics, because the situation may change any time. For example, for some reasons that we are unable to foresee now, an illness like "chalcosis" can become widespread in a couple of years and the web will be inundate by documents about this illness. This is just an example of why a corpus of this kind should be extendible and flexible.

After this preprocessing phase, we applied BootCat[31] (Baroni & Bernardini, 2004) using the advanced settings (i.e. *url seeds*) to create the web corpus.

We handed out documents downloaded with BootCat to two native Swedish speakers (both academics), one lay person (i.e. not working in the medical field) and one specialized person (working with medical-related subjects). They proceeded with the annotation by applying a lay or specialized label to each text in the corpus.

eCare_sv_01 in a Nutshell

eCare_Sv_01 was bootstrapped using 228 terms indicating chronic diseases, namely 13 unigrams and 215 bigrams. The number of unigrams is much lower than multi-word n-grams. This seems to indicate that medical language prefers multiword expressions also in Swedish, which is a compound language.

After the preprocessing, 843 urls (112 for unigrams and 731 for bigrams) were factored out and used as *url-seeds* in BootCat. Some of the urls were automatically discarded by BootCat (e.g. bilingual documents were not included) and some downloaded documents were empty. Finally, 801 documents were successfully bootcat-ed with 155 seeds[32]. Table 2 shows the corpus statistics.

Both annotators pointed out that the quality of the writing was poor in some documents, mainly because they had been machine translated, and not written by humans. Some of the web documents explicitly stated "Översatt från engelska av Microsoft" (English: Translated from English by Microsoft). Out of 801 web documents, 339 have received comments by the lay annotator, e.g. "Machine Translated" or "it is about animals and not about humans", and the expert annotator flagged 23 documents as medically "irrelevant". By 'irrelevant', the annotators meant that these documents contained the seed terms, but the genre was a schedule or a conference program, or the described illnesses was on animals rather than humans.

Essentially, we can observe that the corpus is noisy. The annotators' comments help us understand the different types of noise and emphasize a crucial issue that is underexplored in corpus- and computational linguistics, i.e. the reliability and the quality of corpora bootstrapped from the web. The automatic discrimination of "good" documents from "bad" ones is an important problem, especially in sensitive domains like the medical or legal domains. In the medical domain, recent research shows that the reliability, readability and quality of patient-oriented websites are still open issues for the scientific community. It has been pointed out that this kind of resources are easily accessed by patients, but they might contain information that are less rigorous than the information provided by scientific literature or healthcare practitioner websites and can inconveniently cause "misinformation" in patients (Soobrah and Clark, 2012; Küçükdurmaz et al., 2015). These issues will certainly be explored more extensively in future research. However, in the experiments that we present in this chapter, we took another perspective and investigated to what extent lay-specialized text classification is robust to a number of disturbing factors. Since cleaning or refining a corpus might be prohibitive in many projects, our challenge is to see whether noisy corpora can be used in Language Technology without affecting the performance of LT applications. For this reason, the noisy documents have been left in the corpus, but they are flagged so they can be easily included or bypassed, according to the purpose of the project at hand. Other types of research that can benefit from the inclusion of "disturbing" texts in the corpus include the automatic

Table 2. Corpus statistics

	# initial seeds	# retrieved seeds	# bootcat-ed urls	# urls per seed (mean)	# urls per seed (median)	# urls per seed (st dev)	# words
Unigrams	13	13	112	8.61	9.3	3.37	91 118
Bigrams	215	142	689	4.85	4	3.16	618 491
Total	228	155	801	5.16	5	3.35	709 609

analysis of MT "translationese" (Volansky et al., 2015) and the automatic quality assessment of text writing[33].

Proposed Corpus and Text Metadata

Corpus and text metadata are important elements of the whole corpus design since they characterize the corpus and allow us to extract "virtual sub-corpora" matching some criteria.

In Figure 3, the pseudo-annotation by sublanguage is shown. The tags <sublangs> and </sublangs> surround information about how the lay annotator and the expert annotator labelled each text in the corpus[34]. In the example in Figure 3, the lay- and the expert annotator DO NOT agree about the sublanguage of a text in the corpus.

Having the corpus annotated in this way is convenient not only for the linguistic/textual descriptions of the individual texts, but also to quickly extract datasets for text classification according to the sublanguage textual dimension. As a matter of fact, the datasets that we use for the experiments in Section 8 are extracted from this annotated corpus using a simple R script[35].

Human Annotation and Interrater Agreement

The annotation of documents in the corpus as being *lay* or *specialized* was carried out by two native speakers who participate in the project. They are both academics but operating in different research fields: namely the lay annotator works in Language Technology while the expert annotator works in Health Informatics.

The purpose of the manual annotation is to prove that there is no need to decide beforehand the sources of lay and specialized documents but crawling the web indistinctly will return a mixture of lay and specialized comments. The annotators were to follow their spontaneous linguistic instinct for assessing the language and no training was provided. The "lay" annotator has high education, but no familiarity with medical terminology, either personally or professionally. The expert annotator works with medical terminology. At this stage, we did not involve the potential users of the final system because we first wanted to observe to what extent medical expertise affects the agreement on two highly-educated persons. It is normal that the judgement on specialization/technicality of documents varies with the expertise of the annotators. Other factors like the education level can strongly influence the assessment.

We measured the inter-annotator agreement in two steps, first on approximately 1/3 of the documents, and then on the whole corpus, to see if the size of the corpus creates a bias in the agreement. The sample of 1/3 was random. No consensus step was taken to reach a final agreement between the two annotators,

Figure 3. Metadata describing the sublanguage and the annotators' expertise

```xml
<?xml version="1.0" encoding="UTF-8"?>
<document>
    <sublangs>
        <sublang>
            <lay-annotator-evaluation>specialised</lay-annotator-evaluation>
            <specialised_annotator-evaluation>lay</specialised_annotator-evaluation>
        </sublang>
    </sublangs>
</document>
```

since at this stage we are not focusing on that. As shown in experiment 3 in Section 5.2, we argue that there is no need to any further step because a regular classifier can establish the consensus itself. This streamlines and accelerates the construction of supervised LT applications.

To have an idea of the agreement between a lay annotator and an expert annotator, we carried out two interrater-agreement calculations. First, we measured the agreement on a random sample (348 out of 801 documents), then on the whole corpus (801 documents) and observed whether the two calculations returned similar coefficients or not. The rationale of this decision was to determine whether the size of the corpus to be annotated plays a role in the agreement.

Several inter-rater agreement measures exist (Artstein and Poesio, 2008). All the inter-rater agreement measures have their strong points and their drawbacks and the use of one over the other depends on the data, the task and the situation. In our case, we wish to measure to what extent two members belonging to two different user groups (i.e. the lay and the expert) spontaneously agree when assessing the "domain-specificity" of medical language. Our expectation is that a lay person tends to label as "specialized" a larger number of medical documents than an expert person, who, conversely, tends to see as "lay" many documents that laypeople would consider to be "specialized". In order to test this assumption, we measured the inter-rater agreement by using percentage (i.e. the proportion of agreed upon documents in relation to the whole without chance correction), the classic unweighted Cohen's *kappa* (Cohen 1960) and Krippendorff's *alpha* (Krippendorff, 1980) to get a straightforward indication of the raters' tendencies. Cohen's *kappa* assumes independence of the two coders and is based on the assumption that "if coders were operating by chance alone, we would get a separate distribution for each coder" (Artstein and Poesio, 2008). This assumption intuitively fits our expectations. Krippendorff's *alpha* is similar to Cohen's *kappa*, but it also takes into account the extent and the degree of disagreement between raters (Artstein and Poesio, 2008).

Table 3 shows the breakdown of the inter-rater agreement on the sample, while Table 4 shows the overall inter-rater agreement on the whole corpus[36]. The breakdown of Table 3 reveals that, interestingly, annotators tend to disagree more on documents harvested with unigrams (Row 1), while they agree more on documents harvested with bigrams (Row 2).

Overall, Table 3 shows that both *kappa* and *alpha* coefficients are approx. 0.5, and both these values indicate a "moderate" agreement according to the magnitude scale for *kappa* (Sim and Wright, 2005), and the *alpha* range (Krippendorff, 2011).

Table 3. Breakdown: inter-rater agreement on the sample (348 documents)

# documents	Percentage	Cohen's *Kappa*	Krippendorff's *Alpha*
112 (unigram seeds)	75.9%	0.52	0.51
238 (bigram seeds)	82.2%	0.60	0.60
348 (total)	80.2%	0.57	0.57

Table 4. Interrater agreement on the whole corpus (801 documents)

Whole Corpus	Percentage	Cohen's *Kappa*	Krippendorff's *Alpha*
801 documents	78.8%	0.51	0.51

The interrater coefficients computed for the whole corpus (see Table 4) are in line with the coefficients calculated on the sample, although the coefficients for the whole corpus are slightly lower than those for the sample. However, all coefficients confirm that the agreement between the lay and the expert annotator is *moderate*.

Table 5 shows the distribution of labels per annotator. We can observe that the lay annotator tends to apply fewer lay labels than the expert annotator, who conversely perceive as "lay" more documents than the lay annotator. Interestingly, the expert annotator is also much more selective than the lay annotator and flags 23 documents as medically "irrelevant".

Discussion

These results seem to endorse our hypothesis that there exists a *user group bias*, which indicates that the annotation may be biased by the annotator's domain expertise. If we contextualize the results, this finding means that patients (who usually have a "lay" perspective) tend to perceive many documents as "specialized", while physicians would assess these documents simply as "normal". This has a linguistic implication that might affect certain LT applications in the eHealth field, and we encourage more in-depth investigation about this topic in the future.

Intrinsic Evaluation: Supervised Lay-Specialized Text Classification

In this section, we validate the reliability of the corpus. We investigate how reliable a small and noisy corpus is for LT applications. We present three experiments based on lay-specialized text classification. We apply fully-supervised machine learning methods to explore how well supervised algorithms learn the labels applied by the lay annotator (Experiment 1 and Experiment 2), and how sensitive a LT task, such as text classification, is to the disagreement between the lay annotator and expert annotator (Experiment 3). Technically speaking, Experiment 1 focuses on corpus scalability, and help us understand whether the size of the corpus has an impact on the classification results. In Experiment 2, we explore to what extent lay-specialized text classification is affected by noisy documents. Both in Experiment 1 and 2, we use the labels applied by the lay annotator because we focus on the patients' perspective on language, which is presumably *lay*. In Experiment 3, we investigate whether text classification is sensitive to the user group bias, i.e. the different ways of labelling documents.

Corpus scalability refers to the capability to identify the critical mass of corpus size that ensures a satisfactory performance of a specific algorithm for a specific task. With supervised machine-learning algorithms, the normal assumption is that classification performance improves when more data is available. However, since we are after a minimalist approach, we wish to identify the minimum data requirement to get a "good enough" performance.

Table 5. Number of labels by annotator

	Lay labels	Specialized Labels	NA	Total
Lay Annotator	246	555	0	801
Expert Annotator	279	499	23	801

In these experiments, we relied on the Weka Machine Learning Workbench, Explorer and Experimenter interfaces (Witten et al., 2016).

Quick-and-Dirty: Features and Noisy Texts

The first question to answer when performing lay-specialized text classification is: which features are most appropriate to represent lay and specialized medical sublanguages? We decided to take a Bag-of-Words approach. Only two attributes were declared, namely *the textual content of the document* defined as "string", and the *sublanguage label* (either "lay" or "specialized") defined as "nominal".

Experiment 1: Lay-Specialized Text Classification and Corpus Scalability

The rationale of this experimental setting is to observe whether and to what extent the performance of the classifiers deteriorates when increasing the corpus size.

We converted four subsets of the whole corpus into four datasets. The first dataset contains 156 documents; the second one 220 documents; the third one 337 documents; the fourth datasets includes the whole corpus and contains 801 documents. The datasets were created randomly and they contain some overlapping data since we wish to simulate the progressive expansion of the corpus over time by appending more documents to the original corpus. Since we did not know in advance which type of machine learning modelling would be more suitable for this kind of data, we applied three standard algorithms that have very different inductive biases, namely *Decision Trees*, *Naive Bayes* and SVM. We took a bag-of-word approach, and construct vectors from strings using a filter (see below).

We used Weka's implementations of the algorithms, namely J48, *Naive Bayes* and *SMO*. All the algorithms were run with standard parameters.

We ran each of the algorithms via a metaclassifier[37]. Recent developments in computational learning theory have led to methods that enhance the performance or extend the capabilities of these basic learning schemes. Those learning schemes have been called "meta-learning schemes" or "meta-classifiers" because they operate on the output of other learners or filters.

We selected in turn each of the pre-decided classifiers together with the *StringToWordVector* filter (standard parameters). StringTOWordVector is the filter class in Weka which filters strings into n-grams. Besides just tokenizing, it also provides other functionalities like removing stopwords, weighting words with TFIDF[38], output word count rather than just indicating if a word is present or not, pruning rate, stemming, lowercase conversion of words, etc. Basically, it provides basic functionalities which helps us to fine-tune the training set according to requirements before training.

We applied 10-fold-crossvalidation. Results are shown in Table 6 (values have been truncated to two decimal places).

For the first dataset (156 documents), J48 seems to be less suitable than Naive Bayes and SMO. J48's k statistic is low, indicating that most of the corrected classifications happen by chance. The confusion matrix for J48 shows that lay texts are quite confusing for this classifier (only 48 TP vs 35 misclassified cases), while specialized texts are more clearly set apart (110 TP[39] vs 27 misclassifications). Naive Bayes and SMO do a better job on this dataset: their averaged ROC area[40] values are much higher than 0.5 (0.5 would mean that a classifier is random).

Table 6. Experiment 1: performance on datasets of different sizes

DATASET 1: 156 DOCUMENTS

	k	Acc.	Avg. P	Avg. R	Avg. F	ROC A.	Avg TP	Avg FP
J48	0.14	62.8	0.62	0.62	0.62	0.63	0.62	0.42
NB	0.46	75.6	0.77	0.75	0.76	0.80	0.75	0.26
SMO	0.43	75.6	0.75	0.75	0.75	0.71	0.75	0.32

DATASET 2: 220 DOCUMENTS

	k	Acc.	Avg. P	Avg. R	Avg. F	ROC A.	Avg TP	Avg FP
J48	0.38	71.8	0.71	0.71	0.71	0.69	0.71	0.33
NB	0.45	72.7	0.75	0.72	0.73	0.78	0.72	0.25
SMO	0.36	70.9	0.70	0.70	0.70	0.67	0.70	0.35

DATASET 3: 337 DOCUMENTS

	k	Acc.	Avg. P	Avg. R	Avg. F	ROC A.	Avg TP	Avg FP
J48	0.38	72.1	0.71	0.72	0.71	0.71	0.72	0.33
NB	0.46	73.5	0.76	0.73	0.74	0.80	0.73	0.23
SMO	0.50	77.1	0.77	0.77	0.77	0.75	0.77	0.27

DATASET 4: ALL 801 DOCUMENTS

	k	Acc.	Avg. P	Avg. R	Avg. F	ROC A.	Avg TP	Avg FP
J48	0.38	74.15	0.74	0.74	0.74	0.66	0.74	0.37
NB	0.45	73.9	0.78	0.73	0.74	0.83	0.73	0.23
SMO	0.49	78.6	0.78	0.78	0.78	0.74	0.78	0.29

On the second dataset (220 documents), J48's performance values are equivalent to Naive Bayes's and SMO's. On the third dataset (337 documents), SMO shows better figures. The performance on the fourth dataset is similar to the third dataset.

In order to compare the performance of the three classifiers on the four datasets, we applied the Corrected Paired T-Test (two tailed)[41] provided by Weka's Experimenter interface. Statistical significance was measured on the results of the three classifiers per dataset, and on the performance of each classifier for the four datasets. Statistical significance was measured at significance level of $p < 0.001$ on the weighed averaged F-measure. The test did not detect any statistically significant variation due to the sample[42]. We interpret these findings as a sign of stability since results show the robustness of the models to corpus scalability issues. This experiment supports our claim that a corpus can be extended without causing any deterioration of the performance of LT applications.

Experiment 2: Lay-Specialized Text Classification With and Without Noise

In Experiment 2, we explored whether there exists a performance gap between text classification models trained on a collection containing noisy documents and text classification models trained on a collection containing only noise-less documents.

Results are shown in Table 7. In order to compare the two sets of results, we measured the performance of the same algorithm on the two datasets. As in Experiment 1, statistical significance was measured at significance level of $p < 0.001$ on the weighted averaged F-measure. The test did not detect any statistically significant variation. We interpret these findings as a sign of resistance to noise in the lay-specialized text classification task. This experiment supports our claim that noise does not always negatively affect classification performance.

Table 7. Datasets with and without noise

DATASET 4: ALL 801 DOCUMENTS

	k	Acc.	Avg. P	Avg. R	Avg. F	ROC A.	Avg TP	Avg FP
J48	0.38	74.15	0.74	0.74	0.74	0.66	0.74	0.37
NB	0.45	73.9	0.78	0.73	0.74	0.83	0.73	0.23
SMO	0.49	78.6	0.78	0.78	0.78	0.74	0.78	0.29

DATASET WITHOUT NOISY TEXTS: 462 DOCUMENTS

	k	Acc.	Avg. P	Avg. R	Avg. F	ROC A.	Avg TP	Avg FP
J48	0.36	72.29	0.72	0.72	0.72	0.69	0.72	0.35
NB	0.57	79.22	0.82	0.79	0.79	0.88	0.79	0.16
SMO	0.57	80.95	0.81	0.81	0.81	0.78	0.81	0.23

Experiment 3: Lay vs. Specialized Annotation

The expertise of the annotators does not affect the performance. Essentially, there is no need to reach a high agreement between raters because a moderate agreement caused by different expertise is enough to ensure similar classification results. In practical terms, this means, that we do not to worry so much about the expertise or non-expertise of the annotators in a case like this. This will result in a more streamlined corpus annotation.

In this experiment, we compared the performance of the SMO algorithm on the documents labelled by the lay annotator (801 documents) against the documents labelled by the expert annotator (778 documents. The expert annotator left 23 documents unlabelled since they were considered as medically "irrelevant"). Results on the two datasets (see Table 8) show that the performance is basically the same, since no statistical significance variation has been detected. Apparently, the expertise of the annotators, although their agreement is moderate, does not affect automatic text classification. (To confirm this finding, we are currently cross-testing these classifiers by training a classifier on the corpus labelled by the expert annotator and testing this classification model on the corpus labelled by the lay annotator, and vice versa.)

Table 8. Text classification performance: comparing Lay vs Specialized Annotation

	k	Acc.	Avg. P	Avg. R	Avg. F	ROC A.	Avg. TP	Avg. FP
SMO	0.49	78.6	0.78	0.78	0.78	0.74	0.78	0.29

801 documents labelled by the lay annotator

	k	Acc.	Avg. P	Avg. R	Avg. F	ROC A.	Avg. TP	Avg. FP
SMO	0.54	79.5	0,79	0,79	0,79	0,77	0,79	0,25

778 documents labelled by the expert annotator

Discussion

Results of Experiment 1 are in line with previous research. The big advantage with our approach is that we can achieve a competing performance with a noisy corpus and bag-of-words features, certainly the easiest ones to extract automatically.

Experimental results show that lay-specialized classification performance is good (averaged F-measure is above 0.70 in most cases) and stable across classifiers and across datasets of different sizes.

In our view, these results are promising for several reasons. The first reason is *corpus scalability*: Experiment 1 shows that results are essentially equivalent across samples of different sizes since we observe no statistically significant degeneration in the performance when scaling up the size of the corpus. This is reassuring: we can imagine a scenario where we design a dynamic and extensible corpus whose size can be increased over time, and this will not affect the expectation of efficiency and reliability of LT applications when scaling up. We expect SVM to perform better than the other classifiers because this algorithm has been designed to handle large feature sets (which is the case here). Decision Trees (DT) might be disturbed by the presence of many features to build the tree and Naive Bayes (NB) can be negatively affected by the independence assumption. We observe that while the performance of DT is consistently lower than the other two classifiers, the Naive Bayes performs slightly better when the corpus size is smaller, while SVM overperforms NB when the corpus increases. Interestingly, the performance of SVM changes negligibly from 337 to 801 documents, which indicates that a size of about 350 documents can be the "critical mass" to get a reliable performance in this task.

The second reason is resilience to noise: removing noisy documents from a corpus can be prohibitive in some contexts. Arguably, not all LT applications require high quality texts to ensure a good performance and reliable results, as we have shown in Experiment 2.

Another reason is highlighted by Experiment 3 which shows that the disagreement between annotators is flattened out and does not affect the performance of certain LT applications. Essentially, this means that we do not have to worry too much about the agreement or disagreement of different annotators. This finding might have a positive practical consequence since it might contribute to speed up and streamline the construction of certain LT applications.

Additionally, the experiments show that for this kind of text classification, there is no need of linguistically rich features to achieve good results. The word to vector conversion is a ready-made and standard approach that is available in several packages and programming languages, not only in the Weka workbench. It can be easily applied and optimized to achieve better results with little effort and time gain. Again, the process is streamlined.

Whatever the size of the corpus the approach returns good results: the supervised algorithms can detect features which permit to make the distinction between the two categories without any problem. These results indicate that it can be safe to use bag-of-words filtered features and a small corpus with SVM to get a good enough performance.

Arguably these findings are important to streamline automatic lay-specialized text classification, an useful task for document filtering and information retrieval.

The Nitty-Gritty of a Distributional Thesaurus

Term extraction methods based on distributional semantics are very popular and effective (for a thorough evaluation of the offspring of distributional semantic modelling, see Baroni et al., 2014). Meaningful results are returned when the underlying corpora are large, especially when using the most advanced models based on word embeddings.

By contrast, as argued above, our challenge is to find the most effective approaches with the smallest possible corpus. In this experiment, we use a slightly extended version of eCare_Sv_01, known as eCare_Sv_01+, to test the robustness of a simple distributional approach for the extraction of words related to 15 medical terms indicating chronic illnesses and we evaluate the results using an online survey. This approach can be useful to quickly extract synonyms or related terms from a small domain-specific document collection and to enrich existing resources with additional words and to create new resources. Collections of synonyms and of words related to specific terms are useful in LT applications such as, indexing, information extraction, text simplification, question and answering, synonyms expansion, or fine-grained domain-specific ontologies or medical dictionaries.

Expanding the Corpus: eCare_Sv_01+

For expanding the corpus, the software BootCat was used. The corpus was expanded by adding documents related to 10 SNOMED CT medical terms indicating to common ailments (we took inspiration from the 1177 Vårdguiden portal[43]) that were not included in the original list of 155 seed terms. The following 10 term seeds were used to expand the corpus: "*anemi, bronkit, cystit, depression, dermatit, eksem, hepatit, hypotoni, mastit, urtikaria.*" The rationale of such a choice was to foster possible distributional word associations between common diseases and targeted terms (listed below) since a target group of the *E-care@home* project is multimorbid patients.

The search was limited to only .se domains and to sv.wikipedia.org, to avoid foreign and machine translated texts. Furthermore, the domain 1177.se was excluded from the search, to enable evaluation against this site at a later stage. After the corpus was downloaded and cleaned, it was smoothly concatenated with the original corpus, which was increased by 174 new documents. This first corpus expansion proved to be unproblematic (for further details, see Cederblad, 2018).

Methodology

It was decided not to create a full co-occurrence matrix, in order to streamline and accelerate the process. Only context windows were extracted for the desired target terms. For this extraction, a built-in function in the "quanteda" R package, namely KWIC (Key Word In Context), was used. This function provides the possibility to input text, keyword, and window size, getting the desired windows as output.

The 15 target terms chosen for the evaluation are nouns selected from the list of 155 term seeds, namely "*artrit, bronkit, depression, dermatit, emfysem, faryngit, hemicrania, hyperglykemi, hypotoni, pneumoni, prostatit, rinit, schizofreni, sinuit, tonsillit*". For this experiment, all non-nouns were filtered out (the Stagger morphological tagger was used for this task, Östling, 2013) based on the assumption that normally synonyms and related words always belong to the same part-of-speech.

To find synonyms or semantically related words, the textstat_simil function of the Quanteda R package was used to calculate a variety of different similarity measures.

The similarity metrics compared were cosine, Jaccard, eJaccard, Dice, and eDice. For every synonym, the method received two points, and for every related word it received one point. All words were evaluated against 1177.se, to know whether they were synonyms or related. There were, in total, 100 words being evaluated for every method. Results are shown in Table 9.

The settings that have been used for the final results are the following:

- Window size: 10
- Similarity metric: Dice
- Weighting scheme: TFIDF
- Number of output words: 5

In Figure 4, all the steps in extracting the candidate related terms can be seen.

Although two words may have a high statistical similarity, it is not certain that they, in fact, are synonyms or even semantically related. To check whether two words are synonyms or related, a questionnaire was created. The questionnaire was structured in a way similar to that of Kann and Rosell (2005).

The words in the questionnaire were the output of the system described above. For each of the 15 SNOMED CT terms, five related words were considered reasonable for evaluation. There was also a need for controlling whether the users were guessing and answering without knowing the meaning of the words being evaluated. A participant who consistently answers that the control word has a similar meaning to the word being evaluated might not be reliable. Therefore, a randomly chosen word from the corpus was assigned to each set of five words. It was decided that each rating should have an explicit definition, to make it easier for the participants. Thus, the definitions agreed upon was as follows:

1. The words have entirely different meanings (ex: nästäppa & ryggbesvär, en: nasal congestion & back problem)

Table 9. The comparison of similarity measures

Cosine	Jaccard	eJaccard	Dice	eDice
58	79	67	80	68

Figure 4. A description of the procedure of extracting the candidate related terms

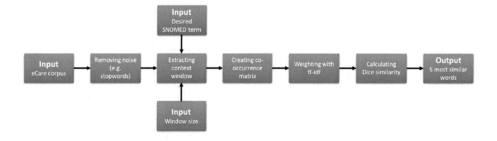

2. The words can be related to each other (ex: nästäppa & symptom; en: nasal congestion & symptom)
3. The words are related and are often used together (ex: nästäppa & förkylning; en: nasal congestion & cold)
4. The words are strongly related and can sometimes replace each other (ex: nästäppa & snuva; en: nasal congestion & rhinitis)
5. The words are synonyms and often replaces each other (ex: nästäppa & nasalobstruktion; en: nasal congestion & nasal obstruction)

The questionnaire was distributed to the participants through an URL published in a Facebook group for nurses in Sweden providing also the possibility to submit the answers through a smartphone. The questionnaire was accessible for seven days.

The SNOMED CT terms chosen for evaluation were considered too specialized for lay people to answer. It has to be stressed that the purpose of the questionnaire is not to find out whether people know the meaning of the terms. Rather, its purpose is to evaluate whether the words extracted by the distributional systems were related to the target terms. This requires some basic knowledge of the medical domain. For this reason, the participants were chosen with respect to their putative medical knowledge. That is, people with occupations exposing them to medical terminology were considered suitable. A control question was placed at the beginning of the questionnaire, to check whether the participants were or had been working in healthcare, or if they were studying or had studied a healthcare related subject. Since the questionnaire was published in a Facebook group for nurses in Sweden, it is reasonable to assume that most of the participants were nurses, although this was not further investigated. The total number of participants was 239, out of which 16 had to be excluded for not having completed the questionnaire.

Knowing the reliability of the raters (i.e. participants in the evaluation) is crucial for comparing their answers with the system output's Dice similarity. For calculating inter-rater reliability, Fleiss Kappa was used. Fleiss kappa is used for measuring the agreement of several raters (Fleiss, 1971). Landis and Koch (1977) propose a way of interpreting Kappa values. The proposal is as in Table 10. It is worth noting that this proposal contains a large portion of arbitrariness and in no way provides exact definitions. Despite this, it can be a useful tool when discussing the results. The agreement among the participants, calculated using Fleiss kappa, was k=0.28. According to the proposed interpretation in Table 10, this is a fair agreement.

The system output for all the 15 SNOMED CT terms chosen for evaluation and their Dice similarity can be seen in Table 11, with the candidate related term in the left column and its corresponding Dice similarity in the right column. The similarity calculated in R was, in general, rather low. As much as

Table 10. Landis and Koch (1977) proposal of Kappa interpretation

Kappa Statistic	Strength of Agreement
< 0.00	Poor
0.00-0.20	Slight
0.21-0.40	Fair
0.41-0.60	Moderate
0.61-0.80	Substantial
0.81-1.00	Almost perfect

91% of the words had a Dice similarity that was less than 0.50. The word with the highest similarity was the word pair "hemicrania-continua." The lowest found similarity was 0.17, and three word-pairs got a similarity this low.

There is a difference in how much text the corpus contains for each SNOMED CT term. When extracting the context window for each word, this difference becomes salient and is shown in Table 12. There was a difference of agreement among the categories, shown in Table 13, where the highest agreement was in the lowest rating category. The category with the lowest agreement was the one stating that the words were synonyms.

The most similar words to every SNOMED CT term, based on their average user rating, was extracted and is presented in Table 14 together with the corresponding Dice similarity.

The average rating of all the words, with the control words excluded, was 2.48 (St. Dev. = 0.80).

Table 15 shows the ten word-pairs with the highest number of participants answering "I don't know." Out of these word pairs, five belong to the SNOMED CT term "hemicrania."

Table 11. System output

artrit		bronkit		depression		dermatit	
reumatoid	0.56	luftväg	0.35	liv	0.28	hud	0.52
psoriasisartrit	0.21	kol	0.28	person	0.22	eksem	0.43
knä	0.19	lunga	0.27	ångest	0.18	atopisk	0.37
symptom	0.17	pneumoni	0.25	symtom	0.18	perioral	0.33
barn	0.17	luftvägsinfektion	0.24	episod	0.17	utslag	0.22

emfysem		faryngit		hemicrania		hyperglykemi	
lunga	0.48	hals	0.50	continua	0.90	glukos	0.41
lungsjukdom	0.34	slemhinna	0.27	huvudvärk	0.59	diabetes	0.37
obstruktiv	0.30	sjukdom	0.25	paroxysmal	0.56	insulin	0.32
lungemfysem	0.29	svalg	0.25	info	0.46	mmol	0.27
lungvävnad	0.21	behandling	0.23	indomethacin	0.41	måltid	0.24

hypotoni		pneumoni		prostatit		rinit	
blodtryck	0.61	crp	0.27	prostata	0.59	näsa	0.33
ortostatisk	0.38	bronkit	0.25	prostatakörtel	0.29	nästäppa	0.29
postural	0.28	kol	0.25	besvär	0.27	nässlemhinnan	0.25
hjärtfrekvens	0.24	otit	0.18	bäckenbotten	0.24	allergi	0.21
blodvolym	0.21	pneumoniae	0.18	bakterie	0.23	polyp	0.19

schizofreni		sinuit		tonsillit	
psykos	0.28	bihåleinflammation	0.29	tonsill	0.53
beteende	0.20	otit	0.29	halsfluss	0.38
tonår	0.18	öli	0.26	halsont	0.18
hjärnvolym	0.18	polyp	0.23	gas	0.18
mathalon	0.18	karies	0.22	polyp	0.18

Table 12. The size of the extracted context windows

Word	Number of words in window
artrit	5542
bronkit	5174
depression	11544
dermatit	7377
emfysem	3667
faryngit	8270
hemicrania	1101
hyperglykemi	2180
hypotoni	758
pneumoni	2465
prostatit	3482
rinit	2551
schizofreni	1153
sinuit	1402
tonsillit	2426

Table 13. The agreement rate of each category

Category	Agreement
The words have entirely different meanings	0.29
The words can be related to each other	0.24
The words are related and are often used together	0.25
The words are strongly related and can sometimes replace each other	0.08
The words are synonyms and often replaces each other	0.06
I don't know	0.08

For correlation, Kendall's tau was used. This choice is motivated by the data not being normally distributed. Kendalls's tau uses the difference between the number of concordant and discordant pairs. This is divided by the total number of pairs (Kendall, 1938). There was a significant relationship between the average rating of the words and their Dice similarity. A Kendall's tau coefficient test showed the following: tau=.28, p<.001.

Discussion

The correlation between the average human rating and the average Dice similarity was significant, but rather weak. What this correlation means is that the higher Dice similarity a word gets, the higher aver-

Table 14.

SNOMED term	Candidate related term	Average user rating	Dice similarity
artrit	psoriasisartrit	3.28	0.21
bronkit	luftvägsinfektion	3.84	0.24
depression	ångest	2.94	0.18
dermatit	eksem	3.51	0.43
emfysem	lungemfysem	4.35	0.29
faryngit	svalg	2.93	0.25
hemicrania	huvudvärk	3.26	0.59
hyperglykemi	diabetes	3.22	0.37
hypotoni	blodtryck	3.32	0.61
pneumoni	pneumoniae	3.95	0.18
prostatit	prostatakörtel	2.85	0.29
rinit	nästäppa	3.47	0.29
schizofreni	psykos	3.09	0.28
sinuit	bihåleinflammation	4.72	0.29
tonsillit	halsfluss	4.39	0.38

Table 15. Percentage of "I don't know" answers

SNOMED term	Candidate related term	Percentage of "I don't know" answers
hemicrania	indomethacin	72%
hemicrania	continua	68%
schizofreni	mathalon	61%
hemicrania	paroxysmal	52%
hemicrania	info	45%
hemicrania	huvudvärk	40%
hypotoni	postural	33%
dermatit	perioral	14%
sinuit	öli	9%
sinuit	polyp	8%

age human rating it gets. However, much can be said about these results. Firstly, the Dice similarity was in general rather low (91% of all word pairs got a Dice similarity less than 0.50, see Table 17). Words that are synonyms, or at least by the participants considered closely related should have a Dice similarity closer to 1 than 0. The overall quite low Dice similarity may be a reason for the weak correlation. An example of the low Dice similarity is for the word pair "emfysem-lungemfysem" (en: emphysema-pulmonary emphysema), where the average user rating is 4.35, whereas the Dice similarity was only 0.29. What this rating means it that the participants perceived the similarity as somewhere in between "The words are strongly related and can sometimes replace each other", and "The words are synonyms and often replaces each other". The word "lungemfysem" is a compound of the two words; "lunga" and "emfysem." Thus "lungemfysem" is a certain kind of emphysema, which makes it clear that they have a strong semantic relationship. It is difficult to decide on whether they are synonyms or just strongly related, but what is clear is that the participants were more accurate on rating these words than the system was.

Table 14 shows the highest rated candidate related term for every SNOMED CT term. Among these, the word pair which was least similar according to the participants, with an average rating of 2.85, was "prostatit-prostatakörtel" (en: prostatitis-prostate gland). The word "prostatit" means inflammation of the prostate gland and has the synonym "blåshalskörtelinflammation". In a best-case scenario, the system would have found this synonym. However, the word "blåshalskörtelinflammation" only occurs twice in the context window extracted around "prostatit". The word "prostatakörtel" on the other hand occurs 116 times. A comparison with the highest rated word pair, "sinuit-bihåleinflammation" (en: sinusitis-sinus infection) emphasizes how the word occurrence affects the similarity. "Bihåleinflammation" occurs 68 times together with "sinuit". A reason for "blåshalskörtelinflammation" rarely occurring might be that it is not, in general, being used that often. It might be that "prostatit" more often is described with an expression containing several words, and by limiting the analysis to unigrams, this definition is impossible to catch. Section 5.3, Table 12 shows that there was a considerable size difference of the context windows, where the window for "depression" was more than 15 times the size of that of "hypotoni." The fewer words in a context window, the more impact each word has on the similarity measure. Preferably, there would have been a more even distribution of texts among all the SNOMED CT terms.

Limiting the system only to handle unigrams may have decreased the overall performance of the system. Some of the terms might have to be described by more than one word. An example of this is "hyperglykemi" (en: hyperglycemia) which does not have a synonym. Instead, it is best described as "onormalt hög blodsockernivå" (en: abnormally high blood glucose level). This is a trigram and would therefore not be found by the system in this work. In the case of "onormalt hög blodsockernivå," the words "onormalt" and "hög" would have been removed in the noise removal stage, which is reasonable since they, taken out of context, have no apparent relation to "hyperglykemi." The fact that there is no synonym to "hyperglykemi" explains why none of the candidate related terms got a higher human rating than 3.22. There are other medical terms to which there are no synonyms, only correctly described by multiple-word expressions. This lack of synonyms emphasizes the need for a model that can manage n-grams larger than unigrams.

It was decided only to keep the nouns. However, some of the more complicated medical adjectives were left in the corpus. An example of this is the word "atopisk" (en: atopic) that often occur together with "dermatit" (en: dermatitis) as the expression "atopisk dermatit." Stagger did not manage to tag "atopisk" correctly. All 88 occurrences of this word were tagged with "NN," making it mistakenly included in the analysis. This inaccurate tagging was also the case with a few other words. As mentioned earlier, synonyms always belong to the same part of speech. If an adjective is included in the results, one can be certain that this is not a synonym. Had these words been excluded from the analysis, it is entirely possible that the results would have been more accurate.

Asking humans to put a rating on something always entails some arbitrariness. It is not certain that they know the meaning of the words, nor that they perceive the similarity rating in the same way. For each rating in the rating scale, an example was provided. These examples, however, was evidently not enough for the participants to be sure of what to answer. The highest, on average, rated word pair was "sinuit-bihåleinflammation" with an average rating of 4.72 (St. Dev. = 0.66). Although this is a rather clear case of synonymy, 49 participants did not rate them as synonyms. This mean that as much as a fifth of the participants, either did not know the meaning of the word or how to interpret the questionnaire.

The participants' knowledge in Swedish was not investigated. Since a majority of the participants are nurses in Sweden, it is possible to assume that their knowledge in Swedish is sufficient for performing their work. However, it would have been good to include a question about the participants' native language.

Table 15 shows that some words tended to get a lot of "I don't know" answers. Among the top ten, word pairs with "hemicrania" occur five times. The fact that "hemicrania" occurs so many times makes it reasonable to conclude that the participants, in general, had trouble with understanding the meaning of this word. The opaque meaning of the term "hemicrania" even for healthcare professional was confirmed by our domain expert. This is somewhat surprising since even the Swedish Mesh indicates that "huvudvärk" (en: "headache") and "hemicrania" are synonyms[44].

Generally speaking, according to our domain expert (who is a nurse specialized in health informatics), some answers from the participants were quite unexpected. Arguably, the cause was in the interpretation of the task. Looking directly at the question - "To what extent do the following words have a linguistic meaning similar to XXX" - one might be quite "hard" in his/her assessment. But if one takes into account the initial text that not only "capturing synonyms, but also words used in similar contexts", one seems to have made another assessment. Therefore, it might be possible that the questionnaire contained some unforeseen or veiled ambiguities in the formulation. However, what is relatively problematic at this stage is indeed informative, since we can build on these findings when we proceed on to the next step of development.

The purpose of this work was to extract synonyms and related words from a medical corpus. It was indeed possible to extract related words from the given E-care corpus. The evaluation showed that although the nitty-gritty distributional thesaurus needs improvements, it was able to extract words that are related to each other. The average human rating of the extracted words was 2.48, i.e. somewhere in between "The words can be related to each other" and "The words are related and are often used together". Enhancements can certainly include bigrams or multi-grams and not only unigrams since many medical terms (also in Swedish) are expressed as multi-words. Future work aims at a more in-depth investigation about the medical knowledge and the language proficiency of the evaluation study participants, as well as additional distributional semantic models and several corpus sizes. Although this experiment was not focused on the lay-ness of term, we can certainly observe that some of the related words are indeed lay, such as "hud" (en: "skin") extracted with "dermatit" (from Ancient Greek "derma", (en: skin) +ʹ-itis)[45], or "luftväg" (en: "windpipe") (from Ancient Greek ("brónkhos" (= "windpipe") +ʹ-itis.)[46]. Considering the small size and the noisiness of the corpus and the open issues about the human evaluation, these results of these experiments are certainly promising.

Growing Up: Creation and Evaluation of eCare_En_02

In this experiment (see also Strandqvist et al. 2018), we extend *the E-care@home Corpus* by adding web documents in English. For this expansion we used a two-step approach, namely:

1. Automatic extraction and evaluation of term seeds from *use cases, personas/scenarios*;
2. Creation and validation of specialized and domain-specific web corpora bootstrapped with term seeds automatically extracted in step 1.

In the first step, we build a term extraction algorithm that can automatically identify term candidates in project-specific *use cases, personas/scenarios*. These texts are narratives that describe a "system's behavior under various conditions as the system responds to requests from stakeholders" (Cockburn, 2000) and are nowadays normally included in many language technology projects (e.g. see Henkel et al. 2015). *Use cases, personas/scenarios* are relatively short texts - only a few dozen pages (see Pressmann, 2005:657) - normally written by domain experts who know how to correctly use terms in their own domain. For this reason, we argue that they are a convenient textual resource (when available) to automatically extract term seeds to bootstrap specialized web corpora, thus overriding any tedious and sometimes controversial or arbitrary process normally required to compile term lists (e.g. see Vivaldi et al., 2007; Loginova et al., 2012). In our study, we focus on the medical terms that occur in use cases, personas/scenarios written in English for *E-care@home*. We complete this step with the evaluation (Precision and Recall metrics) of the term extractor against a gold standard made of SNOMED CT terms. The challenge of this phase is to create an accurate term extractor based on a relatively small textual resource, a task that is still under-investigated since most of existing term extractors are based on large corpora (e.g. Park et al., 2002; Nazarenko and Zargayouna, 2009).

In the second step, we use the term seeds extracted in the previous step to *bootcat* (Baroni and Bernardini, 2004) a medical web corpus and evaluate the quality of the corpus. Leveraging on the web as a textual source for language technology applications is a well-established idea (e.g. Kilgarrif et al. 2010) and many general- or special-purpose corpora have already been created. While bootstrapping a web corpus is common practice (many tools exist, either based on crawling or on search engine queries), the validation of web corpora is still a grey area. Currently, there is little research available on this topic (among the few who address the issue, see: Ciaramita & Baroni, 2006; Eckart et al., 2012; Schäfer et al. 2013; Kilgariff, 2014). It follows that approaches are not standardized; thus it is not possible to compare results. In our study, we analyze and test several corpus profiling measures (e.g. Rayson and Garside, 2000; Oakes, 2008; Nanas and De Roeck, 2008, Rayson, 2008) and propose answers to the following questions: What is meant by "quality" of a web corpus? How can we assess the quality of a corpus automatically bootstrapped from the web? What if a bootstrapped web corpus contains documents that are *not* relevant to the target domain? Can we measure the domain-specificity of a corpus?

eCare Term Extractor

Generally speaking, automatic term recognition (ATR) deals with the extraction of domain-specific lexical units from text. Normally, the input of ATR is a large collection of documents, i.e., a special corpus, and the output is a vocabulary that is used for communicating specialized knowledge (L'Homme, 2014). Terms, extracted by an ATR system, represent a broad spectrum of concepts that exist in a domain knowledge. (Zadeh, 2016). In contrast, keyword extraction focuses on the extraction of topical words from individual documents for indexing (Hasan & Ng, 2014).

In this experiment, we conflate the two foci of ATR and keyword extraction and implement a term extractor from individual documents. The challenge of this step is to create a "good enough" term extractor based on a relatively small textual resource, a task that is still under-investigated since most of existing term extractors are based on large corpora (e.g. see Nazarenko and Zargayouna, 2009).

Arguably, the use of personas and use cases/scenarios, when available, is a good starting point to automatize the manual process of term seeds selection. The E-care term extractor developed for this purpose includes three main components. The first component (terminology extractor) uses a shallow syntactic analysis of the text to extract candidate terms. The second component (terminology validator) compares each of the candidate terms and their variations to SNOMED CT to produce candidate terms. The third component is a seed validator.

The terminology extractor uses the Stanford Tagger (Toutanova, Klein, Manning, & Singer, 2003) to assign a part-of-speech (POS) tag to each word in the texts. The tagged text is then searched sequentially with each of the syntactic patterns (Pazienza, Pennacchiotti, & Zanzotto, 2005) presented in Table 16.

The terminology validator takes the candidate terms produced in the previous step and matches them against SNOMED CT. If an exact match is not found, each word is stemmed. The stemmed words are permuted, and each permutation is then matched against SNOMED CT once again, this time using wildcards between the word, to allow for spelling variations. Matches are then ranked by TFIDF scores (cutoff = 200).

The seed generator generates three terms (i.e. triples) from the cutoff list when they occurred in the same document.

The E-care term extractor performance is summarized in Table 17. The terminology extractor has an extraction recall of 81.25% on the development set. When evaluated, the terminology validator achieves the following performance: Precision = 34.2%, Recall = 71%, F1 = 46.2%. These results are promising if compared with the state of the art of keyword extraction methods, but are moderate if compared with term-extractor based on large corpora.

Extrinsic Evaluation: Assessing Domainhood

Intrinsic evaluation is when the quality of a system is assessed by direct analysis of the system's characteristics, and how they relate to some given criteria, as shown above. Often, the hope is that good results in an intrinsic evaluation will be telling of a system's quality and of its aptness for further use in downstream tasks (however, this assumption might not always be true).

Unlike intrinsic evaluation, extrinsic evaluation does not assess or inspect the system directly. Rather, the system is assessed by using its output as input of another downstream task. The results of this downstream, task is then indicative of the quality of the original system. For instance, Kilgarriff et al., (2014) describe a method for extrinsic evaluation of web corpora by extracting collocations for lexicography, while Biemann et al. (2013) evaluate web corpora on two collocation identification tasks that focus on

Table 16. Syntactic patterns used for term recognition

Patterns
(noun)+
(adjective)(noun)+
(noun)(prep)(noun)+

Table 17. Current performance of E-care term extractor

	Metrics	**%**
Term candidate extraction	Extraction recall	81
Term validation	Precision	34.2
	Recall	71
	F1	46.2

different aspects of multiword expressions and different types of data. It must be stressed, however, that good results in one task do not necessarily imply good results in another task.

In this experiment, we evaluate how good the performance of the eCare term extractor is to bootstrap a web corpus based on the domain of the use cases. We measure the domainhood (or domain-specificity) against a reference corpus representing general language (see also Santini et al., 2018).

For corpus evaluation, we use metrics based on word frequency lists, namely rank correlation coefficients (Kendall and Spearman), KL divergence, log-likelihood. It makes sense to use domain-specific terms for both bootstrapping the web corpus and for evaluating its domainhood because the terms used as seeds (source terms) should be found in non-trivial proportions in the final corpus to be sure that the corpus is domain-representative. Estimating domainhood may be a useful preliminary check for domain adaptation (e.g. see Cuong et al., 2016; Hoang & Sima'an 2014; McClosky, 2010), ie when porting NLP applications from one domain to another.

1. **Correlation Coefficients:** The Kendall correlation coefficient (Tau) and Spearman correlation test (Rho) are non-parametric tests. They both measure how similar the order of two ranks is. (We used the R function "cor.test()" with method="kendall, spearman" to calculate the tests).

2. **Kullback–Leibler (KL) Divergence:** (a.k.a. relative entropy) is a measure of the "distance" between two distributions. The KL divergence quantifies how far-off an estimation of a certain distribution is from the true distribution. The KL divergence is non-negative and equal to zero if the two distributions are identical. In our context, the closer the value is to 0, the more similar two corpora are. (We used the R package "entropy", function "KL.empirical()" to compute KL divergence).

3. **Log-Likelihood (LL-G2):** LL-G2 (Dunning, 1993) has been used for corpus profiling (Rayson and Garside, 2000). The words that have the largest LL-G2 scores show the most significant word-frequency difference in two corpora. LL-G2 is not affected by corpus size variation.

For the evaluation, we use three web corpora, namely:

- **ukWaCsample (872 565 words):** A random subset of ukWaC, a general- purpose web corpus (Ferraresi et al., 2008).
- **Gold (544 677 words):** A domain-specific web corpus collected with hand-picked term seeds from the E-Care personas and use cases/scenarios.
- **Auto (492 479 words):** A domain-specific web corpus collected with automatically extracted term seeds from the E-Care personas and use cases/scenarios.

Measuring Rank Correlation

We computed the normalized frequencies of the three corpora (words per million) and ranked them (with ties). The plots of the first 1000 top frequencies of the three corpora are shown in Figure 5. From the plots, we can see that UkwaCsample has very little in common with both Gold and Auto (boxes 1 and 2), while Gold and Auto (box 3) are similar.

When testing the rank correlation (Kendall and Spearman), we observe a statistically significant positive rank correlation between Gold and Auto (see Figure 6, box 3; Figure 3, box 3), which means that words in Gold and in Auto tend to have similar ranks. Conversely, the correlation between ukWaCsample

Figure 5. Plotting 1000 top ranks: (from left to right): ukWaCsample and Gold (box 1), ukWaCsample and Auto (box2), and Gold and Auto (box 3)

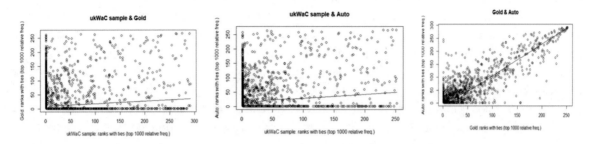

Figure 6. Kendall Tau: (from left to right):): ukWaCsample and Gold (box 1), ukWaCsample and Auto (box 2), and Gold and Auto (box 3)

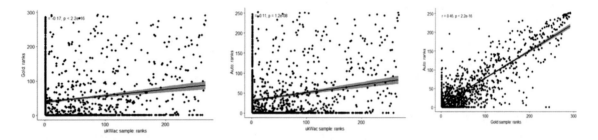

and Gold and ukWaCsample and Auto is weak (see Figure 7, box 1 and box 2; Figure 6, box 1 and box 2), which essentially means that their ranks follow different distributions.

Kullback-Leibler Divergence

Before calculating KL divergence, a smoothing value of 0.01 was been added to the normalized frequencies. Results are shown in Table 18. The scores returned by KL distance for ukWacSample vs Gold (row 1) and ukWacSample vs Auto (row 2)- 7.544118 and 6.519677, respectively- are (unsurprisingly) large and indicate a wide divergence between the general-purpose ukWacSample and the domain-specific Gold and Auto. On the contrary, the KL score of 1.843863 indicates that Gold vs Auto (row 3) are similar to each other.

Figure 7. Spearman Rho: (from left to right):): ukWaCsample and Gold (box 1), ukWaCsample and Auto (box 2), and Gold and Auto (box 3)

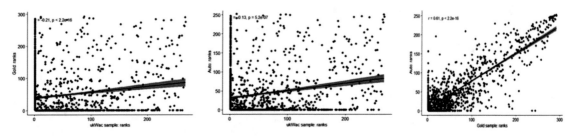

Table 18. KL scores

Corpora	KL Scores
ukWacSample vs Gold	7.544118
ukWacSample vs Auto	6.519677
Gold vs Auto	1.843863

Log-Likelihood (LL-G2)

We computed LL-G2 scores on smoothed word frequencies. The total LL-G2 scores for the three web corpora (top 1000 words) are shown in Table 19. The larger the LL-G2 score of a word, the more different its distribution in two corpora. The large LL-G2 scores for ukWaCsample vs Gold (453 441.6) and for ukWaCsample vs Auto (393 705.9) indicate that these corpora are remarkably dissimilar if compared to the much smaller LL-G2 score returned for Gold vs Auto (114 694.2), which suggests that Gold and Auto are more similar to each other.

It is also possible to assess the statistical significance of the individual LL-G2 scores. Normally, a LL-G2 score of 3.8415 or higher is significant at the level of $p < 0.05$ and a LL-G2 score of 10.8276 is significant at the level of $p < 0.001$ (Desagulier, 2017). Figure 8 shows the breakdown of the top-ranked LL-G2 scores of three corpora. We take 3.8415 ($p < 0.05$) as a threshold and observe that ukWaCsample vs Gold (box 1) differs very much in the use of words such as "patient" or "patients" and "blood", and in ukWaCsample vs Auto (box 2) these words have a similar behavior. Conversely, these words are not in the top list of Gold vs Auto (box 3). Additionally, the LL-G2 scores in box 3 are much smaller in magnitude, which indicates that the difference between words is less pronounced.

Table 19. LL G2 scores of the three corpora

Corpora	Total LL-G2 Scores
ukWacSample vs Gold	453 441.6
ukWacSample vs Auto	393 705.9
Gold vs Auto	114 694.2

Figure 8. Top-ranked LL-G2 scores (from left to right): ukWaCsample and Gold (box 1), ukWaCsample and Auto (box 2), and Gold and Auto (box 3)

patients	6162.61		blood	5825.56		headache	1040.9
blood	5092.01		risk	3847.85		parkinson's	967.5
patient	4120.3		patients	3827.24		valve	680.56
symptoms	3803.51		diabetes	3725.77		aortic	677.53
disease	3654.71		heart	3657.2		milk	535.3
treatment	3326.27		pressure	2868.36		ltot	453.59
risk	3121.56		pain	2867.39		eggs	426.37
heart	2959.02		oxygen	2730.52		administration	420.84
stroke	2733.91		symptoms	2581.23		stenosis	402.16
diabetes	2712.8		patient	2286.48		memory	396.69
			disease	2198.23		online	396.11
			glucose	2071.23			

Discussion

Interestingly, this performance of the current version of the E-care term extractor did not affect detrimentally the quality of the resulting web corpus. This means that our approach is effective and help create a domain-specific corpus without any manual intervention. The corpus bootstrapped with the candidate terms returned by the term extractor is indeed domain-specific and it contains both lay and specialized terminology in the previous figures.

We have shown that it is possible to create a fairly accurate term extractor for relatively short texts written by domain experts. When used to bootstrap a web corpus, the automatically extracted term seeds create a corpus whose domain-specificity quality is similar to a corpus bootstrapped with hand-picked term seeds. This is an added value because corpus construction can be accelerated and standardized.

We have seen that well-established measures– such as rank correlation, KL divergence and log-likelihood (LL-G2 scores)– *do* give a coarse but grounded idea of domain-specificity. Essentially, they allow for an evaluation of the quality of a domain-specific web corpus and can also be used to pre-assess the portability of NLP tools from one domain-specific corpus to a different corpus belonging to another domain. Similar experiments have also been carried out on Swedish corpora with much the same results (Santini et al., 2018), showing that our approach may become a language-independent standardized step in corpus evaluation practice (intrinsic evaluation metrics).

We can now provide some empirical answers, namely: (1) in these experiments, "quality" means high density of medical terms related to certain illnesses described in the personas and use cases/scenarios; (2) we can assess the quality of a corpus automatically bootstrapped from the web by using metrics that are well-established and easily replicable; (3) we can get a coarse but robust indication of the similarities across corpora; (4) we can measure the domain-specificity of a corpus and assess whether it is satisfactorily domain-specific or whether the corpus needs some amends before being used for LT applications.

CONCLUSION AND FUTURE DIRECTIONS

In this chapter, the design, the creation and current use of the *E-care@home Corpus* was presented. More than a single corpus, it has been conceived to be a family of domain-specific sub-corpora. The domain of interest is the medical field of chronic diseases. The current version of the corpus, *eCare_Sv-En_03,* has been bootstrapped from the web via search engines using a selection of SNOMED CT medical terms. The corpus includes web texts written in Swedish (namely those included in *eCare_Sv_01* and *eCare_Sv_01+*) and in English (*eCare_En_02*). A further expansion is currently in progress in both languages.

The *E-care@home Corpus* proposes a new corpus design. This design is centered upon the idea of a flexible and extensible textual resource, where additional documents and additional languages will be appended over time. The main purpose of the corpus is to be used for building and training LT applications for the "layfication" of specialized sublanguages, namely the medical jargon used by professional staff working in eHealth and eCare. Although a case study based on the ongoing project *E-care@home* is presented here, it is claimed that this design is applicable to any kind of corpora and domains.

Exploratory experiments that leverage on subparts of *the E-care@home Corpus* were presented. Namely, supervised "lay-specialized" classification of Swedish web documents (subcorpus *eCare_Sv_01*), automatic extraction of words semantically related to medical terms (*eCare_Sv_01+*) and the assessment of the domain specificity of a corpus (*eCare_En_02*).

In these experiments, the focus was on the development of corpus-based LT applications that are simple but robust enough to disturbing factors, such as noise and corpus size variations.

It was argued that, for layfication tasks, the creation of a parallel or comparable corpus of specialized and lay documents is not needed. Aligning corpora, documents, sentences or words is a daunting task that takes time and engineering. The proposed approach was aimed to investigate whether a "regular" corpus bootstrapped with technical terms as seeds (Section 5.1) can also be used for layfication tasks. The answer is positive since off-the-shelf classifiers built with easy to extract bag-of-word features show promising performance (Section 5.2) and a simple model based on distributional semantics can extract sensible set of related terms (Section 5.3). The corpus can be easily expanded by adding more documents and additional languages (Section 5.4). Each increment of the corpus is annotated with metadata, so it is easy to extract sub-corpora based on specific attributes. It was also shown that the domain-specificity of a corpus bootstrapped with term seeds automatically extracted from use cases (i.e. single documents rather than a corpus) is equivalent to the domain-specificity of a corpus built with hand-picked seeds. This means that the seed selection phase (which is usually a delicate task that needs the knowledge of a domain expert and several iterations) can be streamlined and accelerated.

As stressed several times along the chapter, the corpus is conceived as work-in-progress, and future expansions are scheduled. For instance, to expand the Swedish part, a new corpus expansion has been bootstrapped by translating use case seeds (originally in English) into Swedish. To expand the English part, we used the SNOMED CT Swedish translations of chronic diseases.

Future experiments will include bilingual lay terminology induction, ontology creation from text, text simplification, or simplified summarization, i.e. tasks that all involve a layfication of technical terminology.

ACKNOWLEDGMENT

This research was supported by *E-care@home*, a "SIDUS – Strong Distributed Research Environment" project, funded by the Swedish Knowledge Foundation [kk-stiftelsen, Diarienr: 20140217]. Project website: <http://ecareathome.se/>. *E-care@home Corpus* website: <http://santini.se/eCareCorpus/home.htm>.

REFERENCES

Abrahamsson, E., Forni, T., Skeppstedt, M., & Kvist, M. (2014). Medical text simplification using synonym replacement: Adapting assessment of word difficulty to a compounding language. *Proceedings of the 3rd Workshop on Predicting and Improving Text Readability for Target Reader Populations (PITR)@ EACL*, 57–65. 10.3115/v1/W14-1207

Åhlfeldt, H., Borin, L., Daumke, P., Grabar, N., Hallett, C., Hardcastle, D., . . . Willis, A. (2006). *Literature review on patient-friendly documentation systems?* Technical Report 2006/04, Department of Computing, Faculty of Mathematics and Computing, The Open University, Milton Keynes, UK.

Alirezaie, M. (2015). *Bridging the semantic gap between sensor data and ontological knowledge* (Ph.D. dissertation). Örebro University.

Alirezaie, M., Hammar, K., & Blomqvist, E. (2018a). SmartEnv as a network of ontology patterns. *Semantic Web, 9*(6), 903–918.

Alirezaie, M., Hammar, K., Blomqvist, E., Nyström, M., & Ivanova, V. (2018b). *SmartEnv Ontology in E-care@home.* 9th Workshop on Semantic Sensor Networks (SSN) held in conjunction with ISWC 2018, Monterey, CA.

Antoine, E., & Grabar, N. (2017). Acquisition of Expert/Non-Expert Vocabulary from Reformulations. *Studies in Health Technology and Informatics, 235*, 521–525. PMID:28423847

Artstein, R., & Poesio, M. (2008). Inter-coder agreement for computational linguistics. *Computational Linguistics, 34*(4), 555–596. doi:10.1162/coli.07-034-R2

Band, J., & Gerafi, J. (2015). *Fair Use/Fair Dealing Handbook.* Retrieved from http://infojustice.org/wp-content/uploads/2015/03/fair-use-handbook-march-2015.pdf

Barbaresi, A. (2015). Ad hoc and general-purpose corpus construction from web sources (PhD thesis). École Normale Supérieure de Lyon (Université de Lyon), France.

Barbaresi, A. (2016). Efficient construction of metadata-enhanced web corpora. In *10th Web as Corpus Workshop* (pp. 7-16). Academic Press. 10.18653/v1/W16-2602

Barbu, E. (2016). *D3.2: Multilingual Corpus. Project Deliverable. EXPERT (Exploiting Empirical approaches to Translation), Project funded by the People Programme.* Marie Curie Actions.

Baroni, M., & Bernardini, S. (2004). BootCaT: Bootstrapping Corpora and Terms from the Web. *LREC 2004 - Fourth International Conference On Language Resources And Evaluation.*

Baroni, M., Bernardini, S., Ferraresi, A., & Zanchetta, E. (2009). The WaCky wide web: A collection of very large linguistically processed web-crawled corpora. *Language Resources and Evaluation, 43*(3), 209–226. doi:10.100710579-009-9081-4

Baroni, M., Dinu, G., & Kruszewski, G. (2014). Don't count, predict! A systematic comparison of context-counting vs. context-predicting semantic vectors. In *Proceedings of the 52nd Annual Meeting of the Association for Computational Linguistics* (*Vol. 1*, pp. 238-247). Academic Press. 10.3115/v1/P14-1023

Baroni, M., Kilgarriff, A., Pomikálek, J., & Rychlý, P. (2006). WebBootCaT: instant domain-specific corpora to support human translators. In *Proceedings of EAMT* (pp. 247-252). Academic Press.

Basili, R., Pazienza, M. T., & Velardi, P. (1993). Acquisition of selectional patterns in sublanguages. *Machine Translation, 8*(3), 175–201. doi:10.1007/BF00982638

Biemann, C., Bildhauer, F., Evert, S., Goldhahn, D., Quasthoff, U., Schäfer, R., ... Zesch, T. (2013). Scalable Construction of High-Quality Web Corpora. *JLCL, 28*(2), 23–59.

Biemann, C., Heyer, G., Quasthoff, U., & Richter, M. (2007). The Leipzig Corpora Collection-monolingual corpora of standard size. *Proceedings of Corpus Linguistic.*

Bigeard, E., Grabar, N., & Thiessard, F. (2018). Detection and Analysis of Drug Misuses. A Study Based on Social Media Messages. *Frontiers in Pharmacology, 9*, 2018. doi:10.3389/fphar.2018.00791 PMID:30140224

Borin, L., Grabar, N., Gronostaj, M. T., Hallett, C., Hardcastle, D., Kokkinakis, D., . . . Willis, A. (2007). Semantic Mining Deliverable D27. 2: Empowering the patient with language technology. Technical Report Semantic Mining, NOE 507505), 1–75. Göteborg: Göteborg University.

Branco, A., Cohen, K. B., Vossen, P., Ide, N., & Calzolari, N. (2017). Replicability and reproducibility of research results for human language technology: Introducing an LRE special section. *Language Resources and Evaluation*, *51*.

Burnard, L. (2007). *Reference guide for the British National Corpus (XML edition)*. Retrieved from http://www.natcorp.ox.ac.uk/XMLedition/URG/

Cardillo, E. (2015). *Medical terminologies for patients. Annex 1 to SHN Work Package 3 Deliverable D3.3*. Retrieved from http://www.semantichealthnet.eu/index.cfm/deliverables/

Cardillo, E., Tamilin, A., & Serafini, L. (2011). A Methodology for Knowledge Acquisition in Consumer-Oriented Healthcare. *Knowledge Discovery, Knowledge Engineering and Knowledge Management*, *249*.

Cederblad, G. (2018). *Finding Synonyms in Medical Texts – Creating a system for automatic synonym extraction from medical texts* (Bachelor thesis). Linköping University, Department of Computer Science.

Chapman, K., Abraham, C., Jenkins, V., & Fallow, L. (2003). Lay understanding of terms used in cancer consultations. *Psycho-Oncology*, *12*(6), 557–566. doi:10.1002/pon.673 PMID:12923796

Chmielik, J., & Grabar, N. (2009) Comparative study between expert and non expert biomedical writings: their morphology and semantics. In *Medical Informatics in a United and Healthy Europe: Proceedings of MIE 2009, the XXII International Congress of the European Federation for Medical Informatics* (Vol. 150, p. 359). IOS Press.

Ciaramita, M., & Baroni, M. (2006). A Figure of Merit for the Evaluation of Web-Corpus Randomness. *EACL 2006 - 11th Conference of the European Chapter of the Association for Computational Linguistics*.

Claveau, V., Hamon, T., Maguer, S. L., & Grabar, N. (2015). Health consumer-oriented information retrieval. *Studies in Health Technology and Informatics*, *210*, 80–84. PMID:25991106

Cockburn, A. (2000). *Writing effective use cases, The crystal collection for software professionals*. Addison-Wesley Professional Reading.

Cocoru, D., & Boehm, M. (2016). An analytical review of text and data mining practices and approaches in Europe Policy recommendations in view of the upcoming copyright legislative proposal. *OpenForumEurope*. Retrieved from http://www.openforumeurope.org/wp-content/uploads/2016/05/TDM-Paper-Diana-Cocoru-and-Mirko-Boehm.pdf

Cohen, J. (1960). A coefficient of agreement for nominal scales. *Educational and Psychological Measurement*, *20*(1), 37–46. doi:10.1177/001316446002000104

Coradeschi, S., Cesta, A., Cortellessa, G., Coraci, L., Gonzalez, J., Karlsson, L., . . . Pecora, F. (2013). Giraffplus: Combining social interaction and long term monitoring for promoting independent living. In *Human system interaction (HSI), 2013 the 6th international conference on* (pp. 578-585). IEEE.

Coradeschi, S., Cesta, A., Cortellessa, G., Coraci, L., Galindo, C., Gonzalez, J., ... Loutfi, A. (2014). GiraffPlus: a system for monitoring activities and physiological parameters and promoting social interaction for elderly. In *Human-Computer Systems Interaction: Backgrounds and Applications 3* (pp. 261–271). Cham: Springer.

Costa, Â., Castillo, J. C., Novais, P., Fernández-Caballero, A., & Simoes, R. (2012). Sensor-driven agenda for intelligent home care of the elderly. *Expert Systems with Applications, 39*(15), 12192–12204. doi:10.1016/j.eswa.2012.04.058

Cuong, H., Sima'an, K., & Titov, I. (2016). Adapting to all domains at once: Rewarding domain invariance in SMT. *Transactions of the Association for Computational Linguistics, 4*, 99–112. doi:10.1162/tacl_a_00086

Dalianis, Henriksson, Kvist, Velupillai, & Weegar. (2015). Health bank-a workbench for data science applications in healthcare. *CAiSE Industry Track*, 1–18.

Dalianis, H., Hassel, M., & Velupillai, S. (2009). The stockholm epr corpus–characteristics and some initial findings. *Women, 219*(906), 54.

Davies, M. (2009). The 385+ million word Corpus of Contemporary American English (1990–2008+): Design, architecture, and linguistic insights. *International Journal of Corpus Linguistics, 14*(2), 159–190. doi:10.1075/ijcl.14.2.02dav

Deléger, L., Cartoni, B., & Zweigenbaum, P. (2013). *Paraphrase detection in monolingual specialized/lay corpora*. Building and Using Comparable Corpora. doi:10.1007/978-3-642-20128-8_12

Deléger, L., & Zweigenbaum, P. (2009). Extracting lay paraphrases of specialized expressions from monolingual comparable medical corpora. In *Proceedings of the 2nd Workshop on Building and Using Comparable Corpora: from Parallel to Non-parallel Corpora*. Association for Computational Linguistics. 10.3115/1690339.1690343

Desagulier, G. (2017). *Corpus Linguistics and Statistics with R*. Springer. doi:10.1007/978-3-319-64572-8

Doing-Harris, K. M., & Zeng-Treitler, Q. (2011). Computer-assisted update of a consumer health vocabulary through mining of social network data. *Journal of Medical Internet Research, 13*(2), e37. doi:10.2196/jmir.1636 PMID:21586386

Dunning, T. (1993). Accurate methods for the statistics of surprise and coincidence. *Computational Linguistics, 19*(1).

Eckart, T., Quasthoff, U., & Goldhahn, D. (2012). The Influence of Corpus Quality on Statistical Measurements on Language Resources. In LREC (pp. 2318-2321). Academic Press.

Elhadad, N., & Sutaria, K. (2007). Mining a lexicon of technical terms and lay equivalents. In *Proceedings of the Workshop on BioNLP 2007: Biological, Translational, and Clinical Language Processing*. Association for Computational Linguistics. 10.3115/1572392.1572402

Escartin, C. P., & Torres, L. S. (2016). *D6. 3: Improved Corpus-based Approaches. Project Deliverable. EXPERT (Exploiting Empirical appRoaches to Translation), Project funded by the People Programme*. Marie Curie Actions.

Falkenjack, J., Mühlenbock, K. H., & Jönsson, A. (2013). Features indicating readability in swedish text. In *Proceedings of the 19th Nordic Conference of Computational Linguistics (NODALIDA 2013)*. Linköping University Electronic Press.

Ferraresi, A., Zanchetta, E., Bernardini, S., & Baroni, M. (2008). Introducing and evaluating ukWaC, a very large Web-derived corpus of English. *Proceedings of the 4th Web as Corpus Workshop (WAC-4) "Can we beat Google?"*

Fleiss, J. L. (1971). Measuring nominal scale agreement among many raters. *Psychological Bulletin, 76*(5), 378–382. doi:10.1037/h0031619

Fotokian, Z., Mohammadi Shahboulaghi, F., Fallahi-Khoshknab, M., & Pourhabib, A. (2017). The empowerment of elderly patients with chronic obstructive pulmonary disease: Managing life with the disease. *PLoS One, 12*(4), e0174028. doi:10.1371/journal.pone.0174028 PMID:28369069

Gao, Q., & Vogel, S. (2011). Corpus expansion for statistical machine translation with semantic role label substitution rules. In *Proceedings of the 49th Annual Meeting of the Association for Computational Linguistics: Human Language Technologies: short papers* (vol. 2, pp. 294-298). Association for Computational Linguistics.

Glavaš, G., & Štajner, S. (2015). Simplifying lexical simplification: do we need simplified corpora? In *Proceedings of the 53rd Annual Meeting of the Association for Computational Linguistics and the 7th International Joint Conference on Natural Language Processing* (*Vol. 2*, pp. 63-68). Academic Press. 10.3115/v1/P15-2011

Goldberg, L., Lide, B., Lowry, S., Massett, H. A., O'Connell, T., Preece, J., ... Shneiderman, B. (2011). Usability and accessibility in consumer health informatics: Current trends and future challenges. *American Journal of Preventive Medicine, 40*(5), S187–S197. doi:10.1016/j.amepre.2011.01.009 PMID:21521594

Goldhahn, D., Eckart, T., & Quasthoff, U. (2012). Building Large Monolingual Dictionaries at the Leipzig Corpora Collection: From 100 to 200 Languages. In LREC (Vol. 29, pp. 31-43). Academic Press.

Grabar, N., Chauveau-Thoumelin, P., & Dumonet, L. (2015). *Study of Subjectivity in the Medical Discourse: Uncertainty and Emotions Advances in Knowledge Discovery and Management* (Vol. 5). Springer.

Grabar, N., & Hamon, T. (2014). Automatic extraction of layman names for technical medical terms. In *Healthcare Informatics (ICHI), 2014 IEEE International Conference on* (pp. 310-319). IEEE. 10.1109/ICHI.2014.49

Grabar, N., & Hamon, T. (2014). Unsupervised method for the acquisition of general language paraphrases for medical compounds. In *Proceedings of the 4th International Workshop on Computational Terminology (Computerm)* (pp. 94-103). Academic Press. 10.3115/v1/W14-4812

Grabar, N., & Hamon, T. (2017). Understanding of unknown medical words. In *Proceedings of the Biomedical NLP Workshop associated with RANLP* (pp. 32-41). Academic Press. 10.26615/978-954-452-044-1_005

Grabar, N., Hamon, T., & Amiot, D. (2014). Automatic diagnosis of understanding of medical words. In *Proceedings of the 3rd Workshop on Predicting and Improving Text Readability for Target Reader Populations (PITR)* (pp. 11-20). Academic Press. 10.3115/v1/W14-1202

Grabar, N., Krivine, S., & Jaulent, M. C. (2007). Classification of health webpages as expert and non expert with a reduced set of cross-language features. *AMIA ... Annual Symposium Proceedings - AMIA Symposium. AMIA Symposium, 2007*, 284. PMID:18693843

Grabar, N., van Zyl, I., de la Harpe, R., & Hamon, T. (2014). The Comprehension of Medical Words. In *Proceedings of the International Joint Conference on Biomedical Engineering Systems and Technologies* (vol. 5, pp. 334-342). SCITEPRESS-Science and Technology Publications, Lda.

Greenes, R. A. (2001). eCare and eHealth: The Internet meets health care. The Journal of medical practice management. *MPM, 17*(2), 106–108. PMID:11680134

Gries, S. Th. (2013). Elementary statistical testing with R. In M. Krug & J. Schlüter (Eds.), *Research methods in language variation and change*. Cambridge University Press. doi:10.1017/CBO9780511792519.024

Grifoni-Waterman, R. (2016). *International fair use developments: Is fair use going global?* Retrieved July 2018. https://www.authorsalliance.org/2016/02/25/international-fair-use-developments-is-fair-use-going-global/

Grigonyte, G., Kvist, M., Wirén, M., Velupillai, S., & Henriksson, A. (2016). Swedification patterns of latin and greek affixes in clinical text. *Nordic Journal of Linguistics, 39*(01), 5–37. doi:10.1017/S0332586515000293

Grishman, R., & Kittredge, R. (2014). *Analyzing language in restricted domains: sublanguage description and processing*. Psychology Press.

Habernal, I., Zayed, O., & Gurevych, I. (2016). C4Corpus: Multilingual Web-size corpus with free license. In *Proceedings of the 10th International Conference on Language Resources and Evaluation (LREC 2016)* (pp. 914–922). Portorož, Slovenia: European Language Resources Association (ELRA).

Handke, C., Guibault, L., & Vallbé, J. J. (2015). *Is Europe falling behind in data mining? Copyright's impact on data mining in academic research*. Academic Press.

Hasan, K. S., & Ng, V. (2014). Automatic keyphrase extraction: A survey of the state of the art. In *Proceedings of the 52nd Annual Meeting of the Association for Computational Linguistics* (*Vol. 1*, pp. 1262-1273). Academic Press. 10.3115/v1/P14-1119

Haslerud, V., & Stenström, A.-B. (1995). The bergen corpus of london teenager language (colt). Spoken English on Computer, 235–42.

Heffer, C., Rock, F., & Conley, J. (Eds.). (2013). *Legal-Lay Communication: Textual Travels in the Law*. Oxford University Press. doi:10.1093/acprof:oso/9780199746842.001.0001

Henkel, M., Perjons, E., & Sneiders, E. (2015). Supporting Workflow and Adaptive Case Management with Language Technologies. In WorldCIST (pp. 543-552). Academic Press. doi:10.1007/978-3-319-16486-1_53

Heppin, K. F. (2010). *Resolving Power of Search keys in Medeval a Swedish Medical Test Collection with User Groups: Doctors and patients* (Ph.D. dissertation). University of Gothenburg.

Hoang, C., & Sima'an, K. (2014). Latent domain translation models in mix-of-domains haystack. In *Proceedings of COLING 2014, the 25th International Conference on Computational Linguistics: Technical Papers* (pp. 1928-1939). Academic Press.

Hole, W. T., & Srinivasan, S. (2000). Discovering missed synonymy in a large concept-oriented Metathesaurus. In *Proceedings of the AMIA Symposium* (p. 354). American Medical Informatics Association.

Humphreys, B. L., McCray, A. T., & Cheh, M. L. (1997). Evaluating the coverage of controlled health data terminologies: Report on the results of the NLM/AHCPR large scale vocabulary test. *Journal of the American Medical Informatics Association, 4*(6), 484–500. doi:10.1136/jamia.1997.0040484 PMID:9391936

Huo, H., Xu, Y., Yan, H., Mubeen, S., & Zhang, H. (2009, June). An elderly health care system using wireless sensor networks at home. In *Sensor Technologies and Applications, 2009. SENSORCOMM'09. Third International Conference on* (pp. 158-163). IEEE. 10.1109/SENSORCOMM.2009.32

Jackson, G. L., Powers, B. J., Chatterjee, R., Bettger, J. P., Kemper, A. R., Hasselblad, V., ... Gray, R. (2013). The patient-centered medical home: A systematic review. *Annals of Internal Medicine, 158*(3), 169–178. doi:10.7326/0003-4819-158-3-201302050-00579 PMID:24779044

Jiang, L., & Yang, C. C. (2013). Using co-occurrence analysis to expand consumer health vocabularies from social media data. *2013 IEEE International Conference on Healthcare Informatics (ICHI)*, 74-81. 10.1109/ICHI.2013.16

Jimison, H., Gorman, P., Woods, S., Nygren, P., Walker, M., Norris, S., & Hersh, W. (2008). Barriers and drivers of health information technology use for the elderly, chronically ill, and underserved. *Evidence Report/technology Assessment, 175*, 1–1422. PMID:19408968

Johansson, V., & Rennes, E. (2016). Automatic extraction of synonyms from an easy-to-read corpus. *Proceedings of the Sixth Swedish Language Technology Conference (SLTC-16).*

Kann, V., & Rosell, M. (2005). Free construction of a free Swedish dictionary of synonyms. In *Proceedings of the 15th Nordic Conference of Computational Linguistics (NODALIDA 2005)* (pp. 105-110). Academic Press.

Kilgarriff, A. (2001). Comparing corpora. *International Journal of Corpus Linguistics, 6*(1), 97–133. doi:10.1075/ijcl.6.1.05kil

Kilgarriff, A. (2005). Language is never, ever, ever, random. *Corpus Linguistics and Linguistic Theory, 1*(2), 263–276. doi:10.1515/cllt.2005.1.2.263

Kilgarriff, A. (2007). Googleology is bad science. *Computational Linguistics, 33*(1), 147–151. doi:10.1162/coli.2007.33.1.147

Kilgarriff, A. (2014). *How to evaluate a corpus. Slides. 15th lecture of the Fred Jelinek Seminar series.* Institute of Formal and Applied Linguistics Charles University, Czech Republic Faculty of Mathematics and Physics.

Kilgarriff, A., Avinesh, P. V. S., & Pomikálek, J. (2011). BootCatting comparable corpora. In *9th International Conference on Terminology and Artificial Intelligence* (p. 123). Academic Press.

Kilgarriff, A., Reddy, S., Pomikálek, J., & Pvs, A. (2010). *A corpus factory for many languages.* In LREC workshop on Web Services and Processing Pipelines, Malta.

Kilgarriff, A., Reddy, S., & Pomikálek, J. and PVS A. (2010). A corpus factory for many languages. *Proceedings of the Seventh International Conference on Language Resources and Evaluation (LREC'10).*

Kim, J., Joo, J., & Shin, Y. (2009). An exploratory study on the health information terms for the development of the consumer health vocabulary system. *Studies in Health Technology and Informatics, 146,* 785.

Kittredge, R. (2003). Sublanguages and controlled languages. In R. Mitkov (Ed.), *The Oxford Handbook of Computational Linguistics* (pp. 430–447). Oxford, UK: Oxford University Press.

Kittredge, R., & Lehrberger, J. (Eds.). (1982). *Sublanguage: Studies of language in restricted semantic domains.* Walter de Gruyter. doi:10.1515/9783110844818

Koch, S., & Hägglund, M. (2009). Health informatics and the delivery of care to older people. *Maturitas, 63*(3), 195–199. doi:10.1016/j.maturitas.2009.03.023 PMID:19487092

Kokkinakis, D. (2006). Developing resources for Swedish Bio-Medical text mining. *Proceedings of the 2nd International Symposium on Semantic Mining in Biomedicine (SMBM).*

Kokkinakis, D. (2012). *The Journal of the Swedish Medical Association - A Corpus Resource for Biomedical Text Mining in Swedish.* In The Third Workshop on Building and Evaluating Resources for Biomedical Text Mining (BioTxtM), an LREC Workshop.

Kokkinakis, D., & Gronostaj, M. T. (2006). Comparing lay and professional language in cardiovascular disorders corpora. *WSEAS Transactions on Biology and Biomedicine, 3*(6), 429.

Krippendorff, K. (1980). *Content analysis. Beverley Hills* (Vol. 7). Sage Publications.

Krippendorff, K. (2011). *Computing Krippendorff's alpha-reliability.* Available: http://repository.upenn.edu/asc_papers/43

Kristoffersen, K. B. (2017). *Common Crawled Web Corpora: Constructing corpora from large amounts of web data. Thesis submitted for the degree of Master in Informatics: Programming and Networks (Language Technology group).* Department of Informatics, Faculty of mathematics and natural sciences, University of Oslo. Retrieved from http://urn.nb.no/URN:NBN:no-60569

Kristoffersson, A., & Lindén, M. (2017). *Understanding users of a future E-care@home system.* Retrieved from http://oru.diva-portal.org/smash/get/diva2:1073710/FULLTEXT01.pdf

Kucera, H., & Francis, W. (1979). *A standard corpus of present-day edited American English, for use with digital computers* (revised and amplified from 1967 version). Academic Press.

Küçükdurmaz, F., Gomez, M. M., Secrist, E., & Parvizi, J. (2015). Reliability, Readability and Quality of Online Information about Femoracetabular Impingement. *Archives of Bone and Joint Surgery, 3*(3), 163–168. PMID:26213699

Kunz, M., & Osborne, P. (2010). A Preliminary Examination of the Readability of Consumer Pharmaceutical Web Pages. *Journal of Marketing Development and Competitiveness, 5*(1), 33–41.

L'Homme, M. C. (2014). Terminologies and taxonomies. In J. R. Taylor (Ed.), The Oxford Handbook of the Word. Oxford University Press.

Landis, J. R., & Koch, G. G. (1977). The measurement of observer agreement for categorical data. *Biometrics*, 159-174.

Lee, D. W. Y. (2001). Genres, Registers, Text Types, Domains, And Styles: Clarifying The Concepts And Navigating A Path Through The Bnc Jungle. *Language Learning & Technology, 5*(3), 37–72.

Leroy, G., Helmreich, S., Cowie, J. R., Miller, T., & Zheng, W. (2008). Evaluating online health information: Beyond readability formulas. *AMIA ... Annual Symposium Proceedings - AMIA Symposium. AMIA Symposium, 2008*, 394. PMID:18998902

Lewin, S., Munabi-Babigumira, S., Glenton, C., Daniels, K., Bosch-Capblanch, X., van Wyk, B. E., ... Scheel, I. B. (2010). Lay health workers in primary and community health care for maternal and child health and the management of infectious diseases. *Cochrane Database of Systematic Reviews*, (3): CD004015. PMID:20238326

Lilly, C. M., Zubrow, M. T., Kempner, K. M., Reynolds, H. N., Subramanian, S., Eriksson, E. A., ... Cowboy, E. R. (2014). Critical care telemedicine: Evolution and state of the art. *Critical Care Medicine, 42*(11), 2429–2436. doi:10.1097/CCM.0000000000000539 PMID:25080052

Lin, D., Zhao, S., Qin, L., & Zhou, M. (2003). Identifying synonyms among distributionally similar words. IJCAI, 3, 1492-1493.

Lind, L., & Karlsson, D. (2018). The eHealth Diary – tailoring a solution for elderly, multimorbid homecare patients. Presented at Medical Information Europe (MIE2018), Gothenburg, Sweden.

Lindberg, B., Nilsson, C., Zotterman, D., Söderberg, S., & Skär, L. (2013). Using Information and Communication Technology in Home Care for Communication between Patients, Family Members, and Healthcare Professionals: A Systematic Review. *International Journal of Telemedicine and Applications, 2013*, 1–31. doi:10.1155/2013/461829 PMID:23690763

Lippincott, T., Séaghdha, D. Ó., & Korhonen, A. (2011). Exploring subdomain variation in biomedical language. *BMC Bioinformatics, 12*(1), 212. doi:10.1186/1471-2105-12-212 PMID:21619603

Loginova, E., Gojun, A., Blancafort, H., Guégan, M., Gornostay, T., & Heid, U. (2012). Reference lists for the evaluation of term extraction tools. *Proceedings of the Terminology and Knowledge Engineering Conference (TKE'2012)*.

Loutfi, Jönsson, Karlsson, Lind, Lindén, Pecora, & Voigt. (2016). *Ecare@Home: A Distributed Research Environment on Semantic Interoperability*. Presented at the 3rd EAI International Conference on IoT Technologies for HealthCare (HealhtyIoT 2016), Västerås, Sweden.

Lüdeling, A., Evert, S., & Baroni, M. (2007). Using web data for linguistic purposes. *Language and Computers, 59*, 7.

Malá, M. (2017). A Corpus-Based Diachronic Study of a Change in the Use of Non-Finite Clauses in Written English. *Prague Journal of English Studies, 6*(1), 151–166. doi:10.1515/pjes-2017-0009

McClosky, D. (2010). *Any domain parsing: automatic domain adaptation for natural language parsing* (PhD dissertation). Department of Computer Science at Brown University, Providence, RI. Retrieved from https://pdfs.semanticscholar.org/1c6e/e895c202a91a808de59445e3dbde2f4cda0e.pdf

McEnery, T., Xiao, R., & Tono, Y. (2006). *Corpus-based language studies: An advanced resource book.* Taylor & Francis.

McGregor, B. (2005, January). Constructing a concise medical taxonomy. *Journal of the Medical Library Association: JMLA, 93*(1), 121–123. PMID:15685285

Merilampi, S., & Sirkka, A. (2016). *Introduction to smart eHealth and eCare technologies.* CRC Press. doi:10.1201/9781315368818

Messai, R., Zeng, Q., Mousseau, M., & Simonet, M. (2006). *Building a bilingual French-English patient-oriented terminology for breast cancer.* Toronto, Canada: MedNet.

Miller, T., & Leroy, G. (2008). Dynamic generation of a Health Topics Overview from consumer health information documents. *International Journal of Biomedical Engineering and Technology, 1*(4), 395–414. doi:10.1504/IJBET.2008.020069

Miller, T., Leroy, G., Chatterjee, S., Fan, J., & Thoms, B. (2007). A Classifier to Evaluate Language Specificity in Medical Documents. *Hawaii International Conference on System Sciences.* 10.1109/HICSS.2007.6

Nanas, N., & De Roeck, A. (2008). Corpus profiling with Nootropia. In *Proceedings of Workshop on Corpus Profiling for Information Retrieval and Natural Language Profiling.* London: BCS-IRSG.

Nazarenko, A., & Zargayouna, H. (2009). Evaluating term extraction. In *International Conference Recent Advances in Natural Language Processing (RANLP'09)* (pp. 299-304). Academic Press.

Nilsson, C., Öhman, M., & Söderberg, S. (2006). Information and communication technology in supporting people with serious chronic illness living at home–an intervention study. *Journal of Telemedicine and Telecare, 12*(4), 198–202. doi:10.1258/135763306777488807 PMID:16774702

Norman, G. R., Arfai, B., Gupta, A., Brooks, L. R., & Eva, K. W. (2003). The privileged status of prestigious terminology: Impact of "medicalese" on clinical judgments. *Academic Medicine, 78*(10Supplement), S82–S84. doi:10.1097/00001888-200310001-00026 PMID:14557104

Nyström, M., Merkel, M., Ahrenberg, L., Zweigenbaum, P., Petersson, H., & Åhlfeldt, H. (2006). Creating a medical english-swedish dictionary using interactive word alignment. *BMC Medical Informatics and Decision Making, 6*(1), 35. doi:10.1186/1472-6947-6-35 PMID:17034649

Nyström, M., Merkel, M., Petersson, H., & Åhlfeldt, H. (2007). Creating a medical dictionary using word alignment: The influence of sources and resources. *BMC Medical Informatics and Decision Making, 7*(1), 37. doi:10.1186/1472-6947-7-37 PMID:18036221

O'Brien, S. (1993). *Sublanguage, text type and machine translation* (Doctoral dissertation). Dublin City University.

Oakes, M. P. (2008). Statistical measures for corpus profiling. *Proceedings of the Open University Workshop on Corpus Profiling.*

Östling, R. (2013). Stagger: An open-source part of speech tagger for Swedish. *Northern European Journal of Language Technology, 3*, 1–18. doi:10.3384/nejlt.2000-1533.1331

Ownby, R. L. (2005). Influence of vocabulary and sentence complexity and passive voice on the readability of consumer-oriented mental health information on the internet. In *AMIA 2005 Symposium Proceedings*. AMIA.

Park, Y., Byrd, R. J., & Boguraev, B. K. (2002). Automatic glossary extraction: beyond terminology identification. In *Proceedings of the 19th international conference on Computational linguistics* (vol. 1, pp. 1-7). Association for Computational Linguistics.

Pazienza, M., Pennacchiotti, M., & Zanzotto, F. (2005). Terminology extraction: an analysis of linguistic and statistical approaches. In *Terminology Extraction: An Analysis of Linguistic and Statistical Approaches*. Springer. doi:10.1007/3-540-32394-5_20

Pearson, J. (1998). *Terms in context* (Vol. 1). John Benjamins Publishing. doi:10.1075cl.1

Pieterse, A. H., Jager, N. A., Smets, E. M., & Henselmans, I. (2013). Lay understanding of common medical terminology in oncology. *Psycho-Oncology, 22*(5), 1186–1191. doi:10.1002/pon.3096 PMID:22573405

Pomikálek, J., Rychlý, P., & Kilgarriff, A. (2009). Scaling to billion-plus word corpora. *Advances in Computational Linguistics, 41*, 3–13.

Poprat, M., Markó, K., & Hahn, U. (2006). A language classifier that automatically divides medical documents for experts and health care consumers. *Studies in Health Technology and Informatics, 124*, 503. PMID:17108568

Pressman, R. S. (2005). *Software engineering: a practitioner's approach*. Palgrave Macmillan.

Quintas, J. M. L. (2018). *Context-based Human-Machine Interaction Framework for Artificial Social Companions* (Doctoral dissertation). Universidade de Coimbra.

Quirk, C., Brockett, C., & Dolan, B. (2004). Monolingual machine translation for paraphrase generation. *Proceedings of the 2004 Conference on Empirical Methods in Natural Language Processing, EMNLP 2004, A meeting of SIGDAT, a Special Interest Group of the ACL, held in conjunction with ACL 2004.*

Rayson, P. (2008). From key words to key semantic domains. *International Journal of Corpus Linguistics, 13*(4), 519–549. doi:10.1075/ijcl.13.4.06ray

Rayson, P., & Garside, R. (2000). Comparing corpora using frequency profiling. In *Proceedings of the workshop on Comparing Corpora* (pp. 1-6). Association for Computational Linguistics.

Remus, S., & Biemann, C. (2016). Domain-Specific Corpus Expansion with Focused Webcrawling. LREC.

Rudd, R. E. (2013). Needed action in health literacy. *Journal of Health Psychology, 18*(8), 1004–1010. doi:10.1177/1359105312470128 PMID:23349399

Santini, M. (2006). *Common Criteria for Genre Classification: Annotation and Granularity.* Workshop on Text-based Information Retrieval (TIR-06), In Conjunction with ECAI 2006, Riva del Garda, Italy.

Santini, M., Jönsson, A., Nyström, M., & Alirezai, M. (2017). A Web Corpus for eCare: Collection, Lay Annotation and Learning - First Results. Workshop LTA'17 (Language Technology Applications 2017) co-located with FedCSIS 2017, Prague. In M. Ganzha, L. Maciaszek, & M. Paprzycki (Eds.), *Position Papers of the 2017 Federated Conference on Computer Science and Information Systems, Proceedings,* (Vol. 12, pp. 71-78). Academic Press.

Santini, M., Strandqvist, W., Nyström, M., Alirezai, M., & Jönsson, A. (2018). *Can we Quantify Domain-hood? Exploring Measures to Assess Domain-Specificity in Web Corpora.* TIR 2018 - 15th International Workshop on Technologies for Information Retrieval.

Schäfer, R. (2016). CommonCOW: Massively Huge Web Corpora from CommonCrawl Data and a Method to Distribute them Freely under Restrictive EU Copyright Laws. LREC.

Schäfer, R., Barbaresi, A., & Bildhauer, F. (2013). The good, the bad, and the hazy: Design decisions in web corpus construction. *Proceedings of the 8th Web as Corpus Workshop.*

Schäfer, R., Barbaresi, A., & Bildhauer, F. (2014). Focused web corpus crawling. In *Proceedings of the 9th Web as Corpus workshop (WAC-9)* (pp. 9-15). Academic Press. 10.3115/v1/W14-0402

Schäfer, R., & Bildhauer, F. (2012). Building large corpora from the web using a new efficient tool chain. In LREC (pp. 486-493). Academic Press.

Schäfer, R., & Bildhauer, F. (2013). Web corpus construction. *Synthesis Lectures on Human Language Technologies, 6*(4), 1–145. doi:10.2200/S00508ED1V01Y201305HLT022

Scott, N., & Weiner, M. F. (1984). "Patientspeak": An exercise in communication. *Journal of Medical Education.* PMID:6492107

Seedor, M., Peterson, K. J., Nelsen, L. A., Cocos, C., McCormick, J. B., Chute, C. G., & Pathak, J. (2013). Incorporating expert terminology and disease risk factors into consumer health vocabularies. In *Pacific Symposium on Biocomputing. Pacific Symposium on Biocomputing.* NIH Public Access.

Seedorff, M., Peterson, K. J., Nelsen, L. A., Cocos, C., McCormick, J. B., Chute, C. G., & Pathak, J. (2013). Incorporating expert terminology and disease risk factors into consumer health vocabularies. In Biocomputing 2013 (pp. 421-432). Academic Press.

Seljan, S., Baretić, M., & Kučiš, V. (2014). Information Retrieval and Terminology Extraction in Online Resources for Patients with Diabetes. *Collegium Antropologicum, 38*(2), 705–710. PMID:25145011

Sharoff, S., Rapp, R., Zweigenbaum, P., & Fung, P. (Eds.). (2013). *Building and using comparable corpora.* Springer. doi:10.1007/978-3-642-20128-8

Sim, J., & Wright, C. C. (2005). The kappa statistic in reliability studies: Use, interpretation, and sample size requirements. *Physical Therapy, 85*(3), 257. PMID:15733050

Sioutis, M., Alirezaie, M., Renoux, J., & Loutfi, A. (2017). *Towards a Synergy of Qualitative Spatio-Temporal Reasoning and Smart Environments for Assisting the Elderly at Home.* 30th International Workshop on Qualitative Reasoning (held in conjunction with IJCAI 2017), Melbourne, Australia.

Smith, C. A., & Wicks, P. J. (2008). PatientsLikeMe: Consumer health vocabulary as a folksonomy. *AMIA ... Annual Symposium Proceedings - AMIA Symposium. AMIA Symposium, 2008*, 682. PMID:18999004

Soergel, D., Tse, T., & Slaughter, L. A. (2004). Helping healthcare consumers understand: an "interpretive layer" for finding and making sense of medical information. In Medinfo (pp. 931-935). Academic Press.

Soobrah, R., & Clark, S. K. (2012). Your patient information website: How good is it? *Colorectal Disease, 14*(3), e90–e94. doi:10.1111/j.1463-1318.2011.02792.x PMID:21883807

Strandqvist, W., Santini, M., Lind, L., & Jönsson, A. (2018). Towards a Quality Assessment of Web Corpora for Language Technology Applications. In *Proceedings of TISLID18: Languages For Digital Lives And Cultures.* Ghent University.

Suryadevara, N. K., Gaddam, A., Rayudu, R. K., & Mukhopadhyay, S. C. (2012). Wireless sensors network based safe home to care elderly people: Behaviour detection. *Sensors and Actuators. A, Physical, 186*, 277–283. doi:10.1016/j.sna.2012.03.020

Tchami, O. W., & Grabar, N. (2014). Towards automatic distinction between specialized and non-specialized occurrences of verbs in medical corpora. In *Proceedings of the 4th International Workshop on Computational Terminology (Computerm)* (pp. 114-124). Academic Press. 10.3115/v1/W14-4814

Toutanova, K., Klein, D., Manning, C. D., & Singer, Y. (2003). Feature-rich part-of-speech tagging with a cyclic dependency network. *Proceedings of the 2003 Conference of the North American Chapter of the Association for Computational Linguistics on Human Language Technology, 1.* 10.3115/1073445.1073478

Versley, Y., & Panchenko, Y. (2012). Not just bigger: Towards better-quality Web corpora. In *Proceedings of the seventh Web as Corpus Workshop (WAC7)* (pp. 44-52). Academic Press.

Vivaldi, J., & Rodríguez, H. (2007). Evaluation of terms and term extraction systems: A practical approach. Terminology. *International Journal of Theoretical and Applied Issues in Specialized Communication, 13*(2), 225–248.

Volansky, V., Ordan, N., & Wintner, S. (2015). On the features of translationese. *Digital Scholarship in the Humanities, 30*(1), 98–118. doi:10.1093/llc/fqt031

Vydiswaran, V. V., Mei, Q., Hanauer, D. A., & Zheng, K. (2014). Mining consumer health vocabulary from community-generated text. In *AMIA Annual Symposium Proceedings.* American Medical Informatics Association.

Wang, Y. (n.d.). Automatic Recognition of Text Difficulty from Consumers Health Information. *19th IEEE Symposium on Computer-Based Medical Systems (CBMS'06).*

Williams, N., & Ogden, J. (2004). The impact of matching the patient's vocabulary: A randomized control trial. *Family Practice, 21*(6), 630–635. doi:10.1093/fampra/cmh610 PMID:15520032

Wong, W., Liu, W., & Bennamoun, M. (2011). Constructing specialized corpora through analysing domain representativeness of websites. *Language Resources and Evaluation, 45*(2), 209–241. doi:10.100710579-011-9141-4

Zadeh, B. Q. A. (2016). Study on the Interplay Between the Corpus Size and Parameters of a Distributional Model for Term Classification. In *Proceedings of the 5th International Workshop on Computational Terminology (Computerm2016)* (pp. 62-72). Academic Press.

Zeng, Q., Kim, E., Crowell, J., & Tse, T. (2005). A text corpora-based estimation of the familiarity of health terminology. In *International Symposium on Biological and Medical Data Analysis* (pp. 184-192). Springer. 10.1007/11573067_19

Zeng, Q., Tse, T., Divita, G., Keselman, A., Crowell, J., Browne, A. C., … Ngo, L. (2015). Term Identification Methods for Consumer Health Vocabulary Development. *Journal of Medical Internet Research, 9*(1), 4.

Zeng, Q. T., & Tse, T. (2006). Exploring and developing consumer health vocabularies. *Journal of the American Medical Informatics Association, 13*(1), 24–29. doi:10.1197/jamia.M1761 PMID:16221948

Zeng-Treitler, Q., Kim, H., Goryachev, S., Keselman, A., Slaughter, L., & Smith, C. A. (2007). Text characteristics of clinical reports and their implications for the readability of personal health records. In Medinfo. MEDINFO (2nd ed.; vol. 12, pp. 1117-1121). Academic Press.

Zheng, J., & Yu, H. (2017). Readability formulas and user perceptions of electronic health records difficulty: A corpus study. *Journal of Medical Internet Research, 19*(3), e59. doi:10.2196/jmir.6962 PMID:28254738

Zheng, W., Milios, E., & Watters, C. (2002). Filtering for medical news items using a machine learning approach. In *Proceedings of the AMIA Symposium* (p. 949). American Medical Informatics Association.

ENDNOTES

[1]   iWeb: The Intelligent Web-based Corpus has been released in May 2018. For further details, see <<https://corpus.byu.edu/iweb/help/iweb_overview.pdf>> and the list of corpora available at BYU (Brigham Young University, Utah, USA) <<https://corpus.byu.edu/>>. URLs retrieved July 2018.

[2]   See <<https://www.sics.se/projects/digital-inkludering-i-det-uppkopplade-samhallet-for-grupper-med-speciella-behov>>. In Swedish. Retrieved July 2018.

[3]   <<http://ecareathome.se/>>.

[4]   SEMANTICMINING: Semantic Interoperability and Data Mining in Biomedicine <<https://cordis.europa.eu/project/rcn/71155_en.html>>. Retrieved July 2018.

[5]   <<http://www.semantichealthnet.eu/>>. Retrieved July 2018. This project has contributed to give to the establishment of the European Institute for Innovation through Health Data (i~HD) <<https://www.i-hd.eu/>>, a permanent organization aimed to "develop and promote best practices in the governance, quality, semantic interoperability and uses of health data, including its reuse for research".

6 One of Accurat's main objectives was to "To develop methods and tools for automatic acquisition of comparable corpora from the Web" <<http://www.accurat-project.eu/index.php-p=about.htm>>. Retrieved July 2018.

7 TTC (Terminology Extraction, Translation Tools and Comparable Corpora) developed and adapted tools for "gathering and managing comparable corpora, collected from the web, and managing terminologies" <<https://cordis.europa.eu/docs/projects/cnect/5/248005/080/publishing/readmore/TTC-public-annual-report-2012.pdf>>. Retrieved July 2018.

8 "EXPERT (EXPloiting Empirical appRoaches to Translation) aims to train young researchers, namely Early Stage Researchers (ESRs) and Experienced Researchers (ERs), to promote the research, development and use of hybrid language translation technologies. The overall objective of EXPERT is to provide innovative research and training in the field of Translation memory and Machine Translation Technologies". <<http://expert-itn.eu/?q=content/deliverables>>. Retrieved July 2018.

9 <<https://dkpro.github.io/dkpro-c4corpus/>>. Retrieved July 2018.

10 <<https://en.wikipedia.org/wiki/Blekko >>. Retrieved July 2018.

11 <<http://agilemanifesto.org/ >> Retrieved July 2018.

12 <<https://www.nhs.uk/conditions/iron-deficiency-anaemia/ >>. Retrieved July 2018.

13 <<https://www.health24.com/Medical/Anaemia/Anaemia-20130216-3>>. Retrieved July 2018.

14 <<https://www.1177.se/>>. Retrieved July 2018.

15 "Applied in the context of machine learning, this means that if two algorithms have broadly similar performance for the criteria identified as the most important for a particular project — accuracy and stability, say — we should always prefer the "simpler" one." <<https://www.teradata.com/Blogs/Occam%E2%80%99s-razor-and-machine-learning#/>>. Retrieved July 2018.

16 Review <<https://telepresencerobots.com/reviews/giraff/giraff-plus-revolutionizing-remote-patient-care>>. Retrieved July 2018.

17 "Healthcare Is Coming Home With Sensors And Algorithms" in The Medical Futurist <<http://medicalfuturist.com/healthcare-is-coming-home/ >>. Retrieved July 2018.

18 For example, see the recently funded project (2016-2019) led by M. Popescu: *Linguistic Summarization of Sensor Data for Early Illness Recognition in Eldercare*" <<https://www.eldertech.missouri.edu/projects/linguistic-summarization-of-in-home-sensor-data-trends/ >>. Retrieved July 2018.

19 For instance, CARRE (Personalized patient empowerment and shared decision support for cardiorenal disease and comorbidities) <<https://www.carre-project.eu/>>; Designing for People with Dementia: designing for mindful self-empowerment and social engagement <<https://cordis.europa.eu/project/rcn/199934_en.html>>. Retrieved July 2018.

20 Several initiative exist at present. For instance, the Open Access, Collaborative Consumer Health Vocabulary Initiative<<http://consumerhealthvocab.chpc.utah.edu/CHVwiki/>>; Flashcards on consumer health terminology <<https://quizlet.com/70547741/chapter-1-consumer-health-vocab-flash-cards/>>. Retrieved July 2018.

21 The concept of "register" has numberless definitions and characterizations in linguistics and related fields. <<https://en.wikipedia.org/wiki/Register_(sociolinguistics)>>. Retrieved July 2018.

22 This is a registry for registering linguistic terms used in various fields of translation, computational linguistics and natural language processing and defining mappings both between different terms and the same terms used in different systems. The registers identified are: bench-level register,

dialect register, facetious register, formal register, in house register, ironic register, neutral register, slang register, taboo register, technical register, vulgar register, <<https://en.wikipedia.org/wiki/Register_(sociolinguistics)>>. Retrieved July 2018.

23   <<https://plainlanguage.gov/guidelines/words/avoid-jargon/ >>. Retrieved July 2018.

24   <<https://skillcrush.com/2015/03/26/99-tech-terms/>>. Retrieved July 2018.

25   For instance, see "Small Data and Big Health Benefits" <<https://research.cornell.edu/news-features/small-data-and- big-health-benefits >>. Retrieved July 2018.

26   The UMLS integrates and distributes key terminology, classification and coding standards, and associated resources to promote creation of more effective and interoperable biomedical information systems and services, including electronic health records. <<https://www.nlm.nih.gov/research/umls/>>. Retrieved July 2018.

27   "The deCODEme service was discontinued in January 2013 and deCODE genetics stopped selling personal genetic tests altogether." <<https://en.wikipedia.org/wiki/DeCODE_genetics#deCODEme>>. Retrieved July 2018.

28   "GeneWiki+ is a mirror of the Gene Wiki project on Wikipedia, running on top of the Semantic Mediawiki framework. Content from Wikipedia is mirrored in near-real time by our server and modified to work with Semantic Mediawiki's special semantic links. This allows you, the user, to ask simple queries that exploit the huge amount information in Wikipedia." <<https://archive.is/4Aqhp#selection-255.0-267.253>>. Retrieved July 2018.

29   "PharmGKB is a comprehensive resource that curates knowledge about the impact of genetic variation on drug response for clinicians and researchers." <<https://www.pharmgkb.org/ >>. Retrieved July 2018.

30   <<https://en.wikipedia.org/wiki/Agile_software_development>>. The principles of the Agile strategy is explained in the Agile Manifesto <<http://agilemanifesto.org/>>. Retrieved July 2018.

31   "The BootCaT front-end is a graphical interface for the BootCaT toolkit (Baroni & Bernardini 2004). It automates the process of finding reference texts on the web and collating them in a single corpus". Read more here: <<https://bootcat.dipintra.it/>>. Retrieved July 2018.

32   228 initial URL seeds; 155 retrieved URLs; 73 URLs discarded either because they were empty documents or containing non-Swedish text. The list of 155 url seeds are available on the corpus website.

33   Arguably, also the project "Text-based measures of information quality in online health information", recently funded in the UK, will address some of these issues.

34   The annotated corpus has a xml format and is available here <http://santini.se/eCareCorpus/home.htm>. Also accessible from <<http://ecareathome.se/>>.

35   See: <<http://santini.se/eCareCorpus/home.htm>>. Also accessible from <<http://ecareathome.se/>>.

36   All calculations of intercoder/interrater reliability coefficients for lay-specialized labels (nominal data) coded by two annotators have been computed using the ReCal2 online calculator <<http://dfreelon.org/utils/recalfront/recal2/>>. Retrieved July 2018.

37   Options: Classify - Meta – FilteredClassifiers. See: Weka Explorer Interface. <<http://weka.sourceforge.net/doc.dev/weka/classifiers/meta/FilteredClassifier.html>>. Retrieved July 2018.

[38] "In information retrieval, tf–idf or TFIDF, short for term frequency–inverse document frequency, is a numerical statistic that is intended to reflect how important a word is to a document in a collection or corpus". <<https://en.wikipedia.org/wiki/Tf%E2%80%93idf>>. Retrieved July 2018.

[39] "TP / True Positive: case was positive and predicted positive". <<https://www.kdnuggets.com/faq/precision-recall.html >>. Retrieved July 2018.

[40] "A receiver operating characteristic curve, i.e. ROC curve, is a graphical plot that illustrates the diagnostic ability of a binary classifier system as its discrimination threshold is varied.". <<https://en.wikipedia.org/wiki/Receiver_operating_characteristic>>. Retrieved July 2018.

[41] Corrected Paired t-test is a statistical hypothesis testing method for comparing the result of measuring one group twice (here with two different classifiers). By taking into account both mean and variance of the differences between these two measures over several runs, it calculates a t-value. Using this value and desired significance level (normally 5%), the probability that these two measurements are significantly different can be obtained by looking it up from a t-distribution table. Consequently, one can say that these classifiers with a certain degree of confidence (100 - significance level) are significantly different or not. Paired t-test wrongly assumes that these differences between accuracy of two classifiers are independent and therefore has normal distribution (which is in fact not true because test sets and training sets overlap). The corrected resampled paired t-test boosts the paired t-test by entering the fraction of data used for testing and training into t-calculation formula (see <<http://imagej.net/Trainable_Weka_Segmentation_-_How_to_compare_classifiers >>. Retrieved July 2018.; Witten et al., 2016).

[42] "Statistical significance helps quantify whether a result is likely due to chance or to some factor of interest,". When a finding is significant, it simply means you can feel confident that it is real, not that you just got lucky (or unlucky) in choosing the sample.

[43] <<https://www.1177.se/ >>. Retrieved July 2018.

[44] <<https://mesh.kib.ki.se/Mesh/search/?searchterm=hemicrania >>. Retrieved July 2018.

[45] <<https://en.wiktionary.org/wiki/dermatitis>>. Retrieved July 2018.

[46] <<https://en.wiktionary.org/wiki/bronchitis>>. Retrieved July 2018.

Chapter 7
Merging Realities in Space and Time:
Towards a New Cyber–Physical Eco–Society

Lyuba Alboul
Sheffield Hallam University, UK

Martin Beer
https://orcid.org/0000-0001-5368-6550
Sheffield Hallam University, UK

Louis Nisiotis
Sheffield Hallam University, UK

ABSTRACT

The rapid developments in online technology have provided young people with instant communication with each other and highly interactive and engaging visual game playing environments. The traditional ways of presenting museum and heritage assets no longer, therefore, hold their attention and provide them with an exciting and dynamic visitor experience. There is considerable interest in the use of augmented reality to allow visitors to explore worlds that are not immediately accessible to them and relating them to the real worlds around them. These are very effective in providing much needed contextual information, but appear rather static when compared with multi-player games environments where players interact with each other and robotic characters (non-player characters) in real time. By fusing these technologies, the authors postulate a new type of conceptually-led environment (cyber museum) that fuses real (physical), virtual worlds and cyber-social spaces into a single dynamic environment that provides a unique experience of exploring both worlds simultaneously.

DOI: 10.4018/978-1-5225-7879-6.ch007

INTRODUCTION

Custodians of historic, cultural and other important sites have had to develop new methods of engaging the current generation of visitors who are influenced by their exposure to modern technology such as social media and visual games. No longer is it sufficient to simply display artefacts in glass cabinets with typed tables or provide written guide books that describe the area visited. Visitors want a more dynamic experience that lets them feel that they are part of the key events that took place in the location, or which are associated with the objects that they are viewing.

One way to achieve this is to provide interpretation boards that describe the history and location. These are relatively easy to produce using modern printing technology and can be mounted in such a way as to withstand all but the worst excesses of the weather.

Early attempts were to provide audio guides, basically pre-recorded texts with suitable sound effects, pictures and videos which the visitor could play at specified locations as their visit progressed. Initially cassette tapes were used and later CDs or internal memory, which do not deteriorate in quality, and allow the stations to be visited in any order[1]. Whilst it is possible to provide customised tours for different types of visitor, these tours are essentially standard presentations with little automatic personalisation, based mainly on the order which visitors visit marked locations, and the sections of the pre-recorded material that the visitors decide to view. It is also common to provide different tours where appropriate, for children or other special groups. More recent developments are to use tablets and include more interactive navigation guidance to further enhance the information provided in the audio.

In recent years museums have developed new strategies to attract visitors and enhance their experience. This commenced when visitors started to expect similar facilities to those provided by the growing entertainment industry, including the reality TV, on-demand movies, the Internet and games. In order to avoid the negative financial and cultural implications of falling visitor numbers museums turned to these types of technology to attract visitors and retain them. One of the tools adopted by some museums is augmented reality, which re-creates a real-world environment where the sensory input is increased by the means of the computer (ARTutor, Lytridis. C and Tsinakos. A). It is different from virtual reality which is 'invented' reality. In augmented reality one sees what is really there, but the experience of seeing it is reinforced by adding additional personalised components to help better understand the places and displays that they are visiting (Young & Smith, 2016).

Similar techniques can be used to provide visitors to cultural spaces much more interactive and personalized experiences where they can interact with objects, characters and each other to better understand the meaning of the spaces that they are visiting. This may be to view them in a historical context, such as walking down a street in an archaeological site and seeing it as it was in its prime or taking part in a virtual procession by walking along its route as if one is part of the procession. This gives the visitor a much clearer impression of the importance of museum artefacts that due their fragility can only be displayed behind glass, in controlled environments. Similar systems are already in use to aid the understanding of future developments (Wang, Wang, Shou, & Xu, 2014).

This chapter discusses the development of cyber-social systems to provide a more engaging and information rich environment for visitors of all ages and interests to interact throughout their visit. It gives a brief outline of how information has been presented in the past and current developments, discusses the limitations of current methods in the context of three different scenarios:

1. A museum specifically built to display the artefacts used in a Spanish religious procession.
2. Providing information to visitors to a very popular beauty spot in the Peak District of Derbyshire which has a long and complicated geological and historical past that many visitors wish to explore to a greater or lesser degree.
3. Understanding the terrific forces and terror as Pompeii was overcome by the eruption of 79AD and understanding the context of the finds discovered.

These three scenarios are very different and demonstrate how cyber-physical and the more recently defined cyber-physical-social systems can be deployed to enhance the enjoyment of all visitors and the issues raised by them.

BACKGROUND

With the changing ways in which particularly young people interact with others and their environment, museums have turned to modern technologies to attract visitors and retain them. It is no longer sufficient to display a range of artefacts in glass cases and expect visitors to read complex descriptions to find out about them. They need to compete with the entertainment industry and stay modern. Some museums have therefore used augmented reality around storytelling. When one enters the museum, the experience becomes more pleasurable if there is a story around the artefacts. This allows the visitor to develop an emotional relationship with what they are viewing and better understand how each forms part of the story and how this has changed over the years. As the following Guardian article highlights, storytelling lies at the forefront of museum experience:

...storytelling is certainly not absent from museums. It's one of the most important factors behind the emergence of the so-called new museology doctrine, which brought storytelling to the forefront of the museum experience through audio guides, video and by placing more emphasis on thematic organization and different perspectives, such as varying cultural interpretations. (Ioannidis, Balet, & Pandermalis, 2014)

Using augmented reality to make the storytelling even more alluring is what seems to attract more visitors to the museums, and especially the young audiences, which are primordial in order to maintain the cultural heritage of different countries and arts. Thus, museums increasingly adopt so-called museology doctrine to make the experience of visiting a museum more personalized.

There are a number of national and international projects which promote augmented reality across the whole cultural sector. The EU project, Chess (which stands for Cultural Heritage Experiences through Socio-personal Interactions) wants to bring the experience of augmented reality to the entire museum world. The project aims to take visiting a museum to a totally new level by matching visitors with their own personalized museum experience in augmented reality. As the site of project explains:

it aims to integrate interdisciplinary research in personalization and adaptivity, digital storytelling, interaction methodologies, and narrative-oriented mobile and mixed reality technologies, with a sound theoretical basis in museological, cognitive, and learning sciences. (CHESS, 2016).

All new visitors will complete a visitor survey and depending on the result will be guided through the museum with the help of technological tools. The newly designed system is supposed to follow the space of the visitor. For instance, if the visitor lingers longer around an artefact, the system will adjust a story and might offer to go to another artefact than that initially programmed.

Smart Museum aims to create a future smart museum environment. It plans to develop a platform for innovative services enhancing on-site personalized access to digital cultural heritage through adaptive and privacy preserving user profiling (Smart Museum Consortium, n.d.).

The project's aim is to increase interaction between visitors and cultural heritage objects by "using on-site knowledge databases, global digital libraries and visitors' experiential knowledge" (Smart Museum Consortium, n.d.).

With the goal to create innovative multilingual services and by "taking full benefit of digitized cultural information" (Smart Museum Consortium, n.d.).

Similarly, the meSch project (Material Encounters with digital Cultural Heritage) also wants to increase the experience of visitors to cultural sites, but by connecting "the physical dimension of museums and exhibitions with relevant digital cross-media information in novel ways" (2018).

And as the site explains:

A wealth of digital cultural heritage is currently available in on-line repositories and digital archives. It is however accessed only in a limited way and utilized through rather static modes of delivery. meSch will bridge the gap between visitors' cultural heritage experience on-site and on-line by providing a platform for the creation of tangible smart exhibits. (meSch, 2018)

As a technology platform and interaction style, AR is still in its infancy. Many applications are mere proof-of-concept rather than robust solutions integrated into museums' existing programmes and interpretative strategies. But this does not diminish its potential for creating engaging and meaningful experiences for visitors. AR may have been over-hyped to begin with but we are now entering a more serious phase during which its usefulness will become evident. (Museum Ideas London, 2019).

It is possible to bring these technologies together to provide an engaging and interactive environment that brings the exhibits displayed in glass cabinets to preserve them in a much more informative and accessible way. Recently, there have been several attempts to interact with visitors of various types emotionally in order to modernise museums and overcome the old principles of traditional museology (Barbieri et al, 2018). This is more challenging as it is necessary to continuously interact with the users and adapt to their changing feelings.

The purpose of a museum is to help people who are not experts to understand information and context in regards to a topic that took place in history with the use of exhibits, artefacts and/or short multimedia interactions. The main aim is to present accurate complex information in engaging and entertaining ways, and the use of technology to enable these affordances has started to be implemented over the last few years, with mediums known as Virtual Museums (Jensen & Konradsen, 2018). Over the years, many scholars have provided a range of definitions to explain what a Virtual Museum is, and many of those had differences as to the status of information conveyed and the technology utilised (Shaw 1991; Schweibenz, 1998; Carlucci, 2002; Jones & Christal 2002; Petridis, et al. 2005; Styliani et al 2009; Jensen & Konradsen, 2018). Pujol & Lorente (2010: 46) have considered some of the available definitions and have proposed that the term Virtual Museum refers to *"digital spatial environment, located in the WWW or in the exhibition, which reconstructs a real place and/or acts as a knowledge of a metaphor, and in which visitors can communicate, explore and modify spaces and digital or digitalized objects"*. Virtual museums combine a mixture of traditional museum practices, a range of semiotics communication modes, trends and technologies (Lorente & Kanellos, 2010).

Among the wide range of technologies adopted to implement Virtual Museums, the use of Virtual Reality has been gaining a lot of attention and acceptance in the field of cultural heritage, conservation and restoration, education and digital storytelling (Carrozino & Bergamasco, 2010).

VR is a mature technology in our days and it has been increasingly been used due to its unique affordance of immersion and presence (Carrozino & Bergamasco, 2010; Jensen & Konradsen, 2017). Immersion relates to the experience of an immersive technology that exchanges sensory input from reality with digitally generated input, i.e. audio and graphics (Ott & Freina, 2015). Presence relates to the potential subsequent reaction to immersion, which leads to the users brain reacting to the virtual environment in the same way as if it would behave in the real world (Slater, 2003), and is defined as *"the subjective experience of being in one place or environment, even when one is physically situated in another"*(Witmer & Singer, 1998: 255). The ability of VR systems to provide an immersive first person experience to the user with a unique sense of presence in the virtual environment and the ability to experience situations that may be difficult or even impossible to experience in the real world are affordances that support motivations for technology adoption (Mikropoulos and Natsis, 2011).

METHODS USED

A powerful method of investigating how new and disruptive applications can be utilized effectively is to develop several scenarios to investigate potential applications and then analyse them for commonalities which would allow a general application to be developed. At this stage the practicalities of implementation are not considered as this is likely to lead to a development of an existing, rather than determining the hardware and software needed to meet the needs of the application and the exploration of novel solutions which may come from different, unfamiliar areas, or may not yet be available. It is important that the scenarios are developed either by, or with significant input from, the subject specialists, in this case museum and tourism staff, who know the objectives they wish to achieve. In this way a novel approach can be achieved, which is not simply a development of existing practice. The process is iterative so that ideas developed in one scenario are shared with the others. This approach was used, for example, by Tim Berners-Lee in his original semantic web article when much of the technology that was needed to implement his ideas was not yet available.

The three key issues that we want to explore are:

1. To what extent virtual reality could be used to demonstrate how the articles on display are or were used or the landscape had changed over time, so giving a clearer understanding of their context
2. Whether emotional engagement was possible and would enhance visitor experience, and
3. The role of robots in an augmented environment where the robots provide the link between the virtual and real worlds.

This chapter discusses the first round of developments of the proposed scenarios where proposals were made as to what a future visit might appear to the visitor. These were used to develop a small demonstrator – the virtual robot museum. This was considered as it did not require a large space and it allowed visitors to observe the robots 'in action', which would not be always possible because of safety concerns. Review of this and the scenarios will now be analysed to develop a refined scenario that can be used to test whether the objectives of the museum and tourism professionals can be met in practice and what technologies will need to be developed to meet their requirements.

INVESTIGATING SCENARIOS

The scenarios chosen to explore further were as follows:

- A Spanish religious procession and how the artefacts associated with it are used
- A popular beauty spot that has multiple levels of history for the visitor to explore
- Touring the Pompeii ruins and seeing what it would be like standing where you are during the eruption

The first scenario provides an opportunity to investigate how a coherent collection of artefacts can be brought to life by placing them in the ceremonial context in which they are used for visitors who are unable to witness the procession in person. The second scenario shows how the ways that cultural and heritage information are presented to visitors may change as visitor expectations and technology have developed together with the need to use new technologies to better explain the world around them in a more engaging way. The third scenario develops the theme by showing how the technology can be used to show what the scene that the visitor is looking at may has looked like at various times in the past and how it came to be in the state that it is in now.

Putting Museum Artefacts in Their Cultural Context

The city of Elche (near Alicante in southern Spain) has a long and varied cultural history. Having been occupied by the Moors it was recaptured by the Spanish who built the cathedral on the location of the Moorish mosque. This cathedral has been rebuilt several times. Elche is famous because of its mystery play, the Misterio de Elx, dating back to the Middle Ages. This is a sacred musical drama of the death, assumption and crowning of the Virgin. It has been performed since the 15th century in the Basilica of Saint Mary of Elche with special permission from the Pope. The play is living testimony to European religious theatre from the Middle Ages; as well as the medieval culture of devotion to the Virgin which was influenced by Byzantine rites. The mystery play, which is entirely sung, is presented in two acts played on 14 and 15 August. The text, conserved in collections dating from 1625, is written in the Valencian language, with several parts in Latin. Medieval songs alternate with songs from the Renaissance and Baroque periods. The stage is organized horizontally for the earth and vertically for heaven, a characteristic of medieval mysteries. The play, reflecting the cultural and linguistic identity of the people of Valencia, involves about 300 volunteers each year and attracts the entire population. A special museum called the Museum of Virgin of Assumption of Elche, are linked to the Misteri d'Elx (Masterpieces of the Oral and Intangible Heritage of Humanity) has been established next to the cathedral to house some of the historical and artistic artefacts associated with the play. It also includes a video and graphic display to introduce visitors to the play whenever they visit the city.

As will be seen the important locations are split with the visual depiction of the play in one place, the collection of the artefacts in the museum and the basilica each in their own spaces. The objective of Cyber Museum is to bring them all together so that the visitor will be able to appreciate them as a whole. So for example when looking at artefacts in the museum the visitor can see exactly what part they perform in the play and equally when standing in the basilica they can see how it would look when the play is being performed. Translations can be provided from the old Valencian language used in the play to the language of the visitor and there will be the capability to add comments and one's own pictures and to ask questions that can either be answered autonomously by a question-answering system or if they are too difficult they can be referred to an appropriate expert. One of the important aspects of preserving this type of cultural heritage is the maintenance of the skills. The Cyber Museum concept brings together the artefacts, their location and the skills necessary to preserve, maintain and replace them. The visitor (or pupil) will be able to review all the material available about objects and spaces so that the future of the mystery play is secured.

The Cyber Museum will also have an important part to play at the time of the performance of the play. It will allow visitors to view the important artefacts and learn about their function in the play and their relationships with each other. Visitors will be able to discuss the different parts of the play and share their own photographs etc. There will be a facility that will allow the posting of 'virtual post-it notes' that can be viewed by other visitors allowing one to leave comments and ask questions about the

Figure 1. Photographs of the procession and individual items as displayed in the museum [2]

Figure 2. The museum displays

play and the artefacts that form part of the performance. These notes link through to the real and virtual worlds and for example to the artefacts when viewing either the real play or the virtual rendition of it.

The system developed in the Cyber Museum will enrich a visitor experience by 'mapping' an object on display to the performance of the Misterio de Elx. This can be achieved in various ways, depending on the preferences of a visitor: from just a video demonstration on a screen to full immersion into the virtual reality recreating the actual scenes of the Elche play.

Mam Tor

The Cyber Museum can also be used effectively in many environments, not just strictly in museum situations. One of the examples of potential application of the Cyber Museum concept outside a 'strict' museum environment is to assist and inform visitors to a major countryside visitor attraction. Visitors have come to Mam Tor near Castleton in the Peak District of Derbyshire, UK for many years both to enjoy walks through spectacular scenery and to explore the complex history of the area. Figure 4 gives a general view of the area. Access is along the ridges that form the skyline and to the base of the landslip in the centre of the picture. This area has attracted visitors for many years because of the unspoilt countryside and the evidence of many layers of human activity. The scene has however changed considerably as the landslip is continuously moving, and indeed the main Sheffield-Manchester road, which climbed out of the valley under it has now completely disappeared and travellers must use other routes. There are the remains of an Iron Age hill fort on the summit, part of which has been lost by the land slip and there is evidence all-around of mining activity both for Blue John, which is semi-precious form of fluorite with

Figure 3. The statue of the Madonna, as displayed in the museum

bands of a purple-blue or yellowish colour and only found in England under Mam Tor. There is therefore a lot to explore beyond enjoying the open countryside.

Guidance has been given in many ways over the years, making use of the technology available at the times and the fashions and interests of the visitors. This allows one to follow the development of guides and visitor support.

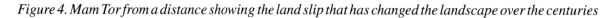

Figure 4. Mam Tor from a distance showing the land slip that has changed the landscape over the centuries

For example, Daniel Defoe, the author of Robinson Crusoe, in the early eighteenth century wrote the following to describe the area (the spelling etc. is as near as possible to the original):

The first of these is Mam Tor, or, as the word in the mountain jargon signifies, the Mother Rock, upon a suggestion that the soft crumbling earth, which falls from the summit of the one, breeds or begets several young mountains below. The sum of the whole wonder is this, That there is a very high hill, nay, I will add (that I may make the most of the story, and that it may appear as much like a wonder as I can) an exceeding high hill. But this in a country which is all over hills, cannot be much of a wonder, because also there are several higher hills in the Peak than that, only not just there.

The south side of this hill is a precipice, and very steep from the top to the bottom; and as the substance of this hill is not a solid stone, or rocky, as is the case of all the hills thereabouts, but a crumbling loose earth mingled with small stones, it is continually falling down in small quantities, as the force of hasty showers, or solid heavy rains, loosens and washes it off, or as frosts and thaws operate upon it in common with other parts of the earth; now as the great hill, which is thick, as well as high, parts with this loose stuff, without being sensibly example with the quantity that falls down; the space where it is received being small, comparatively to the height and thickness of the mountain: Here the pretended wonder is form'd, namely, that the little heap below, should grow up into a hill, and yet the great hill not be the less for all that is fallen down; which is not true in fact, any more than, as a great black cloud pouring down rain as it passes over our heads, appears still as great and as black as before, though it continues pouring down rain over all the country. But nothing is more certain than this, that the more water comes down from it, the less remains in it; and so it certainly is of Mama Tor, in spite of all the poetry of Mr. Cotton or Mr. Hobbes, and in spite of all the women's tales in the Peak.

This gives a basic description of the hill at a time when the only means of providing images was painting or drawing. There is little emotional engagement between the reader and the landscape being described, although the actual text gives a highly evocative description, which can be enjoyed whether one visits the area or not. Over the following more than two centuries many guides have been published, some very general and others that give detailed descriptions of specific characteristics. So, by the mid nineteenth century there were many examples of guidebooks that advised visitors not only of the sites but where to stay etc. (Jewitt, 1857), as well as guides to specific areas of interest such as archaeological sites and the geology of the area (Taylor, 1862). In the twentieth Century an increased emphasis on exploring the countryside and improving health and fitness has led to a wide range of walking guides, giving routes of different lengths and required levels of fitness (Richards, 2012; Ford, 1986). Attempts have been made to bring forward a combination of the traditional guidebook approach brought forward into modern technology by, for example, the National Trust's online walking guide (Peak District National Park, n.d.). This gives clear instructions for the walk by providing an audio commentary to be listened to at a series of markers but does little to help the visitor understand the history and geography of the wider area. The latest audio guides to other local sites are much more clearly focused on particular areas of interest and therefore provide a much more interesting and educational experience. The Cyber Museum approach is intended to enhance this experience by using feedback from the user to add to the experience by customising the information provided and tailoring the walk to the needs and interests of the visitor.

More detailed descriptions give a bigger problem as they need to be targeted at specific audiences. Figure 5 is a good example that attempts to explain the reasons for the landslip, it is highly technical and gives a good description of the geological situation and can be considered to attempt to explain the loss of a major road. In the small area available it cannot explain how the overall landscape has changed and its effect on the remains of the hill fort over time.

Figure 6 shows a totally different approach where the site of an old mine is marked, but no description of the remains is given. It does however attempt to explain the importance of mining in the area. These information boards are placed a few yards apart, but serve different purposes, and appeal to different audiences. The first is an explanation for the more technically minded who is likely to know a good deal about the background already, and the second is for the more general visitor who may not know much about the history of the area. The object is to cater for both types of visitor, so all can gain the most out of their visit.

Figure 7 is a general view of the remains of the hill fort as it is today. The scenario considered was a walk to the summit from this side, following the footpath that starts in the gap in the ridge on the left of the picture. The object is to allow the visitor to identify their interests, such as:

- A pleasant hill walk admiring the view;
- Exploring the history of the hill fort and the reason for it being in such an exposed location;
- The changes in the landscape as the landslip has developed over more than a thousand years;
- The effect of mining on the area since Roman times.

Figure 5. A display board which attempts to describe the land slip

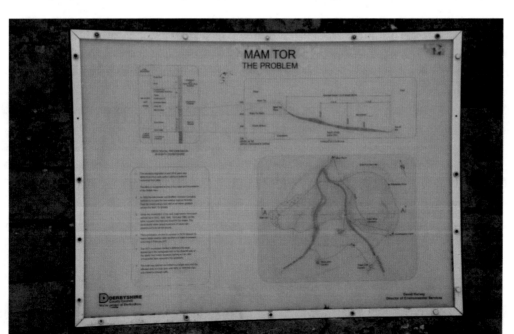

Figure 6. Another example of a display board that draws visitors' attention to the mining history of this particular site

They are also invited to enter their level of expertise and whether they wish to contact other visitors and see previous comments that have been left at each location on the walk.

Pompeii at the Time of the Eruption

A different approach can be taken with an area of extensive ruins, such as Pompeii (Figure 8). It is quite difficult for the casual visitor to envisage a bustling city with many citizens navigating streets filled with shops and public buildings, particularly as many of the key features were destroyed by the eruption.

It would be possible to represent the city as it was before the eruption and to fill the space with automated characters which would only be seen in the 3D environment. This would confuse the viewer as they would be other visitors wandering around, viewing the sites, who would not be represented. This would interfere with the "suspension of belief" that is essential for the graphical representation to be fully appreciated and the visitor to become emotionally engaged with what they know is about to happen. All the visitors can be tracked with motion sensors, which are essential for the system to follow everyone's movement anyway, and avatars can then represent them as citizens in the city going about their normal business. Additional automated characters can be added to represent characters performing special roles. These would need to be able to move around the scene missing the representations of real people. Special attention would also need to be taken of twenty first century activities that would have no place in a first century roman city, such as push chairs, wheelchairs, iPhones etc.

Figure 7. Another view of Mam Tor showing surviving evidence of the hill fort in the form of a ditch and how much has disappeared because of multiple land slips over the centuries, making it difficult to visualize its size and complexity when occupied

Figure 8. Ruins of Pompeii, Forum[3]

Figure 9. Garden of the Fugitives

POSSIBLE APPROACHES

Cyber-Physical-Social Systems

'Cyber Museum' is an example of Cyber-Physical-Social Systems (CPSS) which integrate the computational physical elements that interact with, reflect and influence each other with the systems and information exhibited by humans' social behaviour (Sheth, Anantharam, & Henson, 2013). The integration of cyber-physical systems and social networks as proposed in 'Cyber Museum' provides a novel platform with which to address the challenges in cyber-physical-social interactions and human-centric technology development through the use of powerful tools such as social computing, social cooperation, and social sensing, etc. The scenarios chosen to demonstrate the power of CPSS systems are just a small fraction of their potential and have been chosen to illustrate this potential in a controlled and readily observed environment. Further examples of employing mobile computing in CPSS include command and control (Liu et al., 2011), search and rescue (Ghosh et al., 2014), disaster relief (Gao et al., 2011), friend recognition (Yu et al., 2011), transport (Lau, Tham, & Luo, 2011) etc. Museums and cultural heritage sites are typical examples, which have embraced mobile and interactive devices for visitor information and learning (Ardito et al., 2009), they have been less able to harness the power of social networks to enhance the visitor experience. There are many areas where this can be done with advantage: related items are often spread over a number of often disparate sites, which can be linked through a virtual world, individual items may have to be removed from their original position for conservation and security reasons, or the physical requirements of display may hinder the understanding of the items. Interaction with other visitors can also help understanding, both interactively in real time, and by the comments provided, in a similar way to recommendations on sales and travel sites. Continuous monitoring of visitor flows can be used to manage traffic and encourage visitors to spread their activities in such a way that they are better able to enjoy the most popular exhibits. 'Cyber Museum' provides the interface between the visitor, the real and the virtual worlds. Several robots and their virtual avatars work as a swarm to assist the visitors to obtain the best from their visit.

The introduction of social elements into CPS systems brings new system design challenges and open research issues. The safety and reliability requirements of the physical components are qualitatively different from general-purpose distributed computing infrastructures and currently lack effective consistent and unified system modelling and design principles. Resources in data centres and cloud infrastructures have to be efficiently managed and scheduled to optimize reliability and scalability of CPSS under a range of new constraints. Also, CPSS are expected to deal safely and securely with data transmitted directly from trans-domain applications, which could be in a variety of forms such as local or universal location coordinates, environmental information, robot speed and direction, information requests, etc. Another important challenge is to coordinate the various applications of heterogeneous systems and facilitate a deeper integration, interaction and personalization of the physical, cyber, and social domains.

The evolution from cyber space to cyber-physical-socio space is shown in Figure 10. Figure 10(a) illustrates two types of the cyber space in that it allows users to:

- Read information in the cyber space like the Web, and
- Read and write information in the cyber space as with Web 2.0.

Both rely on humans to add information so that it can be shared with others.

Figure 10(b) extends cyber space to physical space using appropriate sensors. This allows information in physical space to be automatically 'sensed', stored and transmitted through cyber space. The 'Cyber Museum' robot provides this sensor capability in that it can sense its local environment and transmit this information to remote real and virtual worlds.

Figure 10(c) provides an important extension of (b):

- It allows user behaviours to be sensed and fed back to the cyber space for analysis of behaviour patterns, and
- Humans can remotely control the actuators (in other words, the robots) to behave in the physical space through the cyber space. (or vice versa)

Cyber space can then adapt services according to the feedback provided from the human participants since behaviour change may indicate some psychological change. For example, this enables a museum system to capture visitor behaviours during their visit so that their itinerary can be adapted in real time according to their reactions. So, if they appear bored, they can be guided to other areas which they are likely to find more interesting, based on their developing profile, or if they are showing particular interest in a particular topic they can be provided with more detailed information.

The final sketch in Figure 10 shows a simple cyber-physical-social space. In addition to each individual's behaviours being communicated back into cyber space, their social interactions are fed back as well. This means that the user's social characteristics and relations can be used to develop their individual profile, rather than just information about their activities based on sensor data. Sensors are limited in their ability to collect complete information about the physical space they are monitoring, so users will need to directly collect the significant information (for them) place it in the cyber space. Users can also change physical objects in the physical space, which can also be fed back into the cyber space to reflect the current situation. Users' status, interests and knowledge evolve as they interact socially and move about in the cyber space.

Figure 10. Cyber-physical-socio space
(Zhuge, 2011)

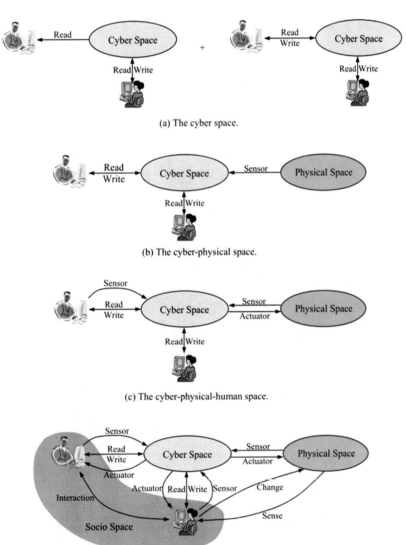

(a) The cyber space.

(b) The cyber-physical space.

(c) The cyber-physical-human space.

Virtual Storytelling

The 'Cyber Museum' offers an opportunity to critically explore the relationship of curatorial decisions to the formation of historical narrative. The informed, but subjective, editing and selection of contextual references to artefacts, testimony and exhibitions can have a profound impact on the reading of the theses being advanced. While responsible curatorial approaches can offer an authoritative narrative, the limitations of location, collections, audience attention and contextual specificity necessitates that any articulated narrative has to exist as a partial representation of the pluralism of experience, rather than a comprehensive vision. While 'Cyber Museum' cannot offer a solution to the impossibility of infinite pluralism within historical representations, it does offer a critical framework to enable considered reflection on the manner in which narratives are formed and a heightened awareness of the potential validity of parallel alternate truths and analysis. The interweaving of multiple real and virtual worlds with the auto reactive interpretations of professional staff and those of other visitors creates a new way of discovering validity within the chosen domain.

Robots as Guides and Curators

Robots are usually associated in popular press with either impressive Hollywood humanoid characters or with machines who are capable to do repetitive tasks. In reality, however, the recent research in the domain of robotics has allowed for robots to become complex creations used in complicated contexts, where robots help to understand humans themselves or assist humans to engage in cultural environments in new and exciting ways. In this respect, robots are used more and more in interaction with people, where humans and robots 'literally' learn from each other. For instance, at the Robotville Festival (Shute, 2011) several projects showed examples of this interaction. One robot (IURO project) can learn information by talking with humans, while another project (Concept) studies how people react to the face of a robot. In response, the robot also learns from the reaction of humans.

In other situations robots are assisting people in real life, where they become guides of humans, and help them with such tasks as crossing the road, finding their destination, shopping and cleaning. One such robot, named 'I', is being tested in Japan at the train stations, where it can help customers by showing information on his chest and can even contact customer services for assistance (Melanson, 2006).

Robots are also increasingly used in cultural environments, such as at museums and exhibitions, where the interaction between humans and robots adds a totally new dimension to the experience of engaging with culture and society around us. In Tokyo Science Museum robot guides who look very much like humans show visitors around the museum (Demetriou, 2014), while in 2014 in London the robot called 'Linda' greeted visitors when they first arrived to the Natural History Museum in London (Szondy, 2014). This experience is also now possible to be done from the comfort of one's own home, where thanks to new technologies one can visit a museum remotely. For instance, in 2014 the public was able to use the After Dark web application in order to visit the Tate museum in London from their homes (Tate, 2014).

The implications of being able to attend the museums remotely with the help of the robots are huge. Not only will they enable to enjoy a totally new 'virtual' experience of being immersed in a cultural context, but they will also help to allow access to exhibits to all those who, otherwise, are unable to do so, due, for instance, to a disability. There are already some examples of robots who help people in unfortunate circumstances to enjoy the world of art. Thus, telepresence robots (Kelvey, 2014) help people who can't leave their homes or hospital beds to see museums around the world, showing how the collaboration between new technology and science can become a wonderful thing.

There has been interest in the development of robot guides for over twenty years. Some of the first guide robots were Rhino, developed by Burgard et al. (1999), its successor Minerva developed by Thrun et al. (1999), and the robots used in the Mobot Museum experiment by Nourbakhsh et al.(2003). The key feature of these robots was the development of autonomous navigation and collision avoidance systems.

As the concept of a robotic guide has developed more emphasis has been placed on human-robot interaction. For example, RoboX used a series of 11 robots that were developed by Jensen et al. (2005), to guide visitors at the Swiss National Exhibition Expo.02. These robots used dynamic scenarios to manage visitor flow. Two robots in the science museum in Osaka, developed by Shiomi et al. (2006), engaged in personalized interaction with visitors. The Robovie tour guide developed by Yamazaki et al. (2008) adopted typically human interaction cues to focus the attention of the visitors. These robots were equipped with guiding behaviours to guide visitors to several exhibits and present information about exhibits. In other words, the robots provided routing help and provide canned information. They were not helping in developing the overall story of the visit. Nourbakhsh et al. also note that the robot's awareness of the people close by is an important way to attract their attention. Clodic et al. (2006) report that in order to keep the interest of the visitors, the robot Rackham continuously gave feedback to them so that they understood that it knew where they were, what it did, where it went and what its intentions were. All these robot guides of course worked in a single physical space with their visitors and could interact in a number of different ways. Within 'Cyber Museum' we have both real and virtual robots that need to interact effectively whether they are local or remote. This will primarily be done either by speech or by either means of communication such as graphical signs or messages.

The system may consist of a team of mobile and stationary networking robots positioned in a museum. Mobile robots will act as physical curators that will guide a visitor in the museum physical space. They should be capable to navigate safely to the locations of interest.

Via the 'Cyberguides' network each guide can access information required by a visitor. The information can be communicated by using various modalities: by projecting on the screen, by speech or by text. Stationary robots will be positioned by the prominent artefacts and will provide information in depth related to the artefact in question.

The potentialities offered by the use of Robotic Systems for Cultural Heritage are extremely appealing and represent a challenge for scientists and entrepreneurs who want to experiment new ideas and new products; however, only in a few cases the enormous potentialities offered by the Robotic Systems were exploited, particularly for Museums.

The robotic agents thus will play role as a physical link between real and virtual worlds in that while they are physically located in the real world, their avatars will act as virtual guides in virtual spaces.

Physical robots together with their avatars and other virtual and physical objects of interest form an innovative integrated multi-agent system.

In order to achieve communication with visitors as well as ensure integration links between real and virtual worlds, we propose a modular User-Interface System. The system will consist of several modules that can be used separately depending on the user requirements.

The resulting networking system will represent a new multi-genre networking system.

Why robots?

Robots will be able to access large databases in a short amount of time

Robots will form a network consisting of mobile and static robots, and robot-avatars in virtual realities (potentially involving human curators), that will allow for a visitor 'travel' through museum collections and heritage sites, and related events in time and space.

They can provide remote access to restricted areas in the museums where visitor are not allowed, for example to elevated spaces or areas where it would be too dangerous to allow visitors access. They can act as drone-guides for people that are unable to leave their homes, or for visitors to view items that they could not otherwise see because of accessibility issues.

The previous point can be enhanced further. Ideally, the robot networks in one site will be connected to the network in other sites, and a visitor in one site can be connected to the physical robot in the other site and be guided by that robot through that site.

In a large and important city like Pompeii there would be a large amount of ceremonial and civic activity. This would involve individuals, such as giving speeches and groups, such as military marches etc.

It is often difficult to engage visitors emotionally with, for example, hustings for an election, and CGI type simulations are too unresponsive to allow this. One way to overcome this is for robots to play the part of the candidates and give the speeches and potentially argue with each other and respond to the audience of visitors. The characters present, both robot and human are replicated in the virtual world in Roman dress, bringing the scene to life. Since the human characters will behave differently for each enactment, the visitors' attention should be enhanced.

ROBOTICS MUSEUM

One of the ways to develop immersive experiences that are difficult to reproduce in the real world is with the use of 3D virtual worlds. These are computer simulated graphical environments in which users are represented as Avatars and can coexist, communicate with the environment and each other, in the same shared space at the same time. The Avatar is the visual representation of the user and the viewpoint of the environment, enables navigation, and acts as a mean of social interaction (Bell, 2002; Dickey, 2005). In virtual worlds anything is possible (Warburton & Garcia, 2016) and such environments allows developing and experiencing situations that can be difficult, expensive, hazardous, or even impossible to experience in the real world (Dieterle & Clarke, 2016). Over the past few years, virtual worlds have been utilised for many purposes including marketing, e-commerce, training, teaching and learning, events, meetings, as well as exhibitions (Minocha & Hardy, 2016). With the technological advancement of software and hardware over the past few years, the desktop virtual worlds can now be experienced in Virtual Reality (VR) modes for a more immersive and interactive user experience, using Head Mounted Displays (HMD) such as Oculus Rift Oculus Rift[4], HTC Vive[5], or even through smart phones using Google VR[6] using Google Daydream[7] or Cardboard[8].

At SHU we have developed a virtual world named 'VirtualSHU' (See Figure 11) to support students in their learning. This environment is successfully used for teaching an undergraduate computing module (Introduction to ICT), to support students final year projects, hold exhibitions, conduct empirical research and for other educational purposes. 'VirtualSHU' has been developed using the Opensimulator Multi User Virtual Environment platform. This is an open source platform that allows deploying virtual worlds for multiple users to connect and co-exist in the same virtual setting at the same time, allowing them to interact with each other and the environment. VirtualShu is designed a way that represents a common didactical setting with recognizable facilities to help users understand and orientate in the environment.

The layout of VirtualShu features many buildings and areas for teachers and students to utilize for a wide range of educational activities and relevant purposes. A central campus building is provided featuring a series of areas and classrooms equipped with different functionality each.

An orientation area where students can learn the basic functionalities and navigation features of the environment is provided, as well as a courtyard for students to meet, and a number of classrooms and collaborative areas dedicated to different topics each. Each classroom was designed to provide access to PowerPoint slides, website loaders, YouTube videos and information boards. In addition, sandbox areas where the environment building and flying restrictions are lifted and a quiet area for students who are away from keyboard but still logged in the environment are also provided. The VirtualSHU also features the Robotics museum, which is located on the upper floor of the main building (see Figure 12). The museum provides information around the history or robotics, general information about the research conducted by the Sheffield Robotics group and the Robotics department at Sheffield Hallam University, as well as featuring many artefacts and robot models that students developed.

Users can connect to the environment using specific software (the Firestorm[9] and CtrlAltStudio[10] Viewers) that have to be installed on their computers and to configure it accordingly by using a few simple steps. An account creation is necessary for each user to connect and interact with the environment. Each account is attached to an Avatar, which is the user's virtual embodiment and viewpoint of the virtual world. Using their Avatars, users can interact with the environment and communicate with other users. Communication can be established through text and audio channels. Text channels include 'the nearby chat', Instant Message (IM) and Group Messages. The nearby chat allows avatars within close proximity to exchange messages that everyone within that proximity can read and reply. IM's and Group Messages are private messages that only the participating avatars can read and reply. Users can also interact using voice over IP, and broadcasted audio is audible within close proximity.

Figure 11. VirtualSHU

Figure 12. The Robotics Museum in VirtualSHU

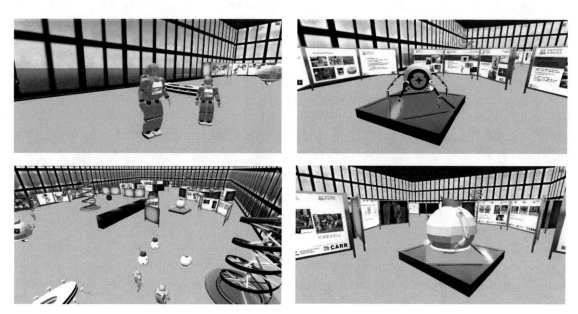

The environment can be experienced in two modes; virtual reality (using CtrlAltStudio Viewer, see Fig 13) and desktop mode (see Figure 14). In virtual reality mode, users are using the Oculus Rift head mounted display and a joystick to navigate in the environment. When in desktop mode, users are using their keyboard and mouse to navigate and interact, and their computer monitor to experience the visual aspect of the environment.

Below in the series of snapshots, a potential interaction in the virtual Robotics Museum between two avatars is illustrated. Bear in mind that the people behind the avatars can be in different locations around the world.

Future work is focusing on the deployment of a dedicated environment to host the Robotics Museum. Furthermore, we aim to keep developing the museum with the help of students and scholars, and make it accessible from several platforms that will include computers, smartphones and VR hardware.

FUTURE RESEARCH DIRECTIONS

For the proposals in this chapter to become a reality a number of technologies need to be developed and enhanced. Whilst there have been experiments linking activities in the real world with those in a virtual world, they are mainly in the games environment. Very little has been done where the very close linkage proposed here, particularly where groups of robots, acting in a swarm, have to act in a swarm with the real people and represent both in the virtual world. It is also necessary to investigate the devices that are suitable for visitors to use when engaging with the virtual and real worlds. It is clear that the current generation of VR headsets are unsuitable as they transport the viewer to the virtual world but block out the real world around them. The use of tablets or the visitors' own mobile phones needs to be investigated. The use of virtual storytelling may provide the necessary link to engage the visitor emotionally in the exhibits.

Figure 13. Robotics Museum in VirtualSHU, view from the Oculus Rift Virtual Reality headset

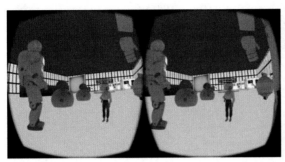

Figure 14. Robotics Museum in VirtualSHU, view from the Firestorm Viewer: examples of users interacting in the VirtualSHU

Currently, such a system would be extremely expensive to set up as it would require considerable effort by a wide range of museum or tourism specialists, computing professionals, video artists etc. The resulting system would be specific for the application in hand and would be very difficult to update or replicate. A framework needs to develop that allows subject specialists to develop applications faster and more cheaply so suitable visitor interpretations can be provided at many applications in a timely manner.

CONCLUSION

The use of augmented reality to help explain complex historical sites is becoming much more common. It is even being used by general broadcasters, such as the BBC in programs on the history of ancient cities such as Constantinople11. Not only does this programme use the technique very effectively to take the viewer to areas, such as the dome of Santa Sophia, which would otherwise be inaccessible but mixes areal fly through with actual aerial film to illustrate the theme of the story. This is of course extremely expensive to produce, is intended for the viewer to view remotely and requires extensive use of presenters to replace the feeling of actually being there. It is likely that the programme will only be viewed once as there is little or no emotional engagement with between the viewer and the objects being viewed.

Previous work has shown that much greater engagement has been achieved by providing extensive facilities for groups with similar interests to interact online within virtual spaces (Beer et al., 2001, Nisiotis et al., 2017, Jalil, Beer & Crowther, 2016). These experiments clearly demonstrated the increased levels of emotional engagement engendered by social interaction within cyber space. This was used to assist learners navigate teaching material and to connect with others who were working on the same topics. This led to the formation of dynamic tutorial groups who would work together for a topic, and then reform as needed for future learning activities. The object of this chapter is to develop a similar environment which links objects, virtual worlds and visitors so that they can gain the maximum benefit from their visit. This linkage means that every visit will be a different experience which will encourage visitors to return and contribute their own thoughts. Since museum and other cultural visits are essentially ad hoc, with visitors deciding their own activities, there is much less opportunity to manage the user experience than in an online learning environment. This chapter has shown how social interaction within an augmented reality environment can be developed to provide a dynamic and engaging visit.

ACKNOWLEDGMENT

The authors would like to thank their colleagues, in particular, Professor David Cotterrell, for useful comments. We are also very grateful to the members of the 'Interwoven Spaces' proposal team, discussions with whom inspired the current article.

REFERENCES

Ardito, C., Buono, P., Costabile, M. F., Lanzilotti, R., & Piccinno, A. (2009). Enabling interactive exploration of cultural heritage: An experience of designing systems for mobile devices. *Knowledge, Technology & Policy*, *22*(1), 79–86. doi:10.100712130-009-9079-7

Barbieri, L., Bruno, F., & Muzzupappa, M. (2018). User-centered design of a virtual reality exhibit for archaeological museums. *International Journal on Interactive Design and Manufacturing*, *12*(2), 561–571. doi:10.100712008-017-0414-z

Beer, M., Armitt, G., Van Bruggen, J., Daniels, R., Ghyselen, L., Green, S., ... Sixsmith, A. (2001). Running a European Internet school - OTIS at work. In *Advanced Learning Technologies, 2001. Proceedings. IEEE International Conference on.* IEEE.

Bell, M. (2008). Toward a Definition of "Virtual Worlds". *Journal of Virtual Worlds Research*, *1*(1). doi:10.4101/jvwr.v1i1.283

Burgard, W., Cremers, A. B., Fox, D., Hähnel, D., Lakemeyer, G., Schulz, D., ... Thrun, S. (1999). Experiences with an interactive museum tour-guide robot. *Artificial Intelligence*, *114*(1), 3–55. doi:10.1016/S0004-3702(99)00070-3

Carlucci, R. (Ed.). (2002). *Archeoguide: Augmented reality-based cultural heritage on-site guide.* Lemmer.

Carrozino, M., & Bergamasco, M. (2010). Beyond virtual museums: Experiencing immersive virtual reality in real museums. *Journal of Cultural Heritage*, *11*(4), 452–458. doi:10.1016/j.culher.2010.04.001

CHESS. (2016). *Cultural Heritage Experiences Through Socio-Personal Interactions and Storytelling.* Retrieved from http://www.chessexperience.eu/

Clodic, A., Fleury, S., Alami, R., Chatila, R., Bailly, G., Brèthes, L., ... Montreuil, V. (2006). Rackham: an interactive robot-guide. *2006 IEEE ROMAN*, 502–509. doi:10.1109/ROMAN.2006.314378

Demetriou, D. (2014). *Humanoid Robots Join Staff at Tokyo Science Museum.* Retrieved from http://www.telegraph.co.uk/news/worldnews/asia/japan/10924594/Humanoid-robots-join-staff-at-Tokyo-science-museum.html

Dickey, M. D. (2005). Three-dimensional virtual worlds and distance learning: Two case studies of Active Worlds as a medium for distance education. *British Journal of Educational Technology*, *36*(3), 439–451. doi:10.1111/j.1467-8535.2005.00477.x

Dieterle, E., & Clarke, J. (2007). Multi-User Virtual Environments for Teaching and Learning. *Encyclopedia of multimedia technology and networking*, 2, 1033-44.

Ford, T. D. (1986). Geological excursion guide 3: The Peak District. *Geology Today*, *2*(4), 112–116. doi:10.1111/j.1365-2451.1986.tb01045.x

Gao, H. (2011). Harnessing the crowdsourcing power of social media for disaster relief. *IEEE Intelligent Systems*, *26*(3).

Ghosh, A., Alboul, L., Penders, J., Jones, P., & Reed, H. (2014). Following a Robot using a Haptic Interface without Visual Feedback. *Seventh International Conference on Advances in Computer-Human Interactions, ACHI 2014*.

Ioannidis, Y., Balet, O., & Pandermalis, D. (2014). *Tell Me a Story: Augmented Reality Technology in Museums*. Retrieved from https://www.theguardian.com/culture-professionals-network/culture-professionals-blog/2014/apr/04/story-augmented-reality-technology-museums

Jalil, A., Beer, M., & Crowther, P. (2016). Improving design and functionalities of MOBIlearn2 application: A case study of mobile learning in metalwork collection of Millennium Gallery. In *Proceedings IEEE Eighth International Conference on Technology for Education*. IEEE. 10.1109/T4E.2016.013

Jensen, B., Tomatis, N., Mayor, L., Drygajlo, A., & Siegwart, R. (2005). Robots meet Humans interaction in public spaces. *IEEE Transactions on Industrial Electronics*, *52*(6), 1530–1546. doi:10.1109/TIE.2005.858730

Jensen, L., & Konradsen, F. (2018). A review of the use of virtual reality head-mounted displays in education and training. *Education and Information Technologies*, *23*(4), 1515–1529. doi:10.100710639-017-9676-0

Jewitt, L. (Ed.). (1857). *Black's Tourist's Guide to Derbyshire* (2nd ed.). Edinburgh, UK: Adam and Charles Black.

Jones, G. & Christal, M. (2002). The future of virtual museums: On-line, immersive 3-D environments. *Created Realities Group, 2002*(9), 1-12.

Kelvey, J. (2014). *A Quick Reminder That Technology Can Be Wonderful*. Retrieved from http://www.slate.com/articles/technology/future_tense/2014/07/telepresence_robots_make_museums_accessible_to_everyone.html

Lau, Tham, & Luo. (2011). Participatory cyber physical system in public transport application. In *Utility and Cloud Computing (UCC), 2011 Fourth IEEE International Conference on*. IEEE.

Liu, Z., Yang, D., Wen, D., Zhang, W., & Mao, W. (2011). Cyber-physical-social systems for command and control. *IEEE Intelligent Systems*, *26*(4), 92–96. doi:10.1109/MIS.2011.69

Lorente, G. A., & Kanellos, I. (2010). What do we know about on-line museums? A study about current situation of virtual art museums. In *International Conference in Transforming Culture in the Digital Age* (pp. 208-219). Academic Press.

Melanson, D. (2006). *I Robot Coming to a Train Station Near You*. Retrieved from http://www.engadget.com/2006/08/29/i-robot-coming-to-a-train-station-near-you

meSch. (2018). *Project Goal*. Retrieved form http://www.mesch-project.eu/About/

Mikropoulos, T. A., & Natsis, A. (2011). Educational virtual environments: A ten-year review of empirical research (1999–2009). *Computers & Education*, *56*(3), 769–780. doi:10.1016/j.compedu.2010.10.020

Minocha, S., Hardy, C. (2016). Navigation and Wayfinding in Learning Spaces in 3d Virtual Worlds. *Learning in Virtual Worlds: Research and Applications.*

Museum, S. (n.d.). *Deliverable D4.1 SMARTMUSEUM Report of Architecture of Web Services.* Retrieved from http://www.smartmuseum.eu/del/D4.1_FINAL_v1.03.pdf

Museum Ideas London. (2019). *Museum.* Retrieved from https://museum-id.com/augmented-reality-museums-beyond-hype-shelley-mannion/

Nisiotis, L., Loizou, K., & Styliani, B. (2017). The use of a Cyber Campus to Support Teaching and Collaboration: An Observation Approach. In Immersive Learning Research Network (iLRN) Conference, Coimbra, Portugal.

Nourbakhsh, I. R., Kunz, C., & Willeke, T. (2003). The mobot museum robot installations: a five year experiment. *2003 IEEE/RJS International Conference on Intelligent Robots and Systems*, 3636–3641. 10.1109/IROS.2003.1249720

Ott, M., & Freina, L. (2015). *A literature review on immersive virtual reality in education: state of the art and perspectives.* Paper presented at the conference proceedings of eLearning and software for education (eLSE).

Peak District National Park. (n.d.). *Audio Trails.* Retrieved from https://www.peakdistrict.gov.uk/visiting/trails/audio-trails

Pennington, R. (1877). *Notes on the Barrows and Bone-caves of Derbyshire: With an Account of a Descent Into Elden Hole.* Macmillan and Company.

Pennington, R. (1877). *Notes on the Barrows and Bone-caves of Derbyshire: With an Account of a Descent Into Elden Hole.* Macmillan and Company.

Petridis, P., White, M., Mourkousis, N., Liarokapis, F., Sifniotis, M., Basu, A., & Gatzidis, C. (2005). Exploring and interacting with virtual museums. *Proceedings of the 33rd Annual Conference of Computer Applications and Quantitative Methods in Archaeology (CAA).*

Pujol, L., & Lorente, A. (2012). The Virtual Museum: a Quest for the Standard Definition. *Archaeology in the Digital Era, 40.*

Richards, M. (2012). *White Peak Walks: The Northern Dales: 35 walks in the Derbyshire White Peak.* Cicerone Press Limited.

Schweibenz, W. (1998). The "Virtual Museum": New Perspectives for Museums to Present Objects and Information Using the Internet as a Knowledge Base and Communication System. Proceedings des 6° Internationalen Symposiums für Informationswissenschaft ISI, 185-200.

Shaw, J. (1991). *The Virtual Museum. Installation at Ars Electrónica.* Linz, Austria: ZKM, Karlsruhe.

Sheth, A., Anantharam, P., & Henson, C. (2013). Physical-cyber-social computing: An early 21st century approach. *IEEE Intelligent Systems, 28*(1), 78–82. doi:10.1109/MIS.2013.20

Shiomi, M., Kanda, T., Ishiguro, H., & Hagita, N. (2006). Interactive humanoid robots for a science museum. *Proceedings of the 1st ACM SIGCHI/SIGART conference on Human-robot interaction*, 305–312.10.1145/1121241.1121293

ShuteS. (2011). *Robotville in Pictures*. Retrieved from https://blog.sciencemuseum.org.uk/robotville-in-pictures/

Slater, M. (2003). A note on presence terminology. *Presence Connect, 3*(3), 1–5.

Styliani, S., Fotis, L., Kostas, K., & Petros, P. (2009). Virtual museums, a survey and some issues for consideration. *Journal of Cultural Heritage, 10*(4), 520–528. doi:10.1016/j.culher.2009.03.003

Szondy, D. (2014). *Robot to Meet the Public at London's Natural History Museum*. Retrieved from https://newatlas.com/linda-robot-self-learning-museum/32267/

Tate. (2014). *IK Prize 2014: After Dark*. Retrieved from http://www.tate.org.uk/whats-on/tate-britain/special-event/after-dark

Taylor, J. (1862). Geology of Castleton, Derbyshire. In The Geologist. Cambridge University. doi:10.1017/S135946560000321X

Thrun, S., Bennewitz, M., Burgard, W., Cremers, A. B., Dellaert, F., Fox, D., ... Schulz, D. (1999). MINERVA: a second-generation museum tour-guide robot. *Proceedings of the 1999 IEEE International Conference on Robotics and Automation, 3*, 1999–2005.

Wang, J., Wang, X., Shou, W., & Xu, B. (2014). Integrating BIM and augmented reality for interactive architectural visualisation. *Construction Innovation, 14*(4), 453–476. doi:10.1108/CI-03-2014-0019

Warburton, S., & García, M.P. (2016). Analyzing Teaching Practices in Second Life. *Learning in Virtual Worlds: Research and Applications*.

Witmer, B. G., & Singer, M. J. (1998). Measuring presence in virtual environments: A presence questionnaire. *Presence (Cambridge, Mass.), 7*(3), 225–240. doi:10.1162/105474698565686

Yamazaki, A., Yamazaki, K., Kuno, Y., Burdelski, M., Kawashima, M., & Kuzuoka, H. (2008). Precision timing in human-robot interaction: coordination of head movement and utterance. *Proceedings of the SIGCHI Conference on Human Factors in Computing Systems*, 131–139. 10.1145/1357054.1357077

Young, T. C., & Smith, S. (2016). An Interactive Augmented Reality Furniture Customization System. In S. Lackey & R. Shumaker (Eds.), *VAMR 2016: Virtual, Augmented and Mixed Reality. LNCS* (Vol. 9740, pp. 662–668). Springer. doi:10.1007/978-3-319-39907-2_63

Yu, X. (2011). Geo-friends recommendation in GPS-based Cyber-Physical Social network. In *Advances in Social Networks Analysis and Mining (ASONAM), 2011 International Conference on*. IEEE.

Zhuge, H. (2011). Semantic linking through spaces for cyber-physical-socio intelligence: A methodology. *Artificial Intelligence, 175*(5-6), 988–1019. doi:10.1016/j.artint.2010.09.009

ENDNOTES

[1]   A useful collection of audio tours can be downloaded from http://www.peakdistrict.gov.uk/visiting/trails/audio-trails, which shows how such services have developed over time.

[2]   Courtesy of MUVAPE, Museum of the virgin of the Assumption, Patron Saint of Elche

[3]   Images of Pompeii (Figure 8 and 9)- Courtesy of Mr Tiberio Gracco, http://www.pompeionline.net/

[4]   Oculus Rift: http://www.oculus.com

[5]   HTC Vive: https://www.vive.com

[6]   GoogleVR: https://vr.google.com/

[7]   Google Daydream: https://vr.google.com/daydream/

[8]   Google Cardboard: https://vr.google.com/cardboard/

[9]   Firestorm Viewer: http://www.firestormviewer.org

[10]   CtrlAltStudio Viewer: http://ctrlaltstudio.com/

[11]   https://www.bbc.co.uk/programmes/b0bkz22l

Chapter 8
Digitization and Preservation of Digital Resources and Their Accessibility for Blind People

Galina T. Bogdanova
Bulgarian Academy of Sciences, Bulgaria

Nikolay Genchev Noev
Bulgarian Academy of Sciences, Bulgaria

ABSTRACT

This chapter explores digital technologies and their use in social applications for blind people. The digitization, creation, and indexing of digital resources aimed at using these resources for the needs of visually impaired people are presented. Standards for digitization, metadata, digital media storage, and media resources are presented. Internet technologies, semantic networks, and ontologies are of particular importance and can be used for blind learners. 3D technologies and 3D models are particularly suitable tools and give new opportunities for blind people. Website standards and website accessibility standards, as well as accessibility technologies for people with disabilities, are a means and a way of socializing. Both digital resources and robots are considered inaccessible to people with visual limitations. They are widespread on a global scale, but their use is rather limited in people with disabilities and in their special education. Particular attention is paid to the interdisciplinary use of digital technologies and social robots as training tools.

INTRODUCTION

The creation of new digital objects in the present time of a dynamically evolving digital society does not seem to be a difficult task. Using modern, generally available technologies, object capture is perceived as a child's play. But it misses the fact that besides color image digital object brings information about the process of its creation; about the person who digitizes the object; about file characteristics; about the reason is designed for; about the nature of the object and many other important information hidden under color image. Often an object is shot with multiple images and multimedia recordings, which themselves

DOI: 10.4018/978-1-5225-7879-6.ch008

are multiple digital recordings of the same subject, but systematized and unified with single knowledge are transformed into a digital copy of an object with multiple digital recordings.

Digitizing and storing digital resources and knowledge, as well as accessibility and use for visually impaired people are an interesting issue.

DIGITALIZATION AND CREATING OF DIGITAL RESOURCE

Digitalize

Digital objects are "digital images" of different type of objects or content (text content, images, photos, documents, audio or video recordings and etc.). Digital objects can be made by two main approaches: creating a new digital content or digitalizing of real object or signal into digital one. Different type of content required a different equipment and methodology. For example, text content may enter by operator or may be scanned. It depends by the purpose of creation of the resource, whether it is a priority the content of the document or its authentic layout. Before digitization should be analyzed specifics of the objects and seeking goals of creation of digital resources:

- **A digital resource is created to spread or to preserve:** By this depends the quality of the resulting recordings.
- **The digital resource will be used for further analysis:** By that depends a requirement of the content.
- **Is the subject endangered of harm:** By that depends the choice of technology of digitizing – contact or contactless, in a secure environment.
- **And so long.**

The preparations for the digitization of objects from the cultural and historical area include the following processes:

- Planning of working procedures.
- Selection of objects for digitization.
- Review of intellectual property rights.
- Choosing hardware and software.
- Selection of digital formats and standards.
- Digital processing of surrogates obtained.
- Indexing of digital resources.
- Adhering to standards and accessibility criteria for people with disabilities if they are acceptable.
- Design of storage space.

The Standards for Digitization, Metadata, Digital Media Storage and Media Resources are presented with emphasis on their use by people with visual deficits.

Next is listed some methods of digitalizing objects:

- **Digitization of document (text or image):** Text or image digitization is a process in which content printed on document is reproduced in digital form as a digital image. In the digitization of texts and images of objects, the content of the document is essential, which must be interpreted correctly in the digital copy. Typically, digitization is performed by scanning with a scanner or by digital photographing of documents. Often, these images are not available to visually impaired people, so it is advisable to add annotations explaining the content of the images.
- **Text input:** An operator recreates text content using a computer, keyboard, and text editor. It requires basic computer knowledge of the operator and time for copying text content. In this method, the operator determines how to visualize (format) the text and resembles the original recording as much as possible. As far as possible, the text accessibility criteria should be met and the text should be in recognizable format and for visually impaired people.
- **Scanning with a flatbed scanner of documents:** An operator scans a document or image using a computer and flatbed scanner. If possible, the criteria and accessibility conditions must be respected so that the document can also be understood by visually impaired people.
- **Photographing documents:** Photographing of documents and images is a common way for digitization because of the speed, affordability and relatively good quality of digital copies received. Unfortunately, this process is not very reliable when scanning negatives or slides. The result of photographing text is an unmovable image. The results obtained are excellent, but some features have to be respected:
  - Shot with the largest possible resolution of the camera.
  - If there is enough light, there is no need to use the flash. If the photo carrier is exposed to photography, there is a risk of glare from the surface, especially if the photo paper is glossy. If not, the flash power is set according to the camera. It should not be either very illuminated or very dark.
  - Shot from a distance to fill the entire frame. If a tripod is available, it is best to increase the distance and use zoom.
  - After photographing or scanning text documents, Optical character recognition (OCR) technology can be applied to convert images into text editing documents.
  - With this method, digital copies are not available to people with visual problems, so it's a good idea to provide an additional text or sound annotation of the digitized image.
- **Digitization of analog audio and video streams:** The process of digitizing analog audio and video streams is the conversion of this signal into a digital copy recorded on an electronic medium. The analog signal digitization is usually performed in real time by a suitable analogue-computer system, where the analogue part reproduces the signal being recorded and processed digitally.

A digital audio copy is available that is accessible and can be heard by visually impaired people (if the software and the interface are accessible to everyone).

Digital 3D Models

The creation of digital 3D models of voluminous objects aims to recreate the object digitally in space, while retaining more information of the shape and geometry of the object, and the texture of its surface and its location in space. A digital 3D object is a digital representation of an object or surface in a three dimensional space where, in addition to height and width, each point carries depth information as well (Bogdanova, Noev, Stoffel, & Todorov, 2011). In addition, color, texture, surface material can be added.

Three-dimensional images and their copies, if comfortable to touch, are available to visually impaired people and can provide an approximate picture of the originals. It is also good to provide additional audio and text annotations for a more complete presentation of the original.

There are several principled methods of building a three-dimensional image:

- **Computer 3D modeling:** This is a process in which an operator-specialist through a specialized computer application, point by point, surface after a surface builds a three-dimensional object. This method is mainly used in the field of architecture, geodesy, computer animation, computer restoration, and more. In this method, the skills of the operator (3D designer or others) are decisive for the qualities of the 3D image and it is possible to obtain voluminous digital objects with a small amount of digital information.
- **Computer 3D generation:** A process where a computer application generates a three-dimensional image of a set of images or other information. The quality of 3D object generated depends on some subjective factors: the quality of the input images; enough images from different angles to cover the entire object volume; enough contrast elements from the object so the software can assemble the individual images and more.
- **3D scanning:** This is a process that creates a three-dimensional digital model of an existing object or surface by capturing and/or measuring. The purpose of 3D scanning is to create a cloud of points of geometric shapes located in the space to reconstruct the surface of the scanned object. These points, besides providing information about their spatial positioning, also have information about the color and, in some cases, about the material on the surface of the object. The digital three-dimensional object model obtained through the three-dimensional scan process is created by multiple scans at different object positions that make up a complete 3D digital image/copy of the object.

Digital 3D model contains digital information about the surface of the volume object or scene in 3-dimensional virtual space by building a mesh of points and surfaces. Elements of mesh of 3D model are:

- **Vertex or points:** It's containing details about position in space and may contain some other information about color, texture, etc.
- **Edges or lines:** Connecting two positional points (vertex).
- **Face (surface):** Closes edges in a geometric figure, usually triangles, squares or polygons.
- **Polygon:** Not always used because it is built from several triangles.
- **United surfaces:** Complex geometric figures combined into one face surface.

There are a variety of technologies of 3D scanning to digitally recreate the shape of the object. Classification of 3D scanners starts with a division into two types - contact and non-contact. Contact 3D scanners use probe to touch the surface of the object to determine the position of each point and hence the shape of the object. Non-contact scanners are divided into two main types: active and passive. Passive scanners are capturing multiple images of an object and according to them, determine spatial location of individual points on the surface of the object. One of the passive methods is stereo recording, which is shooting simultaneously with two or more cameras of the object from different angles, and according to the differences in the images is determined position of individual items (recreates human vision). Active 3D scanners use radiation of some kind of light, sound, ultrasound or other and capture the reflection of this radiation. Usually active 3D scanners use several types of measurements:

- **Time-of-flight:** This is a type of measurement, where 3D scanner emits a laser beam, and by measure a time of that beam reaches the surface of the object and reflected beam to return to the sensor, calculate the distance to the point of reflection. This type of scanner is crawling with beam entire visible surface to determine its form and shape. The technology allows scanning large areas at long distance.
- **Triangulation:** This method determines the distance to a point of surface of object by trigono-metric functions. The mode of action of this method is as follows: 3D laser scanner emits in a line laser beam. Sensor or camera at a certain distance from the line of the laser, detects the point of reflection. These formed three lines: line of emitted laser beam, line of reflected beam and line between laser and sensor, form a triangle. Triangulation is shown below on next figure and explains at next section.
- **3D imaging modeling:** Method in which, a set of two-dimensional images (sections or slices) on a short distance between then, computer builds three-dimensional image through a special algorithms (called: isosurface extraction algorithms). This method is very well developed in the medical field, using the superimposition of X-ray, ultrasound images of CT or MRI slices at a small distance to build 3D full image.

Triangulation in 3D area is a method of determining the position of a point by measure orientation of line of reflection beam by trigonometric functions. More precisely, scheme of triangulation is shown on figure 1, where 3D scanner "knows": position of laser device (point A), orientation of laser beam (line AB), position of camera or sensor (point C), orientation of reflected beam (line BC), distance and orientation of line between laser and camera (line AC). And position of point of reflection at surface of object (point B) can be found by applying trigonometric functions at formed triangle ABC. On figure 1 is shown also second position of object and different formed triangle AB1C.

Structured light technology for three-dimensional scanning use method of triangulation to determine the position of the points at the surface of the scanned object, with the difference that do not use a laser beam but use projection of light patterns. On a figure 2 is shown an example of projection of light pattern on spherical object (round vase) and its reflection (Todorov & Noev, 2014).

The main objective in three-dimensional scanning is getting the digital spatial model of the scanned object, which means that not all scanners measure color, texture, material, hardness, etc. of the surface of the scanned object. For an example: Contact scanning devices can determine the relative hardness of the surface. Devices that use cameras to capture the object can determine the color and texture of it. But those devices that use laser technology can determine only the location of the points of the surface in space, and you should further capture the texture of the object.

Size and distance to the object can range from centimeters to kilometers, depending on the technology used for 3D scanning. Technology "Time-of-flight" is measure time that laser beam travel to surface of object and back through air, which can give a tolerance of precision, but allows scanning of large objects such as buildings, terrestrial elevation at kilometers away. Contact scanning technology by the method of touch of object is much more accurate in capturing spatial surface (measured position of each point with an accuracy of fractions of a millimeter), but the objects must be of such size and location that the

Figure 1. Scheme of laser triangulation system

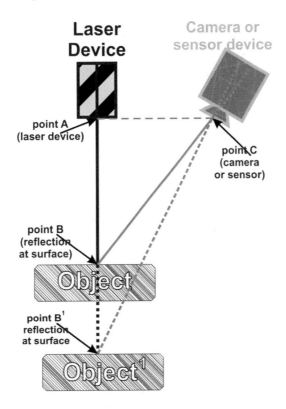

Figure 2. Staging of projection of light on a round vase

scanning device can reach it. Scanning devices using structured light capture portion size which projected schemes of the focal length of the camera, but allow mounting of separate surveys in an image, which means that the size of the object can exceed the size of the staging scan.

Accuracy when scanning bulky objects is measured in deviation from the actual location in space of a point on the surface of the scanned object to the other points. In technology for contact scanning and technology used method of triangulation accuracy is very high (fractions of a millimeter). While technology Time-of-flight has less accuracy because there is deviation due to the measurement of the time for which the beam is go to the surface of the scanned object and go back, with the influence of light speed through air.

Due to the high accuracy of the contact scanners and systems using triangulation reflection density scanning the surface of the object is very large. For example, scanned image of one side of the object, approximately 10 cm by 10 cm using system DAVID SLS-1 with structure light scanning of the surface are of the order of 50 000 to 150 000. For contact scanners density scanning depends on the sensitivity crawl shoulder.

Shortcomings and challenges facing different types of technology are:

- Upon contact scanners drawback is the contact of the device with the scanned object, may lead to deformation of the object.
- At technology Time-of-flight inaccuracy due time measure of beam relative to the light speed in air.
- At 3D scanner devices using technology of reflection of light should also consider the influence of ambient light to the object, which is neutralized when working in a light controlled environment. It should also be borne in mind and the reflective properties of the surface of the scanned object. Scanning of reflective surfaces such as metal, glass and other have difficulties in capturing the reflection of projected schemes. This challenge can be avoided with the use of anti-glare spray or powder-coated pigment on the scanned object. An example of 3D image of reflective surface is shown figure 3 bellow, where there are holes of non-scanned parts of surface of metal historical artifact.

Figure 3. Part of 3D scanned image of a historical artifact (metal dagger), with non-scanned parts of surface caused by blinks of light reflection

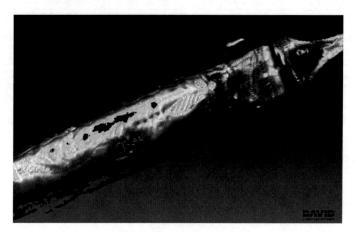

Indexing the Digital Resources

Indexing of separate digital recordings has been done by entering the metadata into objects, as it is consistent with international standards applicable to objects of cultural heritage. The choice of these standards should be consider where the resources will perform in the global network. Good practice is to use the Dublin Core standard and technology of adding text boxes (metadata). For all digital objects is generated XML attached file. That file includes text annotations in metadata form, which helps the various archives, library systems and Internet agents to index and process the content of those digital artifacts. The description of digital resources is necessary as part of the method of building digital archive, supporting activities such as classification, searching, filtering and etc. of artifacts in a wide array of resources. After research was formed two lines of organization of metadata (the use of two lines simultaneously is recommended):

- **Indexing of Characteristics of Resources:** Brief descriptions of recordings with purpose of fast processing of computer systems.
- **Indexing of Content of Resources:** Descriptions in detail of the content of the digitized object in order to detect information in that content.

The presence of metadata with correctly placed points of connection ensures speed and accuracy of the application, and user interaction. Main problem is the lack of standards for exchange of metadata between systems. The standards are developing in major two main groups. The first is proposal by Microsoft, supported by the Meta Data Coalition, which unites fifty companies. Competitive specification was proposed consortium Object Management Group of the companies IBM, Oracle, Unisys and others. Metadata is classified according to the functions they support:

- **Metadata to Describe:** Describe resources and facilitate extraction. May be useful for cultural institutions to create the metadata describing several categories of resources such as: physical objects that are digitized, digital objects created during the process of digitization, new resources created using these digital objects, etc.
- **Metadata Protection and Storage:** Handle activities related to archiving, preservation and storage.
- **Administrative Metadata:** Managing digital resources and provide information on their creation and all restrictions governing their use. Such metadata may include: technical metadata (describing the hardware/software used in the creation of digital resources, formats, standards, and others), metadata sources describing the original object, metadata about the origin of the digital object, metadata rights.
- **Structural Metadata:** Describes the physical or logical connections between parts of one whole. Metadata standard for encoding and transmission provides a format for describing the coding, administrative and structural metadata and is intended to serve as the management of digital objects and their delivery and exchange between different systems.

Other metadata categories: Education, geography, and other metadata.

Metadata should be available to people with visual limitations, and it is advisable to add appropriate annotations to explain what they will not see.

Protection of Digital Resources

A major stage in the creation of digital resources is the protection of information in them from unauthorized dissemination. Research in this area is related to the search for effective methods for embedding characters, serial numbers, and more in the original data proving their origin. The introduction of more and more restrictive measures by some governments on encryption services motivates the search for methods to hide information in the original data. Studies in this area are developed in several sub-disciplines. One of the most important of these is cryptography in the field of coding theory and steganography.

Steganography in literal translation from Greek means "secret type". Like the other subterfuges involved in hiding information and steganography, it conceals the message that we want to remain hidden. Unlike other subregions such as cryptography, for example, dealing with the concealment of the message itself, steganography attempts to conceal the fact that such an embedded message exists at all. Embedding must be done in such a way that a third party having access to the site is unable to detect the presence of the record. In an "ideal" system, the object to be covered must not be different from the object, man, nor through statistical computerized search methods. Theoretically, the cover object could be any type of computer-processed data such as static images, video, sound, and text.

Steganographic methods for embedding information use redundant data on a digital object to record secret information. And the modifications made during the embedding process must be inconspicuous for anyone not involved in the communication. This makes it necessary for the overlay to contain a sufficient amount of redundant information to be replaced by the secret data. For example, any type of data that results from some kind of physical scanning contains a stochastic component called noise. Such random changes can be used in the secret communication process.

The aim of steganography and watermarking is to conceal hidden information. However, there are also significant differences between the two approaches. Steganography refers to hidden communication between two parties. Steganography methods typically are not resistant to modification of the data or have limited stability and protection of the built-in information for technical modifications that may occur during transmission or storage as conversion, compression, transformation of the digital to analog signal (Berger & Todorov, 2008), (Ivanova, 2011).

Watermark protection on the other hand has additional resistance against attempts to remove embedded information. Thus, watermark protection is applicable in cases where the cover object is accessible to third parties who know about the presence of hidden data in it and have an interest in removing hidden data. One of the most popular applications of watermark protection is proof of copyright on digital data by embedding hidden information into them. Another application is to monitor data dissemination in order to collect data from a marketing point of view. Known applications include adding backup data to an archive and signing when trying to modify the data.

Steganography conceals the very fact of the existence of the secret message. Digital steganography can be divided primarily into four directions:

- Embedding information for the purpose of hiding and transmitting.
- Embed a digital watermark.
- Embed ID numbers.
- Embedding titles.

The digital watermark is a visible or preferably invisible identification code that is permanently embedded in digital data and retains its presence in it after retrieval. It is a special sign imperceptibly embedded in an image, text, or other signal in order to control the use of this signal. All watermark protection methods have the same basic building blocks: watermark embedding system and watermarking system. The input data for the embedded system are the watermark, the cover object, and an optional public or secret key. The watermark may be of any type such as number, text, or image. The key is used to prevent unauthorized extraction and manipulation of the watermark. In combination with a public or secret key, watermark techniques refer to secret or public watermark protection. The output of the scheme is data protected by a watermark.

Protective methods do not affect accessibility and their use by visually impaired people for whom protection is invisible, and it is most important to add appropriate annotations that explain what they will not see.

Methods to protect text and images with watermark:

- Methods for concealing information in the spatial area.
- Spread spectrum watermark.
- Coding by line offset.
- Word-by-word encoding.
- Characteristic encoding.

In order for a watermark system to be resistant to attacks, it is necessary to meet basic requirements such as:

- **Unobtrusive:** The modifications caused by the embedding of the watermark must be below the threshold of notice. This means that a criterion is needed to be used not only in designing the watermark, but also to determine the changes that are being made. Because of the need for such an inconspicuity, the individual elements that are modified change with an optimal small amount.
- **Excessity:** To ensure sustainability despite the few allowable changes, the information composing the watermark must be distributed over the many elements of the cover object to ensure global sustainability, i.e. the information can only be restored by small parts of the watermarked data.
- **Keys:** Watermarking systems use one or more cryptographic secure keys to ensure security against manipulation or removal of the watermark.
- **Resilience:** The ideal watermark system must be resistant to any kind of change caused by standard or malicious data processing. Since such a practical system has not been found, a compromise is made between sustainability on the one hand and invisibility and capacity on the other. Depending on the purpose of the particular application, the desired stability affects the design of the watermark. For example, for a watermark used for images, if we want it to resist JPEG compression with high compression factor, it is better to use a method that works in the transformation area than in the spatial one. Conversely, if we want greater resistance to geometric transformations such as rotation, translation, scaling, etc., it is better to use the spatial area.

These principles apply to watermark systems that use all types of data such as audio, video, formatted text, etc. The input parameters to the extraction system are data protected by a watermark, secret or public key, and depending on the watermark method, the original data, and the original watermark.

The output is either the extracted watermark W or some measure of the possibility that the watermark submitted at the entrance is present in the data under consideration.

Watermarking systems can be divided into three types:

- **Private Watermark:** Such systems require at least the original data. Type I systems retrieve the watermark W from the changed data and use the original data to determine if the watermark is present. Type II systems also require a copy of the embedded watermark and give a "yes" or "no" decision to the question: whether the watermark.
- **Received Watermark:** They do not use the original recognition data, but they answer the same question.
- **Public Watermark:** This is the problem with the most challenges because in this case neither the original data nor the built-in watermark.

According to the changes to which a watermark could be subjected (deliberately or unintentionally), two sets of interventions differ. The first includes interferences that add some extra noise to the data, while the second is spatial modifications and geometric changes that aim to induce a discrepancy between the watermark and the key used in embedding. These two groups of attacks are known as destructive attacks and synchronizing attacks.

Depending on the application and the watermark requirement, the list of possible attacks includes the following main types of interference:

- Changes in the signal (contrast changes, luminance, color correction, gamma corrections).
- Additive and multiplicative noise (Gaussian, even, etc.).
- Linear filtering (low-frequency, high-frequency, etc.).
- Non-linear filtering.
- Loss Compression (JPEG, H.261, H.263, MPEG-2, MPEG-4, MP3, MPEG-4, G.723).
- Local and global affinities (translation, rotation, scaling).
- Cutting data (cut, histogram modifications).
- Blending data (inserting a logo or frame).
- Transcoding (H.263 - MPEG-2, GIF - JPEG).
- D/A and A/D conversion.
- Multiple watermarks.
- Collision attack.
- Statistical averaging.
- Mosaic attack.

For embedding information in audio signals, methods adopted with other types of steganographs can be used. Information can be embedded, replacing at least the significant bits based on the characteristics of the audio signals or the human hearing system.

Methods to protect audio files:

- Spectrum Encoding Method.
- Modification of the audio signal phase.
- Embedding information at the expense of changing the echo alert time.

- Masquerade method of hidden information.

In terms of network-based scenarios (Internet space) and applications, there are five main areas of multimedia data hide scaling technology, which are listed below. The first two areas of application fall within the steganography research sphere, while the other three are the subject of a digital signage study (Cox, Miller, Bloom, Fridrich, & Kalker, 2008).

- **Secret Communication (Steganography):** Views the transmission of sensitive messages across the global network using digital media. The purpose of secret communication is similar to the transmission of encrypted data - ensuring the confidentiality of personal communication between two parties. The added advantage of steganographic techniques in this area is that they hide the very existence of a communication process by embedding messages into arbitrary multimedia content. The two communicators use multimedia data whose content is visible to arbitrary third parties (for example, photos on the Internet blog) and is not confidential. The presence and meaning of secret messages embedded in the media remain undetectable by unauthorized third parties.
- **Confidential Data Storage (Steganography):** Invisible storage of confidential data such as credit card numbers, bank accounts, passwords, and more. The security of this data storage can be enhanced by multimedia data embedding technology. They can make encrypted personal data invisible by embedding them in multimedia. In this way, the level of protection is increased - an additional layer of protection (complementing cryptographic protection) is added between confidential data and potential hackers.
- **Proof of Authorship (watermarking):** It affects the protection of intellectual property and allows proofing of copyright on a particular media. Hidden technologies can embed information about the true author directly into the multimedia content. Thus, when copyright disputes arise on the work, the legitimate author can prove and defend his rights.
- **Authentication Check (watermarking):** It refers to the protection of multimedia content against unauthorized changes. Through hidden data technologies, individual regions of rich media content that have been tampered with can be recognized and, depending on the method used, the original content can even be restored to a certain extent.
- **Marking of Multimedia Recordings (Watermarking):** It also affects the protection of copyright. Similar to authorship proofing applications, data hiding methods embed information that identifies the buyer or legitimate user of the multimedia content. Thus, if action is taken that violates the author's rights - such as the illegal distribution of multimedia content on the Internet - the offender can be identified through the hidden information embedded in the illegally distributed copies.

Each media recording is marked with interpolation of identification code in its content. This is done in order to guarantees its authenticity, identification and copyright. For images is used insertion of visible and invisible watermark in it. Marking of audio tracks is done by insertion of an identification code in at least significant channels adapted to human hearing. For videos are used combined methods of image and sound marking (Bogdanova, Trifonov, Todorov, & Georgieva, 2007).

DIGITAL MEDIA STORAGE FOR MEDIA RESOURCES

Digital Archive

The essence of archives during the time of development of human culture is to collect, classify and preserve the accumulated knowledge, as these principles are also the main challenges in building and exploiting them.

Digital archives are a collection of recordings of different kinds of information - visual, sound, spatial, etc., stored and classified in the form of digital recordings using electronic technologies. The digital archive is, by its very nature, an archive that takes advantage of digital technologies.

According to the development of digital technology and the trend of building the information society at local and global level, quite naturally is building a new digital storage or conversion of existing archives into electronic storage of information. The advantages of digital archives can be listed in a number of ways: flexibility of stored records, accessibility of information, etc.

In digital technology, there is a separation between the physical media of the record and the information contained therein which determines the independence of the digital archive from the material storage of electronic records. For example, a collection of digital images may be stored on one or more computer stations, divided into one or more servers, on a plurality of electronic media (CD, DVD, Blu-ray, HDD, etc.) at an independent location or another building in one or other country, continent), etc. An advantage is the ability to copy, move or restructure the records without changing their contents. Besides the physical independence of the stored records, there is also the independence of the format of the information contained, such as the file format, coding mode, etc. For example, an image can be recorded under the Bit Map Picture file format, or the same image may be recorded with JPEG encoding with different parameters that carries the same information value but with a different file structure.

The benefits of accessibility to digital archive information compared to conventional ones are undeniable. In seconds, with the technology of the Internet, it is possible to get the information from the digital archive from anywhere in the world. Also the same content can be presented in various ways with detailed information content or a summary sample, with applications for facilitating people with disabilities, with different exposure techniques or different coding methods. The fastness within seconds that filters the bank with information to retrieve the content you are looking for is undeniable.

Possible challenges and problems with the operation of digital archives are similar to conventional ones. For example: data storage without being damaged by the physical environment; protection of content from malicious intrusion; intellectual property and unauthorized copying and distribution; etc.

The repository applies the rules of good content organization established in the archive, whether paper or paper. That is, the content is arranged, processed, described and indexed unambiguously. To organize and build a digital repository, must be analyzed the necessary steps in content organization and the necessary processing and preparation of the content. Systematization of content meets the following requirements:

- **Content Ordering:** for faster access to the requested data.
- **Systematization:** To uniquely identify each element of the content.
- **Protection:** Every content item must be protected against unauthorized access and unauthorized use.
- **Reliability:** Store content on trusted media in multiple locations.

- **Functionality:** Implementing additional content processing modules, processing multiple content items, filtering content, accessing content by specific features, and more.

The following conditions were defined for processing and preparing content for inclusion in the digital repository:

- The file format is an established worldwide standard suitable for use and content delivery purposes.
- The file format is hardware and software-independent.
- Possibility to protect intellectual property.
- Parameters of digital recordings allow for free and fast transmission over the network space.
- The quality-quantity ratio of saved information to the size of the recording is appropriate.
- Describe and index content to improve storage organization, search for digital repository.
- Maintenance of well-established mass metadata indexing technologies - XML, XMP, and others.

Building a Digital Repository

When creating a digital repository, a traditional tree file system is used, where surrogates are divided into separate branches. First, they are divided into the type of media - photo, audio, video, historical references, technical data, etc., then divided by a specific signature of the objects - on the date of creation of the digital samples - to facilitate the processing teams information and location of sites - location and geographical coordinates. Finally, the digital samples are divided into surrogate and processed material.

As soon as materials are loaded into the repository, they are indexed using the program environment using the metadata properties to describe digital resources. It is not accidental that metadata technology is preferred because these are text fields embedded in media files or are additional text files (XML, XMP) for writing information about the essence of the digital resource. In other words, meta data is "data" describing any electronic or non-electronic source of information according to a predefined standard. The use of a standard for describing information contributes to its compatibility, although it may have been generated by different information systems. Thus, the use of metadata and the provision of information with information from other information systems make it possible to locate and exchange it, no matter what the original source of this information is. Meta data contribute to finding and sharing information. In other words, this is the final stage of information management. Once digitized (electronically) and structured (arranged in a certain order and order), the information is visualized in the appropriate form. In order to fully justify the efforts of the information management stages so described, it needs to be found and used by as many users as possible.

When examining the possibilities of choosing file formats for the construction of the experimental digital archive and building an internet portal with presented results from the collection and processing of digital samples of church bells, the following case study was made: selection between reduced volume digital media records with priority of (compressed media file formats), or digital volumetric content (uncompressed or poorly compressed formats). In line with the above principles, two strands of digital storage have been identified: digital archive for collected information, media records with priority storage of as detailed and complete information as possible (poor compression for media files) and the direction for creating a digital library with media resources for their use of Internet technologies, with priority performance (compressed media to reduce the volume of the digital resource). The following file formats for retaining the collected information were used to build the experimental digital archive with the relevant sample parameters (Bogdanova, Todorov, & Noev, Digitalization and security of "Bulgarian folklore heritage" archive, 2010), (Paneva-Marinova, Goynov, & Luchev, Multimedia digital library: Constructive block in ecosystems for digital cultural assets. Basic functionality and services., 2017) and (Todorov, Bogdanova, & Noev, 2016),.

KNOWLEDGE FOR DIGITAL OBJECTS

Semantic Web

Semantic Web is a technology that aims to expand access to information resources. It introduces semantic tagging of data on the Internet. In this way, semantically-connected and easily computer-readable information is created and more precise searching, analysis, mixing and presentation of different types of data is allowed. The Semantic Web concept was introduced by Tim Berners-Lee (Berners-Lee & Fischetti, 2008), and identifies the next generation of Internet, which describes how to upgrade the conventional network space and expand information, published there. It is used as a term describing the possibility that information used by computers is understandable both for machines and for people in the sense that machines directly or indirectly interpret and process the meaning and purpose of the information resources of the network. Semantic Web refers to knowledge bases, such as knowledge to be accessible to computers - not only to be cultivated as in databases but also "understandable", meaning that machines will also be able to make an intelligent interpretation of knowledge.

The technologies used in the construction of the semantic web are designed to provide a formal description of concepts, terms and relationships within a given area of knowledge needed in the creation of ontology.

Semantic web and ontologies can be handy tools and offer opportunities to create an accessible environment for visually impaired people. There are many ways to refer and build appropriate annotations that explain and conform to what they will not see.

Definition of Ontology

At the core of the Semantic Web are ontologies, which are the main technology for describing and semantically marking data on the Internet and enabling them to build machine-processable knowledge.

The term ontology comes from philosophy, where according to the definition which gives Aristotle ontology is "science as beings". Generally speaking, ontology studies the being - both the beginning of everything that exists, its basic principles and its categorical expression.

The word "ontology" is borrowed from philosophy, where there are two basic meanings:

- A philosophical discipline that studies the most common characteristics of being and essence.
- It is an artifact, characteristic, structure, describing the meanings of the elements of a system.

In modern philosophical literature, the term is used to denote a particular system of categories that is a consequence of a certain system of views (a certain point of view) for the world. In the literature of artificial intelligence, the term is used to mean formally presented knowledge based on some conceptualization.

Informal ontology is a description of a worldview brought to a particular area of interest. This description consists of conditions, terms and rules for the use of these terms, limiting their significance in the particular subject area. At the formal level, ontology is a system consisting of a set of concepts and a set of assertions of these concepts, on the basis of which we can describe classes, relationships, functions and elements.

One of the most well-known definitions of ontology is given by Tom Gruber (Gruber, 1995), which sounds like this: "Ontology - this is an exact specification of conceptualization". Conceptualization - this is a structure of reality, considered independently of the vocabulary of the subject area and the specific situation. For example, to look at a simple subject area describing table dice, then conceptualization is the set of possible positions of the dice and not their actual placement at the current moment.

Some definitions reflect the way the authors construct or use ontologies, for example: Ontology - this is a hierarchically structured set of terms describing a subject area that can be used as the baseline structure of knowledge bases.

Contents of Ontology

Regardless of the description languages they use, ontologies share common characteristics in order to make the possible tasks of presenting knowledge and drawing conclusions. Often, the set of assumptions comprised of ontology has the form of a first-order logic theory in which vocabulary terms are the names of unicorn and binary predicates, respectively called concepts and properties (relationships or relationships). In the simplest case, ontology describes a hierarchy of concepts related to categorization relations. In more complex cases, appropriate axioms are added to it to express other links between the concepts and to limit the supposed interpretations of their meanings. In this sense, ontology is a knowledge base describing facts that are supposed to always be true within a particular mutual community based on the commonly accepted meaning of the vocabulary used.

The data described by ontology is interpreted as a set of "objects" and a set of "allegations of belonging" with which these "objects" interact with one another.

Ontology also contains a set of axioms that put restrictions on "individuals" and the type of allowed relationships between them. These axioms provide a part of semantics of ontological systems that allows machine agents to infer from additional information to explicitly requested data.

Main components of ontology are:

- Classes (or concepts).
- Relationships (or properties, characteristics).
- Functions.
- Axioms.
- Specimens (or individuals).

Classes (or concepts) are used in a broad sense. Concept can be any statement, which can give some information is a kind description of the essence, the common feature that many individuals possess something for someone / something a variant, functionality, activity, course of action, etc., as long as it is directly related to the planned objectives of ontology. The idea behind concepts in ontology can be seen as similar to that of the paradigm of object-oriented modeling. Each concept has a name, a description of a natural language and a variety of properties. In addition, sub-concepts (its elements) and their limitations can be defined. Classes - these are abstract groups, collections, or a set of objects. They may include specimens, individuals, other classes or a combination thereof. Classes in ontologies are usually organized into taxonomy - a hierarchical classification of inclusion terms. For example, the "Male" and "Female" classes are subclasses of the "Man" class, which in turn is included in the "Mammals" class.

Relationships (i.e., more properties and characteristics) represent the type of interaction between concepts in the subject area, characterizing them and helping to identify them. They can be used to link specimens to different classes or to attribute attributes. Properties are a way of presenting existing links between concepts in an area. They are the basis of the hierarchical (is-a relational) and network structure of ontology. Two types of relationships are particularly important: taxonomy and metrology. The taxonomy of concepts defines the main "superclass-subclass" relations in the subject area. The inheritance of the properties of the concepts in taxonomy is modeled in different ways through the various ontology presentation languages. The metrological relationship is defined in the ontological models to express a situation in which the whole is composed of parts.

Formally n-torque is defined as a subset of a product of n sets: $R: C1 \times C2 \times ... \times Cn$. Example of the binary relationship – Part-Whole. Relationships may be organized into inclusion taxonomy: for example, the relationship "to be a father of" "to be a mother of" many people are contained in the "to be a parent of".

Axioms are used to record statements that are always true. They can be included in ontology for a variety of purposes, such as defining complex attribute value restrictions, relationship arguments, validating the information described in the ontology, or displaying new information.

For example, in the framework of axiom ontology, the next situation can be brought in and formally expressed in a tongue for predictive first-order calculus:

"An employee (who is) project manager works in the project."

We introduce the variables E (Employee) and P (Project manager). Then the axiom can be written as follows:

"Forall(E,P) Employee(E) and Project manager(E,P) => Works-At-Project(E,P).

There are different ways of designating portions of a complete structure listed in the following list (Artale, Franconi, Guarino, & Pazzi, 1996):

- **Component / Object:** The object has its own structure and its components have their own specific functions – "Wheels are parts of a car".
- **Article / Collection:** Members do not play any special role with respect to the whole, they are only separate parts of it – "The tree is part of a forest".
- **Part / Multiple:** The whole (the set) is a homogeneous aggregate and the parts are similar to it but are also separable from it – "This slice is part of the lemon".
- **Component / Object:** The idea of the "made from" relationship is expressed, where the component components cannot be separated from the object and have no particular role – "The bicycle is made of steel".
- **Act / Activity:** Indicates a phase of activity. The phase as a component has a functional role but is not separable – "Understanding the essence of a concept is part of its consideration".
- **Place / Province:** Expresses a spatial relationship between regions occupied with different objects – "The oasis is part of the desert".

Concurrent use of different types of "part-of" relationships determines them to be defined without allowed transit in many ontologies and thus to avoid false conclusions.

Axioms are involved in determining limitations in the interpretation of ontological elements. They define facts and rules that are always in place and are useful for verifying the correctness of input data. Two types of axioms are used:

- **Structural Axioms:** Place restrictions on the structure of ontology. For example, "Concepts A and B do not overlap", i.e., there are no individuals who are both A and B specimens.
- **Nonstructural Axioms:** Restrict the interpretation of a concept by terms for its attributes.

The specimens of ontology are individuals of defined concepts (classes) and facts representing relationships between them.

Classification of Ontologies

When developing ontology, it is important to determine in advance what type and purpose and scope. There are currently many classifications depending on different signs. Some authors view ontologies as orientated to the underlying concepts, others to the subjects in the subject area. The literature talks about the dependence and independence of ontology from a specific subject area or task, more types of ontologies are defined according to the different roles they can play in the process of building knowledge-based systems. A basic classification, presented by Fensel (Fensel, 2004), separates the ontologies as:

- General ontologies.
- Ontology oriented to a specific area.
- Ontologies for a particular task.
- Ontologies for metadata.
- Representative ontologies.
- Applied ontologies and others.

For authors who support the conceptual idea, the degree of detail used to describe concepts in ontologies is of particular importance. Those with a more detailed description are better, but they need a richer vocabulary. Simplified ones can be developed to share between different users, adopt and agree in advance on the conceptualization underlying ontology.

Another classification supported by some authors is based on the type of the ontology glossary of terms. Depending on the type of dictionary, ontologies are divided into four types:

- **Highly Informal:** Expressed in free form of natural language.
- **Semi-Informal:** Expressed in a limited and specially structured form of natural language.
- **Semi-Formal:** Expressed in terms of artificially created language.
- **Formal:** Expressed in precisely defined terms and formally described semantics, with theorems of completeness and relevant evidence.

Ontological data can be represented by digital multimedia libraries. They contain multimedia records and ontological annotations, dictionaries and semantic links between concepts. Such are: BellKnow;

Virtual Encyclopedia of Bulgarian Icons; Bulgarian Folklore Digital Library and Bulgarian Ethnographic Treasure (Goynov, Paneva-Marinova, & Pavlov, 2012), (Paneva-Marinova, Goynov, Luchev, & Pavlov, Solution for content interoperability among digital libraries for orthodox artefacts and knowledge, 2015), (Paneva-Marinova, Pavlov, & Goynov, Two Integrated Digital Libraries for Knowledge and Iconography of Orthodox Saints, 2012).

USING OF DIGITAL RESOURCES AND KNOWLEDGE AND THEIR ACCESSIBILITY FOR PEOPLE WITH VISUAL DEFICITS

Accessibility for People With Disabilities

The idea is to use digital and access technology with computer and robotic systems to help teach people with sensory deficits and the use of technology access systems to become an effective interface. The design should be well and professionally structured and allow the user to easily navigate and discover what they are looking for. Here are some accessibility issues: consumer health issues: visual: e.g. Complete or partial blindness, myopia, distorted vision, color perception; Hearing; Trauma: The keyboard or mouse cannot be used. People with disabilities should have equal opportunities to use Information and Communication Systems (ICT), but there are studies showing that no more than 5-10% of websites are publicly available. Accessibility is an essential condition for the equality of people with disabilities and their social participation and is included in the UN Convention on the Rights of Persons with Disabilities as a basic prerequisite for the inclusion of people in the Convention on the Rights of Persons with Disabilities (http://ec.europa.eu/programmes/horizon2020/en/news/first-future-and-emerging-technologies-fet-proactive-projects-under-horizon-2020-framework). The described in the chapter concept for wide access to digital resources is in line with the EU and national higher-education priorities (Blagoeva-Hazarbassanova, 2016). Websites and accessibility standards for websites and accessibility technologies for people with disabilities are a means and a way to socialize them. Research has been done on public websites and digital applications in specific areas and their accessibility for people with disabilities targeted at people with visual deficits (Bogdanova, Georgieva-Tsaneva, & Sabev, Characteristics ofInteractivity and Using the Interactive Technologies in System North+, 2017), (Sabev, Bogdanova, & Georgieva-Tsaneva, 2018). Accessibility and use of digital resources and knowledge by disadvantaged people is a common problem, especially for people with visual deficits. Lack of digital accessibility particularly discriminates against people with reduced vision. They are the smallest part of people with disabilities, but they most need access to digital knowledge and their use for different needs (social applications, special education, etc.). Ensuring accessibility in the field of special education for visually impaired people is often considered very expensive and inefficient for such a small group of people who also have a very limited learning capacity. But they can change with the emergence of modern accessibility technologies that can be used in the special education of this social group as accessible tools for people with poor vision (Sabev N., 2017). Internet access standards and accessibility and criteria for websites for people with disabilities are considered. Principles, guidelines and criteria for accessibility standard in WCAG 2.0: Contains 12 guidelines, organized on 4 principles: visibility, operability, comprehensibility, sustainability. For each guideline, there are success criteria that can be tested and they are on three levels: A, AA, AAA.

Digital accessibility standards for people with disabilities also set accessibility conditions on public sites. Therefore, developers should take into account the WCAG 2.0 standards and accessibility criteria for websites for people with disabilities.

Web accessibility of public websites is recommended to be AA class.

Applications of Digitized Knowledge in Socially-Based Cyber-Physical Systems With Accessibility for People With Disabilities

The effectiveness of digital social applications, and specifically the cyber-physical system in specific areas, and their accessibility to people with disabilities, with a focus on people with visual deficits, have been studied from many authors.

When designing a socially-based cyber-physical system, semantically grounded and organized digital cultural objects can be applied in various thematic fields with interdisciplinary focus (including in the field of robotics, social and human sciences). They are a good addition to new types of socially-based cyber-physical systems with accessibility features for people with disabilities. In this respect, many researchers have conducted a research on applied research with aspects of fundamental conceptualization of a cyber-physical system accessible to people with visual impairments. Such applications are cyber-physical education and pedagogical rehabilitation systems that can be integrated through information and robotic technologies into schools, clinics and special education (Benitti, 2012), (Haque, Aziz, & Rahman, 2014) and (Dimitrova, et al., 2016). The application of the concept of cybernetic systems in education and pedagogical rehabilitation has recently been developed within the framework of the "Bulgaria and Norway Free Grants Project" – "METEMSS: Methods and Technologies for Improvement of Motor and Social Skills of children with developmental problems", Contract N° D03-90 / 27.05.2015 with Ministry of Education and Science (http://www.iser.bas.bg/metemss/en/index.html).

Areas of application of cyber-physical systems such as creativity, art, social communication / media and entertainment relate to professions, activities [e.g. social theater (https://www.workaway.info/829265455839-en.html), and the industries involved in the distribution of entertainment, educational and socializing, which are increasingly important in modern times, including as a method of coping with conflicts in society. In these industries, robot behavior is comparable to that of man - composing and performing music, painting or dancing (Zappi, Pistillo, Calinon, Brogni, & Caldwell, 2012). Some journalistic articles, such as business or sports, are already being generated by intelligent web agents (https://www.ue-varna.bg/Uploads/AdminUploads/izdatelstvo_textbooks/Inteligentni-agenti-2015.pdf) and (http://journal.ue-varna.bg/uploads/0150220092110_180614095154e6fc866f060.pdf).

Moreover, despite the great technological possibilities, robotics is still very poorly represented in social-intensive communicative art such as the theater. A conceptual design was developed from a cyber-physical system perspective. The model will be the so-called "Forum Theater", presenting interactive performances on cutting-edge topics from the present, with an open end and no strict overall scenario. They are released from the traditional scene and can be performed both in closed and open spaces, depending on the purpose of the show. The cybernetic system can collect digital data, store it, analyze processes, and make recommendations within the theory of decision support systems (Aronson, Liang, & Turban, 2005), (COST Action IC1404, http://www.cost.eu/COST_Actions/ict/IC1404). In this way, we strive to acquire new and socially meaningful knowledge of future situations in which people and robots are present in a variety of contexts - from routine help and co-participation to creative and entertaining endeavors.

New generation robotic systems can be human assistant in a number of intellectual activities, including pedagogy, special education, and psychotherapy / counseling (https://www.igi-global.com/newsroom/archive/can-robot-successful-assistant-teacher/3307/). The cyber-physical systems methodology combines both aspects - the virtual, realized in the network and the real - physically present in the human environment. Through them, even in the case of sensory deficit, the understanding and perception of theatrical art can be enhanced as an interactive way of communication in time and space at a new technological level (Rabbitt, Kazdin, & Scassellati, 2014).

The interdisciplinary use of digital technologies and social robots, such as robots as training tools, is widespread globally but is rather limited in people with disabilities and in special education. Digital resources and robots are considered inaccessible to people with visual limitations. Pilot studies demonstrate the effectiveness and accessibility of social applications and social robots.

CONCLUSION

Digitization and the wide and accessible use of digital resources is an important for all consumer groups and social problem. The use of digital resources and robotic systems as training tools is quite widespread on a global scale but is quite limited in special education.

REFERENCES

Aronson, J., Liang, T., & Turban, E. (2005). *Decision Support Systems and Intelligent Systems*. Pearson Prentice-Hall.

Artale, A., Franconi, E., Guarino, N., & Pazzi, L. (1996). Past-whole relations in object centered systems: An Overview. *Data & Knowledge Engineering*, *20*(3), 347–383. doi:10.1016/S0169-023X(96)00013-4

Benitti, F. (2012). Exploring the Educational Potential of Robotics in Schools: A Systematic Review. *Computers & Education*, *58*(3), 978–988. doi:10.1016/j.compedu.2011.10.006

Berger, T., & Todorov, T. (2008). Improving the Watermarking Process With Usage of Block Error-Correcting Codes. *Serdica Journal of Computing*, *2*, 163–180.

Berners-Lee, T., & Fischetti, M. (2008). *Weaving the Web: The Original Design and Ultimate Destiny of the World Wide Web by Its Inventor*. Paw Prints.

Blagoeva-Hazarbassanova, E. (2016). How "Hard Times" Stimulate Reforms – The Case of the Bulgarian Higher Education. *International Journal Knowledge, 11*(1), 71-75.

Bogdanova, G., Georgieva-Tsaneva, G., & Sabev, N. (2017). Characteristics ofInteractivity and Using the Interactive Technologies in System North+. *Digital Presentation and Preservation of Cultural and Scientific Heritage*, *VII*, 133–142.

Bogdanova, G., Noev, N., Stoffel, K., & Todorov, T. (2011). 3D Modeling of Valuable Bulgarian Bells and Churches. Mathematica Balkanica, 25(5), 475-482.

Bogdanova, G., Todorov, T., & Noev, N. (2010). Digitalization and security of "Bulgarian folklore heritage" archive. In *11th International Conference on Computer Systems and Technologies, CompSysTech'10* (pp. 335-340). Sofia, Bulgaria: Institute of Mathematics and Informatics, Bulgarian Academic of Science, Bulgaria. 10.1145/1839379.1839438

Bogdanova, G., Trifonov, T., Todorov, T., & Georgieva, T. (2007). Analyzing and protecting audio and video archives of unique Bulgarian bells. Analyzing and protecting audScientific conference "Europe as a cultural space".

Cox, I. J., Miller, M., Bloom, J., Fridrich, J., & Kalker, T. (2008). *Digital Watermarking and Steganography* (2nd ed.). Morgan Kaufmann Publishers.

Dimitrova, M., Lekova, A., Kostova, S., Roumenin, C., Cherneva, M., Krastev, A., & Chavdarov, I. (2016). A Multi-Domain Approach to Design of CPS in Special Education: Issues of Evaluation and Adaptation. In *Proceedings of the 5th Workshop of the MPM4CPS COST Action, 24-25 November, 2016*, (pp. 196-205). Malaga, Spain: Academic Press.

Fensel, D. (2004). Ontologies: A Selver Bullet for Knowledge Management and Electronic Commerce (2nd ed.). Academic Press. doi:10.1007/978-3-662-09083-1

Goynov, M., Paneva-Marinova, D., & Pavlov, R. (2012). Content interoperability between digital libraries for Orthodox heritage. *ACM International Conference Proceeding Series, CompSysTech '12 Proceedings of the 13th International Conference on Computer Systems and Technologies*, 201-207. 10.1145/2383276.2383307

Gruber, T. R. (1995). Toward principles for the design of ontologies used for knowledge sharing. *International Journal of Human-Computer Studies*, *43*(5–6), 907–928. doi:10.1006/ijhc.1995.1081

Haque, S. A., Aziz, S. M., & Rahman, M. (2014). Review of Cyber-Physical System in Healthcare. *International Journal of Distributed Sensor Networks*, *10*(4), 217415. doi:10.1155/2014/217415

Ivanova, K. (2011). *A Novel Method for Content-Based Image Retrieval in Art Image Collections Utilizing Colour Semantics*. Hasselt, Belgium: Hasselt University.

Paneva-Marinova, D., Goynov, M., & Luchev, D. (2017). *Multimedia digital library: Constructive block in ecosystems for digital cultural assets. Basic functionality and services*. Berlin, Germany: LAP LAMBERT Academic Publishing.

Paneva-Marinova, D., Goynov, M., Luchev, D., & Pavlov, R. (2015). Solution for content interoperability among digital libraries for orthodox artefacts and knowledge. *ACM International Conference Proceeding Series, CompSysTech '15 Proceedings of the 16th International Conference on Computer Systems and Technologies*, 168-175. 10.1145/2812428.2812474

Paneva-Marinova, D., Pavlov, R., & Goynov, M. (2012). Two Integrated Digital Libraries for Knowledge and Iconography of Orthodox Saints. Progress in Cultural Heritage Preservation. EuroMed 2012. Lecture Notes in Computer Science, 7616, 684-691.

Rabbitt, S., Kazdin, A., & Scassellati, B. (2014). Inegrating socially assistive robotics into mental health-care interventions: Applications and recommendations for expanded use. *Clinical Psychology Review*, *35*, 35–46. doi:10.1016/j.cpr.2014.07.001 PMID:25462112

Sabev, N. (2017). The Usefulness of diversity: the utility and accessibility analysis for people with disabilities. In Scientific Conference "Harmony in Differences", About the Letters - О писменехь, (pp. 459-466). Academic Press. (in Bulgarian)

Sabev, N., Bogdanova, G., & Georgieva-Tsaneva, G. (2018). Negoslav Sabev, Galina Bogdanova, Galya Georgieva-Tsaneva. Creating a Software System with Functionality to Help Make it Accessible for People with a Visual Deficit. In *CBU International Conference on Innovations in Science and Education*. Central Bohemia University.

Todorov, T., Bogdanova, G., & Noev, N. (2016). Information Management: Database Design for a Cultural Artifact Repository. In *Encyclopedia of Information Systems and Technology*. Taylor & Francis Inc.

Todorov, T., & Noev, N. (2014). Technology of Three-Dimensional Scanning "Structured Light". In R. Pavlov, & P. Stanchev (Ed.), *International conference Digital Preservation and Presentation of Cultural and Scientific Heritage - DiPP`14. IV*, (pp. 87-94). Veliko Tarnovo, Bulgaria: Institute of Mathematics and informatics - BAS.

Zappi, V., Pistillo, A., Calinon, S., Brogni, A., & Caldwell, D. (2012). Music expression with a robot manipulator used as a bidirectional tangible interface. *EURASIP Journal on Audio, Speech, and Music Processing*, *2*, 1–11.

Chapter 9
Information Security Problem and Solution Approaches in Social Applications

Mamata Rath

https://orcid.org/0000-0002-2277-1012

Birla Global University, India

ABSTRACT

A social network is a portrayal of the social structure between actors, mostly individuals or organizations. It indicates the ways in which they are connected through various social familiarities ranging from casual acquaintance to close familiar bonds. This chapter exhibits an exhaustive review of various security and protection issues in social networks that directly or indirectly affect the individual member of the network. Furthermore, different threats in social networks have been focused on that appear because of the sharing of interactive media content inside a social networking site. Additionally, the chapter also reports current cutting-edge guard arrangements that can shield social network clients from these dangers.

1. INTRODUCTION

From simple communication network currently there are evolution of the Social Networks which are based on emerging technology that stand their base very strong with formation of social sites with group members which have high influential capability to control and communicate the social networks as per their own strategy. Therefore design issues are going to be very tedious by considering all the emerging challenges in such a magnificent network. Social networks such as Facebook has attracted millions of users in recent past and the members are increasing day by day (Rath et.al, 2014). People use social networks to communicate information with other people located at different geographical distance within fraction of time and to spread the relevant information globally sometimes for marketing purpose too. Smart mobile devices and a large number of social mobile applications are currently emerging that encourage distinctive associations amongst users of the social networks (Rath et.al, 2018). Though this is a developing collaborative force in digital social networks, but privacy issue is a major concern among

DOI: 10.4018/978-1-5225-7879-6.ch009

the clients. The expanding number of users of such applications is a challenge and threat for users as well as the developers. This is because of the growing number of clients of such applications and the idea of setting up trust among such users. In this exploration, we will address such protection concerns considering the clients' perspectives and their acknowledgment of such applications. The exploration will illustrate a portion of the recommended components to support clients' trust in social communications.

A social network is a explanation of the social structure involving members, mostly individuals or associations. It represents the ways in which they are connected throughout various social familiarities ranging from casual social contact to close familiar bonds. The informal organization is an entangled structure made out of social individuals and connections between them. Vast scale online interpersonal organizations like Sina Weibo, Tencent Wechat and Facebook have pulled in a large number of clients as of late People might want to utilize interpersonal organizations to convey or diffuse data. For instance, an organization builds up another item, they need to promote the item in a specific informal community (Rath et.al, 2015). The organization has a restricted spending so they can just give free example items to few clients. They trust that the underlying clients could infuence their companions to utilize the items, and their companions could impact theirs companions. Through the verbal impact, countless at last receive the products. Influence boost is an essential research issue in interpersonal organizations. It chooses an arrangement of k hubs as seeds with a specific end goal to boost the engendering of thoughts, conclusions and items.

The chapter has been organized as follows. Section 2 presents a brief literature review on various application aspects of social network and utility tools used in social network development and maintenance such as big data perspective, soft computing techniques etc. Section 3 presents various security issues and challenges in social network. At last section 4 concludes the chapter.

2. LITERATURE REVIEW

This section of chapter presents study of some important contributions in social networking area of researchers by eminent research people. Educational contribution to social networks between peer groups

Figure 1. Common activities in a social network site

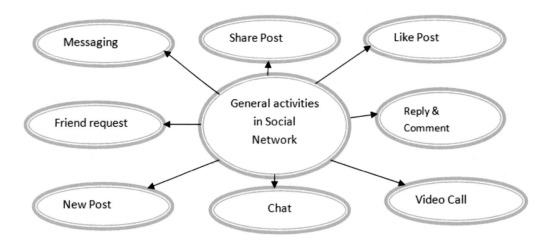

and members has been a challenge to researchers. Notwithstanding, the likelihood that associate gatherings ruled by either low-or high-accomplishing youth can have substantively extraordinary impacts on accomplishment has been to a great extent overlooked (R. Bond et.al, 2017). Social networks are exceptionally well known in this day and age. A large number of individuals utilize different types of social networks as they enable people to associate with loved ones and offer private data. Be that as it may, issues identified with keeping up the protection and security of a client's information can happen, particularly when the client's transferred content is sight and sound, for example, photographs, recordings, and sounds (Rath et.al, 2017) . Transferred media content conveys data that can be transmitted virally and quickly inside a social networking site and past. In such manner (S. Rathore et.al, 2017) exhibit an exhaustive review of various security and protection dangers that objective each client of social networking locales. The issue of influence maximization (IM) in a social system is to decide an arrangement of hubs that could amplify the spread of influence (J. Zhu et.al, 2017). The IM issue has been indispensably connected to promoting, publicizing, and general supposition checking. Albeit late investigations have considered the IM issue, they are for the most part covetous or heuristic-based calculations, which are tedious for reasonable use in substantial scale social systems. As a moving hub in a city, a vehicle has its own dataset of directions. On every direction, remote connections can be worked between various clients and the vehicle (F. Meng et.al, 2017) Since every vehicle is related with a particular territory that covers certain potential client gatherings, such portable vehicles have turned into the premise of a Vehicle Social Network (VSN) for prescribing items to potential clients in present day society. Crowdsourcing has turned into a well-known administration registering worldview for requesters to coordinate the omnipresent human-insight administrations for errands that are troublesome for PCs however unimportant for people (W. Wang et.al, 2017). This concept nconcentrates on crowdsourcing complex assignments by group development in Social Networks (SNs) where a requester associates with an expansive number of laborers. A decent pointer of proficient group coordinated effort is the social association among specialists.

In this section some of the literature reassess have been placed that are reviewed to get some idea for associated concepts used in social networking sites and during their design. M. Sarwar et.al, (2017) project on a Map reduce framework towards met genomic data classifier. Map reduce has been utilised in big data techniques for refinement of extracted data from social network sites using various data mining methods. A new model of storage and access of big data and applications are presented (H. Matallah et.al, 2017). Data storage design and repository layout is another major critical task for handling the social network information. A competency based behavioural interview has been designed (D. V. Timar et.al, 2016) that helps to review customers or members of social groups during conducting various survey on current security issues, political or elective issues. Mediline text mining (W. Abdessalem et.al, 2015) and UML(Unified Modelling Language) generation technique for better project management has been proposed (W. Karaa et.al, 2015). These act as a part of project design which may be helpful during execution of some common projects, contest or project layout design requirements. Statistical rough set computing (D. Acharya et.al, 2017) and Map reduce approach to decrease imbalanced parameters in big data is suggested (S. Kamal et.al, 2016) . Management of big data and their analysis using SNA techniques are more important as far as social polling or social nomination is concerned.These are carried out to perform survey on social issues, to select better choice in competitions, opinion mining etc. Swarm intelligent technique for protein classification (S. Kamal et.al, 2017) has been carried out and Exon separati on process using neural skyline (S. Kamal et.al, 2016) has been planned. These techniques follow some important soft computing approaches for classification and problem solving techniques.

Individual based computer models demonstrate that basic heuristic overseeing individuals' conduct may do the trick to create complex patterns of social conduct (I. Gonzalez et.al, 2017) at the gathering level, for example, those saw in creature social orders. 'GrooFiWorld' is a case of such sort of computer models. In this model, self-association and straightforward behavioral principles produce complex patterns of social conduct like those depicted in tolerant and narrow minded social orders of macaques. Social many-sided quality outcomes from the socio-spatial structure of the gathering, the nature of which is, thusly, a symptom of force of animosity. An informal organization model in ((I. Gonzalez et.al, 2017) demonstrates that a comparable system may offer ascent to complex social structures in macaques. It is, in any case, obscure if the spatial structure of the model and that of macaques are surely comparable. I. Gonzalez et.al, (2017) utilized informal organizations examination as an intermediary for spatial structure of the gathering.

Development of cooperation in social issues is a basic marvels for the working of various multilevel and complex frameworks (A. Bandopadhyaya et.al, 2018). The confirmation of cooperation ranges from the rudimentary natural living beings to the most modern human social orders. Despite the fact that development of cooperation is broadly experienced, yet its advancement isn't all around clarified, since normal choice commonly advances egotistical practices which are frequently not socially ideal. Evolution of system structure and rise of cooperation is contemplated in four classes of social situations, speaking to the detainee's problem, Hawk– Dove, snowdrift and coordination classes of amusements, in organized populaces characterized by weighted complex systems. The quality of interaction between two individuals is spoken to by organize (edge) weight, which changes as per individuals' inclination through the developmental system elements. Utilizing developmental dynamic system based re-enactments of the recreations model on haphazardly weighted finish systems(Rath et.al, 2018). A definite investigation of the advancement of dynamic complex system through the development of the auxiliary properties of a system, for example, grouping coefficient, assortativity coefficient, entropy of degree appropriation, normal quality of interaction and the advancement of agreeable conduct in each of the four classes of diversions. The impact of changing the cost-to-profit proportion on these system properties and development of cooperation is additionally revealed.

The examination inspects the gendered talk patterns on a prominent online informal community, The Marker Café, utilizing interpersonal organization investigation (T. Hayat et.al, 2017). Generally, the discoveries reinforce past examinations that report confirmation of men's decisive and overwhelming talk style and social part versus ladies' more agreeable and strong talk style. Men composed more posts, while ladies remarked on other individuals' posts all the more regularly. Ladies' posts gotten higher rankings than men's posts, fortifying the thought that ladies get more confirmations on online informal organizations. The investigation additionally inspected the exchange between the structure of the TheMarker Café organize and gendered talk patterns. Discoveries of this concept likewise affirmed a connection between action arrange structure and ladies content fame.

Receiving a socio-semantic point of view, this examination expects to check the connection between social impact and talk similitude organizes in workgroups and investigate its change over time (J. Charles et.al, 2018). Information comprise of video transcripts of 45 3-h aggregate gatherings and week by week sociometric surveys. Connection between tie quality, performing artist centrality inside the impact organize, and shared components of talk between aggregate individuals are analyzed after some time. Watched connections bolster the theory of a connection between social impact and talk likeness. Changes after some time propose a closeness limit above which the connection amongst comparability and impact is turned around.

3. PROSPECTIVE ISSUES AND SECURITY DISPUTE IN SOCIAL NETWORKING

Social Network Analysis demonstrates that performance of a social network site can be measured by parameters such as degree centrality, between centrality and closeness centrality. Degree centrality refers to direct connections a member of social network has with other members (Rath et.al, 2015). This is important to measure the influence of message passing from one source to many source. Between centrality refers that a member or node is present in between two or more number of nodes. This factor has great influence in a social network to know what flows in the network and which node is the single point of failure. Closeness centrality is a measure of how close one member is to another in order to know the frequency of message transmission in a social network. Other important issues which have been technically analysed and presented in this article are as follows.

3.1 Security Threat in Educational Social Network

Educational contribution to social networks between peer groups and members has been a challenge to researchers. Notwithstanding, the likelihood that associate gatherings ruled by either low-or high-accomplishing youth can have substantively extraordinary impacts on accomplishment has been to a great extent overlooked. View of digital libraries in social media is a major source of student learning system. Hyper text, hyper media are hugely used for providing education links to users of social sites. Information storage and retrieval, knowledge management, machine learning, multimedia, personal information management, and Web 2.0. Applications have included managing not only publications, but also archaeological information, educational resources, fish images, scientific datasets, and scientific experiments/ simulations.

3.2 Social Ontology and Semantic Actions (SOSA)

End-clients are limited by the social networking stages that they put exertion in to set up their social contacts and connections. The brought together, cornered, and storehouse approach of the present social networking suppliers debilitate interoperability crosswise over stages. Endeavors try to locate a typical social networking way to deal with manage the decent variety of social networking stages of decision of their clients. Despite the fact that every social networking stage gives their very own APIs to externalizing clients' social information, they are not intended to interoperate with different stages. J. W. Ng (2013) propose Social Ontology and Semantic Actions (SOSA) as a tool to bring together, between operable social networking model and runtime administrations that ventures can use as social networking middleware segments for interoperability of social networking stages of their clients. SOSA gives stage freethinker develop to contacts; relationship aphorism relationship with contacts, with inalienable inductions to process participations given a relationship saying. SOSA additionally empowers official with big business benefits as semantic activities of a given relationship maxim. Social relationship can likewise be utilized in context with big business benefits and circulated web entrusting.

3.3 Spammers in Social Networks With Active Honeypots

Y. Zhou et. al, (2012) presents their examination on the microblog spammers with tests pulled in by 50 honey spots from two prominent Chinese microblogging networks: Sina Weibo (weibo.com), and Ten penny Weibo (t.QQ.com) in seven months. Their highlights, for example, social data, action, account age and spamming system were considered and dissected. A few distinctive qualities of spammers on these two social network networks are watched, which can be useful to the further examination on programmed recognition of microblog spammers. This is the first of its sort on the investigation of highlights of Chinese micloblog spammers.

3.4 Retweeting on Weibo and Paying on CrossFire

Social influence has been a generally acknowledged wonder in social networks for quite a long time. C. Zhang et.al, (2016) had examined influence from the point of view of structure, and spotlight on the most straightforward gathering structure - set of three. Two distinct classes of conduct: Retweeting on Weibo and Paying on CrossFire were examined. There were a few captivating perceptions from these two networks. To begin with, various inside structures of one's companions show noteworthy heterogeneity in influence designs. Second, the quality of social relationship assumes an essential job in affecting one's conduct, and all the more strikingly, it isn't really emphatically connected with the quality of social influence. It is joined that the triadic influence designs into a prescient model to anticipate client's conduct. Investigation results demonstrate that this technique can altogether enhanced the forecast precision.

3. 5 Community Evolution in Social Networks

These days, supported improvement of various social media can be watched around the world. One of the significant research areas seriously investigated as of late is examination of social networks existing in social media and in addition expectation of their future advancement considering gathered chronicled development chains. These development chains proposed (S. Saganowski et.al, 2015) contain gather states in the past time spans and its authentic advances that were recognized utilizing Group Evolution Discovery (GED) technique. In light of the watched advancement chains of different length, auxiliary network highlights are separated, approved and chose and in addition used to learn grouping models. The test thinks about were performed on three genuine datasets with various profile: DBLP, Facebook and Polish blogosphere. The procedure of gathering expectation was dissected as for various classifiers and also different spellbinding capabilities extricated from development chains of various length. The outcomes uncovered that, when all is said in done, the more drawn out advancement chains the better prescient capacities of the order models. Notwithstanding, chains of length 3 to 7 empowered the GED-based strategy to nearly achieve its most extreme conceivable expectation quality.

Figure 2 shows the communication in social network where people of different profession communicate in a social site for different activities. All the data are stored in a central computer called as a server.

3.6 Communication in Vehicle Social Network

As a moving hub in a city, a vehicle has its own dataset of directions. On every direction, remote connections can be worked between various clients and the vehicle Since every vehicle is related with a particular territory that covers certain potential client gatherings, such portable vehicles have turned into the premise of a Vehicle Social Network (VSN) for prescribing items to potential clients in present day society .However, little research has concentrated on publicizing through a VSN . For VSN-based publicizing, the advertiser normally situated in a remote Central Office (CO)chooses certain vehicles to

Figure 2. Communication among people in a social network

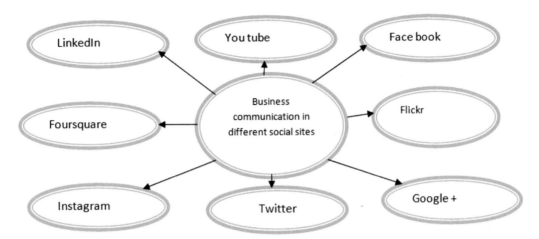

go about as recommenders as indicated by their scope territories. Data about the vehicles' scope zones will be sent from the VSN to the advertiser working at the CO i.e., information backhauling. Moreover, the advertiser will sent the outcomes in regards to the picked recommenders to all vehicles in the VSN, i.e., information front hauling. Naturally, a compelling correspondence framework(Rath et.al, 2016) is desperately required to help information back-/front hauling amongst COs and VSNs.

3.7 Crowd Sourcing Complex Task

Crowd sourcing has turned into a well known administration registering worldview for requesters to coordinate the omnipresent human-insight administrations for errands that are troublesome for PCs however unimportant for people . This concept concentrates on crowd sourcing complex assignments by group development in Social Networks (SNs) where a requester associates with an expansive number of labourers.

A decent pointer of proficient group coordinated effort is the social association among specialists. Most past social group arrangement approaches, in any case, either expect that the requester can keep up data of all labourers and can straightforwardly speak with them to construct groups or accept that the specialists are agreeable and join the particular group worked by the requester, both of which are unrealistic in numerous genuine circumstances. Inside the no cooperative SNs, a conveyed transaction-based group development component is intended for the requester to choose which specialist to employ and for the laborer to choose which group to join and what amount ought to be paid for his expertise benefit arrangement. The proposed social group development approach can simply construct communitarian groups by permitting colleagues to frame an associated chart with the end goal that they can cooperate proficiently. At long last, it leads to an arrangement of tests on genuine dataset of laborers to assess the viability of our approach. The trial comes about demonstrate that our approach can save impressive social welfare by looking at the benchmark concentrated methodologies and frame the beneficial groups inside less arrangement time by contrasting the customary conveyed approaches, making our approach a more financial alternative for certifiable applications. Table 2 describes details of the survey on different themes that focus on social networking issues.

Table 1. Social networking design and focused challenges

Sl. No	Literature	Year	Highlighted Topics
1	R. M. Bond *et.al*	2017	Effect of social networks on academic outcomes
2	S.Rathore *et.al*	2017	Survey of security and privacy threats of social network users
3	J.Zhu *et.al*	2017	Influence maximization in social networks
4	F.Meng *et.al*	2017	Data communication between vehicle social network
5	W.Wang *et.al*	2017	Crowd sourcing complex tasks by team formation in social network
6	V.Amelkin *et.al*	2017	Polar opinion dynamics in social network
7	R. Schlegel *et.al*	2017	Privacy preservation location sharing
8	C.Joshi *et.al*	2017	Security threats in Educational Social network
9	J.Kim *et.al*	2018	Social network in disaster management
10	A.Ahmad *et.al*	2017	Authentication of delegation of resource use in social networking
11	B.Tarbush *et.al*	2017	Dynamic model of social network formation
12	R.Rau *et.al*	2017	Financial outcome of social networks
13	D.Quick *et.al*	2017	Pervasive social networking forensic
14	S.Janabi *et.al*	2017	Privacy as a concern among social network users
15	L.C.Hua *et.al*	2017	Cooperation among members of social network in VANET

Table 2. Details of the survey on themes that focus on social networking issues

Sl.No	Literature	Year	Subject of Discussion on Social Network
1.	Davidekova & Greguš	2017	Emergency social network approach that uses emergency posting through Application Program Interface.
2.	Marche et al.	2017	Object navigation in social network as per distance from one node to other
3.	Merini, Uricchio, & Caldelli	2017	Image tracing in social network using CNN approach
4.	Santi	2012	Analysis of mobile social network based on mobility model for the purpose of next generation network
5.	Nie, Song, & Chua	2016	Learning and Teaching from Multiple Social Networks
6.	Hargitai & Sandvig	2016	Investigation on Social network analysis based on big data, big problems and Internet Log Data
7.	Zhao, Yang, Lu, & Weninger	2018	Recommendation of movie for social awareness through multi modal network learning
8.	Mitra, Paul, Panda, & Padhi	2016	Analytical study of dynamic models in social network
9.	Mady & Blumstein	2017	Focus on positive aspects of social security measures
10.	Kamal, Dey, Ashour, & Balas	2016	An automated system for Monitoring of facebook data

A most noticeable resources for Universities are the information and must be shielded from security break. The security dangers particularly develop in University's network, and with thought of these issues, proposed data security structure for University network condition. The proposed structure decreases the danger of security rupture by supporting three stage exercises; the primary stage sur(C. Joshi et.al, 2017) conveys the dangers and vulnerabilities with a specific end goal to distinguish the frail point in instructive condition[8], the second stage concentrates on the most noteworthy hazard and make significant remediation design, the third period of hazard appraisal display perceives the helplessness administration consistence necessity so as to enhance University's security position. The proposed structure is connected on Vikram University Ujjain India's, processing condition and the assessment result demonstrated the proposed system upgrades the security level of University grounds network. This model can be utilized by chance investigator and security administrator of University to perform dependable and repeatable hazard examination in practical and reasonable way.

4. CONCLUSION

The offered article presents an extensive survey on various critical issues that have been considered and carefully identified during the review process. After observation in most of the contribution, it was found that the major challenges lie in the area of security and smart communication among members of the social network. The Chief challenge lies in authentication of delegation for proper use of resources in social network and design of dynamic models for correct network formation. Similarly, where role of financial outcome of the sub-networks under a social group is very significant, in the same time cooperation among members of social network is considered equally important during the above study and analysis. Topic of how to maximize the influence of social network system was discussed with few proposed models as well as the educational outcome of the social networks as a key part of educational improvement was also elaborated with problem solution. The above research piece of work reports most of the practical and social issues of the most recent and emergent technology of current age with their positive aspects with scope of further development for optimization.

REFERENCES

Abdessalem, W., Ashour, A. S., Ben Sassi, D., & Dey, N. (2015). *MEDLINE Text Mining: An Enhancement Genetic Algorithm based Approach for Document Clustering, Applications of Intelligent Optimization in Biology and Medicine: Current Trends and Open Problems*. Springer.

Acharjya, D., & Anitha, A. (2017). A Comparative Study of Statistical and Rough Computing Models in Predictive Data Analysis, April 2017. *International Journal of Ambient Computing and Intelligence*, *8*(2), 32–51. doi:10.4018/IJACI.2017040103

Ahmad, A., Whitworth, B., Zeshan, F., Bertino, E., & Friedman, R. (2017). Extending social networks with delegation. In *Computers & Security* (Vol. 70, pp. 546–564). Elsevier.

Al-Janabi, Al-Shourbaji, Shojafar, & Shamshirband. (2017). Survey of main challenges (security and privacy) in wireless body area networks for healthcare applications. *Egyptian Informatics Journal, 18*(2), 113-122.

Amelkin, V., Bullo, F., & Singh, A. K. (2017). Polar Opinion Dynamics in Social Networks. *IEEE Transactions on Automatic Control, 62*(11), 5650–5665. doi:10.1109/TAC.2017.2694341

Balas-Timar, Balas, Breaz, Ashour, & Dey. (2016). Technique for scoring competency based behavioural interviews: a fuzzy approach. *Conference: congresului internaţional cercetarea modernă în psihologie.*

Bandyopadhyay, A., & Kar, S. (2018). Coevolution of cooperation and network structure in social dilemmas in evolutionary dynamic complex network. *Applied Mathematics and Computation, 320*, 710-730.

Bond, Chykina, & Jones. (2017). Social network effects on academic achievement. *The Social Science Journal, 54*(4), 438-449.

Creating and Connecting//Research and Guidelines on Online Social - and Educational – Networking. (2007). National School Boards Association.

Dávideková, M., & Greguš, M. (2017). Social Network Types: An Emergency Social Network Approach - A Concept of Possible Inclusion of Emergency Posts in Social Networks through an API. *2017 IEEE International Conference on Cognitive Computing (ICCC)*, 40-47. 10.1109/IEEE.ICCC.2017.13

Hargittai, E., & Sandvig, C. (2016). *Big Data, Big Problems, Big Opportunities: Using Internet Log Data to Conduct Social Network Analysis Research. In Digital Research Confidential:The Secrets of Studying Behavior Online, 1* (p. 288). MIT Press.

Hayat, Lesser, & Samuel-Azran. (2017). Gendered discourse patterns on online social networks: A social network analysis perspective. *Computers in Human Behaviour, 77*, 132-139. doi:10.1016/j.chb.2017.08.041

He, Z., Cai, Z., & Yu, J. (2018). Latent-Data Privacy Preserving With Customized Data Utility for Social Network Data. IEEE Transactions on Vehicular Technology, 67(1), 665-673.

Hua, L. C., Anisi, M. H., & Yee, P. L. (2017). Social networking-based cooperation mechanisms in vehicular ad-hoc network—a survey. In *Vehicular Communications*. Elsevier.

Jiang, J., Wen, S., Yu, S., Xiang, Y., & Zhou, W. (2018). Rumor Source Identification in Social Networks with Time-Varying Topology. *IEEE Transactions on Dependable and Secure Computing, 15*(1), 166–179. doi:10.1109/TDSC.2016.2522436

Joshi, C., & Singh, U. K. (2017). Information security risks management framework – A step towards mitigating security risks in university network. *Journal of Information Security and Applications, 35*, 128-137.

Kamal, Dey, Ashour, & Balas. (2016). FbMapping: An Automated System for Monitoring Facebook Data. *Neural Network World.*

Kamal, Ripon, Dey, & Santhi. (2016). A MapReduce Approach to Diminish Imbalance Parameters for Big Deoxyribonucleic Acid Dataset. *Computer Methods and Programs in Biomedicine.* PMID:27265059

Kamal, Nimmy, Hossain, Dey, Ashour, & Sathi. (2016). ExSep: An Exon Separation Process using Neural Skyline Filter. *International Conference on Electrical, Electronics, and Optimization Techniques (ICEEOT)*.

Kim, J., & Hastak, M. (2018). Social network analysis: Characteristics of online social networks after a disaster. *International Journal of Information Management, 38*(1), 86-96.

Mady & Blumstein. (2017). Social security: are socially connected individuals less vigilant? *Animal Behaviour, 134*, 79-85.

Marche, C., Atzori, L., Iera, A., Militano, L., & Nitti, M. (2017). *Navigability in Social Networks of Objects: The Importance of Friendship Type and Nodes' Distance. In IEEE Globecom Workshops* (pp. 1–6). Singapore: GC Workshops.

Matallah, H., Belalem, G., & Bouamrane, K. (2017). Towards a New Model of Storage and Access to Data in Big Data and Cloud Computing. *International Journal of Ambient Computing and Intelligence, 8*(4), 31–44. doi:10.4018/IJACI.2017100103

Meng, F., Gong, X., Guo, L., Cai, X., & Zhang, Q. (2017). Software-Reconfigurable System Supporting Point-to-Point Data Communication Between Vehicle Social Networks and Marketers. *IEEE Access: Practical Innovations, Open Solutions, 5*, 22796–22803. doi:10.1109/ACCESS.2017.2764098

Merini, T. U., & Caldelli, R. (2017). Tracing images back to their social network of origin: A CNN-based approach. *2017 IEEE Workshop on Information Forensics and Security (WIFS)*, 1-6.doi: 10.1109/WIFS.2017.8267660

Mitra, A., Paul, S., Panda, S., & Padhi, P. (2016). A Study on the Representation of the Various Models for Dynamic Social Networks. *Procedia Computer Science, 79*, 624-631.

Ng, J. W., & Lau, D. H. (2013). Social Ontology and Semantic Actions: Enabling Social Networking Services for Distributed Web Tasking. *2013 IEEE Ninth World Congress on Services*, 131-135. 10.1109/SERVICES.2013.23

Nie & Song. (2016). Learning from Multiple Social Networks. In *Learning from Multiple Social Networks*. Morgan & Claypool.

Puga-Gonzalez & Sueur. (2017). Emergence of complex social networks from spatial structure and rules of thumb: a modelling approach. *Ecological Complexity, 31*, 189-200.

Quick, D., & Choo, K.-K. R. (2017). Pervasive social networking forensics: Intelligence and evidence from mobile device extracts. *Journal of Network and Computer Applications, 86*, 24-33. doi:10.1016/j.jnca.2016.11.018

Rath, Pati, & Pattanayak. (2018). An Overview on Social Networking: Design, Issues, Emerging Trends, and Security. *Social Network Analytics: Computational Research Methods and Techniques*, 21-47.

Rath, M. (2017). Resource provision and QoS support with added security for client side applications in cloud computing. *International Journal of Information Technology, 9*(3), 1–8.

Rath, M., & Panda, M. R. (2017). MAQ system development in mobile ad-hoc networks using mobile agents. *IEEE 2nd International Conference on Contemporary Computing and Informatics (IC3I)*, 794-798.

Rath, M., & Pati, B. (2017). *Load balanced routing scheme for MANETs with power and delay optimisation. International Journal of Communication Network and Distributed Systems* , 19.

Rath, M., Pati, B., Panigrahi, C. R., & Sarkar, J. L. (2019). QTM: A QoS Task Monitoring System for Mobile Ad hoc Networks. In P. Sa, S. Bakshi, I. Hatzilygeroudis, & M. Sahoo (Eds.), *Recent Findings in Intelligent Computing Techniques. Advances in Intelligent Systems and Computing* (Vol. 707). Singapore: Springer. doi:10.1007/978-981-10-8639-7_57

Rath, M., Pati, B., Panigrahi, C. R., & Sarkar, J. L. (2019). QTM: A QoS Task Monitoring System for Mobile Ad hoc Networks. In P. Sa, S. Bakshi, I. Hatzilygeroudis, & M. Sahoo (Eds.), *Recent Findings in Intelligent Computing Techniques. Advances in Intelligent Systems and Computing* (Vol. 707). Singapore: Springer. doi:10.1007/978-981-10-8639-7_57

Rath, M., Pati, B., & Pattanayak, B. K. (2016). Inter-Layer Communication Based QoS Platform for Real Time Multimedia Applications in MANET. Wireless Communications, Signal Processing and Networking (IEEE WiSPNET), 613-617. doi:10.1109/WiSPNET.2016.7566203

Rath, M., Pati, B., & Pattanayak, B. K. (2017). Cross layer based QoS platform for multimedia transmission in MANET. *11th International Conference on Intelligent Systems and Control (ISCO)*, 402-407. 10.1109/ISCO.2017.7856026

Rath, M., & Pattanayak, B. (2017). MAQ:A Mobile Agent Based QoS Platform for MANETs. *International Journal of Business Data Communications and Networking, IGI Global, 13*(1), 1–8. doi:10.4018/IJBDCN.2017010101

Rath, M., & Pattanayak, B. (2018). Technological improvement in modern health care applications using Internet of Things (IoT) and proposal of novel health care approach. *International Journal of Human Rights in Healthcare*. doi:10.1108/IJHRH-01-2018-0007

Rath, M., & Pattanayak, B. (2018). Technological improvement in modern health care applications using Internet of Things (IoT) and proposal of novel health care approach. *International Journal of Human Rights in Healthcare*. doi:10.1108/IJHRH-01-2018-0007

Rath, M., & Pattanayak, B. K. (2014). A methodical survey on real time applications in MANETS: Focussing On Key Issues. *International Conference on, High Performance Computing and Applications (IEEE ICHPCA)*, 1-5, 22-24. 10.1109/ICHPCA.2014.7045301

Rath, M., & Pattanayak, B. K. (2018). Monitoring of QoS in MANET Based Real Time Applications. In Information and Communication Technology for Intelligent Systems Volume 2. ICTIS. Smart Innovation, Systems and Technologies (vol. 84, pp. 579-586). Springer. doi:10.1007/978-3-319-63645-0_64

Rath, M., & Pattanayak, B. K. (2018). SCICS: A Soft Computing Based Intelligent Communication System in VANET. Smart Secure Systems – IoT and Analytics Perspective. *Communications in Computer and Information Science, 808*, 255–261. doi:10.1007/978-981-10-7635-0_19

Rath, M., Pattanayak, B. K., & Pati, B. (2017). *Energetic Routing Protocol Design for Real-time Transmission in Mobile Ad hoc Network. In Computing and Network Sustainability, Lecture Notes in Networks and Systems* (Vol. 12). Singapore: Springer.

Rathore, Sharma, Loia, Jeong, & Park. (2017). Social network security: Issues, challenges, threats, and solutions. *Information Sciences, 421*, 43-69.

Rau, R. (2017). Social networks and financial outcomes. *Current Opinion in Behavioral Sciences, 18*, 75-78.

Rtah, M. (2018). Big Data and IoT-Allied Challenges Associated With Healthcare Applications in Smart and Automated Systems. *International Journal of Strategic Information Technology and Applications, 9*(2). doi:10.4018/IJSITA.201804010

Saganowski, S. (2015). Predicting community evolution in social networks. *IEEE/ACM International Conference on Advances in Social Networks Analysis and Mining (ASONAM)*, 924-925.

Saint-Charles & Mongeau. (2018). Social influence and discourse similarity networks in workgroups. *Social Networks, 52*, 228-237.

Santi, P. (2012). *Mobile Social Network Analysis. In Mobility Models for Next Generation Wireless Networks: Ad Hoc, Vehicular and Mesh Networks, 1* (p. 448). Wiley Telecom. doi:10.1002/9781118344774

Sarwar Kamal, M. (2017). De-Bruijn graph with MapReduce framework towards metagenomic data classification. *International Journal of Information Technology, 9*(1), 59–75. doi:10.100741870-017-0005-z

Sarwar Kamal, M., Golam Sarowar, M., Dey, N., & Joao Manuel, R. S. T. (2017). Self-Organizing Mapping based Swarm Intelligence for Secondary and Tertiary Proteins Classification. *International Journal of Machine Learning and Cybernetics*.

Schlegel, R., Chow, C. Y., Huang, Q., & Wong, D. S. (2017). Privacy-Preserving Location Sharing Services for Social Networks. *IEEE Transactions on Services Computing, 10*(5), 811–825. doi:10.1109/TSC.2016.2514338

Tarbush, B., & Teytelboym, A. (2017). Social groups and social network formation. *Games and Economic Behavior, 103*, 286-312.

Wahiba, B. A. K., Ben Azzouz, Z., Singh, A., Dey, N., Ashour, A. S., & Ben Ghazala, H. (2015, November). Automatic builder of class diagram (ABCD): an application of UML generation from functional requirements, Software: Practice and Experience. *Wiley Online Library, 46*(11), 1443–1458.

Wang, W., Jiang, J., An, B., Jiang, Y., & Chen, B. (2017). Toward Efficient Team Formation for Crowdsourcing in Noncooperative Social Networks. *IEEE Transactions on Cybernetics, 47*(12), 4208–4222. doi:10.1109/TCYB.2016.2602498 PMID:28113391

Zhang, C., Gao, S., Tang, J., Liu, T. X., Fang, Z., & Cheng, X. (2016). Learning triadic influence in large social networks. *2016 IEEE/ACM International Conference on Advances in Social Networks Analysis and Mining (ASONAM)*, 1380-1381. 10.1109/ASONAM.2016.7752421

Zhao, Z., Yang, Q., Lu, H., Weninger, T., Cai, D., He, X., & Zhuang, Y. (2018). Social-Aware Movie Recommendation via Multimodal Network Learning. *IEEE Transactions on Multimedia*, *20*(2), 430–440. doi:10.1109/TMM.2017.2740022

Zhou, Y., Chen, K., Song, L., Yang, X., & He, J. (2012). Feature Analysis of Spammers in Social Networks with Active Honeypots: A Case Study of Chinese Microblogging Networks. *2012 IEEE/ACM International Conference on Advances in Social Networks Analysis and Mining*, 728-729. 10.1109/ASONAM.2012.133

Zhu, J., Liu, Y., & Yin, X. (2017). A New Structure-Hole-Based Algorithm For Influence Maximization in Large Online Social Networks. *IEEE Access: Practical Innovations, Open Solutions*, *5*, 23405–23412. doi:10.1109/ACCESS.2017.2758353

Section 2
Engineering and Mathematical Foundations of Cyber-Physical Systems for Social Applications

Chapter 10
Geometric Simplification of Cyber–Physical Systems

T. V. Gopal
Anna University, India

ABSTRACT

Human beings are always attracted to patterns, designs, and shapes. Even infants are attracted to the geometry around them. Angles, shapes, lines, line segments, curves, and other aspects of geometry are ubiquitous. Even the letters are constructed of lines, line segments, and curves. Nature also has an abundance of geometry. Patterns can be found on leaves, in flowers, in seashells, and many other places. Even the human bodies consist of patterns, curves, and line segments. Therefore, like many professions, the cyber-physical systems also require at least a foundational understanding of geometry. This chapter elucidates the use of geometry to simplify the design and analysis of cyber-physical systems to enhance the efficiency in social applications. The knowledge learned through the understanding of geometric principles provides not only an increase in safety but also an increase in the creation of tools, skill level enhancement, and aesthetically pleasing arrangements.

INTRODUCTION

Philosophy is written in this grand book - I mean the universe - which stands continually open to our gaze. But it cannot be understood unless one first learns to comprehend the language and interpret the characters in which it is written. It is written in the language of mathematics, and its characters are triangles, circles, and other geometric figures, without which it is humanly impossible to understand a single word of it. - Galileo Galilei, Il Saggiatore, 1623

Geometry roughly translates in Greek as "Earth Measurement". It is a practical guide for measuring lengths, areas, and volumes.

Geometry is an original field of mathematics, and is indeed the oldest of all sciences, going back at least to the times of Euclid, Pythagoras, and other "natural philosophers" of ancient Greece. Initially, geometry was studied to understand the physical world we live in, and the tradition continues to this

DOI: 10.4018/978-1-5225-7879-6.ch010

day. However, geometry transcends far beyond physical applications, and it is not unreasonable to say that geometric ideas and methods have always permeated every field of mathematics.

Cyber-Physical Systems (Gopal, 2015a) is an emerging discipline that eludes a clear structuring of a code or a protocol that can be deemed correct. They are combinations of physical devices controlled by software systems. The primary requirement is high dependability assurance. However, a key challenge is to determine not only correct but also cost-effective dynamic operation (Lyndon, 2010, Partha, 2007) of all physical devices in the system in the context of real world constraints. The evolving complex software and its behavior in the Cyber - Physical Systems (Gopal, 2015b) are not readily amenable to a typical engineering code or a protocol that can simply be deployed and assumed safe if not correct. This chapter uses geometry to simplify the processing in the Cyber – Physical Space in a manner which reflects the natural thinking of human beings to provide the necessary assurance in their actions.

BACKGROUND

Roughly 2400 years ago, Euclid of Alexandria wrote Elements which served as the world's geometry textbook until recently. Studied by Abraham Lincoln in order to sharpen his mind and truly appreciate mathematical deduction, it is still the basis of what we consider a first year course in geometry.

Euclidean Geometry is the study of geometry based on definitions, undefined terms (point, line and plane) and the assumptions of the mathematician Euclid. While many of Euclid's findings had been previously stated by earlier Greek mathematicians, Euclid is credited with developing the first comprehensive deductive system. Euclid's approach to geometry consisted of proving all theorems from a finite number of postulates (axioms).

Euclid introduced the idea of an axiomatic geometry when he presented his 13 chapter book titled *The Elements of Geometry*. The Elements he introduced were simply fundamental geometric principles called axioms and postulates. The most notable are Euclid five postulates which are stated in the next passage.

1.   Any two points can determine a straight line.
2.   Any finite straight line can be extended in a straight line.
3.   A circle can be determined from any center and any radius.
4.   All right angles are equal.
5.   If two straight lines in a plane are crossed by a transversal, and sum the interior angle on the same side of the transversal is less than two right angles, then the two lines extended will intersect.

Euclidean Geometry is the study of flat space. We can easily illustrate these geometrical concepts by drawing on a flat piece of paper or chalkboard. In flat space, we know such concepts as:

●   The shortest distance between two points is one unique straight line.
●   The sum of the angles in any triangle equals 180 degrees.
●   The concept of perpendicular to a line can be illustrated as seen in the picture at the right.

Geometry is the study of figures in a space of a given number of dimensions and of a given type. The most common types of geometry are plane geometry (dealing with objects like the point, line, circle, triangle, and polygon), solid geometry (dealing with objects like the line, sphere, and polyhedron), and spherical geometry (dealing with objects like the spherical triangle and spherical polygon). Geometry was part of the quadrivium [crossing of four roads or Chaurastha: arithmetic, astronomy, geometry, and music] taught in medieval universities.

Historically, the study of geometry proceeds from a small number of accepted truths (axioms or postulates), then builds up true statements using a systematic and rigorous step-by-step proof. However, there is much more to geometry than this relatively dry textbook approach, as evidenced by some of the beautiful and unexpected results of projective geometry (not to mention Schubert's powerful but questionable enumerative geometry).

The branch of geometry dealing with the properties and invariants of geometric figures under projection. In older literature, projective geometry is sometimes called "higher geometry," "geometry of position," or "descriptive geometry".

The conservation of number principle asserts that the number of solutions of any determinate algebraic problem in any number of parameters under variation of the parameters is invariant in such a manner that no solutions become infinite. Schubert called the application of this technique the calculus of enumerative geometry.

The concepts in Euclid's geometry remained unchallenged until the early 19th century. At that time, other forms of geometry started to emerge, called non-Euclidean geometries. Four names - C. F. Gauss (1777-1855), N. Lobachevsky (1792-1856), J. Bolyai (1802-1860), and B. Riemann (1826-1866) - are traditionally associated with the discovery of non-Euclidean geometries. It was no longer assumed that Euclid's geometry could be used to describe all physical space. The essential difference between Euclidean and non-Euclidean geometry is the nature of parallel lines.

Carl Friedrich Gauss was apparently the first to arrive at the conclusion that no contradiction may be obtained this way. In a private letter of 1824 Gauss wrote:

The assumption that (in a triangle) the sum of the three angles is less than 180° leads to a curious geometry, quite different from ours, but thoroughly consistent, which I have developed to my entire satisfaction.

From another letter of 1829, it appears that Gauss was hesitant to publish his research because he suspected the mediocre mathematical community would not be able to accept a revolutionary denial of Euclid's geometry. Gauss invented the term "Non-Euclidean Geometry" but never published anything on the subject.

Lobachevsky was first to publish a paper on the new geometry. His article appeared in *Kazan Messenger* in Russian in 1829 and, naturally, passed unnoticed. Trying to reach a broader audience, he published in French in 1837, then in German in 1840, and then again in French in 1855. In the geometry of Gauss, Bolyai and Lobachevsky, parallels are not unique.

The number of parallel lines that can be drawn through a given point to a given line is one in Euclid's geometry, none in Riemann's, and an infinite number in the geometry of Lobachevsky.

Usually, the set of solutions of a system of partial differential equations has the structure of some high dimensional manifold. Understanding the "geometry" of this manifold often gives new insight into the nature of these solutions, and to the actual phenomenon that is modeled by the differential equations (Maxwell, 1967, Rajaraman, 1971), whether it comes from physics, economics, engineering, or any other quantitative science.

Today, there are many different subfields of geometry that are actively studied. Some of them are:

- **Riemannian Geometry:** This is the study of manifolds equipped with the additional structure of a Riemannian metric, which is a rule for measuring lengths of curves and angles between tangent vectors.

- **Hyperbolic Geometry:** This is the study of a **saddle shaped space**. Consider what would happen if instead of working on the Euclidean flat piece of paper, you work on a curved surface shaped like the outer surface of a saddle or a Pringle's potato chip. Hyperbolic geometry has applications to certain areas of science such as the orbit prediction of objects within intense gradational fields, space travel and astronomy. Einstein stated that space is curved and his general theory of relativity uses hyperbolic geometry.

- **Algebraic Geometry:** This is the study of algebraic varieties, which are solution sets of systems of polynomial equations.

- **Symplectic Geometry.** This is the study of manifolds equipped with an additional structure called a symplectic form. A symplectic form is in some sense (that can be made precise) the opposite of a Riemannian metric, and symplectic manifolds exhibit very different behaviour from Riemannian manifolds.

- **Complex Geometry.** This is the study of manifolds which locally "look like" ordinary n-dimensional spaces that are modeled on the complex numbers rather than the real numbers.

Another very important area of geometry is the study of connections (and their curvature) on vector bundles, also commonly called "gauge theory". This field was independently developed by both physicists and mathematicians around the 1950's. When the two camps finally got together in the 1970's to communicate, led by renowned figures such as Atiyah, Bott, Singer, and Witten, there resulted a spectacular succession of important new advances in both fields.

All geometries are based on some common presuppositions in the axioms, postulates, and/or definitions. Non-Euclidean geometries can be constructed by substituting alternative versions of Euclid's parallel postulate; but they begin by keeping some axioms fixed. Keeping some aspects of the axiomatic structure fixed is what makes the different systems all *geometries*. Unifying the various geometric systems is the fact that they determine the possible constructions, or objects, in space.

Pure geometry is studied from the standpoint of its axioms and postulates rather than its objects. Pure geometry is an intuitive understanding of space in general. **Synthetic geometry** (sometimes referred to as axiomatic geometry or even **pure geometry**) is the study of geometry without the use of coordinates.

Synthetic geometry is that which studies figures as such, without recourse to formulas, whereas analytic geometry consistently makes use of such formulas as can be written down after the adoption of an appropriate system of coordinates. – Felix Klein

Euclidean geometry is the quintessential example of the use of the synthetic method. Euclid made the study of geometry into an axiomatic form.

Henri Poincare proposed that there is an a priori intuitive basis for geometry in general, upon which the different metric geometries can be constructed in pure mathematics. Once constructed, they can then be applied depending on empirical and theoretical need.

In the Preface to the *Principia* (1687) Newton famously states that "geometry is founded on mechanical practice". There is no doubt that close study of Rene Descartes' three-book *Geometrie* (1637) helped shape Newton's early researches into mathematics.

The Ancients so assiduously distinguished [arithmetic and geometry] from the other that they never introduced arithmetical terms into geometry; while recent people, by confusing both, have lost the simplicity in which all elegance in geometry consists. Accordingly, the arithmetically simpler is indeed that which is determined by simpler equations, while the geometrically simpler is that which is gathered by a simpler drawing of lines – and in geometry what is simpler on geometrical grounds ought to be first and foremost. – Isaac Newton

In classical mathematics, **Cartesian geometry**, also known as **coordinate geometry**, or *analytic geometry*, is the study of geometry using a coordinate system. Following the methods delimited by Descartes, only the so-called "algebraic" curves, those with a corresponding closed polynomial, are to be included in the sphere of geometry. In contrast, so-called "transcendental" curves are rendered geometrically unintelligible. Rene Descartes created the concept of analytical geometry. It is one of the driving forces for the development of calculus.

Computational geometry is a branch of computer science devoted to the study of algorithms which can be stated in terms of geometry. Some purely geometrical problems arise out of the study of computational geometric algorithms, and such problems are also considered to be part of computational geometry. The main impetus for the development of computational geometry as a discipline was progress in computer graphics and computer-aided design and manufacturing (CAD/CAM), but many problems in computational geometry are classical in nature, and may come from mathematical visualization.

The focus on perspective resulted in projective geometry. Geometry has strong ties with physics, and is an integral part of new physical concepts such as relativity and string theories.

Geometry has two great treasures: one is the theorem of Pythagoras, the other the division of a line into mean and extreme ratios, that is, the Golden Mean. The first way may be compared to a measure of gold, the second to a precious jewel. – Johannes Kepler, an astronomer (1571-1630)

Pythagoreans introduced numbers in geometry in the form of numerical values of lengths and areas. Numbers are further utilized when Descartes was able to formulate the concept of coordinates. Geometry of numbers is the branch of number theory that studies number-theoretical problems by the use of geometric methods. The starting point of this science, which subsequently became an independent branch of number theory, is the fact that certain assertions which seem evident in the context of figures in an n-dimensional Euclidean space have far-reaching consequences in number theory.

Professions such as medicine benefit from geometric imaging technologies such as CT scans and MRIs which are used both for diagnosis and surgical aids. Such methods enable doctors to do their job better, safer, and simpler.

Computer imaging for creating animations, video games and designing, are created using geometric concepts. Geometry is used in mapping. Mapping is an essential for in surveying, navigation, and astronomy. The aim of modeling is to study and argue about the physical objects in the real world. They can also be abstract objects and classes. A mathematical model is a geometric model that has a clear and intuitive connection with its physical counterpart. Mathematical models are suitable for human reasoning but often inappropriate for computer manipulation. A representation scheme is a set of rules defining the mapping from a mathematical model to another model suitable to computer manipulation (Nambiar, 1999). Such geometric model is called representation and consists of a finite collection of basic elements called symbols. The domain is the set of mathematical models that can be represented with a representation scheme. The extension of the domain depends on the expressive power of the representation scheme.

Rapid advances in Computer Architecture have resulted in "Graphics Processing Units" and the method for processing matches the way human eye processes. Geometry is used in the following application domains.

- Graphics and Visualization
- Information Systems
- Medicine and Biology
- Physical Sciences
- Robotics
- Character recognition
- Compiler design
- Control theory
- Signal processing
- Sociology
- Earth sciences
- Metallurgy
- Telecommunication
- Timber processing
- Typography
- Windowing systems
- Smart Cities

Trigonometry helps in solving geometrical problems. In its most basic form, trigonometry helps in determining the relationships between angles in a triangle and the lengths of the sides of the triangle. It does this by defining six functions: sine, cosine, tangent, cotangent, secant, and cosecant. The function is one of the most fundamental concepts in mathematics. Functions are one of the uniting features of all the different fields of mathematics. More advanced trigonometry leaves classical geometry behind.

Topology is one branch of Geometry that is concerned only with "connectness", in which there are no notions as distance, curvature and corners. While both geometry and topology examine shapes and spaces, Topology makes no distinction between two shapes if the one can be made from the other by stretching or twisting. Squares and circles are very different geometric objects, but they are topologically the same. A metric space can admit different distance functions; one can study the different geometries induced by the distances.

The intersections of the three domains of mathematics namely Geometry, Trigonometry and Topology are found in everyday life. They simplify the way one comprehends the Cyber – Physical Systems to get on with the daily activities.

The view which we shall explore is that mathematics is the language of size, shape and order and that it is an essential part of the equipment of an intelligent citizen to understand this language. If the rules of mathematics are the rules of grammar, there is no stupidity involved when we fail to see that a mathematical truth is obvious. The rules of ordinary grammar are not obvious. They have to be learned.

They are not eternal truths. They are conveniences without whose aid truths about the sorts of things in the world cannot be communicated from one person to another. - Lancelot Hogben, Mathematics for the Million, 1936

SACRED GEOMETRY

Sacred Geometry is the blueprint of Creation and the genesis of all form. It is an ancient science that explores and explains the energy patterns that create and unify all things and reveals the precise way that the energy of Creation organizes itself. On every scale, every natural pattern of growth or movement conforms inevitably to one or more geometric shapes.

Many of the **Sacred Geometry** principles of the human body (Wickham, 2008, Wilkinson, 2005) and of ancient architecture have been compiled into the Vitruvian Man drawing by Leonardo Da Vinci, itself based on the much older writings of the roman architect Vitruvius.

The ancient Egyptians considered certain numbers as "sacred", for example numbers 1, 2, 3, 4, 7, and their multiples and sums.

The basic belief is that geometry and mathematical ratios, harmonics and proportion are also found in music, light, and cosmology.

Another aspect of sacred geometry is that all figures could be drawn or created using a straight line (not even necessarily a ruler) and compass, i.e. without measurement (dependent on proportion only).

The three main systems of proportion in architecture are given below.

1. A system based on the musical ratios
2. A system based on the golden ratio
3. A system based on the square, Sacred Cut Square and Octagon

Therefore since nature has proportioned the human body so that its members are duly proportioned to the frame as a whole, in perfect buildings the different members must be in exact symmetrical relations to the whole general scheme. – Vitruvius

In sacred geometry, a straight line is considered male and a curved line, female.

Geometry as a contemplative practice is personified by an elegant and refined woman, for geometry functions as an intuitive, synthesizing, creative yet exact activity of mind associated with the feminine principle. But when these geometric laws come to be applied in the technology of daily life they are represented by the rational, masculine principle: contemplative geometry is transformed into practical geometry. - Robert Lawlor, Sacred Geometry – Philosophy and Practice, 1982

Sacred Geometry charts the unfolding of number in space. It differs from mundane geometry purely in the sense that the moves and concepts involved are regarded as having symbolic value, and thus, like good music, facilitate the evolution of the soul. - Miranda Lundy, Sacred Geometry, 2001

Sacred geometry, or spiritual geometry, is the belief that numbers and patterns such as the divine ratio have sacred significance. Pythagoras taught that each number had its own peculiar character, virtues, and properties.

There are three classical problems in Greek mathematics which were extremely influential in the development of geometry. These problems were those of squaring the circle, doubling the cube and trisecting an angle. The most famous of these problems, is the problem of squaring the circle or the quadrature of the circle as it is sometimes called.

There is no place that can take away the happiness of a man, nor yet his virtue or wisdom. Anaxagoras, indeed, wrote on the squaring of the circle while in prison. - Plutarch, On Exile

Anywhere in this cosmos, the Circle, Triangle, Square, Hexagon and so on remain the same unchanging archetypes.

As far back as Greek Mystery schools 2500 years ago, we as a species were taught that there are five perfect 3-dimensional forms -The tetrahedron, hexahedron, octahedron, dodecahedron, and icosahedron. Collectively these are known as The Platonic Solids -- and are the foundation of everything in the physical world. Modern scholars ridiculed this idea until the 1980's, when Professor Robert Moon at the University of Chicago demonstrated that the entire Periodic Table of Elements – literally everything in the physical world -- is based on these same five forms!

Clear examples of Sacred Geometry in Nature and matter are found in the following examples.

- All types of crystals, natural and cultured.
- The hexagonal geometry of snowflakes.
- Creatures exhibiting logarithmic spiral patterns: e.g. snails and various shell fish.
- Birds and flying insects, exhibiting clear Golden Mean proportions in bodies & wings.
- **The way in which lightning forms branches.**
- The way in which rivers branch.
- The geometric molecular and atomic patterns that all solid metals exhibit.
- The way in which a tree spans out so that all its branches receive sunlight
- The Pyramid has a connection with the human form.

The Cosmos is an utterly malleable experience that feeds back to us what we want to perceive. - Chris Ladue

Chris Ladue is a Renaissance man with accomplishments in technological and artistic endeavors.

The Olympic Mountains make up a small corner of earth, battered by winds and washed with ocean rain. Yet this small, rugged range encloses the beauty of a newly born earth, and like the brushstrokes in a painting by Sesshu or van Gogh, traces the magic by which it was brought to life. The Wisdom of Nature speaks to the Heart, and Nature's first language is beauty - Tim McNulky

Beauty, like supreme dominion Is but supported by opinion - Benjamin Franklin, Poor Richard's Almanack, 1941

Fractal geometry will make you see everything differently. There is a danger in reading further. You risk the loss of your childhood vision of clouds, forests, flowers, galaxies, leaves, feathers, rocks, mountains, torrents of water, carpet, bricks, and much else besides. Never again will your interpretation of these things be quite the same. - Michael F. Barnsley, Fractals Everywhere, 2000

Hence, this chapter is not based on Fractal Geometry. Isaac Newton and his Calculus provide an expression to adequate detail for the solution to appear and more importantly making garnering other details clearly appear unnecessary. The world of mathematics and hence science began capturing the minds of many.

MAIN FOCUS OF THE CHAPTER

The primary uses of "continuous" higher mathematical disciplines like calculus (Joel, 1977, David, 1981) and differential equations in software engineering are in developing algorithms for modeling real-world phenomena.

A vector is a mathematical object that has magnitude and direction, and satisfies the laws of vector addition. Vectors are used to represent physical quantities that have a magnitude and direction associated with them. Rene Descartes specified the method of subjecting vector quantities to scalar algebra by resolution into three components. The manipulative power of algebra can thus be brought to bear upon geometry. And, conversely, algebraic equations can be interpreted as representing geometric shapes—the loci of their solutions – whose properties reflect those of the equations .The need of a calculus directly operating on the vectors has been strongly felt. Also, giving geometrical representation of complex numbers has attracted plenty of attention.

In practice, we almost always describe 3 dimensional vectors by specifying their components in a Cartesian basis. Specifying the components of a vector is a lot like stating the position of a point on a map. Principles of Vectors, Geometry of the plane and sphere and Newtonian Mechanics are very useful in the context of evolving complex Cyber-Physical Systems (Katherine, 2010).

However, engineers typically do not use higher level mathematics (Gopal, 2016a, Gopal, 2016b) because the code or protocol specifications are written specifically to avoid this need. This is also done to limit the possible sources of errors. This way the engineer that uses the code or protocol later does not have to worry about it being correct. Usually, just referencing a code or protocol is enough to "prove" that an answer is correct.

Geometry is significantly different from the typical engineering practices such as codes and protocols (Theodore, 2011) . The behavior of a purely mechanical system does not depend on electrical, electronic, nuclear, biological, chemical or magnetic principles. Specific subjects that are part of engineering mechanics include statics, dynamics, stress analysis, fluid mechanics, heat transfer and so on.

Man is the measure of all things: of the things that are, that they are, of the things that are not, that they are not – Protagoras

Plato interpreted the statement by Protagoras to mean that there is no absolute truth, but that which individuals deem to be the truth.

As civilization developed, so too did the need for units of measurement. These were required for numerous tasks such as: constructing dwellings of an appropriate size and shape, fashioning clothing, or bartering food or raw materials. **Weights and measures** have taken a great variety of forms over the course of history, from simple informal expectations in barter transactions to elaborate state and supranational systems that integrate measures of many different kinds.

An aspect of the human brain function that is very interesting is the modeling of abstract concepts like numbers within the brain. It may look less like an evenly segmented ruler and more like a logarithmic slide rule on which the distance between two numbers represents their ratio (when divided) rather than their difference (when subtracted). The mathematical idea of a **[Roman]** number line - a line of numbers placed in order at equal intervals—is a simple yet surprisingly powerful tool, useful for everything from taking measurements to geometry and calculus. **"Our Innate Sense of Numbers is Logarithmic, Not Linear"**. Common [Base 10] and natural logs [Base e] are pretty much the only logs that are used "in real life".

In general, $a^b = c$ can be rewritten as $log_a c = b$

Euler's number is named after Leonhard Euler. The number *e* is a famous **irrational number**, and is one of the most important numbers in mathematics. *e* is irrational (not the ratio of two integers). *e* is the base of the Natural Logarithms (invented by John Napier). e is also a transcendental number [**not an Algebraic Number**] All rational numbers are algebraic, but an irrational number may or may not be algebraic.

e and the natural log are indispensable and surprisingly natural. The derivative is an operation that takes a function, f, and yields a new function, f', that tells what the slope of f is. e^x has the remarkable property that the derivative doesn't change it, so at every point on its graph the value of e^x is also the slope of e^x at that point. Fixed points are tremendously important for things like chaos theory and a lot of computer algorithms, and eigenvalues and eigenspaces are about the only way to do linear algebra. An **eigenvector** or **characteristic vector** of a **linear transformation is a non-zero vector** whose direction does not change when that linear transformation is applied to it.

Natural logarithm is widely used in pure mathematics specially calculus. It gives the time needed to reach a certain level of growth. The natural logs are preferred because, as described above, coefficients on the natural-log scale are directly interpretable as approximate proportional differences: with a coefficient of 0.06, a difference of 1 in x corresponds to an approximate 6% difference in y, and so forth. It is simplification in the context of linear regression in the social sciences.

ISSUES, CONTROVERSIES, PROBLEMS

Recognition, Reasoning and Retrieval (Ivan, 2015) are three fundamental operations in a cyber-physical space [Cyberspace] that is capable of identifying and tracking the emerging dynamics. *Cyberspace* describes an emerging environment in which most information about physical objects such as manufactured products, buildings, processes, organizations, artifacts, human beings, and dialog between human beings, is accessible on-line through computer-based communication systems. Further, it is expected that in *Cyberspace* both the user and the environment will be able to analyze, synthesize and evaluate information in a virtual reality environment that couples to the human senses through, at the very least, sound, speech synthesis, three-dimensional space, and animation. The Calculus of Variations is the basis for modeling this space.

The Calculus of Variations based on the difference between dynamic and static is called "The Lagrangian" is a useful model. Addition of the dynamic and static gives the total effect (Gheorghe, 2006). It is a key component in the Euler-Lagrange equations to find the path according to the "principle of least action". However, this is quite complex (Klaus, 2007) for typical social applications that work on good approximations.

A Lagrange Point is a location in space where the combined gravitational forces of two large bodies, such as Earth and the sun or Earth and the moon, equal the centrifugal force felt by a much smaller third body. The interaction of the forces creates a point of equilibrium where a spacecraft may be "parked" to make observations.

The equivalent of Lagrangian Points of L-Points in the Cyber – Physical Space can be modeled as a relationship between the "Attractors". In the mathematical field of dynamical systems, an **attractor** is a set of numerical values toward which a system tends to evolve, for a wide variety of starting conditions of the system. Geometry is a simplifier in computing the pointes to be included, the patterns of interactivity and the context. Tensors can provide us a mathematical basis dependability and stability of the Cyber – Physical Space. This is very much natural to a human being.

Dynamics in time consists of alternating birth and death of patterns with spatial phases transformed from one stage of activity to another. Some pragmatic attractors for the stated purpose are indicated in the Figure 1.

The L-Points in the Cyber – Physical Space are thus computed.

Figure 1. Some pragmatic attractors in the four quadrants

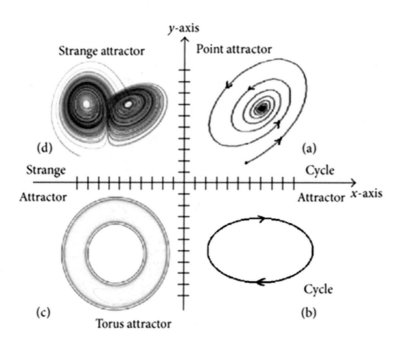

BODYNET AS HUMAN – IN – THE - LOOP

Bodynet is an array of technology attached to the body. Geometry simplifies the way of detecting and leveraging a Bodynet that could be a Human – in – the – Loop or a Golem.

Wearable "on-body" and implanted "intra-body" sensors may enable continuous monitoring of physiological parameters of human beings (e.g., heart rate, blood pressure, glucose level, and respiratory rate), physical activities (e.g., calorie expenditure), and activity patterns (e.g., sleep). The availability of smartphones equipped with multiple sensors may enable inference of complex human activities. Even more intriguing scenarios involve the development of intra-body cyber-physical systems, where implanted sensing and actuating devices communicate within the human body (Kohei, 2011, Lee, 2011)..

The advances of Body Area Networks [BANs], mobile computing, wireless networking and cloud computing offer tremendous opportunities in providing newer and better cyber-physical systems (CPS). The CPS-enabling technologies include body area networks, sensor-actuator networks, machine-to-machine (M2M) communication, RFID and the Internet of Things (IoT).

Due to the huge potential of Wireless Body Area Networks (WBANs) in terms of applications, it is expected in the future that a considerable number of people will wear such WBANs. Interference could then become an issue that would slow down their development. Recent years have witnessed a growing interest by the ICT community on the use of millimeter – waves for WBANs. Given higher propagation loss, their limited coverage would truly permit the coexistence of several WBANs within a given area. It would also contribute to solve privacy issues that are crucial with such technology.

Human Body Communication (HBC) uses human body itself as a communication route to transmit data. It usually operates at dozens of kHz to dozens of MHz, because at these frequencies the propagation loss along the human body (Leonardo and Grant, 2011) is smaller than that through the air. This feature makes it be especially promising in the healthcare, medical diagnoses, consumer electronics and user identification applications, and be also suitable to establish a body area network.

Body Area Network [BAN] uses the surface of the human body as a network transmission path. Communication starts when the skin comes in contact with a transceiver and ends with physically separation. The system works through shoes and clothing as well. The human body becomes a secure communication channel even in a Cloud Based infrastructure (Paul et al, 2014)..

Potential advantages include:

- Services tailored to the individual needs of the user;
- As communication is triggered by natural human actions, there is no need to insert smart cards, connect cables, tune frequencies;
- Setup, registration, and configuration information for an user can all be uploaded to a device the instant the device is touched, eliminating the need for the device to be registered or configured in advance;
- Tables, walls, floors and chairs can act as conductors and dielectrics, turning furniture and other architectural elements into a new class of transmission medium. For example, one could have instant access to the Internet by placing a laptop onto a conductive tabletop.
- The system could be installed on any locations calling for secure access, such that each secure access could be initiated and authenticated with a simple touch.

Let us remember that the automatic machine is the precise economic equivalent of slave labor. Any labor which competes with slave labor must accept the economic consequences of slave labor. - Norbert Wiener, Cybernetics

THE GOLEM

In Jewish folklore, a golem is an animated anthropomorphic being, created entirely from inanimate matter. The word was used to mean an amorphous, unformed material (usually out of stone and clay) in Psalms and medieval writing.

The word *golem* occurs once in the Bible in Psalms 139:16, which uses the word *galmi* - my golem), meaning "my unshaped form", connoting the unfinished human being before God's eyes. The Mishnah uses the term for an uncultivated person: "Seven characteristics are in an uncultivated person, and seven in a learned one". In Modern Hebrew, *golem* is used to mean "dumb" or "helpless".

The Mishnah or Mishna (Hebrew: "repetition", from the verb *shanah* or "to study and review", also "secondary;" derived from the adj. *shani*) is the first major written redaction [a form of editing in which multiple source texts are combined and altered slightly to make a single document] of the Jewish oral traditions called the "Oral Torah". It is also the first major work of Rabbinic literature. Geometry is a simple way of including even golems in the Cyberspace (Raghunathan, 2010).

HEMPELS'S DILEMMA

The Bull of Hempel's Dilemma Charges: Which Horn Will Catch You?

The First Horn: Metaphysics Is What Current Physics Cannot Explain

With this choice the boundary is clear, but it is likely that some phenomena that you would classify as metaphysical will eventually find a sound physical explanation. According to 20th century quantum physics an object can be at two positions simultaneously. Should a 19th century scientist have classified this as a case of magic bilocation?

The Second Horn: Metaphysics Is What Future Physics Will Not Be Able to Explain

With this choice the boundary is so vague that it is not of much use. Who knows what discoveries some 21st century Einstein will make — so where should we draw the line today?

SOLUTIONS AND RECOMMENDATIONS

During language processing, humans form complex embedded representations from sequential inputs. A geometrical language with recursive embedding also underlies the human ability to encode sequences of spatial locations. Geometry facilitates fast comprehension akin to human adults and preschoolers (Marie et al, 2017). The representation of visio-spatial sequences in humans, involves the minimization of the complexity of the structured expressions that capture them (Andrew and Jennifer, 2007) . Please see Figures 2,3 and 4.

The application of tensor analysis to the problems of electrical engineering results in a great simplification of the mathematics involved in such a complicated system as that of a rotating machine, for tensor analysis provides the ability to generalize from simple individual cases to complicated groups and systems. Tensor analysis finds extensive applications in many other fields including the Cyber – Physical Space.

Processing streamed images in a Cyber – Physical Space (Bernard, 1980) is now a reality in the hands of anyone with a smart phone. The conclusions ought to align with the innate natural sense of processing the stream. The Graphical Processing Unit and Tensor analysis are valuable tools to enable the natural appeal of the processed result which can provide the necessary assurance and dependability in the actions initiated by the users of these social applications who are not necessarily well qualified in the mathematics of computing. Location based social networking systems are also simplified in this approach.

Figure 2. Typical geometry for inclusion, connectedness

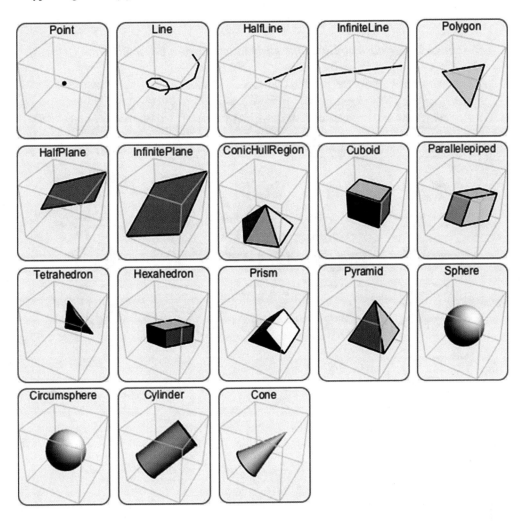

Figure 3. Typical geometry for context that is amenable for formulae

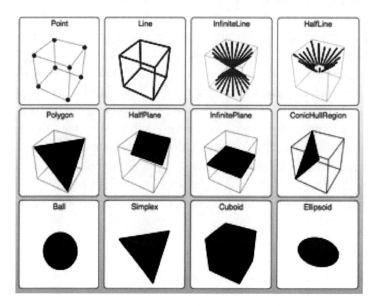

Figure 4. The solids to study the stability of the structures in cyber: physical space

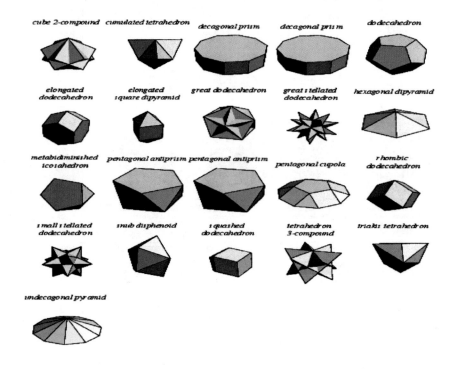

Eigenvectors and Eigenvalues are natural ways of visualizing the ellipsoid attractors using Tensors. It aligns well with the way the Human Brain processing pathways are found in the MRI Scans.

The most effective processor architecture is the Graphical Processor Unit. A **graphics processing unit (GPU)** is designed to rapidly manipulate the creation of images in a frame buffer intended for output to a display device. GPUs are used in embedded systems, mobile phones, personal computers, workstations, and game consoles. Modern GPUs are very efficient at manipulating computer graphics and image processing, and their highly parallel structure makes them more efficient than general-purpose CPUs for algorithms (David, 2011) where the processing of large blocks of data is done in parallel.

GPU is the ideal architecture for processing in the Cyber – Physical Space in a manner where even the novice user readily associates with the output and decides more naturally.

FUTURE RESEARCH DIRECTIONS

Developing necessary formal methods (Gopal, 2016c) for Human-directed proof is a challenging domain of research. Sometimes, the motivation for proving the correctness of a system is not the obvious need for reassurance of the correctness of the system, but a desire to understand the system better. A "good" proof is one which is readable and understandable by other human readers. Social proof is considered prominent in ambiguous social situations where people are unable to determine the appropriate **mode of behavior**, and is driven by the assumption that the surrounding people possess more knowledge about the current situation. Uncertainty is a major factor that encourages the use of social proof. The theory is underspecified by evidence. It becomes necessary to draw upon social and political interests to explain the successes and failures of the theory. Adequate formalism is necessary to negotiate the possible social proof (Gopal, 2017). At the foundation of such negotiation is persuasion.

Geometry has a natural appeal to the mind and hence it is possible to arrive at the basic principles of acceptability in future. Geometric simplification (Carlos, 1999) of the Cyber – Physical Space based on the figures 2,3 and 4 have reasonably well researched and structured formal proofs, theorems and lemmas. However, it is L-points and the pertinent aspects of inclusivity, connectness and context that remain as core challenges (William, 2008) in providing formal methods.

CONCLUSION

The successful application of such large volumes of scientific and engineering data from the Cyber – Physical Space hinges on the user's ability to access the data through phone lines or network connections and to manipulate significant portions of these 3D models interactively on the screen for scientific discovery, teaching, collaborative design, or engineering analysis. Algorithms which eliminate unnecessary or un essential rendering steps, may lead to dramatic performance improvements and hence reduce hardware costs for graphics.

Simplification (Carlos, 1999) takes a polyhedral surface model S and produces a model S' that resembles S, but has significantly less vertices and faces. This process blends the geometric and visual processing of the human brain and facilitates better and more efficient integration of the Human – in – the – Loop or even Golem. Graphics Processing Units facilitate the faster processing of the massively parallel algorithms based on the possible geometric simplifications.

ACKNOWLEDGMENT

Sincere thanks are due to Anna University, Chennai, the members of the Steering Committee of the Series of Annual Conferences on Theory and Applications of Models of Computation [TAMC] and the Conference Chairs of the IEEE Series of Conferences on Norbert Wiener in the 21st Century.

REFERENCES

Amalric, M., Wang, L., Pica, P., Figueira, S., Sigman, M., & Dehaene, S. (2017). The language of geometry: Fast comprehension of geometrical primitives and rules in human adults and preschoolers. *PLoS Computational Biology, 13*(1), e1005273. doi:10.1371/journal.pcbi.1005273 PMID:28125595

Andujar, C. (1999). Geometry Simplication. Technical Report, Department of Computer Science, Universitat Politecnica De Catalunya, Barcelona, Spain.

Brading, K. (2010). On composite systems: Descartes, Newton, and the law-constitutive approach. University of Notre Dame.

de Moura & Passmore, (2010). *Computation in Real Closed Infinitesimal and Transcendental Extensions of the Rationals.* Report supported by EPSRC [grant numbers EP/I011005/1 and EP/I010335/1].

Evans, D. (2011). *Introduction to Computing Explorations in Language.* Logic, and Machines, CreateSpace Independent Publishing Platform.

Frankel, T. (2011). The Geometry of Physics – An Introduction. Cambridge University Press.

Gelman & Hill. (2007). *Data Analysis using Regression and Multilevel/Hierarchical Models.* Cambridge, UK: Cambridge University Press.

Gilliland. (1967). Handbook of Analog Computation. Systron – Donner Corporation.

Glotfelter, Eichelberger, & Martin. (2014). *PhysiCloud: A Cloud-Computing Framework for Programming Cyber-Physical Systems.* Report supported by US National Science Foundation through grant CNS-1239221.

Gopal, T. V. (2015a). The Physics of Evolving Complex Software Systems. *International Journal of Engineering Issues, 2015*(1), 33-39.

Gopal, T. V. (2015b). Modeling Cyber - Physical Systems for Engineering Complex Software. *International Journal of Engineering Issues, 2015*(2), 73-78.

Gopal, T. V. (2016a). Engineering Software Behavior in Cyber – Physical Systems. *International Journal of Engineering Issues, 2016*(1), 44-52.

Gopal, T. V. (2016b). Engineering Logic for Cyber – Physical Systems. *International Journal of Engineering Issues, 2016*(3), 112-120.

Gopal, T. V. (2016c). Beautiful code – circularity and anti-foundation axiom. *Int. J. Computing Systems in Engineering, 2*(3), 148–154. doi:10.1504/IJCSYSE.2016.079001

Gopal, T. V. (2017). Communicating and Negotiating Proof Events in the Cyber – Physical Systems. *International Journal of Advanced Research in Computer Science and Software Engineering*, 7(3), 236–242. doi:10.23956/ijarcsse/V7I3/0184

Guha, P. (2007, February 1). Metriplectic structure, Leibniz dynamics and dissipative systems. *Journal of Mathematical Analysis and Applications*, 326(1), 121–136. doi:10.1016/j.jmaa.2006.02.023

Hadley. (2008). *A Layered Grammar of Graphics*. Report Supported by the National Science Foundation under grant 0706949.

Ivan, G., & Opri, D. (2006). Dynamical systems on Leibniz algebroids, Differential Geometry -. *Dynamical Systems*, 8, 127–137.

LaRouche, Jr. (2010). What Leibniz Intended. *EIR Dynamics*, 44 – 49.

Lee, E. A., & Seshia, S. A. (2011). *Introduction to Embedded Systems - A Cyber-Physical Systems Approach*. LeeSeshia.org.

Magnani & Dossena. (2003). Perceiving the Infinite and the Infinitesimal World: Unveiling and Optical Diagrams in the Construction of Mathematical Concepts. *Proceedings of the 25th Annual Meeting of the Cognitive Science Society*.

Mainzer, K. (2007). *Thinking in Complexity*. Springer.

Nambiar, K. K. (1999). Intuitive Set Theory. Computers and Mathematics with Applications, 39(1-2), 183–185.

Perry. (2008). *Grand Challenges in Engineering*. National Academy of Engineering, Report.

Rajaraman, V. (1971). *Analog Computation and Simulation*. Prentice-Hall of India.

Rajkumar. (2010). *Cyber-Physical Systems: The Next Computing Revolution*. Design Automation Conference 2010, Anaheim, CA.

Ruchkin, I., Schmerl, B., & Garlan, D. (2015). Analytic Dependency Loops in Architectural Models of Cyber-Physical Systems. *8th International Workshop on Model-based Architecting of Cyber-Physical and Embedded Systems (ACES-MB)*.

Schutz, B. (1980). *Geometrical Methods of Mathematical Physics*. Cambridge University Press. doi:10.1017/CBO9781139171540

Suenaga & Hasuo. (2011). Programming with Infinitesimals: A WHILE-Language for Hybrid System Modeling. *Automata, Languages and Programming, 6756*, 392-403.

Tall, D. (1981). Infinitesimals constructed algebraically and interpreted geometrically. *Mathematical Education for Teaching*, 4(1), 34–53.

Tropp, J. A. (1997). *Infinitesimals: History & Application, Plan II Honors Program, WCH 4.104*. The University of Texas at Austin.

Wilkinson, L. (2005). The Grammar of Graphics (2nd ed.). New York: Springer.

Chapter 11
Photoplethysmographic Sensors in Automatized Diagnosis of the Cardiovascular System:
New Guidelines in Computer–Based Medical Diagnostics

Mitko Gospodinov
Bulgarian Academy of Sciences, Bulgaria

Galya Nikolova Georgieva-Tsaneva
Bulgarian Academy of Sciences, Bulgaria

Evgeniya Gospodinova
Bulgarian Academy of Sciences, Bulgaria

Krasimir Cheshmedzhiev
Bulgarian Academy of Sciences, Bulgaria

ABSTRACT

The implementation of photoplethysmographic sensors in the data capture and data storage to analyze the cardiovascular condition of the patient is a new direction in automatized diagnosis of the cardiovascular system. This chapter contains a description of the use of photoplethysmographic sensors in a computerized patient cardiac monitoring system. The system consists of a portable device for collection of patient's cardiac data by applying photopletithysmographic method and software for mathematical analysis. An important diagnostic parameter that can be determined by the photoplethysmographic signal is the heart rate variability. The current application of the photoplethysmographic sensors in portable automatized system is of particular importance because the results of cardiac data analysis with these methods can provide not only detailed information about the cardiovascular status of the patients but also provide the opportunity to generate new knowledge about the diagnosis, and the prevention of pathology in cardiovascular diseases.

DOI: 10.4018/978-1-5225-7879-6.ch011

INTRODUCTION

In recent years, photoplethysmographic sensors have found new applications as sources of information in physiological non-invasive human studies (Allen, 2007). They are constructed as portable photo sensors, measuring the change in the density of the light flow passing through the peripheral organs of the human body - finger, ear and others (Kim & Lee, 2010). Because of these characteristics, photoplethysmographic sensors are increasingly engaging in portable, mobile capture and recording systems for medical research on the human body (Allen, 2007). From the point of view of diagnostic and clinical medicine, one important application is the heart rate variability (HRV) study by capturing and processing the heart rate data of the patient over a prolonged period of time (Buccelletti, Bocci, Gildardi, Fiore, Calcinaro, Fragnoly, Maviglia, & Franceschi, 2012) . Such a study of the cardiovascular system is a difficult task because of the need to process a large amount of information. For example, in the daytime (24 hours) the heart makes about 100,000 beats. For the analysis of the HRV in 100,000 registered pulse cycles, a variety of diagnostic mathematical methods are developed that are applied in modern automated systems using low-cost remote diagnostic devices and equipment, easy to use at home, using the latest computerized technologies.

One way to achieve this is to develop customized medical devices that would allow patients to collect their own physiological data and use wireless technologies to pass this information to specialist physicians or to medical centers. Consequently, the most up-to-date devices must be reliable, accurate, fast, safe, and of course inexpensive. This will provide patients with more mobility and reduce their physical and psychological stress by helping to improve the quality of life.

HRV is a useful biomarker that measures characteristics of the autonomic nervous system (ANS), which regulates the internal organs, including the heart. This parameter is an informative and non-invasive, showing a lot of information regarding the quantification and characterization of ANS (Ernst, 2014). Low parameters of HRV indicate poor health, not only associated with cardiovascular diseases but also with diseases such as diabetes, oncological diseases, etc. (Mirza & Lakshmi, 2012; Soni, Shukla, Dube, Shukla, Soni, & Soni, 2014). The advantage of this research method (HRV) is its ability to detect minor cardiovascular abnormalities, so its use is particularly effective in assessing the body's overall functional abilities as well as early disease abnormalities which, in the absence of the necessary preventive measures, can lead at serious illnesses.

This chapter presents the application of the photoplethysmographic sensors in portable automatized systems for cardiovascular diagnostics. Such systems consist of:

1. Sensors and computerized devices to capture information about the patient's current health condition by applying a photoplethysmographic method, suitable for prolonged study, with advantage of providing better comfort to the observed individuals than conventional (electrocardiographic) methods. The use of sensory devices improves the ability to monitor and control risk groups of patients suffering from cardiovascular disease. They are easy to operate throughout the day without the need for specialized medical staff.
2. Software for the analysis of registered photoplethysmographic signals using linear (time and frequency analysis) and non-linear mathematical methods. The graphical capabilities of the attached software are a helpful tool for physicians to diagnose the health condition of patients.

BACKGROUND

In the field of the clinical medicine, various methods and devices are used to research the health condition of the human body, including cardiovascular diseases. The timely, accurate and rapid diagnosis by the medical specialists of the disease, preferably in the early stages of the disease, is of paramount importance for the effective treatment of the patients. There are different methods for assistance of the diagnosis of the heart diseases, which are basically divided into invasive and non-invasive. Invasive methods for assessing cardiac processes are used in extreme situations when widely implemented non-invasive methods cannot be applied.

Recently widely used photoplethysmographic (PPG) sensors in portable monitoring and diagnosis systems are based on the PPG technology for detection of the physical signals and conversion in electrical signals entered the electronic devices used in the clinical and diagnostic medicine (Allen, 2007; Anderson & Parrish, 1981). Such devices can be used to assess heart and respiratory activity (Nakajima, Tamura, Ohta, Miike, & Oberg, 1996), vasomotor function, thermoregulation, blood pressure (Ernst, 2014), blood oxygen saturation (Hasan & Cáceres, 2015) physiological monitoring (Tarniceriu, Harju, & Vehkaoja, 2018). The developed specialized devices and automatized systems assist in achievement of an objective view of the processes of aging in the arteries and in the human body (by quantifying the viability of the tissues), to examine the variability of the heart rate and the variability of blood pressure.

PPG technology can be seen as an alternative to traditional methods of cardiac monitoring by means of electrocardiographic devices. In the ECG process, it is necessary to place electrodes in the heart (chest) area to monitor the electrical activity of the heart, which leads to some discomfort for the patient and is therefore mainly applicable in medical settings. In PPG technology, using non-contact sensors, no conductive gel is required to make good contact with the skin surface (Tamura, Maeda, Sekine, & Yoshida, 2014).

The monitoring via PPG sensors can be performed in peripheral areas of the human body (wrist, forehead, hand, nose, ear, etc.). This gives a significant advantage to the PPG sensor method and brings it into small intelligent portable devices and makes it the preferred way for continuous cardiac observation. Performing cardiac monitoring using the PPG method can be performed without the observed individuals changing their daily activities such as walking, running, even in the practice of various types of physical games.

Unprocessed PPG signals are heavily influenced by various artifacts that result from patient movement. The reason for this is the relative displacement between the PPG light source / detector and the surface of the individual in the movement of the body (Webster, 2009). These artifacts are superimposed on the basic, carrying the essential card information signal. For these reasons, a substantial part of the preprocessor processing of PPG data is filtering disturbances and removing artefacts caused by motion and other reasons (Nakajima, Tamura, & Miike, 1996; Yoon & Yoon, 2009). To date, a number of signal processing techniques have been proposed in the scientific literature to separate PPG data from various artifacts (Schäfer& Vagedes, 2013).

One of the important diagnostic parameters that can be determined by the PPG sensor is HRV by taking into account the time difference between consecutive heart beats over a sufficiently long period of time. The heart rate is not absolutely even, even in a state of rest, and is influenced by various factors: health, age, gender, environmental conditions, body temperature, physical and mental load, body position, daytime running rhythms and other factors (Ernst, 2014).

Changing HRV may be an indicator of a number of disease states. Stress also has a negative impact on this parameter as well as the emotional state, with positive emotions increasing the HRV and the negative ones decreasing (Cho, Ham, Oh, Park, Kim, Lee, & Lee, 2017; Malik, 1996). In 1996, the European Cardiological and North American Electrophysiological Society gave recommendations for the clinical use of the HRV method, which could assess the risk of various cardiac diseases such as angina, heart attack, life-threatening arrhythmias, etc. (Malik, 1996).

Heart rhythm sensors used in the cardiac device result in nonlinear and non-stationary signals, with a significant portion of the required patient information encoded in the dynamics of their fluctuations at different times.

Mathematical methods for HRV analysis can be divided into the following 3 classes (Ernst, 2014; Kumar, Prasannakumar, Sudarshan, & Jayadevappa, 2013):

- Methods of analysis in the time domain for the study of the common HRV;
- Methods of analysis in the frequency domain for the study of the periodic components of the HRV;
- Methods for non-linear analysis to study the internal structure of cardio-intervals.

The norm-pathology limits, according to the introduced standard in 1996, are known for the quantitative dimensions of the parameters using the analysis methods in the time and frequency domain (Malik, 1996). The application of conventional (linear) mathematical methods in HRV analysis can lead to the omission of some important properties of cardiac signals because these signals are non-stationary and have both periodic and non-periodic components. Fundamental theoretical research on the development and application of new nonlinear mathematical methods in the portable automated system allows the detection of fluctuations resulting from the HRV.

The current application of the PPG sensors in portable automatized systems is of particular importance because the results of the mathematical analysis of the recorded data can provide not only detailed information about the physiological state of the patient over a prolonged period of time but also create the ability to generate new knowledge on the diagnosis, prognosis and prevention of pathology in cardiovascular diseases. Prevention in medicine is important not only for every person but also for society as a whole.

PORTABLE PHOTOPLETHYSMOGRAPHIC CARDIO SIGNALS REGISTERING SYSTEM

Continuous monitoring of the human health status is one of the most promising guidelines for prevention of the cardiovascular diseases and the maintenance of human health all around the day. One of the ways for achieving this aim is creation and using portable devices containing LEDs and photodetectors for reliable monitoring of the heart rhythm by the non-invasive approach (Hasan & Cáceres, 2015; Mainsah & Wester, 2007). The requirements for new advanced systems based of PPG technology are: maximum miniaturization, patient's comfort, reliability of the surveyed indicators and low cost.

The principle of the medical devices based on PPG-signals is the using of a sensor-based system that tracks the smallest changes in the intensity of light transmitted or reflected by human tissue (Allen, 2007). The changes in intensity are an indication of blood flow, passing through the tissue and are a source of information for heart rate rhythm. PPG devices can also be used effectively for remote monitoring of cardiovascular activity of patients as well as for observations in extreme situations.

The portable photoplethysmographic system developed and described in the chapter includes: a portable photosensitive signaling computerized device and signal processing software. The software performs the determination of the P peaks of the signal taken by the device, removes the artefacts, and determines the intervals between the individual pulse waves. These intervals correspond to the RR intervals determined by an electrocardiogram signal.

Essence of the Photoplethysmographic Method

The photoplethysmographic method is based on the principle of counting changes in blood volume in the human body through skin perfusion. The property of the materials (in this case, the blood and surrounding tissues) is used to swallow differently the light emitted by the LED used for this purpose. The difference between the emitted light and the photodetected light is a means of measuring the volume of the blood. The PPG method can be used to measure different physiological parameters: pulse, breathing (Leonard, Grubb, Addison, Clifton, & Watson, 2004), blood pressure (Chon, Dash, & Ju, 2009; Fleming & Tarassenko, 2007).

The blood pressure from the heart during a contraction of the heart muscle (systole), create a higher pressure wave, spreading throughout the body from the aorta to the smallest blood vessels (capillaries). As a result, the light emitted by the LED is absorbed strongly by the tissues. Changing of the absorption of light radiation from tissues affects the shape of the impulse wave. The shape of the impulse wave is determined by the condition of the large and small blood vessels so that its parameters allow for an examination and objective assessment of the condition of the cardiovascular system. From the impulse waveform, the functional state and structural changes in the peripheral vascular system can be assessed.

Photoplethysmographic method therefore provides valuable information about the condition of the blood vessels, which cannot be obtained by another non-invasive method, and supplements the data obtained from the electrocardiographic method.

Figure 1 shows a general plan of a photoplethysmogram with the main elements of the pulse wave corresponding to the basic phases of the heart cycle consisting of coordinated consecutive shrinks and disruptions of the heart. Point A1 corresponds to the beginning of the heart cycle - the beginning of the phase called the systole, with the characteristic maximal expansion of the heart muscle at point A2. Point A3 marks the moment of the Dicrotic notch period when the heart is relaxed and its valves closed. Point A4 shows the Diastolic peak and A5 completes the heart cycle.

The pulse wave of the photoplethysmogram consists of alternating pulsatile (AC) and non-pulsatile (DC) components (Allen, 2007). The PP portion of the PPG signal is caused by differences in the local blood volume obtained during the two phases of systole and diastole. The AC component is small and depends on arterial blood pulsation, which changes with the change in heart rate and therefore the AC component can be used to determine heart rate ripples. The second component - DC is larger, relatively constant and depends on the optical properties of the fabric. The DC component corresponds to the absorption or reflection of light from the soft tissues in the human body and the mean blood content in the arteries and veins. It changes a bit about changes in venous blood flow (Rao & Ram, 2006), thermoregulation and vasomotor activity (Schäfer & Vagedes, 2013).

There are two methods for pulse wave measurement using PPG sensor technology:

Figure 1. PPG waveform

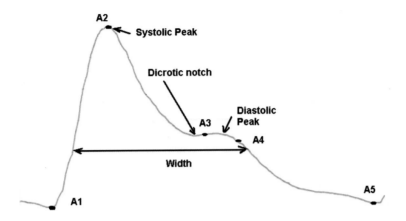

1.   transmission mode.
2.   reflection mode.

The light source, in the first method, is located on one side of the test site and the photodetector on the other, whereas in the second method, the light source and the photodetector are located on the same side of the test site.

Description of a Photoplethysmographic Sensing Device for Recording Cardiac Signals

The described photoplethysmographic sensor device uses a method, based on recording and processing the peripheral arterial blood pulsation signal using the photoplethysmographic method.

Figure 2 shows a block diagram of the created photoplethysmographic device. It consists of the following distinct functional modules:

Power: The power supply unit contains two main components:

- Battery charging circuit that provides required voltage and current for charging internal Li-ION or Li-Pol battery.
- Switch mode DC-DC converter to create a voltage of 3.3V to power the entire electronic part of the device. A buck-boost converter topology is used to make better use of the battery.

When using a USB cable, the built-in battery is charged automatically.

Integrated HR/SPO2 Sensor: The Integrated circuit (Figure 3) is a complete solution for measuring pulse and oxygen content in the blood by using a photoplethysmographic method (Koblenski, 2015). This IC is chosen because of its small size and low power consumption. The main components of the scheme are:

Figure 2. Block diagram of the proposed PPG device

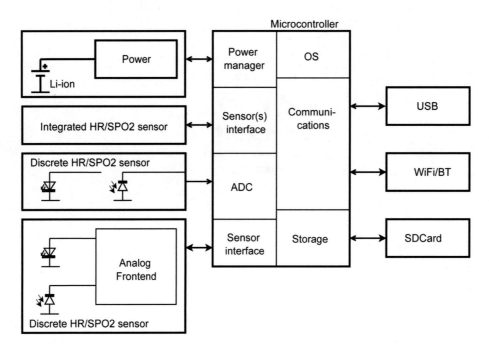

- Red and infrared LEDs. They provide the necessary light for pulse and oxygen content measurements. These LEDs work at different wavelengths. The red LED works at 660nm wavelength and the infrared LED is 880nm;
- The photosensor detects the strength of the red and/or infrared LEDs. The current through them is controlled by PWM (Pulse Width Modulator), which reduces energy consumption;
- Ambient Light Cancellation system to reduce the impact of side light;
- Built-in temperature sensor for compensation of SPO_2 readings, when ambient temperature changes;
- Analogue-to-digital converters for digital signal digitization from photocopiers;
- Digital Filtering Module;
- Interface module for connection to a microcontroller.

Discrete HR/SPO2 Sensor: For experimental purposes, the device also provides the possibility of using a simple red LED and a photodiode as shown in Figure 4(a) or using a sensor with an output voltage proportional to its illumination Figure 4(b) (Pulse Sensor, n.d.). In these cases, the entire analogue processing of the received signal is performed by the microcontroller.

Analog Input/Output for Discrete HR/SPO2 Sensor: A special integrated circuit - AFE4490 (Texas Instruments, 2014) for initial processing and conversion of the analog signals obtained, using a Discrete HR/SPO2 sensor, is used to enable the operation of various discrete sensors (eg Nellcor DS-100A or compatible) of a photoplethysmographic method. Figure 5 shows the simplified block diagram of the analog frontend for the Discrete HR/SPO2 sensors. The block diagram contains the following modules:

Figure 3. Integrated HR/SPO2 sensor
(Maxim Integrated Products Inc., 2018)

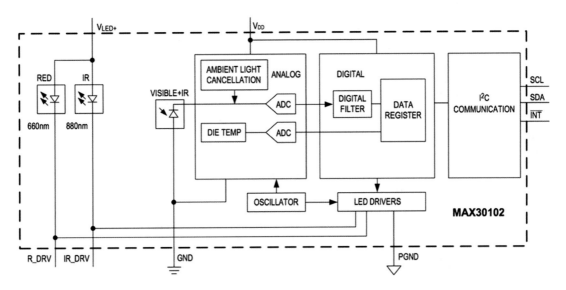

Figure 4. Discrete HR/SPO2 sensor

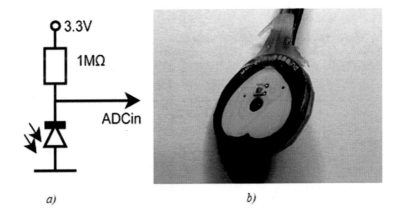

1. Module for processing and digitalization of the input signal obtained from a photo sensor - current-voltage converter, adjustable amplifier (PGA), analogue-to-digital converter.
2. Module for control the red and infrared LEDs - a system for regulating the current through them, a digital-to-analog converter.
3. Interface module for connection to external microcontroller or other equipment via SPI bus.
4. Clock generator and control circuit.
5. Logic for diagnosis.

Microcontroller: The used microcontroller is ARM, Cortex-M4 having a maximum operating frequency of 120MHz (Microchip, ATSAM4S16C) (Microchip, n.d.). The use of a relatively high performance microcontroller will allow the add functionality without a substantial change to the basic scheme. It performs the following tasks:

1. Managing and receiving sensor data.
2. Connection to a personal computer and exchange of information.
3. Record the received data in non-volatile memory.
4. Optimization and management of power consumption from the power source.

A prototype of the photoplethysmographic device in development stage is shown in Figure 6. The device can be positioned at different locations of the human body: finger, wrist, ear, etc. The resulting PPG data is transmitted via a USB interface to a computer for mathematical processing and analysis.

Figure 7a and Figure 7b shows the different types of sensors used in the photoplethysmographic cardiac data capture devices.

A finished version of the device placed in a small lightweight and portable box is shown in Figure 8a and Figure 8b.

The device consists of the following elements:

1. USB interface for PC connection;
2. LED showing the current status (on / off);

Figure 5. Analog Input/Output Block for Discrete HR/SPO2 sensor, simplified diagram adapted from AFE4490 Datashett
(Texas Instruments, 2014)

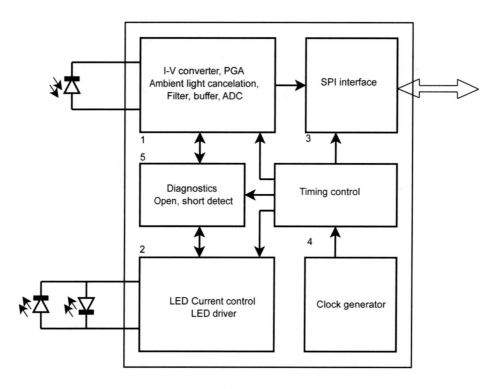

Figure 6. Prototype of the photoplethysmographic device
(the image was shot by the authors)

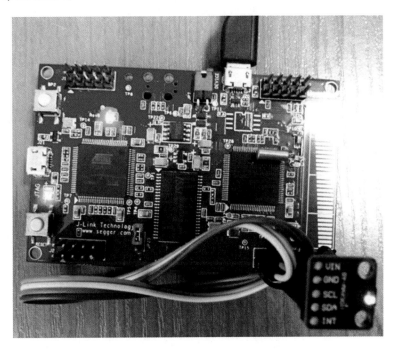

Figure 7. a) Integrated sensor for pulse and oxygen content, b) Discrete sensor, in the form of a clip
(the images was shot by the authors)

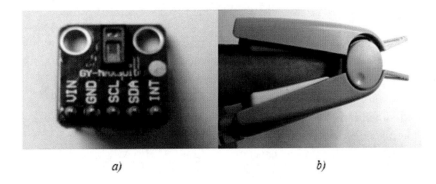

3. Integrated sensor;
4. Interface for disconnection of discrete sensors.

Algorithm for Preprocessing of PPG Signals

The algorithm for preprocessing PPG signals includes the following main steps:

- Determination of the P peaks;
- Determination of PP intervals;

Figure 8. PPG device
(the images was shot by the authors)

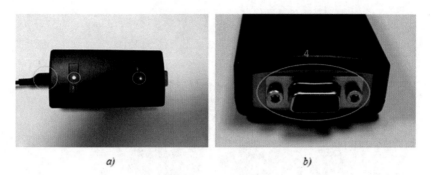

a) *b)*

- Removal of artefacts;
- Creating normalized PP intervals.

Various algorithms exist for the detection of maximum amplitude variations in the photoplethysmographic signal (Nenova & Illiev, 2010; Nenova-Baylova, 2011; Nikolova, 2008).

The block diagram of the proposed algorithm is shown in Figure 9. The basic steps of the algorithm are as follows:

1. Receiving input data (signals) from:
   a. The integrated digital sensor;
   b. The discrete sensor after analogue-to-digital conversion.
2. Removing the constant component of the signal - the signal received by the sensors contains two components: constant and variable. For the determination of the P peaks, only the variable part is needed. A filter is programmatically implemented based on the information from (DC Blocker, n.d.; Microchip, n.d.).
3. Elimination the noise from the input data by applying an averaging filter.
4. Removing individual large deviations in the input data by applying a medial filter.
5. Removing the high frequency components from the input signal through a low pass filter. If the maximum heart rate is 220 bpm, the heart rate is about 3.7 Hz. Any higher frequency signal should be suppressed to prevent further processing.
6. Investigation the slope of the signal curve by checking the increase:
   a. If the value obtained is greater than the previous one, the maximum value is updated and the process continues to process the next received data.
   b. If the received value is less than the previous one, the current position is memorized in an internal buffer of about 0.5 - 0.6 seconds.
7. Second checking in order to determine whether the maximum is incorrectly determined by researching the last 0.5 second data to determine the exact position of the P peak.
8. Determination the PP intervals.
9. Removing of artefacts and PP intervals that are 25% shorter and 25% longer than the median of the previous five PP intervals, as well as PP intervals shorter than 333ms and longer than 2 s.

10. If no more processing data are available, the data are stored in the local memory or send for further processing, including mathematically linear (time and frequency domain analysis) and non-linear (Poincaré plot, DFA, etc.) analysis.

A Microsoft Visual C ++ software program was created for the preprocessing of the registered data through the photoplethysmographic device.

Experimental Studies

Under the same conditions (at rest), PPG signals were taken with the proposed device for a young (17 year) and adult subject (72 years). The experiment lasts 20 minutes and the measurement is performed with the discrete sensor of the device. Figure 10 and Figure 11 show PPG signals of young and adult subjects.

Figure 9. Block diagram of the algorithm for preprocessing PPG signals

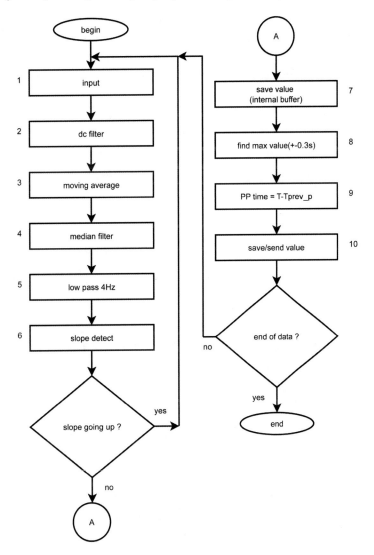

Through the algorithm described above for preprocessor processing of PPG signals, the PP intervals of the subjects studied are shown in Figure 12. From the behavior of the PP intervals, one can judge for the HRV. In this case, the HRV in the adult subject is significantly lower than that of the young subject.

MATHEMATICAL ANALYSIS OF PHOTOPETITISMOGRAPHIC SIGNALS

The variability of cardiac activity can be estimated by the time intervals between the P vertices in the PPG signal. The PPG signal is measured from the surface of human tissue and reflects the change in blood volume in peripheral blood vessels (Webster, 2009). Because changes in blood volume depend on the action of the heart muscle, the sequence of peaks of the PPG signal are almost completely similar to the time intervals obtained by localizing the QRS complexes in the ECG signal (Yoon & Yoon, 2009).

Time-Domain Analysis of HRV

The obtained values of the parameters analyzed in the time domain analysis of the PPG signals give a quantitative assessment of the changes occurring in the normal cardio inserts using the statistical methods validated in the scientific literature. The calculated time parameters give a complete picture of the onset of changes in heart rate over time. The parameters for estimating the heart rate variability in the time domain are presented in Table 1 (Malik, 1996).

Figure 10. PPG signal of young subject

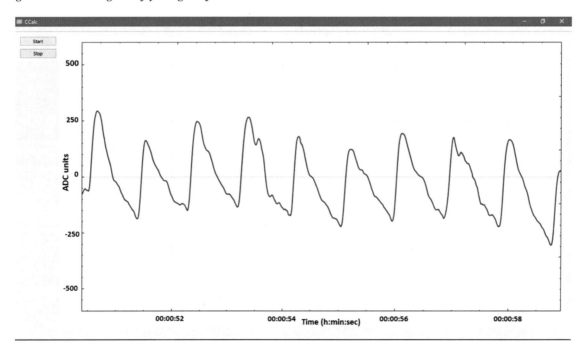

Figure 11. PPG signal of elderly subject

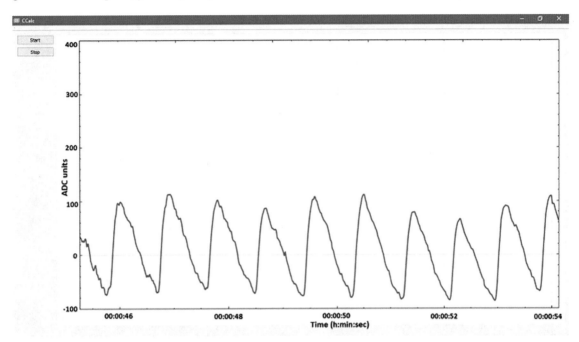

Figure 12. PP interval series of young and elderly subjects

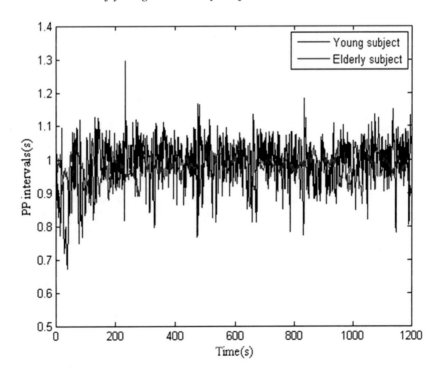

Table 1. Parameters for assessing the heart rate variability in the time domain

Parameter	Description	Formula
HR_{mean}	Mean value of heart rate	$HR_{mean} = \dfrac{1}{N}\sum_{i=1}^{N} HR_i$
NN_{mean}	Mean value of normal intervals	$NN_{mean} = \dfrac{1}{N}\sum_{i=1}^{N} NN_i$
SDNN [ms]	Standard deviation of normal intervals	$SDNN = \sqrt{\dfrac{1}{N}\sum_{i=1}^{N}(RR_i - \overline{RR})}$ Where: $\overline{RR} = \dfrac{1}{N}\sum_{i=1}^{N} RR_i$
SDANN [ms]	Standard deviation of averages normal intervals (over five-minute series)	$SDANN = \sqrt{\dfrac{1}{N}\sum_{i=1}^{N}(\overline{RR_i} - \overline{\overline{RR}})^2}$ $\overline{RR_i}$ - mean of RR intervals in 5 min segment, $\overline{\overline{RR}} = \dfrac{1}{M}\sum_{i=1}^{M} RR_i$
SDNN index [ms]	Mean value of SD of all normal intervals for all five-minute segments of the whole series	$SDNN_{index} = \dfrac{1}{N}\sum_{i=1}^{N} SDNN_i$
RMSSD [ms]	Mean of the SD of all normal intervals for all five-minute segments of the whole series	$.RMSSD = \sqrt{\dfrac{1}{N-1}\sum_{i=1}^{N-1}\left(RR_{i+1} - RR_i\right)^2}$

Frequency-Domain Analysis of HRV

The heart rate standard recommends that the frequency analysis of the cardiac data under investigation be performed on five-minute segments of patients' records (Malik, 1996). The frequency ranges and their corresponding boundary frequencies in which the spectral analysis is performed are given in Table 2. Frequency analysis also includes the determination of the LF / HF parameter known as the sympathetic balance index.

Non-Linear Analysis of HRV

In recent years, non-linear methods of HRV analysis have become increasingly prevalent because the fact, that cardiac signals are non-stationary, having both periodic and non-periodic components (Ar-

Table 2. Spectral analysis frequency ranges

Frequency range	Frequency (Hz)
Total power, ms^2	0-0.4
Power in the ultra low frequency range (ULF), ms^2	0-0.003
Power in very low frequency range (VLF), ms^2	0.003-0.04
Power in low frequency range (LF), ms^2	0.04-0.15
Power in high frequency range (HF), ms^2	0.15-0.4

charya, Suri, Spaan, & Krishnan, 2007; Smith et al., 2009). The mathematical analysis of HRV using non-linear methods provides not only detailed information about the physiological state of the patient but also generates new knowledge for the prediction, prognosis and prevention of pathological conditions in cardiovascular diseases.

Poincaré Plot

The Poincaré plot is a relatively new approach for analyzing the non-linear dynamics of HRV. It is a geometric model in which each of the PP (RR) intervals is represented as a function of the previous interval and is applied to the coordinate system (Tayel & AlSaba, 2015) Each pair of PP (RR) intervals (past and subsequent) has coordinates (x, y), where x is the value of the PP_n (RR_n) interval and y is the value of PP_{n+1} (RR_{n+1}). When the chart is formed, a "cloud" is created from points whose center is located on the line of identity. The line of identity is the graph of the function x = y ($PP_n = PP_{n+1}$). If the point is above the identity line, it means that x <y ($PP_n < PP_{n+1}$). Accordingly, if the dot is located below the line of identity, this indicates that the interval PP_{n+1} is shorter than the PP_n interval. Therefore, the form of the "cloud" of points (PP_n; PP_{n+1}) on the Poincaré graph reflects the change in the duration of the PP intervals.

If on the graph built by the Poincaré method (Figure 13) an ellipse with a longitudinal and transverse axis is placed, the following indicators can be derived:

- Length of the ellipse (SD2 [ms] parameter) - this indicator corresponds to the long-term variability of the PP intervals and reflects the total HRV;
- Ellipse Width (SD1 [ms] parameter) - This metric represents the scattering of the points along the straight line of the line of identity and is associated with rapid variations between individual heart attacks;
- SD1/SD2 ratio - this parameter reflects the relationship between short-term and long-term HRV;
- Area of the ellipse - the area of the ellipse is defined by the formula: S = (SD1 * SD2 * pi) / 4.

Figure 13. Poincaré plot of PP intervals

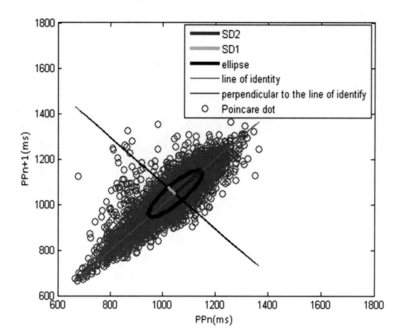

Characteristics of Poincaré Plot Method

The main features that are used for HRV visual analysis using the Poincaré method are: the shape, size, and location of the main cloud of points, localization, and symmetry of the cloud points.

The shape of the "cloud" is categorized for the different functional states of a person (Ernst, 2014; Khandoker, Karmakar, Brennan, Voss, & Palaniswami, 2013):

- The chart of the healthy subject has one main "cloud" of points to which even more points can be evenly scattered. The main "cloud" has the shape of a comet with a narrow lower part and gradually expanding towards the top (Figure 14a).
- The chart of the diseased subject takes the form of a torpedo (Figure 14b), a fan (Figure 14c) or a complex form (consisting of several "cloud") depending on the type of disease (Figure 14d).

Localization and Symmetry of the "Cloud" Points

If there are other clusters in the graph that are substantially separate from the main "cloud", arrhythmia may be expected. As a rule, these clusters indicate the presence of extrasystoles (Khandoker et al., 2013).

The cloud point symmetry is determined by the identity line. Symmetry shows the absence of rhythm disturbances, and the asymmetry - for the presence of rhythm disturbances.

Experimental Results Received

The data used in this study were captured by the PPG device for patients with various cardiac diseases, which were made and annotated holter records in specialized medical centers. The data are accompa-

Figure 14. Visual patterns of Poincaré plot depending on the shape of the "cloud"

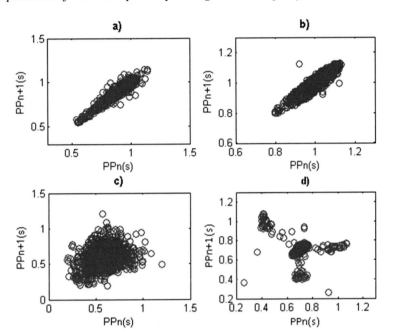

nied by a diagnosis by a physician cardiologist. Recordings made via a PPG device last for 20 minutes, in which the study patients are placed in rest, resting. All analyzed records in this study were made in connection with solving the tasks of research projects funded by scientific funds.

For software analysis, the author developed software that includes time domain analysis, frequency domain, and nonlinear analysis. The software is implemented using the programming languages: C++, MATLAB. It allows analysis of both short (5, 10 minute) ECG or PPG records as well as long (24, 48 hour) holter ECG or PPG records. Patient data (digital electrocardiograms or photoplethysmogram) can be read/written from/on a local computer or from a remote server.

The analyzes were made on records of three groups of individuals: 20 patients diagnosed with heart arrhythmia, 20 patients diagnosed with heart failure and 20 healthy subjects (control group).

Experimental Results in Time Domain Analysis

The photoplethysmographic records were analyzed in the time domain by determining the statistical parameters described in Table 1. All obtained results are presented as *mean±std*. In order to determine the statistical significance of the studied parameters ANOVA statistical analysis was carried out and parameter q was determined. The results are statistically significant, when p have values <0.05. The results are presented in Table 3.

The table shows that the SDNN, SDANN and SDNN index parameters are of statistical significance (the parameter p holds values <0.05). These parameters can be used to assess the cardiac activity of the human organism and to distinguish healthy individuals from those with arrhythmia and heart failure.

Table 3. Values of the parameters studied in the time domain

Parameter	Arrhythmia (n=20)	Heart failure (n=20)	Healthy (n=20)	p-value
	mean±sd	mean±sd	mean±sd	
Mean NN (ms)	690.01±283.47	876.89±318.81	822±114.37	0.067
Mean HR(bpm)	86.96±31.07	68.42±23.81	72.99±17.22	0.055
SDNN (ms)	182.62±19.09	138.21±45.73	152.16±24.07	<0.0001
SDANN (ms)	124.71±25.86	158.29±43.66	168.07±44.18	<0.005
SDNNindex (ms)	46.16±11.08	81.53±51.9	64.04±26.93	<0.05
RMSSD (ms)	47.04±36.11	31.82±19.3	32.41±16.8	0.112

Experimental Results in Frequency Domain Analysis

The analysis of photoplethysmographic data in the frequency domain was performed on a 20-minute signal, divided into 5-minute segments according to the recommendations of the heart rate standard (Malik, 1996). The spectral components in the field of the very low frequencies, in the low frequency and the high-frequency area were investigated and the sympathetic balance index was determined.

The statistical analysis was performed of the studied parameters (Table 4) and the parameter p was determined. The research on the three groups of individuals showed statistical significance of the parameters in the low-frequency and high-frequency area and the sympathetic balance index ($p < 0.05$).

The analysis performed in the frequency domain is illustrated with graphical results presented in Figure 15, Figure 16, and Figure 17. The graphs in the figures show roughly the same spectra of Power Spectral Density (PSD) at the very low frequencies of the three photoplethysmographic records. In the low-frequency and high-frequency areas, PSD has lower values in patients with arrhythmia compared to PSD healthy controls and even lower values in patients with heart failure.

Table 4. Values of the parameters studied in the frequency domain

Parameter	Arrhythmia (n=20)	Heart failure (n=20)	Healthy (n=20)	p-value
	mean±sd	mean±sd	mean±sd	
VLF (ms^2)	10648.57±420.73	10983.72 ±487.16	11001.12±648.31	0.067
LF (ms^2)	598.51±186.29	481.84±206.65	1246.24±209.73	<0.0001
HF (ms^2)	783.22±236.82	586.88±143.16	761.85 ±311.46	<0.05
LF/HF	0.76±0.24	0.82±0.51	1.64 ±0.82	<0.0001

Figure 15. Power spectral density of healthy subject

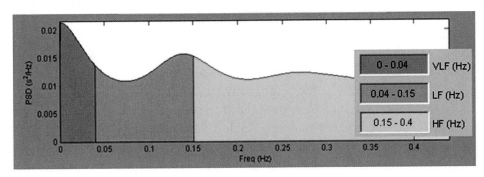

Figure 16. Power spectral density of patient with arrhythmia

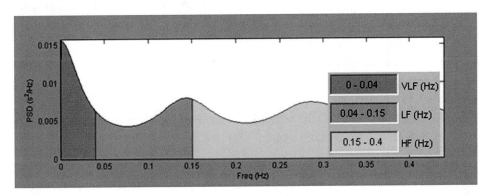

Figure 17. Power spectral density of patient with of heart failure

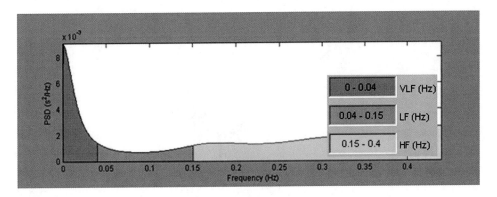

Experimental Results in Non-Linear Analysis

Based on the investigated values of the PP intervals of 20-minute PPGs. on Figure 18, Figure 19 and Figure 20 are showed the graphical illustration of the analysis by using of Poincaré method for a healthy subject, for patient with arrhythmia and for patient with heart failure. The graph of the healthy subject (Figure 18) has the shape of a comet with a sharpened lower part and gradually expanding towards the top. Graphs (Figure 19 and Figure 20) of patients with cardiovascular disease have the form of a fan (arrhythmia) and a complex form (heart failure). For each diagram an ellipse with a longitudinal and transverse axis is built. In healthy patients, the shape of the ellipse is clearly expressed, whereas in patients with diseases the length and width of the ellipse are approximately equal and the ellipse approaches a circle. In the patient with heart failure, the dots on the graph are asymmetric with respect to the line of identity, which is evidence of the presence of rhythm disorders. In the other 2 cases (healthy subject and patient with arrhythmia), the points in the graph are symmetrical.

The quantitative characteristics of the Poincaré method are significantly altered in patients with cardiovascular disease compared to healthy subjects. Table 5 shows the values of parameters SD1 and SD2, the relationship between them and the faces of the ellipses of the groups surveyed. SD1 decreased in patients with arrhythmia (Group 1) and heart failure (Group 2) as compared to healthy controls (Group 3). This decrease was statistically significant (p <0.05). The SD2 value is almost double in patients compared to healthy controls, and this decrease is statistically significant (p <0.0001). Lower values of SD1 and SD2 parameters in patients have reduced HRV. The ratio of SD2 / SD1 is at least in healthy subjects and also has statistical significance (p <0.005). The reduction of the SD1 and SD2 parameters leads to a reduction in the ellipse faces of the patients.

HRV analysis based on non-linear methods, such as the method of Poincaré, can provide important information about the physiological condition of the patients and assess the risk of sudden death. The Poincaré method is a special tool that allows physicians to view the entire study at a glance (in this case 20 minutes, but it could be 24 hours). This method is unique because it allows rapid detection of cardiovascular disorders that cannot be detected using traditional linear methods of HRV analysis.

Figure 18. Poincaré plot of the healthy subject

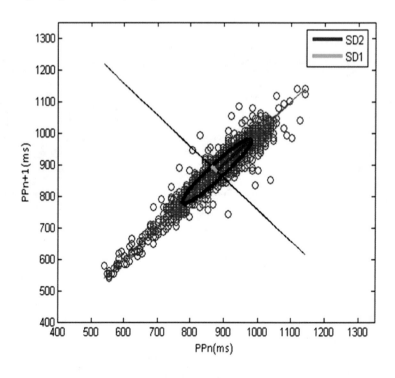

Figure 19. Poincaré plot of patient with arrhythmia

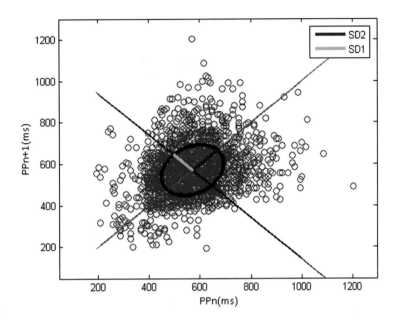

Figure 20. Poincaré plot of patient with heart failure

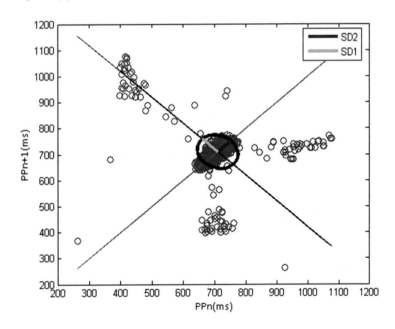

Table 5. Values of the parameters studied by the Poincaré plot

Parameter	Arrhythmia (Group 1) (n=20)	Heart failure (Group 2) (n=20)	Healthy (Group 3) (n=20)	p-value
	mean±sd	mean±sd	mean±sd	
SD1(ms)	63.2±10.2	44.5±12.8	46.94±17.5	<0.01
SD2(ms)	260.1±27.8	101.3±22.1	110.2±21.6	<0.0001
SD1/SD2	0.25±0.08	0.61±0.2	0.52±0.29	<0.002
S(ms²)	13 062±52	3 532±31	3 600±45	<0.0001

CONCLUSION

Modern medical devices based on PPG technology, which measure heart rate by optical methods, can be used to adequately and accurately assess the activity of the cardiovascular system during the day-to-day activities of individuals as well as in extreme situations such as: mental and physical load, stress, etc. These devices are useful for monitoring of cardiovascular disease as well as other changes in the patients' health status as result of the processes of aging in the human body. PPG technology has the potential to provide alternative measurement of a number of functional indicators, long-term monitoring activity, fast, cheap, reliable and secure. PPG based devices can be designed to be worn on the wrist, finger-like ring, on the forehead like a band, can be integrated into a man's garment, etc., thereby providing the monitoring of their health. The presented photoplethysmographic device may be used in medical clinical practice to monitor the condition of patients with cardiac symptoms, and other similar diseases. The development of wireless digital PPG based devices would contribute to the complete comfort of the monitored individuals, which is the future direction of the scientific researches.

The significance of the presented new automatized registration system for photoplethysmographic signals through the portable device and software for linear and nonlinear cardiac analysis is the formation of parametric and graphical assessment of patients' health status. An important diagnostic parameter that can be determined by PPG signals is a HRV that can be used in addition to the diagnosis of cardiovascular diseases, but also in the diagnosis of various internal, nerve, mental and other diseases. The quantitative dimensions of the investigated parameters in the use of linear mathematical methods of analysis are of significant clinical use because the norm-pathology limits are known, according to the standard introduced in 1996 by the European Cardiological and North American Electrophysiological Societies. The material analyzes in detail different methods for the study of the phenomenon of heart rate variability: time analysis, frequency analysis and non-linear analysis. There are presented the parameters that are tested in the time domain and their formulas; the parameters that are defined in the frequency domain and the frequency domains that are characteristic of the heart rate variability analysis. The methods investigated have been applied to records of patients with various cardiac diseases. The researches are part of the work on a project of National Science Fund of Republica Bulgaria. The analysis of HRV using non-linear methods can provide not only detailed information about the patient's physiological state but also provide the opportunity for predicting and preventing pathological conditions in cardiovascular diseases. Prevention in medicine is important not only for the individual, but also for society as a whole.

ACKNOWLEDGMENT

This research was carried out as part of the project "Investigation of the application of new mathematical methods for the analysis of cardiac data" № KP-06-N22/5, 07.12.2018, founded by National Science Found, Bulgaria.

REFERENCES

Acharya, U., Suri, J., Spaan, J., & Krishnan, S. (2007). *Advances in Cardiac Signal Processing*. Berlin: Springer. doi:10.1007/978-3-540-36675-1

Allen, J. (2007). Photoplethysmography and its application in clinical physiological measurement. *Physiological Measurement*, *28*(3), R1–R39. doi:10.1088/0967-3334/28/3/R01 PMID:17322588

Anderson, R., & Parrish, J. (1981). The optics of human skin. *The Journal of Investigative Dermatology*, *77*(1), 13–19. doi:10.1111/1523-1747.ep12479191 PMID:7252245

Blocker, D. C. (n.d.). *DSP Related*. Retrieved from https://www.dsprelated.com/freebooks/filters/DC_Blocker.html

Buccelletti, F., Bocci, M., Gilardi, E., Fiore, V., Calcinaro, S., Fragnoly, C., ... Franceschi, V. (2012). Linear and Nonlinear HRV Indexes in Clinical Practice. *Computational and Mathematical Methods in Medicine*, *2012*.

Cho, D., Ham, J., Oh, J., Park, J., Kim, S., Lee, N., & Lee, B. (2017). Detection of Stress Levels from Biosignals Measured in Virtual Reality Environments Using a Kernel-Based Extreme Learning Machine. *Sensors (Basel)*, *17*(10), 2435. doi:10.339017102435 PMID:29064457

Chon, K., Dash, S., & Ju, K. (2009). Estimation of respiratory rate from photoplethysmogram data using time-frequency spectral estimation. *IEEE Transactions on Biomedical Engineering*, *56*(8), 2054–2063. doi:10.1109/TBME.2009.2019766 PMID:19369147

Ernst, G. (2014). *Heart Rate Variability*. London: Springer-Verlag. doi:10.1007/978-1-4471-4309-3

Fleming, S., & Tarassenko, L. (2007). A comparison of signal processing techniques for the extraction of breathing rate from the photoplethysmogram. *International Journal of Biological and Medical Sciences*, *2*(4), 232–236.

9.   Hasan, E., & Cáceres, I. (2015). Heart Rate Variability Analysis Based on Photoplethysmographic Signals. *Revista Cubana de Informática Médica*, *7*(2), 113–121.

Khandoker, A., Karmakar, C., Brennan, M., Voss, A., & Palaniswami, M. (2013). *Poincare Plot Methods for Heart Rate Variability Analysis*. New York: Springer. doi:10.1007/978-1-4614-7375-6

Kim, Y., & Lee, J. (2010). Cuffless and non-invasive estimation of a continuous blood pressure based on PTT. *2nd International Conference on Information Technology Convergence and Services*. 10.1109/ITCS.2010.5581266

Koblenski, S. (2015). *Everyday DSP for Programmers: DC and Impulsive Noise Removal*. Retrieved from http://sam-koblenski.blogspot.com/2015/11/everyday-dsp-for-programmers-dc-and.html

Kumar, D., Prasannakumar, S., Sudarshan, B., & Jayadevappa, D. (2013). Heart Rate Variability Analysis: A Review. *International Journal of Advanced Technology in Engineering and Science*, *1*(6), 9–24.

Leonard, P., Grubb, N., Addison, P., Clifton, D., & Watson, J. (2004). An algorithm for the detection of individual breaths from the pulse oximeter waveform. *Journal of Clinical Monitoring and Computing*, *18*(5-6), 309–312. doi:10.100710877-005-2697-z PMID:15957620

Mainsah, B. & Wester, T. (2007). *Design of a Dual Heart Rate Variability Monitor*. Worcester Polytechnic Institute.

Malik, M. (1996). Heart Rate Variability: Standards of Measurement, Physiological Interpretation, and Clinical Use: Task Force of the European Society of Cardiology and the North American Society for Pacing and Electrophysiology. *Annals of Noninvasive Electrocardiology*, *1*(2), 151–181. doi:10.1111/j.1542-474X.1996.tb00275.x

Maxim Integrated. (n.d.). *MAX30102 Datasheet*. Retrieved from https://datasheets.maximintegrated.com/en/ds/MAX30102.pdf

Microchip. (n.d.). *Microchip Technology ATSAM4S16C Datasheet*. Retrieved from https://www.microchip.com/wwwproducts/en/ATSAM4S16C

Mirza, M., & Lakshmi, A. (2012). A comparative study of Heart Rate Variability in diabetic subjects and normal subjects. *International Journal of Biomedical and Advance Research*, *03*(08), 640–644. doi:10.7439/ijbar.v3i8.542

Nakajima, K., Tamura, T., & Miike, H. (1996). Monitoring of heart and respiratory rates by photoplethysmography using a digital filtering technique. *Medical Engineering & Physics*, *18*(5), 365–372. doi:10.1016/1350-4533(95)00066-6 PMID:8818134

Nakajima, K., Tamura, T., Ohta, T., Miike, H., & Oberg, P. (1993). Photoplethysmographic measurement of heart and respiratory rates using digital filters. In *Proceedings of the 15th Annual International Conference of the IEEE Engineering in Medicine and Biology Society* (Vol. 15, pp. 1006–1007). San Diego, CA: IEEE. 10.1109/IEMBS.1993.978978

Nenova, B. & Iiliev, I. (2010). An automated algorithm for fast pulse wave detection. *Bioautomation*, *3*(14), 203–216.

Nenova-Baylova, B. (2011). *Determination of Cardiac Activity in Extreme Situations*. Autoreferate. (in Bulgarian)

Nikolova, R. (2008). The Time to Distribute the Pulse Wave - a Method for the Study of the Functional Status of the Cardiovascular System [in Bulgarian]. *Bulgarian Medical Journal*, *2*(1), 9–13.

Nutt, G. (2018). *NuttX operating system user's manual*. Retrieved from www.nuttx.org

Pulse Sensor. (n.d.). Retrieved from https://pulsesensor.com/

Rao, M., & Ram, R. (2006). Photoplethysmography: A noninvasive tool for possible subtle energy monitoring during yogic practices. *Subtle Energies & Energy Medicine*, *17*(2), 163–179.

Schäfer, A., & Vagedes, J. (2013). How accurate is pulse rate variability as an estimate of heart rate variability? A review on studies comparing photoplethysmographic technology with an electrocardiogram. *International Journal of Cardiology*, *166*(1), 15–29. doi:10.1016/j.ijcard.2012.03.119 PMID:22809539

Smith, R., Wathen, E., Abaci, P., Bergen, N., Law, I., Dick, I. I. M., ... Dove, E. (2009). Analyzing Heart Rate Variability in Infants Using Non-Linear Poincare Techniques. *Computers in Cardiology*, *36*, 673–876.

Soni, R., Shukla, J., Dube, A., Shukla, A., Soni, R., & Soni, S. (2014). A Comparative Study of Heat Rate Variability in Obese and Healthy Young Adults (18 – 25 Years). *Research Journal of Pharmaceutical, Biological and Chemical Sciences*, *5*(3), 1111–1117.

Tamura, T., Maeda, Y., Sekine, M., & Yoshida, M. (2014). Wearable photoplethysmographic sensors-past and present. *Electronics (Basel)*, *3*(2), 282–302. doi:10.3390/electronics3020282

Tarniceriu, A., Harju, J., & Vehkaoja, A. (2018). Detection of Beat-to-Beat Intervals from Wrist Photoplethysmography in Patients with Sinus Rhythm and Atrial Fibrillation after Surgery. *Proceeding of IEEE International Conference on Biomedical and Health Informatics*. 10.1109/BHI.2018.8333387

Tayel, M., & AlSaba, E. (2015). Poincaré Plot for Heart Rate Variability. *International Journal of Biomedical and Biological Engineering*, *9*(9), 708–711.

Texas Instruments. (2014). *AFE4490 Datasheet*. Retrieved from http://www.ti.com/lit/gpn/afe4490

Webster, J. (2009). *Medical instrumentation: application and design*. John Wiley & Sons.

Yoon, J., & Yoon, G. (2009). Non-constrained blood pressure monitoring using ECG and PPG for personal healthcare. *Journal of Medical Systems*, *33*(4), 261–266. doi:10.100710916-008-9186-0 PMID:19697692

Chapter 12
Mathematical Processing of Cardiological Signals and Organization of Access to Holter Databases:
Guide for Accessing Data From People With Visual Deficits

Galya Nikolova Georgieva-Tsaneva
Bulgarian Academy of Sciences, Bulgaria

ABSTRACT

The study of human cardiovascular activity is one of the main methods for assessing the health of the human. It is performed in clinical conditions via electrocardiographic devices and in the daily life of a individuals through Holter monitoring. An important diagnostic parameter that can be determined by an electrocardiogram, taking into account the difference between successive heartbeat is heart rate variability – a widely used non-invasive method of measuring heart rate. This parameter makes it possible to assess the risk of various cardiac diseases such as angina, cardiac infarction, life-threatening arrhythmias, etc. This chapter presents the morphological bases of the cardio records, heart rate variability, and its impact on the healthy status of the individual. It describes the created cardiology base of prolongated Holter recordings for the purposes of scientific research project. Presented are internationally approved standards to provide web accessibility to internet-based data bases and other resources for people with disabilities.

DOI: 10.4018/978-1-5225-7879-6.ch012

INTRODUCTION

The work on this Chapter is closely related to work of a team of young scientists on tasks of a scientific project: "Investigation of Mathematical Techniques of Analysis of Physiological Data with Functionality for People with Visual Deficit", funded by Fund for Scientific Research at Ministry of Education and Science of Republic of Bulgaria.

Two of team's tasks for given project, which are presented in Chapter, are following:

1. The main task of this project is study the modern mathematical technologies for processing and analysis of prolonged time sequences of physiological data (specifically cardiological data). The investigations will be performed on real patient prolonged data by conducting holter monitoring of patients' cardiac activity.

2. The second task is to explore the possibilities of modern information technologies to provide resources, conditions, ways in this scientific activity can include people with visual deficits - ie. people with visual deficits can participate in research itself - they themselves research data, they analyze data, they use data processing software and analyze data. The assignment of such a task results from the fact that in project team has involved participant with visual deficit, who conducts scientific activity.

In this Chapter (in order to accomplish the first task), the morphological bases of cardiological data (basic elements in an electrocardiogram and its graphic appearance) are presented, the means for obtaining these patient data are described, and mathematical technologies for their analysis are examined.

The two main ways of obtaining cardiological data are described: via standard stationary device of the human body and by conducting Holter monitoring in which one performs his usual work.

In this Chapter concept of Heart Rate Variability (reflecting the variability of cardiac intervals over the time) is presented, the way it is received and studied, and the methods for its evaluation. Both types of Heart Rate Variability (HRV) are shown graphically: normal and abnormal.

One of the tasks assigned to the project team is to inform the public in Bulgaria and around the world on the issues of accessibility of data bases in Web (e.g. information bases of cardiological data that are being studied using modern mathematical technologies). The goal is to give publicity of problems encountered by People with Visual Deficit (as well all people with special needs), accessing information resources on the web, and showing ways and methods to address these issues. This Chapter examines established international Standards designed to help developers of web-based information resources and shows how to implement them.

The guidance given in the latest version of the internationally accepted Web Accessibility Standard will be used in the design, creation and maintenance of information databases containing annotated prolonging cardiological data and software programs for data analysis.

BACKGROUND

Cardiovascular diseases throughout the world continue to increase over the last decades, despite remarkable advances in their prophylaxis and treatment. They are the number one cause of death among European populations. Bulgaria is among the countries in the European Union with the highest morbidity and mortality from cardiovascular diseases. According to data from the Bulgarian Cardiology Society, 60% of mortality in Bulgaria is the result of heart disease. These diseases are also a major factor in disabling the population, which leads to a decrease in the quality of life. Research studies in this area indicate that cardiovascular disease can be reduced by early detection, prognosis and prevention.

Electrocardiography is one of leading medical non-invasive methods to study the condition of the cardiovascular system of the human body. The electrocardiogram (ECG) is a linear graphic recording of electrical activity of heart muscle during cardio cycles and is a standard procedure in medicine. The first human ECG was published in 1887 by British physiologist Waleer, and the first ECG record on paper was carried out in 1903 by the Dutch physiologist Willem Einthoven. The development of methods of processing, analysis and compression of cardiological data goes through several stages during years and continues to be improved in Nowdays. In the study of long-term electrocardiogram data are generates a huge amount of data, and therefore it is preferable to use automated processing and analysis methods.

Currently there are a number of directions for research, processing and analysis of cardiological data (signals):

- recognition of the basic characteristics of the electrocardiogram - QRS cardiological complex (QRS is a name for combination of three basic points: Q, R and S of electrocardiogram);
- P and T wave;
- Morphological analysis of QRS complex;
- Morphological analysis of T wave;
- Modeling of the ECG signal;
- High resolution ECG analysis;
- HRV analysis;
- Heart Rate Turbulence analysis;
- Analysis of the fetal ECG;
- Reduction of noise in the ECG data;
- Removing the drift of zero line;
- Compression of ECG data;
- Rhythmic analysis;
- Measuring the heart rate and marking the deviations;
- Classification of ventricular contractions, normal QRS complexes, premature extrasystoles and others.

HRV analysis is scientific direction, which has been developing at a rapid pace in recent years. Bulgarian researchers in their works (Gospodinov, Gospodinova, 2017; Gospodinova & Gospodinov, Domuschiev et al., 2015; Gospodinova, 2014; Simov, Matveev, Milanova, Krasteva & Christov, 2014) receive interesting scientific results using various mathematical methods.

An integral part of modern medical services are program-medical complexes performing diagnostic and functional examination of human health. Together with stationary unit modules, recording short - term (duration from 3 to 5 minutes), cardiological data, portable Holter monitoring systems are also used recording continuous (24 hours to 72 hours; some modern models of holter devices can record the heart activity of the patient within 2 weeks) ECG data.

The scheme of these systems includes: a cardiological data recorder, a data processing computer (located in a healthcare facility), and a channel for transmitting cardiological data from registrar to computer. The situation is similar in systems where remote monitoring and patient control is performed. Critical parameters of these systems are the bandwidth of connection channel and

the internal memory of the data logger. These features can be improved by using effective program compression of registered cardiological data.

MORPHOLOGICAL BASES OF CARDIOLOGICAL DATA

Electrocardiogram is a graphical recording of electrical activity of the heart during cardio cycles (in depolarization and repolarization of atrium and heart chamber) from different points of body and is an effective means of analyzing and diagnosing the functioning of heart. The electrical activity of heart is detected by electrodes attached to the human skin. Typically, the frequency range of cardiological signal is 0.05 to 125 Hz (Sarmiento et al., 2013); dynamic range is from 1 to 10 mV (Sasikala & Wahidabanu, 2010). The required resolution for correct analysis - 5 µV. The real cardiological signals have a number of interferences overlapped and it is important to separate them before the analysis is performed.

Registration of cardiac activity is performed in several leads - clinical practice usually involves 12 standard leads. Figure 1 shows a schematic diagram of a typified ECG signal which corresponds to a second standard output with its characteristic points. The following basic elements of a cardio cycle are noted:

- P-wave - smooth low-amplitude wave due to the excitation (depolarization) of the atrium.
- QRS complex - a highly amplitude part with steep slopes forming during the reduction of normally excited heart chambers. It consists of a negative peak Q, follows a high positive peak R and ends with a negative S peak.
- T wave - medium amplitude smoothing wave due to repolarization of the cameras.
- U wave - after T wave there may be a low amplitude wave, visible in 50 to 75% of cases, of undetermined origin.

Figure 1. Scheme of the typical electrocardiogram

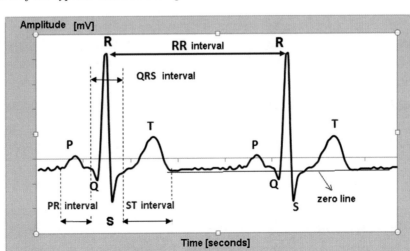

The morphology of the ECG signal is different even in healthy individuals. P or T waves may dominate or fuse with QRS complex, in some electrocardiograms R peak may be negative.

When electrical activity of the heart is not detected, ECG represents a straight line called isolation (zero line). A normal heart rate for a person ranges from 60 to 100 beats per minute. From form of ECG record can determine the status of cardiac activity (normal, abnormal and type of anomaly). Figure 2 shows a schematic diagram of a real ECG signal.

HEART RATE VARIABILITY

Cardiological Intervals

The time from one beat of the heart to next (from one recognized R peak to next R peak in the electrocardiogram) is called a cardiological interval and is usually marked with a RR interval. Cardiological intervals change their duration as a result of different processes in the human body: respiratory activities, blood pressure, physical and mental load, day-night rhythms, thermoregulation, health condition, etc. The change of heart rhythm is a response of human organism to effects of the external environment.

Changing the duration of cardiological intervals over time is a dynamic, non-static variable and is referred to in the scientific literature with the term HRV. The HRV study is based on measurement of RR intervals, building on their basis rhythms, tachographs and subsequent analysis with various mathematical methods. For this purpose, QRS complexes are recognized in the continuous ECG record, the intervals between them are measured and the instantaneous HR is calculated.

In 1996 it has established Standard, regulating clinical use of parameters for evaluation of HRV (Malik, 1996). Currently HRV is not sufficiently investigated and is the subject of increasing scientific interest.

The duration from peak R of one QRS complex to peak R of next QRS complex determines duration of given cardiological interval. This duration varies in individual cycles in all individuals regardless of their health status. Instantaneous heart rate is reciprocal value of RR interval, and accordingly also varies. The sequence of times { $t_i, i = 1, 2, \ldots n$ }, obtained after successful recognition of all R peaks in electrocardiogram, forms an RR cardiological time series in which each i-th RR interval is determined by:

$$RR_i = t_i - t_{i-1}$$

Figure 2. Scheme of the real ECG signal (second lead)

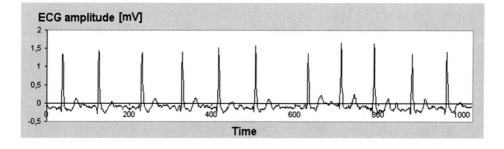

The sequence of instantaneous heart rates is defined as:

$$f_i = \frac{1}{RR_i}$$

The ECG data according to their duration is divided into:

- Short-term (from 5 to 30 minutes) - are performed with specialized device that perform electrocardiography (electrocardiograph);
- Long-term (up to 24, 48 or 72 hours) – are performed with specialized Holter monitoring device.

Several well-conducted studies of HRV have shown that in time domain, high HRV (Figure 3) is an indicator of good overall health, whereas low HRV (Figure 4) indicates a high risk of cardiac death (Clifford et al., 2006) myocardial infarction, heart failure, diabetes and others. Decreased HRV is an unfavorable prognostic sign following a myocardial infarction (Clifford et al., 2004).

Spectral analysis of cardiological intervals presents the distribution of frequencies present in RR intervals. In the spectral analysis of long-term HRV data in total frequency range of 0 to 0.4 Hz, four subbands are distinguished for physiological reasons (Table 1). The spectrum of short-time HRV data covers the frequencies of high frequency, low frequency and ultra low frequency range. Of great importance for clinical practice in the study of short-term cardiological data are the low frequency and the high frequency range.

Figure 3. High (normal) Heart Rate Variability

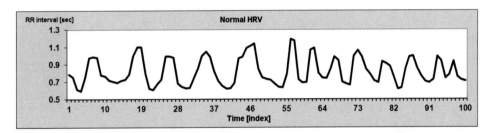

Figure 4. Low (abnormal) Heart Rate Variability

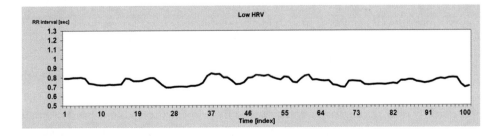

Table 1. Frequency ranges for Heart Rate Variability analysis of long-term records

Frequency range	Frequency (Hz)	Physiological reason
Common Frequency Spectrum Total power of the heart rate spectrum	0 – 0.4	The variation at all normal intervals. Reflects the overall activity of regulatory systems.
Ultra Low Frequency (ULF)	0-0.003	Influence of the cycle day and night.
Very Low Frequency range (VLF)	0.003-0.04	It reflects the sympathetic activity of the nervous system.
Low Frequency Range (LF)	0.04-0.15	Refers to the sympathetic and parasympathetic activity of the nervous system.
High Frequency Range (HF)	0.15-0.4	Respiratory and parasympathetic activity of the nervous system
LF / HF ratio	-	Reflects the balance between the two parts of the nervous system - sympathetic and parasympathetic

Heart rate is a non-stationary signal (Acharya et al., 2006) and is influenced by sympathetic and parasympathetic activity of autonomic nervous system (ANS) (Malik, Camm, 2004). The ANS is as part of nervous system, involuntary and autonomously controls activity of cardiovascular system. The sympathetic and parasympathetic nervous systems are parts of ANS and have opposite effect. Research conducted in frequency domain of HRV indicates that when the effect of sympathetic nervous system active in situations of physical exercise (running, wrestling) or emotional stress, HR can accelerate to 180 beats / minute, it also increases the spectral power of variable in low frequency range. The sympathetic system is responsible for narrowing the blood vessels, raising blood pressure, expanding the airways in the lungs, enlarging the pupil. Under the sympathetic impulses the body is mobilized.

The other part of ANS, parasympathetic nervous system is opposite of sympathetic - it slows down the functions of the body. It acts in a state of rest, sleep, cooling and can reduce heart rate to 60 beats / minute. The research studies carried out show an increase of the spectral power of the HRV in high frequency range respectively.

The parasympathetic system is consistent with the respiratory rate, and this effect is known as Respiratory Sinus Arrhythmia (RSA).

In the study of healthy individuals are observed two typical peaks in frequency spectrum (McSharry et al., 2003):

- 0.1 Hz (in the LF area) - is related to Meyer's wave due to changes in blood pressure;
- 0.25 Hz (in the HF area) - RSA oscillations show the peak in the HF spectrum, which corresponds to a breathing rate of 15 breaths per minute.

Based on the studies of HRV spectrum, scientists have reached the following conclusion: the ratio between low frequency components and high frequency components in the spectrum is an indicator of the cardiological sympatheticvagal balance in human body (Matveen et al., 2012).

In healthy individuals the influence of LF and HF ranges is changing periodically, with the influence of low frequency components predominating during the day and the influence of high frequency components prevailing over the night. Scientists prove that, under the influence of various factors, the spectral power of HF and LF ranges can be increased to judge different human conditions, pathological disorders or to be a predictor of certain diseases.

Cardiological Database With Patient Records

For research purposes of a scientific project a cardiological database was created by project team. About a period of nine months, over 1100 prolonged cardiological data records for various patients have collected and processed. Data patient's records have made from January to September 2018. The project team also received ECG recordings have made in previous periods. Records have transferred from the data carriers located in hospital to external storage devices by the team. These cardiological data represent records have made on patients visiting a hospital and diagnosed with cardiovascular disease. ECG records are long-term, usually about 24 hours. The purpose of continuous monitoring is to capture rare cardiac anomalies that cannot be detected in traditional 3-minute study under stationary conditions.

The investigated database has obtained with assistance of cardiology department of Multiprofile District Hospital for Active Treatment MOBAL "Dr. Stefan Cherkezov", V. Tarnovo, Bulgaria. Each cardiological data record has made using Holter monitoring performed for approximately 24 hours at 200 Hz frequency and consists of one to four channels Leads. The monitoring Holter device used for obtaining the records is produced by company SignaCor, Sofia, Bulgaria. This device has ability to continuously record of cardiological signal with duration of up to 72 hours, as well to record only in certain epochs. The monitoring device is placed on patient in hospital conditions - in cardiology department, usually in morning about 10 hours, after which individual returns to his usual way of life. The next day, a doctor removes Holter from the patient and cardiological data from device for analysis. The recorded ECG data reflect he actual state of activity of cardiovascular system of investigated individual, placed in his everyday environment. By comparison, the 3 minute records are made in the stationary position of individual. The Holter device can work in a WINDOWS environment.

The created cardiology base of long-term Holter record contains over 1100 entries, which are analyzed in detail for research objectives of project with specially created software procedures from the project collective. The MATLAB R2015b (MathWorksInc.) and Microsoft Visual C ++ programming environments have been used.

The collected physiological records are of study population (men, women and children) with varying degrees of cardiac morbidity in the age range of 8 to 92 years, among which there are records of healthy people. Each ECG Holter record is accompanied by an annotation from the treating physician cardiologist. The database thus created allows for extensive comparative analyzes.

One of most important conditions for the success of holter observation is accurate and detailed diary of patient's subjective complaints during the recording.

Advantages of Holter monitoring:

1. The patient does not need to remain in hospital conditions.
2. Through Holter, asymptomatic conditions, problems with cardiac conduction can be diagnosed.
3. Holter helps to compare patient's symptoms and abnormalities in heart rhythm (with care keeping of diary).

Disadvantages of Holter Monitoring:

1. Holter is not much pleasant to wear.
2. Some people may get an allergy from constantly wearing of electrodes on the skin.

3. Sometimes 24 or even 72 hours of recording are not enough to detect some rare arrhythmias. When wearing the holter for 1 week, twice as many recurrences of atrial fibrillation were detected.
4. During Holter monitoring, the patient should not bathing, cannot swimming.

Despite its disadvantages, Holter monitoring is a proven tool for detecting a number of cardiovascular anomalies such as: syncope, palpitations, changes in the ST segment, complicated for diagnosis arrhythmias, heart conduction problems, etc.

Application of Wavelet Theory for Cardiological Data Analysis

Wavelet Theory is a modern mathematical technology for exploring and processing processes of a different nature. Created in the early 1980s by Morley, Grossman and others (Grossman, Morlet, 1984) it continues to be developed to Nowdays. Unlike of traditional Fourier analysis, Wavelet Analysis (WA) has great information and is a way of directly processing some signal features that are difficult to analyze with traditional Fourier transforms. WA offers simultaneous localization in the time domain and frequency domain, so it is a suitable means of analyzing non-stationary signals. According to (Xiong, Qi, Nattel & Comtois, 2015) Fourier analysis, based on the spectral properties of stationary signals, cannot directly provide information about the spectrum changes in terms of time. In his work (Aldonin, Soldatov & Cherepanov, 2018), researches used wavelet analysis as a suitable means of detecting various cardiac diseases. Zoltan German-Sallo in his work (German-Sallo, 2014) uses Wavelet Packet Transform to evaluate the HRV, calculates the frequency ranges resulting from the Wavelet decomposition and determines the sympathovagal balance index. Methods are traditional and are often used by HRV researchers.

Wavelet transforms introduce an additional degree of freedom in the processing of signals and the ability to locate the essential moments of data being studied. WA is successfully applied for frequency-time analysis of signals, filtration and separation of beneficial components against background noise, signal recognition and classification, interpolation, approximation and random casualty assessment as well as in medical applications. Due to these characteristics WA is suitable for processing and analyzing cardiological signals.

Basic functions of wavelet transform can be various functions with compact carrier - modulated impulse sinewave, level change functions, etc. selected for the specific application so as to best describe character of signal, its jumps, interruptions, etc. local peculiarities. In each application, appropriate waveform transformat of thesignal is sought to give themaximum information equivalence of spectrum of time representation of signal and uniformity of its right and inverse transform, tasks with which the orthogonal and biorthogonal wavelets. An important task of selected basic function is possibility of transform realized through it to evaluate the information content of signal and dynamics of its change.

Summary characteristic of basic types of base wavelets is given in table 2.

In wavelet analysis of physiological signals may be used continuous wavelet transform or discrete wavelet transform. A comparative characteristic between the continuous Wavelet analysis and the discrete Wavelet analysis, according to their advantages and disadvantages, in the treatment of cardiological data is presented in Figure 5.

Table 2. Characteristics of basic wavelet functions

Wavelet type	Basic function	Properties
Rough	Derivatives of Gaussian function of Morley	Simplexing feature - they do not. The detail function is not compact carrier. Symmetrical. The detailing function is set to clear. Performing a non-orthogonal analysis. Fast computational algorithms - do not. Exact data reconstruction - impossible.
Orthogonal with compact carrier	Haar Daubechies	Approximating function - they have. The detailing and the approximating function - have a compact carrier. They have a certain number of zero moments. They can perform orthogonal analysis. Fast computational algorithms have been developed. Exact data reconstruction - possible.
Infinitely regular	Meyer wavelet	Approximating function - they have. The detailing and approximation function is not set explicitly. Symmetrical. The detailing and approximation feature is not compact carrier. Performing an Orthogonal Analysis. Fast computational algorithms - do not.
Biorthogonal with compact carrier	Biorthogonal	Approximating function - they have. The detailing and approximation feature has a compact media. Performing a biotogonal analysis. The detailing and approximation function has zero moments.
Complex	Gauss, Morley, Shannon, Frequency	Approximate function - they do not. The detailing and approximation feature does not have a compact media. Perform non-orthogonal analysis. Reconstruction of the data is not guaranteed. Fast algorithms - not developed.

Comparison Between Continuous Wavelet Analysis and Discrete Wavelet Analysis

1. The continuous wavelet transform comprises a large amount of information that is suitable for signal analysis; for expressing the periodic dependencies of local disturbances. The calculation is labor-intensive and takes a significant processing time. For some applications, not all wavelet transform can be calculated, but only values within a certain range, making inverse transform impossible. Effective for tasks where parts of a wave image are calculated without reversing the process.

2. The discrete wavelet transform contains relatively little information, and the continuous signal being investigated is placed in accordance with a discrete function. Information is sufficient to perform inverse transform. Suitable for applications where signal reconstruction is needed (non-stationary signal processing, compression of information). The possibilities of Discrete Wavelet Transform in the area of signal analysis are significantly smaller than that of Continuous Wavelet Transform.

3. The using of Wavelet Analysis opens new data processing capabilities by shortening processing time. The presentation of Wavelet functions in analytical form increases performance. This is not the case with complex wavelength functions and wavelets described with iterative expressions.

Figure 5. Comparison between continuous wavelet analysis and discrete wavelet analysis

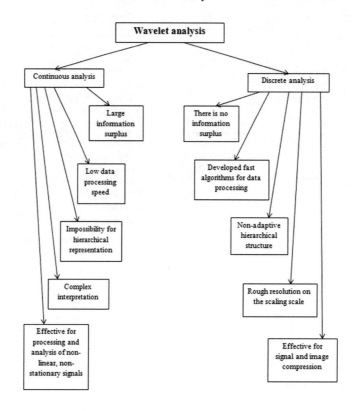

Of those conclusions outline the advantages of using the Discrete Wavelet Transform in development of fast-running computational methods, reducing time of analysis, processing and compression of cardiological data.

Mathematical Methods for Analysis of Heart Rate Variability

In cardiological sequences are detected cardiological complexes (so-called QRS complexes), time sequences from cardiological intervals were created. In the next step, ectopic intervals are excluded and the time-series of normal-to-normal intervals is formed. The data is processed by interpolation. The resulting HRV sequence is analyzed by various mathematical methods (Figure 6).

Methods for analysis of HRV can be divided into following groups:

- Linear methods:
  ○ Methods for time domain analysis. They are mainly used to obtain statistical estimates of the variability.
  ○ Methods for frequency domain analysis. They provide a general spectral analysis of the variability.
- Non-linear methods. Through them, specific information on the behavior of the variability can be derived. They are often used to detect cardiac anomalies. Some commonly used nonlinear methods are:

◦ Detrended Fluctuation Analysis;

◦ Measurement of Capacity dimension;

◦ Measurement of Correlation dimension;

◦ Measurement of Entropy;

◦ Measurement of Fractal dimension.

- Fractal methods. Used to evaluate self-similarity of the time series by computing the Hurst exponent.
- Methods using WA. The methods use Continuous WA and Discreet WA. The use of this technology has increased in recent years.

figure 6. Heart rate variability data processing

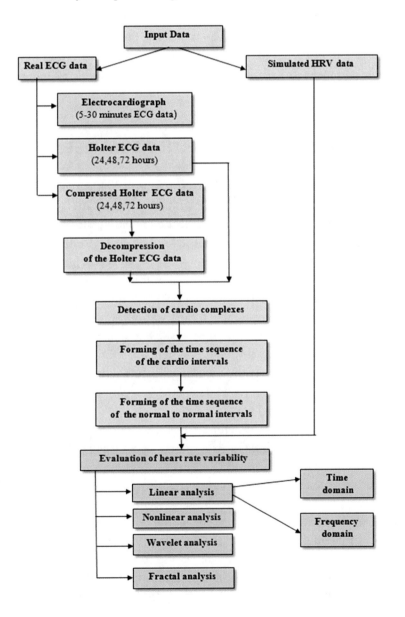

Lem point out in (Lem, 2016) as a good practice the pre-planning of research. Research should be considered in advance: what data will be conducted on the research, how many records will be, what the sample size of these records will be and what criteria this sample will determine. Once set up, these rules should be followed throughout the study.

In cardiovascular research, it is necessary to maintain a solid, carefully thought-out and well-written protocol; it is better to describe the conditions under which the data were obtained; to provide the information needed to conduct the specific surveys. It is necessary to apply statistical methods for assessing the results obtained, which methods are well known, accepted and validated in the specific field where the scientific studies are carried out. The author of (Lem, 2016) detail statistical methods for evaluation of cardiology results.

In research studies currently conducted by project team and in presentation of results, researchers adhere to these methods in results-based publications (results obtained are evaluated using ANOVA-based statistical analysis). This is a guarantee of objectivity of presented results, whether they support or reject original hypotheses of researcher on a given issue. The presentation of results in field of cardiac data research should receive relevant biostatistical support due to importance of healthcare research to people. It is a good idea to make statistical analyzes as simple as possible so that results are supported by transparent and easy to obtain statistical values.

USING WEB RESOURCES BY PEOPLE WITH VISUAL DEFICIT

This chapter focuses on the main tasks of project " Investigation of Mathematical Techniques of Analysis of Physiological Data with Functionality for People with a Visual Deficit ".

The leading task of project is study of mathematical technologies for analysis of cardiac data, on which previous sections were dedicated. One of other tasks of project is to study and, if possible, improve conditions for study of cardiological data from people with special needs, particularly people with visual deficits. This is a non-standard task at first glance, and for this reason is a bit difficult to understand. People with special needs want to participate fully in common life of all people. The development of information technology makes this desire possible for realization. Among people with special needs (for example, people with visual deficits) there are people who want to do science, be researchers, work with information, analyze it and process it. In team of project, there is a PhD student at Institute of Mathematics and Informatics of the Bulgarian Academy of Sciences with 100% visual impairment. He wants to be a researcher, to use vast amounts of information in databases. People with reduced vision or blind people can not use information in databases and software applications that are created for data analysis in the way people do without visual impairment. Therefore, it is necessary to make software tools specifically available to them to facilitate their handling of data from databases and software information programs for processing and analysis of data.

The next section of the chapter discusses web accessibility standards designed to make it easier for web developers to provide resources to improve the accessibility of people with special needs to information databases and applied software products. The author of this chapter is convinced that informing an increasing number of people, especially researchers and people who set up information databases and software products, is of great importance in addressing this issue, which has been on the agenda in recent years - creating resources, technologies and conditions for people with special needs to integrate them successfully into our technology society. Therefore, the issues that this chapter views from here on, apart from their scientific significance, also contribute to science, its leading role and indisputable technological advantages of today, to tackle pressing social issues of our society.

Creating Web Accessibility for People With Visual Deficit

The availability of information databases, the use of digital libraries in Internet for learning purposes gives users great opportunities to increase their knowledge (Paneva-Marinova, Goynov & Pavlov, 2017; Paneva-Marinova, Pavlov & Kotuzov, 2017; Paneva-Marinova, Goynov, Luchev & Pavlov, 2015). The implementing principles of Web Accessibility for People with Visual Deficit to public web sites and useful information in them, to internet-based user systems and information resources is a difficult task. This issue has a social aspect - creation of Internet access conditions by certain groups of people with special needs means placing on agenda of problems associated with these people. Society is obliged to take into consideration these different people, who have their own specificities, but who wish to enjoy the contemporary achievements of information technologies in equal measure with rest of people. Addressing the problems of accessing web-based resources from people with visual deficits, as well as from other specific groups of people, such as elderly people or people with hearing impairment, means caring for these people. Ensuring real equality between people means taking certain actions to implement it.

The public Web sites in the Republic of Bulgaria today are not sufficiently accessible for people with disabilities. In recent years Institute of Mathematics and Informatics of Bulgarian Academy of Sciences, Horizons Foundation and other researchers have been working on topic of web accessibility in Bulgaria. To solve the issues related to the implementation of the regulations and the implementation of the European Union Directive 2016/2102 on accessibility of websites and mobile applications of public sector organizations in 2017, an Interministerial Commission was established in Bulgaria at the Ministry of Transport, Information Technology and Messages.

When research into the availability of 100 public websites in Bulgaria, results show that these websites are largely unavailable to people with special needs. The principles in web accessibility standard and accessibility on 100 websites of public institutions in Bulgaria are investigated in (Bogdanova, Sabev, 2016; Sabev, Bogdanova, 2017; Bogdanova, Sabev, 2018).

For software developers, implementing Web Accessibility for people with visual deficits is a task that has following difficulties:

- Understanding the problems encountered by people with specific needs when working in a web environment;
- Creating real conditions for easy access to information in a web environment;
- Taking consideration the ways of accessing different types of information - text, audio, video, etc .;
- Taking consideration the different types of specific needs of different groups of people and adjusting the software applications to them.

Definition of Term Web Accessibility

According adopted in December 2010 Convention of United Nations Organization for the rights of persons with disabilities must be guaranteed all human rights and freedoms of people with disabilities.

According to data from National Statistics Institute in Republic of Bulgaria since last census in 2011, 475 267 people are disabled and number is actually more. Data from the 2011 National Insurance Institute in Bulgaria shows that an even higher number of invalid pensions are being paid. The majority of people with disabilities are women. The largest is age group of over fifty years.

Web developers work to create Internet-based resources, software systems, databases that are user-friendly for all.

The words "easy to use" are often used to indicate the characteristics of the resources created for people with specific problems, but the technical term is "usability".

The ISO 9241 Standard created in 1998, on "Ergonomics of Human Systems Interaction" gives the following definition of usability:

The extent to which a product [service or environment] can be used by specified users to achieve specified goals with effectiveness, efficiency and satisfaction in a specified context of use".

The following definitions are also given:

- Effectiveness – "the accuracy and completeness with which users achieve specified goals";
- Efficiency – "the resources expended in relation to the accuracy and completeness with which users achieve those goals;
- Satisfaction - "freedom from discomfort, and positive attitudes towards the use of the product [system, service or environment]".

The question of Web Accessibility in the scientific circles was put in place in 1996. From then until the present 2018 this issue has been discussed in a number of reports, articles, specially developed Standards, books, Internet-based sources, etc. Accessibility issues over the years are based on researchers from over twenty countries around the world. In the scientific literature, many definitions of the term Web Accessibility are given. Almost all definitions include a description of the people for whom this concept refers by identifying groups of users or giving a characteristic of the specific needs of these people. Some of these definitions include the group of older people. These definitions also address information technology issues that make accessibility available.

Accessibility can be defined as universal principle with very significant influence. According to Tim Berners-Lee, Director of World Wide Web Consortium (W3C) and inventor of the World Wide Web, Internet network is designed to be used by all people and therefore: "The power of the Web is in its universality. Access by everyone regardless of disability is an essential aspect". The specific characteristics of users such as: reduced vision or complete blindness; reduced hearing or missing hearing; restrictions on physical movements; different cognitive abilities must not be a barrier to the use of the web. The Internet as a global information network should remove barriers rather than set new ones to facilitate communication between people. Information technology with all its power, using all the modern advances of science and technology, must serve all people today. Thus, the principle of equal standing between people can be realized. Web Accessibility is a matter that seeks solutions from web developers and web tools that provide accessibility for all users can guarantee the use of web-based resources and products by all people, regardless of their specific needs.

The most comprehensive definition of Web Accessibility is given by the Web Accessibility Initiative (WAI) in the article "Strategies, Standards, resources to make the Web accessible to people with disabilities" (available on the web address: https://www.w3.org/WAI/fundamentals/accessibility-intro/#what). The definition is as follows: " Web Accessibility means that websites, tools, and technologies are designed and developed so that people with disabilities can use them. More specifically, people can: perceive, understand, navigate, and interact with the Web; contribute to the Web". In this definition is allowed the possibility for people with disabilities not only to use web-based information for their needs but also to use them themselves, such as delivering their information on the Web. This makes consumers with specific needs on an equal footing with other users. In his book (Harper, S., Yesilada, Y., 2008) authors also pay attention to this issue.

WAI points to what disabilities it is targeted Web Accessibility: "audory, cognitive, neurological, physical, speech, visual". Of particular interest is the fact that achieving of Web Accessibility for people with disabilities contributes to better networking and other groups of people, for example: "people using mobile phones, smart watches, smart TVs and other devices with small screens, different input modes; older people with changing abilities due to age; people with "temporary disabilities" such as a broken arm or lost glasses; people with "situational limitations" such as in bright sunlight or in an environment where they can not listen to audio; people using a slow internet connection or who have limited or expensive bandwidth".

World Wide Web Consortium (W3C) gives the following definition of Web Accessibility: „Web Accessibility means that people with disabilities can use the Web. More specifically, Web Accessibility means that people with disabilities can perceive, understand, navigate, and interact with the Web, and that they can contribute to the Web. Web Accessibility also benefits others, including older people with changing abilities due to aging".

The authors Helen Petrie, Andreas Savva and Christopher Power (Helen P. et al., 2015) give the following generalized and comprehensive definition of Web Accessibility on the Internet: „all people, particularly disabled and older people, can use websites in a range of contexts of use, including mainstream and assistive technologies; to achieve this, websites need to be designed and developed to support usability across these contexts".

Web Accessibility Standards

The world-famous World Wide Web Consortium (W3C) creates detailed technical guidelines for implementing Web Accessibility, which sets and validates an internationally recognized Standard: Web Content Accessibility Guidelines (WCAG). This is a guide in the form of guidelines that has changed over the years since its first establishment in the direction of addressing all the problems of people with disabilities. The guidelines in Standard are very well structured. They aim to increase the level of accessibility of the web resource and to be useful to the people who develop it.

The establishment of Standard is a long process involving many global organizations. The first version of the Standard came out in 1999. The Web Content Accessibility Guidelines, version 2.0, was adopted at the end of 2008 (published on 11 December 2008), and from 2012 is ISO Standard (ISO / IEC 40500: 2012).

The latest version of this Standard was released in June 2018: WCAG 2.1 containing the latest guidelines for improving the accessibility of three groups of users: individuals with cognitive or learning disabilities low-visually impaired people, and motor-disabled users.

The last editing of Standard aims to help developers of Web resources, Developers of Web site development tools, developers of Web Accessibility evaluation tools, and users who need Web Accessibility Standards. The WCAG 2.1 Standard (published on 5 June 2018) contains four principles (perceivable, operable, understandable, and robust) to which a total of 12 guidelines have been created. For each guideline, testable success criteria (at 3 levels: A, AA and AAA) are provided - a total of 78 success criteria.

The WCAG 2.1 Standard (compared to WCAG 2.0) provides 17 additional success criteria to improve the accessibility of the following people with special needs to the web:

- Users with motor disabilities;
- Visually impaired users;
- Users with cognitive and learning disabilities.

Principles in Web Accessibility Standards

In the created Web Accessibility Standards set the following four principles:

- **Perceivable**: User interface information and components must be presented to the user in a user-friendly way.
  - ○ Guidelines: Provide an alternative to the text, for example: Enlarged Text, Braille, Speech, Symbols, or Simplified Language. For each video record, to provide descriptive text of what's happening; for the audio tracks to give a detailed text. The content of the web site can be represented in different ways.
- **Operable**: Ensure user interface management and navigation.
  - ○ Guidelines: All elements of the website can be accessed via the keyboard. Give users enough time to read the relevant text or use the content. Do not interfere with user actions (e.g.: „Web pages do not contain anything that flashes more than three times in any one second period". Give users the right way to navigate. Allow users to work with other incoming devices other than the keyboard.
- **Understandable**: The information and user interface management must be understandable to consumers.
  - ○ Guidelines: The text content must be clear. Web pages must work in a way that is predictable. Users should be helped to prevent mistakes.
- **Robust**: The content must be robust enough to be reliably interpreted by a wide range of consumer agents, assistive technologies. Ensure compatibility with user agents, including the assistive technologies those users with disabilities use. Disabled users use Internet access tools (Kurt S., 2011), tailored to the level of their disabilities. For completely blind users, screen readers are suitable, individuals with low vision use screen magnifiers. The individuals who cannot distinguish colors use display-adaptive operating system options.

Assistive Technology for People With Disabilities

Different technology tools that help people deal with problems they face due to their disabilities have been created to access Internet-based information bases and software systems for people with disabilities. Assistive technologies should be tailored to the level of human disability (Kurt S., 2011).

One of the affected groups of people with disabilities regarding the use of information (scientific, entertainment, etc.) on the web is group of blind users.

People with impaired vision reach information resources on Internet through support tools such as:

- Screen magnifiers, magnifiers - increase text and images to such an extent that they allow the user to perceive and interact with the operating system and user applications – suitable for partially sighted individuals;
- "Screen reader" specialized software - software that visually converts screen content into a different form in the form of a synthesized dictionary or braille text - Suitable for completely blind users. The blind man hears with his ears or reads the information provided on the Braille display;
- Adaptable to the display options of the operating system - suitable for the Daltonists (with color differentiation problems);
- Computer-based augmentative and alternative communication systems for people with speech and language disabilities (Cook, A.M., Polgar, J.M., 2015).

News in the Latest Version of Web Accessibility Standard

The following success criteria presented in Table 3 are new in WCAG 2.1.

The necessary conditions for people with disabilities, including people with visual deficits, to use Internet-based resources are: the availability of a screen reader and the ability to work with it; installed software on the computer that the screen reader can handle.

According to the authors of research [https://webaim.org/projects/screenreadersurvey7/] The biggest barriers to using the web of people with disabilities are:

- Completely Automated Public Turing Test to Tell Computers and Human Apart - CATCHA;
- Parts of the screen that unexpectedly change;
- Buttons and links that do not understand the purpose;
- Inaccessible Flash content;
- Lack of keyboard;
- Complicated forms;
- Using images that are not explained;
- Headlines that are not well-chosen or totally missing;
- Many navigation elements;
- Complexly organized tables;
- Inaccessible search functionality;
- Poor navigation.

Study of Availability of Web-Based Information Resources

Before being put to use by users, each created information product must be tested for use. The best option to determine whether an Internet-based information resource is accessible to people with special needs is to have access to this resource to be tested by people with the appropriate type of disability. It is a good idea to have a questionnaire filled in with appropriate questions, the answers to which will give a good idea of the availability of the web resource. One of the most basic issues that developers themselves can answer are:

Table 3. New success criteria in WCAG 2.1

Guideline	Level	Success criteria	Description
1.3 Adaptable	AA	1.3.4 Orientation	Content does not restrict its view and operation to a single display orientation, such as portrait or landscape, unless a specific display orientation is essential.
	AA	1.3.5 Identify Input Purpose	The purpose of each input field collecting information about the user can be programmatically determined.
	AAA	1.3.6 Identify Purpose	In content implemented using markup languages, the purpose of User Interface Components, icons and regions can be programmatically determined.
1.4 Distinguishable	AA	1.4.10 Reflow	Content can be presented without loss of information or functionality, and without requiring scrolling in two dimensions. Possibility to increase the text size by 400%.
	AA	1.4.11 Non-Text Contrast	The visual presentation of the User Interface Components and Graphical Objects have a contrast ratio of at least 3:1 against adjacent colors.
	AA	1.4.12 Text Spacing	The criteria allows for change of the following text style properties: - Line height (line spacing); - Spacing following paragraphs; - Letter spacing (tracking) ; - Word spacing to at least.
	AA	1.4.13 Content on Hover or Focus	When additional content is triggered,to provide for the possibility of: - Reject additional content; - Trigger additional content; - The additional content remains visible until the user rejects it.
2.1 Keyboard Accessible	A	2.1.4 Character Key Shortcuts	Providing an opportunity to exclude Key Shortcuts.
2.2 Enough Time	AAA	2.2.6 Timeouts	Users are warned of the duration of any user inactivity that could cause data loss, unless the data is preserved for more than 20 hours when the user does not take any actions.
2.3 Seizures and Physical Reactions	AAA	2.3.3 Animation from Interactions	Motion animation triggered by interaction can be disabled, unless the animation is essentian to the functionality or the information being conveyed.
2.5 Input Modalities	A	2.5.1 Pointer Gestures	All functionality that uses multipoint or path-based gestures for operation can be operated with a single pointer without a path-based gesture, unless a multipoint or path-based gesture is essential.
	A	2.5.2 Pointer Cancellation	Improving prevention against accidental or erroneous activation of functionality by touch or mouse.
	A	2.5.3 Label in Name	For user interface components with labels that include text or images of text, the name contains the text that is presented visually.
	A	2.5.4 Motion Actuation	Functionality that can be operated by device motion or user motion can also be operated by user interface components and responding to the motion can be disabled to prevent accidental actuation.
	AAA	2.5.5 Target Size	Ensuring all existing controls in web content and providing a sufficiently large field for their easy activation even on a small screen area.
	AAA	2.5.6 Concurrent Input Mechanisms	Web content does not restrict use of input modalities available on a platform except where the restriction is essential, required to ensure the security of the content, or required to respect user settings.
4.1 Compatible	AA	4.1.3 Status Messages	The user must be notified for content changes, without them accepting a focus, disturbing his work.

- Can information resources be used only by means of the keyboard?
- Is a screen reader allowed?
- Can I use a screen magnifier (zoom) and keep the content at this magnification?
- Is the web resource easy to use?
- Is there comprehensible content created?
- Are there any appropriate explanations for the graphic material?
- Can a blind user enter the information resource site?

When designing and building data databases, Internet based software products, resources and services, it is best to use the guidelines of the internationally recognized Web Content Accessibility Guidelines 2.1. The Standard should be well studied as it is quite extensive and covers the greatest possible number of accessibility problems encountered by people with disabilities when working on the web.

Using Accessibility Principles to Create Holder Database

The established database of physiological data consists of consistently stored information for each of the patients studied. The information contains:

- Headline, with information about:
  - Patient's name
  - Physiological data for the patient: age, sex, etc.
  - Diagnosis of disease;
  - History of disease;
  - Accompanying diseases;
  - Medical establishment where the recording was made;
  - Name of the treating cardiologist;
  - Time of beginning and end of recording;
  - Duration of recording
  - Index to the numeral of the record.
- Actual numerical data of the record:
  - ECG Signal Value;
  - Time in which the value is recorded.

The created Holter database consists of over 1100 records of cardiac patients obtained by conducting prolonged Holter monitoring in the normal living conditions of individuals. When creating the database is realized protection of information from external unauthorized access. When solving the task of accessing this physiological database of People with Visual Deficit, the guidelines of the internationally approved Standards for accessibility of information (Figure 7) are applied.

The author of this chapter has previous research on accessibility of people with visual deficits on information databases and custom software products (Georgieva-Tsaneva, 2018; Georgieva-Tsaneva, Sabev 2018). To solving issues of facilitating accessibility of people with visual deficits to databases with information, including the cardiological databases created by the project, and to facilitating the use of software program for processing and analyzing this data, which is in process of creating, the following methods based on web accessibility standards are applied:

Figure 7. Application of Standards for Accessibility of information to databases

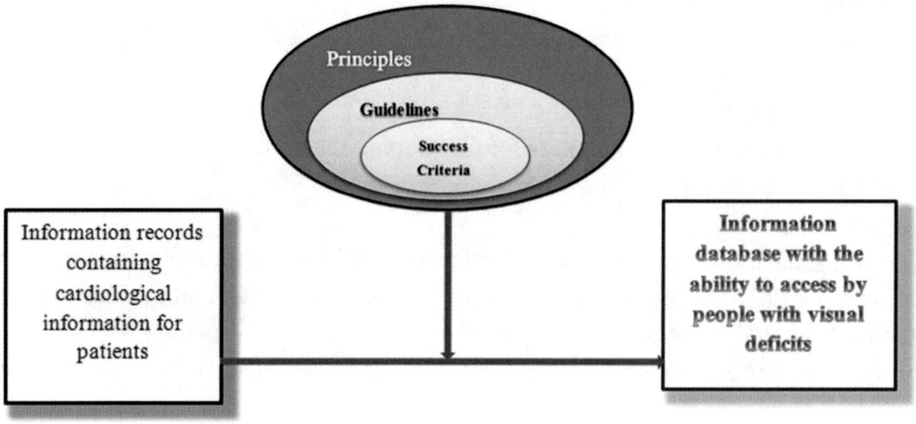

1. When creating the software analysis system, create a user interface that is suitable for use by all users. Persons with visual deficits should be able to use software system without much effort (Sabev, Georgieva-Tsaneva, Bogdanova, 2018).
2. Creating program tools to increase font sizes, creating audio files with explanations of places that are incomprehensible or that can not be read by an electronic reader (Njanji & Nggada, 2011).
3. Providing assistive technologies: screen readers, specialized keyboards, and more aids that facilitate the use of computer technology by people with special needs.
4. If software produces results in the form of graphics, they shall be accompanied by appropriate textual or audio explanations.
5. For improving access and readability of information in cardiac database, software for increasing font size (for users with reduced vision) and using an electronic reader for blind users are applied.
6. If there are links in database, these must comprehensible.

Future Work to Solve Project Tasks

The collected over 1100 prolonged cardiological recordings during a Holter monitoring of patients with various cardiac diseases will be systemized according to type of disease. To cardiological database whit physiological data records, functionalities will be created by which database records can be accessed by different characteristics: type of cardiac disease, age, gender, patient name, name of the treating physician, etc. The guidance given in the latest version of the internationally-validated Web Accessibility Standard WCAG 2.1 will be used to design, create and maintain an information database containing annotated prolonged cardiological records.

CONCLUSION

The creation of a comprehensive data base of long-term cardiological data obtained through a Holter monitoring of patients with various cardiac diseases will help to carry out thorough studies and analyzes of cardiovascular diseases, which are one of the most common diseases in Bulgaria and in the world. The created cardiological database of ECG data includes annotated patient records containing a diagnosis from a physician treating a cardiologist, patient information, cardiac count values, and some scientific research made on these data using established software procedures.

The chapter has explored the tools and the methods that can facilitate the interaction of people with visual deficits with information technology, to ensure their work in the global Internet space, to facilitate their operation with user software products. The work on the project concerned includes a doctoral student, an individual with visual impairment. His recommendations, tips are taken into account when working on tasks of project. Our aspiration is to maximally involve it in the work of the scientific team.

Today, attitudes towards people with different types of disability are different from those of several decades ago, the aim is to socially integrate people with disabilities, and their integration into society is not based solely on financial support. Therefore, the policies and programs relating to these people need to be completely changed. People with disabilities must be socially involved in our society. The research in this chapter aims to take into account the specificities of people with disabilities in the use of different information databases and to contribute to the creation of annotated physiological databases that can be used by people with disabilities and - especially People with Visual Deficit. The work in this direction has its social element - the social inclusion of people with disabilities in scientific process of processing and analysis of physiological data through modern mathematical technologies.

ACKNOWLEDGMENT

This research was supported by the National Science Fund of Bulgaria [Research project N° DM 12/36/20.12.2017: "Investigation of Mathematical Techniques of Analysis of Physiological Data with Functionality for People with Visual Deficit" under the tasks: Task 2.5 Establish a model to provide access to the database of people with sensor deficits; Task 3.1 Examining existing technology for sequence analysis of Heart Rate Variability; Task 3.3 Investigation of wavelet analysis methods and the possibilities for their effective application in the analysis of sequences of Heart Rate Variability; Task 4.3 An analysis of current trends, the methods and means by which issues of access to information products for people with visual deficits are addressed; Task 5.1: Dissemination of project results].

REFERENCES

W3C. (1999). *Web content accessibility guidelines 1.0.* W3C Recommendation. Cambridge, UK: W3C. Retrieved from https://www.w3.org/TR/WAI-WEBCONTENT/

Acharya, U. R., Joseph, K. P., Kannathal, N., Lim, C. M., & Suri, J. S. (2006). Heart rate variability: A review. *Medical & Biological Engineering & Computing, 44*(12), 1031–1051. doi:10.100711517-006-0119-0 PMID:17111118

Aldonin, G. M., Soldatov, A. V., & Cherepanov, V. V. (2018, July). Wavelet Analysis of Cardiac Electrical Activity Signals. *Biomedical Engineering, 52*(2), 120–124. doi:10.100710527-018-9796-x

Bogdanova, G., & Sabev, N. (2017). The first principle in the standard for web accessibility "Web Content Accessibility Guidelines". In *Science Days 2016*. USB branch Veliko Tarnovo, Faber.

Bogdanova, G., & Sabev, N. (2017). The second principle of operability in the standard for web accessibility WCAG 2.0. *XV-National Conference with international participation "Libraries - reading - communications" - Digital conversion of literary and cultural heritage*, 302-314.

Clifford, G., Azuaje, F., & McSharry, P. (Eds.). (2006). *Advanced Methods and Tools for ECG Data Analysis*. Boston: Artech House, Inc.

Clifford, G., & Tarassenko, L. (2004). Segmenting Cardiac-Related Data Using Sleep stages Increases Separation between Normal Subjects and Apnoeic Patients. *IOP Physiol. Means, 25*(6), N27–N35. doi:10.1088/0967-3334/25/6/N03 PMID:15712732

Cook, A. M., & Polgar, J. M. (2015). Principles of assistive technology: introducing the Human Activity Assistive Technology model. In *Assistive technologies: Principles and practice* (pp. 1–15). St. Louis, MO: Elsevier.

Georgieva-Tsaneva, G. (2018). Increasing the Quality of Education for Blind Students, through Improving Web Accessibility to Digitized Libraries, Software Systems and Databases. In *Proceedings of EDULEARN18 Conference*. IATED Academy. 10.21125/edulearn.2018.1123

Georgieva-Tsaneva, G., & Sabev, N. (2018). *Technologies, Standarts and Approaches to Ensure Web Accessility for Visually Impaired People*. Sofia, Bulgaria: Institute of Mathematics and Informatocs-BAS.

German-Sallo, Z. (2014). Wavelet transform based Heart Rate Variability analysis. *Procedia Technology, 12*, 105–111. doi:10.1016/j.protcy.2013.12.462

Gospodinov, M., & Gospodinova, E. (2017). The effect of obesity on heart rate variability in healthy subjects. *International Journal of Biological & Medical Research, 8*(4), 6153-6157.

Gospodinova, E. (2014). Graphical Methods for Nonlinear analysis of ECG signals. *International Journal of Advanced Research in Computer Science and Software Engineering, 4*(12), 40-44.

Gospodinova, E., Gospodinov, M., Domuschiev, I., Dey, N., Ashour, A., & Sifaki-Pistolla, D. (2015). Analysis of Heart Rate Variability by Applying Nonlinear Methods with Different Approaches for Graphical Representation of Results. *International Journal of Advanced Computer Science and Applications, 6*(8), 38–45. doi:10.14569/IJACSA.2015.060805

Grossman, A., & Morlet, J. (1984). Decomposition of Hardy functions into square interable wavelets of sonstant shape. *SIAM Journal on Mathematical Analysis, 15*(4), 723–736. doi:10.1137/0515056

Harper, S., & Yesilada, Y. (Eds.). (2008). *Web Accessibility*. Heidelberg, Germany: Springer Berlin. doi:10.1007/978-1-84800-050-6

Helen, P., Savva, A., & Power, C. (2015). Towards a unified definition of Web Accessibility. *W4A '15 Proceedings of the 12th Web for All Conference Article No. 35*. Available from: https://www.research-gate.net/publication

Kurt, S. (2011). The Accessibility of university websites: The case of Turkish universities. *Universal Access in the Information Society, 10*(1), 101–110. doi:10.100710209-010-0190-z

Lem, M. (2016). Statistical Methods for Cardiovascular Researchers. *Circulation Research, 118*(3), 439–445. doi:10.1161/CIRCRESAHA.115.306305 PMID:26846639

Malik, M., Bigger, J. T., Camm, A. J., Kleiger, R. E., Malliani, A., Moss, A. J., & Schwartz, P. J. (1996). Heart Rate Variability. Standards of measurement, physiological interpretation, and clinical use. *European Heart Journal, 17*(3), 354–381. doi:10.1093/oxfordjournals.eurheartj.a014868 PMID:8737210

Malik, M., & Camm, A. J. (Eds.). (2004). *Dynamic Electrocardiography*. New York: Futura Division. doi:10.1002/9780470987483

Matveen, M., Krasteva, V., Jekova, I., Georgiev, G., Milanov, St., Prokopova, R., & Todorova, L. (2012). Profile of Autonomic Cardiac Control in Patients who are Not Considered Ready for Weaning from Mechanical Ventilation. *Computers in Cardiology, 39*, 625–628.

McSharry, P. E., Clifford, G., Tarassenko, L., & Smith, L. A. (2003). A dynamical model for generating synthetic electrocardiogram signals. *IEEE Transactions on Biomedical Engineering, 50*(3), 289–294. doi:10.1109/TBME.2003.808805 PMID:12669985

Nganji, J., & Nggada, S. (2011). Disability-Aware Software Engineering for Improved System Accessibility and Usability. *International Journal of Software Engineering and Its Applications, 5*(3), 47–62.

Paneva-Marinova, D., Goynov, M., Luchev, D., & Pavlov, R. (2015). Solution for content interoperability among digital libraries for orthodox artefacts and knowledge. In *CompSysTech '15, Dublin, UK. Proceedings of the 16th International Conference on Computer Systems and Technologies*. ACM. 10.1145/2812428.2812474

Paneva-Marinova, D., Goynov, M., & Pavlov, R. (2017). Personalized Observation and Enhanced Learning Experience in Digital Libraries. In *ICERI2017 Proceedings. 10th annual International Conference of Education, Research and Innovation, ICERI2017*. IATED Academy.

Paneva-Marinova, D., Pavlov, R., & Kotuzov, N. (2017). Approach for Analysis and Improved Usage of Digital Cultural Assets for Learning Purposes. *Cybernetics and Information Technologies, 17*(3), 140-151.

Sabev, N., & Bogdanova, G. (2018). Accessibility of National Tourist Sites for People with Disabilities. In *Cultural and Historical Heritage: Preservation, Presentation, Digitalization* (pp. 38-98). Public Library. Retrieved from http://www.math.bas.bg/vt/kin/book-5/04-KIN-5-2018.pdf

Sabev, N., Georgieva-Tsaneva, G., & Bogdanova, G. (2018). Creating a Software System with Functionality to Help Make it Accessible for People with a Visual Deficit. In *CBU International Conference on Innovations in Science and Education*. Prague, Czech Republic: CBU Research Institute. 10.12955/cbup.v6.1241

Sarmiento, S., Garcria-Manso, J., Martrin-Gonzralez, J., Vaamonde, D., Calderron, J., & Da Silva-Grigoletto, M. (2013). Heart Rate Variability During High-Intensity Exercise. *Journal of Systems Science and Complexity, 26*(1), 104–116. doi:10.100711424-013-2287-y

Sasikala, P., & Wahidabanu, R. (2010). Robust R Peak and QRS detection in Electrocardiogram using Wavelet Transform. *International Journal of Advanced Computer Science and Applications*, *1*(6), 48–53. doi:10.14569/IJACSA.2010.010608

Screen Reader User Survey #7 Results. (n.d.). Retrieved from https://webaim.org/projects/screenreadersurvey7/

Signa Cor Laboratory. (1991). Retrived October 16, 2018, from http://www.signacor

Simov, D., Matveev, M., Milanova, M., Krasteva, V., & Christov, I. (2014). Cardiac autonomic innervation following coronary artery bypass grafting evaluated by high resolution heart rate variability. *Computing in Cardiology Conference*, 1013-1016.

WCAG 2.0. (2008). Retrieved from http://www.w3.org/TR/WCAG20/

WCAG 2.1. (2018). Retrieved from https://www.w3.org/TR/WCAG21/#requirements-for-wcag-2-1

Web Content Accessibility Guidelines (WCAG) Overview. (1999). Retrieved from https://www.w3.org/WAI/intro/wcag

Xiong, F., Qi, X., Nattel, S., & Comtois, P. (2015). Wavelet analysis of cardiac optical mapping data. *Computers in Biology and Medicine*, *65*(C), 243–255. doi:10.1016/j.compbiomed.2015.06.022 PMID:26209111

Chapter 13
Introduction to Human Electroencephalography:
Recording, Experimental Techniques, and Analysis

Gagandeep Kaur
Indian Institute of Technology Kanpur, India

ABSTRACT

This chapter is a general introduction to electroencephalography and popular methods used to manipulate EEG in order to elicit markers of sensory, cognitive perception, and behavior. With development of interdisciplinary research, there is increased curiosity among engineers towards biomedical research. Those using signal processing techniques attempt to employ algorithms to the real-life signals and retrieve characteristics of signals such as speech, echo, EEG, among others. The chapter briefs the history of human EEG and goes back to the origins and fundamentals of electrical activity in brain, how this activity reaches the scalp, methods to capture this high temporal activity. It then takes the reader through design methodology that goes behind EEG experiments, general schema for analysis of EEG signal. It describes the concept of early evoked potentials, which are known responses for study of sensory perception and are used extensively in medical science. It moves on to another popular manipulation of EEG technique used to elicit event related potentials.

BACKGROUND

Hans Berger, a German psychiatrist is known to have recorded the first human EEG. He joined the university Psychiatric clinic after finishing his medical degree from the University of Jena, Germany in 1897. Interestingly in one of his earlier pursuits, Berger was working to discover the physiological basis of psychic phenomena but initial results were disappointing. It was around this time that he drew inspiration from Richard Caton's work on cortical electrical activity in animals and turned his attention to investigate the electrical activity of human brain. Subsequently, Berger characterized the wave patterns including popularly known alpha and beta waves and coined the term 'electroencephalogram'.

DOI: 10.4018/978-1-5225-7879-6.ch013

Using a string galvanometer, Berger made recordings on moving photographic paper with a wavy spot of light. Later, with the support of Carl Zeiss foundation, he repeated his experiments with electronic amplifiers and oscilloscopes and extended the spectrum of inquiries by working with people who suffered from Alzheimer's, multiple sclerosis, epilepsy, schizophrenia, bipolar illness, melancholia, and speech loss among other disease. He further studied EEG among, young children as well as infants. In 1934, using copper gauze electrodes in saline soaked lint, Edgr Adrian and B.H.C. Matthews of Cambridge physiological laboratory confirmed Berger's research, thus giving the due acknowledgment for a discovery which would alter the course of brain studies for ever after, Millett, (2001). Berger's studies gave a fresh impetus to the study of human brain and its functioning. The non-invasive procedure through which electrical rhythms representing the brain activities are recorded gave rise to enormous data. This in turn facilitated the quest to understand and define brain functions, in particular human behavior.

ELECTRICAL ACTIVITY OF HUMAN BRAIN

There are two types of cells in human brain, Glial cells also known as Glia and the nerve cells also known as Neurons. Glia cells are termed as support cells of neurons and there are up to 50 times more glia cells than neurons in the central nervous system of vertebrates. Oligodendrocytes and Schwann cells are two types of glia cells that produce insulating myelin sheath which insulates cell outgrowths known as axons that conducts electrical signals. Glia cells play the important role of maintenance by removing debris after cell death. Third types of Glia cells, Astrocytes form the blood-brain barrier. The blood brain barrier aids the mechanism which restricts the movement of ions protects the neuronal tissue from toxins (Daneman & Prat, 2015). Some of glia cells also promote the release of growth factors and help nourish the nerve cells.

Neurons, also known as nerve cells play the fundamental role in transmission of electrical signals in nervous system. Soma or cell body, axon and dendrites and pre-synaptic terminals constitute the structural units of a neuron. Each part of the neuron plays specific roles in the electrical activity which it takes part. The neuronal membrane is bimolecular lipoprotein structure creating a barrier for free movements of ions such as sodium, potassium, chloride among others into and out of cell body. The concentration of ions within the cell body and in the interstitial space is critical in maintaining the resting state potential of neuron. Within the cell, the concentration of sodium and chloride ions in low and of potassium ions is high. The interstitial space has just the opposite and in a balanced state the resting state potential of the cell is measured to be around 80mV. The cell membrane regulates the ion exchange through its complex lipoprotein layers, which helps to maintain this resting state potential.

If the resting state potential is disturbed, in other words the membrane permeability is disturbed; it can lead to negative or positive changes in cell potential depending on the changes in the concentration of negative or positive ions. If the membrane potential is sufficiently positive beyond a threshold level the orchestrated movement of ions inside the cell body can be observed. This current is known as action potential which propagates along the cell fibres and spread throughout the dendritic branches. This phenomenon is commonly referred as spiking/firing of neuron. The axon fibre also has membrane along its length till the fibre terminates at the cell body and it is further protected by myelin sheath with nodes of ranveir in between. The myelin sheath and the gaps provide the necessary insulation from dissipation as well as controlled ion source for unattenuated propagation of action potential within the fibre and through the axon. The amplitude of the action potential is around 100mV, remains constant along the

Figure 1. The cell body is the metabolic centre of the cell, has the nucleus which stores genetic information of cell. The apical dendrites or dendrites are short extensions connected to the soma that act as receptor of electrical signals from other neurons. While the axon extends away from the cell body carrying the electrical signals to be transmitted to neighbouring neurons through synaptic terminals. Figure source (Somov, P.G., 2012).

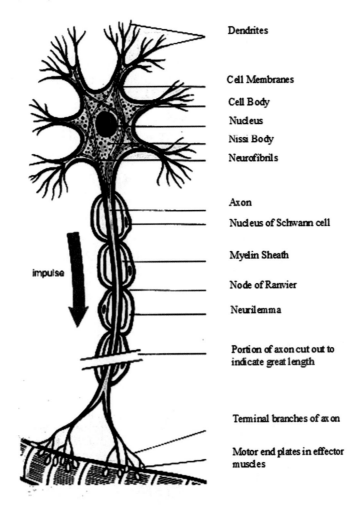

length of axon and can last for 1millisecond; hence neuronal spikes are transient events in general. The axons terminate at the synapse of the pre-synaptic neuron and when the action potential reaches here, synaptic vesicles release the neurotransmitters which bind to the receptors at the post synaptic neuron. If the transmitter substance is excitatory, it causes the membrane potential to become more positive or less negative and there is a high probability of receptor neurons producing spikes of their own. If the transmitter substance is inhibitory, it will lead to more negative membrane potential and the postsynaptic neuron fires with much less probability. The feeble, transient current produced by single neurons in the cortex will not reach the scalp. But at the same time EEG equipment successfully records the collective electrical activities of neurons using the electrodes placed at scalp. This is explained by the principle of volume conduction. Volume conduction can be envisaged as an electric spread depicting passive resistance, where the intensity of measured neuronal activity decreases as distance from cortex; the source, increases. It is called a passive resistance, since no active component is placed to restrict the current. It is rather distance from source of current, the neurons which act as resistance.

Working mechanism of volume conduction is illustrated in Figure-2 and can be comprehended as follows: At point A, the waves of depolarization (build-up of Na+ ions inside the neurons) are moving away from the current source; they are also slightly against the movement of electrode-towards extreme side of electrode A. By convention it will produce a downward deflection in the oscilloscope. At B, current flows toward the sink resulting in upward deflection; this provides rising edge of positive peak. At C, the lines of depolarizing wave front reverse their direction, giving rise to the falling edge of peak. After crossing the equipotential line it enters D, within D, the fanning out of current lines gradually begins to move in the same direction as the electrode, producing an upward deflection on oscilloscope and returning tracing to the baseline. As the distance from axon increases, level 2 and 3, edges of peaks appear more negligent. The EEG records obtained at the scalp are differential currents; the electrical activity

Figure 2. A nerve cell at equilibrium has electric field around it, the resting cell potential, analogous to a unit charge at rest. As the neurons begin to fire in accord, the ion flow generates an electro-magnetic field. This field is strong enough to be detected at the scalp via electric spread- essentially magnetic field strength is measured. In the above figure, the levels 1, 2, 3 represent the distance as recording electrodes move away from source of conduction, the cortex. A, B, C and D represent position of electrodes along the depolarized axon.

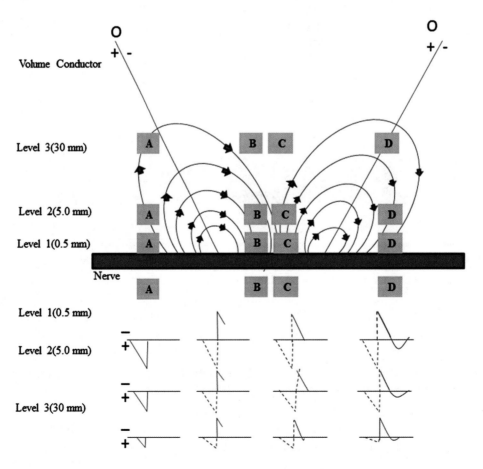

at site of interest is computed relative to another electrode site. The former is called active electrode, 'V1' and latter is the reference electrode, 'V2'. There are two configurations to record differential currents, referential and bipolar. They are based on whether the source of neural activity is near the cortex leading to near-field recording or much beneath as in case of signals originating from the brain stem or hippocampus leading to far-field recordings. The choice of these configurations is part of design of EEG experiment which the following section describes.

1. **Design of EEG Experiment:** The sequence of steps taken for design of EEG experiment in general, is as follows:

   a. Like any other proper scientific inquiry, an EEG experiment must begin with a hypothesis which will be addressed in the subsequent study. An appropriate hypothesis must be formed considering the limitations and scopes of EEG equipment in hand and related theoretical constraints. For example, accurate source localization at neuronal level of a specific brain activity is beyond the scope any EEG experiment at present.

   b. A minimum number of electrodes would be necessary to use certain kinds of analytical techniques to process the acquired data, and hence the specifications of EEG equipment plays a role in formulating a valid hypothesis.

   c. Once a testable hypothesis is formulated, experimental tasks need to be designed in accordance with the hypothesis and may include physical, mental engagements and responses.

   d. Primary objective of such a task is to provide suitable stimuli to elicit a particular brain activity.

      i. Generally, faculties such as visual, aural, sensory and imaginary are used individually or in combination, for stimulation.

      ii. A visual stimulus which may be in motion or fixed, may trigger a variety of cognitive, affective processes, sensory responses.

   e. These probable responses are important to decide locations for electrode placement on the scalp, settings of EEG amplifier at the time of acquisition and the procedure to be followed for data analysis post acquisition.

      i. For instance response to a visual sensation shall require less number of active channels while cognitive response will require more number of electrodes.

      ii. A minimum 8 electrodes are used for ERP studies which may be extended to a dense mesh of 256 for studies demanding higher spatial resolution.

      iii. The number of channels also depends on the type of post-acquisition analysis as to employ independent component analysis, a minimum 16 channels are recommended.

   f. Selection of appropriate set of subjects is the next step.

      i. In fact, the hypothesis formulation and design of experimental tasks must be performed by keeping in mind a specific set of human or animal subjects.

      ii. Another factor which affects selection of appropriate subjects is whether it will be within subjects study or between subjects study.

      iii. A statistical study will require more number of subjects compared to a empirical observation.

   g. As there are various ethical issues involved in experimenting with humans and animals, a clearance from ethical committee of institution must be obtained prior to the start of the experiments.

h. Experiment preparation must begin by informing the subject(s) in written about the tasks, the scope of study, role of subject, risks if any involved and restrictions which subject(s) has(ve) to follow.

i. Written consent from subject(s) should be taken with an option to quit the procedure anytime in case of any discomfort.

    i. In case of visual stimulus based experiments, there could be restrictions on blinks, gaze shifts, facial expressions and bodily movements.

    ii. In case of tasks involving mental load, restrain from non-prescription drugs that could interfere with cognitive ability may be required. Thus, relevant information about the health of subject(s) must be collected and checked against with the required criteria.

j. When the subject(s) are prepared, attention needs to be given to suitably arrange the EEG equipments.

k. Special care to be given for the specifications related to space where the equipments will be situated. This includes, necessary noise insulation from electric and non-electric sources, facility for presentation of stimulus, seating of subject, and experimenter. These procedures may vary according to the research questions.

l. Once all the preparations are in order, the experiment can begin.

    i. The subject should be seated on a comfortable chair at a suitable distance from the screen which has to be fixed for all subsequent sessions.

    ii. The information sheet has to be briefed to the subject and it should be reiterated that the subject has option to quit the experiment anytime.

    iii. Additional instructions relevant to task must be given to subject to avoid artifact such as eye blinks, swallowing, movement etc.

    iv. If subject agrees to continue, the electrode cap must be carefully mounted and the electrodes must be carefully placed over selected locations.

    v. The gel should be applied in case of wet electrodes, impedance checked.

    vi. At this point amplifier settings such as bandpass filter, sampling rate, montage, notch and other filters should be laid down. These setting should remain same throughout the experiment.

    vii. A dry run should be performed before actual data recording.

    viii. The trigger pulses should be ready to mark the beginning and end of trial and also the onset of events, as required by the task.

2. The EEG Signal Processing

a. Pre-processing essentially includes cleaning the EEG data post acquisition and preparing it for further processing using algorithms fed to digital computers.

    i. Part of pre-processing requires artifact removal, which when present within epochs require epoch rejection, and it leads to loss of data. Informing the subject about the periods to avoid movements and to be more attentive during the trials may lead to cleaner epochs.

    ii. Filters are used to mitigate baseline shifts, line noise, DC shifts among others. The key is to apply filters before sampling and digitizing the data, else the noise present in signal will also get amplified.

    iii. Mains frequency is sinusoidal and displays simple harmonic motion. While working with higher frequencies present in EEG e.g.; gamma band, to mitigate line frequency effect, the filter should be able to remove the fundamental frequency and its higher harmonics.

Figure 3. The general procedure to process raw EEG signal and retrieve information is depicted in the above block diagram. The raw EEG signals are fed to the pre-processing module in order to separate artifacts, down sample signal, create epochs among other functions as desired by the aim of enquiry. Feature vector is created using Amplitude, frequency, power spectral density or statistical moments of signal. An appropriate algorithm is used to classify given epochs into different classes based on differences in features. The classified signal is ready for whichever further application.

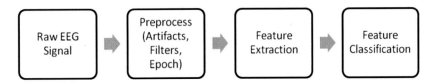

     iv.   Also instead of using a sharp filter, a narrow band stop filter should be considered in order to avoid ringing effect.

     v.   Yet another distortion in EEG is a flat waveform, caused by skin potentials. This distortion can be corrected by using high pass filters, usually while working with adults a high pass filter of 0.01 cut-off frequency should be used.

  b. Feature extraction: Amplitude, frequency, phase, statistical moments are defining characteristics of EEG signal, at this stage of processing, these features are isolated and a feature matrix is created.

     i.   It is common practice to extract features in time, frequency and time-frequency domain. In case of analysis of event related potentials time domain features such as amplitude and latency have been frequently used.

     ii.   The ERP is a measure of neuronal activity related to cognitive processing of stimuli and this activity is observed in form of ERP components. These components are elicited each time the stimulus is presented. The time domain analysis of ERP uses averaging to extract ERP buried within the ongoing EEG, it assumes that every time the stimulus elicits same components at the same time. The neuronal activity on the other hand may not be exactly the same for each of the subsequent trials. Thus averaging trials gives out a blurred view of actual neuronal responses. The latency, amplitude and duration of latent components may vary across trials. Additionally, ERP phase can also shift across trials, which would imply, that the signal to noise ratio will deteriorate after ensemble averaging.

     iii.   Frequency domain analysis and issues: the most used frequency domain analysis includes power spectral density. For a real signal such as EEG, which is discontinuous beyond the interval of measurement, a tool such as Fourier transform assumes that the signal repeats itself. Also, the sharp discontinuities have broad frequency spectra, thus for signals with finite measurement time, the frequency spectra would spread leading to spectral leakage. To mitigate spectral leakage, windowing can be done wherein; the finite signal is multiplied by some function that smoothly reduces the signal to zero at the end points hence avoiding discontinuities.

iv. Time-frequency analysis: Wavelet coefficients have been commonly used features for analysis of real life signals such as speech, ECG, EEG. Analysis of ERP waveform can be carried out by choosing appropriate mother wavelets and bases function. Using wavelet packet decomposition can separate given epochs into frequency bands which make it possible to analyze ERPs in terms of rhythmic activity.

c. Classifiers are algorithms designed to extract information from the feature vector and categorizing them into various classes. Individual classes may represent different components of event related responses. The classifiers can be adaptive, based on deep learning and transfer learning. Choice of classifiers, their function, limitation and advantages is itself a broad area of deliberation which will not be detailed in present study.

3. Manipulating EEG in a Controlled Environment:

Spontaneous EEG activity is non-linear and non-stationary in nature; this can be corroborated by a small exercise of calculating moments of EEG signal across trials. In order to make sense of information contained within this continuous and highly non-linear signal, some experimental manipulations are necessary. One such manipulation includes stimulation of sensory pathways of nerves, the early latency responses thus elicited after stimulus onset is known as evoked potentials (Allison T., Goff W.R., Wood C.C., 1979). By designing complex mental tasks changes in neuronal activity have been observed during execution; these responses are known to have late latencies and are commonly known as event related potentials (Brown W.S., & Lehmann D., 1979). Evoked potential refers to the electrical activity in response to deliberate external stimulation of sensory nerve pathways. Evoked potential tests are used for diagnosis of neurodegenerative disorders such as multiple sclerosis wherein demyelination of the nerve pathways may cause inadvertent delays in neuronal processing of sensory perception.

Davis Hallowell a paediatrician, with specialization in otolaryngology was born in 1896, New-york city, to a lawyer father. He graduated from Harvard College where he had become a devoted chemist, a physiologist during his tenure at Harvard medical school and a neurophysiologist during his postdoctoral year 1922-23 (Galambos, 1998). In 1939, Hallowell along with Pauline Davis, were the first in history to have recorded the human cortical evoked brain potentials. His pioneering work on animal cochlear potentials, improved stimulus generation and response recording equipment led to the present-day audiometer.

Sutton's work on evoked potentials/event related potentials in humans became recognized as pioneering in cognitive neuroscience. His work addressed the functional relevance of sensory evoked potentials. His experiments largely manipulated subject's expectation of stimulus and observed possible changes in response under variations in stimuli (Sutton et al., 1964 & Sutton et al., 1967). The study of ERP though initially limited to purview of cognitive scientists further expanded in realm of neuroscientists trying to address the human brain/ mind and further into application of brain computer interface systems. This caught the attention of engineers who applied vivid algorithms for analysis of event related potentials.

The human brain is always active; this can be observed on an electroencephalograph (EEG). The EEG represents neural centres of voluntary function of body like breathing, heartbeat, eye-blinking, smelling, swallowing, motion, seeing and, that of cognitive activities such as perception, decision, selection, navigation among many other. During early phase, study of response to sensory perception to visual, somatosensory stimulus, selective attention; reflected in EEG activity was referred as evoked response or evoked potential. Much later the differentiation between EP and ERP has been made; the obligatory responses to a stimulus are referred as Evoked potentials and the non-obligatory responses are referred to as Event related potentials (Luck, S.J., 2005). The response to external stimuli which may be auditory, somatosensory or visual can be seen as consecutive phenomenon. First, it appears as early latency responses that imply registry by the sensory neurons of brain with subcortical and cortical origin. It is followed by late latency responses associated with cognitive realm. The responses that represent neuronal activity corresponding to mental processes are event related potentials.

As an illustration, consider a typical ERP waveform. Figure 4 has labels P1, P2, N1, N2, and P3. The P1 peak appears between 100-130 ms after the stimulus onset, it begins to appear approx. 60 ms after stimulus onset. This component is prominent at the occipital electrode, (Hillyard and Munte, 1984) established that this component is not sensitive to whether or not stimulus evoked cognitive load.

In order to model the neuronal pathways during executing of simple and complex tasks experiments are designed. The tasks are usually part of stimulus given through visual, aural or somatosensory pathways. The discussion in following paragraph assumes visual stimulus based task. It has been observed that most of processing occurs after the stimulus onset. The initial early latency components have subcortical and cortical origins depicting sensory perception. It is followed by late latency components associated with cognitive processing. These responses last for a little over a second. Further, neuronal activity before the stimulus onset has also been reported. This activity is related to preparation of incoming stimulus. Thus, overall response to the stimulus can be divided broadly into three phases. It begins with peaks of anticipation, followed by early latency components or the peaks of sensory perception and subsequently by late latency components depicting cognitive tasks.

The first of ERP components are indicators of underlying anticipation and they appear as a complex, known as contingent negative variations (CNV). If a short lived warning stimulus is presented, a CNV is a large negative deflection that occurs between a short-lived warning stimulus and a much persistent target stimulus, it is a manifestation of expectation and its reinforcement by the aforesaid stimuli, re-

Figure 4. Kaan, E. (2007). Event-Related Potentials and Language Processing: A Brief Overview. Language and Linguistics Compass, 1, 571-591.

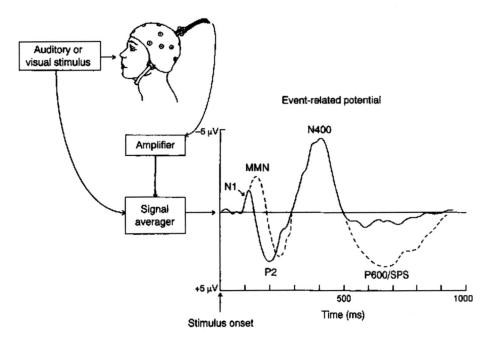

spectively. CNV is a summation of readiness potential (RP) and stimulus preceding negativity (SPN). The user attitude has shown to have a marked effect on existence and behaviour of CNV (Walter et al., 1964). The readiness potentials (RP) also known as Brietschaftspotentials (BP) are a demonstration of anticipation of a voluntary movement. Movement plays a vital role. For instance the user has a predefined task, here movement such as a button press, after every n seconds, which in turn elicits the process of anticipation which manifests itself in form of BP. The amplitude of BP can be controlled by reducing time between consecutive responses. In case it is movement/button press; the shorter the time between two consecutive movements, the stronger the BP [Deecke and Kornhuber, 2003].

As an illustration, consider a typical ERP waveform, Figure 4. The visual nature of stimulus evokes subcortical and cortical activity which is sensitive to change in luminance and change in pattern. This activity can be seen in form of ERP components and when multiple trials are averaged the peaks and troughs give a glimpse of these components.

- Very early latency visual evoked potentials have been observed as early as 30 ms and lasting till 90 ms. Most of these components have periocular, optic nerve origins as reported by some studies. While components occurring between 35 and 70ms are reported to have occipital origins, the components beyond 70 ms have generators located in the visual and associative cortex (Luck, S.J. & Kappernman E.S., 2012).
- Among long latency components, there is generally a negative peak C1around 70ms that arises due to excitation of primary visual cortex.
  - It is followed by the P1 component, which is most prominent on the lateral occipital sites. Typically P1 commences between 60ms and 90ms after stimulus onset and latency peaks between 100-130 ms though the latencies may vary due to differences in stimulus contrast as well as across subjects.
  - Because of its overlap with the C1 component, its onset is difficult to assess. Early portion of P1 arises from middle occipital gyrus, later portions from ventrally fusiform gyrus (Di Russo et al., 2003).
  - Stimulus contrast, selective attention and subject's state of arousal which depends on difficulty of given task, are known to have affects on P1 (Hillyard, Vogel & Luck 1998, Luck, woodman & Vogel, 2000, Vogel &Luck, 2000).
  - The P1 amplitude is not sensitive to whether stimulus matches a task defined target category [Hillyard, Munte, 1984].
- The earliest onset of N1 subcomponent can be observed between 100-150 ms after the stimulus onset, over frontal electrode sites. The posterior N1 subcomponent peaks around 150-200ms after stimulus onset over parietal and occipital areas. The N1 subcomponents are affected by spatial attention.
- The functional P3 components peaks between 350 and 600 ms, when it was first noticed by (Sutton et al., 1965) its peak latency was 300 ms and hence it was named P300. Subsequent studies found multitude of variation in latency thus this component is known as third major positive peak, P3 after stimulus onset.

The prominence and subjugation of one or more component reflects mental processes evoked by stimulus. The oddball paradigm or rare/frequent manipulation of stimulus is designed to isolate P300 component of ERP. Among the study related to late latency ERP components, P3 and N6 have found a wider popularity. The conventional way to draw these components from raw EEG has been averaging across multiple trials which have some limitations. While this draws out overall ERP responses to trials within a session, by cancelling the background EEG activity, it leaves little information to observe the variations in components that might have occurred across individual trials (Luck, S.J., 2003).

The ERP experiments are designed to capture neuronal activity corresponding to external behavior by setting up simple tasks in controlled environment. The fundamental aim is to device methods that can distinguish the subtle variations in neural activities within related tasks. As these changes are buried within the much stronger ongoing EEG activity averaging is one viable option. But due to the limitations of averaging such as necessity of multiple trials, reduction in amplitude of components due to habituation, alternative analysis in time-frequency domain has been explored to mitigate effects of amplitude variation and to reduce number of trials.

The time frequency analysis includes using wavelet analysis which isolates frequency bands within single epochs. These frequency bands can be chosen equivalent to the well known bands of human EEG activity such as delta (0.5-4Hz), theta (4-8Hz), alpha (8-12Hz), beta (12-30Hz) and gamma(30-100Hz). How these bands can help in determining the event related responses is described in following lines.

- The most well-known representation of alpha rhythm is observed over the frontal and occipital lobes with eyes closed and as the subject opens eyes the alpha rhythm disappears. There are some widely observed variants of alpha rhythm across the scalp.
  - Mu rhythms: Also known as rolandic rhythms for their presence around the rolandic fissure/ and by the name of sensory motor rhythms for being controlled by muscles movements. These rhythms appear between frequency ranges of 9-13Hz in humans and are observed over motor cortex at C3-C4 positions. Muscle relaxation will enhance these while hand movement will depress them with Eyes Open. Occipital Alpha observed at O1-O2, is known to have strong presence around10Hz. The synchronization between O1 and O2 is seen by blocking the visual input to occipital areas. Hence this variant of alpha is also known as idling rhythm of occipital area. This rhythm can be independent at O1 and O2 also. The frequency of occipital rhythm changes with age. Children around 7 years of age have higher power occipital alpha compared to young adults. Variance is wider for subjects with age 25+. Occipital alpha frequency lowers than 7>5 Hz is considered as mild abnormality for instance, in eyes closed condition, alpha frequency should appear at the occipital lobe, absence of such activity indicates abnormality (Kropotov, J., 2008).
  - Parietal Alpha rhythm is mostly present, during eyes closed condition with maximum at Pz. In rare cases, opposite effect is seen. The Alpha at the parietal during task is high. Higher the task load, greater the overall power of Alpha rhythm. This parietal alpha is present in few subjects and mostly this alpha is dominated by the occipital alpha rhythm, hence not fully understood. This generates an opportunity to study it over increased number of trials and ascertain claims.
  - Alpha rhythms are driven by regular thalamic activity. The alpha rhythms that occur in bursts are normal during sleep (sleep spindles) and during anesthesia also, they last for about >5-3seconds and recur after 3-10 seconds. They are spread across channels. The alpha rhythm during wakefulness (relaxed wakeful) are more localized not spread, they are more persistent

- ○ Alpha has lower frequency than the sleep spindles. In response to tasks, alpha reacts in form of Event related desynchronization and synchronization.
- Beta rhythm in humans can be anywhere between 14-30Hz, it is typical to find it swinging at 20Hz, which is twice that of alpha activity, hence rightly named as second order activity by Hans Berger. While the former has its origins in the somatosensory cortex, the later has it's in the motor cortex. It can be observed during eyes open as well as eyes closed condition over sensory motor area. With smaller amplitudes and wider peaks the amplitude of frontal beta rarely exceeds 20 microvolt; the patterns are also more irregular.
- Delta rhythms can have cortical or subcortical origins. When the thalamo cortical neurons are hyperpolarised at the deepest level, delta rhythms are generated. The clinical relevance of delta waves was famously established by Grey Walter who demonstrated use of delta rhythms for detection of tumours in brain and loci of epileptic seizures. Food and sexual arousals have been related to increase in delta activity. Fatigue leading to urgent need for rest and sleep onset are also related to increase in delta activity. Delta is also been associated with subcortical sources, mostly associated with reward system.
- Theta activity in humans appears between frequency range of 4-8 Hz. Among writing, sitting and walking, frequency of hippocampal theta was higher during writing task. Silent mental activity also contributes to increased theta activity. A separate study during a navigation task conferred that frequent theta activity occurred while navigating through complex mazes. During sleep studies, the lower end of theta activity was prominent for rapid eye movement periods, suggesting hippocampal origins. Theta usually occurs in bursts, the duration of bursts lengthens as memory load increases within a given task.

4. Design and Execution of an ERP Experiment:
   a. If the task involves a significant element buried within insignificant element; and expects a response at elicitation of significant element. Then the neural activity related to the event begins much earlier than the event itself; in anticipation. Almost immediately after the stimulus onset markers of sensory perception of stimulus emerge and later markers of neuronal activity corresponding to cognitive perception, such as differentiation between significant event and insignificant-event. Event related potentials depict such traces that can be successfully retrieved using multi trail data. These traces are known as components of ERPs.
   b. Among the many aspects concerning stimulus design is duration of stimulus and inter-stimulus interval (ISI) between two flashes. ISI should sufficient to allow the late latency response to earlier stimulus to fade off. This duration varies according to the nature of stimulus, whether it is the attention based or task based, and if a cognitive process are evoked while attending to stimulus.
   c. Currently, there is no standard protocol fixing the number of trials. It is a decision that depends on the signal to noise characteristics of the data, how big the effect is and the type of analysis under the purview of study.
   d. The choice of number of electrode positioning depends largely on enquiry. When the sensory response is to be traced, such as a visually evoked response, less number of channels is sufficient.
   e. For analysis requiring use of spatial filters, spatial resolution is of concern, topographic distribution of results, brain source localization are needed, more electrodes are desired.

f.   At the same time, more the electrodes, more cumbersome is task of subject preparation considering the gel filling between scalp and electrode to create a conducting bridge between the signal and scalp. While the other option of using dry electrodes or salt water sponges between electrodes makes the task easier, these options are available with limited EEG setups.

g.   Most of present day EEG amplifiers come with the viable sampling rate options according to popular enquiries, that satisfying the nyquist criterion. The sampling rate must be at least twice the highest frequency component present in the signal but practice shows that the sampling rate should be much higher in order to capture higher frequency components in the EEG signal. For instance a sampling rate of 64Hz won't be sufficient to capture the gamma activity of 40 Hz. At the same time, a sampling rate as high as a 2048 Hz won't give much additional information compared to working with 512 Hz. Unless one wants to work with very low frequencies and wants to monitor extremely subtle changes within them.

h.   The volume of data generated is direct function of sampling rate. Hence, care should be taken to ensure data handling capability of computing machine with respect to size of data and algorithm complexity.

i.   In order to process the raw EEG data and draw meaningful interpretation around specific time instances, event markers are used. Markers can be generated to identify the beginning of an event of significance, such as stimulus onset. They are imperative to time lock the EEG data for offline analysis. These are short lived square wave pulses that are generated by the recording device to mark the start, end of trial. The length of marker or its temporal duration should be chosen in conjunction with the sampling rate, this is to ensure that marker is recorded. For instance, a 1 milliseconds long sample may not get recorded if the sampling rate is 1024Hz.

CONCLUSION

The present chapter introduces a systematic approach to enquiries based on Human EEG. This approach can be followed to create models that mimic human interactions, cognition and can be extended to model human emotions. The application of this schema to understand human affect becomes relevant for design of social interaction modules such as cobots, and intelligent systems within the social sphere.

REFERENCES

Allison, T., Goff, W. R., & Wood, C. C. (1979). Auditory, Somatosensory and Visual Evoked Potentials in the Diagnosis of Neuropathology: Recording Considerations and Normative Data. *Human Evoked Potentials*, 9. 10.1007/978-1-4684-3483-5_1

Brown, W. S., & Lehmann, D. (1979). Linguistic Meaning-Related Differences in ERP Scalp Topography. In *Human Evoked Potentials* (vol. 9, pp. 31-42). Springer. 10.1007/978-1-4684-3483-5_3

Courchesne, E., Hillyard, S. A., & Galambos, R. (1975). Stimulus novelty, task relevance and the visual evoked potential in man. *Electroencephalography and Clinical Neurophysiology*, *39*(2), 131–143. doi:10.1016/0013-4694(75)90003-6 PMID:50210

Cracco, R. Q., & Cracco, J. B. (1976). Somatosensory evoked potential in man: Far field potentials. *Electroencephalography and Clinical Neurophysiology*, *41*(5), 460–466. doi:10.1016/0013-4694(76)90057-2 PMID:61849

Daneman, R., & Prat, A. (2015). The Blood-Brain Barrier. *Cold Spring Harbor Perspectives in Biology*, *7*(1), a020412. doi:10.1101/cshperspect.a020412 PMID:25561720

Deecke, L., & Kornhuber, H. H. (2003). Human Freedom, Reasoned Will, and the Brain: The Bereitschaftspotential Story. In M. Jahanshahi & M. Hallett (Eds.), *The Bereitschaftspotential* (pp. 283–320). Boston, MA: Springer. doi:10.1007/978-1-4615-0189-3_17

Di Russo, F., Martínez, A., Sereno, M. I., Pitzalis, S., & Hillyard, S. A. (2003). Cortical sources of the early components of the visual evoked potential. *Human Brain Mapping*, *15*(2), 95–111. doi:10.1002/hbm.10010 PMID:11835601

Galambos, R. (1998). Hallowell Davis: August 31, 1896-August 22, 1992. In Biographical Memoir (Vol. 75, pp. 117-37). National Academy of Science.

Hillyard, S. A., & Münte, T. F. (1984). Selective attention to color and location: An analysis with event-related brain potentials. *Perception & Psychophysics*, *36*(2), 185–198. doi:10.3758/BF03202679 PMID:6514528

Hillyard, S. A., Squires, K. C., Bauer, J. W., & Lindsay, P. H. (1971). Evoked potential correlates of auditory signal detection. *Science*, *172*(3990), 1357–1360. doi:10.1126cience.172.3990.1357 PMID:5580218

Kropotov, J. (2008). *Quantitative EEG, Event related potentials and neurotherapy*. London: Elsevier.

Luck, S. J. (2003). Ten Simple Rules for Designing and Interpreting ERP Experiments. In T. C. Handy (Ed.), *Event Related Potentials: A Methods Handbook* (pp. 17–32). Cambridge, MA: The MIT Press.

Luck, S. J. (2005). *An Introduction to Event-Related Potentials and Their Neural Origins*. Cambridge, MA: MIT Press.

Millett, D. (2001). Hans Berger: From psychic energy to the EEG. *Perspectives in Biology and Medicine*, *44*(4), 522–542. doi:10.1353/pbm.2001.0070 PMID:11600799

Phillips, D. K. (2015). *Speed of the Human Brain*. Retrieved October 1, 2018 from https://askabiologist.asu.edu/plosable/speed-human-brain

Sutton, S., Braren, M., Zubin, J., & John, E. R. (1965). Evoked-potential correlates of stimulus uncertainty. *Science*, *150*(3700), 1187–1188. doi:10.1126cience.150.3700.1187 PMID:5852977

Sutton, S., Tueting, P., Zubin, J., & John, E. R. (1967). Information delivery and the sensory evoked potential. *Science*, *155*(3768), 1436–1439. doi:10.1126cience.155.3768.1436 PMID:6018511

Chapter 14

Towards the Real–Life EEG Applications:
Practical Problems and Preliminary Solutions

Guangyi Ai
Neusoft Institute Guangdong, China

ABSTRACT

Electroencephalogram (EEG) is one of the most popular approaches for brain monitoring in many research fields. While the detailed working flows for in-lab neuroscience-targeted EEG experiments conditions have been well established, carrying out EEG experiments under a real-life condition can be quite confusing because of various practical limitations. This chapter gives a brief overview of the practical issues and techniques that help real-life EEG experiments come into being, and the well-known artifact problems for EEG. As a guideline for performing a successful EEG data analysis with the low-electrode-density limitation of portable EEG devices, recently proposed techniques for artifact suppression or removal are briefly surveyed as well.

INTRODUCTION

Understanding how the brain works and responds to stimuli of interest under specified contexts plays a significantly important role in various research fields from fundamental neuroscience researches to complicated social behavioral topics. In many researches, since no clear answers can be effectively obtained, a deep-going analysis based on objective, quantitative, and context-dependent brain states turns into the key for further uncovering the essential parts of the research topics. Yet, monitoring brain states and activities is still remaining a challenge. While brain monitoring techniques and corresponding standard working flows have been well established for in-lab neuroscience researches, when carrying out social or behavioral tasks under a real-life condition, special care must be kept in mind because of a number of practical and technical limitations. This chapter reviews the techniques targeted to the real-life applications of EEG, and briefly marks the practical problems should be aware of, thus makes a preliminary guideline for the EEG applications under real-life environments.

DOI: 10.4018/978-1-5225-7879-6.ch014

Background

In conjunction with the rapid development of sensors and electronic systems, epoch-making techniques for brain state monitoring have been brought onto the frontal stage and widely used in various research fields. Relying on disparate principles, brain states and neuron activities can be observed from different viewpoints. Among those techniques, EEG has gained increasing attention and become popular in various research topics. However, the use of EEG also has its own limitations. In practice, the experimental condition for EEG applications under an open real-world environment is hugely different from the in-lab setups for standard neuroscience researches, and portable EEG measurements are usually preferred. Thus, the practical issues and solutions to real-life portable EEG applications should be taken into account.

Why EEG?

To measure brain activities or responses to specific stimuli, a number of techniques can be adopted. In dependence on the fact that neuronal activities are associated with changes in cerebral blood flow, functional magnetic resonance (fMRI) measures brain activity using blood-oxygen-level dependent (BOLD) contrast. In comparison with a predefined control state, detections for increased brain activities can be obtained with a high spatial resolution. Magnetoencephalography (MEG) is another leading neuroimaging technique to specify activated brain regions deep inside using sensitive magnetometers that can catch magnetic field changes caused by electrical activities taking place inside the brain. These techniques provide extraordinary information for brain states estimation, and have been widely used in various brain related researches. However, both of them must be taken with unportable, huge, expensive apparatus, which imposes strong constraints to its applications and experimental task design. Near-infrared spectroscopy (NIRS) is a new optical imaging technology, which is possible to be miniaturized for portable use and having an extra advantage of interference-free against other electric activities, such as activities caused by muscle movements. But its conspicuous disadvantages of limited spatial and temporal resolutions are usually negatively concerned as a limitation to real-life portable applications. Electroencephalography (EEG), which is firstly recorded by Hans Berger in 1929, so far, is still one of the most prominent and dominant technologies to observe brain activities, especially for monitoring brain responses or state changes when a high time resolution is needed. Due to its principle relying on the detection of electric potential changes on scalp, EEG data sampling can be performed from DC to several kilohertz (depending on the device specification), and provides a great benefit for temporal feature analysis. Moreover, devices for EEG measurement are easy to miniaturize for portable uses. Thus, EEG technique can release the subjects from highly constrained conditions and provide significant freedom for brain-related experiments, hence extremely enlarges its possible applications. Although, EEG also faces its own inevitable problems as every other technology has, its advantages of low cost, portability, and high time resolution makes it one of the most prospective methods for the researches under real-life conditions.

EEG Recording in Real-World

For most neuroscience researches, standard EEG recording devices are tacitly approved. These devices are usually a set of cable connected modules (e.g. battery, amplifier, recording PC or laptop, electrode set with head-cap and so on), thus constrains subjects to keep still in a range no further than the cables could reach. On the other hand, continuously growing research interests that need EEG to be measured under out-lab conditions greatly hastened the development of portable EEG techniques. As a result, wearable EEG acquisition techniques came into being and started playing a key role in various researches, such as social interaction, neuromarketing, human factors, and so on. With those techniques, experiments can be easily moved from laboratories into the real and meaningful life space.

A number of companies released their representative portable EEG recording systems for various applications. In many portable EEG researches, g.Nautilus wireless EEG acquisition system from g.tec (http://www.gtec.at/) is adopted. Excitingly, OpenBCI (https://openbci.com/) also released a low-cost open source solution for portable EEG applications. Furthermore, it is also worth of mention that Emotiv (https://www.emotiv.com/) portable EEG headset has been developed as a commercialized solution for entertainment and daily EEG uses, and has been successfully applied in a number of researches as well.

While portable EEG systems can utilize real-life environment experiments, the practical EEG acquisition is not an easy-to-go task. To obtain high signal quality, many factors should be taken care with, for example, oily hairs and head skin surface and tight electrode touch. In practice, most EEG systems have impedance check utilities, and usually the impedance is expected to be lower than 15 kiloohms for satisfactory EEG acquisition. For more serious occasions (i.e. neuroscience researches) a lower than 5 kiloohms impedance condition is preferred (skin preparation is usually needed). As a result, portable EEG systems are usually doubted to be low-performance and incapable of recording precise EEG potentials, since they are generally optimized for portable properties whereas sacrifices a certain signal acquisition performance. However, comparison studies (Badcock et al., 2013; Melnik et al., 2017) between standard research-grade products and portable EEG devices suggested that competitive performance can be obtained by portable EEG systems and enlightened possible scientific research applications using portable EEG devices.

Techniques Popularly Adopted for Wearable EEG Acquisition

1. Dry/Half-Dry Electrode

Electrode setup for EEG experiment can be quite annoying, since the process of injecting gel or attaching paste for electrodes needs the subject to keep still and to tolerate the discomfort as much as possible until all EEG channels are completely attached and well-adjusted for low impedance. A long-time tiring electrode setup process before experiments may seriously influence subjects' physical and mental conditions, even inflicts intolerable fatigue on subjects.

To get over this practical problem, dry/half-dry electrode techniques are proposed. Both techniques can dramatically reduce setup time for electrode montage by canceling the need of carefully putting conducting gel or paste onto electrodes one by one after mounting.

To a obtain a firm contact with the head for dry electrodes, comb-like electrode designs are commonly adopted, because the separated pins of the comb-like electrodes can easily pass through hair layer and obtain a stable contact with head skin. Whereas half-dry electrode takes advantage of conducting liquid solution, which is instilled into hydrophilic-material electrodes to maintain the conductivity between head skin and sampling circuits. In this way, the conductance can remain a period of time, so that EEG acquisition tasks can be performed until the electrodes dry out.

2. Active Electrode

Active electrodes are designed with a built-in amplifier circuit inside before the cabling to the main amplifier box (Xu et al., 2017). Thus, differing from passive electrodes which picks up noise over the all the paths before the final amplifier node in the main amplifier box, active electrodes inherently have a low output impedance and are robust to environmental interferences, without having to sample all interferences with EEG signals together and then amplify them simultaneously by the same coefficient. Active electrode technique is quite suitable for dry electrodes if the extra power consumption is not a critical problem. Note, not all the systems have an impedance check utility for active electrodes, but active electrodes are usually supposed to have sufficiently high input impedance and low output imped-ance in the signal capture circuits. Hence, for the lack of impedance check, a little experience of EEG signal collection is needed to ensure the signal quality. Observing artificially made signals (e.g. blink, eye-movement) is one of the frequently applied empirical methods.

3. Wireless Data Transfer

To free subjects from the constrained range of moving which is limited by the cabling (i.e. from the main amplifier to the electrodes, and from the main amplifier to a PC or laptop), the main amplifier or amplifier box for portable EEG devices is usually downsized and attached onto the head-cap or fasten to somewhere stable on subjects' body. Data transfer for portable EEG devices is usually realized via wireless communication. The best merit of wireless data transfer is to eliminate the cable connection from the main amplifier to the PC or laptop which stores and displays the real-time data series. The wireless connection is usually utilized by Bluetooth for Wi-Fi. Notably, EEG sampling rate under a wire-less connection is usually much slower than cabled connections. Although the theoretical bandwidth for wireless connections remarkable high, as applying a relatively low data rate may improve the signal to noise rate (SNR) and the robustness for the cable-free communication, a low data rate is usually applied. Commonly, the sampling rate of a wireless EEG devices is no more than 512 Hz.

Informational EEG Features and Basic Analysis Techniques

Making use of EEG, it is important to understand the meaningful EEG features that reflect brain dynam-ics. While the internal mechanisms that generate the complicated brain dynamics and EEG potential changes remain unclear, a number of EEG components had been found as informational markers related to cognition process, emotional states, and brain dynamic process. Those features are fundamentally used for EEG analysis.

Event-related potential (ERP) is deemed as the direct brain response to a specific stimulus or event. Therefore, it can be used as the feature reflecting sensory process, cognitive process and so on. ERP technique benefits from the high time resolution of EEG, which is difficult to obtain with other brain monitoring methods such as fMRI and NIRS. The calculation of ERP can be done with simple signal averaging method. Since ERP reliably occurs over time with respect to the stimulus onset, as long as adequate trials can be collected, summing up all the trials can monotonically increase the reliable time-locked responding EEG components meanwhile suppress the uncorrelated components (e.g. noise), and finally obtains a result in which the pure ERP is finely approximated. The final result highly depends on both the number of trials and the signal quality of each trial. Thus, trials that are contaminated badly should be rejected for a better ERP calculation before summing and averaging. Because the statistical properties of bad trials are usually distinctly different from normal trials, statistical solutions to reject bad trials can be realized. Yet, collecting a significantly large number of trials is impractical for EEG experiments. Both the time limitation and the comfort issue of subjects must be carefully considered. Hence, the balance between the maximum number of trials that can be obtained in an experiment and the time limitation for the whole experiment should be well established in experiment design stage. Usually, a number of trials over 20 is preferred.

Power spectrum and its changes over time can reveal brain activities from another viewpoint. According to the Nyquist sampling theorem, a frequency range from DC to half of the sampling rate of EEG can be effectively collected and analyzed. The frequency band in EEG is divided into several sub-bands in practice. Depending on the purpose of data analysis, the definition of these sub-bands can be slightly different. A common division to the sub-bands:

- **Delta:** < 4Hz
- **Theta:** 4-7Hz
- **Alpha:** 8-15Hz
- **Beta:** 16-31Hz
- **Gamma:** >32Hz

Specially, for sensorimotor related researches a Mu band is defined and used to show the rest-state for motor neurons in motor imaginary tasks (Tang et al., 2016).

Each band of them has been found related to a number of brain states. Consequently, analyzing the spectral power changes turns into one of the main tasks for EEG analysis. The spectral power of each band can be investigated independently in most tasks. On the other hand, combination of two or more bands may be applied to show the results of interest, for example, the beta-to-alpha ratio which is defined by beta power divided by alpha power. In addition, change of time-related power spectrum is also deemed to reflect the dynamic process of brain, hence the event-related spectral perturbation (ERSP) (Makeig, 1993) in ongoing EEG signals also plays an important role in many studies, especially for the cases that non-phase-locked potential of brain activities take place.

Different from the basic Fourier transform analysis, analyzing power spectrum of EEG generally employs time-frequency analysis techniques. One of the simplest examples is the analysis based on short-time Fourier transform. However, such technique treats the time information and frequency information with the same resolutions respectively. Since the high frequency components which covers a larger frequency range change rapidly (i.e. require higher time resolution), whereas the low frequency components whose center-frequency slightly differ from each other change slowly (i.e. require higher frequency resolution), when using the same time-frequency resolution, at least one of the high frequency component and the low frequency component can not get well revealed with the fixed time-frequency resolution.

To solve this problem, a relatively advanced technique --- wavelet (Hazarika et al., 1997) has been intensively studied and applied in EEG analyses. Recently, a Hilbert-Huang transform (HHT) method has been proposed using empirical mode decomposition (EMD) to observe instantaneous frequencies. It has been reported effective and successfully adopted in EEG related works (Mandic et al., 2013; Zhuang et al., 2017).

3N Nature of EEG

To effectively make use of EEG, the '3N' nature which is the shorthand for 'Nonstationary, Nonlinear, and Noisy' of EEG should be kept in mind. EEG signals, similar to the other bio-signals, is nonstationary. This implies that EEG signal's statistical characteristics vary over time, so that the long-term statistical properties such as the mean value or variance of an EEG time series may not be stable enough to reveal related brain states or activities. In practice, EEG signals are usually truncated into short epochs for analysis, because the local stationarity holds for EEG signals (i.e. statistical properties remain nearly stable in a short period of time). Furthermore, human brain is quite complex and is deemed to act as a nonlinear system, but as long as the period is short enough (e.g. as for truncate epochs) linear methods may work perfectly well for EEG analysis. When it comes to large time scales the nonlinearity must be concerned. These two problems mentioned above have been studied over decades, thus are not aimed to be further discussed in this chapter. The third problem --- noisy, as is highly related to practical EEG uses, will be the main target in the following contents.

EEG signal is noisy in many senses. Generally, a number of systemic errors are inevitable. For example, the quantization error which results from analog to digital conversion (ADC). This kind of noise monotonically decreases when the ADC resolution increases, hence devices with a high resolution are preferred in most cases. On the other hand, EEG signal itself is always inevitably contaminated by other electric activities called artifacts. EEG signals are considerably weak and are recorded in micro-volt level. Along with the true EEG components, other electric potentials that are not related to brain activities also mix in and contaminate brain sourced EEG signals. These artifacts are usually large in amplitude and dominant in EEG recordings. Hence, a successful artifact rejection or removal is significantly vital for EEG analysis.

Artifacts come into being through various ways, typical ones are summarized as follow:

- **Line Noise:** Line noise emerges in form of regular sinusoidal oscillation at 50 or 60 Hz depending on the AC electric frequency of power supply. This kind of artifact may exhibit in all channels or a part of them. It is quite easy to recognize, and can be effectively suppressed by establishing a good earthing condition before the experimental setting up. For the residual line noise remains in EEG recordings, notch filters can be applied to filter out all this constant frequency component and its harmonic components when analysis.

- **Electrocardiography (ECG):** ECG is sourced from heartbeat and circulation. Periodical spikes synchronized with the pace of heartbeat is the distinct appearance of this kind of artifact. As human heartbeat is relatively slow in frequency (around 1Hz), for researches in which such low frequency components are not needed, a simple high pass filter can be applied to solve this problem perfectly. Note, electrode montage with average reference may effectively suppress ECG artifacts as well.

- **Electrode Artifact:** Electrode artifact is the most troublesome artifact. It is usually caused by bad electrode contact or electrode popping. When electrode artifacts take place, the EEG recording is severely contaminated and almost no meaningful EEG data sourced from brain activities can be extracted until it recovers. When necessary, a part or the whole EEG data recorded from those channels should be rejected. Manually or automatically data rejection to bad epochs or data segment even the whole EEG data from the channel is the only solution for data analysis.

- **Electromyography (EMG):** EMG indeed is one of the most common sources of noise in EEG recordings. It is actually a kind of muscle movement sourced potential captured by EEG electrodes, and is quite high in amplitude in almost all EEG recordings. Because of the fact that EMG usually shows a greatly higher amplitude than EEG signals and has considerably wide spectral distribution, EEG recordings are severely contaminated and blurred. Furthermore, the topographical distribution for EMG is irregular and changes from time to time, so that the signal correction for EMG contamination is quite intractable. So far, in spite of the fact that algorithm-based attempts against EMG contamination have been proposed (Weidong Zhou & Gotman, 2004), trying to avoid muscle movements is still one of best solutions.

- **Ocular Artifact:** Ocular artifacts are induced by eye movements, such as blinks and muscular activities of eyes. Because eye movements are physiological activities, it is not possible to eliminate ocular artifacts from the source. Forcing the subjects to keep staring at a fixed point and not to blink for the whole experiment is physically impossible. Besides, trying to avoid eye movements may ruin the purpose of collecting EEG data from an experiment that induces subjects' natural reactions. Thus, ocular artifacts turn into the most common and non-separable artifacts which contaminates EEG signals. The amplitude of ocular artifacts is usually more than 100 μV (Keren et al., 2010), which is much higher than common EEG signals. Its frequency spans from DC to about 20 Hz in common, thus, the frequency band of ocular artifacts overlaps the most meaningful EEG bands (i.e. delta, theta, alpha and a part of beta). The existence of ocular artifacts mainly causes following problems:

  ○ **Obscuring ERPs**: Ocular artifacts that take place near stimulation onsets badly distort EEG baselines and the invoked potentials. Although signal averaging technique can improve the signal-to-noise ratio and expected to cancel out all kinds of artifacts, as the brain related invoked potentials are usually very weak (e.g. less than 10 μV), if ocular artifacts are involved, much more trials are needed to average out the influences of them.

  ○ **Contaminating Low-Frequency EEG Signals**: Because their frequency band is overlapped, during EEG spectrum analysis it is unclear that the low-frequency power changes are caused by ocular artifacts or brain activities. This problem becomes even more serious in real-life EEG applications, because in such kind of EEG experiments eye movements are irregular, spontaneous and frequent. In comparison with in-lab neuroscience experiments real-life EEG applications are special because subjects' view sights and ranges are not highly constrained. In other words, real-life EEG applications are basically performed in a completely free-viewing condition without any artificial fixation lockers/points to guide the subjects' visual actions. Furthermore, the frequency and magnitude of eye movements may be greatly higher than those from traditional in-lab neuroscience researches, because of the complicated stimulations in real-life environments. Hence, ocular artifacts turn into one of the biggest challenges to boost in-lab EEG achievements into reliable EEG applications in real-life.

Simple practical solutions such as using a more flexible head-cap to proof loose of electrode contact (i.e. suppress electrode artifacts) and lightly constraining subjects' unnecessary muscle movements to decrease EMG would never work on ocular artifacts because the presence of ocular artifacts are caused by spontaneous actions. Therefore, dealing with ocular artifacts is a vital task for real-life EEG applications. The following parts of this chapter mainly focus on the solutions to ocular artifacts.

Electrical Model of Eyes and Ocular Artifacts Removal

In human eyeballs, there exists a differential potential between cornea and retina (Marmor & Zrenner, 1993). The electrolysis process inside eyes is deemed as the reason why this potential exists. When lights pass through eyeballs, the cornea and racial parts of eyeballs are charged positively and negatively respectively. The electrical potential difference can be measured between the frontal and back sides. In practice, a related potential is usually collected by electrodes placed near eyes and the collected potential is named as electrooculography (EOG).

Generally, eyes act similarly to charged batteries in a 3-D dimension space, which cause electric field changes and potential propagation over scalp by the volume conductance of brain. Croft and Barry (2002) suggested that the amplitude of the propagated potential is inversely related to the distance from eyeballs to the electrode positions on scalp, and the propagation coefficient (i.e. a number represents how strongly the potential propagated) remains nearly still in tens of minutes.

Although, EOG potential itself is not static due to the influences from inconstant light conditions and the dynamical electrolysis processes taking place inside eyeballs and brain, the relationship between EOG and the propagated potentials over scalp is generally linear. Hence it is possible to obtain a linear coefficient to represent their relationship. Once the linear coefficients between all EEG channels and EOG have been obtained, since in a period of time they are supposed to be fixed (usually the time is long enough to carry out an EEG experiment), the whole EEG recording can be corrected using simple subtraction calculations to each EEG channel for ocular artifacts removal. The calculation can be expressed as follow:

$$estEEG = mEEG - \vec{b} * \overrightarrow{EOG}$$

where $estEEG$ represents the estimated pure EEG in an EEG channel without ocular artifacts; $mEEG$ represents the measured EEG signal; $\vec{b}$ stands for the linear coefficients presenting how strongly each EOG component (usually two or three components are taken into the correction) propagated onto the electrode position, and finally $\overrightarrow{EOG}$ represents the EOG vector which is comprised of vertical EOG component and horizontal EOG component in common. In most cases, two EOG components (i.e. horizontal and vertical) are used for the calculation, but in some studies three EOG components (with a radical component included) are used to obtain the correction. The formalization of this heuristic turns into a classical and widely used technique --- the linear regression-based ocular artifact removal.

Linear regression-based ocular artifact removal method commonly takes two EOG components into account, as mentioned previously the horizontal eye movement related EOG component named as hEOG which can be collected by two electrodes placed near outer canthi, and the vertical eye movement related component named as vEOG which can be collected by two electrodes below and above one of the eyes. Both the vEOG and hEOG should be recorded simultaneously with EEG signals. In an extra calibration stage (i.e. the stage to obtain the propagation coefficients for EOGs) before the real EEG tasks, subjects are asked to perform a number of large eye movements vertically and horizontally, then from the collected data the propagation coefficients for both vEOG and hEOG can be calculated using linear regression algorithm for each EEG channel.

The coefficient calculation is usually obtained in an ordinary least squares (OLS) sense, which optimizes the results by minimizing the sum of square errors between the EEG and the product of EOGs and their corresponding coefficients. There are two classical strategies for the linear coefficient calculation process: Gratton style (Gratton et al., 1983) and AAA style (Croft & Barry, 1998). In both styles, data collected in the calibration stage is firstly cut into short epochs near eye movement onsets, so that the nonstationarity of both EEG and EOG can be suppressed. The AAA style coefficient calculation process is depicted in figure 1.

It is reported that the AAA style shows a better performance for ocular artifact removal (Croft & Barry, 1998). Recently, revised strategies have been proposed as well, for example, lately developed Bayesian adaptive regression splines (BARS) methods (Dimatteo et al., 2001; Wallstrom et al., 2004) and so on. The advantages of regression-based technique are quite obvious: simplicity, low computational consumption, and easy to carry out for online EEG processing. On the other hand, its disadvantages are clear as well --- the need of extra EOG electrodes.

By the work of Picton et al. (2000), a topographical perspective on ocular artifacts removal and brain source separation was suggested. This topographic view boosted the application of component-based artifact rejection approaches. Principal component analysis (PCA) (Sadasivan & Narayana Dutt, 1996) and independent component analysis (ICA) (Jung et al., 2000) are two typical techniques in component-based approaches. Both of them belong to blind source separation (BSS) family, and assume EEG signal as a linear mixture of different EEG components. PCA decomposes EEG signals into orthogonal components, whereas ICA decomposes EEG signals into independent ones and is deemed to outperform PCA algorithm for EEG source separation in practice. The number of components can be separated by both PCA and ICA equals the number of EEG channels. As a result, a projection matrix which describes how strongly each component projects into all EEG channels can be obtained. The projection matrix is comprised of projection vectors and each projection vector can be explained topographically with a head map which graphically describes how a component propagate over scalp. By observing the head map for each component, whether or not a component reflects ocular artifact can be determined. Then, the artifact rejection can be done by replacing the identified artifact component with an all-zeros data series meanwhile leaving all the other components untouched. After clearing the artifact component, artifact-free EEGs can be obtained using the same projection matrix inversely with the updated components. Note,

Figure 1. AAA style propagation coefficient calculation

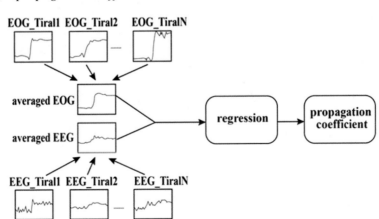

to identify artifact components, manual operations and some hand-on experience are needed. Yet there are no clearly defined rules for determining ocular artifact components since the polarity and scale of components are vague in separated components and several similar topographical components may appear on head maps as well. Hence, at a certain this approach may not fit beginner's hand very well. Figure 2 shows an example of ocular artifact topographies, and in practice similar topographies can be observed. With a little investigation to the components' corresponding temporal data series (e.g. searching for the eye-movements-like temporal features) whether or not they are ocular artifacts can be determined. Note, because ICA can not determine the polarity of components, in practice the topographies may show the topographies in reversed colors.

The advantages of component-based approaches are: (1) no need of EOG collection by extra electrodes, (2) reliable performance when sufficient electrodes are provided, and (3) the topographically meaningful separation to EEG sources for further analysis. However, to obtain an effective decomposition by component-based approach, the number of EEG channels must be no less than the number of sources assumed to form up the EEG signals under linear mixture assumption. Using less channels may also obtain similar result, but actually the approximation sacrifice precision and pure components may not be obtained in the results. Thus, the performance of these component-based approaches is directly limited by the available EEG channels in practical applications.

So, limited number of EEG channels in portable EEG applications severely degrades the performance of component-based methods. To overcome this problem, new alternative algorithms and techniques have been continuously proposed. In recent studies, single channel source separation techniques which separate latent sources by BSS has gained great attention with respect to portable EEG uses. These techniques usually combine PCA or ICA with time-frequency methods such as wavelet and HHT.

Figure 2. Typical topographies for ocular artifact components obtained from ICA. In case of PCA, similar patterns can be observed as well. They are the basic topographical patterns of ocular artifacts. (a) represents the component corresponding to vertical eye movements. As shown in the topography this component propagated from frontal side to the backside with a gradually decreasing pattern. (b) shows a typical topography for the component corresponding to horizontal eye movements. Generally, this kind of component form a dipolar pattern horizontally, thus, represents the horizontally changing potentials. (c) represents an eyelid sourced component. Eyelid movements not only take place when blinking, when the subject moving their eyes, eyelid movements are observed as well. The component concentrates on the frontal sides on a head map.

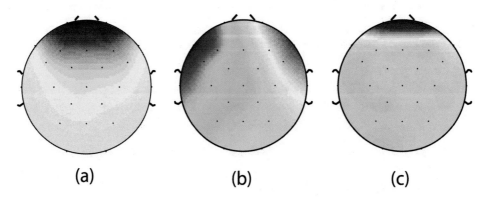

(a)　　　　　　(b)　　　　　　(c)

Teixeira (2006) proposed a singular spectrum analysis (SSA) method for single channel EEG processing, and suggested its effectiveness on high-amplitude artifacts removal. The algorithm is suitable for ocular artifacts suppression with portable EEG devices that have very low-density electrode distribution. It has also been reported that by combining EMD and ICA an effective source separation method can be realized (Mijović et al., 2010), and the algorithm outperforms two other ICA-based single channel methods named as single-channel ICA (SCICA) (Davies & James, 2007) and wavelet-ICA (WICA) (Lin & Zhang, 2005) by comparison. Nonnegative matrix factorization (NMF) is another technique for single channel source separation, and a study suggested that it can be applied for EEG artifact removal as well (Kanoga & Mitsukura, 2014). In the study NMF was applied for one of the EEG channels to reject ocular artifacts, meanwhile a standard ICA algorithm was performed on the original multichannel EEG signals as well. The results showed an over 99% correlation between NMF method and standard ICA method for a low-density EEG device.

Although not all the newly proposed methods haven't been fully approved and widely adopted in neuroscience related fields, their appearance highly enlightened EEG signal processing with portable devices, and enlightened the future researches with portable EEG solutions. Yet, more sophisticated methods and algorithms are still urgently expected for real-life researches using portable EEG devices.

CONCLUSION

This chapter gave a brief overview to the natures of EEG and its practical limitations in real-life experiments. In addition to the basic EEG analyzing techniques, several practical problems are pointed out with the recommended solutions. Finally, to serve practical EEG under real-life conditions, the ocular artifacts problem and techniques to solve them are briefly reviewed. Thus, the technical statements in this chapter and the heuristics form up a preliminary guideline for the real-life EEG researches.

ACKNOWLEDGMENT

This research received no specific grant from any funding agency in the public, commercial, or not-for-profit sectors.

REFERENCES

Badcock, N. A., Mousikou, P., Mahajan, Y., de Lissa, P., Thie, J., & McArthur, G. (2013). Validation of the Emotiv EPOC ® EEG gaming system for measuring research quality auditory ERPs. *PeerJ*, *1*, e38. doi:10.7717/peerj.38 PMID:23638374

Croft, R. J., & Barry, R. J. (1998). EOG correction: A new aligned-artifact average solution. *Electroencephalography and Clinical Neurophysiology*, *107*(6), 395–401. doi:10.1016/S0013-4694(98)00087-X PMID:9922084

Croft, R. J., & Barry, R. J. (2002). Issues relating to the subtraction phase in EOG artefact correction of the EEG. *International Journal of Psychophysiology, 44*(3), 187–195. doi:10.1016/S0167-8760(01)00201-X PMID:12031294

Davies, M. E., & James, C. J. (2007). Source separation using single channel ICA. *Signal Processing, 87*(8), 1819–1832. doi:10.1016/j.sigpro.2007.01.011

Dimatteo, I., Genovese, C. R., & Kass, R. E. (2001). Bayesian curve-fitting with free-knot splines. *Biometrika, 88*(4), 1055–1071. doi:10.1093/biomet/88.4.1055

Gratton, G., Coles, M. G., & Donchin, E. (1983). A new method for off-line removal of ocular artifact. *Electroencephalography and Clinical Neurophysiology, 55*(4), 468–484. doi:10.1016/0013-4694(83)90135-9 PMID:6187540

Hazarika, N., Chen, J. Z., Tsoi, A. C., & Sergejew, A. (1997). Classification of EEG signals using the wavelet transform. *Signal Processing, 59*(1), 61–72. doi:10.1016/S0165-1684(97)00038-8

Jung, T. P., Makeig, S., Humphries, C., Lee, T. W., McKeown, M. J., Iragui, V., & Sejnowski, T. J. (2000). Removing electroencephalographic artifacts by blind source separation. *Psychophysiology, 37*(2), 163–178. doi:10.1111/1469-8986.3720163 PMID:10731767

Kanoga, S., & Mitsukura, Y. (2014). Eye-Blink Artifact Reduction Using 2-Step Nonnegative Matrix Factorization for Single-Channel Electroencephalographic Signals. *Journal of Signal Processing, 18*(5), 251–257. doi:10.2299/jsp.18.251

Keren, A. S., Yuval-Greenberg, S., & Deouell, L. Y. (2010). Saccadic spike potentials in gamma-band EEG: Characterization, detection and suppression. *NeuroImage, 49*(3), 2248–2263. doi:10.1016/j.neuroimage.2009.10.057 PMID:19874901

Lin, J., & Zhang, A. (2005). Fault feature separation using wavelet-ICA filter. *NDT & E International, 38*(6), 421–427. doi:10.1016/j.ndteint.2004.11.005

Makeig, S. (1993). Auditory event-related dynamics of the EEG spectrum and effects of exposure to tones. *Electroencephalography and Clinical Neurophysiology, 86*(4), 283–293. doi:10.1016/0013-4694(93)90110-H PMID:7682932

Mandic, D. P., Ur Rehman, N., Wu, Z., & Huang, N. E. (2013). Empirical mode decomposition-based time-frequency analysis of multivariate signals: The power of adaptive data analysis. *IEEE Signal Processing Magazine, 30*(6), 74–86. doi:10.1109/MSP.2013.2267931

Marmor, M. F., & Zrenner, E. (1993). Standard for clinical electro-oculography. International Society for Clinical Electrophysiology of Vision. *Archives of Ophthalmology, 111*(5), 601–604.

Melnik, A., Legkov, P., Izdebski, K., Kärcher, S. M., Hairston, W. D., Ferris, D. P., & König, P. (2017). Systems, Subjects, Sessions: To What Extent Do These Factors Influence EEG Data? *Frontiers in Human Neuroscience, 11*(March), 1–20. PMID:28424600

Mijović, B., De Vos, M., Gligorijević, I., Taelman, J., & Van Huffel, S. (2010). Source separation from single-channel recordings by combining empirical-mode decomposition and independent component analysis. *IEEE Transactions on Biomedical Engineering, 57*(9), 2188–2196. doi:10.1109/TBME.2010.2051440 PMID:20542760

Picton, T. W., Van Roon, P., Armilio, M. L., Berg, P., Ille, N., & Scherg, M. (2000). The correction of ocular artifacts: A topographic perspective. *Clinical Neurophysiology, 111*(1), 53–65. doi:10.1016/S1388-2457(99)00227-8 PMID:10656511

Sadasivan, P. K., & Narayana Dutt, D. (1996). SVD based technique for noise reduction in electroencephalographic signals. *Signal Processing, 55*(2), 179–189. doi:10.1016/S0165-1684(96)00129-6

Tang, Z., Sun, S., Zhang, S., Chen, Y., Li, C., & Chen, S. (2016). A Brain-Machine Interface Based on ERD/ERS for an Upper-Limb Exoskeleton Control. *Sensors (Basel), 16*(12), 2050. doi:10.339016122050 PMID:27918413

Teixeira, A. R., Tomé, A. M., Lang, E. W., Gruber, P., & Martins da Silva, A. (2006). Automatic removal of high-amplitude artefacts from single-channel electroencephalograms. *Computer Methods and Programs in Biomedicine, 83*(2), 125–138. doi:10.1016/j.cmpb.2006.06.003 PMID:16876903

Wallstrom, G. L., Kass, R. E., Miller, A., Cohn, J. F., & Fox, N. A. (2004). Automatic correction of ocular artifacts in the EEG: A comparison of regression-based and component-based methods. *International Journal of Psychophysiology, 53*(2), 105–119. doi:10.1016/j.ijpsycho.2004.03.007 PMID:15210288

Xu, J., Mitra, S., Van Hoof, C., Yazicioglu, R. F., & Makinwa, K. A. A. (2017). Active Electrodes for Wearable EEG Acquisition: Review and Electronics Design Methodology. *IEEE Reviews in Biomedical Engineering, 10*, 187–198. doi:10.1109/RBME.2017.2656388 PMID:28113349

Zhou, W., & Gotman, J. (2004). Removal of EMG and ECG artifacts from EEG based on wavelet transform and ICA. In *The 26th Annual International Conference of the IEEE Engineering in Medicine and Biology Society* (Vol. 3, pp. 392–395). IEEE.

Zhuang, N., Zeng, Y., Tong, L., Zhang, C., Zhang, H., & Yan, B. (2017). Emotion Recognition from EEG Signals Using Multidimensional Information in EMD Domain. *BioMed Research International, 2017*, 1–9. doi:10.1155/2017/8317357 PMID:28900626

318

318

Chapter 15
Morphological Component Analysis for Biological Signals:
A Sophisticated Way to Analyze Brain Activities in Various Movable Conditions

318

Balbir Singh
National Institute for Physiological Sciences, Japan

ABSTRACT

This chapter explains the removal of artifacts from the multi-resource biological signals. Morphological components can be used to distinguish between the brain activities and artifacts that are contaminated with each other in many physical situations. In this chapter, a two-stage wavelet shrinkage and morphological component analysis (MCA) for biological signals is a sophisticated way to analyze the brain activities and validate the effectiveness of artifacts removal. The source components in the biological signals can be characterized by specific morphology and measures the independence and uniqueness of the source components. Undecimated wavelet transform (UDWT), discrete cosine transform (DCT), local discrete cosine transform (LDCT), discrete sine transform (DST), and DIRAC are the orthonormal bases function used to build the explicit dictionary for the decomposition of source component of the biological signal in the morphological component analysis. The chapter discusses the implementation and optimization algorithm of the morphological component analysis.

INTRODUCTION

The computational advancement and mathematical approach have been playing an important role in envision technologies. There has been a great interest in an explicit model that could solve the many fundamental problems in daily life. With the advent of technology, significant progress has been made in understanding the interaction between noninvasive human brain and intelligent peripheral systems. With subsequent problems, intelligent peripheral systems control with feedback in real-time, robot mechanical kinematic, dynamic as well as robot control architecture and behavior, human brain robot interaction refers to many research field of medicine, engineering, psychology and robotics. SSVEP (steady-state

DOI: 10.4018/978-1-5225-7879-6.ch015

visual evoked potential), ERP (event-related potential), MI (motor imagery), and cognitive based EEG BCIs technology is a promising tool. Recently, EEG BCIs technology could be used to enhance the motor rehabilitation devices for elderly or different kind of disabled patients, automated detection system and can be induce neural plasticity. EEG BCIs technology and method have been developed depending on the intelligent peripherals such as wheelchair, manipulator, drone, humanoid robot and many more. To derive these intelligent peripherals, the electrical properties measured from the biological aspects have a great probability to be consider. These electrical properties can be measured in form of electrocardiography (ECG), electromyography (EMG), electrooculography (EOG), electroencephalography (EEG) and many more. Electroencephalography (EEG), a method for measuring electrical activity from the scalp, is a popular method used for a clinical purposes (biomarkers), neuroscientific research and brain-computer-interface (BCI) (Al-Hudhud, 2014; Blasco, Iáñez, Úbeda, & Azorín, 2012; Cecotti, 2011; Nicolas-Alonso & Gomez-Gil, 2012). The very first tool commonly used is EEG to record and analyse the neuronal activity. EEG based methods for neuroscientific research or clinical purposes diagnosis consist of mainly three procedure, namely pre-processing EEG, feature extraction from the EEG in spectral, time, entropy and energy domain to capture spatial and temporal patterns. The third procedure being some machine learning techniques to classify the targeted events. All the procedures plays different but important roles in EEG BCIs system. Preprocessing of EEG segments into different brain wave band is important as EEG is widely distributed over the scalp, depicts the cumulative activities of the underline neuronal mass altogether and dynamically brain activities shows different pattern or changes in different brain wave bands. However, EEG signals are contaminated with other activity called artifacts generated from different active sources other than neurons that propagate the electrical activity and mix with each other in many physical situations. For example, EEG signals could be mixed with EOG, EMG and external noise interference (Kovach, Tsuchiya, Kawasaki, Oya, Howard, & Adolphs. 2011). A serious risk in EEG are the spikes and bumps in the signal caused by EOG artifacts (specific eye movements like blinks and saccades) (Powers, Basso, & Evinger, 2013; Plöchl, Ossandón, & König, 2012). Various precautions could be taken in order to avoid these artifacts. For example, the subjects could fixate on a visual target without moving the eye, or the affected segment of the EEG signal could be excluded from the analysis. However, fixation does not reduce involuntary eye-movements during a physical task. Due to this, the amount of EEG data is reduced which is not acceptable in research or physical systems driven by EEG. Therefore, it is highly desirable to suppress/ remove the artifacts or separate source components that represent the original activities. Several decomposition methods and filters have been used to separate the source components from measured EEG signal in the time-frequency domain, such as fast Fourier transform (FFT), eigenvectors and wavelet transform (WT) (Al-Fahoum, Amjed, & Al-Fraihat, 2014). Fundamentally the signal segment, depending on the windowing method applied, is convoluted with basis function or mother wavelet in wavelet methods to get desired coefficients. In the regression method, the EOG signal is used as a reference for removing EOG artifacts from the EEG signal. Therefore it is canceled out the useful information due to a bilateral effect of EEG. Berg & Scherg (1991) had proposed a spatiotemporal dipole method and many more methods focus on removing ocular artifacts and other artifacts (Urigüen & Garcia-Zapirain, 2015) such as cardiac, muscle, electrode noise and so on. Filtering can be used for artifacts removal but it poses the threat of losing some of the useful information. After getting the EEG preprocessed or filtered, features are extracted in spectral, time, entropy and energy domain which enable the system to capture the specific pattern showing significant difference in the instant of the targeted event. There are non-linear parameters also which are employed to extract the desired pattern. Features have used cautiously otherwise would lead to high dimensionality, outliers causing problem for classification. While using the continuous EEG, feature containing the time information provide vital information of the mental state of the human. Upon these features BCI technology has been implemented to derive intelligent peripheral systems.

The development and utilization of robotic assistive device in daily life become more challenging, means for detection and processing of erroneous robot action as it typically rely on the scalp measured EEG. Therefore the EEG signals decoding is the key issue to identify the human mental states. The distinct EEG patterns such paying attention to a stimulus, performing mental tasks related human cognitive control or MI (motor imagery) require by BCIs to perform specific voluntary tasks. But a number of the issues, such as individual differences among subjects, accuracies, and information transfer rate, still need to be addressed.

In this chapter, the main focus will be on the multiresource biological signals and their morphology, denoising and artifacts removal, source component decomposition and application of the source component that could be used in BCI system. This chapter contains four sections, the first section elaborates EEG and EOG signals contamination model and morphology. In second section elaborates the two-stage wavelet shrinkage for denoising and artifacts removal; in third section, morphological component analysis used for constructive source components decomposition of multiresource biological signals based on their morphology. In fourth section, the application by considering the source components as identify the features from measured signal for the physical system.

1. EOG-EEG SIGNAL AND THEIR MORPHOLOGY

According to the electrophysiological mechanism, it is unclear how underlying EEG signals are mixed with different sources in the brain. The most plausible hypothesis is suggested that the signals are modulated by synchronous spiking activities (Whittingstall & Logothetis, 2009). The most difficult issue is an uncertainty in EEG signals to discriminate the EEG signals having different morphology and noise. The EEG signal contains multiple types of morphologies caused by different internal mechanisms such as EOG caused by eyeballs and eyelids movements, and EMG caused by muscular movements of body parts. EEG signals is characterized by "monomorphic" (consist of one frequency as dominant activity), "polymorphic" (consist of multiple frequencies and form a complex activity) and "transient" (spike has peaked with 20 to 70 msec duration, sharp wave has peaked with 70 to 200 msec duration) (McGill, n.d.). Underlying the brain, electrophysiological mechanism is coupled with myogenic potential evoked by ocular movements (Kovach et al., 2011). The observed potential is approximately 400 µV from EOG recording in the 4-20 Hz range known as corneo-retinal dipole. The generation of the potential depending on the degree of eyeball rotation (Singh & Wagatsuma, 2019; Nilsson & Andersson, 1988; Berg & Scherg, 1991; Ai, Sato, Singh, Wagatsuma, 2016). The EEG and EOG morphologies are shown in Figure 1 (Singh & Wagatsuma, 2017). Figure 2 illustrates the contamination of the EEG and EOG signal as per the biological mechanism (Singh & Wagatsuma, 2019). The individual neuronal spikes in the brain represents the information, which reflects in the EEG signal. The collective information from a specific range of neuronal oscillations is important rather than individual spikes, and the fact has extended the possibility of EEG/MEG measurements (David, Kilner, & Friston, 2006). The signal f can be considered $kf (k<1)$ as an inevitable decay of the amplitude from inside to outside of the scalp. The reduction ratio of EEG signal is estimated as $k \cong 0.25$, when simultaneous recording between the scalp EEG and intracranial EEG (Debatisse et al., 2005; Ray et al., 2007; Ball et al., 2009; Yamazaki et al.,

2012). The EOG signal ranges from 200-500 μV and the scalp EEG signal range is about 10-50 μV in the ERP studies (Plöchl, Ossandón & König, 2012; Singh & Wagatsuma, 2019). It is observed that the scalp EEG measurement is quite less than the intracranial and which implies that the ratio of EOG and scalp EEG is $\frac{\hat{g}}{kf}$. (Long, Burke, & Kahana, 2014). Consistently, the ratio of intracranial EEG and EOG can be estimated in the same manner as k≅0.25 and then f≫g. The measured EEG signal at scalp given as

$$y = k\left(g + f\right) + \eta$$

$$= kg + \left(kf + \eta\right)$$

$$= \hat{g} + \left(kf + \eta\right)$$

The desired signal and noise treated as $(kf + \eta$. and kg. respectively, where EOG $\hat{g}$. ($\sim 500\,\mu V) \gg kf + \eta\left(\sim 10\mu V\right)$. The problem of the true EEG signal is inevitable and it may be solved by the isolation of individual electrophysiological mechanisms. We know that the EEG signal is the most noninvasive tool in particular for clinical diagnosis and neuroscience research, while medical professionals and researchers in related fields have faced the difficulty of the signal contamination. The ocular artifacts i.e. eye movements and eye blinks are the most serious artifacts.

2. TWO-STAGE WAVELET SHRINKAGE FOR ARTIFACTS REMOVAL FROM MULTIRESOURCE BIOSIGNALS

The electrical activity (EEG) measured from scalp is a popular technique for brain related activities which can be used in many directions. The measured EEG signal should be assumed as a linear combination of different components generated from different sources, or the mixing of underlying brain activities and artifacts. The mixing of constructive sources components are lead the measured signal into non-linearity and non-stationary. Therefore the separation of source components from desired measured signal become

Figure 1. Different morphologies in a) EEG signals, b) EOG signals
(Singh & Wagatsuma, 2017)

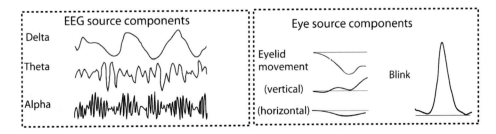

Figure 2. EEG-EOG signal contamination model with respect to the biological mechanism (Singh & Wagatsuma, 2019)

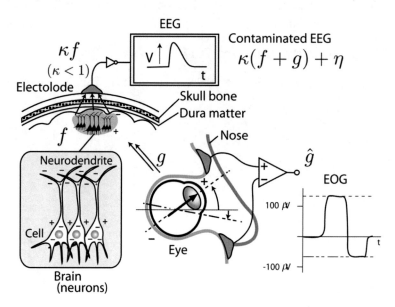

more difficult in the time or frequency domain. A famous approach is blind source separation (BSS) for separating underlying source from a linear mixture of several sources, where mixing source components is unknown. The blind source separation methods have aimed to recover mutually independent source component from unknown linear mixture without knowing the mixing coefficients. Principal component analysis (PCA) and independent component analysis (ICA) are popular methods that have been used for separation of source components or removal of artifacts (Jung, Makeig, Humphries & Lee, 2000; Joyce, Gordonitsky, & Kutas, 2004; Hyvarinen, 1999; Vigário, 1997; Romo-Vázquez et al., 2012; Akhtar, Mitsuhashi, & James, 2012). The PCA and ICA methods work based on a statistical approach and aim to find the statistical independence of the linear projected signals. PCA is a sophisticated method to reduce the artifacts and specify principal components (PC) to reconstruct overall signal structure. In PCA, the signal irregularity occurs while removing the source components with small amplitudes (Berg & Scherg, 1994; Picton et al., 2000) and the representation of remaining PCs of mixed signal is always a difficult challenge, requiring prior knowledge to identify the source components or artifacts. The subspace projection is also used to extract EEG components on time/space basis (Sameni & Gouy-Pailler, 2014). A traditional method ICA decomposes the measured signal into source components by computing the demixing matrix. ICA uses one of the statistical independence criteria such as minimization of mutual information, maximization of non-gaussianity, maximization of likelihood (Hyvarinen, 1999). Whitening has been used in ICA algorithms to make the components of measured signal independent. Whitening strengthen the measured signal at all given frequencies. Mainly, unit variance is the strength of signal, therefore mixing matrix is an orthogonal. If whitening is not sufficient to make measured signal independent then orthogonal transformation is used. ICA amplified the noise therefore the detection of the source components become difficult as gaussian noise spread over the source components in an undesired way. ICA generates spikes and bumps, if the sample size is not sufficient. Several methods and algorithms have been proposed for this purpose. Every method has its own pros and cons which suggests that we have not reached to the stage where the real-time separation of source components occurs. The separation of source components from a signal measured from a single electrode was always a difficult task. ICA works efficiently for multi-electrodes. In case of single electrode ICA works but it required stationary signal and disjoint in frequency domain. Even though a very few methods are available that are the combination of two or three techniques, there is no single approach that could handle this problem.

Wavelet transform is a real time decomposition approach method with less computational costs which has been used to separate the source components. This method preserves the time-frequency characteristics of the original signal and significantly improves the frequency domain. The wavelet denoising performance is widely clarified in signal and image processing (Lang, Guo, Odegard, Burrus, & Wells, 1996). Wavelet transform in biomedical signals remains an investigation challenge because it consists of multiple sources signal that emerge spontaneously. The decomposition of EEG signal using WT is also known as decimated wavelet transform, one of the techniques in analyzing non-stationary EEG signals. The threshold used in denoising has witnessed for loss of information and resulting the improper reconstruction of signals. Discrete wavelet transform (DWT) down-samples the approximation coefficients and details coefficients at each decomposition level but UWDT does not incorporate the down sampling operation, thus the approximation coefficients and details coefficients have the same length as the original at each level. The UWDT up-samples the coefficients of the low pass and high pass filter at each level. The up-sampling operation is equivalent to dilating wavelets. The resolution of the UWDT coefficients decreases with the increasing of the levels of decomposition, therefore proper levels for decomposition have to be selected. UWDT has the translation or shift invariant property. This means that if the two signals have shifted with respect to each other, then the result from UDWT have a shifted signal as well. This does not exist in an ordinary DWT. UWDT gives more amount of information as compared to DWT. The translation invariant property is important for feature extraction in EEG signals. Denoising with UWDT has shift invariant and has better balance between smoothness and accuracy with respect to DWT (Lang et al., 1996; Starck, Fadili & Murtagh, 2007; Gyaourova, Kamath, & Fodor, 2002; Fowler, 2005). UWDT has supported both the real and complex signal used for real signals. The drawback of UWDT is that it requires higher computational memory and redundancy in the coefficients. UDWT modifies the DWT decomposition scheme by changing the low pass and high pass at each level (Fowler, 2005). It has imitated the sub-sampling of the filtered signal by including zeros between each of the filter coefficients to up-sampling the low-pass filter at each level. The UDWT is based on the 'a trous' algorithms. The UDWT used the wavelet filters of a 1-D signal (Starck, Fadili, & Murtagh, 2007; Fowler, 2005).

2.1 Denoising

The measured EEG signal y .is the function f .with white noise z .initially formulated for denoising signal model as described below:

$$y_i = f\left(t_i\right) + \sigma z_i \left(i = 1,\ldots,\eta\right).$$

$$= f_i + \eta_i$$

where $\eta = 2^{j+1}$. the unit interval $t_i = \dfrac{i}{\eta}\left(t \in [0,1]\right)$. gaussian white noise z_i. and noise level σ. The relationship between signal f .and noise η .is unknown. It works if satisfies $f \gg \eta$. The denoising algorithms (Lang et al, 1996; Gyaourova, Kamath, & Fodor, 2002) with adaptive thresholds were designed and three steps can be applied as follows:

Step 1: Pyramid wavelet filtering of Cohen, Daubechies, Jawerth, and Vial (1993) to the coefficients of

signal $\beta_{j+1,k} = \dfrac{y_k}{\sqrt{\eta}}$., yielding noisy wavelet coefficients $w_{j,k}\left(j = j_0,\ldots,J; k = 0,\ldots,2^{j-1}\right)$.

Step 2: Consider the thresholding protocol either soft threshold $s\ (w)$.r hard threshold $h\ (w)$ith certain threshold level λ, applied to the wavelet coefficients and renewed wavelet coefficients $w_{\lambda_{j,k}}$.

Step 3: The renewed coefficients ($j > J$. used for recovered signal $\widehat{f(t)}, (t \in [0,1]$ .by inverting the wavelet transform.

The soft thresholding $s(w)$ .defined as

$$s(w) = \begin{cases} sgn(w)(|w| - \lambda), & |w| \geq \lambda \\ 0, & |w| < \lambda \end{cases}.$$

The hard thresholding $h(w)$ .defined as

$$h(w) = \begin{cases} w, & |w| \geq \lambda \\ 0, & |w| < \lambda \end{cases}.$$

A wavelet coefficient w .can be replaced with an absolute value if $w \geq \lambda$ .and under the threshold λ .replaced by 0 in the hard thresholding $h(w)$. In soft thresholding $s(w)$. coefficients with magnitude above the threshold λ .are shrunken and preserve the smoothness of the signal.

The difference in quantity error with respect to the threshold appears clearly. The serval ways to define the optimal threshold such as minimax, rigorous SURE etc. Minimax threshold is larger than universal threshold as defined $\lambda_{univ} = \sigma\sqrt{2\log(n)}$ .for particular value of n. The threshold according to Donoho and Johnstone [38] can be optimized as

$$\lambda = \sqrt{\log n}.\gamma.\dfrac{\sigma}{\sqrt{n}}.$$

where γ is a constant if the empirical wavelet transform of f is denoted as $W_n^n f$ .that is quasi-orthogonality (Donoho, 1995). The multiple factor of the threshold value depends on the target signal. And the universal threshold (Donoho & Johnstone, 1994) value given as $\lambda_{univ} = \hat{\sigma}\sqrt{\log(n)}$ .with error $\hat{\sigma}$ .defined as

$$\hat{\sigma} = \frac{median\ (|w_{j-1,k}| : 0 \leq k < 2^{j-1})}{0.6745}.$$

The time-frequency characteristics varies among the sources signal. The denoising of signal coefficients by applying the universal hard and soft thresholding creates the problematic situation as sources signal varies. The clinically desired information is lost. Therefore the traditional model is not applicable to such biomedical signal (specifically EEG signal).

2.2 Shift Invariant Effect in UDWT

The shift invariant property is crucial for signal denoising in wavelet transform (Coifman & Donoho, 1995). The discontinuities in the neighboring coefficients reflect the translation invariance in the conventional DWT therefore self-generated artifacts occurs as explained by Gibbs phenomenon. This drawback is effectively suppressed in the UDWT and stationary wavelet transform. The cycle-spinning over the range of all circular shifts in order $n \log 2(n)$ time for denoising equivalent to UDWT and stationary WT. The aliasing effect occurs in DWT in the details coefficients at a different level of decomposition, therefore, the information is lost while denoising based on thresholding and improper reconstruction of coefficients (Starck, Fadili, & Murtagh, 2007; Gyaourova, Kamath, & Fodor, 2002) is taking place. The importance of shift-invariance property in the UDWT was supported by Lang et al. (1996). And the effectiveness of the UDWT was demonstrated in various cases by Starck (2007). The UDWT has an advantage of shift invariant therefore the biomedical signals were tested for iEEG-based validation framework [14]. In the effect, it is simply expected that the quick pursuit has relied on the Hard-thresholding and the smoothness is on the Soft-thresholding as discussed earlier and which needs to be investigated in the real EEG signals. The undecimated wavelet transform (UDWT) shrinkage two-stage model as shown in Figure 3 was used for decomposition/ separation in which signal is contaminated with EEG, EOG and white noise signal (Singh & Wagatsuma, 2019). In general, continuous wavelet transform (CWT) has been used for denoising and how much the original signal can be reconstructed in comparison with the discrete wavelet transform (DWT). As mentioned in EEG-EOG signal contamination models both have different potentials therefore universal threshold is not desirable for denoising or artifacts removal and standard model should be quantitatively validated. In first stage high amplitude fluctuations reflects the EOG signal was reconstructed and second stage provides the significant EEG signal. It is suggested that the threshold value and the level of decomposition/ reconstruction must be carefully determined depending on the target signal which exceeds the conventional shrinkage performance. This method focuses on the actual amplitude-frequency structure in the polygenetic signal and reveals how the standard model enhances the decomposition performance.

Figure 3. Two-stage model for decomposition of f and g with the condition f ≫ .. κ amplitude reduction ratio is used as the single constant but if two signals are contaminated after the amplitude reduction (passing the scalp) κ can be considered as the average of κ 1 for EEGs and κ 2 for EOGs. The same extension can be considered in multiple noise factors on η
(Singh & Wagatsuma, 2019)

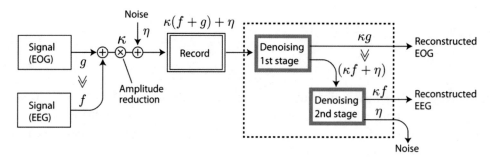

3. MORPHOLOGICAL COMPONENT ANALYSIS

Recently, the decomposition of relevant signal into desired source components has become a trend in research. In signal decomposition, the sparsity is one of the best possible features used for source components separation. Instead of independence of the source components, sparsity can be consider for source components separation. The relation between independence and sparsity has been vaguely understood (Starck, Moudden, Bobin, Elad, & Donoho, 2005). A methodology based on redundant transform to separate the source components, which is called morphological component analysis (MCA) (Starck et al., 2005). Recently, it is used to decompose a measured signal into its desired morphological components and in that sparsity plays an important role. It is unconfined from restriction of independence of source components. The representation of source components of the signal can be estimated by redundant basis or over-complete dictionary. The decomposition of measured signal into its constructed source components and from this the desired source components could have used to derive the rehabilitation device or used for diagnosis the brain disorder. There is an assumption that any given signal/ image is a linear combination of several source components of more coherent origin. Various methods of decomposition, such as ICA, PCA, wavelets and many more, were discussed earlier. Due to the advancement of harmonic analysis and applied mathematics, the morphologically sparse modelling of signals has attracted a lot of interest. It is assumed that each source component can be sparsely decomposed by some basis function, a waveform dictionary or some signal representation. The morphological component analysis (MCA) (Starck et al., 2005) is a method recently developed to decompose the measured signal and image into its constructive source components. It extended the traditional concept of signal decomposition and reconstruction using basis function which not only guarantees accuracy in reconstruction but also requires being independent of each other and uniqueness in representation. MCA is used the basis function (Dictionaries) and creates a redundancy in representations of the signal i.e. a way of decomposition. The over-complete dictionary Φ is a set of redundant transforms /mathematical function that represents the specific waveform/ source component or designed by adapting its coefficient to fit a given set of components that leads to sparse representation (Starck, Donoho, & Elad, 2004). A dictionary/redundant transform can reproduce the specific component of the signal. The concept of sparsity and over-completeness dictionary benefits the signal decomposition and extends to source component separation and more. Separation from the sparse representation is a serious issue that has been extensively investigated in the past few years. The dictionary is usually used for sparse representation or approximation of the signal/image and dictionary learning or training in the signal processing. A dictionary is a collection of elements and n length elements are the real column vector. A finite dictionary can be represented by $n \times L$ matrix of L elements. The dictionary such as discrete sine transform (DST) is a Fourier transform similar to the discrete Fourier transform (DFT) but using a purely real matrix and the dictionary discrete cosine transform (DCT) which is equivalent to a DFT of real and even function. There are various types of transforms such as DCT, orthogonal wavelet transforms, Bi-orthogonal wavelet transforms. Redundant transform such as local DCT, undecimated wavelet transform, isotropic undecimated wavelet transform, ridgelet transform, curvelet transform.

The sparsity can be used for the separation of signal mixtures with varying degrees of success. The morphological component analysis is used to morphologically decompose / separate the building component of the signal. This method relies on the sparsity and over-completeness dictionary; an over-complete dictionary $\Phi \in R^{n \times k}$ where κ morphological component coefficient of signal for $\left\{ \varnothing_k \right\}_{k \in \Gamma}$ Γ is the dictionary index set and a signal X is sparse linear combination of source component (Starck, Donoho, & Elad, 2004). The limitation of traditional tools such as linear systems and Fourier analysis for solving the geometry based problem because they don't directly address the issues of how to quantify the shape and the size of the signals. A complex signal such as the EEG signal is rarely well represented by a few coefficients in single basis, therefore, large dictionaries in cooperating more patterns can increase sparsity and thus improve the application to compression, denoising, inverse problem and pattern recognition. It is crucial to find the set of k dictionary coefficients that approximate a signal with minimum non-deterministic polynomial-time (NP) hard error in redundant dictionaries. The type of dictionary includes a combination of orthonormal basis such as Fourier, Dirac (delta), wavelet DCT and Gabor dictionary. The Gabor dictionary is constructed by scaling, modulating and translating a gaussian window on the signal-sample grid on the basis of time and frequency translation-invariant. The n elements of the waveform $\varnothing_k$ .are discrete time signals. Dictionaries can be classified based on frequency, time and time-frequency. Dictionaries are complete or overcomplete in that case they contain exactly n elements or more than n elements but continuum dictionaries containing an infinity of atoms and under complete dictionaries for special purposes, containing fewer than n elements, many of interesting dictionaries have been proposed over last few years. Suppose that a $\varnothing$ .discrete dictionary of j waveform and we consider all these waveforms as columns of $n \times p$ matrix and the decomposition is given by

$$X = \sum_{k=1}^{j} \varnothing_k \beta_k .$$

When the dictionary provides a basis function, then $\varnothing$. is $n \times n$ non-singular matrix and have unique representation $\beta = \Phi^{-1} X$. when the elements are mutually orthonormal, then $\varnothing^{-1} . \varnothing^{T}$. The difference between the synthesis waveform $X = \Phi \beta$ and analysis waveform $\tilde{\beta} = \Phi^{T} X$. The source components of signal X are sparse over the augmented dictionary Φ and MCA can be determined by the original source components of the signal, where each signal is assumed to be a linear mixture of the sources. The disadvantage is that the source components do not necessarily only contain artifacts, but also underlying

EEG signal therefore removing these source components leads to loss of information. The morphology of signal can be used for recognition of source component and based on that source components can be separate from the measured signal (Starck et al., 2005; Starck, Donoho, & Elad, 2004). The sparsity, morphological diversity play an important role in decomposing (Starck, Donoho, & elad, 2004; Bobin, Starck, Fadili, & Moudden, 2007). It devised the quantitative measures of diversity to extricate between the sources. The signals with different morphology have disjoint significant coefficients in a sparsifying dictionary. The linear mixture with additive gaussian noise and the mixing matrix criterion measures a deviation between the true mixing matrix and estimate source components. To extend the spatial and spectral sparsity constraints. Morphological component analysis consists of mathematical and theoretical concepts for signal analysis, nonlinear signal operator design methodologies and application system that are related to mathematical morphology.

An over-complete dictionary as collection of waveforms $\{ \Phi_k \cdot_{\in \Gamma}$, assume that EEG signal is linear combination of source components that can be represented by basis elements ϕ_k (Starck, Donoho, & Elad, 2004). It would be expressed as one dimension $X \in R_N$ and combination of many signals, $X = x_1 + x_2 + \ldots + x_k$ where x_1 x_2 and x_k have different morphology that represents the source components. The signal X decomposed into its building components can be expressed as

$$X = \sum_{i=1}^{k} \phi_i \beta_i + \eta$$

$$= \phi_1 \beta_1 + \phi_2 \beta_2 + \ldots + \phi_k \beta_k + \eta .$$

$$= x_1 + x_2 + \ldots + x_k + \eta .$$

The above equation can be expressed without external noise as

$$X = \sum_{i=1}^{k} \varnothing_i \beta_i .$$

The above equation can be solved as given below

$$\{ \beta_1^{opt} . \beta_2^{opt} . \ldots, \beta_k^{opt} . = \operatorname*{argmin}_{\beta_1, \ldots, \beta_k} \sum_{i=1}^{k} \beta_{i0} .$$

Subject to: $X = \sum_{i=1}^{k} \varnothing_i \beta_i .$

It suffered with several drawbacks therefore to minimize the drawbacks, the source components can be defined as follows.

$$\{ \beta_1^{opt} . \ \beta_2^{opt} . \ ..., \ \beta_k^{opt} . = \underset{\beta_1,...,\beta_k}{\mathrm{argmin}} \sum_{i=1}^{k} \beta_{i1} .$$

Subject to: $X = \sum_{i=1}^{k} \varnothing_i \beta_i$ .Here, the *l2* norm as the error norm is intimately related to the assumption that the residual behaves like a white zero-mean gaussian noise. The functions in dictionaries subdirectory provide fast implicit analysis and synthesis operation. All dictionaries are normalized such that elements have unit *l2* $_n$orm. To estimate the source components by solving the above equation in iterative manner. The iterative algorithm is used to estimate the sparse source EEG signals as mentioned by Starck, Donoho, and Elad (2004). The mathematical derivation of the methods and algorithms is given in the article (Starck, Donoho, & Elad, 2004).

In the decomposition process, normalizing the threshold has an important impact. The signal processing and function approximation, overcomplete dictionary can achieve a more stable, robust and more compact decomposition than using a basis function. A biological signal decomposition into its building source components based on their morphology is a new aspect (Starck et al., 2005; Starck, Donoho, & Elad, 2004). Figure 4 represents a schematic overview of the MCA methodology that illustrates the decomposition of the measured signal into its morphological components.

An artificially generated sine wave and spikes signal as source components having different morphology are used to elaborate the methodology. A mixed signal X . white noise signal η and the simulated signal Y as shown in Figure 5.

$$Y = X + \eta .$$

The blind source separation (BSS) is an important application of ICA is to estimate and recover the independent source components from mixed signal. Here, ICA and MCA used for simulated mixed signal Y and white noise component 5% of the X amplitude to separate the different source components respectively as shown in Figure 6. ICA has multichannel approach for separating the desire source components such as sine wave, spikes signal and noise component therefore it have more than one measured signal from different electrode position and MCA works on single measured signal as shown Figure 4.

2.1 Decomposition Method

A linear combination of k source components of EEG and artifacts in time domain, the sources can be denoted as $x_1(t)$ $x_2(t)$ up to $x_k(t)$ with potentials x_1 x_2 x_k and time index t respectively. Consider three sources signal for simplicity and the measured signal is given as

$$X_1 = \phi_{11} x_1 + \phi_{12} x_2 + \phi_{13} x_3 .$$

$$X_2 = \phi_{21} x_1 + \phi_{22} x_2 + \phi_{23} x_3 .$$

$$X_3 = \phi_{31} x_1 + \phi_{32} x_2 + \phi_{33} x_3 .$$

Figure 4. A schematic diagram for morphological component decomposition from measured signal

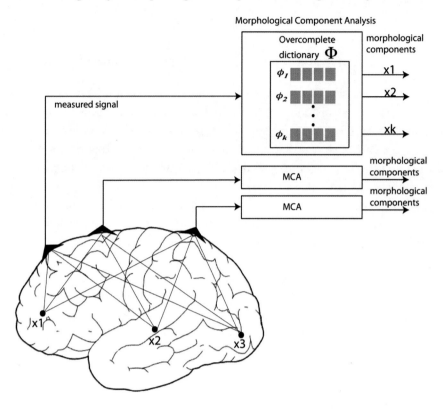

Figure 5. Simulated signal for decomposition, a) the sine wave, b) spikes signal and c) combination of the above two signals

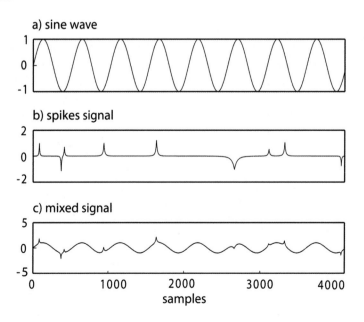

Figure 6. Separated source components by, a) Independent component analysis, b) Morphological component analysis

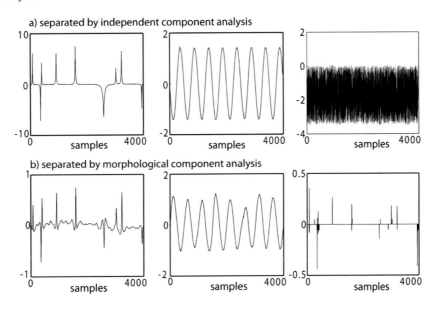

where ϕ_{11} ϕ_{12} ϕ_{13} ϕ_{21} ϕ_{22} ϕ_{23} ϕ_{31} ϕ_{32} and ϕ_{33} are the mixing parameters. And formulate the linear combination of the sources and to separate or remove the artifacts from measured EEG signals. If EEG signals are statistically independent and have non-gaussian distribution than the blind source separation methods like ICA commonly used to decompose or separate the linear combination (Starck et al., 2004). The measured EEG signal can be defined as a sparse linear combination of source signals. The EEG and EOG source signals have specific morphology. The morphologies of eye movements and eye blinks can be considered as slow change with respect to the EEG time scale and a bump shape with a large peak potential (Singh, Ai, & Wagatsuma, 2015). The single bump type morphology to be typical eye blinks and multiple time changes in baseline due to eyeball rotations. The EOG artifacts can be removed by replacing EOG coefficients with zero, when EEG signal is reconstructed. It is very crucial to obtain the final set of sources signal for accurate reconstruction of the original signal. A dictionary (basis function) can reproduce the specific morphology of the source signal if the appropriate iterative method is introduced to pursue the unique sparse representation. The concept of sparsity and over-completeness dictionary has theoretically extended the traditional signal decomposition to feature extractions focusing on the multiple types of morphologies simultaneously. The real problem can be addressed as

1.   What is the best combination of redundant transform or dictionaries to decomposition the EEG and EOG signals?
2.   Which dictionary ϕ .characterize the decomposed morphological component?

Assume three types of dictionaries $k = 3$.(UDWT, DCT and DIRAC) to create over-complete dictionary Φ for decomposing the measured EEG signal (Singh & Wagatsuma, 2017). The three morphological components can be obtained by optimization as explain earlier. Each dictionary represents only one morphological component.

Case 1: An over-complete dictionary ϕ_1 .is represent the morphological component x_1 .:

$$\beta_1^{opt} = \underset{\beta}{\text{argmin}} \, \beta_0 .$$

    Subject to $x_1 = \phi_1\beta$. a sparse solution occurs while solving this equation because $\left(\beta_{1\ 0}^{opt} < \beta_{12\ 0}^{opt}, \beta_{13\ 0}^{opt} \right)$.
And for x_2 .and x_3 .
Subject to and respectively. It gives a non-sparse solution.

Case 2: An over-complete dictionary ϕ_2 .is represent the morphological component x_2 .:

$$\beta_2^{opt} = \underset{\beta}{\text{argmin}} \, \beta_0 .$$

    Subject to $x_2 = \phi_2\beta$. a sparse solution occurs while solving this equation because $\left(\beta_{2\ 0}^{opt} < \beta_{23\ 0}^{opt}, \beta_{21\ 0}^{opt} \right)$.
And for x_3 .and x_1 .
Subject to and respectively. It gives a non-sparse solution.

Case 3: An over-complete dictionary ϕ_3 .is represent the morphological component x_3 .:

$$\beta_3^{opt} = \underset{\beta}{\text{argmin}} \, \beta_0$$

    Subject to $x_3 = \phi_3\beta$, a sparse solution occurs while solving this equation because $\left(\beta_{3\ 0}^{opt} < \beta_{31\ 0}^{opt}, \beta_{32\ 0}^{opt} \right)$.
And for x_1 and x_2
Subject to and respectively. It gives a non-sparse solution.

Morphological component analysis decomposed the measured signal into its components by dictionaries ϕ_1, ϕ_2 and ϕ_3 respectively. It is described mathematically (Singh & Wagatsuma, 2017) as

$$\left\{ \beta_1^{opt}, \beta_2^{opt}, \beta_3^{opt} \right\} = \underset{\beta_1, \beta_2, \beta_3}{\text{argmin}} \, \beta_{10} + \beta_{20} + \beta_{30}$$

    Subject to

$$X = \phi_1\beta_1 + \phi_2\beta_2 + \phi_3\beta_3$$

    The above equation can be formulated to be accurate for representing the morphological components, which is described as:

$$\left\{\beta_1^{opt}, \beta_2^{opt}, \beta_3^{opt}\right\} = \min_{\beta_1,\beta_2,\beta_3} \sum_{k=1}^{3}\beta_{k1} + \lambda X - \sum_{k=1}^{3}\phi_k\beta_{k2}^{2}$$

Consider l_2 to be error norm and λ is the stopping criterion. The block-coordinate-relaxation (BCR) used to solve the above equation (Starck et al, 2005).

MCA validated the decomposition of the real scalp EEG and EOG signal (Singh & Wagatsuma, 2017). The EEG signals shown in Figure 7 taken from five electrodes (Fp1, Fp2, Cz, O1 and O2) which are influenced by EOG signal, electrodes placed on the frontal, central and occipital area of brain scalp. Similarly, the EOG signals taken from left eye as shown Figure 8. MCA decomposed the measured EEG signal into its morphological components, for example, EEG signal Fp1 decomposition shown in Figure 9. The Figure 9 illustrates the separation of morphological components by given dictionaries. Here UDWT, DCT and DIRAC dictionaries used for morphological component separation. It is necessary to evaluate the signal decomposition with complex eye movements, which requires presumably various explicit dictionaries. A fine-tuned design of the DCT or DST dictionary require to remove the baseline fluctuation that denote the persisting of EOG component or other slow frequency artifacts noise.

Figure 7. The real EEG signals
(Singh & Wagatsuma, 2017)

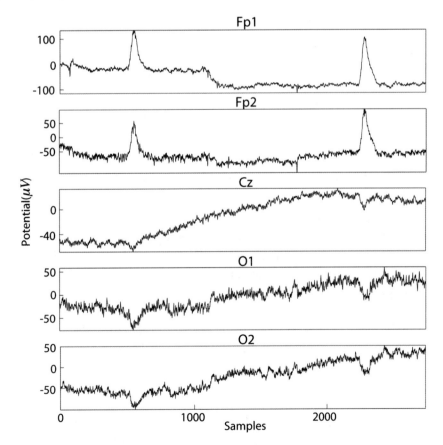

Figure 8. The EOG signal

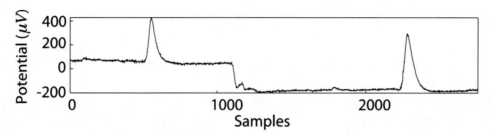

Figure 9. MCA decomposition of the Fp1 EEG signal into three morphological components by a) UDWT, b) DCT, c) DIRAC dictionaries
(Singh & Wagatsuma, 2017)

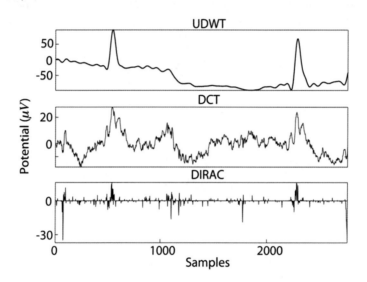

3 IDENTIFY THE FEATURES FOR THE PHYSICAL SYSTEM

Epilepsy is a common neurological disorder in the brain affecting approximately 50 million people of the world population. The manual inspection of patient recorded EEG is a time consuming and not accurate. In this diagnosis requires a continuous monitoring process. Recently EEG recording portable system is quite commonly available therefore seizure diagnosis and detection system discriminating seizure data from non-seizure and interictal is noteworthy. It has the advantage of recording of EEG (without reduction of seizure frequency) signal in the patient's natural condition. The seizure screening from EEG recording across multiple days become a difficult task. Therefore, an automated detection system is extremely useful in this situation. Figure 10 shows a morphological component analysis method that can be used for automated detection system. Seizure detection system mainly consists of two parts, first part is preprocessing, filtering or extraction of desired source components. In second part, the extracted source components are used for detection system. In epilepsy, the commonly observed behavior or morphology is spike train and sharp wave. The sudden transient burst of spikes and high frequency oscillation in interictal recording are also used for localization of the epileptic seizures (Mahapatra,

Singh, Wagatsuma, & Horio, 2018). Both disparity in background activity and EEG paroxysms make automated analysis complicated. Mahapatra et al. demonstrated that the epilepsy EEG morphology can be used for diagnosing and detection of the epileptic seizure (Mahapatra et al., 2018). In this work, MCA used for extraction of the morphological component with composed of UDWT, LDCT and Dirac as over-complete dictionary. The component from Dirac dictionary captured spike morphology of the epileptic seizure used for calculating the root mean instantaneous frequency square (RMIFS) and its consisting parameter ratio. The transient spikes from Dirac dictionary help in localizing the epileptic zone. The RMIFS and center frequency square parameter used for SVM classifier. These features show the high accuracy and sensitivity.

The morphological component of the ERP gives another approach for physical system (rehabilitation device) (Singh, Wagatsuma, & Natsume, 2017; Singh, Wagatsuma, & Natsume, 2016). The systematic approach of MCA that can be used for physical system as shown in Figure 11. However, in recent work of MCA does not require multichannel approach for sources component separation. In order to exploit the maximum amount of information, the explicit dictionary can be used for decomposing the measured ERP signal into morphological based components. The morphological component (feature) that comprised the maximum information is selected. Furthermore, the physical systems are initiated by decoded features from morphological component.

4 SUMMARY AND CONCLUSION

In this chapter, we discussed the artifacts contamination as an important issue in the EEG signal for neurobiological event diagnosis and neuroscientific research. A systematic approach like morphological component analysis has been considered for evaluating the sparsity and non-linearity in the signal. It included the over-complete dictionary/redundant transform such as DCT, DST, LDCT, Dirac and UDWT; EEG and EOG signal have numbers of morphological components. The separation of EEG components doesn't work with unclear dictionary therefore explicit over-complete dictionary is further perspective.

Figure 10. A detection system for epilepsy patients

Figure 11. A diagram that shows MCA approach for physical system

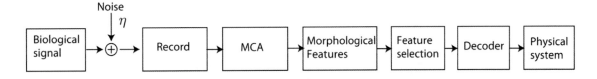

The MCA method has an extended and flexible availability for signal analyses. It gives definite number of morphological components depending on the number of set of basis used in over-complete dictionary. The unique features revealed from the morphological component of the signal and used for prediction of epilepsy. The specific morphological component can be used in the physical system that will assists the patients who have neurological disorder.

REFERENCES

Ai, G., Sato, N., Singh, B., & Wagatsuma, H. (2016). Direction and viewing area-sensitive influence of EOG artifacts revealed in the EEG topographic pattern analysis. *Cognitive Neurodynamics*, *10*(4), 301–314. doi:10.100711571-016-9382-4 PMID:27468318

Akhtar, M. T., Mitsuhashi, W., & James, C. J. (2012). Employing spatially constrained ICA and wavelet denoising, for automatic removal of artifacts from multichannel EEG data. *Signal Processing*, *92*(2), 401–416. doi:10.1016/j.sigpro.2011.08.005

Al-Fahoum, A. S., & Al-Fraihat, A. A. (2014). Methods of EEG signal features extraction using linear analysis in frequency and time-frequency domains. *ISRN Neuroscience*. PMID:24967316

Al-Hudhud, G. (2014). Affective command-based control system integrating brain signals in commands control systems. *Computers in Human Behavior*, *30*, 535–541. doi:10.1016/j.chb.2013.06.038

Ball, T., Kern, M., Mutschler, I., Aertsen, A., & Schulze-Bonhage, A. (2009). Signal quality of simultaneously recorded invasive and non-invasive EEG. *NeuroImage*, *46*(3), 708–716. doi:10.1016/j.neuroimage.2009.02.028 PMID:19264143

Berg, P., & Scherg, M. (1991). Dipole models of eye movements and blinks. *Electroencephalography and Clinical Neurophysiology*, *79*(1), 36–44. doi:10.1016/0013-4694(91)90154-V PMID:1713550

Berg, P., & Scherg, M. (1991). Dipole models of eye movements and blinks. *Electroencephalography and Clinical Neurophysiology*, *79*(1), 36–44. doi:10.1016/0013-4694(91)90154-V PMID:1713550

Berg, P., & Scherg, M. (1994). A multiple source approach to the correction of eye artifacts. *Electroencephalography and Clinical Neurophysiology*, *90*(3), 229–241. doi:10.1016/0013-4694(94)90094-9 PMID:7511504

Blasco, J. L., Iáñez, E., Úbeda, A., & Azorín, J. M. (2012). Visual evoked potential-based brain–machine interface applications to assist disabled people. *Expert Systems with Applications*, *39*(9), 7908–7918. doi:10.1016/j.eswa.2012.01.110

Bobin, J., Starck, J. L., Fadili, J., & Moudden, Y. (2007). Sparsity and morphological diversity in blind source separation. *IEEE Transactions on Image Processing*, *16*(11), 2662–2674. doi:10.1109/TIP.2007.906256 PMID:17990743

Cecotti, H. (2011). Spelling with non-invasive Brain–Computer Interfaces–Current and future trends. *Journal of Physiology-Paris, 105*(1-3), 106-114.

Cohen, A., Daubechies, I., Jawerth, B., & Vial, P. (1993). "Multiresolution analysis, wavelets and fast algorithms on an interval." Comptes rendus de l'Académie des sciences. Série 1. *Mathématique, 316*(5), 417–421.

Coifman, R. R., & Donoho, D. L. (1995). Translation-invariant de-noising. In *Wavelets and statistics* (pp. 125–150). New York, NY: Springer. doi:10.1007/978-1-4612-2544-7_9

David, O., Kilner, J. M., & Friston, K. J. (2006). Mechanisms of evoked and induced responses in MEG/EEG. *NeuroImage, 31*(4), 1580–1591. doi:10.1016/j.neuroimage.2006.02.034 PMID:16632378

Debatisse, D., Pralong, E., Dehdashti, A., & Regli, L. (2005). Simultaneous multilobar electrocorticography (mEcoG) and scalp electroencephalography (scalp EEG) during intracranial vascular surgery: A new approach in neuromonitoring. *Clinical Neurophysiology, 116*(12), 2734–2740. doi:10.1016/j.clinph.2005.08.011 PMID:16256427

Donoho, D. L. (1995). De-noising by soft-thresholding. *IEEE Transactions on Information Theory, 41*(3), 613–627. doi:10.1109/18.382009

Donoho, D.L. & Johnstone, I.M. (1994). Ideal spatial adaptation by wavelet shrinkage. *Biometrika, 81*(3), 425-455.

Fowler, J. E. (2005). The redundant discrete wavelet transform and additive noise. *IEEE Signal Processing Letters, 12*(9), 629–632. doi:10.1109/LSP.2005.853048

Gyaourova, A., Kamath, C., & Fodor, I. K. (2002). Undecimated wavelet transforms for image de-noising. *Report Lawrence Livermore National Laboratory, 12*, 1–12.

Hyvarinen, A. (1999). Fast and robust fixed-point algorithms for independent component analysis. *IEEE Transactions on Neural Networks, 10*(3), 626–634. doi:10.1109/72.761722 PMID:18252563

Joyce, C. A., Gordonitsky, I. F., & Kutas, M. (2004). Automatic removal of eye movement and blink artifacts from EEG data using blind component separation. *Psychophysiology, 41*(2), 313–325. doi:10.1111/j.1469-8986.2003.00141.x PMID:15032997

Jung, T. P., Makeig, S., Humphries, C., Lee, T. W., McKeown, M. J., Iragui, V., & Sejnowski, T. J. (2000). Removing electroencephalographic artifacts by blind source separation. *Psychophysiology, 37*(2), 163–178. doi:10.1111/1469-8986.3720163 PMID:10731767

Kovach, C.K., Tsuchiya, N., Kawasaki, H., Oya, H., Howard, M.A., & Adolphs, R. (2011). Manifestation of Ocular-Muscle EMG Contamination in Human Intracranial Recordings. *NeuroImage, 54*(1), 213–233.

Lang, M., Guo, H., Odegard, J. E., Burrus, C. S., & Wells, R. O. (1996). Noise reduction using an undecimated discrete wavelet transform. *IEEE Signal Processing Letters, 3*(1), 10–12. doi:10.1109/97.475823

Long, N. M., Burke, J. F., & Kahana, M. J. (2014). Subsequent memory effect in intracranial and scalp EEG. *NeuroImage, 84*, 488–494. doi:10.1016/j.neuroimage.2013.08.052 PMID:24012858

Mahapatra, A.G., Singh, B., Wagatsuma, H., & Horio, K. (2018). Epilepsy EEG classification using morphological component analysis. *EURASIP Journal on Advances in Signal Processing, 2018*(1), 52.

McGill. (n.d.). *Biomedical signal.* Retrieved from http://www.medicine.mcgill.ca/physio/vlab/biomed_signals/vlabmenubiosig.htm

Nicolas-Alonso, L. F., & Gomez-Gil, J. (2012). Brain computer interfaces, a review. *Sensors (Basel), 12*(2), 1211–1279. doi:10.3390120201211 PMID:22438708

Nilsson, S.E. & Andersson, B.E. (1988). Corneal DC recordings of slow ocular potential changes such as the ERG c-wave and the light peak in clinical work. *Documenta ophthalmologica, 68*(3-4), 313-325.

Picton, T. W., van Roon, P., Armilio, M. L., Berg, P., Ille, N., & Scherg, M. (2000). The correction of ocular artifacts: A topographic perspective. *Clinical Neurophysiology, 111*(1), 53–65. doi:10.1016/S1388-2457(99)00227-8 PMID:10656511

Plöchl, M., Ossandón, J. P., & König, P. (2012). Combining EEG and eye tracking: Identification, characterization, and correction of eye movement artifacts in electroencephalographic data. *Frontiers in Human Neuroscience, 6*, 278. doi:10.3389/fnhum.2012.00278 PMID:23087632

Powers, A.S., Basso, M.S., & Evinger. C. (2013). Blinks Slow Memory-Guided Saccades. *Journal of Neurophysiology, 109*(3), 734–741.

Ray, A., Tao, J. X., Hawes-Ebersole, S. M., & Ebersole, J. S. (2007). Localizing value of scalp EEG spikes: A simultaneous scalp and intracranial study. *Clinical Neurophysiology, 118*(1), 69–79. doi:10.1016/j.clinph.2006.09.010 PMID:17126071

Romo-Vázquez, R., Vélez-Pérez, H., Ranta, R., Louis-Dorr, V., Maquin, D., & Maillard, L. (2012). Blind source separation, wavelet denoising and discriminant analysis for EEG artefacts and noise cancelling. *Biomedical Signal Processing and Control, 7*(4), 389–400. doi:10.1016/j.bspc.2011.06.005

Sameni, R., & Gouy-Pailler, C. (2014). An iterative subspace denoising algorithm for removing electroencephalogram ocular artifacts. *Journal of Neuroscience Methods, 225*, 97–105. doi:10.1016/j.jneumeth.2014.01.024 PMID:24486874

Singh, B., Ai, G., & Wagatsuma, H. (2015). An electrooculography analysis in the time-frequency domain using morphological component analysis toward the development of mobile BCI systems. In *International Conference on Universal Access in Human-Computer Interaction.* Springer. 10.1007/978-3-319-20681-3_50

Singh, B., & Wagatsuma, H. (2017). A Removal of Eye Movement and Blink Artifacts from EEG Data Using Morphological Component Analysis. *Computational and Mathematical Methods in Medicine.* PMID:28194221

Singh, B., & Wagatsuma, H. (2019). Two-stage wavelet shrinkage and EEG-EOG signal contamination model to realize quantitative validations for the artifact removal from multiresource biosignals. *Biomedical Signal Processing and Control, 47*, 96–114. doi:10.1016/j.bspc.2018.08.014

Singh, B., Wagatsuma, H., & Natsume, K. (2016). The bereitschaftspotential for rise of stand-up towards robot-assist device preparation. In *Society of Instrument and Control Engineers of Japan (SICE), 2016 55th Annual Conference of the.* IEEE. 10.1109/SICE.2016.7749192

Singh, B., Wagatsuma, H., & Natsume, K. (2017). The Detection of the Rise to Stand Movements Using Bereitschaftspotential from Scalp Electroencephalography (EEG). *SICE Journal of Control, Measurement, and System Integration, 10*(3), 149–155. doi:10.9746/jcmsi.10.149

Starck, J.L., Donoho, D.L. & Elad, M. (2004). *Redundant multiscale transforms and their application for morphological component separation.* No. DAPNIA-2004-88. CM-P00052061, 2004.

Starck, J. L., Fadili, J., & Murtagh, F. (2007). The undecimated wavelet decomposition and its reconstruction. *IEEE Transactions on Image Processing, 16*(2), 297–309. doi:10.1109/TIP.2006.887733 PMID:17269625

Starck, J. L., Moudden, Y., Bobin, J., Elad, M., & Donoho, D. L. (2005). *Morphological component analysis. In Wavelets XI* (Vol. 5914). International Society for Optics and Photonics.

Urigüen, J.A. & Garcia-Zapirain, B. (2015). EEG artifact removal—state-of-the-art and guidelines. *Journal of Neural Engineering, 12*(3).

Vigário, R. N. (1997). Extraction of ocular artefacts from EEG using independent component analysis. *Electroencephalography and Clinical Neurophysiology, 103*(3), 395–404. doi:10.1016/S0013-4694(97)00042-8 PMID:9305288

Whittingstall, K., & Logothetis, N. K. (2009). Frequency-band coupling in surface EEG reflects spiking activity in monkey visual cortex. *Neuron, 64*(2), 281–289. doi:10.1016/j.neuron.2009.08.016 PMID:19874794

Yamazaki. (2012). Comparison of dense array EEG with simultaneous intracranial EEG for interictal spike detection and localization. *Epilepsy Research, 98*(2-3), 166-173.

Chapter 16
Attitude and Heading Reference System for Unmanned Aerial Vehicles

Blagovest Hristov
Bulgarian Academy of Sciences, Bulgaria

ABSTRACT

The methods that have been used in navigation over the centuries have changed as have the goals they serve. One of these methods is inertial navigation. Nowadays inertial navigation offers many advantages over other types of navigation. A major advantage is the lack of dependence on external transmitters or other devices, which means independence of the system. With the development of new technologies, the accuracy of these systems is increasing, which increases their applicability. An important aspect is the reduction in the price of sensors, which is a prerequisite for their application in new areas where they have not yet been offered. An important advantage of inertial navigation is the ability to give in real-time information about acceleration, speed, and location and the possibility of autonomous operation of the object.

INTRODUCTION

The Attitude and heading reference system (AHRS) will be build over inertial measurement unit (IMU) sensor based on MEMS technology, consisting of a 3 axis accelerometer, a 3 axis gyroscope, a 3 axis magnetometer and an Atmega microcontroller. Before we can use the data from the sensors, they have to be transformed into a common coordinate system, which in this case is connected to the ground. The co-ordinate system rotates with the ground with center that matched the center of the earth. The measurements obtained in the inertial system by accelerometers and gyroscopes have to be transformed into a common coordinate system (Titterton, D. H., 2004). An important step is to know the nature of the errors of these sensors and to take measures for their compensation and filtration.

DOI: 10.4018/978-1-5225-7879-6.ch016

In the chapter I present various methods of crossing between the coordinate systems (Euler, Quaternions, DCM) and their drawbacks, a linear Kalman filter will be considered, calibration and navigation algorithms will be proposed and experimental results will demonstrate the performance of the system and its accuracy .

Coordinate Systems

Earth Centered, Earth Fixed (ECEF)

Its origin is in the center of the earth and rotates with it. Oz is parallel to the main axis of rotation of the ground, Ox points to the main meridian, Oy completes a right-oriented orthogonal frame

Earth Surface North-East-Down (NED)

The origin of the coordinate system coincides with the instrumental frame, but Ox always points to the geodesic north, Oz pointing to the start point of the Earth-oriented coordinate system, Oy completes a right-oriented orthogonal frame. It is also called the North-East-Down system.

Inertial Coordinate System (ICS)

In this coordinate system, Newton's laws of motion are applied and it is not accelerating. It can be chosen arbitrarily, but it is more convenient to start and coincide with the Earth-connected system (it becomes pseudo-inertial).

Connected Coordinate System (CCS)

This coordinate system matches the center of body gravity with Ox pointing forward, Oz is pointing down to the lower body, and Oy is oriented in a way that form a right-oriented orthogonal system. If the instrument platform is not aligned with the body frame, additional transformation must be done.

Navigation Coordinate System (NCS)

The center of this system is the particular object that been studying, the axes are orientated in the directions east / west, north / south and respectively vertically/ zenith / nadir state. The rotation speed of the navigation coordinate system relative to the Earth's fixed is determined by the motion of the object relative to the ground.

Switching Between Coordinate Systems

The state of the unmanned aerial vehicle (UAV) referenced to the reference coordinate system can be written as a sequence of numbers. The saved state is updated with each UAV rotation using gyro measurements.

Changing the state of a body is the consist of a series of rotations around different axes and a function of the angles through which it rotates.

Different mathematical models can be used to determine the state of a body relative to the coordinate frame (Titterton, D. H. 2004).

Directioncosinematrix

The Transition Matrix (DCM) C_b is a 3×3 matrix whose columns are singular vectors in the coordinate axes projected along the reference axes. C_b^n is presented as follows:

$$C_b^n = \begin{bmatrix} c_{11} & c_{12} & c_{13} \\ c_{21} & c_{22} & c_{23} \\ c_{31} & c_{32} & c_{33} \end{bmatrix} \tag{1}$$

The i-row and the j-column element represent the cosine of the angle between i-axes of reference frame and z-axes of connected frame.

The value of the vectors in the connected axes r ^{b} can be represented in the reference axes by multiplying it with DCM:

$$r^n = C_b^n . r^b \tag{2}$$

The rate of change of C_b^n over time is:

$$\dot{C}_b^n = \lim_{\delta t \to 0} \frac{C_b^n}{\delta t} = \lim_{\delta t \to 0} \frac{C_b^n\left(t + \delta t\right) - C_b^n\left(t\right)}{\delta t} \tag{3}$$

where $C_b^n\left(t\right)$ and $C_b^n\left(t + \delta t\right)$ represent DCM at time t and t + δt, respectively. $C_b^n\left(t + \delta t\right)$ can also be written as:

Figure 1. Coordinate axes and angular speed direction

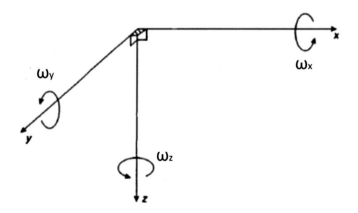

$$C_b^n \left(t + \delta t\right) = C_b^n \left(t\right).A\left(t\right) \tag{4}$$

where A (t) is DCM referenced to connected frame at t time and at time t + δt. For small rotations A (t) can be written:

$$A\left(t\right) = \left[I + \delta\Psi\right] \tag{5}$$

where I is the 3 × 3 singular matrix

$$\delta\Psi = \begin{bmatrix} 0 & -\delta\psi & \delta\theta \\ \delta\psi & 0 & -\delta\varphi \\ -\delta\theta & \delta\varphi & 0 \end{bmatrix} \tag{6}$$

In which δδ, δθ and δφ are small angles of rotation through which a connected coordinate system has rotated for a time interval δt around the axis of yaw, pitch and roll, respectively.

When δt is tuned to zero, small angular approximations are valid and the order of rotation is irrelevant. Substituting for $C_b^n \left(t + \delta t\right)$ in equation 3 we get:

$$\dot{C}_b^n = \lim_{\delta t \to 0} \frac{\delta\Psi}{\delta t} \tag{7}$$

In the range δt → 0, ΔΨ / δt is the inclined symmetrical shape of the angular velocity vector $\omega_{nb}^n = \left[\omega_x \, \omega_y \, \omega_z\right]^T$ which represents the rotational speed of the coordinate system relative to the navigation or in the connected axes:

$$\lim_{\delta t \to 0} \frac{\delta\Psi}{\delta t} = \Omega_{nb}^b \left(8\right) \tag{8}$$

By replacing in equation 7 we get:

$$\dot{C}_b^n = C_b^n \Omega_{nb}^b \tag{9}$$

where:

$$\Omega_{nb}^b = \begin{bmatrix} 0 & -\omega_z & -\omega_y \\ \omega_z & 0 & -\omega_z \\ -\omega_y & \omega_x & 0 \end{bmatrix} \tag{10}$$

Equation 9 is presented in a computer-friendly manner:

$$\dot{c}_{11} = c_{12}\omega_z - c_{13}\omega_y \quad \dot{c}_{12} = c_{13}\omega_x - c_{11}\omega_z \quad \dot{c}_{13} = c_{11}\omega_y - c_{12}\omega_x$$

$$\dot{c}_{21} = c_{22}\omega_z - c_{23}\omega_y \quad \dot{c}_{22} = c_{23}\omega_x - c_{21}\omega_z \quad \dot{c}_{23} = c_{21}\omega_y - c_{22}\omega_x$$

$$\dot{c}_{31} = c_{32}\omega_z - c_{33}\omega_y \quad \dot{c}_{32} = c_{33}\omega_x - c_{31}\omega_z \quad \dot{c}_{33} = c_{31}\omega_y - c_{32}\omega_x \tag{11}$$

Euler Angles

Transformation from one coordinate system to another is defined by three consecutive turns around the different axes. This presentation is popular because of the physical importance of the Euler angles corresponding to the angles that will be measured from a stabilized inertial navigation platform.

The three rotations can be described mathematically as three different directional cosine matrices:

$$C_1 = \begin{bmatrix} \cos\psi & \sin\psi & 0 \\ -\sin\psi & \cos\psi & 0 \\ 0 & 0 & 1 \end{bmatrix} \tag{12}$$

$$C_2 = \begin{bmatrix} \cos\theta & 0 & -\sin\theta \\ 0 & 1 & 0 \\ \sin\theta & 0 & \cos\theta \end{bmatrix} \tag{13}$$

$$C_3 = \begin{bmatrix} 1 & 0 & 0 \\ 0 & \cos\varphi & \sin\varphi \\ 0 & -\sin\varphi & \cos\varphi \end{bmatrix} \tag{14}$$

Thus, a transformation from the reference axes to the connected axes can be described as follows:

$$C_n^b = C_3 C_2 C_1 \tag{15}$$

The reverse transformation from connected to reference axes is given:

$$C_b^n = C_n^{bT} = C_1^T C_2^T C_3^T \tag{16}$$

$$C_b^n = \begin{bmatrix} \cos\psi & \sin\psi & 0 \\ -\sin\psi & \cos\psi & 0 \\ 0 & 0 & 1 \end{bmatrix} \begin{bmatrix} \cos\theta & 0 & -\sin\theta \\ 0 & 1 & 0 \\ \sin\theta & 0 & \cos\theta \end{bmatrix} \begin{bmatrix} 1 & 0 & 0 \\ 0 & \cos\varphi & \sin\varphi \\ 0 & -\sin\varphi & \cos\varphi \end{bmatrix} =$$

$$\begin{bmatrix} \cos\theta\cos\psi & -\cos\varphi\sin\psi + \sin\varphi\sin\theta\cos\psi & \sin\varphi\sin\psi + \cos\varphi\sin\theta\cos\psi \\ \cos\theta\sin\psi & \cos\varphi\cos\psi + \sin\varphi\sin\theta\sin\psi & -\sin\varphi\cos\psi + \cos\varphi\sin\theta\sin\psi \\ -\sin\theta & \sin\varphi\cos\theta & \cos\varphi\cos\theta \end{bmatrix} \quad (17)$$

This is DCM represent by Euler Angles.

For small rotations $\sin\varphi \xrightarrow{yields} \varphi$, $\sin\theta \xrightarrow{yields} \theta$, $\sin\psi \xrightarrow{yields} \psi$ and the cosines of these three angles are approaching one. Replacing in Equation 17 and ignoring the values of these angles, which also become small, the directional cosine matrix present by the Euler rotation is reduced to:

$$C_b^n \approx \begin{bmatrix} 1 & -\psi & \theta \\ \psi & 1 & -\varphi \\ -\theta & \varphi & 1 \end{bmatrix} \quad (18)$$

The angles φ, θ, ψ are the measured angles and φ, θ, ψ, ψ are angular velocities.

$$\begin{bmatrix} \omega_x \\ \omega_y \\ \omega_z \end{bmatrix} = \begin{bmatrix} \dot{\varphi} \\ 0 \\ 0 \end{bmatrix} + C_3 \begin{bmatrix} 0 \\ \dot{\theta} \\ 0 \end{bmatrix} + C_3 C_2 \begin{bmatrix} 0 \\ 0 \\ \dot{\psi} \end{bmatrix} \quad (19)$$

This can be rearranged and described in the component form as follows:

$$\dot{\varphi} = \left(\omega_y \sin\varphi + \omega_z \cos\varphi\right)\tan\theta + \omega_z \quad (20)$$

$$\dot{\theta} = \omega_y \cos\varphi - \omega_z \sin\varphi \quad (21)$$

$$\dot{\psi} = \left(\omega_y \sin\varphi + \omega_z \cos\varphi\right)\sec\theta \quad (22)$$

Equations of this kind can be solved in a connected system for the renewal of the Euler 's body rotations relative to a selected coordinate system. There use is limited because the decision of φ and ψ becomes indefinite when $\theta = \pm 90\,°$.

Quaternions

The quaternion is a four-parameter representation based on the idea that a transformation from one co-ordinate system to another can be presented as a single rotation around a vector μ defined in the initial coordinate system. Quaternion is a four-dimensional vector whose elements are a function of this vector and the magnitude of rotation:

$$q = \begin{bmatrix} a \\ b \\ c \\ d \end{bmatrix} = \begin{bmatrix} \cos(\mu/2) \\ (\mu_x/\mu)\sin\mu \\ (\mu_y/\mu)\sin\mu \\ (\mu_z/\mu)\sin\mu \end{bmatrix} \tag{23}$$

where μ_x, μ_y, μ_z is the components of the vector and the magnitude is μ.

Quaternion with components a, b, c and d can also be described as a complex number with four parameters with a real component a with three imaginary components:

$$q = a + ib + jc + kd \tag{24}$$

The vector value described in the associated axes r^b can be defined in the initial axes r^n directly using quaternions. First we define quaternion r^b where the complex components are equal to the components of r^b and with zero scalar component:

$$r^b = ix + jy + kz \tag{25}$$

$$r^{b'} = 0 + ix + jy + kz$$

In the initial axes:

$$r^{n'} = q.r^{b'}.q^* \tag{26}$$

where q * = (a-ib-jc-kd) is complexly fused to q.

Therefore,

$$r^{n'} = \left(a + ib + jc + kd\right)\left(0 + ix + jy + kz\right)\left(a - ib - jc - kd\right) = 0 +$$
$$\left[\left(a^2 + b^2 - c^2 - d^2\right)x + 2\left(bc - ad\right)y + 2\left(bd + ac\right)z\right]i +$$
$$\left[2\left(bc + ad\right)x + \left(a^2 - b^2 + c^2 - d^2\right)y + 2\left(cd - ab\right)z\right]j$$
$$+\left[2\left(bd - ac\right)x + 2\left(cd + ab\right)y + \left(a^2 - b^2 - c^2 + d^2\right)\right]k$$

(27)

Or $r^{n'}$ described in the matrix form:

$$r^{n'} = C' r^{b'}$$

(28)

where $C' = \begin{bmatrix} 0 & 0 \\ 0 & C \end{bmatrix}$, $r^{b'} = \begin{bmatrix} 0 \\ r^b \end{bmatrix}$ and:

$$C = \begin{bmatrix} a^2 + b^2 - c^2 - d^2 & 2\left(bc - ad\right) & 2\left(bd + ac\right) \\ 2\left(bc + ad\right) & \left(a^2 - b^2 + c^2 - d^2\right) & 2\left(cd - ab\right) \\ 2\left(bd - ac\right) & 2\left(cd + ab\right) & \left(a^2 - b^2 - c^2 + d^2\right) \end{bmatrix}$$

(29)

$$r^n = C.r^b$$

(30)

Comparison with equation 2 shows that C is equal to the directional cosine matrix C_b^n.
Quaternion changes over time according to the equation:

$$\dot{q} = 0.5q.p_{nb}^b$$

(31)

This equation can also be expressed in a matrix form as a function of the components of q and $p_{nb}^b = \begin{bmatrix} 0 & \omega_{nb}^{nT} \end{bmatrix}^T$:

$$q = \begin{bmatrix} \dot{a} \\ \dot{b} \\ \dot{c} \\ \dot{d} \end{bmatrix} = 0.5 \begin{bmatrix} a & -b & -c & -d \\ b & a & -d & c \\ c & d & a & -b \\ d & -c & b & a \end{bmatrix} \begin{bmatrix} 0 \\ \omega_x \\ \omega_y \\ \omega_z \end{bmatrix}$$

(32)

$$\dot{a} = -0.5\left(b\omega_x + c\omega_y + d\omega_z\right)$$

(33)

$$\dot{b} = 0.5\left(a\omega_x - d\omega_y + c\omega_z\right) \tag{34}$$

$$\dot{c} = 0.5\left(d\omega_x + a\omega_y - b\omega_z\right) \tag{35}$$

$$\dot{d} = -0.5\left(c\omega_x - b\omega_y - a\omega_z\right) \tag{36}$$

This equations can be solved in a navigation system to monitor quaternion parameters defining body orientation.

Relationship Between Directional Cosine Matrix, Euler Angles and Quaternions

$$
C_b^n = \begin{bmatrix} c_{11} & c_{12} & c_{13} \\ c_{21} & c_{22} & c_{23} \\ c_{31} & c_{32} & c_{33} \end{bmatrix}
$$

$$
= \begin{bmatrix} a^2 + b^2 - c^2 - d^2 & 2\left(bc - ad\right) & 2\left(bd + ac\right) \\ 2\left(bc + ad\right) & \left(a^2 - b^2 + c^2 - d^2\right) & 2\left(cd - ab\right) \\ 2\left(bd - ac\right) & 2\left(cd + ab\right) & \left(a^2 - b^2 - c^2 + d^2\right) \end{bmatrix}
$$

$$
= \begin{bmatrix} \cos\theta\cos\psi & -\cos\varphi\sin\psi + \sin\varphi\sin\theta\cos\psi & \sin\varphi\sin\psi + \cos\varphi\sin\theta\cos\psi \\ \cos\theta\sin\psi & \cos\varphi\cos\psi + \sin\varphi\sin\theta\sin\psi & -\sin\varphi\cos\psi + \cos\varphi\sin\theta\sin\psi \\ -\sin\theta & \sin\varphi\cos\theta & \cos\varphi\cos\theta \end{bmatrix} \tag{37}
$$

Kalman Linear Filter

The Kalman filter is an optimal algorithm for evaluating the state of a discrete linear dynamic system under the influence of white noise.

In the theory of evaluation, the term conditional mathematical expectation is fundamental. The basic dimensions and equations in the Kalman filter are derived using the operator's conditional mathematical expectation (Welch G., Bishop G. 2001). According to one of the fundamental theorems of the evaluation theory - the Sherman theorem - the optimal assessment of the condition of a linear dynamical system has the form:

$$\hat{x}_{(k|j)} = Ex_{(k)} \mid Z^j \tag{38}$$

where: $Z^j = \left\{ z_{(i)}, \forall i \leq j \right\}$ and all measurements are marked up to the time j. This means that the optimal estimation of the system state vector represents the conditional mathematical expectation of this vector at set measurements up to that point.

The specific look of the Kalman filter depends on the two models that underlie its work - the motion model and the measurement model:

$$x_{(k+1)} = F_{(k)}x_{(k)} + G_{(k)}u_{(k)} + v_{(k)} \tag{39}$$

where:

x _ ((k)) is the system state vector of n-dimensional system;
- F _ ((k)) is a transition matrix with size n × n, which connects the state of the vector x at a moment with its state at the next moment;
-u _ ((k)) control vector;
-v _ ((k)) is a random vector of size n and covariance matrix Q, modeling the system noise;
-e time index.

Accordingly, for the measurement model, we will have:

$$z_{(k)} = H_{(k)}x_{(k)} + w_{(k)} \tag{40}$$

where:

z _ ((k)) is the measurement vector of dimension m;
-H ((k)) is a matrix m × n that connects the state vector to the measurement vector;
-w ((k)) is a random vector of m size and a covariance matrix R modeling the measurement noise.

Methodologically, the first filter equation to be displayed is the equation for determining the predicted state of the system for a time step forward. This state is defined by substituting in equation $x_{(k+1)}$ of Equation 39:

$$Ex_{(k+1)} \mid Z^k = EF_{(k)}x_{(k)} + G_{(k)}u_{(k)} + v_{(k)} \mid Z^k \tag{41}$$

By performing the above operation, for the prediction of the state vector we will get the equation:

$$\hat{x}_{(k+1|k)} = F_{(k)}\hat{x}_{(k|k)} + G_{(k)}u_{(k)} \tag{42}$$

In the same way, we define and calculate the covariance matrix of the predicted state error, which we define in advance as:

$$\tilde{x}_{(k+1|k)} \equiv x_{(k+1)} - \hat{x}_{(k+1|k)} = F_{(k)}\tilde{x}_{(k|k)} + v_{(k)} \tag{43}$$

For the covariance matrix we get:

$$P_{(k+1|k)} \equiv E\left[\tilde{x}_{(k+1|k)}\tilde{x}_{(k+1|k)}^T \mid Z^k\right] = F_{(k)}P_{(k|k)}F_{(k)}^T + Q_{(k)} \tag{44}$$

where $Q_{(k)} = E\left[v_{(k)}v_{(l)}^T\right]\delta_{kl}$ the matrix that adds noise of moving.

Replacing the prediction of Equation 42 with Equation 41, we will get the prediction of the measurement:

$$\hat{z}_{(k+1|k)} = H_{(k+1)}\hat{x}_{(k+1|k)} \tag{45}$$

The difference between the measured value and its predictive value gives a magnitude which is an important measure of the convergence of the Kalman filter. This value is called innovation and is derived from the equation:

$$v_{(k+1)} \equiv z_{(k+1)} + \hat{z}_{(k+1|k)} = z_{(k+1)} - H_{(k+1)}\hat{x}_{(k+1|k)} . \tag{46}$$

The following equation of the filter determines the covariance matrix of innovations:

$$S_{(k+1)} = E\left[v_{(k+1)}v_{(k+1)}^T\right] = H_{(k+1)}P_{(k+1|k)}H_{(k+1)}^T + R_{(k+1)} \quad . \tag{47}$$

The final step before deducting the main recurrent equation of the Kalman filter is to determine the filter gain matrix. For this purpose, we will use the assessment of the minimum mean error of the random vector x, depending on the random vector d, which represents the conditional mathematical expectation of x at set z:

$$\hat{x} = E\left[x \mid z\right] = \bar{x} + P_{xz}P_{zz}^{-1}\left(z - \bar{z}\right) \quad . \tag{48}$$

First matrix in the above equation represents the mutual covariance matrix of the state vector and the measurement vector. Using the equation of error of the predicted equation 43 and the error of the measurement prediction equation 46, for this matrix we get the equation:

$$P_{xx} = E\left[\tilde{x}_{(k+1|k)}\tilde{z}^{T}_{(k+1|k)} \mid Z^{k}\right] = \left[\left\{\tilde{x}_{(k+1|k)}\right\}\left\{H_{(k+1)}\tilde{x}_{(k+1|k)}\right\}^{T} \mid Z^{k}\right] = P_{(k+1|k)}H^{T}_{(k+1|k)} \tag{49}$$

The second matrix in equation 48 (ignoring the step mark) is the covariate matrix of the measurement prediction (innovation) which serves as a weighing factor for the first matrix.

$$P_{zz} = S_{(k+1)} \tag{50}$$

The output of these two matrices is called the gain of the filter:

$$W_{(k+1)} \equiv P_{xz}P^{-1}_{zz} = P_{(k+1|k)}H^{T}_{(k+1|k)}S^{-1}_{(k+1)} \tag{51}$$

Finally, using this vector-matrix equations we present the main recurrent equation of the Kalman filter:

$$\hat{x}_{(k+1|k+1)} = \hat{x}_{(k+1|k)} + W_{(k+1)}v_{(k+1)} \tag{52}$$

Kalman's filter ends by calculating the updated value of the covariate matrix of the error of evaluation:

$$P_{(k+1|k+1)} = P_{(k+1|k)} - W_{(k+1)}S_{(k+1)}W^{T}_{(k+1)} \tag{53}$$

It is clear from the description of the algorithm that it is possible to distinguish two stages - prediction (equation 42, equation 44, equation 45) and correction of the prediction, which is the actual filtration (equation 46, 47, equation51, equation52, equation53). In the process of meeting goals, these two phases are cyclically repeated for each new review when new measurements arrive.

AHRS Algorithm

The operating algorithm starts with the initial sensor settings and their calibration, and then goes to the basic operation mode, including calculating the angular position in space and transmitting the data to the PC for analysis.

Initial Settings and Calibration

In the beginning is required to perform the initialization of the sensor. We can change value in sensor's registers and change their sensitivity and the operating mode.

Each sensor in order to work properly needs an initial calibration to the environment. The IMU sensors have built-in self-test and calibration functions. The magnetometer requires calibration to remove the effect of magnetic soft and magnetic hard iron.

Figure 2. Operating loop

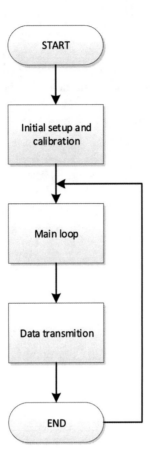

Experimentally was established coefficients correcting the influence of magnetic soft and magnetic hard iron (Caruso, M. J., 2016). The test lasts 10 seconds, during which the device rotates around all axes by 360 °, and collects the readings of the magnetometers. Determine the minimum and maximum values of readings on each axis. The coefficients for correction of magnetic soft iron are calculated using the following formulas:

$$x_{sf} = \frac{\left(max_y - min_y\right)}{\left(max_x - min_x\right)} \tag{54}$$

$$y_{sf} = \frac{\left(max_x - min_x\right)}{\left(max_y - min_y\right)} \tag{55}$$

Figure 3. Initialization and calibration

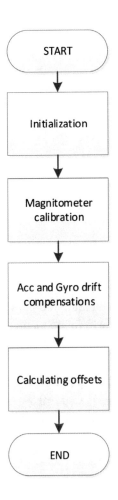

$$z_{sf} = \frac{\left(max_x - min_x\right).x_{sf}}{\left(max_z - min_z\right)} \tag{56}$$

Magnetic hard iron correction coefficients are calculated using the following formulas:

$$x_{hf} = \left(\frac{\left(max_x - min_x\right)}{2} - max_x\right).x_{sf} \tag{57}$$

$$y_{hf} = \left(\frac{\left(max_y - min_y\right)}{2} - max_y\right).y_{sf} \tag{58}$$

$$z_{hf} = \left(\frac{\left(max_z - min_z \right)}{2} - max_z \right) . z_{sf}$$

(59)

The corrected values of the readings of the magnetometer are calculated:

$$x_{corr} = x_{raw} . x_{sf} + x_{hf}$$

(60)

$$y_{corr} = y_{raw} . y_{sf} + y_{hf}$$

(61)

$$z_{corr} = z_{raw} . z_{sf} + z_{hf}$$

(62)

Fifty measurements are performed to calculate the accelerometer and gyroscope drift. The correction coefficient for the drift represents the arithmetic mean of the measurements (Woodman, O., 2007). When calculating the drift coefficient for the accelerometer coordinate z, the earth gravity field must not be compensated.

MEMS sensors are exclusively influenced by temperature changes. For this reason, the manufacturer has incorporated a temperature sensor in the ITG-3200. For calculating the correction coefficients, sensor readings are taken at two different temperatures. It is recommended that the two temperatures have a large difference and opposite signs.

$$temp_{corr} = - \frac{raw_1 - raw_2}{temp_1 - temp_2}$$

(63)

The temperature coefficient is calculated for each sensor and each axis separately.

When starting the system, it must be placed horizontally in the stationary position for the correct calculation of the drift coefficients. We accept all IMU parameters for starting values equal to zero.

Basic Operation/ Main Loop

The operating mode of the system starts with a timer setting that specifies the sampling time, which is reset at each operating mode repeat.

The next step is to read IMU sensors and add correction coefficients. Depending on the selected sensor sensitivity, a scaling factor is applied.

For accelerometer:

$$Acc_X = \frac{\left(Acc_{Xraw} - Acc_{Xdrift} + temp_{accX} . \left(temp - temp_{drift} \right) \right)}{Scale\,Factor\left(256\right)}$$

(64)

Figure 4. Main loop

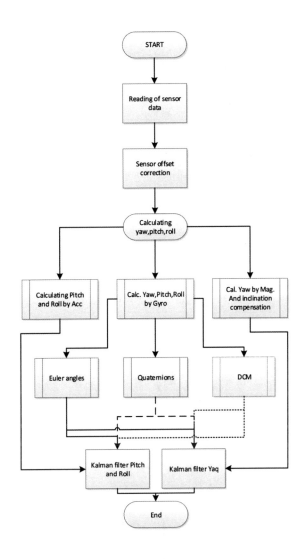

where:

Acc_X is the corrected accelerometer axis X value;

Acc_{Xraw} is the measured value of the sensor;

Acc_{Xdrift} is the pre-calculated sensor drift;

$temp_{accX}$ is a prepaid heat factor;

temp is the current temperature;

$temp_{drift}$ is the temperature at which the drift coefficient is calculated.

For the magnetometer:

$$Mag_X = \frac{\left(Mag_{Xcorr} + temp_{magX} \cdot \left(temp - temp_{drift}\right)\right)}{Scale\,Factor\left(1\right)} \tag{65}$$

where:

Mag_X is the corrected value on the magnetometer axis X.

Mag_{Xcorr} magnetic data with corrections for magnetic soft and magnetic hard iron

$temp_{magX}$ is a correction temperature coefficient

temp is the current temperature

$temp_{drift}$ is the temperature at which the drift coefficient is calculated

For the gyroscope:

$$Gyro_X = \frac{\left(Gyro_{Xraw} - Gyro_{Xdrift} + temp_{gyroX} \cdot \left(temp - temp_{drift}\right)\right)}{Scale\,Factor\left(14.375\right)} \tag{66}$$

where:

$Gyro_X$ is the adjusted gyro axis X value;

$Gyro_{Xraw}$ is the measured value of the sensor;

$Gyro_{Xdrift}$ is the pre-calculated sensor drift;

$temp_{gyroX}$ is a correction heat coefficient;

temp is the current temperature;

$temp_{drift}$ is the temperature at which the drift coefficient is calculated.

The gyroscope values are integrated during the sampling time to obtain the angular velocities on the three axes.

$$\omega_x = Gyro_X \cdot timestep$$

and the other coordinates respectively.

Accelerometer and gyroscope readings pass through a low-pass filter. The accelerometer readings below 0.009g on the three axes are assumed to be zero. For the gyroscope, the angular velocities ω_x, ω_y, ω_z below 0.001 are neglected.

Pitch and Roll Calculation by Accelerometers

$$Pitch_{acc} = \arcsin\left(-Acc_x\right) \tag{67}$$

$$Roll_{acc} = \arcsin\left(\frac{Acc_y}{\cos\left(Pitch_{acc}\right)}\right) \tag{68}$$

Yaw, Pitch and Roll calculation by Gyros and Euler angles

$$Roll_{gyro} = Roll_{gyro} + \left(\left(\omega_y \sin\left(roll\right) + \omega_z \cos\left(roll\right)\right)\tan\left(pitch\right) + \omega_z\right), \tag{69}$$

$$Pitch_{gyro} = Pitch_{gyro} + \left(\omega_y \cos\left(roll\right) - \omega_z \sin\left(roll\right)\right) \tag{70}$$

$$Yaw_{gyro} = Yaw_{gyro} + \left(\omega_y \sin\left(roll\right) + \omega_z \cos\left(roll\right)\right)\sec\left(pitch\right) \tag{71}$$

where: $Pitch_{gyro}$, $Roll_{gyro}$ and Yaw_{gyro} are the current values of the system of pitch, roll and yaw; roll and pitch are the values of $Pitch_{gyro}$ и $Roll_{gyro}$ from the previous iteration.

Yaw, Pitch and Roll Calculation by Gyros and Quaternions

$$\dot{a} = -0.5\left(b\omega_x + c\omega_y + d\omega_z\right) \tag{72}$$

$$\dot{b} = 0.5\left(a\omega_x - d\omega_y + c\omega_z\right) \tag{73}$$

$$\dot{c} = 0.5\left(d\omega_x + a\omega_y - b\omega_z\right) \tag{74}$$

$$\dot{d} = -0.5\left(c\omega_x - b\omega_y - a\omega_z\right) \tag{75}$$

where $\dot{a}$, $\dot{b}$, $\dot{c}$ и $\dot{d}$ are the current values of the quaternion, and a, b, c and d are the values of the previous iteration. From equation 29 we calculate the components of the transition matrix of equation 1.

$$Roll_{gyro} = 0rctan\left(\frac{c_{32}}{c_{33}}\right) \tag{76}$$

$$Pitch_{gyro} = \arcsin\left(-c_{31}\right) \tag{77}$$

$$Yaw_{gyro} = 0rctan\left(\frac{c_{21}}{c_{11}}\right) \tag{78}$$

Yaw Calculation by Magnetometer Using Angles Correction

$$Yaw_{mag} = atan2\left(x_{comp}, y_{comp}\right) \tag{79}$$

where

Yaw_{mag} is the calculated yaw with inclination correction;
atan2 is a modification of the arctan function, which ranges from -π to π;
x_{comp}, y_{comp} are the x and y components of the magnetometer with inclination correction.

$$x_{comp} = Mag_x.\cos\left(Pitch_{acc}\right) + Mag_y.\sin\left(Pitch_{acc}\right).\sin\left(Roll_{acc}\right) - Mag_z.\sin\left(Pitch_{acc}\right).\cos\left(Roll_{acc}\right) \tag{80}$$

$$y_{comp} = Mag_y.\cos\left(Roll_{acc}\right) + Mag_z \sin\left(Roll_{acc}\right) \tag{81}$$

Linear Kalman filter

$$Pitch_{Kalman} = f\left(Pitch_{Acc}, Pitch_{Gyro}\right) \tag{82}$$

$$Roll_{Kalman} = f\left(Roll_{Acc}, Roll_{Gyro}\right) \tag{83}$$

$$Yaw_{Kalman} = f\left(Yaw_{Mag}, Yaw_{Gyro}\right) \tag{84}$$

EXPERIMENTAL RESULTS

For the purposes of the experiment, a test setup was built using an IMU sensor stick (Analog Devices, 2011). consisting of an ADXL345 accelerometer, a HMC5843 magnetometer, and an ITG-3200 gyro communicating with an I2C protocol (Irazabal, J.-M.,2003) with a microprocessor Atmega2560 (Atmel Corporation, 2010) and equipped with a Bluetooth connection for real-time data transmission.

The first test is at a relatively constant temperature and a stationary system. The graphs created by the visualization software use the following markings:

- In the red is the calculated parameter of the gyroscopes by Euler angles without low-pass filter, temperature compensated;
- Green is the computed parameter of the gyroscopes by Euler Angles with low-pass filter, temperature compensated;
- In yellow the calculated parameter of the gyroscopes by quaternions with low-pass filter, temperature compensated;
- Blue shows the combined gyro and accelerometer data (magnetometer for yaw) through a Kalman filter. The parameters of the gyroscopes are calculated by Euler Angles with low-pass filter, temperature-compensated;
- In orange, aggregated gyro and accelerometer data (risk magnetometer) is depicted using a Kalman filter. Gyro parameters are calculated using quaternions with low-pass filter, temperature compensated;

Figure 5. Test setup

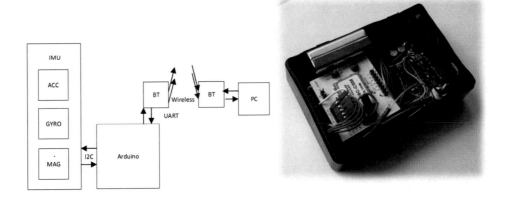

- White is the computed parameter from the gyroscopes by Euler Angles with low-pass filter, temperature uncompensated.

For all experimental data we will show only measurements for Roll angle, because other angles data is changing in similar model.

By letting the sensors over a longer period of time, the good work of the Kalman filter is noticed. At the start time (up to the first 15 s) it is noticeable that the Quaternion-based Kalman filter gives more accurate results. After 100 s the two filtrations are identical. Unfiltered parameters acquire unusable values.

The following graphs show the temperature compensation. The kit remains stationary and the temperature changes from 10 ° C to 25 ° C.

Figure 10 clearly shows how the temperature-uncompensated parameters acquire an extremely large variation in temperature variation. Temperature compensated parameters have deviations and their readings can still be used.

The next attempt involves consecutive rotation of ± 20 ° along the roll and at the pitch at constant temperature.

When rotating on one axis the readings of the remaining axes stay minimally altered.

FUTURE TRENDS

There are several future improvement of the system:

- Using GNSS sensor for more accurate yaw drift compensation
- Using extended Kalman filter
- Add algorithm control actuators for trajectory management

Figure 6. Measuring sensor data for Roll angle

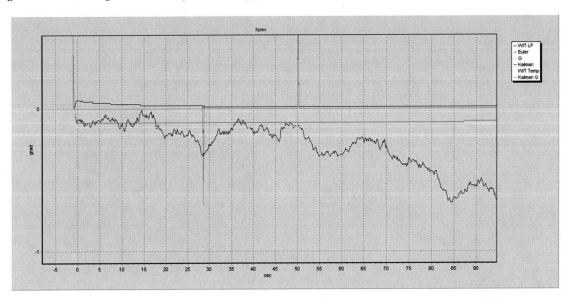

Figure 7. Temperature measurements

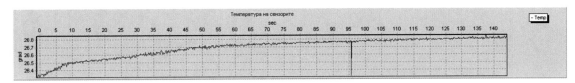

Figure 8. Roll angle by long period

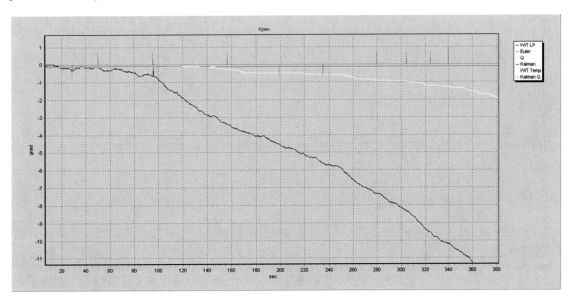

Figure 9. Changing of temperature

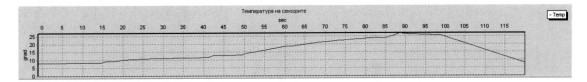

CONCLUSION

The results obtained show the performance of the settings and the calibration and filtration. The similarity of the different methods of crossing between coordinate systems is also seen.

In longer-duration experiments, the robust operation of the Kalman filter is noticeable.

There is a need to complex the navigation data from different navigation systems and sensors. The theoretical and experimental results obtained are categorical in this respect.

A comparative analysis of the accuracy of the system of differential equations for determination of the Euler angles using quaternions and the classical method was made.

Figure 10. Roll angles changing by temperature

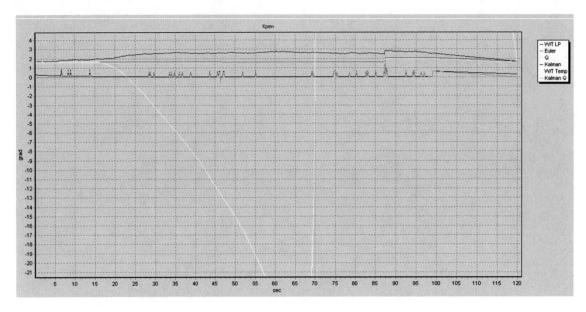

Figure 11. Yaw rotation

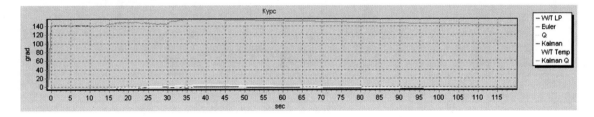

Figure 12. Roll rotation

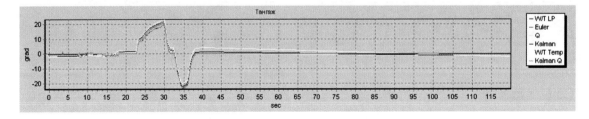

Figure 13. Pitch rotation

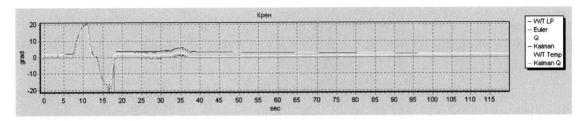

Figure 14. Yaw rotating 360 degree

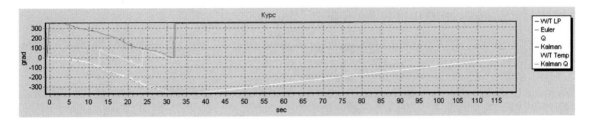

Figure 15. Roll angle by Yaw rotating 360 degree

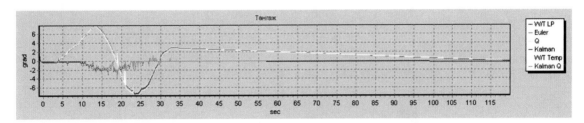

Figure 16. Pitch angle by Yaw rotating 360 degree

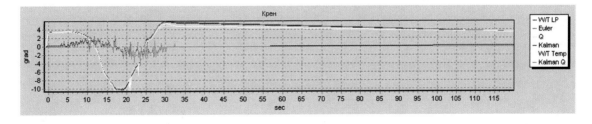

REFERENCES

Analog Devices, Inc. (2011). ADXL345. Norwood, U.S.A. Atmel Corporation. (2010). 8-bit AVR Microcontroller with 64K/128K/256K Bytes In-System Programmable Flash. Preliminary Summary. Atmel Corporation.

Caruso, M. J. (2016). *Applications of Magnetoresistive Sensors in Navigation Systems*. Plymouth: Honeywell Inc.

Irazabal, J.-M. (2003). *I2C MANUAL*. Philips Semiconductors.

Titterton, D. H. (2004). Strapdown Inertial Navigation Technology. Cornwall, UK: The Institution of Electrical Engineers. doi:10.1049/PBRA017E

Welch, G., & Bishop, G. (2001). *An Introduction to the Kalman Filter*. University of North Carolina at Chapel Hill.

Woodman, O. (2007). *An Introduction to Inertial Navigation*. Cambridge, UK: University of Cambridge.

Chapter 17
Control Methods for Bipedal Walking Robots With Integrated Elastic Elements

Sergei Savin

ⓘ https://orcid.org/0000-0001-7954-3144

Innopolis University, Russia

ABSTRACT

In this chapter, the problem of controlling bipedal walking robots with integrated elastic elements is considered. A survey of the existing control methods developed for walking robots is given, and their applicability to the task of controlling the robots with elastic elements is analyzed. The focus of the chapter lies with the feedback controller design. The chapter studies the influence that the elastic elements modelled as a spring-damper system have on the behavior of the control system. The influence of the spring-damper parameters and the inertial parameters of the actuator gear box and the motor shaft on the generated control laws and the resulting peak torques are discussed. The changes in these effects associated with motor torque saturation and sensors nonlinearities are studied. It is shown that the introduction of torque saturation changes the way the elastic drive parameters affect the resulting behavior of the control system. The ways to use obtained results in practice are discussed.

INTRODUCTION

Walking robots are one of the central research topics in mobile robotics, due their wide applicability and their potential for natural integration into social and industrial processes, allowing automating a variety of labor-intensive tasks (Luk et al., 2006; Armada et al., 2005; Buschmann 2010). Particular applications for legged robots range from disaster response and to pipe inspection (Bouyarmane et al., 2012; Savin & Vorochaeva, 2017a).

There had been a lot of research focused on particular types of walking robots, including bipedal robots, quadrupeds and multi-legged robots (Hurmuzlu et al., 2004). Bipedal robots present particular interest due to possibility of using anthropomorphic designs and implementing anthropomorphic mo-

DOI: 10.4018/978-1-5225-7879-6.ch017

tions, which can be beneficial in terms of integrating of this type of robots into the existing processes and infrastructure (Ogura et al., 2006, Khatib et al., 2004). Examples of anthropomorphic biped designs can be found in (Kaneko et al., 2008; Kaneko et al., 2011; Khusainov et al., 2015; Hirose et al., 2007). Non-anthropomorphic bipeds can be found in (Xie et al., 2018; Clary et al., 2018). A separate class of humanoid walkers are active exoskeletons, which are inherently anthropomorphic (Yan et al., 2015; Young et al., 2017; Panovko et al., 2016; Jatsun et al., 2018).

One of the benchmarks for the walking robot technology had been DARPA Robotics Challenge (Johnson et al., 2015; Feng et al., 2015), which demonstrated of the progress in the bipedal robotics and simultaneously revealed a number of problems that still need to be addressed. One of these problems is safe interaction between the robot and the environment, including obstacles, tools, people and other robots. Currently used practical solutions to these challenges are to minimize the robot's interactions with the environment as much as possible, and to act as a stationary manipulator when a manipulation task is present (Atkeson et al., 2015). This leads to stiff and inefficient motions and non-robust control schemes. The capability to operate safely in the scenarios where unplanned contact and collisions are inherently possible has not yet been achieved by humanoid robots.

One of the ways this capability can be achieved is by designing the robots to be less rigid (Pratt, 2002; Robinson et al., 1999). This might allow avoiding damage both to the robot and to the environment in the events of the unplanned contact and collisions. Introduction of elastic elements can also be used for improvement of robots' energy efficiency in particular regimes of operation (Pratt et al., 1997). However, this type of robot design requires changes in the control strategies employed for bipedal robots.

This chapter looks at the problem of controlling bipedal walking robots with integrated elastic elements. It is a broad class of robots with varying structures. This problem can be partially solved by using existing techniques developed for walking robots with rigid structures. This is true for the algorithms based on the robot's kinematics and geometry, rather than their dynamics. However, some of the elements of the control pipeline, including feedback controller design and controller parameters tuning require separate analysis.

BACKGROUND: CONTROL METHODS FOR WALKING ROBOTS

Modern control methods developed for walking robots are generally structured as a pipeline with a hierarchy of tasks. The number of tasks in this structure can vary, and the level of independency between the different elements of this pipeline can be significantly different for different control designs.

One of the common ways to structure the control system of a walking robot is to separate out the walking gait generation task. Walking gait generation can be seen as a problem of finding continuous time functions that determine desired joint-space trajectories for the robot, which would satisfy a set of criteria. The criteria that need to be satisfied include kinematic and dynamic constraints (the motions should be feasible with respect to joint limits, actuator capabilities, contact interactions, etc.), vertical balance (the motion should allow the robot to remain vertically balanced and prevent falling down) and achieving motion objectives (for example, by moving forward or turning). Additionally, the walking gait can be chosen with respect to chosen optimality criteria. These criteria can include specific cost of transport, as defined in (Collins, et al., 2005), stability margins, required motion time (Hong, et al., 2012) and others.

Walking Gait Generation Pipeline

For bipedal walking robots, the gait generation can be broken down to three subtasks: footstep sequence generation, the center of mass trajectory generation and the inverse kinematics. The footstep sequence generation is a problem of constructing a sequence of positions and orientations of the robot's feet contacting the supporting surface, such that the robot can walk placing its feet according to this sequence. This problem is relatively simple for horizontal flat surfaces without obstacles. For the supporting surfaces of general shapes with obstacles this problem becomes more challenging, as was indicated in (Kuffner, et al., 2001; Chestnutt, et al., 2005). In general, choosing the location of a footstep can be seen as a non-convex optimization. These types of problems can be difficult to solve numerically due to present local minima.

Many of the supporting surface classes can be closely approximated by piece-wise linear surfaces with obstacles. This allows decomposing the supporting surface into a set of obstacle-free regions (Deits & Tedrake, 2014). This in turn allows to reformulate the footstep sequence generation problem from a general non-convex optimization to a mixed integer convex program. These types of programs can be efficiently solved using branch and bound methods (Bonami et al., 2008), although they are associated with significant computational loads. The algorithms for generating obstacle-free regions are proposed in (Deits & Tedrake, 2015; Savin, 2017). One is based on the use of semidefinite programming and requires the obstacles to be presented as convex polyhedrons, while the other is based on stereographic projection and requires that the obstacles are presented as point clouds. Both can be used as part of a real-time control system, however they are also associated with non-negligible computational costs.

This highlights the pipeline for the footstep sequence generation for bipedal walking robots. As can be seen, the algorithms discussed here are independent of the robot's dynamics and therefore the introduction of elastic elements in the robot's structure should not affect their work. However, these algorithms rely on a number of assumptions regarding the robot's dynamics. In particular, they assume that the robot is capable of executing generated footstep sequence, as long as it obeys a set of imposed on it constraints associated with the kinematic and dynamics properties of the robot. Since choosing these constraints has to be done with respect to the robots dynamics, they would be affected by the changes resulting from the introduction of the elastic elements.

There are alternative approaches based on rapidly exploring random trees, probabilistic roadmaps and other methods that include random search (Short & Bandyopadhyay, 2018). Some of these formulations allow including the robot's dynamics into the motion planner, which requires considering the effects of the elastic elements directly.

Trajectory Generation

The next step after the footstep sequence generation is trajectory generation. The usual approach is to generate the trajectories for the robot's feet, for its center of mass and to add additional trajectories or constraints depending on the robot's structure, on the desired motion properties and on the requirements of the inverse kinematics algorithms (Wieber, 2006; Jatsun et al., 2017c). Similar approach can be used when the motion does not require a footstep sequence. Examples of the later include sit-to-stand transfer motions and its reverse (Jatsun et al., 2016b, 2016c, 2017a).

Center of mass trajectory generation is linked with the problem of ensuring the vertical stability of the robot. For the case when the robot walks over a flat terrain, the connection is expressed as a zero-moment point (ZMP) principle (Vukobratovic & Borovac, 2004). ZMP principle provides dynamic constraints on the motion of the center of mass of the robot, which allows the robot to remain vertically stable. This principle is the foundation for a number of prevalent trajectory generation and control schemes for bipedal robots, including preview control formulated in (Kajita et al., 2003), auxiliary ZMP control presented in (Kajita et al., 2006) and others.

A common feature of the ZMP-based algorithms is that they first propose a ZMP trajectory such that the ZMP point remains inside the support polygon (the convex hull of all points of contact between the robot and the supporting surface) at all times, and then that trajectory is used to solve for the center of mass trajectory, which is linked with the ZMP trajectory via a set of differential equations. These equations are usually derived from the simplified robot model which captures the essential features of the robot's dynamics and is easy to solve. Examples of such models include linear inverted pendulum (Kajita et al., 2001), cart-table model and others (Zheng et al., 2010).

To generate the center of mass trajectory for a given ZMP trajectory, a number of algorithms had been proposed. One of the examples is treating the trajectory generation as an optimal control problem, formulating the differential constraints imposed on the center of mass trajectory as a linear system and then solving Riccati equation to generate a linear quadratic regulator (LQR) for this system (Kuindersma et al., 2014); this allows soling the center of mass trajectory generation by simulating the obtained control system's dynamics forward. Alternatively, the ZMP equations can be solved analytically. In order to facilitate this, additional assumptions about the robot's dynamics are often made, such as assuming that the center of mass of the robot does not experience vertical accelerations. This results in a particular style of walking, demonstrated by such robots as ATLAS designed by Boston Dynamics and ASIMO designed by Honda.

The approaches discussed here rely on simplified dynamics model which would not change with the introduction of elastic elements. Therefore, it should be possible to use these methods as a part of the control pipeline for walking robots with integrated elastic elements without modifications. However, there are a number of alternative approaches which require more precise dynamics models. For example, this includes some of the methods based on the contact wrench cones (Caron et al., 2015; Hirukawa et al., 2006).

Feedback Control

The feedback control design for walking robots is associated with a number of challenges. Some of these challenges are common to mobile robots, such as limited motor torques, underactuation of the systems and others. The challenges specific to the walking robots arise from the fact that they feature periodic contact with the supporting surface with apply and break mechanical constraints for the system.

Most of the existing controllers are designed for the systems without explicit mechanical constraints. And although it is often possible to change the representation of the system to rid it of the explicit constraints, it is often not desirable. In practice, the walking robots are usually represented using a floating body formulation, which includes constraints. Therefore, the feedback controllers used for walking robots need to take these constraints into account.

One the popular approaches to feedback control design is to formulate it as a quadratic program or convex program (Kuindersma et al., 2016). It allows to explicitly take into account mechanical unilateral constraints, such as friction cones, as well as joint torque limits. The robot's dynamics is then treated as a constraint. In order to make the optimization problem convex, a local linearization of the system dynamics is used. Alternatively, a nonlinear convex approximation of the system's dynamics can be used. To formulate the optimization problem as a quadratic program, the friction cone constraints can be replaced with their polyhedral approximations.

The objective of the optimization can be chosen in a number of ways. This includes using the Lyapunov functions (Galloway et al., 2015), tracking the output of a reference controller (Savin & Vorochaeva, 2017b) and others.

Alternatively, modifications of the linear quadratic regulator had been proposed (Mason et al., 2016). This formulation is based on deriving a constraints projector matrix and using it to convert the linearized dynamics of the original system into a new constraints-free system with a similar dynamical properties. This allows using standard numeric algorithms for solving Riccati equation and calculating the controller gain matrix, which makes it highly efficient. A drawback of this approach is the appearance of static control error (Savin et al., 2017).

As highlighted here, the feedback control design methods developed for walking robots are usually model-based, which means that they have to take the robot's dynamics into account. This means that the changes in the control pipeline which come with introducing integrated elastic elements would manifest mainly in the feedback control.

This chapter studies the problems associated with the feedback control design that arise with the introduction of elastic elements. The following sections will focus on particular issues, such the impact of the elastic elements on the control system performance under torque saturation and the effects the sensors nonlinearity have on these systems.

ROBOT MODEL

In this chapter, a planar bipedal walking robot model is studied. The robot includes seven links total, with every consecutive pair connected via rotary joints. Each of the two legs of the robot consists of serially connected hip, shin and foot links. We assume that the centers of mass of the robot's links are placed in the geometric centers of the links.

Figure 1 shows a diagram of the robot model used in this study.

In figure 1, the following notation is used: O_i are the revolute joints, connecting the links and φ_i are joint angles, determining the orientation of the links. Angles φ_6 and φ_7 determining the orientation of the feet are not shown.

In order to describe the configuration of the robot, a vector of generalized coordinates is introduced:

$$\mathbf{q} = [x_C \quad y_C \quad \varphi_1 \quad \cdots \quad \varphi_7]^{\mathrm{T}}, \tag{1}$$

where x_C and y_C are the coordinates of the center of mass of the torso link of the robot.

Figure 1. Walking robot diagram; 1 is the robot's torso, 2 are the robot's hip links, 3 are the robot's shin links, 4 are the robot's feet

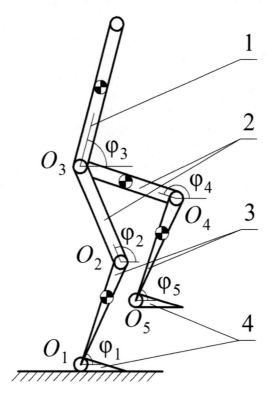

In this study, the case when the robot motion consists of taking a single step is considered. This means that the robot does not acquire or break contact during the simulated motion. This allows to avoid the need for the use of collision modelling, which includes a collision detection algorithms, a model for the instantaneous changes in velocities and others. Although the robot trajectories considered here cover only a single mode of operation of the walking robot, it also requires a minimal number of assumptions, making the simulation results more reliable.

Robot's Dynamics

The full dynamic model of the robot is given by the following equations:

$$\begin{cases} H\ddot{q} + c_1 = F^{\mathrm{T}}\lambda + \tau \\ F\ddot{q} + \dot{F}\dot{q} = 0 \end{cases}, \tag{2}$$

where $\mathbf{H}$ is the generalized inertia matrix, $\ddot{\mathbf{q}}$ is a vector of generalized accelerations, $\mathbf{c}_1$ is a dynamics bias vector, which is a sum of generalized inertial, gravitational and dissipative forces; λ is the vector of Lagrange coefficients, related to the reaction forces, τ is the vector of generalized motor torques and $\mathbf{F}$ is a constraints Jacobian matrix:

$$\mathbf{F} = \partial\mathbf{f}/\partial\mathbf{q}, \tag{3}$$

where $\mathbf{f}(\mathbf{q}) = \mathbf{0}$ are the mechanical constraints equations. The mechanical constraints are imposed on the contact points on the robot's foot which contacts the ground. The constraints are unilateral and the associated reaction forces are normal reaction force and friction. Both of these forces are also constrained by inequalities, known as friction cone constraints. Here we consider the motion regimes that do not break these constraints and do not turn them into equalities, allowing to avoid explicitly including these constraints into the robot model.

The dynamics bias vector $\mathbf{c}_1$ that appears in the equations (2) can be decomposed as follows:

$$\mathbf{c}_1 = \dot{\mathbf{H}}\dot{\mathbf{q}} + \mathbf{c}_0, \tag{4}$$

where $\mathbf{c}_0$ are the components of the bias vector associated with gravitational and dissipative forces.

The system (2) can be viewed as a system of differential-algebraic equations (DAE), which can be solved using methods designed for DAE (Brenan et al., 1996). Numerical solutions of DAE can lead to constraints violations due to the drift effect in the numerical integration schemes, which needs to be accounted for. This can be done with appropriate projection of the position, velocity and acceleration variables.

Integrated Elastic Elements

In this work, the integrated elastic elements are modelled as elastic drives, with a spring-damper system located between the gearbox output shaft and the actuator output shaft. These types of models are studied in (Pratt, 2002; Pratt et al., 2004)

The integrated elastic elements are modelled in the following way:

$$\begin{cases} \tau = -Su_s \\ u_s = K_p(Tq - q_s) + K_d(T\dot{q} - \dot{q}_s), \\ H_s\ddot{q}_s = u + u_s \end{cases} \tag{5}$$

where $\mathbf{u}_s$ is a vector of torques generated by the spring-damper systems (integrated elastic elements), $\mathbf{u}$ is a vector of motor torques, $\mathbf{q}_s$ is a vector of gearbox shafts' orientations, which acts as a vector of generalized coordinates for the elastic elements model, $\mathbf{H}_s$ is a positive-definite diagonal matrix of the inertia associated with the gearboxes and the parts connected to them, $\mathbf{S}$ is a motor matrix dependent on the choice of generalized coordinates and the placement of the motors, $\mathbf{K}_p$ and $\mathbf{K}_d$ are positive-definite diagonal matrices that define the stiffness and dissipative properties of the system and $\mathbf{T}$ is a selector matrix that depends on which generalized coordinates describe joint angles for the joints where the elastic elements are installed.

The expression (5) describes a dynamical system which evolves together with the system (2). This in effect increases the dimensionality of the original system. If the original system had n degrees of freedom and m motors, then after the introduction of the model (5) it will behave as a system with $n + m$ degrees of freedom. It can be treated as such in the control framework, by explicitly taking into account the model (5) when producing the control policy. However, this might not be practical, since this increases the dimensionality of the problem and changes the actuation pattern of the system. In (Robinson et al., 1999) it was indicated that the desirable performance of the control system can be achieved without the explicit model of the elastic drive. In all following simulations, the control system does not have an access to the model of the elastic drive.

For the experiments where the properties of the elastic elements do not need to be taken into account, the following model is used:

$$\tau = Su .$$

(6)

The model (6) describes the connection between motor torques $\mathbf{u}$ and the generalized torques τ as a linear function. In the case of the robot presented in this chapter, $\mathbf{S}$ is a constant matrix.

CONTROL ALGORITHM

In this section, the control system design for the walking robot is presented. The algorithm is based on the constrained linear quadratic regulator (CLQR), presented in (Mason et al., 2016). The algorithms extends the use of linear quadratic regulator to systems with explicit mechanical constraints.

CLQR controller requires the use of a linearized dynamics model of the robot. In order to obtain this linearized model we introduce the following notation:

$$f_d(x, u, \lambda) = \begin{bmatrix} H & \dot{H} \\ F & \dot{F} \end{bmatrix}^{-1} \begin{bmatrix} F^{\mathrm{T}}\lambda + \tau(u) - c_0 \\ 0 \end{bmatrix}.$$

(7)

Then the linearization of the dynamics at the point (x^*, u^*, λ^*) is given by the following expression:

$$\dot{x} = Ax + Bu + c + F_0\lambda ,$$

(8)

where $\mathbf{A}$, $\mathbf{B}$, $\mathbf{F}_0$ and $\mathbf{c}$ are the parameters of the linear model. These parameters can be computed as follows:

$$A = \frac{\partial f_d(x, u, \lambda)}{\partial x}\bigg|_{x=x^*} , \quad B = \frac{\partial f_d(x, u, \lambda)}{\partial \tau}\bigg|_{x=x^*} , \quad F_0 = \frac{\partial f_d(x, u, \lambda)}{\partial \lambda}\bigg|_{x=x^*} ,$$

(9)

$$c = f_d(x^*, u^*, \lambda^*) - (Ax^* + Bu^* + F_0\lambda^*).$$ (10)

In order to implement the CLQR controller the constraints matrix is introduced:

$$\mathbf{C} = \begin{bmatrix} \mathbf{F} & \dot{\mathbf{F}} \\ \mathbf{0} & \mathbf{F} \end{bmatrix}.$$ (11)

The matrix $\mathbf{C}$ can be viewed as a matrix of linear constrains imposed on the values of $\dot{x}$. These constraints take the form $\mathbf{C}\dot{x} = \mathbf{0}$. Let $\mathbf{N}$ be the matrix formed by basis vectors in the null space of $\mathbf{C}$:

$$\mathbf{N} = \mathrm{null}(\mathbf{C}).$$ (12)

The projection matrix $\mathbf{N}$ is the key component of the CLQR formulation presented in (Mason et al., 2016). It is used to project the linear dynamic model (8), producing a new system without explicit mechanical constraints:

$$\dot{\mathbf{x}}_p = \mathbf{N}^\mathrm{T}\mathbf{A}\mathbf{N}\mathbf{x}_p + \mathbf{N}^\mathrm{T}\mathbf{B}\mathbf{u} + \mathbf{N}^\mathrm{T}\mathbf{c},$$ (13)

where $\mathbf{x}_p$ are the state variables of the new system.

System (13) can be used to construct a linear quadratic regulator. To do this, an additive quadratic cost function J is introduced:

$$J = \int (\mathbf{x}_p^\mathrm{T}\mathbf{Q}\mathbf{x}_p + \mathbf{u}^\mathrm{T}\mathbf{R}\mathbf{u})dt,$$ (14)

where $\mathbf{Q}$ and $\mathbf{R}$ are positive-definite weight matrices. The choice of these matrices determines the properties of the obtained controller.

This allows formulating and solving algebraic Riccati equation for the system (13) and cost (14). The solution yields the optimal gain matrix $\mathbf{K}$, which can be used to construct the feedback law for the original system:

$$\mathbf{u} = \mathbf{u}^* - \mathbf{K}\mathbf{N}^\mathrm{T}(\mathbf{x} - \mathbf{x}^*).$$ (15)

where $\mathbf{u}^*$ is the value of control actions obtained by solving the inverse dynamics problem. Solving the inverse dynamics problem for systems with explicit mechanical constraints is discussed in (Mistry et al., 2010).

In the following simulations, the values of weight matrices $\mathbf{Q}$ and $\mathbf{R}$ are chosen as follows: $\mathbf{Q} = 10^3\mathbf{I}_{2n \times 2n}$, $\mathbf{R} = 10^{-2}\mathbf{I}_{m \times m}$, where $\mathbf{I}_{2n \times 2n}$ and $\mathbf{I}_{m \times m}$ are identity matrices of dimensions $2n \times 2n$ and $m \times m$ accordingly; n is the number of elements in the vector $\mathbf{q}$ (number of generalized coordinated) and m is the number of elements in the vector $\mathbf{u}$ (number of actuators).

SIMULATION RESULTS

Study of the Integrated Elastic Elements Model

This sections studies the effects that the elastic elements have on the robot dynamics and on the control system performance. In all simulations in this section the following robot model parameters are used (see table 1).

In the table 1, the lengths of hip and shin links are defined as the distance between the joints, and the lengths of torso and foot are defined as the distance between the joint and the furthest point on the link from the joint.

In the first experiment, the robot's motion for the model without elastic elements is simulated. The controller (15) and the linear torque model (6) are used. Figure 2 shows the torques generated by the actuators.

Table 1. The robot model parameters

Link's name	Parameter	Value	Units
Torso	Mass	20	kg
	Length	0.78	m
Hip	Mass	10	kg
	Length	0.6	m
Shin	Mass	10	kg
	Length	0.6	m
Foot	Mass	5	kg
	Length	0.2	m

Figure 2. The control actions; simulation results for a model without elastic elements

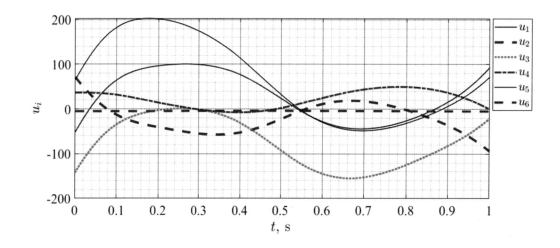

Analyzing the results shown in figure 2, it can be noted that the load is not distributed equally between the actuators. The actuator installed in the joint O_1 (corresponding to the time function $u_5(t)$ in the figure) shows the maximal torques for this experiment, exceeding 200 Nm. As is expected, some of the actuators experience very small loads. An example of the later is the actuator installed in the joint O_5, corresponding to the time function $u_6(t)$ in the figure 2. This actuator is only required to keep the robot's foot level during the stepping motion, which generates comparatively small load on the motor.

From the point of view of the robot design, it is important to consider both the long term and the short term (peak) loads on the actuators. It can be shown that the introduction of elastic elements affects both of these characteristics. For simplicity of analysis, the following discussion is focused on the behavior of a single actuator which demonstrated the largest peak load in the experiment above.

The next series of experiments are conducted with the controller (15) and the elastic drive model (5). For these experiments the following elastic drive model parameters are assumed: $\mathbf{K}_p = 100\mathbf{I}$ and $\mathbf{K}_d = 10\mathbf{I}$, where $\mathbf{I}$ is an identity matrix of appropriate dimensions. The value of the inertia matrix $\mathbf{H}_s$ of the elastic drive model was changing between the simulations and is given as $\mathbf{H}_s = I_s\mathbf{I}$, where I_s is a scalar coefficient. This coefficient can be seen as a reduced moment of inertia for each of the elastic drives.

Figure 3 shows the results of the experiments for different values of I_s.

Figure 3 shows that the increase in value of the reduced moment of inertia I_s of the elastic drives leads to the increase in the peak torque loads for the actuators. However, the effect is limited. It can be shown that further increase of the value of I_s (for example, taking $I_s > 2$) would lead to significant changes in the peak torques. This is related to the fact that the torques requested by the feedback controller are determined by the values of control error accumulated by the system. Larger values of I_s lead to slower control response and higher values of control error, which in turn leads the control system to requesting larger torques.

Figure 3. The control actions; simulation results for a model with elastic elements

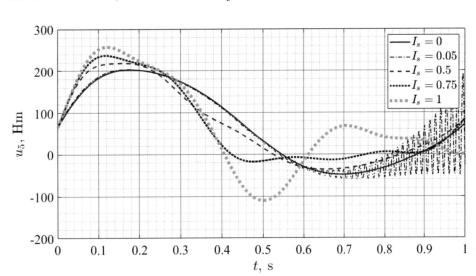

It can also be observed that for smaller values of I_s the torques show oscillatory behavior. This is related to the fact that the simulation becomes poorly conditioned numerically as I_s approaches zero.

It should be noted that the case considered here is simplified, as the inertial parameters and the spring-damper system parameters for each of the elastic drives are taken to be identical. Choosing these parameters individually for each of these actuators and tuning them together with the controller parameters could be beneficial in terms of the optimization of the system's performance. Examples of how such optimization procedure could be executed can be found in (Jatsun et al., 2016a, 2016d, 2017b).

Study of the Effects of Torque Saturation

Previously shown results are achieved for the case when the actuators' output torques were not limited. In practice this is not the case, and motion regimes where the actuators are torque saturated (producing the maximal torque possible) are common. In (Savin, 2018) it was demonstrated that introduction of joint torque limits significantly changes the characteristics of the control system behavior for a walking robot using a number of different controllers, including CLQR. It is of particular interest to investigate how torque saturation affects the robot with integrated elastic elements.

One of the ways to evaluate the performance of the control system is with mean control error. Here, the following criteria is used:

$$e_m = \frac{1}{n(t_f - t_0)} \sum_{i=1}^{n} \int_{t_0}^{t_f} (q_i^* - q_i) dt \,, \tag{16}$$

where q_i are elements of the vector $\mathbf{q}$, t_0 and t_f are the beginning and the end times of the motion, n is the number of generalized coordinated of the system.

To assess the influence of the torque saturation, the following series of experiments are conducted. In the first experiment, 9 simulations different values of $\mathbf{K}_p$, $\mathbf{K}_d$ and $\mathbf{H}_s$ are used and no joint torque limits are applied. The results are shown in the table 2. The second experiment has the same values of $\mathbf{K}_p$, $\mathbf{K}_d$ and $\mathbf{H}_s$ but this time the joint torques are constrained to be less than or equal to u_{min} in absolute values. The results of the second experiment for $u_{min} = 150$ Nm are shown in the table 3.

Comparing the results of the experiments, the following observations can be made. In each case the increase in the values of $\mathbf{K}_p$ and $\mathbf{K}_d$ leads to improvements in the behavior of the control system in terms of the chosen metric. Also, in each case the larger values of $\mathbf{H}_s$ are associated with worse performance of the control system. However, these effects are less pronounced in the system with torque limits. This trend becomes even more apparent for stricter torque limits (not shown here).

It should also be noted that the mean control error higher than a given value might be unacceptable from the safety and precision points of view. These considerations could be based on the safety margins embedded in the trajectory generation algorithm (the ZMP and center of mass trajectory generators in particular). With this in mind, the results shown in tables 2 and 3 can be used to decide the admissible regions of parameters of the elastic drives.

Table 2. Simulation results for the case without joint torque limits

Value of $\mathbf{H}_s$	Value of $\mathbf{K}_p$	Value of $\mathbf{K}_d$	Value of e_m
$\mathbf{H}_s = 0.1\ \mathbf{I}$	$\mathbf{K}_p = 10\ \mathbf{I}$	$\mathbf{K}_d = 1\ \mathbf{I}$	0.015
$\mathbf{H}_s = 0.1\ \mathbf{I}$	$\mathbf{K}_p = 100\ \mathbf{I}$	$\mathbf{K}_d = 10\ \mathbf{I}$	0.0078
$\mathbf{H}_s = 0.1\ \mathbf{I}$	$\mathbf{K}_p = 1000\ \mathbf{I}$	$\mathbf{K}_d = 100\ \mathbf{I}$	0.0076
$\mathbf{H}_s = 1\ \mathbf{I}$	$\mathbf{K}_p = 10\ \mathbf{I}$	$\mathbf{K}_d = 1\ \mathbf{I}$	0.28
$\mathbf{H}_s = 1\ \mathbf{I}$	$\mathbf{K}_p = 100\ \mathbf{I}$	$\mathbf{K}_d = 10\ \mathbf{I}$	0.014
$\mathbf{H}_s = 1\ \mathbf{I}$	$\mathbf{K}_p = 1000\ \mathbf{I}$	$\mathbf{K}_d = 100\ \mathbf{I}$	0.0081
$\mathbf{H}_s = 10\ \mathbf{I}$	$\mathbf{K}_p = 10\ \mathbf{I}$	$\mathbf{K}_d = 1\ \mathbf{I}$	0.39
$\mathbf{H}_s = 10\ \mathbf{I}$	$\mathbf{K}_p = 100\ \mathbf{I}$	$\mathbf{K}_d = 10\ \mathbf{I}$	0.18
$\mathbf{H}_s = 10\ \mathbf{I}$	$\mathbf{K}_p = 1000\ \mathbf{I}$	$\mathbf{K}_d = 100\ \mathbf{I}$	0.018

Table 3. Simulation results for the case with joint torque limits set at 150 Nm

Value of $\mathbf{H}_s$	Value of $\mathbf{K}_p$	Value of $\mathbf{K}_d$	Value of e_m
$\mathbf{H}_s = 0.1\ \mathbf{I}$	$\mathbf{K}_p = 10\ \mathbf{I}$	$\mathbf{K}_d = 1\ \mathbf{I}$	0.034
$\mathbf{H}_s = 0.1\ \mathbf{I}$	$\mathbf{K}_p = 100\ \mathbf{I}$	$\mathbf{K}_d = 10\ \mathbf{I}$	0.02
$\mathbf{H}_s = 0.1\ \mathbf{I}$	$\mathbf{K}_p = 1000\ \mathbf{I}$	$\mathbf{K}_d = 100\ \mathbf{I}$	0.02
$\mathbf{H}_s = 1\ \mathbf{I}$	$\mathbf{K}_p = 10\ \mathbf{I}$	$\mathbf{K}_d = 1\ \mathbf{I}$	0.31
$\mathbf{H}_s = 1\ \mathbf{I}$	$\mathbf{K}_p = 100\ \mathbf{I}$	$\mathbf{K}_d = 10\ \mathbf{I}$	0.033
$\mathbf{H}_s = 1\ \mathbf{I}$	$\mathbf{K}_p = 1000\ \mathbf{I}$	$\mathbf{K}_d = 100\ \mathbf{I}$	0.021
$\mathbf{H}_s = 10\ \mathbf{I}$	$\mathbf{K}_p = 10\ \mathbf{I}$	$\mathbf{K}_d = 1\ \mathbf{I}$	0.55
$\mathbf{H}_s = 10\ \mathbf{I}$	$\mathbf{K}_p = 100\ \mathbf{I}$	$\mathbf{K}_d = 10\ \mathbf{I}$	0.27
$\mathbf{H}_s = 10\ \mathbf{I}$	$\mathbf{K}_p = 1000\ \mathbf{I}$	$\mathbf{K}_d = 100\ \mathbf{I}$	0.036

In order to better illustrate the relations between the performance of the control system and the parameters $\mathbf{H}_s$, $\mathbf{K}_p$ and $\mathbf{K}_d$, the dependency of e_m on $\mathbf{K}_p$ for different constant values of $\mathbf{H}_s$ are calculated and plotted. In each experiment the value of $\mathbf{K}_d$ was chosen to be $\mathbf{K}_d = 0.1\mathbf{K}_p$. The simulations are carried out for $u_{\min} = 120$ Nm. Figure 4 shows the obtained dependencies.

As can be seen from the figure 4, the mean error e_m depend both on $\mathbf{K}_p$ and $\mathbf{H}_s$. However, the influence of $\mathbf{H}_s$ is diminishing as $\mathbf{K}_p$ grows. Choosing the minimal acceptable mean control error allows to use the plots shown in figure 4 to choose the minimal acceptable values of $\mathbf{K}_p$ for a given $\mathbf{H}_s$.

Study of the Effects of Nonlinear Sensors

In (Savin, 2018; Savin et al., 2018) it was observed that the nonlinear joint sensors, in particular sensors that demonstrate signal quantization and white noise, can affect the quality of the control system of walking robots. The effects of these nonlinear sensors show in motor torques commanded by the model-based controllers. The presence of the integrated elastic elements can serve to minimize this effect.

Figure 4. Dependencies of e_m on the parameters of the elastic drives; the horizontal scale in logarithmic

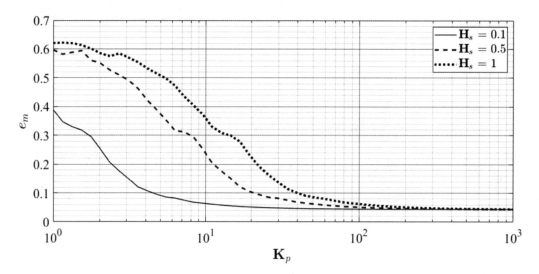

The nonlinear sensor model used here includes white noise with amplitude 1 degree and quantization with a step of 2 degrees. The modelling methods for this type of sensors are discussed in (Savin et al., 2018) in more detail. Figure 5 shows the time functions $u_5(t)$ and $u_{s,5}(t)$ found in simulation with the nonlinear sensor model; $u_5(t)$ and $u_{s,5}(t)$ are the torques produced by the actuator and the spring-damper system installed in the joint O_1 respectively. The joint torques limits are set at $u_{\min} = 180$ Nm.

As can be seen from the figure 5, the torques generated by the actuators demonstrate high frequency components related to the white noise in the sensor model. However, the torques output by the spring-damper system remain smooth. Since the links of the robot experience torque applied to them by the spring-damper system, the oscillations generated by the actuators are not affecting them. This demonstrates one of the advantages of using integrated elastic elements as part of the robot's structure.

Figure 5. The control actions; simulation results for a model with nonlinear sensors

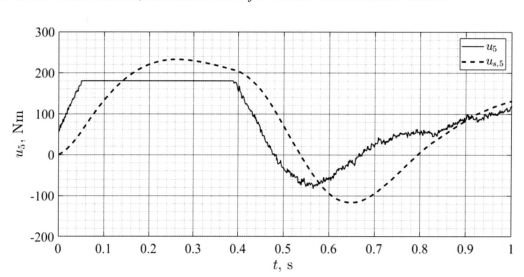

FUTURE RESEARCH DIRECTIONS

There are two major venues for the future research in the control of walking robots with integrated elastic elements: development of the design tools and the methods for choosing the parameters of the elastic drives and the development of new control techniques specific for this type of robots. One of the promising research directions is studying how much of the precise model information is needed for the model-based control techniques to work appropriately with the discussed robots. By their nature, the robots with elastic drives are difficult to model exactly, and as it was shown in this chapter, the exact models are not needed for the control applications. This suggests that there are opportunities to simplify the model-based control formulations, potentially making them more robust and efficient. For example, it is important to study how difficult-to-model effects, such as joint friction, affect the quality of the control system when they are excluded from the robot model available to the feedback controller.

Another promising research direction is dynamic model identification for the robots with integrated elastic elements. It is desirable to have algorithms that can generate and update the robot's model dynamically, as it would mitigate one of the prominent difficulties in the practical walking robotics, namely the need to develop and validate models for individual robots, which slows down the iterative design process often employed in robotics.

CONCLUSION

In this chapter the control methods for walking robots with integrated elastic elements were discussed. The focus of the chapter was on the aspects that are specific to the robots with the elastic elements, rather than the ones that are general for all types of walking robots. In particular, the effects that the introduction of elastic elements has on the feedback control design and the control system performance had been considered.

It was demonstrated that for the case when the actuators are ideal, i.e. have no torque limits, introducing elastic elements increases peak torques. The behavior of the resulting system depends on the inertia of the gearbox and motor shaft as well as on the parameters of the integrated elastic elements modelled here as a spring-damper system. This behavior is persistent for the systems with joint torque limits, however in those cases the individual influences of the mentioned above parameters tend to be smaller.

One of the conclusions that can be made from the results shown in this chapter is that for the systems where the elastic effects are inevitable (which covers a wide range of bipeds, including most of the popular designs that had been successfully tested) it is advantageous to explicitly design the system to have particular spring-damper system parameters, possibly by using elastic drives. Since the motor torques have significant effects on the resulting behavior of the robot, the choice of the elastic elements' parameters needs to be made in accordance to the given motor specifications. Alternatively, both the motors and the elastic drive components can be optimized simultaneously.

An additional result shown in the chapter is the filtering effect of the elastic drives for the case when the noisy nonlinear sensors caused the controller to generate control actions with high frequency components. This last effect is related to the way the control system and the robot are modelled; in particular, the motor current dynamics is omitted from the model. The advantages of using elastic drives related to torque filtering should be studied further, taking into account the motor models.

ACKNOWLEDGMENT

The reported study was funded by Russian Foundation of Basic Research (RFBR) according to the research project Nº18-38-00140\18.

REFERENCES

Armada, M., Prieto, M., Akinfiev, T., Fernández, R., de Santos, P. G., Garcia, E., ... Estremera, J. (2005). On the design and development of climbing and walking robots for the maritime industries. *Journal for Maritime Research*, 2(1), 9–32.

Atkeson, C. G., Babu, B. P. W., Banerjee, N., Berenson, D., Bove, C. P., Cui, X., . . . Gennert, M. (2015, November). No falls, no resets: Reliable humanoid behavior in the DARPA robotics challenge. In *Humanoid Robots (Humanoids), 2015 IEEE-RAS 15th International Conference on* (pp. 623-630). IEEE.

Bonami, P., Biegler, L. T., Conn, A. R., Cornuéjols, G., Grossmann, I. E., Laird, C. D., ... Wächter, A. (2008). An algorithmic framework for convex mixed integer nonlinear programs. *Discrete Optimization*, 5(2), 186–204. doi:10.1016/j.disopt.2006.10.011

Bouyarmane, K., Vaillant, J., Keith, F., & Kheddar, A. (2012, November). Exploring humanoid robots locomotion capabilities in virtual disaster response scenarios. In *Humanoid Robots (Humanoids), 2012 12th IEEE-RAS International Conference on* (pp. 337-342). IEEE. 10.1109/HUMANOIDS.2012.6651541

Brenan, K. E., Campbell, S. L., & Petzold, L. R. (1996). *Numerical solution of initial-value problems in differential-algebraic equations* (Vol. 14). Siam.

Buschmann, T. (2010). *Simulation and control of biped walking robots* (Doctoral dissertation). Technische Universität München.

Caron, S., Pham, Q. C., & Nakamura, Y. (2015, May). Stability of surface contacts for humanoid robots: Closed-form formulae of the contact wrench cone for rectangular support areas. In *Robotics and Automation (ICRA), 2015 IEEE International Conference on* (pp. 5107-5112). IEEE.

Chestnutt, J., Lau, M., Cheung, G., Kuffner, J., Hodgins, J., & Kanade, T. 2005, April. Footstep planning for the honda asimo humanoid. In *Robotics and Automation, 2005. ICRA 2005. Proceedings of the 2005 IEEE International Conference on* (pp. 629-634). IEEE. 10.1109/ROBOT.2005.1570188

Clary, P., Morais, P., Fern, A., & Hurst, J. (2018). *Monte-Carlo Planning for Agile Legged Locomotion*. Academic Press.

Collins, S., Ruina, A., Tedrake, R., & Wisse, M. (2005). Efficient bipedal robots based on passive-dynamic walkers. *Science*, 307(5712), 1082–1085. doi:10.1126cience.1107799 PMID:15718465

Deits, R., & Tedrake, R. (2014, November). Footstep planning on uneven terrain with mixed-integer convex optimization. In *Humanoid Robots (Humanoids), 2014 14th IEEE-RAS International Conference on* (pp. 279-286). IEEE. 10.21236/ADA609276

Deits, R., & Tedrake, R. (2015). Computing large convex regions of obstacle-free space through semidefinite programming. In *Algorithmic foundations of robotics XI* (pp. 109–124). Cham: Springer. doi:10.1007/978-3-319-16595-0_7

Feng, S., Whitman, E., Xinjilefu, X., & Atkeson, C. G. (2015). Optimization-based Full Body Control for the DARPA Robotics Challenge. *Journal of Field Robotics*, *32*(2), 293–312. doi:10.1002/rob.21559

Galloway, K., Sreenath, K., Ames, A. D., & Grizzle, J. W. (2015). Torque saturation in bipedal robotic walking through control Lyapunov function-based quadratic programs. *IEEE Access : Practical Innovations, Open Solutions*, *3*, 323–332. doi:10.1109/ACCESS.2015.2419630

Hirose, M., & Ogawa, K. (2007). Honda humanoid robots development. *Philosophical Transactions of the Royal Society of London A: Mathematical, Physical and Engineering Sciences, 365*(1850), 11-19.

Hirukawa, H., Hattori, S., Harada, K., Kajita, S., Kaneko, K., Kanehiro, F., . . . Morisawa, M. (2006, May). A universal stability criterion of the foot contact of legged robots-adios zmp. In *Robotics and Automation, 2006. ICRA 2006. Proceedings 2006 IEEE International Conference on* (pp. 1976-1983). IEEE. 10.1109/ROBOT.2006.1641995

Hong, Y. D., & Kim, J. H. (2012). An evolutionary optimized footstep planner for the navigation of humanoid robots. *International Journal of Humanoid Robotics*, *9*(01), 1250005. doi:10.1142/S0219843612500053

Hurmuzlu, Y., Génot, F., & Brogliato, B. (2004). Modeling, stability and control of biped robots—A general framework. *Automatica*, *40*(10), 1647–1664. doi:10.1016/j.automatica.2004.01.031

Jatsun, S., Savin, S., & Yatsun, A. (2016). Parameter optimization for exoskeleton control system using Sobol sequences. In *ROMANSY 21-Robot Design, Dynamics and Control* (pp. 361–368). Cham: Springer. doi:10.1007/978-3-319-33714-2_40

Jatsun, S., Savin, S., & Yatsun, A. (2016, August). A Control Strategy for a Lower Limb Exoskeleton with a Toe Joint. In *International Conference on Interactive Collaborative Robotics* (pp. 1-8). Springer. 10.1007/978-3-319-43955-6_1

Jatsun, S., Savin, S., & Yatsun, A. (2016, July). Motion control algorithm for a lower limb exoskeleton based on iterative LQR and ZMP method for trajectory generation. In *International Workshop on Medical and Service Robots* (pp. 305-317). Springer.

Jatsun, S., Savin, S., & Yatsun, A. (2016, October). Comparative analysis of global optimization-based controller tuning methods for an exoskeleton performing push recovery. In *System Theory, Control and Computing (ICSTCC), 2016 20th International Conference on* (pp. 107-112). IEEE.

Jatsun, S., Savin, S., & Yatsun, A. (2017, September). Footstep Planner Algorithm for a Lower Limb Exoskeleton Climbing Stairs. In *International Conference on Interactive Collaborative Robotics* (pp. 75-82). Springer. 10.1007/978-3-319-66471-2_9

Jatsun, S., Savin, S., Yatsun, A., & Gaponov, I. (2017). Study on a two-staged control of a lower-limb exoskeleton performing standing-up motion from a chair. In *Robot Intelligence Technology and Applications 4* (pp. 113–122). Cham: Springer. doi:10.1007/978-3-319-31293-4_10

Jatsun, S., Savin, S., Yatsun, A., & Postolnyi, A. (2017). Control system parameter optimization for lower limb exoskeleton with integrated elastic elements. In Advances in Cooperative Robotics (pp. 797-805). Academic Press.

Jatsun, S. F., Yatsun, A., & Savin, S. (2018). Investigation of Human Locomotion With a Powered Lower Limb Exoskeleton. In *Handbook of Research on Biomimetics and Biomedical Robotics* (pp. 26–47). IGI Global. doi:10.4018/978-1-5225-2993-4.ch002

Johnson, M., Shrewsbury, B., Bertrand, S., Wu, T., Duran, D., Floyd, M., ... Carff, J. (2015). Team IHMC's lessons learned from the DARPA robotics challenge trials. *Journal of Field Robotics*, *32*(2), 192–208. doi:10.1002/rob.21571

Kajita, S., Kanehiro, F., Kaneko, K., Fujiwara, K., Harada, K., Yokoi, K., & Hirukawa, H. (2003, September). Biped walking pattern generation by using preview control of zero-moment point. In *Robotics and Automation, 2003. Proceedings. ICRA'03. IEEE International Conference on* (Vol. 2, pp. 1620-1626). IEEE. 10.1109/ROBOT.2003.1241826

Kajita, S., Kanehiro, F., Kaneko, K., Yokoi, K., & Hirukawa, H. (2001). The 3D Linear Inverted Pendulum Mode: A simple modeling for a biped walking pattern generation. In *Intelligent Robots and Systems, 2001. Proceedings. 2001 IEEE/RSJ International Conference on* (Vol. 1, pp. 239-246). IEEE.

Kajita, S., Morisawa, M., Harada, K., Kaneko, K., Kanehiro, F., Fujiwara, K., & Hirukawa, H. (2006, October). Biped walking pattern generator allowing auxiliary zmp control. In *Intelligent Robots and Systems, 2006 IEEE/RSJ International Conference on* (pp. 2993-2999). IEEE. 10.1109/IROS.2006.282233

Kaneko, K., Harada, K., Kanehiro, F., Miyamori, G., & Akachi, K. (2008, September). Humanoid robot HRP-3. In *Intelligent Robots and Systems, 2008. IROS 2008. IEEE/RSJ International Conference on* (pp. 2471-2478). IEEE. 10.1109/IROS.2008.4650604

Kaneko, K., Kanehiro, F., Morisawa, M., Akachi, K., Miyamori, G., Hayashi, A., & Kanehira, N. (2011, September). Humanoid robot hrp-4-humanoid robotics platform with lightweight and slim body. In *Intelligent Robots and Systems (IROS), 2011 IEEE/RSJ International Conference on* (pp. 4400-4407). IEEE. 10.1109/IROS.2011.6094465

Khatib, O., Sentis, L., Park, J., & Warren, J. (2004). Whole-body dynamic behavior and control of human-like robots. *International Journal of Humanoid Robotics*, *1*(01), 29–43. doi:10.1142/S0219843604000058

Khusainov, R., Shimchik, I., Afanasyev, I., & Magid, E. (2015, July). Toward a human-like locomotion: modelling dynamically stable locomotion of an anthropomorphic robot in simulink environment. In *Informatics in Control, Automation and Robotics (ICINCO), 2015 12th International Conference on* (Vol. 2, pp. 141-148). IEEE. 10.5220/0005576001410148

Kuffner, J. J., Nishiwaki, K., Kagami, S., Inaba, M., & Inoue, H. (2001). Footstep planning among obstacles for biped robots. In *Intelligent Robots and Systems, 2001. Proceedings. 2001 IEEE/RSJ International Conference on* (Vol. 1, pp. 500-505). IEEE. 10.1109/IROS.2001.973406

Kuindersma, S., Deits, R., Fallon, M., Valenzuela, A., Dai, H., Permenter, F., ... Tedrake, R. (2016). Optimization-based locomotion planning, estimation, and control design for the atlas humanoid robot. *Autonomous Robots*, *40*(3), 429–455. doi:10.100710514-015-9479-3

Kuindersma, S., Permenter, F., & Tedrake, R. (2014, May). An efficiently solvable quadratic program for stabilizing dynamic locomotion. In *Robotics and Automation (ICRA), 2014 IEEE International Conference on* (pp. 2589-2594). IEEE. 10.1109/ICRA.2014.6907230

Luk, B. L., Collie, A. A., Cooke, D. S., & Chen, S. (2006). Walking and climbing service robots for safety inspection of nuclear reactor pressure vessels. *Measurement and Control, 39*(2), 43–47. doi:10.1177/002029400603900201

Mason, S., Rotella, N., Schaal, S., & Righetti, L. (2016, November). Balancing and walking using full dynamics LQR control with contact constraints. In *Humanoid Robots (Humanoids), 2016 IEEE-RAS 16th International Conference on* (pp. 63-68). IEEE. 10.1109/HUMANOIDS.2016.7803255

Mistry, M., Buchli, J., & Schaal, S. (2010, May). Inverse dynamics control of floating base systems using orthogonal decomposition. In *Robotics and Automation (ICRA), 2010 IEEE International Conference on* (pp. 3406-3412). IEEE. 10.1109/ROBOT.2010.5509646

Ogura, Y., Shimomura, K., Kondo, H., Morishima, A., Okubo, T., Momoki, S., . . . Takanishi, A. (2006, October). Human-like walking with knee stretched, heel-contact and toe-off motion by a humanoid robot. In *Intelligent Robots and Systems, 2006 IEEE/RSJ International Conference on* (pp. 3976-3981). IEEE. 10.1109/IROS.2006.281834

Panovko, G. Y., Savin, S. I., Yatsun, S. F., & Yatsun, A. S. (2016). Simulation of exoskeleton sit-to-stand movement. *Journal of Machinery Manufacture and Reliability, 45*(3), 206–210. doi:10.3103/S1052618816030110

Pratt, G. A. (2002). Low impedance walking robots. *Integrative and Comparative Biology, 42*(1), 174–181. doi:10.1093/icb/42.1.174 PMID:21708707

Pratt, G. A., Williamson, M. M., Dillworth, P., Pratt, J., & Wright, A. (1997). Stiffness isn't everything. In *Experimental robotics IV* (pp. 253-262). Springer. doi:10.1007/BFb0035216

Pratt, G. A., Willisson, P., Bolton, C., & Hofman, A. (2004, June). Late motor processing in low-impedance robots: Impedance control of series-elastic actuators. In *American Control Conference, 2004. Proceedings of the 2004* (Vol. 4, pp. 3245-3251). IEEE. 10.23919/ACC.2004.1384410

Robinson, D. W., Pratt, J. E., Paluska, D. J., & Pratt, G. A. (1999, September). Series elastic actuator development for a biomimetic walking robot. In *Advanced Intelligent Mechatronics, 1999. Proceedings. 1999 IEEE/ASME International Conference on* (pp. 561-568). IEEE. 10.1109/AIM.1999.803231

Savin, S. (2017, June). An algorithm for generating convex obstacle-free regions based on stereographic projection. In *Control and Communications (SIBCON), 2017 International Siberian Conference on* (pp. 1-6). IEEE. 10.1109/SIBCON.2017.7998590

Savin, S. (2018). *Comparative Analysis of Control Methods for Walking Robots with Nonlinear Sensors*. (Manuscript submitted for publication)

Savin, S., Jatsun, S., & Vorochaeva, L. (2017, November). Modification of Constrained LQR for Control of Walking in-pipe Robots. In Dynamics of Systems, Mechanisms and Machines (Dynamics), 2017 (pp. 1-6). IEEE. doi:10.1109/Dynamics.2017.8239502

Savin, S., Jatsun, S., & Vorochaeva, L. (2018). State observer design for a walking in-pipe robot. In *MATEC Web of Conferences* (Vol. 161, p. 03012). EDP Sciences. 10.1051/matecconf/201816103012

Savin, S., & Vorochaeva, L. (2017, June). Footstep planning for a six-legged in-pipe robot moving in spatially curved pipes. In *Control and Communications (SIBCON), 2017 International Siberian Conference on* (pp. 1-6). IEEE. 10.1109/SIBCON.2017.7998581

Savin, S., & Vorochaeva, L. (2017). Nested Quadratic Programming-based Controller for In-pipe Robots. *Proceeding of the International Conference On Industrial Engineering.*

Short, A., & Bandyopadhyay, T. (2018). Legged Motion Planning in Complex Three-Dimensional Environments. *IEEE Robotics and Automation Letters*, *3*(1), 29–36. doi:10.1109/LRA.2017.2728200

Vukobratovic, M., & Borovac, B. (2004). Zero-moment point—thirty five years of its life. *International Journal of Humanoid Robotics, 1*(1), 157-173.

Wieber, P. B. (2006, December). Trajectory free linear model predictive control for stable walking in the presence of strong perturbations. In *Humanoid Robots, 2006 6th IEEE-RAS International Conference on* (pp. 137-142). IEEE. 10.1109/ICHR.2006.321375

Xie, Z., Berseth, G., Clary, P., Hurst, J., & van de Panne, M. (2018). *Feedback Control For Cassie With Deep Reinforcement Learning.* arXiv preprint arXiv:1803.05580

Yan, T., Cempini, M., Oddo, C. M., & Vitiello, N. (2015). Review of assistive strategies in powered lower-limb orthoses and exoskeletons. *Robotics and Autonomous Systems*, *64*, 120–136. doi:10.1016/j.robot.2014.09.032

Young, A. J., & Ferris, D. P. (2017). State of the art and future directions for lower limb robotic exoskeletons. *IEEE Transactions on Neural Systems and Rehabilitation Engineering*, *25*(2), 171–182. doi:10.1109/TNSRE.2016.2521160 PMID:26829794

Zheng, Y., Lin, M. C., Manocha, D., Adiwahono, A. H., & Chew, C. M. (2010, October). A walking pattern generator for biped robots on uneven terrains. In *Intelligent Robots and Systems (IROS), 2010 IEEE/RSJ International Conference on* (pp. 4483-4488). IEEE. 10.1109/IROS.2010.5653079

ADDITIONAL READING

Aghili, F. (2005). A unified approach for inverse and direct dynamics of constrained multibody systems based on linear projection operator: Applications to control and simulation. *IEEE Transactions on Robotics*, *21*(5), 834–849. doi:10.1109/TRO.2005.851380

Giusti, A., Malzahn, J., Tsagarakis, N. G., & Althoff, M. (2017, May). Combined inverse-dynamics/passivity-based control for robots with elastic joints. In *Robotics and Automation (ICRA), 2017 IEEE International Conference on* (pp. 5281-5288). IEEE.

Kikuuwe, R., Yasukouchi, S., Fujimoto, H., & Yamamoto, M. (2010). Proxy-based sliding mode control: A safer extension of PID position control. *IEEE Transactions on Robotics*, *26*(4), 670–683. doi:10.1109/TRO.2010.2051188

Lakatos, D., Friedl, W., & Albu-Schäffer, A. (2017). Eigenmodes of Nonlinear Dynamics: Definition, Existence, and Embodiment into Legged Robots With Elastic Elements. *IEEE Robotics and Automation Letters*, *2*(2), 1062–1069.

Mazumdar, A., Spencer, S. J., Hobart, C., Salton, J., Quigley, M., Wu, T., ... Buerger, S. P. (2017). Parallel elastic elements improve energy efficiency on the STEPPR bipedal walking robot. *IEEE/ASME Transactions on Mechatronics*, *22*(2), 898–908. doi:10.1109/TMECH.2016.2631170

Posa, M., Kuindersma, S., & Tedrake, R. (2016, May). Optimization and stabilization of trajectories for constrained dynamical systems. In *Robotics and Automation (ICRA), 2016 IEEE International Conference on* (pp. 1366-1373). IEEE. 10.1109/ICRA.2016.7487270

Pratt, G. A. (2000). Legged robots at MIT: What's new since Raibert? *IEEE Robotics & Automation Magazine*, *7*(3), 15–19. doi:10.1109/100.876907

Raibert, M. H. (1986). *Legged robots that balance*. MIT press. doi:10.1109/MEX.1986.4307016

Tomei, P. (1991). A simple PD controller for robots with elastic joints. *IEEE Transactions on Automatic Control*, *36*(10), 1208–1213. doi:10.1109/9.90238

KEY TERMS AND DEFINITIONS

Bipedal Walking Robot: A mobile robot with two legs, which primary mode of operation requires these legs to periodically acquire and break contact with the supporting surface.

Constrained Linear Quadratic Regulator: A modification of the linear quadratic regulator that takes into account the explicit mechanical constraints.

Control Error: The difference between the desired values of the generalized coordinates and their actual values.

Elastic Drive: An actuator with an integrated elastic element installed.

Generalized Inertia Matrix: The matrix of the quadratic form of the kinetic energy of the mechanical system, obtained for the given choice of generalized coordinates.

Integrated Elastic Element: A mechanical system acting as a spring and damper, connected to the output shaft of the actuator's gearbox.

Sensor Model: A mathematical model that describes the relations between the sensor output and the actual values of the measured parameters.

Torque Saturation: An effect that manifests in an electric motor being able to produce torques higher than a given threshold values.

Compilation of References

9.   Hasan, E., & Cáceres, I. (2015). Heart Rate Variability Analysis Based on Photoplethysmographic Signals. *Revista Cubana de Informática Médica, 7*(2), 113–121.

Abdessalem, W., Ashour, A. S., Ben Sassi, D., & Dey, N. (2015). *MEDLINE Text Mining: An Enhancement Genetic Algorithm based Approach for Document Clustering, Applications of Intelligent Optimization in Biology and Medicine: Current Trends and Open Problems.* Springer.

Abrahamsson, E., Forni, T., Skeppstedt, M., & Kvist, M. (2014). Medical text simplification using synonym replacement: Adapting assessment of word difficulty to a compounding language. *Proceedings of the 3rd Workshop on Predicting and Improving Text Readability for Target Reader Populations (PITR)@ EACL,* 57–65. 10.3115/v1/W14-1207

Acharjya, D., & Anitha, A. (2017). A Comparative Study of Statistical and Rough Computing Models in Predictive Data Analysis, April 2017. *International Journal of Ambient Computing and Intelligence, 8*(2), 32–51. doi:10.4018/IJACI.2017040103

Acharya, U. R., Joseph, K. P., Kannathal, N., Lim, C. M., & Suri, J. S. (2006). Heart rate variability: A review. *Medical & Biological Engineering & Computing, 44*(12), 1031–1051. doi:10.100711517-006-0119-0 PMID:17111118

Acharya, U., Suri, J., Spaan, J., & Krishnan, S. (2007). *Advances in Cardiac Signal Processing.* Berlin: Springer. doi:10.1007/978-3-540-36675-1

Admoni, H., Bank, C., Tan, J., Toneva, M., & Scassellati, B. (2011, January). Robot gaze does not reflexively cue human attention. In *Proceedings of the Annual Meeting of the Cognitive Science Society* (*Vol. 33*, No. 33). Academic Press.

Åhlfeldt, H., Borin, L., Daumke, P., Grabar, N., Hallett, C., Hardcastle, D., . . . Willis, A. (2006). *Literature review on patient-friendly documentation systems?* Technical Report 2006/04, Department of Computing, Faculty of Mathematics and Computing, The Open University, Milton Keynes, UK.

Ahmad, A., Whitworth, B., Zeshan, F., Bertino, E., & Friedman, R. (2017). Extending social networks with delegation. In *Computers & Security* (Vol. 70, pp. 546–564). Elsevier.

Ai, G., Sato, N., Singh, B., & Wagatsuma, H. (2016). Direction and viewing area-sensitive influence of EOG artifacts revealed in the EEG topographic pattern analysis. *Cognitive Neurodynamics, 10*(4), 301–314. doi:10.100711571-016-9382-4 PMID:27468318

Ai, G., Shoji, K., Wagatsuma, H., & Yasukawa, M. (2014). A Structure of Recognition for Natural and Artificial Scenes: Effect of Horticultural Therapy Focusing on Figure-Ground Organization. In *Advanced Intelligent Systems* (pp. 189–196). Cham: Springer. doi:10.1007/978-3-319-05500-8_18

Akhtar, M. T., Mitsuhashi, W., & James, C. J. (2012). Employing spatially constrained ICA and wavelet denoising, for automatic removal of artifacts from multichannel EEG data. *Signal Processing*, *92*(2), 401–416. doi:10.1016/j. sigpro.2011.08.005

Aldebaran - SoftBank Robotics. (n.d.). Retrieved from https://www.softbankrobotics.com/emea/ja

Aldonin, G. M., Soldatov, A. V., & Cherepanov, V. V. (2018, July). Wavelet Analysis of Cardiac Electrical Activity Signals. *Biomedical Engineering*, *52*(2), 120–124. doi:10.100710527-018-9796-x

Al-Fahoum, A. S., & Al-Fraihat, A. A. (2014). Methods of EEG signal features extraction using linear analysis in frequency and time-frequency domains. *ISRN Neuroscience*. PMID:24967316

Al-Hudhud, G. (2014). Affective command-based control system integrating brain signals in commands control systems. *Computers in Human Behavior*, *30*, 535–541. doi:10.1016/j.chb.2013.06.038

Alirezaie, M. (2015). *Bridging the semantic gap between sensor data and ontological knowledge* (Ph.D. dissertation). Örebro University.

Alirezaie, M., Hammar, K., Blomqvist, E., Nyström, M., & Ivanova, V. (2018b). *SmartEnv Ontology in E-care@home*. 9th Workshop on Semantic Sensor Networks (SSN) held in conjunction with ISWC 2018, Monterey, CA.

Alirezaie, M., Hammar, K., & Blomqvist, E. (2018a). SmartEnv as a network of ontology patterns. *Semantic Web*, *9*(6), 903–918.

Al-Janabi, Al-Shourbaji, Shojafar, & Shamshirband. (2017). Survey of main challenges (security and privacy) in wireless body area networks for healthcare applications. *Egyptian Informatics Journal, 18*(2), 113-122.

Allen, J. (2007). Photoplethysmography and its application in clinical physiological measurement. *Physiological Measurement*, *28*(3), R1–R39. doi:10.1088/0967-3334/28/3/R01 PMID:17322588

Allison, T., Goff, W. R., & Wood, C. C. (1979). Auditory, Somatosensory and Visual Evoked Potentials in the Diagnosis of Neuropathology: Recording Considerations and Normative Data. *Human Evoked Potentials*, 9. 10.1007/978-1-4684-3483-5_1

Alves-Oliveira, P., Sequeira, P., & Paiva, A. (2016). *The role that an educational robot plays*. Paper presented at the 2016 25th IEEE International Symposium on Robot and Human Interactive Communication (RO-MAN).

Amalric, M., Wang, L., Pica, P., Figueira, S., Sigman, M., & Dehaene, S. (2017). The language of geometry: Fast comprehension of geometrical primitives and rules in human adults and preschoolers. *PLoS Computational Biology*, *13*(1), e1005273. doi:10.1371/journal.pcbi.1005273 PMID:28125595

Amanatiadis, A., Kaburlasos, V. G., Dardani, C., & Chatzichristofis, S. A. (2017, September). Interactive social robots in special education. In *2017 IEEE 7th International Conference on Consumer Electronics-Berlin (ICCE-Berlin)* (pp. 126-129). IEEE. 10.1109/ICCE-Berlin.2017.8210609

Amelkin, V., Bullo, F., & Singh, A. K. (2017). Polar Opinion Dynamics in Social Networks. *IEEE Transactions on Automatic Control*, *62*(11), 5650–5665. doi:10.1109/TAC.2017.2694341

Analog Devices, Inc. (2011). ADXL345. Norwood, U.S.A. Atmel Corporation. (2010). 8-bit AVR Microcontroller with 64K/128K/256K Bytes In-System Programmable Flash. Preliminary Summary. Atmel Corporation.

Anderson, R., & Parrish, J. (1981). The optics of human skin. *The Journal of Investigative Dermatology*, *77*(1), 13–19. doi:10.1111/1523-1747.ep12479191 PMID:7252245

Andujar, C. (1999). Geometry Simplication. Technical Report, Department of Computer Science, Universitat Politecnica De Catalunya, Barcelona, Spain.

Angelov, G., & Zahariev, R. (2017) Research and realization of TCP/IP communication with user interface in service robot, based on ROS node. *Pr. TUSofia, XXVI International Conference ADP-2017*, 304-308.

Antoine, E., & Grabar, N. (2017). Acquisition of Expert/Non-Expert Vocabulary from Reformulations. *Studies in Health Technology and Informatics*, *235*, 521–525. PMID:28423847

Anzalone, S. M., Tilmont, E., Boucenna, S., Xavier, J., Jouen, A. L., Bodeau, N., ... Chetouani, M. (2014). How children with autism spectrum disorder behave and explore the 4-dimensional (spatial 3D+ time) environment during a joint attention induction task with a robot. *Research in Autism Spectrum Disorders*, *8*(7), 814–826. doi:10.1016/j.rasd.2014.03.002

Ardito, C., Buono, P., Costabile, M. F., Lanzilotti, R., & Piccinno, A. (2009). Enabling interactive exploration of cultural heritage: An experience of designing systems for mobile devices. *Knowledge, Technology & Policy*, *22*(1), 79–86. doi:10.100712130-009-9079-7

Aresti-Bartolome, N., & Garcia-Zapirain, B. (2014). Technologies as support tools for persons with autistic spectrum disorder: A systematic review. *International Journal of Environmental Research and Public Health*, *11*(8), 7767–7802. doi:10.3390/ijerph110807767 PMID:25093654

Armada, M., Prieto, M., Akinfiev, T., Fernández, R., de Santos, P. G., Garcia, E., ... Estremera, J. (2005). On the design and development of climbing and walking robots for the maritime industries. *Journal for Maritime Research*, *2*(1), 9–32.

Aronson, J., Liang, T., & Turban, E. (2005). *Decision Support Systems and Intelligent Systems*. Pearson Prentice-Hall.

Artale, A., Franconi, E., Guarino, N., & Pazzi, L. (1996). Past-whole relations in object centered systems: An Overview. *Data & Knowledge Engineering*, *20*(3), 347–383. doi:10.1016/S0169-023X(96)00013-4

Artstein, R., & Poesio, M. (2008). Inter-coder agreement for computational linguistics. *Computational Linguistics*, *34*(4), 555–596. doi:10.1162/coli.07-034-R2

Atkeson, C. G., Babu, B. P. W., Banerjee, N., Berenson, D., Bove, C. P., Cui, X., . . . Gennert, M. (2015, November). No falls, no resets: Reliable humanoid behavior in the DARPA robotics challenge. In *Humanoid Robots (Humanoids), 2015 IEEE-RAS 15th International Conference on* (pp. 623-630). IEEE.

Badcock, N. A., Mousikou, P., Mahajan, Y., de Lissa, P., Thie, J., & McArthur, G. (2013). Validation of the Emotiv EPOC ® EEG gaming system for measuring research quality auditory ERPs. *PeerJ*, *1*, e38. doi:10.7717/peerj.38 PMID:23638374

Baddeley, A. D. (1997). *Human Memory: Theory and Practice*. Psychology Press.

Balas-Timar, Balas, Breaz, Ashour, & Dey. (2016). Technique for scoring competency based behavioural interviews: a fuzzy approach. *Conference: congresului internaţional cercetarea modernă în psihologie*.

Baldassarre, G., & Mirolli, M. (2013). Intrinsically motivated learning systems: an overview. In *Intrinsically Motivated Learning in Natural and Artificial Systems* (pp. 1–14). Berlin: Springer. doi:10.1007/978-3-642-32375-1_1

Ball, T., Kern, M., Mutschler, I., Aertsen, A., & Schulze-Bonhage, A. (2009). Signal quality of simultaneously recorded invasive and non-invasive EEG. *NeuroImage*, *46*(3), 708–716. doi:10.1016/j.neuroimage.2009.02.028 PMID:19264143

Band, J., & Gerafi, J. (2015). *Fair Use/Fair Dealing Handbook*. Retrieved from http://infojustice.org/wp-content/uploads/2015/03/fair-use-handbook-march-2015.pdf

Bandyopadhyay, A., & Kar, S. (2018). Coevolution of cooperation and network structure in social dilemmas in evolutionary dynamic complex network. *Applied Mathematics and Computation, 320*, 710-730.

Barakova, E. I., Bajracharya, P., Willemsen, M., Lourens, T., & Huskens, B. (2015). Long term LEGO therapy with humanoid robot for children with ASD. *Expert Systems: International Journal of Knowledge Engineering and Neural Networks*, *32*(6), 698–709. doi:10.1111/exsy.12098

Barakova, E. I., De Haas, M., Kuijpers, W., Irigoyen, N., & Betancourt, A. (2018). Socially grounded game strategy enhances bonding and perceived smartness of a humanoid robot. *Connection Science*, *30*(1), 81–98. doi:10.1080/0954 0091.2017.1350938

Barakova, E. I., Gillesena, J. C. C., Huskens, B. E. B. M., & Lourens, T. (2013). End-user programming architecture facilitates the uptake of robots in social therapies. *Robotics and Autonomous Systems*, *61*(7), 704–713. doi:10.1016/j. robot.2012.08.001

Barakova, E. I., Kim, M. G., & Lourens, T. (2014, June). Development of a robot-based environment for training children with autism. In *International Conference on Universal Access in Human-Computer Interaction* (pp. 601-612). Springer. 10.1007/978-3-319-07446-7_58

Barbaresi, A. (2015). Ad hoc and general-purpose corpus construction from web sources (PhD thesis). École Normale Supérieure de Lyon (Université de Lyon), France.

Barbaresi, A. (2016). Efficient construction of metadata-enhanced web corpora. In *10th Web as Corpus Workshop* (pp. 7-16). Academic Press. 10.18653/v1/W16-2602

Barbieri, L., Bruno, F., & Muzzupappa, M. (2018). User-centered design of a virtual reality exhibit for archaeological museums. *International Journal on Interactive Design and Manufacturing*, *12*(2), 561–571. doi:10.100712008-017-0414-z

Barbu, E. (2016). *D3.2: Multilingual Corpus. Project Deliverable. EXPERT (Exploiting Empirical appRoaches to Translation), Project funded by the People Programme*. Marie Curie Actions.

Baroni, M., & Bernardini, S. (2004). BootCaT: Bootstrapping Corpora and Terms from the Web. *LREC 2004 - Fourth International Conference On Language Resources And Evaluation*.

Baroni, M., Dinu, G., & Kruszewski, G. (2014). Don't count, predict! A systematic comparison of context-counting vs. context-predicting semantic vectors. In *Proceedings of the 52nd Annual Meeting of the Association for Computational Linguistics* (*Vol. 1*, pp. 238-247). Academic Press. 10.3115/v1/P14-1023

Baroni, M., Kilgarriff, A., Pomikálek, J., & Rychlý, P. (2006). WebBootCaT: instant domain-specific corpora to support human translators. In *Proceedings of EAMT* (pp. 247-252). Academic Press.

Baroni, M., Bernardini, S., Ferraresi, A., & Zanchetta, E. (2009). The WaCky wide web: A collection of very large linguistically processed web-crawled corpora. *Language Resources and Evaluation*, *43*(3), 209–226. doi:10.100710579-009-9081-4

Barraclough, N. E., & Perrett, D. I. (2011). From single cells to social perception. *Philosophical Transactions of the Royal Society of London. Series B, Biological Sciences*, *366*(1571), 1739–1752. doi:10.1098/rstb.2010.0352 PMID:21536557

Barrett, L. F. (2009). The future of psychology: Connecting mind to brain. *Perspectives on Psychological Science*, *4*(4), 326–339. doi:10.1111/j.1745-6924.2009.01134.x

Basili, R., Pazienza, M. T., & Velardi, P. (1993). Acquisition of selectional patterns in sublanguages. *Machine Translation*, *8*(3), 175–201. doi:10.1007/BF00982638

Beach, P., & McConnel, J. (2018). Eye tracking methodology for studying teacher learning: A review of the research. *International Journal of Research & Method in Education*, 1–17. doi:10.1080/1743727X.2018.1496415

Bechara, A., Damasio, H., & Damasio, A. R. (2000). Emotion, decision making and the orbitofrontal cortex. *Cerebral Cortex*, *10*(3), 295–307. doi:10.1093/cercor/10.3.295

Beer, M., Armitt, G., Van Bruggen, J., Daniels, R., Ghyselen, L., Green, S., … Sixsmith, A. (2001). Running a European Internet school - OTIS at work. In *Advanced Learning Technologies, 2001. Proceedings. IEEE International Conference on*. IEEE.

Bell, M. (2008). Toward a Definition of "Virtual Worlds". *Journal of Virtual Worlds Research*, *1*(1). doi:10.4101/jvwr.v1i1.283

Belpaeme, T., Baxter, P., De Greeff, J., Kennedy, J., Read, R., Looije, R., ... Zelati, M. C. (2013, October). Child-robot interaction: Perspectives and challenges. In *International Conference on Social Robotics* (pp. 452-459). Springer. 10.1007/978-3-319-02675-6_45

Benitti, F. (2012). Exploring the Educational Potential of Robotics in Schools: A Systematic Review. *Computers & Education*, *58*(3), 978–988. doi:10.1016/j.compedu.2011.10.006

Berger, T., & Todorov, T. (2008). Improving the Watermarking Process With Usage of Block Error-Correcting Codes. *Serdica Journal of Computing*, *2*, 163–180.

Berg, P., & Scherg, M. (1991). Dipole models of eye movements and blinks. *Electroencephalography and Clinical Neurophysiology*, *79*(1), 36–44. doi:10.1016/0013-4694(91)90154-V PMID:1713550

Berg, P., & Scherg, M. (1994). A multiple source approach to the correction of eye artifacts. *Electroencephalography and Clinical Neurophysiology*, *90*(3), 229–241. doi:10.1016/0013-4694(94)90094-9 PMID:7511504

Berners-Lee, T., & Fischetti, M. (2008). *Weaving the Web: The Original Design and Ultimate Destiny of the World Wide Web by Its Inventor*. Paw Prints.

Biemann, C., Heyer, G., Quasthoff, U., & Richter, M. (2007). The Leipzig Corpora Collection-monolingual corpora of standard size. *Proceedings of Corpus Linguistic*.

Biemann, C., Bildhauer, F., Evert, S., Goldhahn, D., Quasthoff, U., Schäfer, R., ... Zesch, T. (2013). Scalable Construction of High-Quality Web Corpora. *JLCL*, *28*(2), 23–59.

Bigeard, E., Grabar, N., & Thiessard, F. (2018). Detection and Analysis of Drug Misuses. A Study Based on Social Media Messages. *Frontiers in Pharmacology*, *9*, 2018. doi:10.3389/fphar.2018.00791 PMID:30140224

Bjoern, M. (2015). *ISO/TS 15066 - Collaborative Robots - Present Status*. Conference: European Robotics Forum 2015, ABB Germany, Corporate Research, Vienna, Austria.

Bjoern, M., & Reisinger, Th. (2016). *Example Application of ISO/TS 15066 to a Collaborative Assembly Scenario*. 47th International Symposium on Robotics (ISR 2016), Munich, Germany.

Bjork, R. A., Metcalfe, J., & Shimamura, A. P. (1994). *Metacognition: Knowing about knowing*. Academic Press.

Blagoeva-Hazarbassanova, E. (2016). How "Hard Times" Stimulate Reforms – The Case of the Bulgarian Higher Education. *International Journal Knowledge, 11*(1), 71-75.

Blasco, J. L., Iáñez, E., Úbeda, A., & Azorín, J. M. (2012). Visual evoked potential-based brain–machine interface applications to assist disabled people. *Expert Systems with Applications*, *39*(9), 7908–7918. doi:10.1016/j.eswa.2012.01.110

Blocker, D. C. (n.d.). *DSP Related*. Retrieved from https://www.dsprelated.com/freebooks/filters/DC_Blocker.html

Bobin, J., Starck, J. L., Fadili, J., & Moudden, Y. (2007). Sparsity and morphological diversity in blind source separation. *IEEE Transactions on Image Processing, 16*(11), 2662–2674. doi:10.1109/TIP.2007.906256 PMID:17990743

Bogdanova, G., & Sabev, N. (2017). The first principle in the standard for web accessibility "Web Content Accessibility Guidelines". In *Science Days 2016*. USB branch Veliko Tarnovo, Faber.

Bogdanova, G., & Sabev, N. (2017). The second principle of operability in the standard for web accessibility WCAG 2.0. *XV-National Conference with international participation "Libraries - reading - communications" - Digital conversion of literary and cultural heritage*, 302-314.

Bogdanova, G., Noev, N., Stoffel, K., & Todorov, T. (2011). 3D Modeling of Valuable Bulgarian Bells and Churches. Mathematica Balkanica, 25(5), 475-482.

Bogdanova, G., Todorov, T., & Noev, N. (2010). Digitalization and security of "Bulgarian folklore heritage" archive. In *11th International Conference on Computer Systems and Technologies, CompSysTech'10* (pp. 335-340). Sofia, Bulgaria: Institute of Mathematics and Informatics, Bulgarian Academic of Science, Bulgaria. 10.1145/1839379.1839438

Bogdanova, G., Trifonov, T., Todorov, T., & Georgieva, T. (2007). Analyzing and protecting audio and video archives of unique Bulgarian bells. Analyzing and protecting audScientific conference "Europe as a cultural space".

Bogdanova, G., Georgieva-Tsaneva, G., & Sabev, N. (2017). Characteristics ofInteractivity and Using the Interactive Technologies in System North+. *Digital Presentation and Preservation of Cultural and Scientific Heritage, VII*, 133–142.

Bonami, P., Biegler, L. T., Conn, A. R., Cornuéjols, G., Grossmann, I. E., Laird, C. D., ... Wächter, A. (2008). An algorithmic framework for convex mixed integer nonlinear programs. *Discrete Optimization, 5*(2), 186–204. doi:10.1016/j.disopt.2006.10.011

Bond, Chykina, & Jones. (2017). Social network effects on academic achievement. *The Social Science Journal, 54*(4), 438-449.

Borin, L., Grabar, N., Gronostaj, M. T., Hallett, C., Hardcastle, D., Kokkinakis, D., . . . Willis, A. (2007). Semantic Mining Deliverable D27. 2: Empowering the patient with language technology. Technical Report Semantic Mining, NOE 507505), 1–75. Göteborg: Göteborg University.

Borji, A., Sihite, D. N., & Itti, L. (2013). What stands out in a scene? A study of human explicit saliency judgment. *Vision Research, 91*, 62–77. doi:10.1016/j.visres.2013.07.016 PMID:23954536

Boucenna, S., Narzisi, A., Tilmont, E., Muratori, F., Pioggia, G., Cohen, D., & Chetouani, M. (2014). Interactive technologies for autistic children: A review. *Cognitive Computation, 6*(4), 722–740. doi:10.100712559-014-9276-x

Bouyarmane, K., Vaillant, J., Keith, F., & Kheddar, A. (2012, November). Exploring humanoid robots locomotion capabilities in virtual disaster response scenarios. In *Humanoid Robots (Humanoids), 2012 12th IEEE-RAS International Conference on* (pp. 337-342). IEEE. 10.1109/HUMANOIDS.2012.6651541

Brading, K. (2010). On composite systems: Descartes, Newton, and the law-constitutive approach. University of Notre Dame.

Branco, A., Cohen, K. B., Vossen, P., Ide, N., & Calzolari, N. (2017). Replicability and reproducibility of research results for human language technology: Introducing an LRE special section. *Language Resources and Evaluation, 51*.

Breazeal, C. (2002a). *Designing Sociable Robots*. Cambridge, MA: MIT Press.

Brenan, K. E., Campbell, S. L., & Petzold, L. R. (1996). *Numerical solution of initial-value problems in differential-algebraic equations* (Vol. 14). Siam.

Brown, W. S., & Lehmann, D. (1979). Linguistic Meaning-Related Differences in ERP Scalp Topography. In *Human Evoked Potentials* (vol. 9, pp. 31-42). Springer. 10.1007/978-1-4684-3483-5_3

Buccelletti, F., Bocci, M., Gilardi, E., Fiore, V., Calcinaro, S., Fragnoly, C., ... Franceschi, V. (2012). Linear and Nonlinear HRV Indexes in Clinical Practice. *Computational and Mathematical Methods in Medicine, 2012*.

Burgard, W., Cremers, A. B., Fox, D., Hähnel, D., Lakemeyer, G., Schulz, D., ... Thrun, S. (1999). Experiences with an interactive museum tour-guide robot. *Artificial Intelligence, 114*(1), 3–55. doi:10.1016/S0004-3702(99)00070-3

Burnard, L. (2007). *Reference guide for the British National Corpus (XML edition)*. Retrieved from http://www.natcorp.ox.ac.uk/XMLedition/URG/

Buschmann, T. (2010). *Simulation and control of biped walking robots* (Doctoral dissertation). Technische Universität München.

Cabibihan, J. J., Javed, H., Ang, M., & Aljunied, S. M. (2013). Why robots? A survey on the roles and benefits of social robots in the therapy of children with autism. *International Journal of Social Robotics, 5*(4), 593–618. doi:10.100712369-013-0202-2

Cannon, W. B. (1927). The James-Lange theory of emotions: A critical examination and an alternative theory. *The American Journal of Psychology, 39*(1/4), 106–124. doi:10.2307/1415404

Cantoni, V., Galdi, C., Nappi, M., Porta, M., & Riccio, D. (2015). GANT: Gaze analysis technique for human identification. *Pattern Recognition, 48*(4), 1027–1038. doi:10.1016/j.patcog.2014.02.017

Cardillo, E. (2015). *Medical terminologies for patients. Annex 1 to SHN Work Package 3 Deliverable D3.3*. Retrieved from http://www.semantichealthnet.eu/index.cfm/deliverables/

Cardillo, E., Tamilin, A., & Serafini, L. (2011). A Methodology for Knowledge Acquisition in Consumer-Oriented Healthcare. *Knowledge Discovery, Knowledge Engineering and Knowledge Management, 249*.

Carlucci, R. (Ed.). (2002). *Archeoguide: Augmented reality-based cultural heritage on-site guide*. Lemmer.

Caron, S., Pham, Q. C., & Nakamura, Y. (2015, May). Stability of surface contacts for humanoid robots: Closed-form formulae of the contact wrench cone for rectangular support areas. In *Robotics and Automation (ICRA), 2015 IEEE International Conference on* (pp. 5107-5112). IEEE.

Carrozino, M., & Bergamasco, M. (2010). Beyond virtual museums: Experiencing immersive virtual reality in real museums. *Journal of Cultural Heritage, 11*(4), 452–458. doi:10.1016/j.culher.2010.04.001

Caruso, M. J. (2016). *Applications of Magnetoresistive Sensors in Navigation Systems*. Plymouth: Honeywell Inc.

Cecotti, H. (2011). Spelling with non-invasive Brain–Computer Interfaces–Current and future trends. *Journal of Physiology-Paris, 105*(1-3), 106-114.

Cederblad, G. (2018). *Finding Synonyms in Medical Texts – Creating a system for automatic synonym extraction from medical texts* (Bachelor thesis). Linköping University, Department of Computer Science.

Chapman, K., Abraham, C., Jenkins, V., & Fallow, L. (2003). Lay understanding of terms used in cancer consultations. *Psycho-Oncology, 12*(6), 557–566. doi:10.1002/pon.673 PMID:12923796

CHESS. (2016). *Cultural Heritage Experiences Through Socio-Personal Interactions and Storytelling*. Retrieved from http://www.chessexperience.eu/

Chestnutt, J., Lau, M., Cheung, G., Kuffner, J., Hodgins, J., & Kanade, T. 2005, April. Footstep planning for the honda asimo humanoid. In *Robotics and Automation, 2005. ICRA 2005. Proceedings of the 2005 IEEE International Conference on* (pp. 629-634). IEEE. 10.1109/ROBOT.2005.1570188

Chevallier, C., Kohls, G., Troiani, V., Brodkin, E. S., & Schultz, R. T. (2012). The social motivation theory of autism. *Trends in Cognitive Sciences*, *16*(4), 231–239. doi:10.1016/j.tics.2012.02.007 PMID:22425667

Chik, D., Tripathi, G. N., & Wagatsuma, H. (2013, November). A Method to Deal with Prospective Risks at Home in Robotic Observations by Using a Brain-Inspired Model. In *International Conference on Neural Information Processing* (pp. 33-40). Springer. 10.1007/978-3-642-42051-1_5

Chivarov, N., Paunski, Y., Ivanova, V., Vladimirov, V., Angelov, G., Radev, D., & Shivarov, N. (2012). Intelligent modular service mobile robot controllable via internet. *IFAC International Conference "SWIIS 2012"*, 149-153.

Chivarov, N., Penkov, Sv., Angelov, G., Radev, D., Shivarov, N., & Vladimirov, V. (2012). Mixed Reality Server and Remote Interface Communication for ROS Based Robotic System. *International Journal Automation Austria*, 144-155.

Chmielik, J., & Grabar, N. (2009) Comparative study between expert and non expert biomedical writings: their morphology and semantics. In *Medical Informatics in a United and Healthy Europe: Proceedings of MIE 2009, the XXII International Congress of the European Federation for Medical Informatics* (Vol. 150, p. 359). IOS Press.

Cho, D., Ham, J., Oh, J., Park, J., Kim, S., Lee, N., & Lee, B. (2017). Detection of Stress Levels from Biosignals Measured in Virtual Reality Environments Using a Kernel-Based Extreme Learning Machine. *Sensors (Basel)*, *17*(10), 2435. doi:10.339017102435 PMID:29064457

Chon, K., Dash, S., & Ju, K. (2009). Estimation of respiratory rate from photoplethysmogram data using time-frequency spectral estimation. *IEEE Transactions on Biomedical Engineering*, *56*(8), 2054–2063. doi:10.1109/TBME.2009.2019766 PMID:19369147

Ciaramita, M., & Baroni, M. (2006). A Figure of Merit for the Evaluation of Web-Corpus Randomness. *EACL 2006 - 11th Conference of the European Chapter of the Association for Computational Linguistics*.

Clary, P., Morais, P., Fern, A., & Hurst, J. (2018). *Monte-Carlo Planning for Agile Legged Locomotion*. Academic Press.

Claveau, V., Hamon, T., Maguer, S. L., & Grabar, N. (2015). Health consumer-oriented information retrieval. *Studies in Health Technology and Informatics*, *210*, 80–84. PMID:25991106

Clifford, G., Azuaje, F., & McSharry, P. (Eds.). (2006). *Advanced Methods and Tools for ECG Data Analysis*. Boston: Artech House, Inc.

Clifford, G., & Tarassenko, L. (2004). Segmenting Cardiac-Related Data Using Sleep stages Increases Separation between Normal Subjects and Apnoeic Patients. *IOP Physiol. Means*, *25*(6), N27–N35. doi:10.1088/0967-3334/25/6/N03 PMID:15712732

Clodic, A., Fleury, S., Alami, R., Chatila, R., Bailly, G., Brèthes, L., . . . Montreuil, V. (2006). Rackham: an interactive robot-guide. 2006 IEEE ROMAN, 502–509. doi:10.1109/ROMAN.2006.314378

Cockburn, A. (2000). *Writing effective use cases, The crystal collection for software professionals*. Addison-Wesley Professional Reading.

Cocoru, D., & Boehm, M. (2016). An analytical review of text and data mining practices and approaches in Europe Policy recommendations in view of the upcoming copyright legislative proposal. *OpenForumEurope*. Retrieved from http://www.openforumeurope.org/wp-content/uploads/2016/05/TDM-Paper-Diana-Cocoru-and-Mirko-Boehm.pdf

Cohen, A., Daubechies, I., Jawerth, B., & Vial, P. (1993). "Multiresolution analysis, wavelets and fast algorithms on an interval." Comptes rendus de l'Académie des sciences. Série 1. *Mathématique, 316*(5), 417–421.

Cohen, J. (1960). A coefficient of agreement for nominal scales. *Educational and Psychological Measurement, 20*(1), 37–46. doi:10.1177/001316446002000104

Coifman, R. R., & Donoho, D. L. (1995). Translation-invariant de-noising. In *Wavelets and statistics* (pp. 125–150). New York, NY: Springer. doi:10.1007/978-1-4612-2544-7_9

Collins, S., Ruina, A., Tedrake, R., & Wisse, M. (2005). Efficient bipedal robots based on passive-dynamic walkers. *Science, 307*(5712), 1082–1085. doi:10.1126cience.1107799 PMID:15718465

Cook, A. M., & Polgar, J. M. (2015). Principles of assistive technology: introducing the Human Activity Assistive Technology model. In *Assistive technologies: Principles and practice* (pp. 1–15). St. Louis, MO: Elsevier.

Coradeschi, S., Cesta, A., Cortellessa, G., Coraci, L., Gonzalez, J., Karlsson, L., . . . Pecora, F. (2013). Giraffplus: Combining social interaction and long term monitoring for promoting independent living. In *Human system interaction (HSI), 2013 the 6th international conference on* (pp. 578-585). IEEE.

Coradeschi, S., Cesta, A., Cortellessa, G., Coraci, L., Galindo, C., Gonzalez, J., ... Loutfi, A. (2014). GiraffPlus: a system for monitoring activities and physiological parameters and promoting social interaction for elderly. In *Human-Computer Systems Interaction: Backgrounds and Applications 3* (pp. 261–271). Cham: Springer.

Cortiella, C., & Horowitz, S. H. (2014). *The state of learning disabilities: Facts, trends and emerging issues.* New York: National Center for Learning Disabilities.

Costa, Â., Castillo, J. C., Novais, P., Fernández-Caballero, A., & Simoes, R. (2012). Sensor-driven agenda for intelligent home care of the elderly. *Expert Systems with Applications, 39*(15), 12192–12204. doi:10.1016/j.eswa.2012.04.058

Costescu, C. A., & David, D. O. (2014). Attitudes toward Using Social Robots in Psychotherapy. *Transylvanian Journal of Psychology, 15*(1).

Courchesne, E., Hillyard, S. A., & Galambos, R. (1975). Stimulus novelty, task relevance and the visual evoked potential in man. *Electroencephalography and Clinical Neurophysiology, 39*(2), 131–143. doi:10.1016/0013-4694(75)90003-6 PMID:50210

Cox, I. J., Miller, M., Bloom, J., Fridrich, J., & Kalker, T. (2008). *Digital Watermarking and Steganography* (2nd ed.). Morgan Kaufmann Publishers.

Cracco, R. Q., & Cracco, J. B. (1976). Somatosensory evoked potential in man: Far field potentials. *Electroencephalography and Clinical Neurophysiology, 41*(5), 460–466. doi:10.1016/0013-4694(76)90057-2 PMID:61849

Cramer, H., Goddijn, J., Wielinga, B., & Evers, V. (2010). Effects of (in) accurate empathy and situational valence on attitudes towards robots. In *Human-Robot Interaction (HRI), 2010 5th ACM/IEEE International Conference on* (pp. 141-142). IEEE.

Creating and Connecting//Research and Guidelines on Online Social - and Educational – Networking. (2007). National School Boards Association.

Croft, R. J., & Barry, R. J. (1998). EOG correction: A new aligned-artifact average solution. *Electroencephalography and Clinical Neurophysiology, 107*(6), 395–401. doi:10.1016/S0013-4694(98)00087-X PMID:9922084

Croft, R. J., & Barry, R. J. (2002). Issues relating to the subtraction phase in EOG artefact correction of the EEG. *International Journal of Psychophysiology, 44*(3), 187–195. doi:10.1016/S0167-8760(01)00201-X PMID:12031294

Cuong, H., Sima'an, K., & Titov, I. (2016). Adapting to all domains at once: Rewarding domain invariance in SMT. *Transactions of the Association for Computational Linguistics, 4*, 99–112. doi:10.1162/tacl_a_00086

CybSPEED. (2017). *Cyber-Physical Systems for PEdagogical Rehabilitation in Special Education.* Horizon 2020 MSCA-RISE Project no. 777720, 1 Dec 2017 – 30 Nov 2021.

CybSPEED. (2017). *Cyber-Physical Systems for PEdagogical Rehabilitation in Special EDucation.* Horizon 2020 MSCA-RISE Project no. 777720, 1 Dec 2017 – 30 Nov 2021.

Dachkinov, P., Lekova, A., Tanev, T., Batbaatar, D., & Wagatsuma, H. (2019). Design and Motion Capabilities of an Emotion-Expressive Robot, "EmoSan". *Proceedings of the Joint 10th International Conference on Soft Computing and Intelligent Systems (SCIS) and 19th International Symposium on Advanced Intelligent Systems (ISIS) in conjunction with Intelligent Systems Workshop (ISWS).*

Dalgleish, T. (2004). The emotional brain. *Nature Reviews. Neuroscience, 5*(7), 583–589. doi:10.1038/nrn1432

Dalianis, Henriksson, Kvist, Velupillai, & Weegar. (2015). Health bank-a workbench for data science applications in healthcare. *CAiSE Industry Track*, 1–18.

Dalianis, H., Hassel, M., & Velupillai, S. (2009). The stockholm epr corpus–characteristics and some initial findings. *Women, 219*(906), 54.

Damasio, A. R. (1994). *Descartes' error: Emotion, rationality and the human brain.* Academic Press.

Damasio, A. R. (1998). Emotion in the perspective of an integrated nervous system. *Brain Research. Brain Research Reviews, 26*(2-3), 83–86. doi:10.1016/S0165-0173(97)00064-7

Daneman, R., & Prat, A. (2015). The Blood-Brain Barrier. *Cold Spring Harbor Perspectives in Biology, 7*(1), a020412. doi:10.1101/cshperspect.a020412 PMID:25561720

Darwin, C. (2007). *The expression of the emotions in man and animals.* New York: Filiquarian.

Das, D., Rashed, M. G., Kobayashi, Y., & Kuno, Y. (2015). Supporting human–robot interaction based on the level of visual focus of attention. *IEEE Transactions on Human-Machine Systems, 45*(6), 664–675. doi:10.1109/THMS.2015.2445856

Dautenhahn, K. (2007). Socially intelligent robots: Dimensions of human–robot interaction. *Philosophical Transactions of the Royal Society of London. Series B, Biological Sciences, 362*(1480), 679–704. doi:10.1098/rstb.2006.2004 PMID:17301026

Dautenhahn, K., Nehaniv, C. L., Walters, M. L., Robins, B., Kose-Bagci, H., Mirza, N. A., & Blow, M. (2009). KASPAR–a minimally expressive humanoid robot for human–robot interaction research. *Applied Bionics and Biomechanics, 6*(3-4), 369–397. doi:10.1155/2009/708594

Dávideková, M., & Greguš, M. (2017). Social Network Types: An Emergency Social Network Approach - A Concept of Possible Inclusion of Emergency Posts in Social Networks through an API. *2017 IEEE International Conference on Cognitive Computing (ICCC)*, 40-47. 10.1109/IEEE.ICCC.2017.13

David, O., Kilner, J. M., & Friston, K. J. (2006). Mechanisms of evoked and induced responses in MEG/EEG. *NeuroImage, 31*(4), 1580–1591. doi:10.1016/j.neuroimage.2006.02.034 PMID:16632378

Davies, M. (2009). The 385+ million word Corpus of Contemporary American English (1990–2008+). Design, architecture, and linguistic insights. *International Journal of Corpus Linguistics, 14*(2), 159–190. doi:10.1075/ijcl.14.2.02dav

Davies, M. E., & James, C. J. (2007). Source separation using single channel ICA. *Signal Processing, 87*(8), 1819–1832. doi:10.1016/j.sigpro.2007.01.011

de Haas, M., Aroyo, A. M., Barakova, E., Haselager, W., & Smeekens, I. (2016). The effect of a semi-autonomous robot on children. In *Intelligent Systems (IS), 2016 IEEE 8th International Conference on* (pp. 376-381). IEEE. 10.1109/IS.2016.7737448

de Moura & Passmore, (2010). *Computation in Real Closed Infinitesimal and Transcendental Extensions of the Rationals.* Report supported by EPSRC [grant numbers EP/I011005/1 and EP/I010335/1].

Debatisse, D., Pralong, E., Dehdashti, A., & Regli, L. (2005). Simultaneous multilobar electrocorticography (mEcoG) and scalp electroencephalography (scalp EEG) during intracranial vascular surgery: A new approach in neuromonitoring. *Clinical Neurophysiology, 116*(12), 2734–2740. doi:10.1016/j.clinph.2005.08.011 PMID:16256427

Deecke, L., & Kornhuber, H. H. (2003). Human Freedom, Reasoned Will, and the Brain: The Bereitschaftspotential Story. In M. Jahanshahi & M. Hallett (Eds.), *The Bereitschaftspotential* (pp. 283–320). Boston, MA: Springer. doi:10.1007/978-1-4615-0189-3_17

Deits, R., & Tedrake, R. (2014, November). Footstep planning on uneven terrain with mixed-integer convex optimization. In *Humanoid Robots (Humanoids), 2014 14th IEEE-RAS International Conference on* (pp. 279-286). IEEE. 10.21236/ADA609276

Deits, R., & Tedrake, R. (2015). Computing large convex regions of obstacle-free space through semidefinite programming. In *Algorithmic foundations of robotics XI* (pp. 109–124). Cham: Springer. doi:10.1007/978-3-319-16595-0_7

Deléger, L., & Zweigenbaum, P. (2009). Extracting lay paraphrases of specialized expressions from monolingual comparable medical corpora. In *Proceedings of the 2nd Workshop on Building and Using Comparable Corpora: from Parallel to Non-parallel Corpora.* Association for Computational Linguistics. 10.3115/1690339.1690343

Deléger, L., Cartoni, B., & Zweigenbaum, P. (2013). *Paraphrase detection in monolingual specialized/lay corpora.* Building and Using Comparable Corpora. doi:10.1007/978-3-642-20128-8_12

Demetriou, D. (2014). *Humanoid Robots Join Staff at Tokyo Science Museum.* Retrieved from http://www.telegraph.co.uk/news/worldnews/asia/japan/10924594/Humanoid-robots-join-staff-at-Tokyo-science-museum.html

Desagulier, G. (2017). *Corpus Linguistics and Statistics with R.* Springer. doi:10.1007/978-3-319-64572-8

Di Russo, F., Martínez, A., Sereno, M. I., Pitzalis, S., & Hillyard, S. A. (2003). Cortical sources of the early components of the visual evoked potential. *Human Brain Mapping, 15*(2), 95–111. doi:10.1002/hbm.10010 PMID:11835601

Dickey, M. D. (2005). Three-dimensional virtual worlds and distance learning: Two case studies of Active Worlds as a medium for distance education. *British Journal of Educational Technology, 36*(3), 439–451. doi:10.1111/j.1467-8535.2005.00477.x

Diehl, J. J., Crowell, C. R., Villano, M., Wier, K., Tang, K., & Riek, L. D. (2014). Clinical applications of robots in autism spectrum disorder diagnosis and treatment. In *Comprehensive Guide to Autism* (pp. 411–422). New York, NY: Springer. doi:10.1007/978-1-4614-4788-7_14

Diehl, J. J., Schmitt, L. M., Villano, M., & Crowell, C. R. (2012). The clinical use of robots for individuals with autism spectrum disorders: A critical review. *Research in Autism Spectrum Disorders, 6*(1), 249–262. doi:10.1016/j.rasd.2011.05.006 PMID:22125579

Dieterle, E., & Clarke, J. (2007). Multi-User Virtual Environments for Teaching and Learning. Encyclopedia of multimedia technology and networking, 2, 1033-44.

Dimatteo, I., Genovese, C. R., & Kass, R. E. (2001). Bayesian curve-fitting with free-knot splines. *Biometrika, 88*(4), 1055–1071. doi:10.1093/biomet/88.4.1055

Dimiccoli, M. (2016). Figure–ground segregation: A fully nonlocal approach. *Vision Research, 126,* 308–317. doi:10.1016/j.visres.2015.03.007 PMID:25824454

Dimitrova, M., & Wagatsuma, H. (2011). Web agent design based on computational memory and brain research. *Information Extraction from the Internet,* 35-56.

Dimitrova, M., Lekova, A., Kostova, S., Roumenin, C., Cherneva, M., Krastev, A., & Chavdarov, I. (2016). A Multi-Domain Approach to Design of CPS in Special Education: Issues of Evaluation and Adaptation. In *Proceedings of the 5th Workshop of the MPM4CPS COST Action, 24-25 November, 2016,* (pp. 196-205). Malaga, Spain: Academic Press.

Dimitrova, M., Vegt, N. N., & Barakova, E. (2012). Designing a system of interactive robots for training collaborative skills to autistic children. *Interactive Collaborative Learning (ICL), 2012, 15th International Conference,* 1-8.

Dimitrova, M., Wagatsuma, H., Kaburlasos, V., Krastev, A., & Kolev, I. (2018). Towards Social Cognitive Neuropsychology Account of Human-Robot Interaction. *Complex Control Systems, 1,* 12-16. Retrieved from http://ir.bas.bg/ccs/2018/2_dimitrova.pdf

Dimitrova, M., & Wagatsuma, H. (2015). Designing Humanoid Robots with Novel Roles and Social Abilities. *Lovotics, 3*(112), 2.

Dimitrova, M., Wagatsuma, H., Tripathi, G. N., & Ai, G. (2015, June). Adaptive and intuitive interactions with socially-competent pedagogical assistant robots. In *Proc. 6th International Workshop on Interactive Environments and Emerging Technologies for eLearning (IEETeL 2015)* (pp. 1-6). IEEE. 10.1109/ITHET.2015.7218031

Doing-Harris, K. M., & Zeng-Treitler, Q. (2011). Computer-assisted update of a consumer health vocabulary through mining of social network data. *Journal of Medical Internet Research, 13*(2), e37. doi:10.2196/jmir.1636 PMID:21586386

Dolan, R. J. (2002). Emotion, cognition, and behavior. *Science, 298*(5596), 1191-1194.

Donoho, D.L. & Johnstone, I.M. (1994). Ideal spatial adaptation by wavelet shrinkage. *Biometrika, 81*(3), 425-455.

Donoho, D. L. (1995). De-noising by soft-thresholding. *IEEE Transactions on Information Theory, 41*(3), 613–627. doi:10.1109/18.382009

dos Santos, A. S., & Valle, M. E. (2018). Max-plus and min-plus projection autoassociative morphological memories and their compositions for pattern classification. *Neural Networks, 100,* 84–94. doi:10.1016/j.neunet.2018.01.013 PMID:29477916

Dua, D., & Karra Taniskidou, E. (2017). *UCI Machine Learning Repository.* Irvine, CA: University of California, School of Information and Computer Science.

Duncan, J. (2016). Incusive Education for Students who are Deaf or Hard of Hearing. In L. Peer & G. Reid (Eds.), *Special Educational Needs. A Guide for Inclusive Practice* (pp. 250–267). Los Angeles, CA: SAGE.

Dunkels. (2002). *lwIP - A Lightweight TCP/IP stack.* Retrieved from https://savannah.nongnu.org/projects/lwip

Dunning, T. (1993). Accurate methods for the statistics of surprise and coincidence. *Computational Linguistics, 19*(1).

Duquette, A., Michaud, F., & Mercier, H. (2008). Exploring the use of a mobile robot as an imitation agent with children with low-functioning autism. *Autonomous Robots, 24*(2), 147–157. doi:10.100710514-007-9056-5

Eckart, T., Quasthoff, U., & Goldhahn, D. (2012). The Influence of Corpus Quality on Statistical Measurements on Language Resources. In LREC (pp. 2318-2321). Academic Press.

Ekman, P., & Friesen, W. V. (1978). *Facial action coding system: Investigator's guide.* Consulting Psychologists Press.

Elhadad, N., & Sutaria, K. (2007). Mining a lexicon of technical terms and lay equivalents. In *Proceedings of the Workshop on BioNLP 2007: Biological, Translational, and Clinical Language Processing.* Association for Computational Linguistics. 10.3115/1572392.1572402

Emery, N. J. (2000). The eyes have it: The neuroethology, function and evolution of social gaze. *Neuroscience and Biobehavioral Reviews, 24*(6), 581–604. doi:10.1016/S0149-7634(00)00025-7 PMID:10940436

Engelberger, J. (1983). *Robots in Practice: Management and Applications of Industrial Robots.* Berlin: Springer. doi:10.1007/978-1-4684-7120-5

Engelberger, J. (1989). *Robots in Service.* MIT Press.

Ernst, G. (2014). *Heart Rate Variability.* London: Springer-Verlag. doi:10.1007/978-1-4471-4309-3

Escartin, C. P., & Torres, L. S. (2016). *D6. 3: Improved Corpus-based Approaches. Project Deliverable. EXPERT (Exploiting Empirical appRoaches to Translation), Project funded by the People Programme.* Marie Curie Actions.

Eurobarometer, S. (2012). *382 'Public Attitudes Towards Robots'.* Academic Press.

European Commission. (2012). *Special Eurobarometer/Wave EB77.1: Public attitudes towards robots.* Report. Retrieved from http://ec.europa.eu/public_opinion/archives/ebs/ebs_382_en.pdf

Evans, D. (2011). *Introduction to Computing Explorations in Language.* Logic, and Machines, CreateSpace Independent Publishing Platform.

Eyssel, F., De Ruiter, L., Kuchenbrandt, D., Bobinger, S., & Hegel, F. (2012). 'If you sound like me, you must be more human': On the interplay of robot and user features on human-robot acceptance and anthropomorphism. In *Human-Robot Interaction (HRI), 2012 7th ACM/IEEE International Conference on* (pp. 125-126). IEEE.

Falkenjack, J., Mühlenbock, K. H., & Jönsson, A. (2013). Features indicating readability in swedish text. In *Proceedings of the 19th Nordic Conference of Computational Linguistics (NODALIDA 2013).* Linköping University Electronic Press.

Fasola, J., & Mataric, M. J. (2010). Robot exercise instructor: A socially assistive robot system to monitor and encourage physical exercise for the elderly. RO-MAN, IEEE, 416-421.

Feil-Seifer, D., & Mataric, M. J. (2008). B 3 IA: A control architecture for autonomous robot-assisted behavior intervention for children with Autism Spectrum Disorders. In *Robot and Human Interactive Communication, 2008. RO-MAN 2008. The 17th IEEE International Symposium on* (pp. 328-333). Academic Press.

Feil-Seifer, D., & Matarić, M. J. (2011). Automated detection and classification of positive vs. negative robot interactions with children with autism using distance-based features. In *Human-Robot Interaction (HRI), 2011 6th ACM/IEEE International Conference on* (pp. 323-330). ACM. 10.1145/1957656.1957785

Feil-Seifer, D., & Matarić, M. J. (2009). Toward socially assistive robotics for augmenting interventions for children with autism spectrum disorders. In *Experimental robotics* (pp. 201–210). Berlin: Springer. doi:10.1007/978-3-642-00196-3_24

Feng, H., Gutierrez, A., Zhang, J., & Mahoor, M. H. (2013, September). Can NAO robot improve eye-gaze attention of children with high functioning autism? In *2013 IEEE International Conference on Healthcare Informatics* (pp. 484-484). IEEE. 10.1109/ICHI.2013.72

Feng, S., Whitman, E., Xinjilefu, X., & Atkeson, C. G. (2015). Optimization-based Full Body Control for the DARPA Robotics Challenge. *Journal of Field Robotics, 32*(2), 293–312. doi:10.1002/rob.21559

Fensel, D. (2004). Ontologies: A Selver Bullet for Knowledge Management and Electronic Commerce (2nd ed.). Academic Press. doi:10.1007/978-3-662-09083-1

Ferraresi, A., Zanchetta, E., Bernardini, S., & Baroni, M. (2008). Introducing and evaluating ukWaC, a very large Web-derived corpus of English. *Proceedings of the 4th Web as Corpus Workshop (WAC-4) "Can we beat Google?"*

Ferrari, E., Robins, B., & Dautenhahn, K. (2009). Therapeutic and educational objectives in robot assisted play for children with autism. In *Robot and Human Interactive Communication, 2009. RO-MAN 2009. The 18th IEEE International Symposium on* (pp. 108-114). IEEE. 10.1109/ROMAN.2009.5326251

Fleiss, J. L. (1971). Measuring nominal scale agreement among many raters. *Psychological Bulletin, 76*(5), 378–382. doi:10.1037/h0031619

Fleming, S., & Tarassenko, L. (2007). A comparison of signal processing techniques for the extraction of breathing rate from the photoplethysmogram. *International Journal of Biological and Medical Sciences, 2*(4), 232–236.

Fong, T., Nourbakhsh, I., & Dautenhahn, K. (2003). A survey of socially interactive robots. *Robotics and Autonomous Systems, 42*(3), 143–166. doi:10.1016/S0921-8890(02)00372-X

Ford, T. D. (1986). Geological excursion guide 3: The Peak District. *Geology Today, 2*(4), 112–116. doi:10.1111/j.1365-2451.1986.tb01045.x

Fotokian, Z., Mohammadi Shahboulaghi, F., Fallahi-Khoshknab, M., & Pourhabib, A. (2017). The empowerment of elderly patients with chronic obstructive pulmonary disease: Managing life with the disease. *PLoS One, 12*(4), e0174028. doi:10.1371/journal.pone.0174028 PMID:28369069

Fowler, J. E. (2005). The redundant discrete wavelet transform and additive noise. *IEEE Signal Processing Letters, 12*(9), 629–632. doi:10.1109/LSP.2005.853048

Frankel, T. (2011). The Geometry of Physics – An Introduction. Cambridge University Press.

Fridin, M., & Belokopytov, M. (2014). Acceptance of socially assistive humanoid robot by preschool and elementary school teachers. *Computers in Human Behavior, 33*, 23–31. doi:10.1016/j.chb.2013.12.016

Galambos, R. (1998). Hallowell Davis: August 31, 1896-August 22, 1992. In Biographical Memoir (Vol. 75, pp. 117-37). National Academy of Science.

Galloway, K., Sreenath, K., Ames, A. D., & Grizzle, J. W. (2015). Torque saturation in bipedal robotic walking through control Lyapunov function-based quadratic programs. *IEEE Access : Practical Innovations, Open Solutions, 3*, 323–332. doi:10.1109/ACCESS.2015.2419630

Ganter, B., & Wille, R. (1999). *Formal Concept Analysis*. Heidelberg, Germany: Springer. doi:10.1007/978-3-642-59830-2

Gao, H. (2011). Harnessing the crowdsourcing power of social media for disaster relief. *IEEE Intelligent Systems, 26*(3).

Gao, Q., & Vogel, S. (2011). Corpus expansion for statistical machine translation with semantic role label substitution rules. In *Proceedings of the 49th Annual Meeting of the Association for Computational Linguistics: Human Language Technologies: short papers* (vol. 2, pp. 294-298). Association for Computational Linguistics.

Gazzaniga, M. S. (Ed.). (2014). *Handbook of cognitive neuroscience*. Springer.

Gelman & Hill. (2007). *Data Analysis using Regression and Multilevel/Hierarchical Models*. Cambridge, UK: Cambridge University Press.

Georgieva-Tsaneva, G., & Sabev, N. (2018). *Technologies, Standarts and Approaches to Ensure Web Accessility for Visually Impaired People*. Sofia, Bulgaria: Institute of Mathematics and Informatocs-BAS.

Georgieva-Tsaneva, G. (2018). Increasing the Quality of Education for Blind Students, through Improving Web Accessibility to Digitized Libraries, Software Systems and Databases. In *Proceedings of EDULEARN18 Conference.* IATED Academy. 10.21125/edulearn.2018.1123

German-Sallo, Z. (2014). Wavelet transform based Heart Rate Variability analysis. *Procedia Technology, 12*, 105–111. doi:10.1016/j.protcy.2013.12.462

Ghosh, A., Alboul, L., Penders, J., Jones, P., & Reed, H. (2014). Following a Robot using a Haptic Interface without Visual Feedback. *Seventh International Conference on Advances in Computer-Human Interactions, ACHI 2014.*

Gilliland. (1967). Handbook of Analog Computation. Systron – Donner Corporation.

Glavaš, G., & Štajner, S. (2015). Simplifying lexical simplification: do we need simplified corpora? In *Proceedings of the 53rd Annual Meeting of the Association for Computational Linguistics and the 7th International Joint Conference on Natural Language Processing* (Vol. 2, pp. 63-68). Academic Press. 10.3115/v1/P15-2011

Glotfelter, Eichelberger, & Martin. (2014). *PhysiCloud: A Cloud-Computing Framework for Programming Cyber-Physical Systems.* Report supported by US National Science Foundation through grant CNS-1239221.

GNU ARM. (2015). *Embedded Toolchain.* Retrieved from https://launchpad.net/gcc-arm-embedded/4.9/4.9-2015-q3-update

Goan, M., Fujii, H., & Okada, M. (2006). Child–robot interaction mediated by building blocks: From field observations in a public space. *Artificial Life and Robotics, 10*(1), 45–48. doi:10.100710015-005-0375-3

Goldberg, L., Lide, B., Lowry, S., Massett, H. A., O'Connell, T., Preece, J., ... Shneiderman, B. (2011). Usability and accessibility in consumer health informatics: Current trends and future challenges. *American Journal of Preventive Medicine, 40*(5), S187–S197. doi:10.1016/j.amepre.2011.01.009 PMID:21521594

Goldhahn, D., Eckart, T., & Quasthoff, U. (2012). Building Large Monolingual Dictionaries at the Leipzig Corpora Collection: From 100 to 200 Languages. In LREC (Vol. 29, pp. 31-43). Academic Press.

Gopal, T. V. (2015a). The Physics of Evolving Complex Software Systems. *International Journal of Engineering Issues, 2015*(1), 33-39.

Gopal, T. V. (2015b). Modeling Cyber - Physical Systems for Engineering Complex Software. *International Journal of Engineering Issues, 2015*(2), 73-78.

Gopal, T. V. (2016a). Engineering Software Behavior in Cyber – Physical Systems. *International Journal of Engineering Issues, 2016*(1), 44-52.

Gopal, T. V. (2016b). Engineering Logic for Cyber – Physical Systems. *International Journal of Engineering Issues, 2016*(3), 112-120.

Gopal, T. V. (2016c). Beautiful code – circularity and anti-foundation axiom. *Int. J. Computing Systems in Engineering, 2*(3), 148–154. doi:10.1504/IJCSYSE.2016.079001

Gopal, T. V. (2017). Communicating and Negotiating Proof Events in the Cyber – Physical Systems. *International Journal of Advanced Research in Computer Science and Software Engineering, 7*(3), 236–242. doi:10.23956/ijarcsse/V7I3/0184

Gospodinov, M., & Gospodinova, E. (2017). The effect of obesity on heart rate variability in healthy subjects. *International Journal of Biological & Medical Research, 8*(4), 6153-6157.

Gospodinova, E. (2014). Graphical Methods for Nonlinear analysis of ECG signals. *International Journal of Advanced Research in Computer Science and Software Engineering, 4*(12), 40-44.

Gospodinova, E., Gospodinov, M., Domuschiev, I., Dey, N., Ashour, A., & Sifaki-Pistolla, D. (2015). Analysis of Heart Rate Variability by Applying Nonlinear Methods with Different Approaches for Graphical Representation of Results. *International Journal of Advanced Computer Science and Applications, 6*(8), 38–45. doi:10.14569/IJACSA.2015.060805

Goynov, M., Paneva-Marinova, D., & Pavlov, R. (2012). Content interoperability between digital libraries for Orthodox heritage. *ACM International Conference Proceeding Series, CompSysTech '12 Proceedings of the 13th International Conference on Computer Systems and Technologies*, 201-207. 10.1145/2383276.2383307

Grabar, N., & Hamon, T. (2014). Automatic extraction of layman names for technical medical terms. In *Healthcare Informatics (ICHI), 2014 IEEE International Conference on* (pp. 310-319). IEEE. 10.1109/ICHI.2014.49

Grabar, N., & Hamon, T. (2014). Unsupervised method for the acquisition of general language paraphrases for medical compounds. In *Proceedings of the 4th International Workshop on Computational Terminology (Computerm)* (pp. 94-103). Academic Press. 10.3115/v1/W14-4812

Grabar, N., & Hamon, T. (2017). Understanding of unknown medical words. In *Proceedings of the Biomedical NLP Workshop associated with RANLP* (pp. 32-41). Academic Press. 10.26615/978-954-452-044-1_005

Grabar, N., Hamon, T., & Amiot, D. (2014). Automatic diagnosis of understanding of medical words. In *Proceedings of the 3rd Workshop on Predicting and Improving Text Readability for Target Reader Populations (PITR)* (pp. 11-20). Academic Press. 10.3115/v1/W14-1202

Grabar, N., van Zyl, I., de la Harpe, R., & Hamon, T. (2014). The Comprehension of Medical Words. In *Proceedings of the International Joint Conference on Biomedical Engineering Systems and Technologies* (vol. 5, pp. 334-342). SCITEPRESS-Science and Technology Publications, Lda.

Grabar, N., Chauveau-Thoumelin, P., & Dumonet, L. (2015). *Study of Subjectivity in the Medical Discourse: Uncertainty and Emotions Advances in Knowledge Discovery and Management* (Vol. 5). Springer.

Grabar, N., Krivine, S., & Jaulent, M. C. (2007). Classification of health webpages as expert and non expert with a reduced set of cross-language features. *AMIA ... Annual Symposium Proceedings - AMIA Symposium. AMIA Symposium, 2007*, 284. PMID:18693843

Gratton, G., Coles, M. G., & Donchin, E. (1983). A new method for off-line removal of ocular artifact. *Electroencephalography and Clinical Neurophysiology, 55*(4), 468–484. doi:10.1016/0013-4694(83)90135-9 PMID:6187540

Greenes, R. A. (2001). eCare and eHealth: The Internet meets health care. The Journal of medical practice management. *MPM, 17*(2), 106–108. PMID:11680134

Gries, S. Th. (2013). Elementary statistical testing with R. In M. Krug & J. Schlüter (Eds.), *Research methods in language variation and change*. Cambridge University Press. doi:10.1017/CBO9780511792519.024

Griffiths, P. E. (2002). *Emotion is still not a natural kind*. Academic Press.

Griffiths, P. E. (2004). Emotions as natural and normative kinds. *Philosophy of Science, 71*(5), 901–911. doi:10.1086/425944

Griffiths, P. E. (2013). Current emotion research in philosophy. *Emotion Review, 5*(2), 215–222. doi:10.1177/1754073912468299

Grifoni-Waterman, R. (2016). *International fair use developments: Is fair use going global?* Retrieved July 2018. https://www.authorsalliance.org/2016/02/25/international-fair-use-developments-is-fair-use-going-global/

Grigonyte, G., Kvist, M., Wirén, M., Velupillai, S., & Henriksson, A. (2016). Swedification patterns of latin and greek affixes in clinical text. *Nordic Journal of Linguistics, 39*(01), 5–37. doi:10.1017/S0332586515000293

Grishman, R., & Kittredge, R. (2014). *Analyzing language in restricted domains: sublanguage description and processing.* Psychology Press.

Gross, J. J. (2002). Emotion regulation: Affective, cognitive, and social consequences. *Psychophysiology, 39*(3), 281–291. doi:10.1017/S0048577201393198

Grossman, A., & Morlet, J. (1984). Decomposition of Hardy functions into square interable wavelets of sonstant shape. *SIAM Journal on Mathematical Analysis, 15*(4), 723–736. doi:10.1137/0515056

Gruber, T. R. (1995). Toward principles for the design of ontologies used for knowledge sharing. *International Journal of Human-Computer Studies, 43*(5–6), 907–928. doi:10.1006/ijhc.1995.1081

Guha, P. (2007, February 1). Metriplectic structure, Leibniz dynamics and dissipative systems. *Journal of Mathematical Analysis and Applications, 326*(1), 121–136. doi:10.1016/j.jmaa.2006.02.023

Gyaourova, A., Kamath, C., & Fodor, I. K. (2002). Undecimated wavelet transforms for image de-noising. *Report Lawrence Livermore National Laboratory, 12,* 1–12.

Habernal, I., Zayed, O., & Gurevych, I. (2016). C4Corpus: Multilingual Web-size corpus with free license. In *Proceedings of the 10th International Conference on Language Resources and Evaluation (LREC 2016)* (pp. 914–922). Portorož, Slovenia: European Language Resources Association (ELRA).

Hadley. (2008). *A Layered Grammar of Graphics.* Report Supported by the National Science Foundation under grant 0706949.

Hall & Loura. (2016). *NASA Awards $750K in Sample Return Robot Challenge.* Academic Press.

Handke, C., Guibault, L., & Vallbé, J. J. (2015). *Is Europe falling behind in data mining? Copyright's impact on data mining in academic research.* Academic Press.

Han, J., Jo, M., Jones, V., & Jo, J. (2008). Comparative Study on the Educational Use of Home Robots for Children. *Journal Of Information Processing Systems, 4*(4), 159–168. doi:10.3745/JIPS.2008.4.4.159

Haque, S., Aziz, S., & Rahman, M. (2014). Review of Cyber-Physical System in Healthcare. *International Journal of Distributed Sensor Networks, 10*(4), 217415. doi:10.1155/2014/217415

Hargittai, E., & Sandvig, C. (2016). *Big Data, Big Problems, Big Opportunities: Using Internet Log Data to Conduct Social Network Analysis Research. In Digital Research Confidential:The Secrets of Studying Behavior Online, 1* (p. 288). MIT Press.

Harper, S., & Yesilada, Y. (Eds.). (2008). *Web Accessibility.* Heidelberg, Germany: Springer Berlin. doi:10.1007/978-1-84800-050-6

Hasan, K. S., & Ng, V. (2014). Automatic keyphrase extraction: A survey of the state of the art. In *Proceedings of the 52nd Annual Meeting of the Association for Computational Linguistics* (Vol. 1, pp. 1262-1273). Academic Press. 10.3115/v1/P14-1119

Haslerud, V., & Stenström, A.-B. (1995). The bergen corpus of london teenager language (colt). Spoken English on Computer, 235–42.

Hayat, Lesser, & Samuel-Azran. (2017). Gendered discourse patterns on online social networks: A social network analysis perspective. *Computers in Human Behaviour, 77,* 132-139. doi:10.1016/j.chb.2017.08.041

Hazarika, N., Chen, J. Z., Tsoi, A. C., & Sergejew, A. (1997). Classification of EEG signals using the wavelet transform. *Signal Processing, 59*(1), 61–72. doi:10.1016/S0165-1684(97)00038-8

He, Z., Cai, Z., & Yu, J. (2018). Latent-Data Privacy Preserving With Customized Data Utility for Social Network Data. IEEE Transactions on Vehicular Technology, 67(1), 665-673.

Hedgecock, J., Standen, P., Beer, C., Brown, D., & Stewart, D. (2014). Evaluating the role of a humanoid robot to support learning in children with profound and multiple disabilities. *Journal of Assistive Technologies*, *8*(3), 111–123. doi:10.1108/JAT-02-2014-0006

Heffer, C., Rock, F., & Conley, J. (Eds.). (2013). *Legal-Lay Communication: Textual Travels in the Law*. Oxford University Press. doi:10.1093/acprof:oso/9780199746842.001.0001

Helen, P., Savva, A., & Power, C. (2015). Towards a unified definition of Web Accessibility. *W4A '15 Proceedings of the 12th Web for All Conference Article No. 35*. Available from: https://www.researchgate.net/publication

Henkel, M., Perjons, E., & Sneiders, E. (2015). Supporting Workflow and Adaptive Case Management with Language Technologies. In WorldCIST (pp. 543-552). Academic Press. doi:10.1007/978-3-319-16486-1_53

Heppin, K. F. (2010). *Resolving Power of Search keys in Medeval a Swedish Medical Test Collection with User Groups: Doctors and patients* (Ph.D. dissertation). University of Gothenburg.

Hillyard, S. A., & Münte, T. F. (1984). Selective attention to color and location: An analysis with event-related brain potentials. *Perception & Psychophysics*, *36*(2), 185–198. doi:10.3758/BF03202679 PMID:6514528

Hillyard, S. A., Squires, K. C., Bauer, J. W., & Lindsay, P. H. (1971). Evoked potential correlates of auditory signal detection. *Science*, *172*(3990), 1357–1360. doi:10.1126cience.172.3990.1357 PMID:5580218

Hirose, M., & Ogawa, K. (2007). Honda humanoid robots development. *Philosophical Transactions of the Royal Society of London A: Mathematical, Physical and Engineering Sciences, 365*(1850), 11-19.

Hirukawa, H., Hattori, S., Harada, K., Kajita, S., Kaneko, K., Kanehiro, F., . . . Morisawa, M. (2006, May). A universal stability criterion of the foot contact of legged robots-adios zmp. In *Robotics and Automation, 2006. ICRA 2006. Proceedings 2006 IEEE International Conference on* (pp. 1976-1983). IEEE. 10.1109/ROBOT.2006.1641995

Hoang, C., & Sima'an, K. (2014). Latent domain translation models in mix-of-domains haystack. In *Proceedings of COLING 2014, the 25th International Conference on Computational Linguistics: Technical Papers* (pp. 1928-1939). Academic Press.

Höflich, J., & El Bayed, A. (2015). Perception, Acceptance, and the Social Construction of Robots—Exploratory Studies. *Social Robots From A Human Perspective*, 39-51. doi:10.1007/978-3-319-15672-9_4

Höflich, J. R. (2013). Relationships to Social Robots: Towards a Triadic Analysis of Media-oriented Behavior. *Intervalla: Platform for Intellectual Exchange, 1*, 35–48.

Hole, W. T., & Srinivasan, S. (2000). Discovering missed synonymy in a large concept-oriented Metathesaurus. In *Proceedings of the AMIA Symposium* (p. 354). American Medical Informatics Association.

Hong, Y. D., & Kim, J. H. (2012). An evolutionary optimized footstep planner for the navigation of humanoid robots. *International Journal of Humanoid Robotics*, *9*(01), 1250005. doi:10.1142/S0219843612500053

Höök, K. (2008, June). Affective loop experiences–what are they? In *International Conference on Persuasive Technology* (pp. 1-12). Springer.

Höök, K. (2009). Affective loop experiences: Designing for interactional embodiment. *Philosophical Transactions of the Royal Society of London. Series B, Biological Sciences*, *364*(1535), 3585–3595. doi:10.1098/rstb.2009.0202

Hua, L. C., Anisi, M. H., & Yee, P. L. (2017). Social networking-based cooperation mechanisms in vehicular ad-hoc network—a survey. In *Vehicular Communications*. Elsevier.

Humphreys, B. L., McCray, A. T., & Cheh, M. L. (1997). Evaluating the coverage of controlled health data terminologies: Report on the results of the NLM/AHCPR large scale vocabulary test. *Journal of the American Medical Informatics Association, 4*(6), 484–500. doi:10.1136/jamia.1997.0040484 PMID:9391936

Huo, H., Xu, Y., Yan, H., Mubeen, S., & Zhang, H. (2009, June). An elderly health care system using wireless sensor networks at home. In *Sensor Technologies and Applications, 2009. SENSORCOMM'09. Third International Conference on* (pp. 158-163). IEEE. 10.1109/SENSORCOMM.2009.32

Hurmuzlu, Y., Génot, F., & Brogliato, B. (2004). Modeling, stability and control of biped robots—A general framework. *Automatica, 40*(10), 1647–1664. doi:10.1016/j.automatica.2004.01.031

Huskens, B., Verschuur, R., Gillesen, J., Didden, R., & Barakova, E. (2013). Promoting question-asking in school-aged children with autism spectrum disorders: Effectiveness of a robot intervention compared to a human-trainer intervention. *Developmental Neurorehabilitation, 16*(5), 345–356. doi:10.3109/17518423.2012.739212 PMID:23586852

Hyvarinen, A. (1999). Fast and robust fixed-point algorithms for independent component analysis. *IEEE Transactions on Neural Networks, 10*(3), 626–634. doi:10.1109/72.761722 PMID:18252563

Ibrani, L., Allen, T., Brown, D., Sherkat, N., & Stewart, D. (2011). *Supporting students with learning and physical disabilities using a mobile robot platform. In Interactive Technologies and Games* (pp. 84–265). Nottingham, UK: ITAG.

Ichiki, M., Ai, G., Ooi, J. S., & Wagatsuma, H. (2016). A Comparative Analysis of Indexing of Mental Workload by using Neuro-Driving Tools based on EEG Measurements Coupling with the Eye-Tracking System. *Frontiers in Neuroinformatics. Conference Abstract: Neuroinformatics, 2016.* doi:10.3389/conf.fninf.2016.20.00041

Ioannidis, Y., Balet, O., & Pandermalis, D. (2014). *Tell Me a Story: Augmented Reality Technology in Museums.* Retrieved from https://www.theguardian.com/culture-professionals-network/culture-professionals-blog/2014/apr/04/story-augmented-reality-technology-museums

Irazabal, J.-M. (2003). *I2C MANUAL.* Philips Semiconductors.

ISO 10218-1:2011. (2011). *Robots and robotic devices – Safety requirements for industrial robots – Part 1: Robots.* ISO.

ISO 8373:2012. (n.d.). *Robots and robotic devices – Vocabulary.* Retrieved from http://www.iso.org/iso/iso_catalogue/catalogue_tc/catalogu.e_detail.htm?csnumber=55890

ISO/TS 15066:2016. (2016). *Robots and robotic devices – Collaborative robots.* ISO.

Ivan, G., & Opri, D. (2006). Dynamical systems on Leibniz algebroids, Differential Geometry -. *Dynamical Systems, 8,* 127–137.

Ivanova, K. (2011). *A Novel Method for Content-Based Image Retrieval in Art Image Collections Utilizing Colour Semantics.* Hasselt, Belgium: Hasselt University.

Jackson, G. L., Powers, B. J., Chatterjee, R., Bettger, J. P., Kemper, A. R., Hasselblad, V., ... Gray, R. (2013). The patient-centered medical home: A systematic review. *Annals of Internal Medicine, 158*(3), 169–178. doi:10.7326/0003-4819-158-3-201302050-00579 PMID:24779044

Jalil, A., Beer, M., & Crowther, P. (2016). Improving design and functionalities of MOBIlearn2 application: A case study of mobile learning in metalwork collection of Millennium Gallery. In *Proceedings IEEE Eighth International Conference on Technology for Education.* IEEE. 10.1109/T4E.2016.013

James, W. (1884). What is an emotion? *Mind*, *9*(34), 188–205. doi:10.1093/mind/os-IX.34.188

Jatsun, S., Savin, S., & Yatsun, A. (2016, October). Comparative analysis of global optimization-based controller tuning methods for an exoskeleton performing push recovery. In *System Theory, Control and Computing (ICSTCC), 2016 20th International Conference on* (pp. 107-112). IEEE.

Jatsun, S., Savin, S., Yatsun, A., & Postolnyi, A. (2017). Control system parameter optimization for lower limb exoskeleton with integrated elastic elements. In Advances in Cooperative Robotics (pp. 797-805). Academic Press.

Jatsun, S. F., Yatsun, A., & Savin, S. (2018). Investigation of Human Locomotion With a Powered Lower Limb Exoskeleton. In *Handbook of Research on Biomimetics and Biomedical Robotics* (pp. 26–47). IGI Global. doi:10.4018/978-1-5225-2993-4.ch002

Jatsun, S., Savin, S., & Yatsun, A. (2016). Parameter optimization for exoskeleton control system using Sobol sequences. In *ROMANSY 21-Robot Design, Dynamics and Control* (pp. 361–368). Cham: Springer. doi:10.1007/978-3-319-33714-2_40

Jatsun, S., Savin, S., & Yatsun, A. (2016, August). A Control Strategy for a Lower Limb Exoskeleton with a Toe Joint. In *International Conference on Interactive Collaborative Robotics* (pp. 1-8). Springer. 10.1007/978-3-319-43955-6_1

Jatsun, S., Savin, S., & Yatsun, A. (2016, July). Motion control algorithm for a lower limb exoskeleton based on iterative LQR and ZMP method for trajectory generation. In *International Workshop on Medical and Service Robots* (pp. 305-317). Springer.

Jatsun, S., Savin, S., & Yatsun, A. (2017, September). Footstep Planner Algorithm for a Lower Limb Exoskeleton Climbing Stairs. In *International Conference on Interactive Collaborative Robotics* (pp. 75-82). Springer. 10.1007/978-3-319-66471-2_9

Jatsun, S., Savin, S., Yatsun, A., & Gaponov, I. (2017). Study on a two-staged control of a lower-limb exoskeleton performing standing-up motion from a chair. In *Robot Intelligence Technology and Applications 4* (pp. 113–122). Cham: Springer. doi:10.1007/978-3-319-31293-4_10

Jensen, B., Tomatis, N., Mayor, L., Drygajlo, A., & Siegwart, R. (2005). Robots meet Humans interaction in public spaces. *IEEE Transactions on Industrial Electronics*, *52*(6), 1530–1546. doi:10.1109/TIE.2005.858730

Jensen, L., & Konradsen, F. (2018). A review of the use of virtual reality head-mounted displays in education and training. *Education and Information Technologies*, *23*(4), 1515–1529. doi:10.100710639-017-9676-0

Jewitt, L. (Ed.). (1857). *Black's Tourist's Guide to Derbyshire* (2nd ed.). Edinburgh, UK: Adam and Charles Black.

Jiang, J., Wen, S., Yu, S., Xiang, Y., & Zhou, W. (2018). Rumor Source Identification in Social Networks with Time-Varying Topology. *IEEE Transactions on Dependable and Secure Computing*, *15*(1), 166–179. doi:10.1109/TDSC.2016.2522436

Jiang, L., & Yang, C. C. (2013). Using co-occurrence analysis to expand consumer health vocabularies from social media data. *2013 IEEE International Conference on Healthcare Informatics (ICHI)*, 74-81. 10.1109/ICHI.2013.16

Jimison, H., Gorman, P., Woods, S., Nygren, P., Walker, M., Norris, S., & Hersh, W. (2008). Barriers and drivers of health information technology use for the elderly, chronically ill, and underserved. *Evidence Report/technology Assessment*, *175*, 1–1422. PMID:19408968

Johansson, V., & Rennes, E. (2016). Automatic extraction of synonyms from an easy-to-read corpus. *Proceedings of the Sixth Swedish Language Technology Conference (SLTC-16)*.

Johnson, C. P., & Myers, S. M. (2007). Identification and evaluation of children with autism spectrum disorders. *Pediatrics*, *120*(5), 1183–1215. doi:10.1542/peds.2007-2361 PMID:17967920

Johnson, M., Shrewsbury, B., Bertrand, S., Wu, T., Duran, D., Floyd, M., ... Carff, J. (2015). Team IHMC's lessons learned from the DARPA robotics challenge trials. *Journal of Field Robotics, 32*(2), 192–208. doi:10.1002/rob.21571

Johnson, W. L., Rickel, J. W., & Lester, J. C. (2000). Animated pedagogical agents: Face-to-face interaction in interactive learning environment. *International Journal of Artificial Intelligence in Education, 11*(1), 47–78.

Jones, G. & Christal, M. (2002). The future of virtual museums: On-line, immersive 3-D environments. *Created Realities Group, 2002*(9), 1-12.

Jordan, R. (2013). *Autistic spectrum disorders: an introductory handbook for practitioners*. Routledge. doi:10.4324/9780203827352

Joshi, C., & Singh, U. K. (2017). Information security risks management framework – A step towards mitigating security risks in university network. *Journal of Information Security and Applications, 35*, 128-137.

Joyce, C. A., Gordonitsky, I. F., & Kutas, M. (2004). Automatic removal of eye movement and blink artifacts from EEG data using blind component separation. *Psychophysiology, 41*(2), 313–325. doi:10.1111/j.1469-8986.2003.00141.x PMID:15032997

Jung, T. P., Makeig, S., Humphries, C., Lee, T. W., McKeown, M. J., Iragui, V., & Sejnowski, T. J. (2000). Removing electroencephalographic artifacts by blind source separation. *Psychophysiology, 37*(2), 163–178. doi:10.1111/1469-8986.3720163 PMID:10731767

Kaburlasos, V. G. (2004). A device for linking brain to mind based on lattice theory. In *Proceedings of the 8th International Conference on Cognitive and Neural Systems (ICCNS 2004)*. Boston University.

Kaburlasos, V., Bazinas, C., Siavalas, G., & Papakostas, G. A. (2018, June). Linguistic social robot control by crowd-computing feedback. In *Proceedings of the 2018 JSME Conference on Robotics and Mechatronics*. Academic Press. 10.1299/jsmermd.2018.1A1-B13

Kaburlasos, V. G. (2011). Special issue on: Information engineering applications based on lattices. *Information Sciences, 181*(10), 1771–1773. doi:10.1016/j.ins.2011.01.016

Kaburlasos, V. G., Dardani, C., Dimitrova, M., & Amanatiadis, A. (2018, January). Multi-robot engagement in special education: a preliminary study in autism. In *2018 IEEE International Conference on Consumer Electronics (ICCE)* (pp. 1-2). IEEE. 10.1109/ICCE.2018.8326267

Kaburlasos, V. G., & Papakostas, G. A. (2015). Learning distributions of image features by interactive fuzzy lattice reasoning in pattern recognition applications. *IEEE Computational Intelligence Magazine, 10*(3), 42–51. doi:10.1109/MCI.2015.2437318

Kahn, P. H., Freier, N. G., Kanda, T., Ishiguro, H., Ruckert, J. H., Severson, R. L., & Kane, S. K. (2008). Design patterns for sociality in human-robot interaction. In *Proceedings of the 3rd ACM/IEEE international conference on Human robot interaction* (pp. 97-104). ACM. 10.1145/1349822.1349836

Kajita, S., Kanehiro, F., Kaneko, K., Fujiwara, K., Harada, K., Yokoi, K., & Hirukawa, H. (2003, September). Biped walking pattern generation by using preview control of zero-moment point. In *Robotics and Automation, 2003. Proceedings. ICRA'03. IEEE International Conference on* (Vol. 2, pp. 1620-1626). IEEE. 10.1109/ROBOT.2003.1241826

Kajita, S., Kanehiro, F., Kaneko, K., Yokoi, K., & Hirukawa, H. (2001). The 3D Linear Inverted Pendulum Mode: A simple modeling for a biped walking pattern generation. In *Intelligent Robots and Systems, 2001. Proceedings. 2001 IEEE/RSJ International Conference on* (Vol. 1, pp. 239-246). IEEE.

Kajita, S., Morisawa, M., Harada, K., Kaneko, K., Kanehiro, F., Fujiwara, K., & Hirukawa, H. (2006, October). Biped walking pattern generator allowing auxiliary zmp control. In *Intelligent Robots and Systems, 2006 IEEE/RSJ International Conference on* (pp. 2993-2999). IEEE. 10.1109/IROS.2006.282233

Kamal, Dey, Ashour, & Balas. (2016). FbMapping: An Automated System for Monitoring Facebook Data. *Neural Network World*.

Kamal, Nimmy, Hossain, Dey, Ashour, & Sathi. (2016). ExSep: An Exon Separation Process using Neural Skyline Filter. *International Conference on Electrical, Electronics, and Optimization Techniques (ICEEOT)*.

Kamal, Ripon, Dey, & Santhi. (2016). A MapReduce Approach to Diminish Imbalance Parameters for Big Deoxyribonucleic Acid Dataset. *Computer Methods and Programs in Biomedicine*. PMID:27265059

Kanda, T., Hirano, T., Eaton, D., & Ishiguro, H. (2004). Interactive robots as social partners and peer tutors for children: A field trial. *Human-Computer Interaction, 19*(1), 61–84. doi:10.120715327051hci1901&2_4

Kanda, T., Miyashita, T., Osada, T., Haikawa, Y., & Ishiguro, H. (2008). Analysis of humanoid appearances in human–robot interaction. *IEEE Transactions on Robotics, 24*(3), 725–735. doi:10.1109/TRO.2008.921566

Kaneko, K., Harada, K., Kanehiro, F., Miyamori, G., & Akachi, K. (2008, September). Humanoid robot HRP-3. In *Intelligent Robots and Systems, 2008. IROS 2008. IEEE/RSJ International Conference on* (pp. 2471-2478). IEEE. 10.1109/IROS.2008.4650604

Kaneko, K., Kanehiro, F., Morisawa, M., Akachi, K., Miyamori, G., Hayashi, A., & Kanehira, N. (2011, September). Humanoid robot hrp-4-humanoid robotics platform with lightweight and slim body. In *Intelligent Robots and Systems (IROS), 2011 IEEE/RSJ International Conference on* (pp. 4400-4407). IEEE. 10.1109/IROS.2011.6094465

Kang, K. D., & Son, S. H. (2008). Real-time data services for cyber physical systems. In *Distributed Computing Systems Workshops, 2008. ICDCS'08. 28th International Conference on* (pp. 483-488). IEEE. 10.1109/ICDCS.Workshops.2008.21

Kang, W., Son, S. H., Stankovic, J. A., & Amirijoo, M. (2007). I/O-aware deadline miss ratio management in real-time embedded databases. In *Real-Time Systems Symposium, 2007. RTSS 2007. 28th IEEE International* (pp. 277-287). IEEE. 10.1109/RTSS.2007.19

Kang, Z., & Landry, S. J. (2015). An eye movement analysis algorithm for a multielement target tracking task: Maximum transition-based agglomerative hierarchical clustering. *IEEE Transactions on Human-Machine Systems, 45*(1), 13–24. doi:10.1109/THMS.2014.2363121

Kann, V., & Rosell, M. (2005). Free construction of a free Swedish dictionary of synonyms. In *Proceedings of the 15th Nordic Conference of Computational Linguistics (NODALIDA 2005)* (pp. 105-110). Academic Press.

Kanoga, S., & Mitsukura, Y. (2014). Eye-Blink Artifact Reduction Using 2-Step Nonnegative Matrix Factorization for Single-Channel Electroencephalographic Signals. *Journal of Signal Processing, 18*(5), 251–257. doi:10.2299/jsp.18.251

Kaspar, K., & König, P. (2011). Overt attention and context factors: The impact of repeated presentations, image type, and individual motivation. *PLoS One, 6*(7), e21719. doi:10.1371/journal.pone.0021719 PMID:21750726

Kelvey, J. (2014). *A Quick Reminder That Technology Can Be Wonderful*. Retrieved from http://www.slate.com/articles/technology/future_tense/2014/07/telepresence_robots_make_museums_accessible_to_everyone.html

Keren, A. S., Yuval-Greenberg, S., & Deouell, L. Y. (2010). Saccadic spike potentials in gamma-band EEG: Characterization, detection and suppression. *NeuroImage, 49*(3), 2248–2263. doi:10.1016/j.neuroimage.2009.10.057 PMID:19874901

Khandoker, A., Karmakar, C., Brennan, M., Voss, A., & Palaniswami, M. (2013). *Poincare Plot Methods for Heart Rate Variability Analysis*. New York: Springer. doi:10.1007/978-1-4614-7375-6

Khatib, O., Sentis, L., Park, J., & Warren, J. (2004). Whole-body dynamic behavior and control of human-like robots. *International Journal of Humanoid Robotics, 1*(01), 29–43. doi:10.1142/S0219843604000058

Khusainov, R., Shimchik, I., Afanasyev, I., & Magid, E. (2015, July). Toward a human-like locomotion: modelling dynamically stable locomotion of an anthropomorphic robot in simulink environment. In *Informatics in Control, Automation and Robotics (ICINCO), 2015 12th International Conference on* (Vol. 2, pp. 141-148). IEEE. 10.5220/0005576001410148

Kilgarriff, A. (2014). *How to evaluate a corpus. Slides. 15th lecture of the Fred Jelinek Seminar series*. Institute of Formal and Applied Linguistics Charles University, Czech Republic Faculty of Mathematics and Physics.

Kilgarriff, A., Avinesh, P. V. S., & Pomikálek, J. (2011). BootCatting comparable corpora. In *9th International Conference on Terminology and Artificial Intelligence* (p. 123). Academic Press.

Kilgarriff, A., Reddy, S., Pomikálek, J., & Pvs, A. (2010). *A corpus factory for many languages*. In LREC workshop on Web Services and Processing Pipelines, Malta.

Kilgarriff, A. (2001). Comparing corpora. *International Journal of Corpus Linguistics, 6*(1), 97–133. doi:10.1075/ijcl.6.1.05kil

Kilgarriff, A. (2005). Language is never, ever, ever, random. *Corpus Linguistics and Linguistic Theory, 1*(2), 263–276. doi:10.1515/cllt.2005.1.2.263

Kilgarriff, A. (2007). Googleology is bad science. *Computational Linguistics, 33*(1), 147–151. doi:10.1162/coli.2007.33.1.147

Kilgarriff, A., Reddy, S., & Pomikálek, J. and PVS A. (2010). A corpus factory for many languages. *Proceedings of the Seventh International Conference on Language Resources and Evaluation (LREC'10).*

Kim, E., Paul, R., Shic, F., & Scassellati, B. (2012). *Bridging the research gap: Making HRI useful to individuals with autism*. Academic Press.

Kim, J., & Hastak, M. (2018). Social network analysis: Characteristics of online social networks after a disaster. *International Journal of Information Management, 38*(1), 86-96.

Kim, J., Joo, J., & Shin, Y. (2009). An exploratory study on the health information terms for the development of the consumer health vocabulary system. *Studies in Health Technology and Informatics, 146*, 785.

Kim, E. S., Berkovits, L. D., Bernier, E. P., Leyzberg, D., Shic, F., Paul, R., & Scassellati, B. (2013). Social robots as embedded reinforcers of social behavior in children with autism. *Journal of Autism and Developmental Disorders, 43*(5), 1038–1049. doi:10.100710803-012-1645-2 PMID:23111617

Kim, Y., & Lee, J. (2010). Cuffless and non-invasive estimation of a continuous blood pressure based on PTT. *2nd International Conference on Information Technology Convergence and Services*. 10.1109/ITCS.2010.5581266

Kirk, S., Gallagher, J. J., Coleman, M. R., & Anastasiow, N. J. (2011). *Educating exceptional children*. Cengage Learning.

Kittredge, R. (2003). Sublanguages and controlled languages. In R. Mitkov (Ed.), *The Oxford Handbook of Computational Linguistics* (pp. 430–447). Oxford, UK: Oxford University Press.

Kittredge, R., & Lehrberger, J. (Eds.). (1982). *Sublanguage: Studies of language in restricted semantic domains*. Walter de Gruyter. doi:10.1515/9783110844818

Klein, T., Gelderblom, G., de Witte, L., & Vanstipelen, S. (2011). Evaluation of short term effects of the IROMEC robotic toy for children with developmental disabilities. *2011 IEEE International Conference On Rehabilitation Robotics.* 10.1109/ICORR.2011.5975406

Klüver, H., & Bucy, P. C. (1937). Psychic blindness and other symptoms following bilateral temporal lobectomy in Rhesus monkeys. *The American Journal of Physiology.*

Koblenski, S. (2015). *Everyday DSP for Programmers: DC and Impulsive Noise Removal.* Retrieved from http://samkoblenski.blogspot.com/2015/11/everyday-dsp-for-programmers-dc-and.html

Koch, S., & Hägglund, M. (2009). Health informatics and the delivery of care to older people. *Maturitas, 63*(3), 195–199. doi:10.1016/j.maturitas.2009.03.023 PMID:19487092

Kokkinakis, D. (2012). *The Journal of the Swedish Medical Association - A Corpus Resource for Biomedical Text Mining in Swedish.* In The Third Workshop on Building and Evaluating Resources for Biomedical Text Mining (BioTxtM), an LREC Workshop.

Kokkinakis, D., & Gronostaj, M. T. (2006). Comparing lay and professional language in cardiovascular disorders corpora. *WSEAS Transactions on Biology and Biomedicine, 3*(6), 429.

Kokkinakis, D. (2006). Developing resources for Swedish Bio-Medical text mining. *Proceedings of the 2nd International Symposium on Semantic Mining in Biomedicine (SMBM).*

Kory Westlund, J. M., Dickens, L., Jeong, S., Harris, P. L., DeSteno, D., & Breazeal, C. L. (2017). Children use nonverbal cues to learn new words from robots as well as people. *International Journal of Child-Computer Interaction*, 1-9. doi:10.1016/j.ijcci.2017.04.001

Kostova, S., Dimitrova, M. I., Saeva, S., Zamfirov, M., Kaburlasos, V., Vrochidou, E., ... Papić, V. (2018). Identifying needs of robotic and technological solutions for the classroom. *Proceedings of the 26th International Conference on Software, Telecommunications and Computer Networks (SoftCOM 2018), Symposium on: Robotic and ICT assisted wellbeing.* 10.23919/SOFTCOM.2018.8555751

Kovach, C.K., Tsuchiya, N., Kawasaki, H., Oya, H., Howard, M.A., & Adolphs, R. (2011). Manifestation of Ocular-Muscle EMG Contamination in Human Intracranial Recordings. *NeuroImage, 54*(1), 213–233.

Kozima, H., Nakagawa, C., & Yasuda, Y. (2005). Interactive robots for communication-care: A case-study in autism therapy. In *Robot and human interactive communication, 2005. ROMAN 2005. IEEE International Workshop on* (pp. 341-346). IEEE. 10.1109/ROMAN.2005.1513802

Kozima, H., Nakagawa, C., & Yasuda, Y. (2007). Children–robot interaction: A pilot study in autism therapy. *Progress in Brain Research, 164*, 385–400. doi:10.1016/S0079-6123(07)64021-7 PMID:17920443

Krichmar, J. L., & Wagatsuma, H. (Eds.). (2011). *Neuromorphic and Brain-Based Robots.* Edinburgh, UK: Cambridge University Press. doi:10.1017/CBO9780511994838

Krippendorff, K. (2011). *Computing Krippendorff's alpha-reliability.* Available: http://repository.upenn.edu/asc_papers/43

Krippendorff, K. (1980). *Content analysis. Beverley Hills* (Vol. 7). Sage Publications.

Kristoffersen, K. B. (2017). *Common Crawled Web Corpora: Constructing corpora from large amounts of web data. Thesis submitted for the degree of Master in Informatics: Programming and Networks (Language Technology group).* Department of Informatics, Faculty of mathematics and natural sciences, University of Oslo. Retrieved from http://urn.nb.no/URN:NBN:no-60569

Kristoffersson, A., & Lindén, M. (2017). *Understanding users of a future E-care@home system*. Retrieved from http://oru.diva-portal.org/smash/get/diva2:1073710/FULLTEXT01.pdf

Kropotov, J. (2008). *Quantitative EEG, Event related potentials and neurotherapy*. London: Elsevier.

Kucera, H., & Francis, W. (1979). *A standard corpus of present-day edited American English, for use with digital computers* (revised and amplified from 1967 version). Academic Press.

Küçükdurmaz, F., Gomez, M. M., Secrist, E., & Parvizi, J. (2015). Reliability, Readability and Quality of Online Information about Femoracetabular Impingement. *Archives of Bone and Joint Surgery, 3*(3), 163–168. PMID:26213699

Kuffner, J. J., Nishiwaki, K., Kagami, S., Inaba, M., & Inoue, H. (2001). Footstep planning among obstacles for biped robots. In *Intelligent Robots and Systems, 2001. Proceedings. 2001 IEEE/RSJ International Conference on* (Vol. 1, pp. 500-505). IEEE. 10.1109/IROS.2001.973406

Kuindersma, S., Permenter, F., & Tedrake, R. (2014, May). An efficiently solvable quadratic program for stabilizing dynamic locomotion. In *Robotics and Automation (ICRA), 2014 IEEE International Conference on* (pp. 2589-2594). IEEE. 10.1109/ICRA.2014.6907230

Kuindersma, S., Deits, R., Fallon, M., Valenzuela, A., Dai, H., Permenter, F., ... Tedrake, R. (2016). Optimization-based locomotion planning, estimation, and control design for the atlas humanoid robot. *Autonomous Robots, 40*(3), 429–455. doi:10.100710514-015-9479-3

Kumar, D., Prasannakumar, S., Sudarshan, B., & Jayadevappa, D. (2013). Heart Rate Variability Analysis: A Review. *International Journal of Advanced Technology in Engineering and Science, 1*(6), 9–24.

Kunz, M., & Osborne, P. (2010). A Preliminary Examination of the Readability of Consumer Pharmaceutical Web Pages. *Journal of Marketing Development and Competitiveness, 5*(1), 33–41.

Kurt, S. (2011). The Accessibility of university websites: The case of Turkish universities. *Universal Access in the Information Society, 10*(1), 101–110. doi:10.100710209-010-0190-z

L'Homme, M. C. (2014). Terminologies and taxonomies. In J. R. Taylor (Ed.), The Oxford Handbook of the Word. Oxford University Press.

Landis, J. R., & Koch, G. G. (1977). The measurement of observer agreement for categorical data. *Biometrics*, 159-174.

Lange, C. (1885). *The Emotions*. Baltimore, MD: Williams & Wilkins.

Lang, M., Guo, H., Odegard, J. E., Burrus, C. S., & Wells, R. O. (1996). Noise reduction using an undecimated discrete wavelet transform. *IEEE Signal Processing Letters, 3*(1), 10–12. doi:10.1109/97.475823

Langton, S. R., Watt, R. J., & Bruce, V. (2000). Do the eyes have it? Cues to the direction of social attention. *Trends in Cognitive Sciences, 4*(2), 50–59. doi:10.1016/S1364-6613(99)01436-9 PMID:10652522

LaRouche, Jr. (2010). What Leibniz Intended. *EIR Dynamics*, 44 – 49.

Lau, Tham, & Luo. (2011). Participatory cyber physical system in public transport application. In *Utility and Cloud Computing (UCC), 2011 Fourth IEEE International Conference on*. IEEE.

Lazarus, R. S., & Folkman, S. (1987). Transactional theory and research on emotions and coping. *European Journal of Personality, 1*(3), 141–169. doi:10.1002/per.2410010304

LeDoux, J. E., & Phelps, E. A. (1993). Emotional networks in the brain. Handbook of Emotions, 109, 118.

LeDoux, J. E. (1989). Cognitive-emotional interactions in the brain. *Cognition and Emotion, 3*(4), 267–289. doi:10.1080/02699938908412709

Lee, E. A., & Seshia, S. A. (2011). *Introduction to Embedded Systems - A Cyber-Physical Systems Approach.* LeeSeshia.org.

Lee, D. W. Y. (2001). Genres, Registers, Text Types, Domains, And Styles: Clarifying The Concepts And Navigating A Path Through The Bnc Jungle. *Language Learning & Technology, 5*(3), 37–72.

Lee, E. A. (2008). *CyberPhysicalSystems: DesignChallenges.* Electrical Engineering and Computer Sciences University of California at Berkeley.

Lem, M. (2016). Statistical Methods for Cardiovascular Researchers. *Circulation Research, 118*(3), 439–445. doi:10.1161/CIRCRESAHA.115.306305 PMID:26846639

Leonard, P., Grubb, N., Addison, P., Clifton, D., & Watson, J. (2004). An algorithm for the detection of individual breaths from the pulse oximeter waveform. *Journal of Clinical Monitoring and Computing, 18*(5-6), 309–312. doi:10.100710877-005-2697-z PMID:15957620

Leroy, G., Helmreich, S., Cowie, J. R., Miller, T., & Zheng, W. (2008). Evaluating online health information: Beyond readability formulas. *AMIA ... Annual Symposium Proceedings - AMIA Symposium. AMIA Symposium, 2008,* 394. PMID:18998902

Lewin, S., Munabi-Babigumira, S., Glenton, C., Daniels, K., Bosch-Capblanch, X., van Wyk, B. E., ... Scheel, I. B. (2010). Lay health workers in primary and community health care for maternal and child health and the management of infectious diseases. *Cochrane Database of Systematic Reviews,* (3): CD004015. PMID:20238326

Leyzberg, D., Spaulding, S., & Scassellati, B. (2014). *Personalizing robot tutors to individuals' learning differences.* Paper presented at the 2014 ACM/IEEE international conference on Human-robot interaction, Bielefeld, Germany. 10.1145/2559636.2559671

Leyzberg, D., Spaulding, S., Toneva, M., & Scassellati, B. (2012, January). The physical presence of a robot tutor increases cognitive learning gains. In *Proceedings of the Annual Meeting of the Cognitive Science Society* (Vol. 34, No. 34). Academic Press.

Lieberman, M. D. (2012). Education and the social brain. *Trends in Neuroscience and Education, 1*(1), 3–9. doi:10.1016/j.tine.2012.07.003

Lilly, C. M., Zubrow, M. T., Kempner, K. M., Reynolds, H. N., Subramanian, S., Eriksson, E. A., ... Cowboy, E. R. (2014). Critical care telemedicine: Evolution and state of the art. *Critical Care Medicine, 42*(11), 2429–2436. doi:10.1097/CCM.0000000000000539 PMID:25080052

Lin, D., Zhao, S., Qin, L., & Zhou, M. (2003). Identifying synonyms among distributionally similar words. IJCAI, 3, 1492-1493.

Lin, Y., Liu, T., Chang, M., & Yeh, S. (2009). Exploring Children's Perceptions of the Robots. Learning By Playing. *Game-Based Education System Design And Development,* 512-517. doi:10.1007/978-3-642-03364-3_63

Lind, L., & Karlsson, D. (2018). The eHealth Diary – tailoring a solution for elderly, multimorbid homecare patients. Presented at Medical Information Europe (MIE2018), Gothenburg, Sweden.

Lindberg, B., Nilsson, C., Zotterman, D., Söderberg, S., & Skär, L. (2013). Using Information and Communication Technology in Home Care for Communication between Patients, Family Members, and Healthcare Professionals: A Systematic Review. *International Journal of Telemedicine and Applications, 2013,* 1–31. doi:10.1155/2013/461829 PMID:23690763

Lin, J., & Zhang, A. (2005). Fault feature separation using wavelet-ICA filter. *NDT & E International, 38*(6), 421–427. doi:10.1016/j.ndteint.2004.11.005

Lippincott, T., Séaghdha, D. Ó., & Korhonen, A. (2011). Exploring subdomain variation in biomedical language. *BMC Bioinformatics, 12*(1), 212. doi:10.1186/1471-2105-12-212 PMID:21619603

Liu, C., Conn, K., Sarkar, N., & Stone, W. (2008). Online affect detection and robot behavior adaptation for intervention of children with autism. *IEEE Transactions on Robotics, 24*(4), 883–896. doi:10.1109/TRO.2008.2001362

Liu, Z., Yang, D., Wen, D., Zhang, W., & Mao, W. (2011). Cyber-physical-social systems for command and control. *IEEE Intelligent Systems, 26*(4), 92–96. doi:10.1109/MIS.2011.69

Loginova, E., Gojun, A., Blancafort, H., Guégan, M., Gornostay, T., & Heid, U. (2012). Reference lists for the evaluation of term extraction tools. *Proceedings of the Terminology and Knowledge Engineering Conference (TKE'2012)*.

Long, N. M., Burke, J. F., & Kahana, M. J. (2014). Subsequent memory effect in intracranial and scalp EEG. *NeuroImage, 84*, 488–494. doi:10.1016/j.neuroimage.2013.08.052 PMID:24012858

Lord, C., & Bishop, S. L. (2010). Autism Spectrum Disorders: Diagnosis, Prevalence, and Services for Children and Families. *Social Policy Report, 24*(2). doi:10.1002/j.2379-3988.2010.tb00063.x

Lorente, G. A., & Kanellos, I. (2010). What do we know about on-line museums? A study about current situation of virtual art museums. In *International Conference in Transforming Culture in the Digital Age* (pp. 208-219). Academic Press.

Lourens, T., & Barakova, E. (2009, June). My sparring partner is a humanoid robot. In *International Work-Conference on the Interplay between Natural and Artificial Computation* (pp. 344–352). Berlin: Springer. doi:10.1007/978-3-642-02267-8_37

Loutfi, Jönsson, Karlsson, Lind, Lindén, Pecora, & Voigt. (2016). *Ecare@Home: A Distributed Research Environment on Semantic Interoperability*. Presented at the 3rd EAI International Conference on IoT Technologies for HealthCare (HealhtyIoT 2016), Västerås, Sweden.

Luck, S. J. (2003). Ten Simple Rules for Designing and Interpreting ERP Experiments. In T. C. Handy (Ed.), *Event Related Potentials: A Methods Handbook* (pp. 17–32). Cambridge, MA: The MIT Press.

Luck, S. J. (2005). *An Introduction to Event-Related Potentials and Their Neural Origins*. Cambridge, MA: MIT Press.

Lüdeling, A., Evert, S., & Baroni, M. (2007). Using web data for linguistic purposes. *Language and Computers, 59*, 7.

Luk, B. L., Collie, A. A., Cooke, D. S., & Chen, S. (2006). Walking and climbing service robots for safety inspection of nuclear reactor pressure vessels. *Measurement and Control, 39*(2), 43–47. doi:10.1177/002029400603900201

Lytridis, C., Vrochidou, E., Chatzistamatis, S., & Kaburlasos, V. G. (2018). Social engagement interaction games between children with autism and humanoid robot NAO. In *Proceedings of the 9th International Conference on EUropean Transnational Educational*. Springer.

Lytridis, C., Vrochidou, E., & Kaburlasos, V. G. (2018). Emotional Speech Recognition toward Modulating the Behavior of a Social Robot. *Proceedings of the 2018 JSME Conference on Robotics and Mechatronics*. 10.1299/jsmermd.2018.1A1-B14

Macintyre, Ch., & Deponio, P. (2015). Identifying and supporting children with specific learning difficulties. In Looking beyond the label to assess the whole child. Sofia: Iztok-Zapad; Centar za priobshtavashto obrazovanie.

MacLean, P. D. (1949). Psychosomatic disease and the" visceral brain"; recent developments bearing on the Papez theory of emotion. *Psychosomatic Medicine, 11*(6), 338–353. doi:10.1097/00006842-194911000-00003

Mady & Blumstein. (2017). Social security: are socially connected individuals less vigilant? *Animal Behaviour, 134,* 79-85.

Magnani & Dossena. (2003). Perceiving the Infinite and the Infinitesimal World: Unveiling and Optical Diagrams in the Construction of Mathematical Concepts. *Proceedings of the 25th Annual Meeting of the Cognitive Science Society.*

Mahapatra, A.G., Singh, B., Wagatsuma, H., & Horio, K. (2018). Epilepsy EEG classification using morphological component analysis. *EURASIP Journal on Advances in Signal Processing, 2018*(1), 52.

Mainsah, B. & Wester, T. (2007). *Design of a Dual Heart Rate Variability Monitor.* Worcester Polytechnic Institute.

Mainzer, K. (2007). *Thinking in Complexity.* Springer.

Makeig, S. (1993). Auditory event-related dynamics of the EEG spectrum and effects of exposure to tones. *Electroencephalography and Clinical Neurophysiology, 86*(4), 283–293. doi:10.1016/0013-4694(93)90110-H PMID:7682932

Malá, M. (2017). A Corpus-Based Diachronic Study of a Change in the Use of Non-Finite Clauses in Written English. *Prague Journal of English Studies, 6*(1), 151–166. doi:10.1515/pjes-2017-0009

Malik, M. (1996). Heart Rate Variability: Standards of Measurement, Physiological Interpretation, and Clinical Use: Task Force of the European Society of Cardiology and the North American Society for Pacing and Electrophysiology. *Annals of Noninvasive Electrocardiology, 1*(2), 151–181. doi:10.1111/j.1542-474X.1996.tb00275.x

Malik, M., Bigger, J. T., Camm, A. J., Kleiger, R. E., Malliani, A., Moss, A. J., & Schwartz, P. J. (1996). Heart Rate Variability. Standards of measurement, physiological interpretation, and clinical use. *European Heart Journal, 17*(3), 354–381. doi:10.1093/oxfordjournals.eurheartj.a014868 PMID:8737210

Malik, M., & Camm, A. J. (Eds.). (2004). *Dynamic Electrocardiography.* New York: Futura Division. doi:10.1002/9780470987483

Mandic, D. P., Ur Rehman, N., Wu, Z., & Huang, N. E. (2013). Empirical mode decomposition-based time-frequency analysis of multivariate signals: The power of adaptive data analysis. *IEEE Signal Processing Magazine, 30*(6), 74–86. doi:10.1109/MSP.2013.2267931

Marche, C., Atzori, L., Iera, A., Militano, L., & Nitti, M. (2017). *Navigability in Social Networks of Objects: The Importance of Friendship Type and Nodes' Distance. In IEEE Globecom Workshops* (pp. 1–6). Singapore: GC Workshops.

Marmor, M. F., & Zrenner, E. (1993). Standard for clinical electro-oculography. International Society for Clinical Electrophysiology of Vision. *Archives of Ophthalmology, 111*(5), 601–604.

Martin. (2016). Designer's Guide to the Cortex-M Processor Family (2nd ed.). Academic Press.

Martyn Cooper, D. K., & William Harwin, K. D. (1999). Robots in the classroom-tools for accessible education. *Assistive Technology on the Threshold of the New Millennium, 6,* 448.

Mason, S., Rotella, N., Schaal, S., & Righetti, L. (2016, November). Balancing and walking using full dynamics LQR control with contact constraints. In *Humanoid Robots (Humanoids), 2016 IEEE-RAS 16th International Conference on* (pp. 63-68). IEEE. 10.1109/HUMANOIDS.2016.7803255

Matallah, H., Belalem, G., & Bouamrane, K. (2017). Towards a New Model of Storage and Access to Data in Big Data and Cloud Computing. *International Journal of Ambient Computing and Intelligence, 8*(4), 31–44. doi:10.4018/IJACI.2017100103

Matveen, M., Krasteva, V., Jekova, I., Georgiev, G., Milanov, St., Prokopova, R., & Todorova, L. (2012). Profile of Autonomic Cardiac Control in Patients who are Not Considered Ready for Weaning from Mechanical Ventilation. *Computers in Cardiology, 39,* 625–628.

Maxim Integrated. (n.d.). *MAX30102 Datasheet*. Retrieved from https://datasheets.maximintegrated.com/en/ds/MAX30102.pdf

McClosky, D. (2010). *Any domain parsing: automatic domain adaptation for natural language parsing* (PhD dissertation). Department of Computer Science at Brown University, Providence, RI. Retrieved from https://pdfs.semanticscholar.org/1c6e/e895c202a91a808de59445e3dbde2f4cda0e.pdf

McEnery, T., Xiao, R., & Tono, Y. (2006). *Corpus-based language studies: An advanced resource book*. Taylor & Francis.

McGill. (n.d.). *Biomedical signal*. Retrieved from http://www.medicine.mcgill.ca/physio/vlab/biomed_signals/vlabmenubiosig.htm

McGregor, B. (2005, January). Constructing a concise medical taxonomy. *Journal of the Medical Library Association: JMLA, 93*(1), 121–123. PMID:15685285

McSharry, P. E., Clifford, G., Tarassenko, L., & Smith, L. A. (2003). A dynamical model for generating synthetic electrocardiogram signals. *IEEE Transactions on Biomedical Engineering, 50*(3), 289–294. doi:10.1109/TBME.2003.808805 PMID:12669985

Meijer, C. J., Soriano, V., & Watkins, A. (Eds.). (2003). *Special needs education in Europe: Thematic publication*. European Agency for Development in Special Needs Education.

Melanson, D. (2006). *I Robot Coming to a Train Station Near You*. Retrieved from http://www.engadget.com/2006/08/29/i-robot-coming-to-a-train-station-near-you

Melnik, A., Legkov, P., Izdebski, K., Kärcher, S. M., Hairston, W. D., Ferris, D. P., & König, P. (2017). Systems, Subjects, Sessions: To What Extent Do These Factors Influence EEG Data? *Frontiers in Human Neuroscience, 11*(March), 1–20. PMID:28424600

Meng, F., Gong, X., Guo, L., Cai, X., & Zhang, Q. (2017). Software-Reconfigurable System Supporting Point-to-Point Data Communication Between Vehicle Social Networks and Marketers. *IEEE Access: Practical Innovations, Open Solutions, 5*, 22796–22803. doi:10.1109/ACCESS.2017.2764098

Merilampi, S., & Sirkka, A. (2016). *Introduction to smart eHealth and eCare technologies*. CRC Press. doi:10.1201/9781315368818

Merini, T. U., & Caldelli, R. (2017). Tracing images back to their social network of origin: A CNN-based approach. *2017 IEEE Workshop on Information Forensics and Security (WIFS)*, 1-6.doi: 10.1109/WIFS.2017.8267660

meSch. (2018). *Project Goal*. Retrieved form http://www.mesch-project.eu/About/

Messai, R., Zeng, Q., Mousseau, M., & Simonet, M. (2006). *Building a bilingual French-English patient-oriented terminology for breast cancer*. Toronto, Canada: MedNet.

Michaud, F., Salter, T., Duquette, A., Mercier, H., Lauria, M., Larouche, H., & Larose, F. (2007). Assistive technologies and child-robot interaction. AAAI spring symposium on multidisciplinary collaboration for socially assistive robotics.

Michaud, F., & Caron, S. (2002). Roball, the rolling robot. *Autonomous Robots, 12*(2), 211–222. doi:10.1023/A:1014005728519

Michaud, F., Laplante, J. F., Larouche, H., Duquette, A., Caron, S., Létourneau, D., & Masson, P. (2005). Autonomous spherical mobile robot for child-development studies. *IEEE Transactions on Systems, Man, and Cybernetics. Part A, Systems and Humans, 35*(4), 471–480. doi:10.1109/TSMCA.2005.850596

Microchip. (n.d.). *Microchip Technology ATSAM4S16C Datasheet*. Retrieved from https://www.microchip.com/wwwproducts/en/ATSAM4S16C

Mijović, B., De Vos, M., Gligorijević, I., Taelman, J., & Van Huffel, S. (2010). Source separation from single-channel recordings by combining empirical-mode decomposition and independent component analysis. *IEEE Transactions on Biomedical Engineering, 57*(9), 2188–2196. doi:10.1109/TBME.2010.2051440 PMID:20542760

Mikropoulos, T. A., & Natsis, A. (2011). Educational virtual environments: A ten-year review of empirical research (1999–2009). *Computers & Education, 56*(3), 769–780. doi:10.1016/j.compedu.2010.10.020

Miller, G., Church, R., & Trexler, M. (2000). *Teaching diverse learners using robotics.* Morgan Kaufmann.

Miller, T., & Leroy, G. (2008). Dynamic generation of a Health Topics Overview from consumer health information documents. *International Journal of Biomedical Engineering and Technology, 1*(4), 395–414. doi:10.1504/IJBET.2008.020069

Miller, T., Leroy, G., Chatterjee, S., Fan, J., & Thoms, B. (2007). A Classifier to Evaluate Language Specificity in Medical Documents. *Hawaii International Conference on System Sciences.* 10.1109/HICSS.2007.6

Millett, D. (2001). Hans Berger: From psychic energy to the EEG. *Perspectives in Biology and Medicine, 44*(4), 522–542. doi:10.1353/pbm.2001.0070 PMID:11600799

Minocha, S., Hardy, C. (2016). Navigation and Wayfinding in Learning Spaces in 3d Virtual Worlds. *Learning in Virtual Worlds: Research and Applications.*

Minsky, M. (1974). *A Framework for Representing Knowledge.* Retrieved from dspace.mit.edu

Mirza, M., & Lakshmi, A. (2012). A comparative study of Heart Rate Variability in diabetic subjects and normal subjects. *International Journal of Biomedical and Advance Research, 03*(08), 640–644. doi:10.7439/ijbar.v3i8.542

Mistry, M., Buchli, J., & Schaal, S. (2010, May). Inverse dynamics control of floating base systems using orthogonal decomposition. In *Robotics and Automation (ICRA), 2010 IEEE International Conference on* (pp. 3406-3412). IEEE. 10.1109/ROBOT.2010.5509646

Mitchell, R. L. (2012). Robots Move Into Corporate Roles: Active Media's Jeanne Dietsch says mobile robots make good corporate citizens. *Computer World.*

Mitra, A., Paul, S., Panda, S., & Padhi, P. (2016). A Study on the Representation of the Various Models for Dynamic Social Networks. *Procedia Computer Science, 79*, 624-631.

Moon, A., Danielson, P., & Van der Loos, H. M. (2012). Survey-based discussions on morally contentious applications of interactive robotics. *International Journal of Social Robotics, 4*(1), 77–96. doi:10.100712369-011-0120-0

Mori, M. (1970/2012). The uncanny valley (K. F. MacDorman & N. Kageki, Trans.). *IEEE Robotics & Automation Magazine, 19*(2), 98–100. doi:10.1109/MRA.2012.2192811

Movellan, J. R., Tanaka, F., Fortenberry, B., & Aisaka, K. (2005). *The RUBI/QRIO Project: Origins, Principles, and First Steps.* Paper presented at the 4th International Conference on Development and Learning. 10.1109/DEVLRN.2005.1490948

Mubin, O., Stevens, C., Shahid, S., Mahmud, A., & Dong, J. (2013). A review of the applicability of robots in education. *Technology For Education And Learning, 1*(1). doi:10.2316/Journal.209.2013.1.209-0015

Museum Ideas London. (2019). *Museum.* Retrieved from https://museum-id.com/augmented-reality-museums-beyond-hype-shelley-mannion/

Museum, S. (n.d.). *Deliverable D4.1 SMARTMUSEUM Report of Architecture of Web Services.* Retrieved from http://www.smartmuseum.eu/del/D4.1_FINAL_v1.03.pdf

Nakajima, K., Tamura, T., & Miike, H. (1996). Monitoring of heart and respiratory rates by photoplethysmography using a digital filtering technique. *Medical Engineering & Physics*, *18*(5), 365–372. doi:10.1016/1350-4533(95)00066-6 PMID:8818134

Nakajima, K., Tamura, T., Ohta, T., Miike, H., & Oberg, P. (1993). Photoplethysmographic measurement of heart and respiratory rates using digital filters. In *Proceedings of the 15th Annual International Conference of the IEEE Engineering in Medicine and Biology Society* (Vol. 15, pp. 1006–1007). San Diego, CA: IEEE. 10.1109/IEMBS.1993.978978

Nambiar, K. K. (1999). Intuitive Set Theory. Computers and Mathematics with Applications, 39(1-2), 183–185.

Nanas, N., & De Roeck, A. (2008). Corpus profiling with Nootropia. In *Proceedings of Workshop on Corpus Profiling for Information Retrieval and Natural Language Profiling*. London: BCS-IRSG.

Nazarenko, A., & Zargayouna, H. (2009). Evaluating term extraction. In *International Conference Recent Advances in Natural Language Processing (RANLP'09)* (pp. 299-304). Academic Press.

Nenova, B. & Iiliev, I. (2010). An automated algorithm for fast pulse wave detection. *Bioautomation*, *3*(14), 203–216.

Nenova-Baylova, B. (2011). *Determination of Cardiac Activity in Extreme Situations*. Autoreferate. (in Bulgarian)

Nganji, J., & Nggada, S. (2011). Disability-Aware Software Engineering for Improved System Accessibility and Usability. *International Journal of Software Engineering and Its Applications*, *5*(3), 47–62.

Ng, J. W., & Lau, D. H. (2013). Social Ontology and Semantic Actions: Enabling Social Networking Services for Distributed Web Tasking. *2013 IEEE Ninth World Congress on Services*, 131-135. 10.1109/SERVICES.2013.23

Nicolas-Alonso, L. F., & Gomez-Gil, J. (2012). Brain computer interfaces, a review. *Sensors (Basel)*, *12*(2), 1211–1279. doi:10.3390120201211 PMID:22438708

Nie & Song. (2016). Learning from Multiple Social Networks. In *Learning from Multiple Social Networks*. Morgan & Claypool.

Nikolova, R. (2008). The Time to Distribute the Pulse Wave - a Method for the Study of the Functional Status of the Cardiovascular System [in Bulgarian]. *Bulgarian Medical Journal*, *2*(1), 9–13.

Nilsson, S.E. & Andersson, B.E. (1988). Corneal DC recordings of slow ocular potential changes such as the ERG c-wave and the light peak in clinical work. *Documenta ophthalmologica, 68*(3-4), 313-325.

Nilsson, C., Öhman, M., & Söderberg, S. (2006). Information and communication technology in supporting people with serious chronic illness living at home–an intervention study. *Journal of Telemedicine and Telecare*, *12*(4), 198–202. doi:10.1258/135763306777488807 PMID:16774702

Nisiotis, L., Loizou, K., & Styliani, B. (2017). The use of a Cyber Campus to Support Teaching and Collaboration: An Observation Approach. In Immersive Learning Research Network (iLRN) Conference, Coimbra, Portugal.

Norman, G. R., Arfai, B., Gupta, A., Brooks, L. R., & Eva, K. W. (2003). The privileged status of prestigious terminology: Impact of "medicalese" on clinical judgments. *Academic Medicine*, *78*(10Supplement), S82–S84. doi:10.1097/00001888-200310001-00026 PMID:14557104

Norwich, B. (2007). *Dilemmas of difference, inclusion and disability: International perspectives and future directions*. Routledge. doi:10.4324/9780203938867

Nourbakhsh, I. R., Kunz, C., & Willeke, T. (2003). The mobot museum robot installations: a five year experiment. *2003 IEEE/RJS International Conference on Intelligent Robots and Systems*, 3636–3641. 10.1109/IROS.2003.1249720

Nutt, G. (2018). *NuttX operating system user's manual.* Retrieved from www.nuttx.org

Nyström, M., Merkel, M., Ahrenberg, L., Zweigenbaum, P., Petersson, H., & Åhlfeldt, H. (2006). Creating a medical english-swedish dictionary using interactive word alignment. *BMC Medical Informatics and Decision Making, 6*(1), 35. doi:10.1186/1472-6947-6-35 PMID:17034649

Nyström, M., Merkel, M., Petersson, H., & Åhlfeldt, H. (2007). Creating a medical dictionary using word alignment: The influence of sources and resources. *BMC Medical Informatics and Decision Making, 7*(1), 37. doi:10.1186/1472-6947-7-37 PMID:18036221

O'Brien, S. (1993). *Sublanguage, text type and machine translation* (Doctoral dissertation). Dublin City University.

Oakes, M. P. (2008). Statistical measures for corpus profiling. *Proceedings of the Open University Workshop on Corpus Profiling.*

Ochs, M., Pelachaud, C., & Sadek, D. (2008). An empathic virtual dialog agent to improve human-machine interaction. In *Proceedings of the 7th international joint conference on Autonomous agents and multiagent systems* (vol. 1, pp. 89-96). International Foundation for Autonomous Agents and Multiagent Systems.

Ochsner, K. N., & Lieberman, M. D. (2001). The emergence of social cognitive neuroscience. *The American Psychologist, 56*(9), 717–734. doi:10.1037/0003-066X.56.9.717 PMID:11558357

Ogura, Y., Shimomura, K., Kondo, H., Morishima, A., Okubo, T., Momoki, S., . . . Takanishi, A. (2006, October). Human-like walking with knee stretched, heel-contact and toe-off motion by a humanoid robot. In *Intelligent Robots and Systems, 2006 IEEE/RSJ International Conference on* (pp. 3976-3981). IEEE. 10.1109/IROS.2006.281834

Okita, S. Y., & Schwartz, D. L. (2006). Young children's understanding of animacy and entertainment robots. *International Journal of Humanoid Robotics, 3*(3), 393-412.

Okita, S. Y., Ng-Thow-Hing, V., & Sarvadevabhatla, R. (2009). Learning together: ASIMO developing an interactive learning partnership with children. In *Robot and Human Interactive Communication, 2009. RO-MAN 2009. The 18th IEEE International Symposium on* (pp. 1125-1130). IEEE.

Oliva, A., & Torralba, A. (2007). The role of context in object recognition. *Trends in Cognitive Sciences, 11*(12), 520–527. doi:10.1016/j.tics.2007.09.009 PMID:18024143

Oros, M., Nikolić, M., Borovac, B., & Jerković, I. (2014). Children's preference of appearance and parents' attitudes towards assistive robots. In *Humanoid Robots (Humanoids), 2014 14th IEEE-RAS International Conference on* (pp. 360-365). IEEE.

Östling, R. (2013). Stagger: An open-source part of speech tagger for Swedish. *Northern European Journal of Language Technology, 3*, 1–18. doi:10.3384/nejlt.2000-1533.1331

Ott, M., & Freina, L. (2015). *A literature review on immersive virtual reality in education: state of the art and perspectives.* Paper presented at the conference proceedings of eLearning and software for education (eLSE).

Ownby, R. L. (2005). Influence of vocabulary and sentence complexity and passive voice on the readability of consumer-oriented mental health information on the internet. In *AMIA 2005 Symposium Proceedings.* AMIA.

Pachidis, T., Vrochidou, E., Kaburlasos, V. G., Kostova, S., Bonković, M., & Papić, V. (2018). Social Robotics in Education: State-of-the-Art and Directions. *Proceedings of the 27th International Conference on Robotics in Alpe-Adria-Danube Region.*

Paiva, A., Leite, I., & Ribeiro, T. (2014). Emotion modelling for social robots. In R. A. Calvo, S. K. D'Mello, J. Gratch, & A. Kappas (Eds.), *Handbook of affective computing*. Oxford University Press.

Paneva-Marinova, D., Goynov, M., & Pavlov, R. (2017). Personalized Observation and Enhanced Learning Experience in Digital Libraries. In *ICERI2017 Proceedings. 10th annual International Conference of Education, Research and Innovation, ICERI2017*. IATED Academy.

Paneva-Marinova, D., Pavlov, R., & Goynov, M. (2012). Two Integrated Digital Libraries for Knowledge and Iconography of Orthodox Saints. Progress in Cultural Heritage Preservation. EuroMed 2012. Lecture Notes in Computer Science, 7616, 684-691.

Paneva-Marinova, D., Pavlov, R., & Kotuzov, N. (2017). Approach for Analysis and Improved Usage of Digital Cultural Assets for Learning Purposes. *Cybernetics and Information Technologies, 17*(3), 140-151.

Paneva-Marinova, D., Goynov, M., & Luchev, D. (2017). *Multimedia digital library: Constructive block in ecosystems for digital cultural assets. Basic functionality and services*. Berlin, Germany: LAP LAMBERT Academic Publishing.

Paneva-Marinova, D., Goynov, M., Luchev, D., & Pavlov, R. (2015). Solution for content interoperability among digital libraries for orthodox artefacts and knowledge. *ACM International Conference Proceeding Series, CompSysTech '15 Proceedings of the 16th International Conference on Computer Systems and Technologies*, 168-175. 10.1145/2812428.2812474

Panovko, G. Y., Savin, S. I., Yatsun, S. F., & Yatsun, A. S. (2016). Simulation of exoskeleton sit-to-stand movement. *Journal of Machinery Manufacture and Reliability, 45*(3), 206–210. doi:10.3103/S1052618816030110

Papakostas, G. A., & Kaburlasos, V. G. (2018). Modeling in cyber-physical systems by lattice computing techniques: the case of image watermarking based on intervals' numbers. *Proceedings of the World Congress on Computational Intelligence (WCCI) 2018, FUZZ-IEEE Program*, 491-496. 10.1109/FUZZ-IEEE.2018.8491653

Papakostas, G., Sidiropoulos, G., Bella, M., & Kaburlasos, V. (2018). Social robots in special education: current status and future challenges. *Proceedings of the 2018 JSME Conference on Robotics and Mechatronics*. 10.1299/jsmermd.2018.1P1-A15

Papez, J. W. (1937). A proposed mechanism of emotion. *Archives of Neurology and Psychiatry, 38*(4), 725–743. doi:10.1001/archneurpsyc.1937.02260220069003

Park, Y., Byrd, R. J., & Boguraev, B. K. (2002). Automatic glossary extraction: beyond terminology identification. In *Proceedings of the 19th international conference on Computational linguistics* (vol. 1, pp. 1-7). Association for Computational Linguistics.

Partala, T., & Surakka, V. (2004). The effects of affective interventions in human–computer interaction. *Interacting with Computers, 16*(2), 295–309. doi:10.1016/j.intcom.2003.12.001

Pastor, P. N., & Reuben, C. A. (2008). Diagnosed Attention Deficit Hyperactivity Disorder and Learning Disability: United States, 2004-2006. Data from the National Health Interview Survey. Vital and Health Statistics. Series 10, Number 237. Centers for Disease Control and Prevention.

Paunski, Y., & Zahariev, R. (2017). Service robots control system, based on "Arm cortex M" architecture microprocessor system. *Pr. TUSofia, XXVI International Conference ADP-2017*, 300-304.

Pazienza, M., Pennacchiotti, M., & Zanzotto, F. (2005). Terminology extraction: an analysis of linguistic and statistical approaches. In *Terminology Extraction: An Analysis of Linguistic and Statistical Approaches*. Springer. doi:10.1007/3-540-32394-5_20

Peak District National Park. (n.d.). *Audio Trails*. Retrieved from https://www.peakdistrict.gov.uk/visiting/trails/audio-trails

Pearson, J. (1998). *Terms in context* (Vol. 1). John Benjamins Publishing. doi:10.1075cl.1

Pennington, R. (1877). *Notes on the Barrows and Bone-caves of Derbyshire: With an Account of a Descent Into Elden Hole*. Macmillan and Company.

Perry. (2008). *Grand Challenges in Engineering*. National Academy of Engineering, Report.

Petridis, P., White, M., Mourkousis, N., Liarokapis, F., Sifniotis, M., Basu, A., & Gatzidis, C. (2005). Exploring and interacting with virtual museums. *Proceedings of the 33rd Annual Conference of Computer Applications and Quantitative Methods in Archaeology (CAA)*.

Pfeiffer, U. J., Vogeley, K., & Schilbach, L. (2013). From gaze cueing to dual eye-tracking: Novel approaches to investigate the neural correlates of gaze in social interaction. *Neuroscience and Biobehavioral Reviews*, *37*(10), 2516–2528. doi:10.1016/j.neubiorev.2013.07.017 PMID:23928088

Phillips, D. K. (2015). *Speed of the Human Brain*. Retrieved October 1, 2018 from https://askabiologist.asu.edu/plosable/speed-human-brain

Picard, R. W., & Liu, K. K. (2007). Relative subjective count and assessment of interruptive technologies applied to mobile monitoring of stress. *International Journal of Human-Computer Studies*, *65*(4), 361–375. doi:10.1016/j.ijhcs.2006.11.019

Picton, T. W., Van Roon, P., Armilio, M. L., Berg, P., Ille, N., & Scherg, M. (2000). The correction of ocular artifacts: A topographic perspective. *Clinical Neurophysiology*, *111*(1), 53–65. doi:10.1016/S1388-2457(99)00227-8 PMID:10656511

Pieterse, A. H., Jager, N. A., Smets, E. M., & Henselmans, I. (2013). Lay understanding of common medical terminology in oncology. *Psycho-Oncology*, *22*(5), 1186–1191. doi:10.1002/pon.3096 PMID:22573405

Pioggia, G., Ferro, M., Sica, M. L., Dalle Mura, G., Casalini, S., De Rossi, D., & Muratori, F. (2006). Imitation and learning of the emotional behaviour: towards an android-based treatment for people with autism. In *Proc. Sixth Int. Workshop Epigenet. Robot.* (pp. 119-25). Lund, Sweden: LUCS.

Plöchl, M., Ossandón, J. P., & König, P. (2012). Combining EEG and eye tracking: Identification, characterization, and correction of eye movement artifacts in electroencephalographic data. *Frontiers in Human Neuroscience*, *6*, 278. doi:10.3389/fnhum.2012.00278 PMID:23087632

Plutchik, R. (1991). *The emotions*. University Press of America.

Pomikálek, J., Rychlý, P., & Kilgarriff, A. (2009). Scaling to billion-plus word corpora. *Advances in Computational Linguistics*, *41*, 3–13.

Poovendran, R. (2010). Cyber–Physical Systems: Close Encounters Between Two Parallel Worlds. *Proceedings of the IEEE*, *98*(8), 1363–1366. doi:10.1109/JPROC.2010.2050377

Poprat, M., Markó, K., & Hahn, U. (2006). A language classifier that automatically divides medical documents for experts and health care consumers. *Studies in Health Technology and Informatics*, *124*, 503. PMID:17108568

Powers, A.S., Basso, M.S., & Evinger. C. (2013). Blinks Slow Memory-Guided Saccades. *Journal of Neurophysiology*, *109*(3), 734–741.

Pratt, G. A., Williamson, M. M., Dillworth, P., Pratt, J., & Wright, A. (1997). Stiffness isn't everything. In Experimental robotics IV (pp. 253-262). Springer. doi:10.1007/BFb0035216

Pratt, G. A. (2002). Low impedance walking robots. *Integrative and Comparative Biology*, *42*(1), 174–181. doi:10.1093/icb/42.1.174 PMID:21708707

Pratt, G. A., Willisson, P., Bolton, C., & Hofman, A. (2004, June). Late motor processing in low-impedance robots: Impedance control of series-elastic actuators. In *American Control Conference, 2004. Proceedings of the 2004* (Vol. 4, pp. 3245-3251). IEEE. 10.23919/ACC.2004.1384410

Prendinger, H., Mori, J., & Ishizuka, M. (2005). Using human physiology to evaluate subtle expressivity of a virtual quizmaster in a mathematical game. *International Journal of Human-Computer Studies*, *62*(2), 231–245. doi:10.1016/j.ijhcs.2004.11.009

Prescott, T., & Szollosy, M. (2017). Ethical principles of robotics. *Connection Science*, *29*(2), 119–123. doi:10.1080/09540091.2017.1312800

Pressman, R. S. (2005). *Software engineering: a practitioner's approach*. Palgrave Macmillan.

Prinz, J. (2004). Embodied emotions. In R. C. Solomon (Ed.), *Thinking about feeling: Contemporary philosophers on the emotions* (pp. 44–59). Oxford, UK: Oxford University Press.

Puga-Gonzalez & Sueur. (2017). Emergence of complex social networks from spatial structure and rules of thumb: a modelling approach. *Ecological Complexity, 31*, 189-200.

Pujol, L., & Lorente, A. (2012). The Virtual Museum: a Quest for the Standard Definition. *Archaeology in the Digital Era, 40*.

Pulse Sensor. (n.d.). Retrieved from https://pulsesensor.com/

Quick, D., & Choo, K.-K. R. (2017). Pervasive social networking forensics: Intelligence and evidence from mobile device extracts. *Journal of Network and Computer Applications, 86*, 24-33. doi:10.1016/j.jnca.2016.11.018

Quintas, J. M. L. (2018). *Context-based Human-Machine Interaction Framework for Arti ficial Social Companions* (Doctoral dissertation). Universidade de Coimbra.

Quirk, C., Brockett, C., & Dolan, B. (2004). Monolingual machine translation for paraphrase generation. *Proceedings of the 2004 Conference on Empirical Methods in Natural Language Processing, EMNLP 2004, A meeting of SIGDAT, a Special Interest Group of the ACL, held in conjunction with ACL 2004*.

Rabbitt, S., Kazdin, A., & Scassellati, B. (2014). Inegrating socially assistive robotics into mental healthcare interventions: Applications and recommendations for expanded use. *Clinical Psychology Review*, *35*, 35–46. doi:10.1016/j.cpr.2014.07.001 PMID:25462112

Rajaraman, V. (1971). *Analog Computation and Simulation*. Prentice-Hall of India.

Rajkumar. (2010). *Cyber-Physical Systems: The Next Computing Revolution*. Design Automation Conference 2010, Anaheim, CA.

Ramamritham, K., Son, S. H., & Dipippo, L. C. (2004). Real-time databases and data services. *Real-Time Systems*, *28*(2-3), 179–215. doi:10.1023/B:TIME.0000045317.37980.a5

Ramey, C. H. (2006). An inventory of reported characteristics for home computers, robots, and human beings: Applications for android science and the uncanny valley. In *Proceedings of the ICCS/CogSci-2006 long symposium "Toward social mechanisms of android science"* (pp. 21-25). Academic Press.

Rao, M., & Ram, R. (2006). Photoplethysmography: A noninvasive tool for possible subtle energy monitoring during yogic practices. *Subtle Energies & Energy Medicine*, *17*(2), 163–179.

Rath, M., & Panda, M. R. (2017). MAQ system development in mobile ad-hoc networks using mobile agents. *IEEE 2nd International Conference on Contemporary Computing and Informatics (IC3I)*, 794-798.

Rath, M., & Pattanayak, B. (2018). Technological improvement in modern health care applications using Internet of Things (IoT) and proposal of novel health care approach. *International Journal of Human Rights in Healthcare*. doi:10.1108/IJHRH-01-2018-0007

Rath, M., & Pattanayak, B. K. (2014). A methodical survey on real time applications in MANETS: Focussing On Key Issues. *International Conference on, High Performance Computing and Applications (IEEE ICHPCA)*, 1-5, 22-24. 10.1109/ICHPCA.2014.7045301

Rath, M., & Pattanayak, B. K. (2018). Monitoring of QoS in MANET Based Real Time Applications. In Information and Communication Technology for Intelligent Systems Volume 2. ICTIS. Smart Innovation, Systems and Technologies (vol. 84, pp. 579-586). Springer. doi:10.1007/978-3-319-63645-0_64

Rath, M., Pati, B., & Pattanayak, B. K. (2016). Inter-Layer Communication Based QoS Platform for Real Time Multimedia Applications in MANET. Wireless Communications, Signal Processing and Networking (IEEE WiSPNET), 613-617. doi:10.1109/WiSPNET.2016.7566203

Rath, Pati, & Pattanayak. (2018). An Overview on Social Networking: Design, Issues, Emerging Trends, and Security. *Social Network Analytics: Computational Research Methods and Techniques*, 21-47.

Rath, M. (2017). Resource provision and QoS support with added security for client side applications in cloud computing. *International Journal of Information Technology*, *9*(3), 1–8.

Rath, M., & Pati, B. (2017). *Load balanced routing scheme for MANETs with power and delay optimisation. International Journal of Communication Network and Distributed Systems* , 19.

Rath, M., Pati, B., Panigrahi, C. R., & Sarkar, J. L. (2019). QTM: A QoS Task Monitoring System for Mobile Ad hoc Networks. In P. Sa, S. Bakshi, I. Hatzilygeroudis, & M. Sahoo (Eds.), *Recent Findings in Intelligent Computing Techniques. Advances in Intelligent Systems and Computing* (Vol. 707). Singapore: Springer. doi:10.1007/978-981-10-8639-7_57

Rath, M., Pati, B., & Pattanayak, B. K. (2017). Cross layer based QoS platform for multimedia transmission in MANET. *11th International Conference on Intelligent Systems and Control (ISCO)*, 402-407. 10.1109/ISCO.2017.7856026

Rath, M., & Pattanayak, B. (2017). MAQ:A Mobile Agent Based QoS Platform for MANETs. *International Journal of Business Data Communications and Networking, IGI Global*, *13*(1), 1–8. doi:10.4018/IJBDCN.2017010101

Rath, M., & Pattanayak, B. K. (2018). SCICS: A Soft Computing Based Intelligent Communication System in VANET. Smart Secure Systems – IoT and Analytics Perspective. *Communications in Computer and Information Science*, *808*, 255–261. doi:10.1007/978-981-10-7635-0_19

Rath, M., Pattanayak, B. K., & Pati, B. (2017). *Energetic Routing Protocol Design for Real-time Transmission in Mobile Ad hoc Network. In Computing and Network Sustainability, Lecture Notes in Networks and Systems* (Vol. 12). Singapore: Springer.

Rathore, Sharma, Loia, Jeong, & Park. (2017). Social network security: Issues, challenges, threats, and solutions. *Information Sciences, 421*, 43-69.

Rau, R. (2017). Social networks and financial outcomes. *Current Opinion in Behavioral Sciences, 18*, 75-78.

Ravenscroft, J. (2016). Visual Impairment and Mainstream Education: Beyond Mere Awareness Raising. In L. Peer & G. Reid (Eds.), *Special Educational Needs. A Guide for Inclusive Practice* (pp. 232–249). Los Angeles, CA: SAGE.

Ray, A., Tao, J. X., Hawes-Ebersole, S. M., & Ebersole, J. S. (2007). Localizing value of scalp EEG spikes: A simultaneous scalp and intracranial study. *Clinical Neurophysiology, 118*(1), 69–79. doi:10.1016/j.clinph.2006.09.010 PMID:17126071

Rayson, P. (2008). From key words to key semantic domains. *International Journal of Corpus Linguistics, 13*(4), 519–549. doi:10.1075/ijcl.13.4.06ray

Rayson, P., & Garside, R. (2000). Comparing corpora using frequency profiling. In *Proceedings of the workshop on Comparing Corpora* (pp. 1-6). Association for Computational Linguistics.

Reid, G., Lannen, S., & Lannen, C. (2016). Autistic Spectrum Disorder. Challenges, Issues and Responses. In L. Peer & G. Reid (Eds.), *Special Educational Needs. A Guide for Inclusive Practice* (pp. 268–286). Los Angeles, CA: SAGE.

Remus, S., & Biemann, C. (2016). Domain-Specific Corpus Expansion with Focused Webcrawling. LREC.

Richards, M. (2012). *White Peak Walks: The Northern Dales: 35 walks in the Derbyshire White Peak*. Cicerone Press Limited.

Robins, B., Dautenhahn, K., & Dickerson, P. (2009). From isolation to communication: a case study evaluation of robot assisted play for children with autism with a minimally expressive humanoid robot. In *Advances in Computer-Human Interactions, 2009. ACHI'09. Second International Conferences on* (pp. 205-211). Academic Press. 10.1109/ACHI.2009.32

Robins, B., Dautenhahn, K., Te Boekhorst, R., & Billard, A. (2004). Effects of repeated exposure to a humanoid robot on children with autism. *Designing a more inclusive world*, 225-236.

Robins, B., Dautenhahn, K., Te Boekhorst, R., & Billard, A. (2005). Robotic assistants in therapy and education of children with autism: Can a small humanoid robot help encourage social interaction skills? *Universal Access in the Information Society, 4*(2), 105–120. doi:10.100710209-005-0116-3

Robinson, D. W., Pratt, J. E., Paluska, D. J., & Pratt, G. A. (1999, September). Series elastic actuator development for a biomimetic walking robot. In *Advanced Intelligent Mechatronics, 1999. Proceedings. 1999 IEEE/ASME International Conference on* (pp. 561-568). IEEE. 10.1109/AIM.1999.803231

Romo-Vázquez, R., Vélez-Pérez, H., Ranta, R., Louis-Dorr, V., Maquin, D., & Maillard, L. (2012). Blind source separation, wavelet denoising and discriminant analysis for EEG artefacts and noise cancelling. *Biomedical Signal Processing and Control, 7*(4), 389–400. doi:10.1016/j.bspc.2011.06.005

Rtah, M. (2018). Big Data and IoT-Allied Challenges Associated With Healthcare Applications in Smart and Automated Systems. *International Journal of Strategic Information Technology and Applications, 9*(2). doi:10.4018/IJSITA.201804010

Ruchkin, I., Schmerl, B., & Garlan, D. (2015). Analytic Dependency Loops in Architectural Models of Cyber-Physical Systems. *8th International Workshop on Model-based Architecting of Cyber-Physical and Embedded Systems (ACES-MB)*.

Rudd, R. E. (2013). Needed action in health literacy. *Journal of Health Psychology, 18*(8), 1004–1010. doi:10.1177/1359105312470128 PMID:23349399

Sabev, N. (2017). The Usefulness of diversity: the utility and accessibility analysis for people with disabilities. In Scientific Conference "Harmony in Differences", About the Letters - О писменехь, (pp. 459-466). Academic Press. (in Bulgarian)

Sabev, N., & Bogdanova, G. (2018). Accessibility of National Tourist Sites for People with Disabilities. In *Cultural and Historical Heritage: Preservation, Presentation, Digitalization* (pp. 38-98). Public Library. Retrieved from http://www.math.bas.bg/vt/kin/book-5/04-KIN-5-2018.pdf

Sabev, N., Bogdanova, G., & Georgieva-Tsaneva, G. (2018). Negoslav Sabev, Galina Bogdanova, Galya Georgieva-Tsaneva. Creating a Software System with Functionality to Help Make it Accessible for People with a Visual Deficit. In *CBU International Conference on Innovations in Science and Education*. Central Bohemia University.

Sabev, N., Georgieva-Tsaneva, G., & Bogdanova, G. (2018). Creating a Software System with Functionality to Help Make it Accessible for People with a Visual Deficit. In *CBU International Conference on Innovations in Science and Education*. Prague, Czech Republic: CBU Research Institute. 10.12955/cbup.v6.1241

Sadasivan, P. K., & Narayana Dutt, D. (1996). SVD based technique for noise reduction in electroencephalographic signals. *Signal Processing*, *55*(2), 179–189. doi:10.1016/S0165-1684(96)00129-6

Saganowski, S. (2015). Predicting community evolution in social networks. *IEEE/ACM International Conference on Advances in Social Networks Analysis and Mining (ASONAM)*, 924-925.

Saint-Charles & Mongeau. (2018). Social influence and discourse similarity networks in workgroups. *Social Networks*, *52*, 228-237.

Sameni, R., & Gouy-Pailler, C. (2014). An iterative subspace denoising algorithm for removing electroencephalogram ocular artifacts. *Journal of Neuroscience Methods*, *225*, 97–105. doi:10.1016/j.jneumeth.2014.01.024 PMID:24486874

Sanada, M., Ikeda, K., Kimura, K., & Hasegawa, T. (2013). Motivation enhances visual working memory capacity through the modulation of central cognitive processes. *Psychophysiology*, *50*(9), 864–871. doi:10.1111/psyp.12077 PMID:23834356

Santini, M. (2006). *Common Criteria for Genre Classification: Annotation and Granularity*. Workshop on Text-based Information Retrieval (TIR-06), In Conjunction with ECAI 2006, Riva del Garda, Italy.

Santini, M., Jönsson, A., Nyström, M., & Alirezai, M. (2017). A Web Corpus for eCare: Collection, Lay Annotation and Learning - First Results. Workshop LTA'17 (Language Technology Applications 2017) co-located with FedCSIS 2017, Prague. In M. Ganzha, L. Maciaszek, & M. Paprzycki (Eds.), *Position Papers of the 2017 Federated Conference on Computer Science and Information Systems, Proceedings*, (Vol. 12, pp. 71-78). Academic Press.

Santini, M., Strandqvist, W., Nyström, M., Alirezai, M., & Jönsson, A. (2018). *Can we Quantify Domainhood? Exploring Measures to Assess Domain-Specificity in Web Corpora*. TIR 2018 - 15th International Workshop on Technologies for Information Retrieval.

Santi, P. (2012). *Mobile Social Network Analysis. In Mobility Models for Next Generation Wireless Networks: Ad Hoc, Vehicular and Mesh Networks, 1* (p. 448). Wiley Telecom. doi:10.1002/9781118344774

Sarmiento, S., Garcria-Manso, J., Martrin-Gonzralez, J., Vaamonde, D., Calderron, J., & Da Silva-Grigoletto, M. (2013). Heart Rate Variability During High-Intensity Exercise. *Journal of Systems Science and Complexity*, *26*(1), 104–116. doi:10.100711424-013-2287-y

Sarwar Kamal, M. (2017). De-Bruijn graph with MapReduce framework towards metagenomic data classification. *International Journal of Information Technology*, *9*(1), 59–75. doi:10.100741870-017-0005-z

Sarwar Kamal, M., Golam Sarowar, M., Dey, N., & Joao Manuel, R. S. T. (2017). Self-Organizing Mapping based Swarm Intelligence for Secondary and Tertiary Proteins Classification. *International Journal of Machine Learning and Cybernetics*.

Sasikala, P., & Wahidabanu, R. (2010). Robust R Peak and QRS detection in Electrocardiogram using Wavelet Transform. *International Journal of Advanced Computer Science and Applications*, *1*(6), 48–53. doi:10.14569/IJACSA.2010.010608

Savin, S. (2017, June). An algorithm for generating convex obstacle-free regions based on stereographic projection. In *Control and Communications (SIBCON), 2017 International Siberian Conference on* (pp. 1-6). IEEE. 10.1109/SIBCON.2017.7998590

Savin, S., & Vorochaeva, L. (2017, June). Footstep planning for a six-legged in-pipe robot moving in spatially curved pipes. In *Control and Communications (SIBCON), 2017 International Siberian Conference on* (pp. 1-6). IEEE. 10.1109/SIBCON.2017.7998581

Savin, S., Jatsun, S., & Vorochaeva, L. (2017, November). Modification of Constrained LQR for Control of Walking in-pipe Robots. In Dynamics of Systems, Mechanisms and Machines (Dynamics), 2017 (pp. 1-6). IEEE. doi:10.1109/Dynamics.2017.8239502

Savin, S., Jatsun, S., & Vorochaeva, L. (2018). State observer design for a walking in-pipe robot. In *MATEC Web of Conferences* (Vol. 161, p. 03012). EDP Sciences. 10.1051/matecconf/201816103012

Savin, S. (2018). *Comparative Analysis of Control Methods for Walking Robots with Nonlinear Sensors.* (Manuscript submitted for publication)

Savin, S., & Vorochaeva, L. (2017). Nested Quadratic Programming-based Controller for In-pipe Robots. *Proceeding of the International Conference On Industrial Engineering.*

Scassellati, B. (2005). Quantitative metrics of social response for autism diagnosis. In *Robot and Human Interactive Communication, 2005. ROMAN 2005. IEEE International Workshop on* (pp. 585-590). IEEE. 10.1109/ROMAN.2005.1513843

Scassellati, B., Admoni, H., & Matarić, M. (2012). Robots for use in autism research. *Annual Review of Biomedical Engineering*, *14*(1), 275–294. doi:10.1146/annurev-bioeng-071811-150036 PMID:22577778

Schäfer, R. (2016). CommonCOW: Massively Huge Web Corpora from CommonCrawl Data and a Method to Distribute them Freely under Restrictive EU Copyright Laws. LREC.

Schäfer, R., & Bildhauer, F. (2012). Building large corpora from the web using a new efficient tool chain. In LREC (pp. 486-493). Academic Press.

Schäfer, R., Barbaresi, A., & Bildhauer, F. (2014). Focused web corpus crawling. In *Proceedings of the 9th Web as Corpus workshop (WAC-9)* (pp. 9-15). Academic Press. 10.3115/v1/W14-0402

Schäfer, A., & Vagedes, J. (2013). How accurate is pulse rate variability as an estimate of heart rate variability? A review on studies comparing photoplethysmographic technology with an electrocardiogram. *International Journal of Cardiology*, *166*(1), 15–29. doi:10.1016/j.ijcard.2012.03.119 PMID:22809539

Schäfer, R., Barbaresi, A., & Bildhauer, F. (2013). The good, the bad, and the hazy: Design decisions in web corpus construction. *Proceedings of the 8th Web as Corpus Workshop.*

Schäfer, R., & Bildhauer, F. (2013). Web corpus construction. *Synthesis Lectures on Human Language Technologies*, *6*(4), 1–145. doi:10.2200/S00508ED1V01Y201305HLT022

Schilbach, L. (2014). On the relationship of online and offline social cognition. *Frontiers in Human Neuroscience*, *8*, 278. doi:10.3389/fnhum.2014.00278 PMID:24834045

Schlegel, R., Chow, C. Y., Huang, Q., & Wong, D. S. (2017). Privacy-Preserving Location Sharing Services for Social Networks. *IEEE Transactions on Services Computing*, *10*(5), 811–825. doi:10.1109/TSC.2016.2514338

Schutz, B. (1980). *Geometrical Methods of Mathematical Physics*. Cambridge University Press. doi:10.1017/CBO9781139171540

Schweibenz, W. (1998). The "Virtual Museum": New Perspectives for Museums to Present Objects and Information Using the Internet as a Knowledge Base and Communication System. Proceedings des 6° Internationalen Symposiums für Informationswissenschaft ISI, 185-200.

Scott, N., & Weiner, M. F. (1984). "Patientspeak": An exercise in communication. *Journal of Medical Education.* PMID:6492107

Screen Reader User Survey #7 Results. (n.d.). Retrieved from https://webaim.org/projects/screenreadersurvey7/

Seedor, M., Peterson, K. J., Nelsen, L. A., Cocos, C., McCormick, J. B., Chute, C. G., & Pathak, J. (2013). Incorporating expert terminology and disease risk factors into consumer health vocabularies. In *Pacific Symposium on Biocomputing. Pacific Symposium on Biocomputing.* NIH Public Access.

Seedorff, M., Peterson, K. J., Nelsen, L. A., Cocos, C., McCormick, J. B., Chute, C. G., & Pathak, J. (2013). Incorporating expert terminology and disease risk factors into consumer health vocabularies. In Biocomputing 2013 (pp. 421-432). Academic Press.

Seljan, S., Baretić, M., & Kučiš, V. (2014). Information Retrieval and Terminology Extraction in Online Resources for Patients with Diabetes. *Collegium Antropologicum, 38*(2), 705–710. PMID:25145011

Serholt, S., & Barendregt, W. (2016). *Robots Tutoring Children: Longitudinal Evaluation of Social Engagement in Child-Robot Interaction.* Paper presented at the 9th Nordic Conference on Human-Computer Interaction (NordiCHI'16), Gothenburg, Sweden. 10.1145/2971485.2971536

Serholt, S. (2018). Breakdowns in children's interactions with a robotic tutor: A longitudinal study. *Computers in Human Behavior, 81,* 250–264. doi:10.1016/j.chb.2017.12.030

Serpanos, D. (2015). The Cyber-Physical Systems Revolution. *J. Computer, 51*(3), 70-73.

Serpanos, D. (2018). The Cyber-Physical Systems Revolution. *Computer, 51*(3), 70–73. doi:10.1109/MC.2018.1731058

Shamsuddin, S., Yussof, H., Hanapiah, F. A., Mohamed, S., Jamil, N. F. F., & Yunus, F. W. (2015). Robot-assisted learning for communication-care in autism intervention. In *Rehabilitation Robotics (ICORR), 2015 IEEE International Conference on* (pp. 822-827). IEEE. 10.1109/ICORR.2015.7281304

Shamsuddin, S., Yussof, H., Hanapiah, F. A., Mohamed, S., Jamil, N. F. F., & Yunus, F. W. (2015). Robot-assisted learning for communication-care in autism intervention. In *Rehabilitation Robotics (ICORR), 2015 IEEE International Conference,* 822-827.

Sharoff, S., Rapp, R., Zweigenbaum, P., & Fung, P. (Eds.). (2013). *Building and using comparable corpora.* Springer. doi:10.1007/978-3-642-20128-8

Shaw, J. (1991). *The Virtual Museum. Installation at Ars Electrónica.* Linz, Austria: ZKM, Karlsruhe.

Shen, C. C., Srisathapornphat, C., & Jaikaeo, C. (2001). Sensor information networking architecture and applications. *IEEE Personal Communications, 8*(4), 52-59.

Sheth, A., Anantharam, P., & Henson, C. (2013). Physical-cyber-social computing: An early 21st century approach. *IEEE Intelligent Systems, 28*(1), 78–82. doi:10.1109/MIS.2013.20

Shibata, T., Mitsui, T., Wada, K., Touda, A., Kumasaka, T., Tagami, K., & Tanie, K. (2001) Mental commit robot and its application to therapy of children. *Proceedings of the IEEE/ASME International Conference on Advanced Intelligent Mechatronics, 2,* 1053-1058. 10.1109/AIM.2001.936838

Shin, N., & Kim, S. (2007). Learning about, from, and with Robots: Students' Perspectives. *RO-MAN 2007 - The 16Th IEEE International Symposium On Robot And Human Interactive Communication.* doi: 10.1109/roman.2007.4415235

Shin, N., & Lee, S. (2008). The effects of appearance and interface design on user perceptions of educational robots. *Proc. URAI 2008.*

Shiomi, M., Kanda, T., Ishiguro, H., & Hagita, N. (2006). Interactive humanoid robots for a science museum. *Proceedings of the 1st ACM SIGCHI/SIGART conference on Human-robot interaction*, 305–312.10.1145/1121241.1121293

Short, A., & Bandyopadhyay, T. (2018). Legged Motion Planning in Complex Three-Dimensional Environments. *IEEE Robotics and Automation Letters, 3*(1), 29–36. doi:10.1109/LRA.2017.2728200

Shouse, E. (2005). Feeling, emotion, affect. *M/C Journal, 8*(6), 26.

ShuteS. (2011). *Robotville in Pictures*. Retrieved from https://blog.sciencemuseum.org.uk/robotville-in-pictures/

Signa Cor Laboratory. (1991). Retrived October 16, 2018, from http://www.signacor

Sim, J., & Wright, C. C. (2005). The kappa statistic in reliability studies: Use, interpretation, and sample size requirements. *Physical Therapy, 85*(3), 257. PMID:15733050

Simov, D., Matveev, M., Milanova, M., Krasteva, V., & Christov, I. (2014). Cardiac autonomic innervation following coronary artery bypass grafting evaluated by high resolution heart rate variability. *Computing in Cardiology Conference*, 1013-1016.

Singh, B., Wagatsuma, H., & Natsume, K. (2016). The bereitschaftspotential for rise of stand-up towards robot-assist device preparation. In *Society of Instrument and Control Engineers of Japan (SICE), 2016 55th Annual Conference of the*. IEEE. 10.1109/SICE.2016.7749192

Singh, B., Ai, G., & Wagatsuma, H. (2015). An electrooculography analysis in the time-frequency domain using morphological component analysis toward the development of mobile BCI systems. In *International Conference on Universal Access in Human-Computer Interaction*. Springer. 10.1007/978-3-319-20681-3_50

Singh, B., & Wagatsuma, H. (2017). A Removal of Eye Movement and Blink Artifacts from EEG Data Using Morphological Component Analysis. *Computational and Mathematical Methods in Medicine*. PMID:28194221

Singh, B., & Wagatsuma, H. (2019). Two-stage wavelet shrinkage and EEG-EOG signal contamination model to realize quantitative validations for the artifact removal from multiresource biosignals. *Biomedical Signal Processing and Control, 47*, 96–114. doi:10.1016/j.bspc.2018.08.014

Singh, B., Wagatsuma, H., & Natsume, K. (2017). The Detection of the Rise to Stand Movements Using Bereitschaftspotential from Scalp Electroencephalography (EEG). *SICE Journal of Control, Measurement, and System Integration, 10*(3), 149–155. doi:10.9746/jcmsi.10.149

Sioutis, M., Alirezaie, M., Renoux, J., & Loutfi, A. (2017). *Towards a Synergy of Qualitative Spatio-Temporal Reasoning and Smart Environments for Assisting the Elderly at Home*. 30th International Workshop on Qualitative Reasoning (held in conjunction with IJCAI 2017), Melbourne, Australia.

Slater, M. (2003). A note on presence terminology. *Presence Connect, 3*(3), 1–5.

Smith, C. A., & Wicks, P. J. (2008). PatientsLikeMe: Consumer health vocabulary as a folksonomy. *AMIA ... Annual Symposium Proceedings - AMIA Symposium. AMIA Symposium, 2008*, 682. PMID:18999004

Smith, P. (2007). Have we made any progress? Including students with intellectual disabilities in regular education classrooms. *Intellectual and Developmental Disabilities, 45*(5), 297–309. doi:10.1352/0047-6765(2007)45[297:HWMAPI]2.0.CO;2 PMID:17887907

Smith, R., Wathen, E., Abaci, P., Bergen, N., Law, I., Dick, I. I. M., ... Dove, E. (2009). Analyzing Heart Rate Variability in Infants Using Non-Linear Poincare Techniques. *Computers in Cardiology, 36*, 673–876.

Soergel, D., Tse, T., & Slaughter, L. A. (2004). Helping healthcare consumers understand: an "interpretive layer" for finding and making sense of medical information. In Medinfo (pp. 931-935). Academic Press.

Soni, R., Shukla, J., Dube, A., Shukla, A., Soni, R., & Soni, S. (2014). A Comparative Study of Heat Rate Variability in Obese and Healthy Young Adults (18 – 25 Years). *Research Journal of Pharmaceutical, Biological and Chemical Sciences, 5*(3), 1111–1117.

Soobrah, R., & Clark, S. K. (2012). Your patient information website: How good is it? *Colorectal Disease, 14*(3), e90–e94. doi:10.1111/j.1463-1318.2011.02792.x PMID:21883807

Soppit, R. (2016). Attention Deficit Hyperactivity Disorder (or Hyperkinetic Disorder). In L. Peer & G. Reid (Eds.), *Special Educational Needs. A Guide for Inclusive Practice* (pp. 216–231). Los Angeles, CA: SAGE.

Special Needs Education. (2012). European Agency for Development for Special Needs and Inclusive Education. Country Data.

Standen, P., Brown, D., Hedgecock, J., Roscoe, J., Galvez, T., & Elgajiji, E. (2014). *Adapting A Humanoid Robot for Use with Children with Profound and Multiple Disabilities*. 10th Internasional Conference of Disability, Virtual Reality & Associated Technologies, Gothenberg, Sweden.

Standen, P., Brown, D., Roscoe, J., Hedgecock, J., Stewart, D., Trigo, M. J. G., & Elgajiji, E. (2014). Engaging students with profound and multiple disabilities using humanoid robots. In *International Conference on Universal Access in Human-Computer Interaction* (pp. 419-430). Springer. 10.1007/978-3-319-07440-5_39

Stanton, C. M., Kahn, P. H., Severson, R. L., Ruckert, J. H., & Gill, B. T. (2008). Robotic animals might aid in the social development of children with autism. In *Human-Robot Interaction (HRI), 2008 3rd ACM/IEEE International Conference on* (pp. 271-278). ACM. 10.1145/1349822.1349858

Starck, J.L., Donoho, D.L. & Elad, M. (2004). *Redundant multiscale transforms and their application for morphological component separation*. No. DAPNIA-2004-88. CM-P00052061, 2004.

Starck, J. L., Fadili, J., & Murtagh, F. (2007). The undecimated wavelet decomposition and its reconstruction. *IEEE Transactions on Image Processing, 16*(2), 297–309. doi:10.1109/TIP.2006.887733 PMID:17269625

Starck, J. L., Moudden, Y., Bobin, J., Elad, M., & Donoho, D. L. (2005). *Morphological component analysis. In Wavelets XI* (Vol. 5914). International Society for Optics and Photonics.

Strandqvist, W., Santini, M., Lind, L., & Jönsson, A. (2018). Towards a Quality Assessment of Web Corpora for Language Technology Applications. In *Proceedings of TISLID18: Languages For Digital Lives And Cultures*. Ghent University.

Strnadova, I., & Evans, D. (2016). Students with Down Syndrome in Inclusive Classrooms. Using Evidence-Based Practices. In L. Peer & G. Reid (Eds.), *Special Educational Needs. A Guide for Inclusive Practice* (pp. 201–215). Los Angeles, CA: SAGE.

Styliani, S., Fotis, L., Kostas, K., & Petros, P. (2009). Virtual museums, a survey and some issues for consideration. *Journal of Cultural Heritage, 10*(4), 520–528. doi:10.1016/j.culher.2009.03.003

Suenaga & Hasuo. (2011). Programming with Infinitesimals: A WHILE-Language for Hybrid System Modeling. *Automata, Languages and Programming, 6756*, 392-403.

Suryadevara, N. K., Gaddam, A., Rayudu, R. K., & Mukhopadhyay, S. C. (2012). Wireless sensors network based safe home to care elderly people: Behaviour detection. *Sensors and Actuators. A, Physical, 186*, 277–283. doi:10.1016/j.sna.2012.03.020

Sussner, P., & Schuster, T. (2018). Interval-valued fuzzy morphological associative memories: Some theoretical aspects and applications. *Information Sciences, 438*, 127–144. doi:10.1016/j.ins.2018.01.042

Sutton, S., Braren, M., Zubin, J., & John, E. R. (1965). Evoked-potential correlates of stimulus uncertainty. *Science, 150*(3700), 1187–1188. doi:10.1126cience.150.3700.1187 PMID:5852977

Sutton, S., Tueting, P., Zubin, J., & John, E. R. (1967). Information delivery and the sensory evoked potential. *Science, 155*(3768), 1436–1439. doi:10.1126cience.155.3768.1436 PMID:6018511

Szondy, D. (2014). *Robot to Meet the Public at London's Natural History Museum.* Retrieved from https://newatlas.com/linda-robot-self-learning-museum/32267/

Tall, D. (1981). Infinitesimals constructed algebraically and interpreted geometrically. *Mathematical Education for Teaching, 4*(1), 34–53.

Tamura, T., Maeda, Y., Sekine, M., & Yoshida, M. (2014). Wearable photoplethysmographic sensors-past and present. *Electronics (Basel), 3*(2), 282–302. doi:10.3390/electronics3020282

Tanaka, F., Cicourel, A., & Movellan, J. R. (2007). Socialization between toddlers and robots at an early childhood education center. *Proceedings of the National Academy of Sciences of the United States of America, 104*(46), 17954–17958. doi:10.1073/pnas.0707769104 PMID:17984068

Tang, Z., Sun, S., Zhang, S., Chen, Y., Li, C., & Chen, S. (2016). A Brain-Machine Interface Based on ERD/ERS for an Upper-Limb Exoskeleton Control. *Sensors (Basel), 16*(12), 2050. doi:10.339016122050 PMID:27918413

Tan, Y., Vuran, M. C., & Goddarrd, S. (2009). Spatio-Temporal Event Model for Cyber-Physical Systems. *CSE Conference and Workshop Papers*, 147.

Tarbush, B., & Teytelboym, A. (2017). Social groups and social network formation. *Games and Economic Behavior, 103*, 286-312.

Tarniceriu, A., Harju, J., & Vehkaoja, A. (2018). Detection of Beat-to-Beat Intervals from Wrist Photoplethysmography in Patients with Sinus Rhythm and Atrial Fibrillation after Surgery. *Proceeding of IEEE International Conference on Biomedical and Health Informatics.* 10.1109/BHI.2018.8333387

Tate. (2014). *IK Prize 2014: After Dark.* Retrieved from http://www.tate.org.uk/whats-on/tate-britain/special-event/after-dark

Tayel, M., & AlSaba, E. (2015). Poincaré Plot for Heart Rate Variability. *International Journal of Biomedical and Biological Engineering, 9*(9), 708–711.

Taylor, J. (1862). Geology of Castleton, Derbyshire. In The Geologist. Cambridge University. doi:10.1017/S135946560000321X

Taylor, R., Spehar, B., Hagerhall, C., & Van Donkelaar, P. (2011). Perceptual and physiological responses to Jackson Pollock's fractals. *Frontiers in Human Neuroscience, 5*, 60. doi:10.3389/fnhum.2011.00060 PMID:21734876

Tchami, O. W., & Grabar, N. (2014). Towards automatic distinction between specialized and non-specialized occurrences of verbs in medical corpora. In *Proceedings of the 4th International Workshop on Computational Terminology (Computerm)* (pp. 114-124). Academic Press. 10.3115/v1/W14-4814

Teixeira, A. R., Tomé, A. M., Lang, E. W., Gruber, P., & Martins da Silva, A. (2006). Automatic removal of high-amplitude artefacts from single-channel electroencephalograms. *Computer Methods and Programs in Biomedicine, 83*(2), 125–138. doi:10.1016/j.cmpb.2006.06.003 PMID:16876903

Texas Instruments. (2014). *AFE4490 Datasheet*. Retrieved from http://www.ti.com/lit/gpn/afe4490

Thill, S., Pop, C. A., Belpaeme, T., Ziemke, T., & Vanderborght, B. (2012). Robot-assisted therapy for autism spectrum disorders with (partially) autonomous control: Challenges and outlook. *Paladyn: Journal of Behavioral Robotics*, *3*(4), 209–217. doi:10.247813230-013-0107-7

Thrun, S., Bennewitz, M., Burgard, W., Cremers, A. B., Dellaert, F., Fox, D., ... Schulz, D. (1999). MINERVA: a second-generation museum tour-guide robot. *Proceedings of the 1999 IEEE International Conference on Robotics and Automation*, 3, 1999–2005.

Titterton, D. H. (2004). Strapdown Inertial Navigation Technology. Cornwall, UK: The Institution of Electrical Engineers. doi:10.1049/PBRA017E

Todorov, T., & Noev, N. (2014). Technology of Three-Dimensional Scanning "Structured Light". In R. Pavlov, & P. Stanchev (Ed.), *International conference Digital Preservation and Presentation of Cultural and Scientific Heritage - DiPP`14. IV*, (pp. 87-94). Veliko Tarnovo, Bulgaria: Institute of Mathematics and informatics - BAS.

Todorov, T., Bogdanova, G., & Noev, N. (2016). Information Management: Database Design for a Cultural Artifact Repository. In *Encyclopedia of Information Systems and Technology*. Taylor & Francis Inc.

Torta, E., van Heumen, J., Piunti, F., Romeo, L., & Cuijpers, R. (2015). Evaluation of unimodal and multimodal communication cues for attracting attention in human–robot interaction. *International Journal of Social Robotics*, *7*(1), 89–96. doi:10.100712369-014-0271-x

Toutanova, K., Klein, D., Manning, C. D., & Singer, Y. (2003). Feature-rich part-of-speech tagging with a cyclic dependency network. *Proceedings of the 2003 Conference of the North American Chapter of the Association for Computational Linguistics on Human Language Technology*, 1. 10.3115/1073445.1073478

Tripathi, G. N., Chik, D., & Wagatsuma, H. (2013, January). How Difficult Is It for Robots to Maintain Home Safety?– A Brain-Inspired Robotics Point of View. In Neural Information Processing (pp. 528-536). Springer Berlin Heidelberg.

Tropp, J. A. (1997). *Infinitesimals: History & Application, Plan II Honors Program, WCH 4.104*. The University of Texas at Austin.

Ueyama, Y. (2015). A bayesian model of the uncanny valley effect for explaining the effects of therapeutic robots in autism spectrum disorder. *PLoS One*, *10*(9), e0138642. doi:10.1371/journal.pone.0138642 PMID:26389805

UNESCO. (1994). *World Conference on Special Needs Education: Access and Quality*. The Salamanca Statement. Retrieved from http://www.unesco.org/new/en/social-and-human-sciences/themes/

Urigüen, J.A. & Garcia-Zapirain, B. (2015). EEG artifact removal—state-of-the-art and guidelines. *Journal of Neural Engineering, 12*(3).

Valchkova, N., & Zahariev, R. (2016). Cognitive Service Robot For Help Of Disabled People. *Pr. TUSofia, XXV International Conference ADP-2016*, 168-173.

Valle, M. E., & Sussner, P. (2013). Quantale-based autoassociative memories with an application to the storage of color images. *Pattern Recognition Letters*, *34*(14), 1589–1601. doi:10.1016/j.patrec.2013.03.034

van Straten, C. L., Smeekens, I., Barakova, E., Glennon, J., Buitelaar, J., & Chen, A. (2017). Effects of robots' intonation and bodily appearance on robot-mediated communicative treatment outcomes for children with autism spectrum disorder. *Personal and Ubiquitous Computing*, 1–12.

Versley, Y., & Panchenko, Y. (2012). Not just bigger: Towards better-quality Web corpora. In *Proceedings of the seventh Web as Corpus Workshop (WAC7)* (pp. 44-52). Academic Press.

Vigário, R. N. (1997). Extraction of ocular artefacts from EEG using independent component analysis. *Electroencephalography and Clinical Neurophysiology, 103*(3), 395–404. doi:10.1016/S0013-4694(97)00042-8 PMID:9305288

Vivaldi, J., & Rodríguez, H. (2007). Evaluation of terms and term extraction systems: A practical approach. Terminology. *International Journal of Theoretical and Applied Issues in Specialized Communication, 13*(2), 225–248.

Volansky, V., Ordan, N., & Wintner, S. (2015). On the features of translationese. *Digital Scholarship in the Humanities, 30*(1), 98–118. doi:10.1093/llc/fqt031

Vrochidou, E., Najoua, A., Lytridis, C., Salonidis, M., Ferelis, V., & Papakostas, G. A. (2018). Social Robot NAO as a self-regulating didactic mediator: a case study of teaching/learning numeracy. *Proceedings of the 26th International Conference on Software, Telecommunications and Computer Networks (SoftCOM 2018), Symposium on: Robotic and ICT assisted wellbeing.* 10.23919/SOFTCOM.2018.8555764

Vukobratovic, M., & Borovac, B. (2004). Zero-moment point—thirty five years of its life. *International Journal of Humanoid Robotics, 1*(1), 157-173.

Vydiswaran, V. V., Mei, Q., Hanauer, D. A., & Zheng, K. (2014). Mining consumer health vocabulary from community-generated text. In *AMIA Annual Symposium Proceedings.* American Medical Informatics Association.

W3C. (1999). *Web content accessibility guidelines 1.0.* W3C Recommendation. Cambridge, UK: W3C. Retrieved from https://www.w3.org/TR/WAI-WEBCONTENT/

Wada, K., Shibata, T., Saito, T., Sakamoto, K., & Tanie, K. (2005). Psychological and social effects of one year robot assisted activity on elderly people at a health service facility for the aged. *Proceedings of the IEEE International Conference on Robotics and Automation (ICRA),* 2785-2790. 10.1109/ROBOT.2005.1570535

Wagatsuma, H., & Yamaguchi, Y. (2007). Neural dynamics of the cognitive map in the hippocampus. *Cognitive Neurodynamics, 1*(2), 119–141. doi:10.100711571-006-9013-6 PMID:19003507

Wahiba, B. A. K., Ben Azzouz, Z., Singh, A., Dey, N., Ashour, A. S., & Ben Ghazala, H. (2015, November). Automatic builder of class diagram (ABCD): an application of UML generation from functional requirements, Software: Practice and Experience. *Wiley Online Library, 46*(11), 1443–1458.

Wallstrom, G. L., Kass, R. E., Miller, A., Cohn, J. F., & Fox, N. A. (2004). Automatic correction of ocular artifacts in the EEG: A comparison of regression-based and component-based methods. *International Journal of Psychophysiology, 53*(2), 105–119. doi:10.1016/j.ijpsycho.2004.03.007 PMID:15210288

Wang, J., Wang, X., Shou, W., & Xu, B. (2014). Integrating BIM and augmented reality for interactive architectural visualisation. *Construction Innovation, 14*(4), 453–476. doi:10.1108/CI-03-2014-0019

Wang, W., Jiang, J., An, B., Jiang, Y., & Chen, B. (2017). Toward Efficient Team Formation for Crowdsourcing in Non-cooperative Social Networks. *IEEE Transactions on Cybernetics, 47*(12), 4208–4222. doi:10.1109/TCYB.2016.2602498 PMID:28113391

Wang, Y. (n.d.). Automatic Recognition of Text Difficulty from Consumers Health Information. *19th IEEE Symposium on Computer-Based Medical Systems (CBMS'06).*

Warburton, S., & García, M.P. (2016). Analyzing Teaching Practices in Second Life. *Learning in Virtual Worlds: Research and Applications.*

WCAG 2.0. (2008). Retrieved from http://www.w3.org/TR/WCAG20/

WCAG 2.1. (2018). Retrieved from https://www.w3.org/TR/WCAG21/#requirements-for-wcag-2-1

Web Content Accessibility Guidelines (WCAG) Overview. (1999). Retrieved from https://www.w3.org/WAI/intro/wcag

Webster, J. (2009). *Medical instrumentation: application and design.* John Wiley & Sons.

Welch, G., & Bishop, G. (2001). *An Introduction to the Kalman Filter.* University of North Carolina at Chapel Hill.

Wendt, C., & Berg, G. (2009) Nonverbal humor as a new dimension of HRI. *Proceedings of the 18th IEEE International Symposium on Robot and Human Interactive Communication (RO-MAN) 2009*, 183–188. 10.1109/ROMAN.2009.5326230

Werry, I., Dautenhahn, K., Ogden, B., & Harwin, W. (2001). Can social interaction skills be taught by a social agent? The role of a robotic mediator in autism therapy. *Cognitive technology: instruments of mind*, 57-74.

Whittingstall, K., & Logothetis, N. K. (2009). Frequency-band coupling in surface EEG reflects spiking activity in monkey visual cortex. *Neuron, 64*(2), 281–289. doi:10.1016/j.neuron.2009.08.016 PMID:19874794

Wieber, P. B. (2006, December). Trajectory free linear model predictive control for stable walking in the presence of strong perturbations. In *Humanoid Robots, 2006 6th IEEE-RAS International Conference on* (pp. 137-142). IEEE. 10.1109/ICHR.2006.321375

Wiener, N. (1961). *Cybernetics: Or Control and Communication in the Animal and the Machine.* MIT Press.

Wilkinson, L. (2005). The Grammar of Graphics (2nd ed.). New York: Springer.

Williams, J. H., Whiten, A., & Singh, T. (2004). A systematic review of action imitation in autistic spectrum disorder. *Journal of Autism and Developmental Disorders, 34*(3), 285–299. doi:10.1023/B:JADD.0000029551.56735.3a PMID:15264497

Williams, N., & Ogden, J. (2004). The impact of matching the patient's vocabulary: A randomized control trial. *Family Practice, 21*(6), 630–635. doi:10.1093/fampra/cmh610 PMID:15520032

Witmer, B. G., & Singer, M. J. (1998). Measuring presence in virtual environments: A presence questionnaire. *Presence (Cambridge, Mass.), 7*(3), 225–240. doi:10.1162/105474698565686

Wong, W., Liu, W., & Bennamoun, M. (2011). Constructing specialized corpora through analysing domain representativeness of websites. *Language Resources and Evaluation, 45*(2), 209–241. doi:10.100710579-011-9141-4

Woodman, O. (2007). *An Introduction to Inertial Navigation.* Cambridge, UK: University of Cambridge.

Wykowska, A., Anderl, C., Schubö, A., & Hommel, B. (2013). Motivation modulates visual attention: Evidence from pupillometry. *Frontiers in Psychology, 4*, 59. doi:10.3389/fpsyg.2013.00059 PMID:23407868

Xie, Z., Berseth, G., Clary, P., Hurst, J., & van de Panne, M. (2018). *Feedback Control For Cassie With Deep Reinforcement Learning.* arXiv preprint arXiv:1803.05580

Xiong, F., Qi, X., Nattel, S., & Comtois, P. (2015). Wavelet analysis of cardiac optical mapping data. *Computers in Biology and Medicine, 65*(C), 243–255. doi:10.1016/j.compbiomed.2015.06.022 PMID:26209111

Xu, J., Mitra, S., Van Hoof, C., Yazicioglu, R. F., & Makinwa, K. A. A. (2017). Active Electrodes for Wearable EEG Acquisition: Review and Electronics Design Methodology. *IEEE Reviews in Biomedical Engineering, 10*, 187–198. doi:10.1109/RBME.2017.2656388 PMID:28113349

Yamazaki. (2012). Comparison of dense array EEG with simultaneous intracranial EEG for interictal spike detection and localization. *Epilepsy Research, 98*(2-3), 166-173.

Yamazaki, A., Yamazaki, K., Kuno, Y., Burdelski, M., Kawashima, M., & Kuzuoka, H. (2008). Precision timing in human-robot interaction: coordination of head movement and utterance. *Proceedings of the SIGCHI Conference on Human Factors in Computing Systems*, 131–139. 10.1145/1357054.1357077

Yan, T., Cempini, M., Oddo, C. M., & Vitiello, N. (2015). Review of assistive strategies in powered lower-limb orthoses and exoskeletons. *Robotics and Autonomous Systems*, *64*, 120–136. doi:10.1016/j.robot.2014.09.032

Yiu. (2013). Definitive Guide to the ARM Cortex-M3 and Cortex-M4 Processors (3rd ed.). Academic Press.

Yoon, J., & Yoon, G. (2009). Non-constrained blood pressure monitoring using ECG and PPG for personal healthcare. *Journal of Medical Systems*, *33*(4), 261–266. doi:10.100710916-008-9186-0 PMID:19697692

Young, A. J., & Ferris, D. P. (2017). State of the art and future directions for lower limb robotic exoskeletons. *IEEE Transactions on Neural Systems and Rehabilitation Engineering*, *25*(2), 171–182. doi:10.1109/TNSRE.2016.2521160 PMID:26829794

Young, T. C., & Smith, S. (2016). An Interactive Augmented Reality Furniture Customization System. In S. Lackey & R. Shumaker (Eds.), *VAMR 2016: Virtual, Augmented and Mixed Reality. LNCS* (Vol. 9740, pp. 662–668). Springer. doi:10.1007/978-3-319-39907-2_63

Yu, X. (2011). Geo-friends recommendation in GPS-based Cyber-Physical Social network. In *Advances in Social Networks Analysis and Mining (ASONAM), 2011 International Conference on*. IEEE.

Zadeh, B. Q. A. (2016). Study on the Interplay Between the Corpus Size and Parameters of a Distributional Model for Term Classification. In *Proceedings of the 5th International Workshop on Computational Terminology (Computerm2016)* (pp. 62-72). Academic Press.

Zahariev, R., & Valchkova, N. (2004). *Assembly Mechatronic System with Flexible Organisation*. University of Technology.

Zahariev, R., & Valchkova, N. (2009). Perturbation Approach for Trajectory Planning of Technological Robot with Analyze of Task Accuracy Performance. *J. Scientific Announcement, 16*(2), 20-24.

Zappi, V., Pistillo, A., Calinon, S., Brogni, A., & Caldwell, D. (2012). Music expression with a robot manipulator used as a bidirectional tangible interface. *EURASIP Journal on Audio, Speech, and Music Processing*, *2*, 1–11.

Zeng, Q., Tse, T., Divita, G., Keselman, A., Crowell, J., Browne, A. C., … Ngo, L. (2015). Term Identification Methods for Consumer Health Vocabulary Development. *Journal of Medical Internet Research*, *9*(1), 4.

Zeng, Q. T., & Tse, T. (2006). Exploring and developing consumer health vocabularies. *Journal of the American Medical Informatics Association*, *13*(1), 24–29. doi:10.1197/jamia.M1761 PMID:16221948

Zeng, Q., Kim, E., Crowell, J., & Tse, T. (2005). A text corpora-based estimation of the familiarity of health terminology. In *International Symposium on Biological and Medical Data Analysis* (pp. 184-192). Springer. 10.1007/11573067_19

Zeng-Treitler, Q., Kim, H., Goryachev, S., Keselman, A., Slaughter, L., & Smith, C. A. (2007). Text characteristics of clinical reports and their implications for the readability of personal health records. In Medinfo. MEDINFO (2nd ed.; vol. 12, pp. 1117-1121). Academic Press.

Zhang, C., Gao, S., Tang, J., Liu, T. X., Fang, Z., & Cheng, X. (2016). Learning triadic influence in large social networks. *2016 IEEE/ACM International Conference on Advances in Social Networks Analysis and Mining (ASONAM)*, 1380-1381. 10.1109/ASONAM.2016.7752421

Zhao, Z., Yang, Q., Lu, H., Weninger, T., Cai, D., He, X., & Zhuang, Y. (2018). Social-Aware Movie Recommendation via Multimodal Network Learning. *IEEE Transactions on Multimedia, 20*(2), 430–440. doi:10.1109/TMM.2017.2740022

Zheng, Y., Lin, M. C., Manocha, D., Adiwahono, A. H., & Chew, C. M. (2010, October). A walking pattern generator for biped robots on uneven terrains. In *Intelligent Robots and Systems (IROS), 2010 IEEE/RSJ International Conference on* (pp. 4483-4488). IEEE. 10.1109/IROS.2010.5653079

Zheng, J., & Yu, H. (2017). Readability formulas and user perceptions of electronic health records difficulty: A corpus study. *Journal of Medical Internet Research, 19*(3), e59. doi:10.2196/jmir.6962 PMID:28254738

Zheng, W., Milios, E., & Watters, C. (2002). Filtering for medical news items using a machine learning approach. In *Proceedings of the AMIA Symposium* (p. 949). American Medical Informatics Association.

Zhou, W., & Gotman, J. (2004). Removal of EMG and ECG artifacts from EEG based on wavelet transform and ICA. In *The 26th Annual International Conference of the IEEE Engineering in Medicine and Biology Society* (Vol. 3, pp. 392–395). IEEE.

Zhou, Y., Chen, K., Song, L., Yang, X., & He, J. (2012). Feature Analysis of Spammers in Social Networks with Active Honeypots: A Case Study of Chinese Microblogging Networks. *2012 IEEE/ACM International Conference on Advances in Social Networks Analysis and Mining*, 728-729. 10.1109/ASONAM.2012.133

Zhuang, N., Zeng, Y., Tong, L., Zhang, C., Zhang, H., & Yan, B. (2017). Emotion Recognition from EEG Signals Using Multidimensional Information in EMD Domain. *BioMed Research International, 2017*, 1–9. doi:10.1155/2017/8317357 PMID:28900626

Zhuge, H. (2011). Semantic linking through spaces for cyber-physical-socio intelligence: A methodology. *Artificial Intelligence, 175*(5-6), 988–1019. doi:10.1016/j.artint.2010.09.009

Zhu, J., Liu, Y., & Yin, X. (2017). A New Structure-Hole-Based Algorithm For Influence Maximization in Large Online Social Networks. *IEEE Access: Practical Innovations, Open Solutions, 5*, 23405–23412. doi:10.1109/ACCESS.2017.2758353

About the Contributors

Maya Dimitrova received her higher education in psychology from St Petersburg, Russia, in 1985. She obtained her MSc in psychology (by research) (with distinction) from Warwick University, UK, in 1995 and her PhD on Adaptive Human Computer Interface from Institute of Control and Systems Research at BAS in 2002. She is currently Associate Professor at the Institute of Robotics at BAS, working on humanoid robotics for learners with special needs. Since 2017 she engaged with EU funded project of Cyber-physical systems for pedagogical rehabilitation in special education CybSPEED.

* * *

Guangyi Ai received his B.S. degree in communication engineering and M.S. degree in instrument science and technology from Changchun University of Science and Technology, China, in 2007 and 2010 respectively, and the Ph.D. degree in brain science and technology in Kyushu Institute of Technology, Japan, in 2016. He is currently a lecturer at Department of Computer Science, Neusoft Institute Guangdong, China. His research interests include statistic signal analysis, neural signal processing, embedded system, brain computer interface and artificial intelligence.

Lyuba Alboul is a professional mathematician with a strong fundamental training in Pure and Applied Mathematics and a broad research experience in Computer Science, Engineering, Robotics and AI. She is currently a Senior Researcher at the Centre for Automation and Robotics Research at Sheffield Hallam University in Sheffield, UK. Lyuba has been involved in a number of research projects as a primary investigator. She been awarded over 15 research grants (personal and as a member of consortia) from EPSRC, EU, MoD, STW/ NWO (Analogue of EPSRC in the Netherlands), and CNR (Analogue of EPSRC in Italy) on subjects in Mathematics, Computing, 3D modelling, Robotics and AI. Lyuba's current research involves the interplay of discrete and continuous representation of reality, perception and interaction with real and virtual worlds, by both humans and machines

Martin Beer recently retired as a Principal Lecturer in Computer Science from Sheffield Hallam University where his research centred around collaborative online learning using virtual and augmented reality, tailored search algorithms and distributed artificial intelligence.

Krasimir Cheshmedzhiev is an Assistant Professor of computer systems engineering at Institute of Robotics of Bulgarian Academy of Sciences. He received a M.Sc. degree in Electronics and Micro-electronics from the Department of Electronics at the Technical University of Gabrovo, Bulgaria. The major fields of professional and scientific research interests include computer networks and communications, embedded systems, signal processing, HRV analysis. He is a member of the National Union of Automatics and Informatics.

Galya Georgieva-Tsaneva received the M.Sc. degree in Electronical Engineering from the Technical University of Varna, Bulgaria in 1989 and Ph.D. degree on Components and Devices of Automation and Computing Equipment from the Institute of Systems Engineering and Robotics (ISER) of the Bulgarian Academy of Sciences (BAS) in 2016. Up to date she is an Assistant Professor at the Institute of Robotics of BAS, Sofia, Bulgaria. Her scientific research interests include medical information system, investigation of Heart Rate Variability of ECG data, wavelet and fractal analysis, computer networks and communications, coding and compression of information, fractal modeling, teletraffic engineering, web accessibility.

Mitko Gospodinov is an Associate Professor of computer systems engineering at Institute of Robotics at Bulgarian Academy of Sciences. He received M.Sc. degree in Microelectronics from the Department of Electronics at the Technical University of Gabrovo, Bulgaria and Ph.D. degree from the Department of Computer Sciences at the Sankt Petersburg State Electrotechnical University, Russia in 1985. The major fields of his professional and scientific research interests include digital image processing, computer networks and communications, mathematical analysis and design of electronic systems for medical implementation and biomedical research, special instruments for information exchange, fractal modeling and analysis of self-similarity in biomedical systems. He is a member of the National Union of Automatics and Informatics and the National Union of Scientists in Bulgaria.

Evgeniya Gospodinova is an Associate Professor of computer systems engineering at Institute of Robotics of Bulgarian Academy of Sciences. She received a M.Sc. degree in Microelectronics from the Department of Electronics at the Technical University of Gabrovo, Bulgaria and Ph.D. degree from the Technical University of Gabrovo in 2010. The major fields of professional and scientific research interests include digital image processing, computer networks and communications, special instruments for information exchange, fractal modeling and analysis in traffic engineering, medical information systems and investigation of Heart Rate Variability of digital ECG and PPG signals. She is a member of the National Union of Automatics and Informatics.

Blagovest Hristov received his MSc degree in Aviation Engineering from the Technical University of Sofia in 2013. Currently he is finishing his PhD on "Design and control of a multi-axis gimbal for UAV" at the Institute of Robotics - BAS.

Vassilis G. Kaburlasos has received the Diploma degree from the National Technical University of Athens, Greece, in 1986, and the M.Sc. and Ph.D. degrees from the University of Nevada, Reno, NV, USA, in 1989 and 1992, respectively, all in electrical engineering. He has been participant or (principal) investigator in 28 research projects, funded either publicly or privately, in the USA and in the European

Union. He has been a member of the technical/advisory committee or an invited speaker in 39 international conferences and a reviewer of 33 indexed journals. He has (co)authored more than 140 scientific research articles in indexed journals, refereed conferences and books. His research interests include computational intelligence modeling and human-machines interaction applications. Currently, there are more than 2000 citations to his published work corresponding to an h-index of 26 (Google Scholar). Dr. Kaburlasos serves as a Tenured Professor in the Department of Computer and Informatics Engineering at the Eastern Macedonia and Thrace Institute of Technology (EMaTTech), Greece; from 2012 to 2016 he also served as an elected member of the Institution's Council. He is founder and director since 2016 of the HUman-MAchines INteraction (HUMAIN) research Lab at EMaTTech. Dr. Kaburlasos is a member of several professional, scientific, and honor societies around the world including the IEEE, Sigma Xi, Phi Kappa Phi, Tau Beta Pi, Eta Kappa Nu, and the Technical Chamber of Greece.

Gagandeep Kaur is currently a PhD student affiliated with Indian Institute of Technology Kanpur, India. Her research interests have been brain computer interface, experimental neuroscience using evoked potentials and event related potentials. With current focus on empirical analysis of EEG signals using the rhythmic EEG activity and theory of neuroscience with digital signal processing as complementary methodology. She is also interested in history of neuroscience with focus on origin and evolution of phrenology and functional neuroscience.

Annica Kristoffersson received a MSc degree in Media Technology and Engineering from Linköping University, Sweden in 2005 and a PhD degree in Information Technology from Örebro University in 2013. Her research interests span human computer interaction (HCI), human machine interaction (HMI) and human robot interaction (HRI). More specifically, She is interested in: HRI and social robotics, smart homes, and how ICT can be developed to support independent living for an ageing population.

Leili Lind is a senior researcher in medical informatics and leads applied user centred and needs driven research in collaboration with industry. She has lead several patient studies in the area telehealth solutions for elderly multi morbid home care patients.

Louis Nisiotis is a Senior Lecturer in Information Systems and Data Management at Sheffield Hallam University. Louis has been awarded his PhD (2015, Sheffield Hallam University) for contributing on developing an understanding of the extent to which cyber campus environments can support learning for students experiencing barriers hindering their access and participation to Higher Education. He has been awarded his MSc IT in 2010 from Sheffield Hallam University, and achieved his BSc in Computer Information Technology from the University of Derby. His research interests include Educational Virtual Worlds, Virtual Learning Environments, Virtual Reality, Immersive Technologies, Online Learning tools, E-Learning, Technology Enhanced Learning.

Mamata Rath has twelve years of experience in teaching as well as in research and her research interests include Mobile Adhoc Networks, Internet of Things, Ubiquitous Computing, VANET and Computer Security.

Sergei Savin has obtained a bachelor degree in Automation and Control and an engineering degree in Mechatronics at Southwest State University. He finished a postgraduate program in Dynamics and Reliability of Machines and Equipment and obtained a candidate of science degree in 2014. He currently holds a senior researcher position at the Centre of technologies and components for Robotics and Mechatronics at Innopolis University. His areas of interest include walking robotics, in-pipe robots, optimal control, dynamics and machine learning. His current research is focused on exoskeletons, walking in-pipe robots and anthropomorphic bipedal robots. Until 2018 he worked as a docent at the department of Mechanics, Mechatronics and Robotics at Southwest State University where he gave lectures on Mathematical Modelling in Mechatronics and Robotics, Information System in Mechatronics and Robotics and on Information System of Mobile Robots for bachelor and master student programs. He authored more than 70 papers and is a co-author of textbooks on applied simulation methods in Robotics.

Balbir Singh is a postdoctoral researcher at the National Institute for Physiological Sciences. He currently works to develop a methodology for decoding of global (whole brain) and local (specific region) activation patterns from local activation patterns. His primary interest in the EEG signals, fMRI, computational neuroscience, spatiotemporal modeling, feature extraction, classification. He received his Ph.D. from the Kyushu Institute of Technology in 2017. He has worked human EEG study to apply the obtained results to Brain-Computer Interface (BCI).

Gopal Tadepalli is presently teaching Computer Science and Engineering at CEG Campus, Anna University. One of his research areas includes "Science and Spirituality". Dr. T V Gopal has published around 75 Research Papers. He has written four books and Co-Edited Seven Conference Proceedings. He is actively associated with many professional societies such as CSI, IEEE and ACM India Council. He is an Expert Member of the Editorial Advisory Board of the International Journal of Information Ethics. For further details, please visit: https://vidwan.inflibnet.ac.in/profile/57545.

Gyanendra Tripathi received PhD (Engg.) from Kyushu Institute of Technology (March 2016), and Master of Engineering from PEC University of Technology, Chandigarh, India (June 2010). He worked about 2.5 year as Assistant Professor in India (July 2010 to March 2013). His PhD research was focused on motion planning of humanoid robot and trajectory planning of rehabilitation robot based on human motion analysis.

Eleni Vrochidou received the Diploma (Embedded Systems), the M.Sc (Automatic Control Systems) and Ph.D. (Signal Processing) Degrees from the Department of Electrical & Computer Engineering, Democritus University of Thrace (DUTH), Greece, in 2004, 2007 and 2016, respectively. She is currently a part-time lecturer in the Department of Computer & Informatics Engineering at the Eastern Macedonia and Thrace Institute of Technology (EMaTTech), Greece. Her research interests are mainly in intelligent systems, signal processing and pattern recognition. In these areas she has published one book chapter, four international journals and four conferences.

Hiroaki Wagatsuma is an Associate Professor in the Graduate School of Life Science and Systems Engineering, Kyushu Institute of Technology. He is also a visiting scientist at RIKEN Center for Brain Science and a Cross-Appointment Fellow, Artificial Intelligence Research Center, National Institute of Advanced Industrial Science and Technology. His areas of specialization are Nonlinear Dynamics, Emergent Intelligence, Episodic Memory and Emotion, Societal Robot, Computational Neuroscience, Neuroinformatics, Sport Biomechanics, Rehabilitation Support. His current research areas are Biomedical Signal Processing and Sparse Coding, Sport Dynamics and Synergy analysis, Computational Neuroscience and Brain-Inspired Robotics, Neuroinformatics. In addition to being actively involved in interdisciplinary research to develop assistive devices to physically challenged people, he has authored books on Neuromorphic and Brain-Based Robots, and a chapter of the Information Extraction from the Internet.

Index

Recommended Reference Books

ISBN: 978-1-6831-8016-6
© 2017; 197 pp.
List Price: $180

ISBN: 978-1-5225-1034-5
© 2017; 350 pp.
List Price: $200

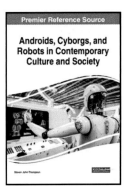

ISBN: 978-1-5225-2973-6
© 2018 ; 286 pp.
List Price: $205

ISBN: 978-1-5225-2589-9
© 2017; 602 pp.
List Price: $345

ISBN: 978-1-5225-2229-4
© 2016; 1,093 pp.
List Price: $465

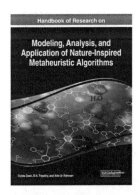

ISBN: 978-1-5225-2857-9
© 2018; 538 pp.
List Price: $265

Do you want to stay current on the latest research trends, product announcements, news and special offers?
Join IGI Global's mailing list today and start enjoying exclusive perks sent only to IGI Global members.
Add your name to the list at **www.igi-global.com/newsletters.**

Publisher of Peer-Reviewed, Timely, and Innovative Academic Research

www.igi-global.com   ✉ Sign up at www.igi-global.com/newsletters   **f** facebook.com/igiglobal   **t** twitter.com/igiglobal   **in** linkedin.com/igiglobal

Ensure Quality Research is Introduced to the Academic Community

Become an IGI Global Reviewer for Authored Book Projects

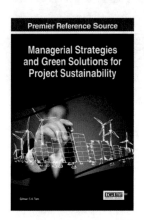

The overall success of an authored book project is dependent on quality and timely reviews.

In this competitive age of scholarly publishing, constructive and timely feedback significantly expedites the turnaround time of manuscripts from submission to acceptance, allowing the publication and discovery of forward-thinking research at a much more expeditious rate. Several IGI Global authored book projects are currently seeking highly qualified experts in the field to fill vacancies on their respective editorial review boards:

Applications may be sent to:
development@igi-global.com

Applicants must have a doctorate (or an equivalent degree) as well as publishing and reviewing experience. Reviewers are asked to write reviews in a timely, collegial, and constructive manner. All reviewers will begin their role on an ad-hoc basis for a period of one year, and upon successful completion of this term can be considered for full editorial review board status, with the potential for a subsequent promotion to Associate Editor.

If you have a colleague that may be interested in this opportunity,
we encourage you to share this information with them.

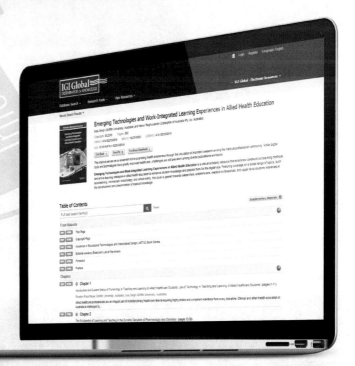

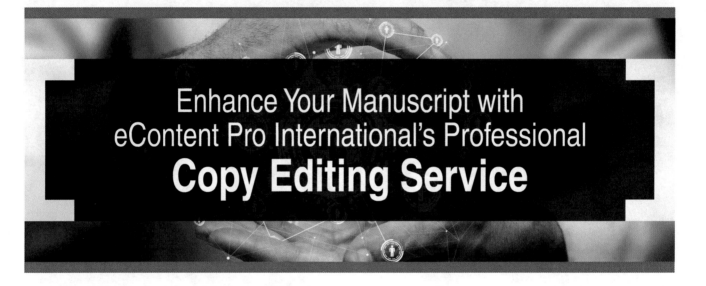

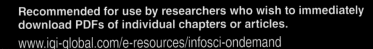

Printed in the United States
By Bookmasters